SOCIAL
PSYCHOLOGY

CONTEXT, COMMUNICATION AND CULTURE

STUART C. CARR

John Wiley & Sons Australia, Ltd

First published 2003 by
John Wiley & Sons Australia, Ltd
33 Park Road, Milton, Qld 4064

Offices also in Sydney and Melbourne

Typeset in 10/12.5 pt Times

© Stuart Carr 2003

National Library of Australia
Cataloguing-in-Publication data

Carr, Stuart C.
Social psychology: context, communication and culture.

Bibliography
Includes index.
ISBN 0 471 34304 8.

1. Social psychology. I. Title.

302

Cover image and images used in internal design:
© 2003 Digital Vision

Printed in Singapore by
CMO Image Printing Enterprise

10 9 8 7 6 5 4 3 2 1

ABOUT THE AUTHOR

Stuart C. Carr is a Senior Lecturer at Massey University in Albany, Auckland. Before this he was the coordinator of psychology at Northern Territory University in Darwin. He has also taught at the University of Newcastle, NSW, and the University of Malaŵi in East Africa. He has consulted on applied social psychology in Thailand, Indonesia and the Pacific region.

Dr Carr has co-authored and edited three books, and has published many book chapters, articles and papers on psychology. He is Editor of the *South Pacific Journal of Psychology.*

BRIEF CONTENTS

CONTENTS

Chapter 6 Everyday explanations   200

Chapter 7 Skilled routines   238

ACKNOWLEDGEMENTS

This book is the fruit of the labour of many people.

I would particularly like to acknowledge the following: At John Wiley & Sons, my thanks to Caroline Hunter and Judith Fox for their early encouragement, and to Lucy Russell for guidance through the proposal process. To Rhonda Black, for your wisdom, foresight and confidence — you provided invaluable motivation when there wasn't even light at the *beginning* of the tunnel. To Catherine Spedding, many thanks indeed for your truly developmental editorship, including detailed feedback on each instalment along the way. To Janine Spencer-Burford, for without your inspiration, verve and vision, as well as vital encouragement and support, this project would never have made it anywhere *near* the finishing line. To Jem Bates, for your humour, political savvy, words of wisdom, and finely crafted sentences and headers. What a team!

For their priceless review work, thanks to all of those John Wiley academics in Australia and New Zealand/Aotearoa who so patiently, constructively and meticulously read and commented on each chapter as it emerged, rough at the edges, out of the rock face. To Ian Purcell, for your mateship and razor-sharp intellect. To Floyd Bolitho, my friend and mentor, who steered me through the minefields and torpedoes. To Don Munro and Jack Schumaker, for all those breaths of fresh air — from Newcastle to Christchurch. To Robbie Sutton, for allowing me to attend his stimulating lecture on love, at Massey University, during a critical juncture in the writing (or rather not writing!) of chapter 9; and to Garth Fletcher, at Canterbury University, for his kind assistance. To Jennifer Stillman, for her advice on Moscovici's minority influence experiments. To all my Malawian, Aussie, Thai and Kiwi students, who over the years have given so much to this volume — and not least, of course, those of you who also read draft chapters. A special mention in that regard to Gillian Long and Margaret Fanning — you are gems.

Last but certainly not least, to my beautiful family, who have put up with so much absence (in body and mind). You have kept me going and are as much in this book as anyone I can think of — no, more than anyone I can think of — metaphorically, at least! Without you, and your unstinting love, support and patience with an irritable old sock, this book would never have come to be. I hope the sacrifices have been worth the effort!

Stuart Carr
September 2002

The author and publisher would also like to thank the following copyright holders, organisations and individuals for permission to reproduce copyright material in this book.

Text

CN 1.1 (p. 22), The Zimbardo study: first appeared in *The Humanist*, September/October 1980; reprinted in *Sociological footprints*, 3rd ed., Wadsworth, CA; reproduced with permission from Philip Zimbardo. CN 2.7 (p. 80), Reversing the cycle: from Robert B Cialdini, *Influence: Science and practice*, 3rd ed.; published by Allyn & Bacon, Boston, MA, © 1993 by Pearson Education. Reprinted by permission of the publisher. CN 3.3 (p. 113), Turbulence at the University of Papua New Guinea:

ETHOS AND DIRECTION

This section of the book is normally called the 'Preface'. Here the author outlines the scope and limits of the work and the values that underpin it — in short, its overall *ethos*. Here, too, the lecturers and students who are its end-users discover how the book interfaces with an overall learning plan — that is, its sense of *direction*. First encounters like these, so the book will argue, are critical for how the semester will proceed. So, to ensure that I consistently practise what I preach, as well as to set the tone for the book and provide the reader with useful material for the opening class of the semester, I have renamed this section 'Ethos and direction'.

Ethos

As its subtitle indicates, this book focuses on three carefully chosen themes. They do not constitute the only possible approach, or *gestalt*, for a book of this nature, nor do they pretend to. Rather, they reflect what I have managed to distil from the study of social psychology after many years of engagement in research, teaching, consultancy and publishing. These three general themes, **context**, **communication** and **culture**, clearly demand some sort of *a priori* working definition.

Context

In a sense, the whole of social psychology is about social context. This is because its core subject area is social influence. Social influence cannot happen without other people; other people *are* social context. Whether these people are the source of influence or its intended target, the study of social psychology is, first and foremost, the study of social context. Admittedly, these people are sometimes imaginary: examples range from internalised feelings of social identity (which influence people to do all sorts of things, as we shall see repeatedly throughout the book), to the jacket left draped over the back of an office chair to fool the boss into thinking we are on the job (thank you, Robbie Sutton, for reminding me about these 'jacket people'). Each of these examples is pregnant with the *symbolic* presence of other people, which in turn is ultimately based on some kind of prior (developmental) experience of them. Thus, social influence inevitably comes back to other people, and so to social context.

Context itself has a variety of meanings that we need to be clear about from the outset. These meanings vary according to the level of analysis that appeals to us most. In social psychology, these levels range from the comparatively psychological to the comparatively sociological. For the 'psychological' social psychologist, social behaviour is motivated by relatively immediate or 'proximal' stimuli. In the case of crowd behaviour, for instance, these stimuli may relate to the size of the crowd; or the particular tide of emotions that their presence generates; or observational learning (modelling effects) that stem from watching how key individuals in the drama behave and what happens to them, if anything, as a consequence of their actions. The 'sociological' social psychologist, on the other hand, might construct the same crowd situation as a socially rational response to years of political oppression. The contextual scope is far wider. Preferred analytical perspective, therefore, influences precisely the kind of social context we perceive, and how we interpret behaviour in it.

Ideally, a book like this should strike a balance between these two perspectives of social psychology. With that balance in mind, I have attempted to be as pluralistic as possible, and to fully recognise that these perspectives are often complementary. However, my particular training has probably predisposed me to being less perceptive of the sociological view. Where I have felt that the balance has tipped away from the sociological view, therefore, I have introduced exercises and readings that explicitly articulate the sociological perspective of the topic. You will find an example of this in chapter 2, in the discussion of crowd behaviour in South Africa, against the background of that nation's pre-democratic, apartheid-based political system.

Whatever the precise focus, one overriding aim in this textbook as a whole is to avoid studying social influence out of context. To give just one illustration of why this is important, an appeal to Australians or New Zealanders for charitable donations to aid agencies in Africa takes on a new meaning following a disaster in East Timor or a tragedy at home in Australia or New Zealand. What has happened here is that the social context has changed. Lines of discourse that may have operated well before this event (being a good Kiwi or Aussie means helping battlers overseas) are out of sync with public consciousness. Now the message that resonates most with the general public's concept of being 'a good Kiwi' or 'a good Aussie' is that charity begins at home.

Communication

Narrative discourses consist of implicit storylines and scripts that we often follow or enact in our everyday lives. For example, they exert influence in workplace teams, within which the cast of characters may include the *resource scavenger*, the *task completer*, the *moral conscience* of the group and the *humorist*. Each of these characters performs a valuable function according to circumstance — for example during times of crisis, when time is short, when ethical issues are involved, or when there is a need to release tension through a cathartic joke or two. Similarly, groups of friends often have their preordained roles and storylines ('Remember that time when . . .'). These roles will probably work well for the group so long as each player accepts the role in which he or she has been implicitly cast by the group. But if 'clowns' do not see themselves that way, then they are liable to become emotionally disaffected, and relationships within the group will become strained or, worse, will break down completely. Such crossed purposes, or discrepancies in the way people are socially positioned, stem from a failure to appreciate one another's perspective. They both predict and reflect a breakdown in *communication*.

Communication, then, is the second major theme in the book. Can *anyone* seriously envisage a social psychology bereft of communication? The treatment of communication in this book is deliberately explicit. Each chapter has a specific section dedicated to it. In chapter 7, for instance, we discuss (a) verbal and (b) non-verbal communication (and failure to communicate), each of which is hugely important in social influence generally. But I have resisted the urge to take this distinction too far, because the perspective in this book is inherently interactive. The verbal and non-verbal are ultimately tangled up together, at least in the social psychological sense. A influences B, and B influences A, and there is not much point or meaning in apportioning 80 per cent of communication to one effect and 20 per cent to the other. Similarly, and taking a wider view on this issue for a moment, there is not much ammunition in this book to support either position in the eternal argument of heredity 'versus' environment, nature 'versus' nurture or biology 'versus' culture.

Culture

Culture is the third and final conceptual plank of the book, and my discussion of it focuses very much on cultural values. One way that these values exert considerable influence is through the competing narrative discourses enacted during everyday communication. For example, health promotion messages are often pitched from a Western 'scientific' perspective towards a community of relatively 'traditional' beliefs about knowledge and expertise, the nature of health and who is entitled to prescribe behavioural norms. Such essentially 'foreign' messages do not always respect the character, roles and, most crucially perhaps, values that underpin the community that is asked to host them. They do not respect the community's sense of who they are and where they come from — that is, their sense of identity. Is it any surprise, then, that messages pitched in this form, implicitly positioning the audience beneath the sender's own cultural and moral high ground, sometimes fail?

Much of the discussion about cultural values, and the cultural landscape that they create for communication and influence generally, is focused on the contrasting values of individualism and collectivism, and the belief (or lack of it) in hierarchy. It is not much use feverishly promoting the self, personal accomplishment and 'tall poppies' when the cultural context eschews these qualities in favour of humility, social cohesion and respect for elders. Much social behaviour, I believe, can be interpreted and perhaps better understood through these lenses, however fuzzy and imperfect the glimpses can be. In this book, these value concepts function as compass points. They are social constructions (like the positioning of Australia and New Zealand at the 'bottom' of the world map instead of at the top where they really belong!) that help us to navigate a wide diversity of cultural landscapes.

At last, then, I come to my values, which — to be consistent — I ought to define according to the same schema. These values and predilections tend towards the collectivist and social, supported by a belief in equality. Conflicts of opinion, not least in university departments, occur between factions who diverge precisely on these very dimensions. Naturally, I hope that any readers who do not share my value orientation will appreciate the opportunity to share another perspective! In the same spirit of pluralism, it is of course fully recognised that we are all sometime individualists, collectivists and taskmasters. Much depends on context, and on the role we are playing at the time.

In writing this book, I have seen my role as a facilitator and equal partner with the students and lecturers who comprise its 'audience'. Given that ethos, I would like to warmly acknowledge the input of many, many students, from the universities of Malaŵi (in East Africa), Newcastle (in New South Wales), Darwin (in the Northern Territory), Srinakharinwirot University (in Thailand), and Massey University (in New Zealand). You have helped me enormously through your intellectual input, practical participation, classroom discussion and of course feedback, and even in reviewing draft chapters of this book. Thanks to you, I am in the privileged position of already knowing that this material *works*; both in the classroom and outside it — in the worlds of your work, social and psychological life. Without you and your good heart, this book would never have happened. I owe you all big time.

I also owe a great debt to my many academic colleagues in New Zealand and Australia, whose invaluable criticisms have contributed to this project at every stage, from the original proposal to the last word of the final draft. Your comments have been consistently helpful and constructive, so I have listened attentively to every word. Here is a potted summary of how.

This project began with a call from academics and students on both sides of the Tasman for a new, fresh approach that would capture for second- and third-year students, who already had a broad, introductory knowledge of social psychology through 101 or 102 courses, some of the big changes experienced in our world, and in social psychology, since the 1970s. These shifts include, to name just a few, globalisation, growing biculturalism and multiculturalism, advances in Internet technology, increasing social inequity, and a possible rise in implicit racism and cultural stereotyping. Students and lecturers had also grown tired of US- and Euro-centric textbooks, and wanted to hear more about research and theory that is being driven from Australia and New Zealand. Naturally, this would relate better to student experiences in this part of the world; in addition, some of the world's best and most relevant research in social psychology has been happening in our region. This book has no cause for cultural cringe!

At the same time, I had to avoid the inherent risk in all such undertakings of throwing out the proverbial baby with the bathwater and becoming affectedly parochial. There is a wealth of fantastically durable, 'classic' social psychology out there, much of it still relevant to today's students, wherever they happen to live. Consequently, this book contains as much classic as leading-edge material from downunder. It is as much vintage Bordeaux as Hunter Valley red.

Above all, I must thank my academic colleagues for their peer reviews of the chapters in this volume. Throughout this process you have kept me on track, helping me to pitch the text at the right level, alerting me to the need for additional references and readings, or for practical examples anchored in the everyday experiences and aspirations of Australian and New Zealand students (a lesson about localisation that I first learned in Africa, from Françoise). As well, you have kept pointing me towards some of the exciting work that is emerging in our own region. As time has passed, I have struck up unique working friendships — still 'anonymous' but increasingly finding ourselves and the text on the same sheet of music. The final ensemble, in fact, jibes extremely well with what the students themselves have been saying. At the core of this book is an infectious energy and passion for the discipline.

This passion and energy has been nourished and nurtured at every turn by the first-class team at John Wiley & Sons Australia. From the very first days of the project, and through thick and thin, this team has provided invaluable input to the book as a whole. The way this has been done is a living testament to what is discussed in the book as 'perspective taking'. At each stage of the task, that is, the various members of the team have, in turn, taken a variety of perspectives on the manuscript. In this way, they have put themselves into the shoes of editors, of student readers, of university lecturers and — most important of all — of social psychologists. We are all purveyors of social psychological wisdoms, and the more we can exchange those perspectives, the better positioned we become to rise to the challenge of better understanding social influence.

One issue deserves special mention. Identifying the level of challenge that students (in this case, those in their second or third year) can rise to is always a balancing act. No one likes to fail; at the same time, no one, in the end, wants to be spoon-fed. For this reason, I have extensively 'road tested' much of the lecture-material and practical exercises in this book, and have listened to the responses of both lecturers and students at every stage. As well, the text draws a lot from Pygmalion effects, and particularly those in the classroom. Students will sense from day one the level of confidence that their instructors have in them, and this impression, this ethos, will influence substantially how much they later achieve. With these effects in mind, as well as the continual quality assurance process used throughout the development of this text, I ask all instructors to give students a fair tilt at this book. The material is not easy, but if student evaluations and the consistently high quality of their work are anything to go by, it will be well worth the effort.

Direction

The text you are about to read has been constructed with a view to building on the more easily absorbed aspects of social psychology, such as crowd behaviour, conformity, obedience and mass persuasion, and progressively introducing more recent and complex material on social cognition and social affect. To some extent, this flow mirrors the historical gradient of social psychology itself, although it also perhaps reflects an increasing complexity (and richness) in the human subject, and social life generally.

This introduction and its counterpart, Chapter 11: Revision, at the end of the semester just before exams, are deliberately designed as bookends for the more 'meaty' material in the main text. This does not, however, mean that they are any less important for the direction of our overall journey. Bookends serve a very valuable function: they enclose and contain the knowledge of the whole bookshelf. Within these confines, the text outlines 12 'weeks' of classes. Based on a 13-week teaching semester, this permits one week of 'teaching time' for mid-term tests, public holidays or other contingencies. In my experience, it is more relaxing, and ultimately more productive, for lecturers and students alike to have this leeway rather than having to squeeze 13 weeks of material into exactly 13 slots.

Each chapter follows a template that conveys about four major ideas per lecture. These major points, along with sub-points and illustrations, are presented on the website of online resources in a series of PowerPoint displays. Each chapter begins with an overview of its content and ends with a summary, following the old teaching adage, 'Say what you will say, say it, and then say that you have said it'. The wisdom of this axiom in the classroom is that it alerts students to what to expect, helping them to absorb new concepts and subsequently to file them accessibly in their memories. As an optional further support, each chapter includes a list of key supplementary readings for students who wish to further pursue topics of interest.

Each chapter also features a series of critical narratives, offering anecdotal stories from a range of acknowledged and referenced sources. These stories are designed to bring the subject area to life using everyday applied examples. They function as 'moving pictures' of the kinds of social influences that have been 'snapshotted' in the laboratory and in survey work. The main strength of such narratives is that they marshal a host of social psychological principles, illustrate for the student how they can interlock in the real world, and above all help to capture the *meaning* of intriguing social psychological phenomena. Critically, these narratives synthesise social psychological analysis into a living *gestalt* to which students can meaningfully relate.

The publisher has produced a dedicated website to support this book (www.johnwiley.com.au/highered/socialpsych). This site provides a wealth of web resources that complement the text, illuminating specific topics and general themes addressed throughout the book. Each chapter has its own, stand-alone section of multiple-choice questions, which are accessible to the instructors through the website online resource. Both lecturers and students can also access the PowerPoint displays for each chapter, along with relevant materials, background and foreground, for the classroom exercises. These exercises have for the most part been timed for 50 minutes, or the average time for one classroom slot. As with the rest of the book, many of them have undergone extensive trial runs with both second- and third-year classes. Any feedback on the website and how it might be improved would always be appreciated. Above all, however, enjoy the journey!

Stuart Carr
Auckland, New Zealand
September 2002

ANALYSIS

CHAPTER 1

Social psychology:
past, present and future

CHAPTER

SOCIAL PSYCHOLOGY: PAST, PRESENT AND FUTURE

LEARNING OBJECTIVES

After reading this chapter, you should be able to:

- define social psychology
- identify key points in its history
- describe the unique research methods on which social psychology is built, including ethics in a global community
- outline new developments in these methods as we enter the twenty-first century.

OVERVIEW

Social psychology is all about the give-and-take of influence — on behaviour, beliefs and feelings — between individuals, between groups, and between an individual and a group. An example of this dynamic today is *glocalisation*, which reflects the interplay between globalisation and its more traditional counterpart, localisation. Historically, social psychological wisdom is found in all societies, although the influences of globalisation are challenging some of these traditional views. The academic discipline of social psychology has a localised origin, too, but it includes a belief in putting all wisdoms to an empirical test. Three of the cornerstones of this discipline are the influence of (a) context, (b) communication and (c) culture. Like footlights, they illuminate and make sense of social behaviour for us, and they can now be trained on the dynamics of glocalisation. As well, the measures we adopt to view these dynamics must move with the dancers themselves. Emergent techniques, such as the *web of meaning* and increased use of *critical narratives*, are being introduced and applied to contemporary issues. A core example of these issues, and one that recurs throughout the book, is the tension between individual and social achievement.

SOCIAL INFLUENCE

The academic discipline of social psychology is, first and foremost, a way of looking at the world. This viewpoint is focused on what we may term social influence, a concept that both encompasses and unifies the whole spectrum of social psychology, and provides us with a compact working definition of the discipline as a whole: *Social psychology seeks to describe and explain the processes of social influence.* The question students invariably ask is, 'Influence on *what*?' In reply, it can be said that influence is exerted on three major domains of everyday life: on each other's *behaviour*; on each other's beliefs, or *cognition*; and on each other's feelings, or social *affect*. But this is still not specific enough. The easiest and most systematic way of illustrating precisely what is influenced in each of these three domains is to briefly preview the journey we will be taking in this book.

Influence on behaviour

If we first consider social behaviour, *crowds* (discussed in chapter 2) can clearly alter the behaviour of each of their individual elements from its usual pattern. Crowds may generate anything from surges of aggression, for example at an international sports match or an anti-globalisation demonstration, to acts of civil defiance and extraordinary individual bravery (such as the Chinese student who stood in the path of a phalanx of armoured tanks approaching Tianenmen Square).

Groups (chapter 3), normally more enduring social entities than crowds, have provided a social context for individual behaviour for eons of social evolution. Today, though, the ante has been upped. Whether as students, healthcare providers or employees, we are increasingly urged to create 'super groups', or 'self-directed teams'. Such teams, many people seem to believe, have the potential to raise levels of individual and group performance; however, if they are not managed carefully they can have the opposite effect. The family, whether nuclear or extended, is another key example of the group. This type of group is always difficult to review as a homogeneous entity or single topic. Its influences are found across so many aspects of everyday life. Accordingly, these influences are discussed throughout the text, from family metaphors in organisations (chapter 3) through to aggression between lovers (chapter 10). Easier to pin down is the mass persuasion capacity of *the media* (chapter 4). Commercial companies (as well as social marketing agencies such as charities) would not be spending significant sums of money to pay for air-time unless they were convinced that these purchases actually changed people's behaviour (for examples of evidence that advertising campaigns change both consumer and charitable behaviour, respectively, see Fernandez & Rosen 2000 and Prottas 1997).

In summary, therefore, we find that social influence on each other's behaviour is ubiquitous, pervading everyday life in multiple ways.

Influence on cognition

The study of social cognition (from the Latin *cognitio*, meaning understanding or knowledge) focuses on how knowledge is influenced by, and influences, behaviour. Sensations from the social world require that we make rapid decisions about what they are and what they represent. 'Does her body language signify anger?' 'Is he lying or telling the truth?' These are important questions of *first impressions*, and thereby social influence on cognition. For example, people often try to make sense of why some individuals or groups are chronically poor. Are they victims of international economic policy or political corruption or the vagaries of nature? Or is it simply that they are too lazy or 'culturally backward' to work themselves out of perpetual crisis? Answers to questions like these will partly determine how 'deserving' of charity these people are perceived to be, and will influence donation behaviour. In their responses to such questions, observers seek to identify the causes of others' behaviour or circumstances; they are forming their own *everyday explanations* of the people around them. If we make these attributions and solutions habitually, we are said to have a cognitive 'schema'. A schema is simply a well-rehearsed mental script, a template held in memory, that we apply to life's everyday events and decisions. For example, we know implicitly how to conduct ourselves in a classroom, in the office or on the production floor. Similarly, people develop mental stereotypes (from the French printing term *stéréotype*, meaning printer's mould or cast) about groups outside their own — 'the poor' for example. The use of stereotypes is often so practised that they roll off the tongue in everyday conversation; paradoxically, they have become *skilled routines* (a defining feature of skills is that they are performed effortlessly). According to this analysis, schema and skill go hand-in-glove. Studying one illuminates and helps manage the other.

Therefore, influence on each other's cognition is pervasive in everyday life and society generally.

Influence on affect

Appeals for aid are based as much on social emotion, or 'affect', as on 'cold' cognitive processes. As we learn at the beginning of part 3, social psychology has traditionally focused first on behaviour, then on cognition, and lastly on the emotional, affective side of social influence. Recent efforts to redress this balance have included greater attention being paid, for example, to 'social intelligence' (a refresher on this concept is provided in chapter 7). Yet even this term suggests a reluctance to take social affect as a domain of influence in its own right; the dominant word is still 'intelligence', which indicates that the schema applied remains anchored in cognition. In this book, 'cold' (cognitive) and 'hot' (affective) systems are weighted equally. Alongside (1) a cognition that our charitable donations to the Third World 'won't get through because of endemic corruption', we can still (2) be moved to tears (experience affect) for the poor themselves. Each of (1) and (2) drives the other; neither is inherently more significant. Indeed, if we deliberately favoured one over the other there would surely be a price to pay — for example if we were social marketers trying to persuade people to reach into their pockets to make a donation to an aid agency or charitable foundation.

Broadly, then, we need to study social emotion on its own terms, not as some 'secondary by-product' of social cognition. Aid petitions, for example, deliberately appeal to a sense of common humanity, and therefore human affiliation. Under what conditions, precisely, are these appeals to social affect successful? This is a legitimate and substantive research domain in its own right. Typically, in fact, our affiliations are differentiated. In everyday life, we feel affiliated to a diversity of other individuals and groups. Social psychologists have extensively studied the factors, such as propinquity (nearness in living space) and similarity (e.g. nearness in emotional temperament) that draw people into these affiliations with each other, or *attraction* (chapter 8). These processes of influence can become central to most people's lives, and nowhere more so than in *love* (chapter 9). This term denotes the various kinds of profound, and often lasting, emotional bonds that form between people. Often equally profound, although potentially far more destructive socially, is *aggression* (chapter 10). This process permeates everyday life, and learning how to manage it has arguably become critical to human survival.

In summary, then, social influence is ubiquitous. There is simply no corner of contemporary life, from its trivia to the most globally portentous issues of the day, that is not touched by social psychology.

Levels of influence

We have just completed a 'Cook's tour' of some classic topics in social psychology. As well as visiting the ideas of behaviour, cognition and affect, the tour makes it clear that social influence occurs between different types of social entity. There are (a) exchanges of influence between individuals, as in a loving interpersonal relationship. There are (b) exchanges between groups, as in the inter-group stereotypes held by rival gangs, sports clubs, software companies, cultural groups or nations. Then there are (c) exchanges of influence between individuals and groups, as manifested in leadership, or by an employee who despises the firm or work team. As these brief examples imply, levels of these forms of influence crisscross the whole of social psychology. Accordingly, they will occur and recur in the chapters that follow. The reason for drawing these distinctions now is to stress the point that the same person *changes* in the way he or she thinks, behaves and feels according to circumstance — whether with a romantic partner, for example, or in a conflict with a rival group or an exploitative employer.

In one sense, then, this is another wake-up call about the importance of context, already discussed in 'Ethos and direction'. Yet in another, equally important sense, the distinction between (a), (b) and (c) presages one of the most basic lessons in the discipline — that in social psychology it is fundamentally mistaken to overestimate the idea of a person as a 'fixed' entity, with a fixed social self.

We can explore this idea further by considering theory.

THEORIES OF SOCIAL BEHAVIOUR: AN EMERGENT PLURALISM

Returning for a moment to our opening definition of social psychology, so far we have discussed it at the level of description rather than explanation. But description is only one half of what social psychology is and what it does. Explanation is the 'why?' domain of theory. In the discipline of social psychology, there are as many theories as there are processes. This apparent mass of information can nonetheless be organised into provisional categories. Given that theories address the question of why, they are frequently a question of motivation. Over the centuries there has been considerable debate about what fundamentally motivates human beings. In psychology, much of this debate has centred on the following question: Is human conduct shaped by (i) its material consequences (rewards and punishments of one kind or another), or is it motivated by (ii) a search for meaning?

This kind of disjunction, in which one type of motive is pitted 'against' the other, and only one is 'true', is increasingly viewed as out of touch with reality (Hermans & Kempen 1998). Just as people are not fixed entities, they are also motivated by both (i) and (ii), neither of which is any more correct than, or necessarily dominant over, the other (Hofstede & Bond 1988). The real task of a social psychological text like this is to mark out when and where one type of motive tends to override the other. With regard to political change, for example, rewards and punishments may be effective in controlling people's behaviour in the short term, but an appeal to their values may be required to retain their support over the longer haul. Dictatorships have a habit of eventually being overthrown; the constraints of rewards (carrots) and coercion (sticks) are often counterproductive in the long run. Also, of course, what is constraining is a question of perspective. Democracy can be a constraint to those who prefer more hierarchically structured systems of governance. These are not necessarily dictatorial; they may just as easily be nurturing. After all, the same people who prefer to be consulted during times of relative calm may prefer firm leadership during times of crisis.

I have suggested a distinction between (i) surface behaviour and (ii) underlying beliefs or feelings (mental processes). In itself, there is nothing new in this distinction (Deutsch & Gerard 1955). But its implications do not seem to have been fully explored in the literature. For example, people are inherently complex, and capable of being motivated in multiple, sometimes conflicting directions at the same time. They may be *in two minds* on an issue — one on what to do or say, and the other on what to think or feel. Today, more than ever, this potential for motivational pluralism poses a serious challenge for social psychology. That challenge has arisen partly because the world is witnessing three powerful new social influences.

New social influence 1: globalisation

Globalisation means many things to many people, including practitioners within the social sciences (Marsella 1998). For its part, social psychology operates at a level of analysis somewhere between the societal (macro) and the individual (micro). From this 'mezzanine', or 'meso', perspective (Rousseau & House 1994), globalisation signifies the diffusion of a uniform mode of acting (behaviour), believing (cognition) or feeling (affect) within groups, between groups, and between an individual and a group. These modes of influence are often, but not only, 'Western' in flavour. They may include, for example, greater acceptance of the idea of self-promotion and the importance of 'me' over 'we'. But they may also include some westward diffusion of 'Eastern' management practices (Posthuma 1995). In this spirit of pluralism, let us also acknowledge that globalisation has been going on, in one form or another, and in a variety of intercultural and geographical directions, for centuries (Rosenau 1998).

What we might legitimately add to this, however, is that the *pace* of global-isation has changed in a fundamental way. It is speeding up prodigiously, and much of this acceleration appears to entail the adoption, however provisionally, of Western-style individualism. For example, globalisation is having widespread impacts on families (e.g. through media penetration of traditional societies and their extended family networks), on schemata concerning Third World poverty (through seemingly endless crisis reporting and consequent 'compassion fatigue') and, potentially, on societal levels of aggression (through violent media role models). From a social psychological point of view, therefore, we are witnessing an influence process of titanic proportions. Social psychology absolutely must engage with this process if it is not to become what one eminent writer once char-acterised as 'journalism in slow motion' (Gergen 1994b, p. 163).

New social influence 2: localisation

A glance at CNN news will tell us that many communities around the world are not taking this pressure lying down. They are 'kicking back', rebounding against what they perceive as constraints in globalisation itself. Fundamentalism and many forms of cultural backlash, including anti-globalisation movements, are pro-liferating. Counter-cultures, reasserting local and traditional values, are finding voice. 'Community development' is back in vogue at both ends of the political spectrum. In the workplace, protests and backlashes are everyday occurrences, as employees brace themselves for the latest management fad from the United States. Individual contracts, for example, undermine union solidarity; they also threaten workplace cultures, many of which reflect societal values that have served groups well in the past. In many cases, the values coming under attack from multiple quarters have been in place for centuries. They are therefore rela-tively tough; they would not have endured *unless* they were robust (MacLachlan 1996b; for a review of culture and evolution, see Plotkin 1998). This inherent toughness is one reason why, across a range of social, community and organ-isational groups, globalisation is not having everything its own way.

New social influence 3: glocalisation

If we now return to our point that people are often pulled in conflicting directions, we see that a major challenge is arising for contemporary social psychology. That challenge stems from the fact that people are experiencing the pushes of global-isation *alongside* the pulls of localisation. In other words, and especially with the massive expansion of travel through work, emigration and immigration, *inter-actions*, including conflicts between different systems of belief, have become the norm. These dynamic tensions, according to the analysis outlined above, will occur across different levels of social life, including (1) within groups (e.g. inside an immigrant community housing estate), between groups (e.g. between ethnic groups within that community), and between an individual and a group (e.g. within that community's leadership). Dramas of various sorts ensue between these individuals and groups. They may be reported, for instance, in the daily news-papers, but they may also be played out (2) as *internalised* versions of the com-peting influences that have been encountered in daily life.

An example of both (1) and (2) that is familiar to many students living in Australia and New Zealand is the experience of being a second- or third-generation immigrant, growing up knowing several, often conflicting codes of acting, thinking and feeling. Young people in these circumstances may find themselves sandwiched uncomfortably between the 'global' culture of youth and the more 'local' values embodied in their caregivers' enduring traditional values. Those conflicts wash back and forth between (1) and (2), as family dynamics create psychological dilemmas and vice versa. One writer evocatively described this experience as being 'caught between two moral worlds' (Mazrui 1990, p. 119). The point, however, is that today, more than ever, people are developing 'multiple cognitive repertoires' (Nsamenang 1994).

Crucially, these multiple repertoires are behavioural and affective as well as cognitive. In addition, they are as often complementary as conflicting. In poorer economies, for instance, the capacity to operate in both modalities — modern (global) *and* traditional (local) — offers distinct advantages, such as extended credit networks that operate on trust rather than collateral (Rugimbana 1996b). These 'human capital' resources can be extremely useful in small business development (for a discussion of this enterprise in an Australian Aboriginal context, see Ivory 1999).

Whatever its value to society generally, this merging of global and local ways of living and earning a living has been termed, appropriately enough, **'glocalisation'** (Robertson 1995). As the examples above are designed to illustrate, the process of glocalisation entails any combination of pushes and pulls that we experience *when local traditions meet global culture*. If glocalisation is truly as revolutionary for the human race as theorists such as Rosenau and Robertson suggest, then our discipline needs more than ever to take stock of its progress and prepare for the challenge ahead. The easiest way of conducting a preliminary audit before reading the book as a whole is to briefly review the historical foundations of the discipline we call Social Psychology.

A BRIEF HISTORY OF SOCIAL PSYCHOLOGY

Books on social psychology often imply, whether intentionally or not, that social psychological wisdom originated in Western Europe and North America through articles published in scientific journals that began appearing around the beginning of the twentieth century. Nothing, of course, could be further from the truth. The wisdom on which the discipline is based is neither the brainchild nor the exclusive property of twentieth-century science. Pre-contact Māori, for instance, had a well-developed psychology for explaining human behaviour (Ritchie & Ritchie 1999). A distinction must be drawn, therefore, between social psychological wisdom and the academic discipline of social psychology. The discipline in the West arose out of relatively localised concerns about war and explanations for genocide. It is, then, partially anchored in time and place; indeed, social psychology is itself a product of social context. It has no inherent monopoly on social wisdom — wisdom that has inevitably arisen in other times and places, and that might well be applicable still in contemporary society. Broadly, therefore, we need to consider two histories, one of social psychological wisdom in wider history; and the other of developing ideas in social psychology the (still relatively new) discipline.

A historical survey is not a major (or practical) focus of this book but, to illustrate the relevance of wider history, it is useful to briefly consider the context of psychological issues that have concerned human society for centuries and continue to do so today. The longevity of these issues underscores how societal wisdoms of the past potentially bear on the present. As two historically astute social psychologists observe, for instance: 'How to maintain a balance between encouraging personal striving and constraining the manner through which personal striving is expressed has been a long-standing problem in almost every social philosophical system' (Chi-yue Chiu & Ying-yi Hong 1997, p. 172). Such evergreen issues are the very stuff of a glocal social psychology, as people everywhere strive to reconcile 'me' with 'we'. The workplace, where many people today spend the largest chunk of their waking lives, offers a living example. Employees the world over are increasingly being urged to work for 'number one', an idea enshrined in workplace incentives like pay for individual performance and individual work contracts. Yet at the same time these employees are expected more than ever to be 'team' players, focused above all on playing and achieving for the group as a whole.

Perched on the shoulders of giants

Given this combination of a timeless dilemma and a time of dilemma, it seems reasonable to take a look at some of the 'advice' that has been offered in the past across a diversity of places and societies. Our twenty-first century is, after all, only a nanosecond in terms of social evolution. The existence of other repositories of knowledge, with their inherent potential for regeneration, is precisely why great historical figures, from Confucius to Machiavelli (two of my personal favourites, among countless others), continue to be read widely today. Sometimes, too, social psychological wisdom is beautifully encapsulated in local proverbs and adages (for a diverse sample, visit www.quotesandsayings.com; for an academic journal devoted entirely to the study of proverbs, visit www.deproverbio.com). To take just one example on the broad issue of individual versus social achievement, traditional wisdom in East Africa asserts that *Kugona pakati nkuyambira*, meaning 'To sleep in the middle [of the group, where it is warmest] is to be first' (Afro-centric Alliance 2001, p. 60). Advice like this reflects what we will later learn from scholarly research about the so-called tall poppy syndrome, and indeed presages what we learn in the book generally (for a discussion of tall poppy syndrome in New Zealand, see Harrington & Liu 2002; in Australia, see Feather 1994).

Given this historical appreciation, the question naturally arises, what can the relatively fledgling academic discipline of social psychology add to existing knowledge? One immediate answer is that the discipline brings a unique attitude to deciding how to evaluate social psychological wisdom. The concept of *attitude* is defined technically in chapter 4. Here, however, the term is used in a colloquial sense, as in describing a teenager who wears a cap with the peak facing backwards — who turns everything around and questions it. In this case, as we shall see shortly, social psychological enquiry includes questioning of traditional proverbs, as well as other forms of folk wisdom, such as 'common sense', by empirically testing the principles they espouse.

Results from these tests support the common suspicion that traditional wisdoms do not always hold water. Sometimes, however, such a conclusion is taken too far, for example when traditions are dismissed as 'inconsistent' and 'unscientific'. Consider the following contradictory adages: 'Two heads are better than one' and 'Too many cooks spoil the broth'; 'The more the merrier' and 'Three's a crowd'; 'Many hands make light work' and 'If you want something done well, do it yourself' (Carron & Hausenblas 1998, p. 7). But such implicitly peremptory dismissals treat folk wisdom too lightly. Of course adages and proverbs can be found that contradict one another when taken too broadly. Most of them, though, have a core of good sense within a range of applicability, however implicit that may be. 'Birds of a feather flock together' and 'Opposites attract' may appear contradictory, but, as we shall see in chapters 8 and 9, each offers reasonable advice for different stages of interpersonal relations. Each of them is thus valid in a particular social context.

Complementarity like this, many of us would agree, means that folk wisdom offers the discipline a store of material worthy of scientific investigation. Some of this traditional wisdom, it turns out, is incredibly robust. The inherent value in the activity of 'perspective sharing' (chapter 7) is found in the traditional wisdom of Native North Americans, which maintains that it is unwise to judge others until you have 'walked a mile in their moccasins'. This principle underlies and helps link together the middle section of this book: it concerns the wisdom of reducing prejudice towards others by finding ways to share their experiences. Such experiences, we learn from theory and evidence, are indeed a major source of enlightenment and of great relevance for contemporary global society.

In addition to testing the wisdom of everyday folk traditions, the social psychology discipline has generated much wisdom of its own. Undoubtedly, some of this learning has come about through studying the contexts in which proverbial wisdoms work and those in which they do not. Yet social psychology has also made its own contribution to our understanding of social influence. This contribution has included, for instance, the discovery that 'commonsense' ideas about what motivates social behaviour are often wrong. A classic example is a tendency to overestimate the role of 'personality' in social behaviour (chapter 6; Choi, Nisbett & Norenzayan 1999). Other discoveries involve ideas that have possibly never been seriously considered by common sense. The clearest way of demonstrating *this* kind of contribution is by reviewing some of the classic studies in social psychology using the themes of context, communication and culture (see 'Ethos and direction').

Context: Triplett and social facilitation

Much of our contemporary understanding of social behaviour can be traced to the study of sporting performance. A prime example of this study is the archival and experimental observations made by Norman Triplett (1897). Triplett, a keen bicycle racing enthusiast, observed from archives that greater speeds were achieved when the racers performed in company and/or in front of a crowd of spectators than when performing solo against the clock. As a scientist, Triplett wondered if this observation might generalise to other settings, and proceeded to test this possibility using a radically different performance setting. He asked children to wind standard lengths of twine onto reels, either alone against the clock, or in the company of another child performing the same task. As with the cycle times, average performance in this activity was improved when the children acted in the company of the smallest possible crowd, rather than alone against the clock. The original observation, then, was not attributable to physical slipstream or the like; improved performance was due to social influence.

Since it held up across diverse settings, Triplett's observation also suggested that the presence of others might have a robust impact on performance when athletes (indeed, performers generally) reach for 'their best'. Subsequently published research, discussed in chapter 2, supported Triplett's basic process, which has since become known as **social facilitation** (for a recent example, see Platania & Moran 2001). This term denotes the facilitation effect that others can have on skilled performance (Zajonc 1965b). In later chapters we will see that social facilitation forms the bedrock for a range of social behaviours, and that it is highly relevant to the wider process of glocalisation. For now, however, there is a more immediate lesson to be grasped. The mere presence of others performing the same activity, for whatever reason, was sufficient to improve performance beyond a solo best, even though the type of social situation was completely nominal — that is, there were no real social ties, no social history, no real social interaction and no 'team' future. Yet the introduction of just one other person still exerted a marked and manifest influence on performance. People could somehow be moved to perform beyond their level best by even the slightest social *context*.

Communication: Sherif and social norms

Muzafer Sherif (1936) and Frederic Bartlett (1932) moved a step beyond this most basic of influencing agencies, which we can term the crowd. Despite the later date of his work, the story begins with Sherif.

Sherif was interested in groups in general and group formation in particular. Groups are pretty much the core business of social psychology. They are more enduring than crowds, for they have a future. Sherif saw the foundation for this future as resting on whether they manage to construct coherent social norms. Norms are the social cement of any group; they apply to any standards of behaviour, beliefs or feelings. In everyday life, we are constantly under the influence of social norms, ranging from those that regulate classroom conduct, to those that give us a sense of who we are. Such implicitly agreed standards help us reduce ambiguity in, and cope with, everyday life. They give it meaning for us. In a word, norms are highly functional. Sherif's logic at the time was that if norms were really so functional, then they would invariably and spontaneously develop whenever (1) people were faced with a totally novel and therefore inherently ambiguous situation, and (2) people were afforded an opportunity to *communicate* with each other.

Sherif created what was surely a wholly novel experimental problem. Seated in a completely darkened room, the subjects were asked to estimate the distance and direction of apparent movement of an apparently labile pinpoint of light. The light was actually physically fixed, and the movement was illusory. When judging the light's movement alone, each individual gradually converged on a stable estimate — a kind of personal standard. These personal norms were initially quite idiosyncratic; however, people were then brought together in the same pitch-dark room and again asked to call out their estimates of distance moved by the light. A degree of verbal communication was therefore introduced. Under these minimal communication conditions, and precisely as Sherif's theory had predicted, a group standard, or norm, spontaneously emerged. A social influence process of **convergence** on a common norm took place.

It is important to note at the outset that at no point in Sherif's procedure was any kind of directive made to the group that they 'should' converge; there was no persuasion. The kind of norm that emerged out of this non-coercive situation reportedly persisted in private, individual judgements made after the group session for up to one year afterwards (Rohrer et al. 1954). In other words, the social experience of unconstrained convergence was sufficient to produce real and lasting personal change. Social influence exerted mutually under minimal constraint was very durable.

What conclusions can we extract from Sherif's classic findings? One of its central points is surely that social interaction generally, and verbal communication in particular, will spontaneously function to solve a problem at hand. In this case, communication helped to establish a consensus (a norm), which then functioned to reassure people that they had found the 'right answer'. When travelling in foreign countries, and experiencing 'culture shock', many of us are quietly relieved to be able to communicate with others from our own, familiar background. In the workplace, too, managers may find comfort in convergence with others when recommending new wage levels (Wilke & Van Knippenberg 1990). Ambiguity is often unsettling and threatening, and establishing norms, through communication with others, helps alleviate this state. To the extent that such norms are one of the defining features of any group, Sherif had indeed managed to capture group formation in flight. But what is also sometimes overlooked is that the process of group formation itself, and thereby the core business of social psychology, depended upon communication.

What was the end product of this communication? Sherif might have said that it resulted in a new norm, and a new form of social reality. He might have concluded that *reality is socially constructed*. This, as we will see, has become a hugely influential idea in the wider social psychological literature — from Festinger (1950, 1954) and Gergen (1973) to Lieberman (1999) and Buunk & Mussweiler (2001).

In Bartlett's most famous study, *The War of the Ghosts*, an indigenous folk story was told and retold along a chain of narrators (Bartlett 1932). As the story progressed along this chain, its form and content were progressively altered to fit more closely with the storytellers' own cultural norms. For example, traditional 'canoes' gradually transformed into twentieth-century 'boats'; and supernatural transcendence from one world to another was reconfigured as the Western idea of 'clinical' death (1932, p. 123). This sort of finding remains very important to this day, for it ties communication to cultural reconstruction, reminding us that life's events are never wholly novel (as Sherif's analogue might implicitly suggest). In real life, we come to every social situation with at least one ready-made set of social constructs that often influences our behaviour considerably (Liu et al. 1999).

Culture: Gergen and cultural influence

Perhaps the foremost advocate of culture's influence on social behaviour is Kenneth Gergen, who in 1973 published a landmark paper that rocked Western social psychology to its core. In it, he dared to propose that social psychology was itself embedded in a particular cultural framework. In his view, this framework severely limited what Western social psychology could say about social processes in other cultures and at other times in human history. According to Gergen, most social processes undergo 'gross modifications' over time and across cultural settings (1973, p. 313). Moreover, once we learn about any social process through social psychology, this knowledge 'increases alternatives to action, and previous patterns of behaviour are modified or dissolved' (p. 313). Therefore, social psychology cannot call itself a science — first, because no theory is universal, and second, because as soon as we learn how an influence process works, we may become at least partially immune to it; that is, the scientific principle may no longer 'work'.

Many people, of course, study social influence precisely because they want to free themselves from the social influence exerted by others. Their aim is to become sufficiently enlightened to sidestep influence processes to which they might otherwise be vulnerable. In this sense, social psychology exists to put itself out of business. Also, and to take up the first of Gergen's themes, cultures vary substantially in terms of what is considered 'normal'. Bartlett's study certainly suggests this, as does Sherif's work (convergence may be anathema to anarchists, for example). Against this, it could be objected that social facilitation (for instance) is based on biological processes of arousal (see chapter 2), rendering it immune to any influence of culture. But even there, cultures vary in the emphasis placed on heeding social context. In more collectivistic societies, for instance, people are taught to pay more attention to the thoughts and feelings of others around them (Nisbett et al. 2001). For these people, we would expect the facilitation effect of a crowd to increase, because being watched by it would mean more. Culture would have an impact after all (for an alternative example related to physiology, temperature and aggression, see Van de Vliert et al. 1999).

Hence, it can be agreed with Gergen that there is always space for culture to modify social processes. Sometimes this means the glass is half empty, because a process often does not travel well across cultures. At other times, however, the glass is half full, since the very space in which culture exerts an influence renders a basic process like social facilitation more relevant, not less.

On balance, it is not difficult to see why Gergen's seminal paper precipitated what became known as 'the crisis' (of confidence) in social psychology. This book, however, takes the position that Gergen (perhaps deliberately) overstated his case. As one of the reviewers of this chapter pointed out, singing on the bus will always 'coerce' many of us into joining in, even though we know and understand the influence dynamics that make us do it, simply to avoid looking like a stick-in-the-mud. Social psychology is beginning to shake off this sense of crisis, although Gergen's work continues to hold valuable lessons for the new millennium. In this book, for instance, we will use one of Gergen's major tests for assessing whether or not a principle is robust — that is, how well it replicates across diverse cultural contexts (this is an extension of Triplett's reasoning, introduced on page 11 and discussed more fully in chapters 9 and 10). We will also test the 'singing on the bus' hypothesis — for example in chapter 2, on helping behaviour among students who had recently studied the social psychology of helping.

Perhaps the most enduring of Gergen's lessons is that the influence of *culture*, and thereby localisation, should never be underestimated. To find out why, we need to briefly review a classic organisational survey, conducted by Hofstede (1980). This study remains crucial today, because it seeks to describe and explain cultural diversity itself, and it is still incredibly influential across the social sciences (Special Commentary 2001). This seminal study undertook a massive poll of some 117 000 sales and service employees at IBM outlets across 53 countries around the world. Because IBM has its own organisational culture, Hofstede argued that any difference he was able to detect between countries would probably constitute a conservative estimate of a more significant phenomenon. He believed that IBM's corporate culture would act, if anything, to stifle and suppress national differences. This argument is somewhat dubious. Prestigious multinationals may recruit and retain people who already fit a certain mould, and those individuals might not be representative of the wider population, either inside a particular host nation or across the company's host nations as a whole. As we will see in chapter 8, organisations do sometimes recruit and retain candidates who resemble themselves in some way. Clearly, therefore, we need to corroborate Hofstede's findings externally by testing them against other studies.

When we apply this yardstick to Hofstede's original work, at least two of his findings appear to be robust. These recurring themes, which have appeared and reappeared in other authors' work, both in different population groups (e.g. Trompenaars 1993) and in different countries (e.g. Schwartz 1996), are the dimensions of *individualism–collectivism* and *power distance*.

Individualism–collectivism

This conceptual continuum signifies the extent to which individuals or groups are oriented towards themselves (individualism) or towards others, such as their extended family and other primary reference groups (collectivism). Individualism means considering 'me' before 'we', while collectivism represents the reverse. In organisational life, for example, a collectivist orientation might mean maintaining in-group relations as the basis for task completion, rather than the other way round. Collectivism, in this sense, may be related to familiar ideas such as mateship and comradeship more generally.

Power distance

Power distance refers to the extent to which it is accepted, within a group, that power should be distributed unequally and hierarchically. People who believe in hierarchies are also likely to prefer to keep a certain distance between themselves and those at other levels within the structure. Power distance signifies feeling comfortable with not coming too close, too often, to those authority figures. It means believing that distance ought to be maintained between legitimately positioned individuals in an established hierarchy. Low power distance, or egalitarianism, means, by contrast, that employees consider themselves as good as each other and their masters (Colling 1992, p. 11). A colleague once encapsulated this idea for me by describing a newspaper cartoon he had seen. In this strip, the driver of a smart-looking car has stopped on a country road to offer a lift to a passing drifter. The drifter, however, takes one look at the besuited driver in his plush car, and slams shut the door with the words, 'Open your *own* ******* gates!' I myself later had one or two experiences like this in Darwin. (In Darwin's defence, see chapter 10 on humidity and aggression.)

The two dimensions of individualism–collectivism and power distance are illustrated in figure 1.1. This 'values grid' actually goes beyond the categorisation attributable to Hofstede. It helps us to see that the same person can occupy different quadrants depending on social context. In figure 1.1 hierarchical individualism on the track and field gives way to horizontal collectivism at the supporters' end of the stadium. People change according to social circumstance. Figure 1.1 shows that everyone is part collectivist and part individualist, favouring power distance or egalitarianism as the occasion demands. This being so, any overall differences between people from different cultural backgrounds, like those dimensions found by Hofstede (1980), simply reflect where those groups, on average, spend most of their time (Kagitçibasi 1992).

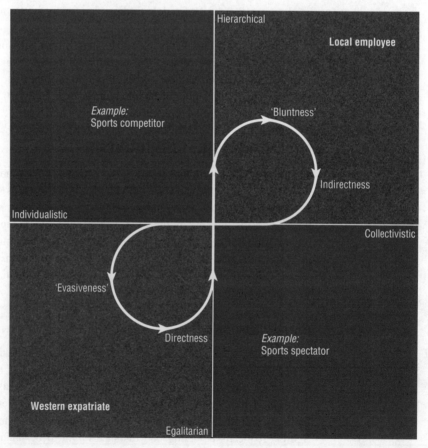

Figure 1.1   A values grid   *Source:* Carr, Bolitho and Purcell (1999).

The values grid

The values grid represented in figure 1.1 will help us to begin thinking about how social parties of differing predominant orientation are liable to interact with each other. One of the most common sources of social conflict is that different people are 'coming from' different quadrants in figure 1.1 during their interactions. Through figure 1.1 we portray what may happen when a relatively individualist and egalitarian manager (say, an Australian or New Zealand expatriate) attempts to appraise the (unsatisfactory) performance of an opposite-minded (host national) employee (Giacalone & Beard 1994). Being relatively individualist and egalitarian, this expatriate tends to believe in one-on-one directness at work, and also in speaking bluntly to individual employees whose performance is perceived to fall short of the norm. Being relatively collectivist and power distant, the host national tends to favour social harmony over individual bluntness, and feels relatively uncomfortable with one-on-one communication with a superior. Unaware of this, the manager speaks directly to the employee, whose first reaction is to attempt to keep matters indirect and so harmonious. To the expatriate, however, this looks like evasiveness. Now, more than ever, he feels that this employee needs 'straightening out'. The expatriate manager therefore becomes even more direct, which again elicits an equal and opposite reaction from the local employee. And so, as figure 1.1 depicts, the dynamics of conflict escalate in a vicious circle that eventually results in a breakdown in work relations. Such dynamics are not unusual in workplaces around the world today, and may be partly responsible for the lack of completion, high turnover and communication failures that reportedly dog international assignments (Muchinsky 2000). The players envisaged in figure 1.1 could be individuals from a range of cultural backgrounds (for some warnings on over-generalising about particular cultural groups, see chapter 6).

The general point here is that we need more than survey snapshots of what different groups tend to value. Photo stills do not inform us about the kind of intercultural interactions that may ensue whenever members of these groups encounter each other — whether in the workplace, the community or an educational institution, or indeed at a holiday destination (for a discussion of these dynamics across different intercultural partnerships, see chapter 7). Today, more than ever, we have to be able to understand intercultural interactions. Indeed, a combination of the values just outlined could equally easily be found within groups, whether cultural, national, community or organisational, as between them (for a discussion of diversity in values within these groups, see Schwartz 1996).

Do individualism–collectivism and power distance, the axes of difference depicted in figure 1.1, really influence people so profoundly? Perhaps the most impressive supporting evidence comes from the numerous replications of another classic in social psychology — what we will term the 'line-length' experiment conducted by Asch (1956).

The line-length study

Solomon Asch, a Jewish emigrant who left Western Europe before the rise of Nazism, sought answers to questions about the Holocaust. One of these was why so many people had apparently remained silent in the face of Nazi atrocities. One way of explaining this was as a gross distortion of reality that many people, rather surprisingly, went along with. In a laboratory representation of how this distortion might have been perpetuated, rather than challenged and so perhaps dispelled, Asch arranged for groups of seven to nine individuals (all but one of them stooges, or 'confederates') to successively call out a manifestly wrong judgement concerning which of three comparison lines matched a standard line in length. In each group sat a lone genuine participant, whose own call was to be made after hearing most of the other, false judgements. Asch's participants were university students in the United States, which would later emerge in Hofstede's survey as ranking highest of all on individualism. Asch expected that such values, especially among 'free-thinking' university students, would assist his participants to speak out against an unacceptable norm. Instead, he found that only one in four students remained completely independent on all of his 12 test trials. In total, these relatively 'free-spirited' undergraduate participants succumbed to a grossly distorted vision of reality on one in every three of the test trials. A major reason for this silence, Asch learned in post-sessional interviews, was the perceived threat of ridicule. The line-length situation had cowed these individuals into public **conformity**.

Given the diversity between the US college sample and the original population of interest to the researcher, a broader implication was now becoming evident. Following the line of reasoning used by both Triplett and Gergen — that result replication across diverse settings indicates durability — alternative points of view, wherever they were represented, might be silenced just the same. Culture would not matter.

Intuition, therefore, even from a scientist of Asch's colossal stature, had apparently been proved wrong. The 'obvious' common sense (his starting hypothesis does 'make sense' to most of us, does it not?) was not so obvious after all. This is one of the most enduring lessons of social psychology, and one of the main reasons we continue to conduct research. In fact, it was research that eventually clarified the role that culture might have in the line-length situation. The evidence for this came much later, through a detailed analysis of 133 global replications of Asch's study (Bond & Smith 1996). This review study aimed to identify the best predictors of precise conformity rate from a wide range of possible candidates. These candidates included the participants' gender; their year of study; the size of the majority; the degree of familiarity among the participants; the anonymity of their responses; and the precise configuration of the visual materials used (layout, line lengths etc.). Buried among these 'material' factors were Hofstede's original indices of individualism–collectivism and power distance, but these were rank outsiders. It would be a tall order indeed to expect such rough estimates of culture-wide values, based on a sample of IBM employees from mostly earlier times, to out-predict clear, intuitive favourites such as gender.

But out-predict them they did. The top predictor of precise conformity rate turned out to be scores on *individualism–collectivism* among IBM employees in that particular country (for an alternative example of testing for this kind of relationship, this time in the domain of love, see Levine et al. 1995). Also related to the level of conformity obtained was national belief in ascribed status, a factor that clearly resembles *power distance*. Overall, therefore, this study provides an impressive demonstration that social behaviour cannot be separated from its cultural context.

We need not go as far with this idea as Gergen did, however. Asch's central finding — that most people complied — was replicated across a range of cultural settings. In fact, if anything, change in behaviour towards the group norm proved to be even more resilient in comparatively collectivist contexts than in the original, relatively individualist one (Smith & Bond 1993). From these data, at least, we cannot infer that social psychology is built on shifting sands. And if we fast-forward for a moment to the process of globalisation, the same point may hold. In an increasingly global culture of 'individual rights', what was once fear of not upsetting the majority has arguably become fear of not upsetting minorities (see chapter 7, on implicit stereotyping). Whether or not such superficial forms of political correctness provide a sustainable basis for social development is currently being tested in various social psychological studies (see chapter 7 on implicit 'rebound' effects). Whatever the outcome of these studies, the point here is that subjective pressures towards uniformity can exist in the most 'unlikely' places, even in a supposedly more tolerant society. In other words, Asch-type effects are historically as well as culturally robust. Peer pressure, after all, is everywhere!

MORALS AND METHODS

Ethics

As well as their philosophical and practical implications, Gergen's arguments also have a sharp moral edge to them. Nowhere is this edge more acute than in the field of research methods. Today, codes of ethics are increasingly arguing for the recognition of cultural diversity, including our own cultural biases (Leach & Harbin 1997). The Australian Psychological Society, for example, has a number of provisos in its Code of Ethics (Australian Psychological Society 2000a), and Ethical Guidelines (Australian Psychological Society 2000b). So, too, does the New Zealand Psychological Society (www.psychology.org.nz/about/code.html). These living documents increasingly address the issue of respect for diverse outlooks, and should be consulted regularly for updates. The Australian guidelines, for example, currently include 'Guidelines for the Provision of Psychological Services for and the Conduct of Psychological Research with Aboriginal and Torres Strait Islander People of Australia' (2000b). In New Zealand, the major document overarching this debate is the 1840 Treaty of Waitangi (http://waitangi.com/index.html). This founding document has led to the acceptance of three principles in the conduct of research: Protection, Participation and Partnership (www.govt.nz/aboutnz/treaty.php3; this site presents both English and Māori versions as signed). A useful New Zealand publication about respecting cultural diversity in everyday practice can be found in Love and Whittaker (1997).

The broader historical context for concerns about diversity is an argument backed by deep-seated feeling. Psychologists and psychological researchers have in the past committed research robbery. Too often, that is, they have taken more 'out' of indigenous communities, by objectifying people in their career-building publications, than they have put back 'in' by way of community service and advocacy (Sanson & Dudgeon 2000; for an alternative, integrative model based on Māori traditional wisdom, see Durie 2000). In the past, then, they may have done significantly more harm than good (Riley 1998). To that extent, psychological research (much of which is at least partly social psychological) has broken the prime ethical directive of preserving **client welfare**.

A concrete example of how easily and insidiously the principle of respecting diversity can be infringed is found in how we name the effect observed by Asch. The literature prefers the term 'conformity', which has assumed the classic definition 'a change in behaviour or belief as a result of real or imagined group pressure'. This term (along with its definition) has derogatory connotations, often carrying the sense of relinquishing individuality under pressure, rather sheepishly, to a group. This is an inherently individualist and egalitarian perspective. Figure 1.1 suggests an alternative model that is more collectivist and power distant. This model helps us to reappraise the line-length situation as it might have appeared to participants in some of the indigenous communities in which the study was run. In Sierra Leone, for instance, one respondent remarked, 'When Temne people choose a thing, we must all agree with the decision. This is what we call *cooperation*' (Berry 1967, p. 417; emphasis added).

As Gergen (1994) reminds us, it is therefore possible to socially construct conformity differently in terms, not of moral torpor, but of social sensitivity (for a discussion of this positive side to conformity in a New Zealand sporting context, see Prapavessis & Carron 1997). The essence of such processes of **construction** is that people tacitly structure their belief systems and ways of experiencing and operating in the world around their core values, like the compass points in figure 1.1. As Sherif (and later Leon Festinger) might have said, reality is socially constructed.

This realisation has serious implications for social psychology. Description is supposed to be the most basic level of carrying out social science, and yet even here it seems impossible to be completely objective. It is all too easy to miss or misconstrue the meaning of social behaviour. The mere act of labelling any social behaviour can make us **ethnocentric**, for example. This is why many codes of ethics today contain repeated and explicit reminders about the dangers of labelling groups or group behaviour, including a requirement to regularly update one's knowledge, through the code, of how best to combat these dangers. Such developments are undoubtedly attributable in no small measure to the enlightening effects of Gergen's work.

Partly through the pressure of globalisation itself, perhaps, the rights of participants are also becoming more salient in research ethics. Some of the classic research studies in social psychology would not pass muster ethically today, because they would violate these rights. A clear example of this is Stanley Milgram's (1963) study of obedience. Milgram, a research assistant student of Asch's, was interested in people's **obedience** to authority figures who gave inhumane orders. In his original study Milgram, like Asch, expected that ordinary US citizens would be relatively resistant to inhumane orders from an authority figure. This thinking squared with what has been termed the 'Germans are different' account of the Holocaust. Once again, however, common sense, as well as expert opinion at the time, proved wrong. Milgram found it very difficult to have his genuine participant do anything *but* obey an inhumane order, in this case to give potentially fatal electric shocks to an apparently innocent victim. As in Asch's study, none of the participants internalised the inhumane acts they thought they were performing. No one came to privately believe that the acts of obedience they had performed were right. Influence was restricted to behaviour change only, or **compliance**. But behaviour was nonetheless radically controlled by the situation in which they found themselves (for discussions of the complementary role of some personality factors even in 'strong' situations like the Milgram simulation, see Blass 1991).

Amid the ethical furore provoked by this study, Milgram argued that the value of his findings outweighed any possible harm to the individuals who had provided them. The greater good was served, because society had become more enlightened, placed on its guard regarding the dangers of 'another Holocaust'. Milgram further argued that his participants were fully debriefed and ultimately simply relieved (not distressed) to find that the so-called 'learner' victim was actually a professional actor (for more details, see Milgram 1964). The issue of client welfare is still controversial, however, and a study like Milgram's would today contravene any number of guidelines across a variety of ethical codes. For example, generic requirements such as **informed consent** (or not deceiving participants and securing their written consent to continue) would likely pre-empt this study from ever taking place. Certainly, mild deception is often permitted in experiments today, provided debriefing feedback is given as soon as the study is completed, but an experimental situation of this severity would probably never be approved in the first place.

Simulation and observation

In methodological terms, Milgram (1963) was attempting to simulate what would happen in the real world if ordinary individuals were faced with a choice between disobeying an authority figure and harming another human being, possibly at the cost of the victim's life. From the participants' point of view, the realism (or fidelity) of the situation seems to have been high. They visibly trembled, sweated and displayed symptoms consistent with mild hysteria, such as nervous, stress-ridden laughter. Despite these indicators of high realism and impact, the situation was also advertised as a 'learning and memory experiment', which would have tilted the representation slightly towards medium fidelity (Blass 1999; Blass & Schmitt 2001). Finally, therefore, the original Milgram study was, and would largely have appeared to be, a university laboratory experiment (see also Milgram 1965).

A clearer example of genuine, high-fidelity **simulation and observation** is Philip Zimbardo's (1982) Stanford Prison study. In this study, Zimbardo took his pursuit of realism to extraordinary lengths. During the first few hours of the study the 'prisoners' were rounded up in their home suburb (no doubt to their great consternation), deloused, given prison numbers and realistically inducted into life in jail. Every attempt was made to faithfully re-create day-to-day life in a real prison. Fidelity to the real world was, therefore, consistently high (for a web-based overview of the methodology and degree of realism it employed, visit www.socialpsychology.org or www.prisonexp.org).

Zimbardo's study was a response to national concern over alleged brutalities in the US prison system at the time. Influenced perhaps by both Milgram and Asch, Zimbardo suspected that much of the blame being levelled at brutality among the guards was misplaced. Rather than personality ('prison guards are different'),

Zimbardo thought that situation influence ('prisons are peculiar places') might be the problem. If this was right, he reasoned, even model citizens, with perfectly 'normal' personalities, could become brutish and warped by working in a simulated prison system. Zimbardo therefore decided to observe what could happen to model citizens who were randomly allocated to the roles of prisoners and guards.

The simulation was originally scheduled to run for a fortnight, but it had to be halted after less than a week. This was primarily because the guards had become more brutal than even Zimbardo had expected ('Power tends to corrupt' — Lord Acton 1887, *Oxford Dictionary of Quotations*). Equally disturbing was the apparent internalisation of their 'low-life' status by the prisoners themselves. Zimbardo described the prisoners as 'conforming in thought and complying in deed' (1982, p. 251).

Again, under today's ethical criteria, and like Milgram's obedience study, the Stanford Prison study would not have been allowed to run. At the time, however, attempts were made to replicate both of these provocative studies in other countries. Australia is one place where both studies were repeated (for a discussion of obedience to authority in a New Zealand context, see Levy 1995). In Hofstede's study, Australia had received a relatively low score on power distance, which, combined with Gergen's psychohistorical perspective (Australia being a former penal colony), suggests that we should see somewhat reduced levels of obedience to authority and less internalisation of roles, at least among those participants playing the role of 'prisoners'.

CRITICAL NARRATIVE

1.1

Dialogues within a prison simulation

The Zimbardo study
Guard A (from his diary), prior to the study: 'As I am a pacifist and non-aggressive individual, I cannot foresee a time when I might maltreat other living things.'
Third day: 'This was my first chance to exercise the kind of manipulative power that I really like.'
Fifth day: 'I harass Sarge, who continues to stubbornly over-respond to commands. I have singled him out for special abuse both because he begs for it and because I simply don't like him.'

Source: McCarthy (1985, p. 339).

The Lovibund study
Officer: 'Get your head in.'
Prisoner: 'Why?'
Officer: 'Because I'm an officer and you're a prisoner and I'm telling you — that's why!'
Prisoner: 'It's an open window and I've got a right to look out.'
Officer: 'In a real prison there wouldn't be an open window, and as such you wouldn't have the right to look out. Now get your head in!'
Prisoner: 'Well, it isn't a real prison is it, and I'll look out when I want to — mate!'
Officer: 'You're on report.'
Prisoner: 'Big deal.'

Source: Lovibund et al. (1979, p. 279). Reproduced with permission.

This 'part reduction' did in fact materialise in reruns of both Milgram's obedience study (Kilham & Mann 1974) and Zimbardo's prison simulation (Lovibund, Mithiran & Adams 1979). These studies were not exact replications. In the Australian study of obedience, for instance, the experimenter was generally less 'authoritative' and more unconventional in appearance, while in the simulated prison different levels of training for the guards were added to the methodology. Those alterations notwithstanding, the broad pattern of findings remains consistent with at least one basic proposal: Many of the 'classics' in social psychology, while travelling reasonably well, are influenced significantly by culture, communication and context. These three themes, and the kinds of influence they can exert, are vividly brought to life in critical narrative 1.1, while the enduring relevance (and controversial nature) of the study is illustrated in critical narrative 1.2.

CRITICAL NARRATIVE 1.2

The continuing relevance of a controversial paradigm

BBC recasts the Stanford Prison experiment

In October 2001, the British Broadcasting Corporation (BBC) announced its plans to replicate the Stanford Prison [study] for television and began recruiting participants for its program ... When filming began ... , 15 volunteers were incarcerated in a television studio converted into a 'social environment' that divided the participants into oppressors and the oppressed; and like its famous model, the psychologists conducting the BBC's study called a halt to the project before it was scheduled to end. On January 24, 2002, the *Guardian* newspaper reported that scientists overseeing the BBC project became concerned that the emotional and physical wellbeing of the participants was in danger of being compromised.

According to the article, 'The BBC study was overseen by two psychologists ... An independent "ethical committee" also monitored the project. This committee, it is thought, in consultation with the psychologists, made the decision to terminate the study, due to last ten days, after eight or nine. Professor [name suppressed] denied the report, stating that the study "was brought to a conclusion but it was not terminated — it had satisfied our scientific goals". He did, however, admit that "there were a few interpersonal tensions and we didn't want it to escalate, but we'd already got a tremendous amount of scientific data and we didn't need to go any further". A BBC spokesman said that everyone was conscious of the impact of the original study, and wanted to ensure that no harm came to the participants. "It was planned that the study would last ten days but, aware of the stresses under which volunteers might find themselves, the BBC was always prepared, if necessary, to withdraw individuals or end it early. The psychologists are confident that the material they have will change the way we think about the nature of power and powerlessness."'

Although the BBC's factual programs department, not its entertainment division, produced it, British critics have questioned whether the study is serious science or 'reality TV gone mad', labelling the project as a cynically ratings-motivated 'Big Brother with even less taste'. Philip Zimbardo, who conducted the original Stanford study, has also expressed his scepticism: 'That kind of research is now considered to be unethical and should not be redone just for sensational TV and survivor-type glamour'. Nevertheless, the BBC plans to televise the program in April or May.

Source: Psychology International (2002).

Laboratory and field experiments

Both Asch (1956) and Milgram (1965) went on to carefully manipulate single aspects of the immediate social context independently of everything else in the original scenario. For example, one of the 'confederates' was instructed to rebel against the group or authority figure. The researchers then observed what happened next, in terms of compliance or obedience levels, compared with their control condition (the original scenario). In so doing, they were investigating the impact of an independent variable (observed rebellion) on a dependent variable (conformity to the group or obedience to authority). Such controlled manipulation of an independent variable (divorced from everything else in the experiment) and noting its effect on a dependent variable (compared with the control condition) is the essence of **experimentation**.

Experimentation may take one of two basic forms, the **laboratory experiment** and the **field experiment**. A difference between laboratory and field experiments is that participants in a field experiment do not know that they are taking part in an experiment. Also, the situation under study is an existing one, rather than being created under laboratory conditions, and the results (although ethically more dubious in terms of the principle of informed consent) may apply more readily to the real world. Laboratory experiments give the experimenter more control. Under these definitions, Asch's and Milgram's variations on their original studies are clearly laboratory experiments. The task and surroundings were essentially artificial and controlled — for example, the researchers could systematically vary the number of complying or obeying 'confederates' without changing anything else in the representation. Sherif's study, too, was a laboratory experiment, to the extent that he carefully introduced the prospect of communication only after personal standards had been established. This is a *repeated measures* design, as distinct from Asch's and Milgram's *between-groups* design, in which one group experienced the independent variable while another did not. Triplett's study also employed the latter design but more closely resembled a field experiment. Being children, the participants would probably have experienced the situation as an everyday competition. The independent variable here was the relatively naturalistic presence of a fellow competitor, while the dependent variable was the spontaneously resulting performance.

From this brief introductory review, we can perhaps discern that a major bone of contention with experimentation, in many people's eyes, is its emphasis on *intervention*. Because of its fundamental concern with *manipulation*, it inevitably collides with issues of people's personal *rights*. By subjecting people to 'manipulation', experimentation inevitably objectifies the person being manipulated. Since these people's rights — not to be objectified and not to be manipulated — are at the forefront of human consciousness today, the culture of experimentation carries with it an ever-present potential to confront and affront ethical principles. This potential is of special concern to university and other research ethics committees. Thus, experimentation is increasingly seen by some groups as both degrading and disrespectful.

Much less ethically 'interventionist' as research tools are the **sample survey** (or survey) and the **case study** (or case).

Surveys and cases

We have seen that Hofstede chose the survey form of research inquiry for his classic cross-cultural study of work values. But no research is perfect, and Hofstede's seminal study can still be criticised for overlooking many of the subtleties of cultural dimensions.

To give one example, Australia ranked as number two (behind the United States) in terms of the individualism dimension depicted in figure 1.1. Yet Australia has many traditions that revolve around 'mateship' and, in that sense, collectivism (Colling 1992). Colling argues that many Australians endorse elements of both individualism (e.g. 'having a go') *and* collectivism (for a fuller discussion of gender and mateship, see chapter 9). Such complexity is by no means new in Australia (Conway 1971). Similarly, New Zealand was sixth (out of 53 countries) in terms of individualism; New Zealanders value highly their individual ingenuity and resourcefulness. Yet they, too, can be strong on mateship. The 'sledge-hammer' approach of the sample survey, therefore, often misses very important cultural nuances, complexities and pluralisms.

Like Hofstede's study, surveys also tend to be on a large scale, which means they have to be heavily structured. This, in turn, means that someone has to structure them, and this inevitably introduces risks that participants will be constrained to respond within the researcher's inevitably localised and potentially biased frame of reference. Such constraints are perhaps especially likely in culturally diverse settings. Accordingly, in studies straddling those kinds of settings, concerted and innovative attempts have been made to address the issue of ethnocentrism and respect for cultural diversity. For example, researchers have worked closely with indigenous groups when generating the survey items at the questionnaire design stage (The Chinese Culture Connection 1987). These improvements have nonetheless tended to remain anchored in one cultural group, rather than from the outset involving all the international stakeholder groups to be surveyed. Thus, the questionnaire design process has tended to fall short of a fully de-centred approach, from the item-generating stage onwards (Aus–Thai Project Team 1998).

Cases may become biased towards the researcher's point of view or towards the participant. When the word 'case' implicitly positions the person or group described in any kind of 'sick', or pathogenic, role, the researcher's point of view is often favoured. A more empowering form of the case would cede centre stage to the participants themselves, allowing them to tell their story in their own words. To signal this, the term **critical narrative** is adopted in place of 'case'. A critical narrative often takes the form of a story, its content focused on particular incidents and its ending being told as either negative or positive (Flanagan 1954). Surveys can approximate this kind of latitude by embracing minimally structured, projective techniques, such as completing sentences or interpreting ambiguous pictures (Liggett 1983). For the most part, however, surveys are still relatively constrained rather than free to allow the equitable construction of reality, as highlighted by Sherif and Bartlett. Narrative, by contrast, is a robust and naturally occurring communication mode across diverse cultures and contexts. Allowing people to 'tell their own stories' is therefore a relatively effective way of respecting cultural diversity.

In being relatively non-interventionist, and overtly respecting the value-laden nature of all social psychology, critical narratives offer a less ethically contentious way of conducting much social research (for an extended discussion of the role of the case study as a research tool for studying organisational groups, see Bryman 1989; Bachiochi & Weiner 2002). Such overtly pro-participant methods are also a means of sharing perspectives (as discussed earlier). In this sense, according to our preceding analysis, they have a potential to serve the valuable enlightenment function described for social psychology by the likes of Gergen (1994b).

Critical narratives allow us to capture influence in motion. The only way to demonstrate fully *how* this is done is to provide an actual example. The one I have chosen for this illustration focuses on the dynamic interplay between individual and social achievement. Critical narrative 1.3 is set in a post-industrial city in Australia, although it might equally have happened in New Zealand. As you read the narrative, consider whether the story, as told by a former employee in the organisation in question, manages to capture some of the subtly interactive, glocal dynamics of achievement. Consider also whether using the same method could help to enlighten us about the social psychology of achievement in other parts of the world (Chi-yue Chiu & Ying-yi Hong 1997). Does the narrative itself help you to think of ways to save other jobs in jeopardy? Such questions might form the basis of a productive and stimulating class exercise. We will be returning periodically in the book to this powerful and disturbing story.

CRITICAL NARRATIVE 1.3

The Buick Bar & Grill

After 18 months of market research, a consortium of North American investors selected a medium-sized Australian coastal city in which they planned to develop the prototype for a chain of entertainment centres throughout the country. The 'Buick Bar & Grill' concept envisaged a multi-purpose complex consisting of a 200-seat restaurant, a night club, a cocktail bar and a 'theme' bar emphasising Australian sporting icons. Facilities were top-of-the-range. No expense was spared on fitting out the venue in order to obtain a uniquely American atmosphere, and to ensure that the staff had the most modern equipment and comfortable working environment.

The manager and part-owner of the complex was an American, Kirk Reed. Reed was still in his early thirties but had already acquired much experience in the US hospitality industry. After leaving school at age 16, Reed got his first job as a kitchen hand in a local restaurant. Four years later he owned it. By the time he was 25 he was also part-owner of two bars. Reed was a self-made man who had worked his way up from the bottom to his current position, and he believed that any individual with motivation and energy was capable of doing the same.

In November 1993 advertisements were run in the local Australian newspaper for applications to positions as bartender, cocktail waiter, bar/food runner, cook and kitchen hand. The ads were visually exciting and emphasised the fact that The Buick Bar & Grill was to be an exciting workplace, 'rapidly expanding ... highly motivated' and full of opportunities. More than 1800 people applied for the 77 vacancies.

Selection interviews were two-tiered. Company trainers, personally recruited by Reed in the United States, carried out a first interview. As well as conducting training, they would later act as temporary managers of specific sections (the kitchen, restaurant

or bar). Reed carried out a second interview. These interviews were fast-paced and informal, with no standard structure or set duration. Previous qualifications were not an issue. The criterion for job selection was to impress Reed with one's own enthusiasm, motivation and desire to succeed. The 77 successful candidates were not informed of the positions they had won. Instead, they were congratulated and invited to attend a two-week training program.

At the outset of the training program, all new staff members received detailed employment manuals and job descriptions. Many staff members were surprised to discover that they had been placed in jobs for which they had no prior experience. Reed then explained the concept of The Buick Bar & Grill in detail. He was an extremely fluent and interesting speaker, who held his audience's attention well. Reed's energy and his desire for success were apparent, and he continually referred to the management and staff of Buick's as a 'family'. He placed great emphasis on teamwork and communication, and he pointed out that the franchising of Buick's would begin within six months. He was therefore looking for 'peak performers ... staff with the little bit more that separated them from the crowd', who would be promoted to trainee managers, with the long-term goal of managing Buick's clubs in various locations around the country.

Reed also explained the pay system at Buick's. Regardless of job description, age, experience or qualifications, every staff member (excluding management, who were on a salary) was to receive a flat rate of $10.00 an hour. Penalty and overtime rates did not apply. It was stressed that all 77 staff members were to start off as 'equals in the family'.

Those who 'soared above the already high standards set at The Buick Bar & Grill' were to be rewarded with pay rises, promotions above the other staff and a variety of other benefits (e.g. free drinks and meals).

Training was intense and combined direct, hands-on work, role-plays and observational learning (modelling). The kitchen, restaurant and bar staff were trained as separate teams by their own trainer. During the training process Reed spent equal time with each of the three groups, to whom he offered words of encouragement, gave pep talks and repeatedly remarked that he was looking for outstanding individuals for promotion.

During training, three of the twenty kitchen staff unexpectedly resigned. All three were qualified chefs and claimed that it was unfair and demeaning to them to do the same tasks as 'unqualified' individuals with no previous experience. Furthermore, they claimed that the dishwasher should not be equal in pay and status with the chefs. These resignations did not seem to worry Reed, who stated that they simply made the task of identifying peak performers in the kitchen team easier — only 17 staff members now needed to be monitored for progress.

Despite these resignations, each of the teams developed into a highly cohesive group. This cohesion was encouraged formally through team-building exercises, games and various initiatives developed by Reed. The groups also became more cohesive outside of work. After the day's training, which finished around 10 p.m., each of the team's leaders took their group out for a 'few quiet drinks'. Friendships were built quickly and, considering the relatively short time the group members had known each other, group cohesion was surprisingly strong.

Opening night was a resounding success. All staff members were rostered on and, except for some first-night jitters, everything went smoothly and professionally. At a staff party afterwards, Reed congratulated the group and reminded everyone that he was looking for individuals who excelled in order to promote them.

(continued)

With the initial orientation, training and opening night out of the way, work began in earnest. Each of the three teams handled its tasks well, and everyone worked competently. Each of the separate teams made decisions on a group basis. In the kitchen, for instance, a decision was not ratified unless every member of the group agreed with it. This further enhanced group cohesion, so that individuals felt uncomfortable receiving praise from Reed in front of their colleagues. Those who received praise in front of the group would often refuse to accept the compliment, insisting that it go to the group as a whole.

Within a month of opening, Reed was placing pressure on the team trainers to identify individual peak performers for the possibility of promotion. The trainers replied that all of the team members were working well, but none seemed to be making any effort to stand out from the group. This, however, was not producing any negative effects on the operations. The team members were close-knit and working well together.

A week later, after much deliberation, Reed called a staff meeting to announce that three staff members had been promoted. Nicholas, a recent university graduate, had received the largest promotion, rising from waiter to trainee manager; Jason, a recent Higher School Certificate graduate, was promoted from food runner to floor supervisor; and Karen, who had worked in the hospitality industry for a number of years, was promoted from card girl to nightclub supervisor. Nicholas, Jason and Karen now had greater responsibilities and the power to delegate tasks to other staff members.

Four other promotions had been offered to various individuals, but none had accepted the offer. Reasons given for this included not wanting to rock the boat; feeling uncomfortable about being in charge of friends and the prospect of no longer being a member of the group. Reed explained that they would still be team players, and put their fears down to an inability to handle responsibility.

Tensions now began to arise between Nicholas, Jason and Karen, on the one hand, and the ordinary staff members on the other. Staff felt that they should not have to answer to them, and many heated arguments ensued. Staff members often ignored Nicholas's and Jason's requests, and those that were heeded were often done under protest. During breaks, Nicholas, Jason and Karen were ignored by the rest of the staff, while much of the informal conversation among staff members consisted of complaints and negative remarks concerning the three new managers.

It soon came to Reed's attention that the separate teams were operating ineffectively under the charge of the new managers compared with under the trainers. Customer orders were often wrong, productivity had dropped, arguments frequently broke out and the teams generally seemed apathetic. Reed had also received numerous anonymous complaints from staff members regarding the three new managers. He began to think that the new managers were ineffective. On close investigation, however, Reed found that Nicholas, Jason and Karen were working extremely hard and within the operational guidelines that he had set for them.

Reed now deduced that the problems being experienced were due to 'troublemakers', and he sacked ten staff members. At a staff meeting he described this sacking as 'cutting out an insidious cancer from within the organisation'. Staff members were now clearly instructed that the slightest form of resistance to requests made by Nicholas, Jason or Karen would be met by instant dismissal.

Within two weeks morale had plummeted among staff at The Buick Bar & Grill. Five staff members had been sacked or resigned, Reed was distrusted and resented by the

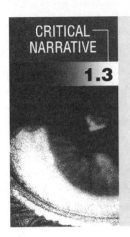

ordinary staff members, and Jason and Karen had both resigned. Their explanation was that they felt ostracised by the majority of the staff members. The low morale and the increasing rate of staff turnover led to a drop in the quality of the work being carried out by remaining staff members. This, in turn, led to frequent customer complaints and dissatisfaction.

In March 1994 poor sales at The Buick Bar & Grill forced the company into the hands of the receivers. Reed wanted to try to trade Buick's out of debt but no longer had either the staff or the finances to do this. Within four months The Buick Bar & Grill had closed down all operations until a new buyer could be found.

Source: McLoughlin & Carr (1994).

Emerging hybrid techniques

Much of the thrust in ongoing critical discourse about social psychology centres on the importance of meaning. Reality is socially constructed, and its construction process is guided by meaning, while the construction itself renders meaning. Thus, belief systems and their associated social norms should be viewed from the inside out, and subjectively shared, if social behaviour is to be reasonably well described and explained. Much of the criticism of surveys and experimental methods hinges on the potential loss of this essential meaning. Some of the most powerful of this criticism has emanated from South American social psychology, which concerns itself more with quality of life and community development than with research data per se (for a rare review in English, see Sánchez 1996; for a recent review of community psychology and Indigenisation in the Australasian region, see Gregory 2001). Others have sought to integrate both ends of the spectrum. Qualitative and quantitative techniques are alternated as the research process progresses. Surveys and other forms of structured interviews are preceded by detailed qualitative groundwork to determine the content of the questionnaire. At a later stage in the research, qualitative data, in the form of comments or illustrative narratives, can be reintroduced to help interpret the quantitative findings.

To illustrate the usefulness of keeping method and meaning together, consider the following innocuous survey option: 'I would rather depend on myself than others' (Rugimbana 1998). Agreement with this statement was found across the relatively individualistic and collectivistic groups in Rugimbana's study (involving Australia and Malaysia). But the statement had two, directly opposite meanings in the two settings — in one case referring to self-reliance, and in the other to not letting the family down. One meaning was profoundly individualist; the other was collectivist (for a detailed discussion of item equivalence issues, see Bartram 2001). As a consequence of this, equal responses on the 7-point measuring scale would miss cultural divergence completely (the same score reflects opposite meanings). If the researcher had not plumbed these opposite meanings beforehand using qualitative techniques, any subsequent cross-cultural comparisons, calculated across whole clusters of such items, would have been downright misleading.

Failure to detect and appreciate the underlying meaning of behaviour can have very practical consequences. In some cultures, the human smile can be used to communicate a range of emotions, depending on the subtleties of social context (Boesch 1994). Intercultural sojourners who are not socially skilled enough to recognise these subtleties may pay a price for their ineptness (for a review of such intercultural issues, including preparatory training, see chapter 7).

One technique that is focused on meaning is called the **web of meaning** (Afro-centric Alliance 2001). This is a hybrid form of measurement and method, based largely on the problem portrait technique (MacLachlan 1997), and leader–manager mapping (Forbes & Farey 1997). Although we apply it here to the workplace, the issues it raises are applicable across a number of other settings (see activity 4). MacLachlan, for instance, applies problem portraits to case management in health and clinical settings. The web of meaning illustrated in figure 1.2, however, is designed to help organisational managers and employees cope with a glocalised and thereby more complex workplace environment. It is thoroughly social, in that it relies on feedback from subordinates, superiors and co-workers in order to gauge and improve self-development as well as organisational development. This emphasis is consistent with what is known in business as developing a 'learning organisation' (Senge 1992). As well as being relevant to practice, the technique can be applied to develop theory.

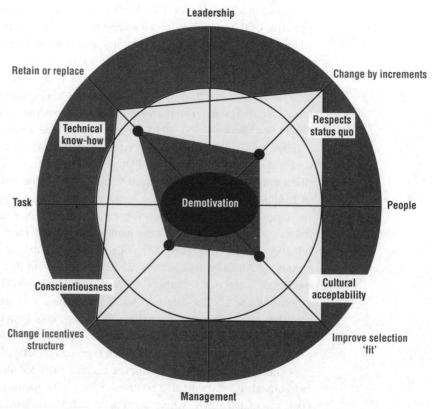

Figure 1.2 A web of meaning   ***Source:*** Afro-centric Alliance (1998, 2001).

Constructing a web of meaning like the one represented in figure 1.2 begins with employee participants relating what they consider to be the major problem facing their organisation or work group. In our fictitious example, set in an offshore branch of a multinational company in a developing economy, the participants have reported that 'demotivation' is the fundamental problem at hand. Participants are then asked to present their own critical narratives, in a group or groups, around their core theme. One of the advantages of using groups is that individuals within them, under some conditions, may feel more 'de-individuated', and thereby freer to give less socially desirable, more candid answers (see chapter 2, on diffusion of responsibility). A careful sifting of their narratives' content will uncover a set of recurring themes. As in figure 1.2, these themes are normally positioned between the four compass points of leadership–management (the north–south axis, with *leadership* meaning being 'change focused' and *management* corresponding to 'administration'), versus task–people (the east–west axis, with *task* relating to the more 'formal' and *people* signifying 'informal' aspects of work). In the particular web represented in figure 1.2, the participating employees' narrative accounts have consistently centred on four particular themes. These are listed inside the circumference of the web. The group is then asked to recommend what it considers the most viable solutions to each of the (four) thematic barriers to organisational development that it has already identified. For this particular organisation, the resulting solutions are identified outside the relevant sector of the web.

In this case, the stories have all pivoted around demotivation arising from expatriates in general, and expatriate–local pay differentials in particular. This kind of differential is proliferating as multinationals globalise into countries that are in the depths of regional or localised economic crisis yet continue to pay expatriates from home countries that are not. Several social psychological theories (see chapter 3) predict that these pay differentials will create demotivation among host national employees, which we might then regard as an example of localised resistance to globalisation. To that extent, the web of meaning may capture, in mid flight, some of the dynamics of glocalisation.

From figure 1.2 we learn that expatriates in this location do not respect the status quo (the way we've always worked around here'); that their ways are not culturally acceptable; and that they are insufficiently conscientious; but that their technical competence is not in question. Solutions to the perceived problems have been identified outside the outer circumference, for example changing the incentives structure so that expatriates are no longer financially 'segregated' and aloof from their local counterparts.

These are the qualitative dimensions of the organisation's problem and its solutions. But to what degree is each problem serious, and to what degree is each solution *viable*? These are important *quantitative* aspects of organisational development. The web technique empowers participants to indicate the degree to which they feel each problem is genuinely problematic, and to what degree each proposed solution is viable. They do this by placing a cross on each inner radius (closer to the origin means more serious) and on each respective outer radius (further from the origin means more viable). The mean position of the cross for each half-radius empowers the group itself to draw out 'windows of opportunity' for its own organisational development (shaded same colour).

Through the particular windows drawn in figure 1.2, we learn that there are three key opportunities for reversing demotivation. The organisation can change its work practices by increments rather than large leaps (expatriates are often sanguine in their expectations for change, in proportion perhaps to their comparative salaries and workplace expectations at home). Managers can improve selection practices to create a better fit between the organisation's work environment and the expatriates they select to work in it. And the organisation can fine-tune its remuneration packages to create greater social equity with local employees.

Because the web-of-meaning technique is essentially grounded in free-flowing and unconstrained narratives (the four compass points are imagined, so could equally well be Hofstede's constructs, for example), webs are also capable of testing *theory* — that is, theoretical barriers to organisational problems. At least one empirical criterion for testing such theories can be found in Gergen's own paper on social construction: 'Although cross-cultural replication is fraught with difficulty, similarity in a given function across widely divergent cultures would strongly attest to its durability across time' (1973, p. 318). This criterion is known as a historicity test (see chapter 9 for a definition of this term). To the extent that open-ended techniques like the web of meaning continue to confirm the same theoretical barriers to development across diverse settings, we would become reasonably confident that the theory predicting them (imaginary now, real by the time we reach chapter 3) is robust too. As Gergen would say, it transcends history. This is really just a cultural variation on what Triplett was doing when he tested his facilitation hypothesis, derived from a context of adult bicycle racing skills, on children reeling in a length of twine.

Pluralistic techniques such as the web of meaning (there are many more) are clearly applicable outside the workplace. Community development projects, for instance, might benefit from webs of meaning derived from the various stakeholders' narratives, by focusing on key barriers to development (development issues), as well as by identifying acceptable solutions to them (development projects). Such applications could be made nationally, through community-based organisations, or internationally, through international aid organisations. In these ways, webs of meaning could have an extremely broad and flexible range of application in social psychology, just as they have had for some time now in organisational settings.

Chapter 4, on the media, explores another of these marriages between qualitative and quantitative methods, narrative positioning. Whatever the particular partnership, however, one of their key strengths for the future is their inherent capacity to capture globalisation and localisation in the same image, and to do so in an essentially non-constraining, ethical and culturally respectful manner. Hybrids like this, which attempt to respect both narrative and number, meaning and mass, may travel relatively well across the diversity of cultures that make up most societies, organisations and communities today.

PATHWAYS

With this flexibility in mind, I will now summarise some of my own practical experiences, which have been gathered across a range of cultural landscapes (MacLachlan & Carr 1994). This summary is intended, not as a 'blueprint' for practising social psychology, but merely as a personal narrative about the kinds of processes that practising social psychologists go through as they develop their own, idiosyncratic approach to the discipline. It is shared in the belief that such critical narratives help to bring to life the discipline for student readers (for a detailed discussion on this region, see Carr, MacLachlan & Schultz 1995; also visit http://spjp.massey.ac.nz).

Realisation

Realisation is not the same process as observation, which for many people denotes the discovery of a new law or principle. Everyday practice of social psychology is more likely to consist of realising, for example, that an essentially unwanted social influence process — one already documented somewhere else — has inadvertently 'broken into' the project at hand and begun to jeopardise it.

Community development projects provide many poignant examples of this. Increasingly, for instance, one hears of hostility being directed towards international aid workers, or against community workers in domestic settings, such as in remote and rural Australia. At first glance, this may look like ingratitude, unwarranted belligerence or disingenuousness on the part of recipient communities. The community response is both vexing and perplexing, and may persuade community development agencies to put human factors in a 'too hard to explain' basket. Social psychologists have not traditionally played a significant role in advising such organisations — ironically because the discipline has not marketed itself to the human services professions generally. If it had, we might have realised that community development activities are not always 'best practice', *in social psychological terms*.

One poignant example stems from my personal experiences in southern East Africa (Carr et al. 1995). During a great drought in 1992 some rather surprising anecdotes (much like critical narratives) began circulating around the wider community. There was, for instance, the story that some villagers had refused to build a well unless they were paid wages to do so by the donating aid agency. There was also an account of town residents refusing to unload a consignment of food relief (maize) from an aid truck unless they were paid. Another rumour featured students refusing to participate in an aid-funded educational survey, designed to improve the school environment, unless participation was paid for. Finally, there were stories of academics refusing to attend aid-funded community health promotion workshops unless the 'per diem' allowance was sufficient for them to make a profit from the occasion.

On the surface, these reactions run directly counter to an often implicit, and occasionally voiced, assumption in aid discourse — namely, that aid is there to 'help people to help themselves'. Instead, the communities in question seemed to be saying, 'Pay me to help myself!' At first, this was especially mystifying, given the circumstances (e.g. a great need for water and food due to the prevailing drought). After a time, however, it began to dawn on us that some social psychological mistakes must be being made in the delivery of aid. Something was being misread. First, and being careful not to take such anecdotes at face value, it was necessary to ascertain whether there was any truth in the rumours. It was decided to survey a sample of participants who would have encountered each type of aid project (water, food, educational and health promotion).

Participants were asked to indicate, based on their own experiences, what reaction would most likely predominate within each type of recipient community — from gratefully rolling up their sleeves, to demanding 'Pay me!' Participants also had the option of indicating the response 'undecided'. Asking participants to estimate how a particular story or scenario might end, or specifically how they think someone *else* might respond to an aid project, normally reduces any tendencies to 'fake good' — that is, to give socially desirable but ultimately superficial responses (Sinha 1989).

Overall, combining responses across all four scenarios, the respondents indicated that a **pay me** response could be realistically expected on 20 per cent of occasions. But there was a significant variation in their predictions across scenarios. The predicted rate of pay me reactions increased progressively from the rural community well scenario (11 per cent pay me, 7 per cent unsure); to the school scenario (14 per cent pay me, 6 per cent unsure); the town food relief scenario (27 per cent pay me, 5 per cent unsure); and the academics' health promotion workshop scenario (with 32 per cent pay me, 17 per cent unsure).

What, then, is the *meaning* of a pay me response? One possible interpretation centres on the interaction between globalisation (of the aid business) and localisation (reassertion of cultural and community identity). Those communities with the highest levels of pay me were also those that typically experienced the greatest amount of contact with international aid agencies and their development projects. Donors may speak of 'donor-' and 'compassion-fatigue', and feel entitled to expect some gratitude for development assistance rendered. But 'recipient' communities are likely to feel fatigued and entitled too. Remember what it feels like to receive too many gifts from someone; it can be humiliating. Communities can experience this reaction too. Apart from severely denting one's sense of community pride, aid and welfare can also hurt and constrain economically. Thus, recipients of forestry projects might prefer, and feel entitled, to conduct their normal business rather than participate in someone else's idea of a development scheme. They might even be justified in expecting *compensation* for their lost time and income.

The great realisation here is that *every gift takes something away*. Viewed in this light, remuneration may actually help to restore the 'balance of payments' in an aid equation. From a recipient's point of view, pay me is perfectly logical (Carr, McAuliffe & MacLachlan 1998). Such restorative processes are especially logical in a global environment that increasingly stresses pay for performance, and in which the importance of maintaining cultural and community pride can never be underestimated (Ah Nee-Benham 2000). Counterintuitively, perhaps, this risk of backlash may be especially high in times of severe hardship, such as drought, when all else is lost or in danger (Carr & MacLachlan 1999). As one prominent indigenous Australian, Mick Dodson, said of domestic welfare, 'We want health, housing, and education; but not at the expense of losing our own soul; our own identity; a say in our lives. We refuse to sacrifice the essence of what makes us Aboriginal people' (1998, p. 8). The social psychological wisdom in this statement is that without a sense of cultural pride, there is no real foundation on which to build sustainable community initiatives; people will neither own nor care about the project; so it will fail.

The gift of giving is clearly something that has to be worked at, especially in a world increasingly tuned to business transactions (global) and cultural identity (local). In this glocal world, we might think about reconstructing both aid and welfare so that they are seen as forms of social negotiation. Perhaps we need to recognise that conventional expectations for aid projects, such as helping people to help themselves, are psychologically naive and ultimately destructive. In a contemporary north Australian setting (Cape York), Aboriginal spokesperson Noel Pearson (1999) has made an analogous point with regard to the 'welfare mentality'. This view is succinctly encapsulated in critical narrative 1.4.

CRITICAL
NARRATIVE

1.4

The welfare mentality in Australia

Narrative discourses are superb examples of influential contextual factors in our everyday lives. Take models of community leadership, for example. In his discussion paper titled 'Our right to take responsibility', the Australian Aboriginal spokesperson Noel Pearson articulates several models of leadership that have 'dominated governance in the communities of the [York] Peninsula' (1999, p. 30).

The 'white dictator' model implicitly assumed that indigenous people should play a role of subservience and obedience to their colonial masters. In the 'black dictator' model, according to Pearson, some indigenous leaders adopt 'Idi Amin'–style roles. The 'white saviour/servant' model, which according to Pearson is now widespread across Australia, supports a cast of 'new age care-givers' anxious to 'consult' and empower, but it still subtly positions Aboriginal people in inferior and passive roles. The 'black saviour/servant' model, despite its foundations in the direct experience of Aboriginal suffering, is ultimately just as demeaning and disempowering, Pearson argues. It, too, does its bit to encourage welfare dependency rather than responsibility.

One of the underlying issues here is that helping others can demean them, lowering their dignity. It acts as a sharp reminder of the 'superior' status and privilege of the helper. This helper also derives a sense of accomplishment out of the act of helping, and in this sense, success keeps going to the successful. The recipient, of course, continues to gain less in this equation. Under such inequitable terms, recipients may reasonably be expected eventually to start resisting, resenting and even rejecting this assistance. Pay me becomes 'pay me back'. Globally, and within countries as much as between them, the gap between rich and poor continues to grow both in reality and in public consciousness (Heredia 1997). We continue to witness local backlashes against what may be felt, sometimes despite the best of intentions, to be exploitation and dehumanisation. Historically, many traditional systems have respected the social psychology of payback, and a 'norm of reciprocity' appears to be relatively robust (although not necessarily universal) across history and culture (Gouldner 1960; for an example in the context of traditional family structures in New Zealand, see Durie 1999). Perhaps, then, we should learn to expect local backlashes against *any* form of development assistance, whether in international aid or domestic welfare.

Source: Extracted, adapted and interpreted from Pearson (1999).

Rejuvenation

The norm of reciprocity is not a new concept, yet it has apparently found a new lease of life with respect to 'doing good' in today's global community. In other words, constructs that have been useful once before can become useful again. This idea of being prepared to recycle a principle whose 'use by' date appears to have expired is called *rejuvenation*. Some of the best examples of this pathway can be found in health promotion. Health problems are constantly evolving and being rejuvenated among the viruses and microbes around us, with globalisation rendering their spread more problematic and difficult to control. Logically, therefore, there will always be scope for rejuvenating social psychology that bears on health.

Promoting awareness of acquired immune deficiency syndrome (AIDS) is a prime need in the 'developing' world. The United Nations recently declared this disease the number one barrier to economic development across Africa, where there are estimated to be more than 22 million victims, with four new infections every minute (Australian Broadcasting Corporation 1999a). In many relatively developed economies, people may already possess most of the information necessary to prevent the disease. Prevention information, then, may indeed be redundant, at least until the next generation. But in certain parts of Africa it is much less safe to assume an informed public. In Malawi until recently, for instance, the acronym 'AIDS' popularly stood for 'American Ideas to Discourage Sex' (MacLachlan 1998). In such contexts, there is clearly a potential for communication about how to prevent infection, to make a difference.

One of the key independent variables in previous Western studies of persuasive communication has been credibility (Hovland & Weiss 1951). In broad terms, this construct has two components, perceived expertise and trust, each of which is vital to communication success. Four decades after the first experimental work on credibility and its component parts, a study in Malawi found that attempts to communicate information about AIDS prevention had been channelled through essentially distrusted mass media channels (controlled by a feared and despised dictator, who has since been ousted). More trusted sources were either too scarce to make a difference (doctors, nurses, psychologists) or, like uncles and aunts in an extended family or members of the numerous popular churches, largely overlooked by the key health promotion agencies at the time (Tembo 1991). Here we see that a *rejuvenated* basic principle, 'Use credible sources for communicating your message', could have made a difference. Its application could have saved young lives.

Refutation

If we are prepared to accept that social psychology, applied somewhere, could sometimes be applied more effectively somewhere else, at another time or place, then we must also be prepared for the reverse to be true. Even the sacred cows of the discipline must be regarded as vulnerable. One of these is arguably found in the work of Leon Festinger (1957). According to Festinger, recognising that we have been inconsistent in our actions, thoughts or feelings is likely to cause psychological discomfort as profound and unsettling as physical hunger itself. Like hunger, this feeling of inconsistency, or 'dissonance', will, according to

Festinger's theory, motivate a keen search to attack the source of the discomfort. In everyday life, the resulting process of **dissonance reduction** is often triggered socially. If somebody accuses you of an 'inconsistency', it can hurt. Science itself is arguably built on this very sensibility. Crucially, too, we are often both accuser and accused. After purchasing a luxury article that we cannot really afford, we may recognise that the article is not really as good as we had expected. There is an inconsistency between knowing that we did x and knowing that we ought not to have done x. So we start to feel uncomfortable or guilty, and so start to convince ourselves that the product is better than it really is. There is the crux of dissonance reduction, as Festinger presented it. It is a process of self-deception, in which we distort our mental states (beliefs and feelings) to fit behaviour. Knowing that we cannot go back and change behaviour (what's done is done; we can't turn back the clock), and that it is inappropriate to confront the shopkeeper, people alter their beliefs and feelings to be consistent with their behaviour ('Doesn't it have some wonderful features, though?'). Such self-deception, according to Festinger, hallmarks an influence process of gargantuan proportions.

One of the most impressive examples of dissonance reduction is provided in a now classic study reported by Brehm and Cohen (1962). This study took place in the wake of a student demonstration that had been broken up with some force by the local police. Participants in the study were members of that same student body, who were understandably critical of the police. They were invited to write essays that supported the police actions and offered varying financial inducements to persuade them to do so. Writing such essays (behaviour) went against their personal beliefs. According to Festinger's theory, such behaviour was bound to precipitate dissonance, and, counterintuitively, especially so if the essays were written for *less* reward. Betraying our principles for less reward creates more dissonance, because it more clearly contravenes the conscience. With greater inducement, it is easier to justify our actions ('I'm a poor student. I needed the money!'). The theory thus leads to a counterintuitive prediction — that a lesser, rather than a greater, inducement will be more successful in changing private opinion.

The evidence that emerged from Brehm and Cohen's study supported the theory and not common sense. Those students who were paid less to argue against their own personal convictions were, at the close of the study, more likely to privately endorse aspects of the police force's conduct. They had changed their personal attitudes, and they had done so under conditions of minimal pressure.

This finding provides the perfect illustration of a founding principle suggested earlier, namely that smaller inducements are often more effective in winning people over in private, and for the longer term. Many of us may recognise, and find meaning in, the process that Festinger articulated. Subsequent research has broadly supported his central proposal, that behaving against our principles is often sufficient to arouse guilt and thereby bring dissonance reduction into play (Croyle & Cooper 1983).

Gergen, however, has argued for caution over any claims that social processes are 'universal'. Indeed, Festinger, too, was wary of such arrogance (Festinger 1954). In Japan, for example, people praise the ability to tolerate inconsistency, considering it a mark of maturity (Moghaddam, Taylor & Wright 1993, p. 12). Similarly, in the field of health promotion there is mounting and widespread evidence that imported 'modern medical' beliefs are tolerated alongside 'traditional' ones. This is so even when a majority of the population have a traditional background (remember that in many 'developing' societies, attempts are being made to supplant traditional systems, rather than simply providing health 'alternatives'). Modern medical beliefs and practices are not necessarily adopted at the expense of traditional beliefs, as Festinger's theory on its own suggests. Many ethnic Chinese, for example, will readily seek multiple forms of treatment, both Western and traditional (Bishop 1994). Traditional medicine thus remains important to these people, and to that extent could be incorporated to a greater extent in messages aiming to promote health services, and increased sustainable use of health services, in these communities.

The pluralistic pragmatism evident in these communities suggests that dissonance reduction is not necessarily universal. It may be in a decline in the face of a wider process, glocalisation. But for the moment, we cannot rule out dissonance reduction. As the Japanese example implies, tolerating inconsistency still requires a certain amount of cognitive work. Evidently, cognitive tolerance is no easier to acquire than dissonance reduction is to perform.

In an age of pluralism like ours, the complete eradication of any influence process, dissonance reduction included, seems improbable. More likely is the possibility that influence processes will be moderated by the local context. Principles of self-promotion, for example, will colonise less successfully where local traditions advocate a counter-culture of group loyalty and humility. To express this in another way, somewhere between rejuvenation (of corporate America) and refutation (of self-promotion) may be found a viable middle way. That middle way can perhaps be thought of as the *restatement* of one principle to respectfully accommodate another.

Restatement

One of the central tenets of globalisation is that the benefits of competition in general, and success in particular, will somehow outweigh all the longer term costs of defeat. But somebody always has to lose. Surely the social psychology of defeat (including notions of honour, respect and 'face') deserves more attention than it is receiving at present. Most of us cannot be winners, and in a global culture that worships success, that may cause conflict. So, counteracting the global pressure to succeed, which we see in the workplace every day in pay-for-performance and individual contracts, is a certain resistance. This resistance is often partially reflected in workplace tensions and unrest (see chapters 3 and 10). Of course, we could analyse these conflicts from a sociological or political level of analysis. A social psychological analysis, however, would focus on the local reassertion of traditional norms, like collectivistic mateship, and underlying values, such as support for equality rather than hierarchy in the group (see critical narrative 1.3; figure 1.1).

What are the glocal dynamics of this resistance? As expressed in figure 1.3, and in much of psychology — including personality, and motivational, cross-cultural and organisational behaviour — there is an implicit assumption: a linear and positive relationship between individual achievement motivation, on the one hand, and individual or group performance on the other. Economic development supposedly partly depends on this human factor. Moreover, so the argument goes, it can be augmented through incremental increases in workplace training and modernising traditional socialisation practices. In psychology, David McClelland has been the foremost advocate of a 'need for achievement' (N. Ach). McClelland has been able to link economic developments across a range of Western European cultures, over historical time, to corresponding changes in the level of N. Ach being sanctioned in each society, for example through their cultural narratives (McClelland 1987b).

There are some problems with McClelland's evidence, however. One of these is its own historicity. The need for achievement lost its power to predict economic growth around 1950 (Lewis 1991). A key reason for this loss appears to have been the economic stirrings of East Asia, and in particular the emergence of a dynamic pattern of Confucian work values at the time (Chinese Culture Connection 1987). That different pattern of values was subsequently linked also to economic growth (Hofstede & Bond 1988). In the wake of the Asian economic crisis, we may witness the birth of another pattern. But the point is that McClelland's formula for economic success worked only in certain, pre-globalisation settings, albeit an impressive range of them (for discussion of the gendered nature of N. Ach, see Ward 2001).

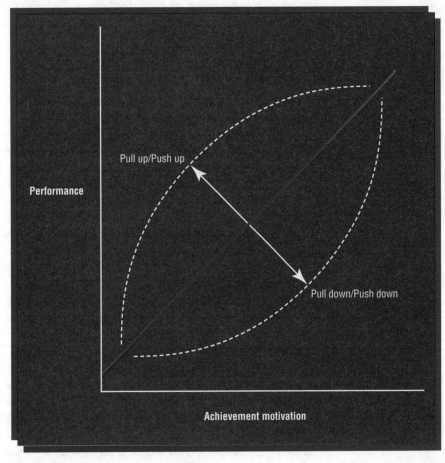

Figure 1.3 The social psychology of achievement

With that restriction in mind, perhaps the current, glocal context is not yet *ready* (or mature enough) for its current obsession with self-promotion. One illustration of how this obsession can go awry was provided in critical narrative 1.3; another is figure 1.3, which graphically summarises the aforementioned theoretical relationship between achievement motivation and performance. As Gergen (1973) accurately warned, it shows how a linear relationship between the two variables can be 'buckled and bent' by social psychological forces outside its control. These social forces together make up a social psychology of achievement (chapter 3). In figure 1.3, they can include envious 'pull-down' intentions from below (e.g. from less successful colleagues and/or 'juniors') as well as jealous 'push-down' intentions from above (e.g. from job insecure and/or prejudiced 'superiors'). The twin issues of envy ('I want what you have') and jealousy (technically the reverse — i.e. 'I have what you want and will act to keep it that way') have always been a social force to contend with. Globalisation, however, has helped to flush these motivations out into the open (Bedeian 1995). Figure 1.3 hints at an additional point, too — that we may wish to start developing an understanding of how to transform these essentially negative social intentions into supportive *push-up* from co-workers and empowering *pull-up* from bosses (chapter 3). Only then will we have learned how to manage the tall poppy syndrome, and its wider parent issue for all societies, namely balancing individual with social achievement (Chi-yue Chiu & Ying-yi Hong 1997).

Reconstitution

Restating known principles to accommodate global and local realities is one means of attempting to cope with the complexities of a glocalised environment. Another is to take pluralism in a more radical direction — to begin to actively borrow from diverse behavioural principles in order to engage more fully with our greater environmental complexity. To do so is to perform a kind of psychological alchemy, applying basic elements so as to transmute old principles into a new one. The concept of alchemy dates back centuries or even millennia, so there is nothing particularly new in evoking the general idea as a metaphor for doing social psychological science. Indeed, it could be argued that science and society alike have always built on this kind of process. What *is* new, perhaps, is the idea of developing a greater readiness to borrow ideas creatively from outside the discipline's conventional borders.

An example of how this might work can be found in the social psychology of community change. Such tasks are firmly based on the change agent's perceived need for change. Perception of the physical world constitutes a fundamental branch of psychology, so it is reasonable to explore the grounds for crossover and the relevance to social psychology. There are, in fact, principles of physical perception that have analogues in social perception. For instance, we tend to group together physical stimuli on the basis of their physical appearance, just as we often do with people (Bowa 1998). Our ability to read distinctive typesetting fonts, or someone else's handwriting, demonstrates how we can readily perform 'closure' on half-completed letters of the alphabet, just as we 'fill in the gaps' in our social memory by using our pre-existing cultural schemata (Bartlett

1932). Negative taste experiences have social parallels, too, in the same way that negative social experiences create indelibly unpleasant memories (Cacioppo, Gardner & Berntson 1999). Thus, some of the principles of perceiving the physical world may apply to the social world (Lewin 1951; for a general recent discussion of the prominence of this idea in social psychology, see Gleitman 1997).

In physical perception, Fechner's Law states that what counts as a 'just noticeable difference' (JND) partly depends on context, in this case the level of background stimulation. Thus, a grey stimulus, when placed against light and dark backgrounds, will appear brighter against the darker setting. As Sherif's study implies, and everyday experience confirms, the illumination from a single candle in an otherwise completely darkened room is considerable, but placing the same candle in a room with 100 other candles will not make a JND.

If we now start to think seriously about this principle in social psychological terms, the implications are both fascinating and relevant. Community changes, for example, often proceed at an uncomfortable or radical pace that is ultimately counterproductive for those who are asked to make the change and to live with its consequences. Quite often the change agent is an outsider from a wealthier, 'faster moving' community or work environment — where, in short, there is the equivalent of 100 candles. He or she is habituated to more material comforts, and indeed the practice of change itself. Change is nothing new and carries no great surprises or — more importantly perhaps — unknown overheads and risks. From a poorer community's perspective, however, the rapid and large changes that these agents freely and, by some accounts, persistently advocate are often liabilities. The latest technology soon requires expensive maintenance or, worse, breaks down completely, leaving the community with nothing to fall back on (their 'old' technology, of course, has been replaced). From a local perspective, smaller, less radical steps might have been more appropriate, if only the outsider had been able to see that. Thus, we might begin to reconstitute principles from physical perception (and JNDs) to help change agents recommend development projects that are more sustainable.

Reflection

Reflection, meaning 'looking back' in an attempt to distil common underlying principles, is as close as we may get to a methodological capstone in the research process. In much of this chapter, for example, the reader may have discerned, in retrospect, a notion that constraint is ultimately counterproductive.

Reflection is nonetheless risky. Consider a poor sleeper who samples a different alcoholic tipple in a nightly glass of milk. At the end of a week, what would this reflecting person conclude? Perhaps that milk is a good somnific substance; or that it gives one a headache the next day! What is missing from this particular reflection is a control condition. An experimentalist would have first tried drinking a glass of milk on its own, and then compared that to various combinations of milk and alcohol to tease out the actual influence of each component in the nightly cocktail.

This anecdote beautifully illustrates one of the fundamental problems with induction and observation generally, as well as the continuing value of experimental methods. It also highlights how no single pathway is sufficient in itself for the practice of social psychology. What is really required is to apply a blend of methods, and for social psychology to keep pace with the developing pluralism of its subject. Social psychology is constantly *becoming*, and this dynamism is more important than ever in a new millennium in which the only constant is change.

This dynamism does *not* mean, as Gergen implied, that social psychology is continuously becoming out of date. On the contrary, we are about to discover that social psychology has produced some very useful findings, theories and methods. Although this book fully agrees with Gergen that many of these have limits, this does not undermine their practical value. At several points since his seminal (1973) paper, Gergen has reiterated that the discipline's greatest potential to make a difference lies in the development of a **generative** and **transformational** social psychology (e.g. Gergen 1994b). By this, he means that social psychology should constantly elevate our consciousness about possible solutions to ongoing social problems. That particular 'enlightenment function' continues to set a benchmark for the discipline as a whole, and therefore also for this book.

SUMMARY

In order to transcend its own inherent historicity, social psychology needs to engage with the duumvirate of globalisation and localisation, and therein with the dynamic complexity of glocalisation. Through its focus on mutual social influences across behaviour, cognition and affect, social psychology is well positioned to contribute towards contemporary global issues in health and education, in the community and at work. The recent history of social psychology contains some glocally relevant lessons that are not immediately evident either in ancient history or in prehistory. These lessons include the facilitating effect of crowds on competitive performance; the convergence of opinion in groups towards a socially constructed reality; and the enlightening effects of studying social psychology in its own right. Scientific research has therefore made substantial contributions to social understanding.

Nonetheless, there has been a general quickening in the extent to which people possess multiple social repertoires. Social psychological methods will not keep pace with these changes unless they, too, become pluralistic. In particular, we need to capture the construction and re-construction of social meaning by research participants, whether through more qualitative techniques or, preferably, through techniques that combine quality *and* quantity, narrative *and* number. Underlying narrative discourse can be analysed using both approaches, as in constructing webs of meaning and combining various methodological pathways towards continuing social development (all societies are 'developing'). Giving social psychology an edge in today's world requires adding value to the highly focused snapshots in experimentation and surveys. Much of this book explores these twin, and in many ways inseparable, landscapes.

Case study. Any mini-narrative, or story, about an individual, organisation or community group. Case studies provide an in-depth look at a particular social phenomenon, often through the eyes of the protagonists themselves. Case studies are therefore able to approximate the full range of contextual factors operating on or in the group in any period of concern. (p. 24)

Client welfare. An overriding ethical principle according to which the wellbeing and best interests of the client are placed before all else (p. 20)

Compliance. Conformity minus any private acceptance (i.e. behavioural change only) (p. 21)

Conformity. A change in behaviour or belief, as a result of real or imagined group pressure (p. 18)

Construction. A social influence process similar to convergence but wider in scope. It entails a series of implicit norms, and thereby potentially comprises an entire way of life. Convergence produces a norm; construction, an edifice. Construction can be a less equitable process than convergence, in which each party concedes about the same distance. It may occur through brainwashing, for instance. (p. 20)

Convergence. The coming together of judgements about reality so as to form a single group norm. Convergence often occurs without fully conscious awareness, accompanied by feelings of reassurance, and tends to become part of a longer term belief system. Because each party concedes about as much as the other, this process is inherently equitable, involving little or no constraint. It constitutes a form of social negotiation. (p. 13)

Critical narrative. A story or vignette from everyday life that contains a critical incident; an event or series of events starkly illustrating the dynamic interplay between various, often competing social psychological influences (p. 25)

Dissonance reduction. The social influence process by which, once we become aware of any inconsistencies between our behaviours, beliefs or feelings, we attempt to resolve that inconsistency (and dissonance) by changing one or more of them to re-establish consistency (and consonance). The essence of this *cognitive dissonance* theory is that people are inherently motivated to avoid inconsistency, finding it fundamentally aversive. (p. 37)

Ethnocentric. Reflecting a perspective on others' beliefs, feelings and behaviour from within a particular worldview, as if that were the only correct view to hold. Such a view fails to recognise its inherent self-centredness. (p. 20)

Experimentation. See **field** and **laboratory experiments**. (p. 24)

Field experiment. A realistic-looking situation that is manipulated by an experimenter. An independent variable is whatever the field experimenter is interested in manipulating (e.g. whether a marketing promoter touches the arm of a prospective buyer in a supermarket campaign), whereas the dependent variable is the behaviour, belief or feeling that might be influenced (e.g. tasting the sample, buying the product). (p. 24)

Generative. This type of social psychology keeps on reinventing itself and so keeps pace with accelerating social development. (p. 42)

Glocalisation. The combined pressures of globalisation and localisation. For example, children of migrants often experience tension between the pushes and pulls of teenage culture (global youth culture) and parental values (local traditional culture). (p. 9)

Informed consent. Before members of the public take part in any social psychological study, they are entitled to be given information about the reasons for the study, what it will entail, and how it will benefit society. Based on this information, they must give their consent to the researcher, usually in writing. (p. 21)

Laboratory experiment. An artificial and overtly contrived environment in which, in theory, everything is carefully controlled. One variable (e.g. number of people believed by the participant to be present in the room) is then manipulated while everything else (in the room) is held constant. This independently manipulated variable may then have an impact on another, dependent variable (e.g. help given by the genuine participant to an apparent victim of a staged accident). (p. 24)

Obedience. A special form of conformity in which the conformer yields to an authority figure rather than to a majority in the group. Like conformity, obedience often takes the form of compliance (i.e. behavioural change without any accompanying change in private opinion). (p. 20)

Pay me. Recipients of aid donations and other forms of charity may feel entitled to remuneration for their participation in the donor's charitable project. They may demand to be paid for their time, effort, inconvenience and loss of community pride. Pay me can be sought as a form of restitution for these injustices, as a form of payback. (p. 34)

Sample survey. A non-interventionist research method by which representatives of a population or social group are asked to complete a questionnaire about their beliefs, feelings or behaviour. The questions contained on the survey form can be answered either during an interactive interview (face-to-face, voice-to-voice, computer-to-computer), or remotely, through e-mail, postal or classroom surveys. (p. 24)

Simulation and observation. In the anthropological tradition, simulations place people in mock-ups of social scenarios, such as a prison, an isolated camp or a biosphere, in order to observe the spontaneous effects on human behaviour, beliefs or feelings. As social and work groups become increasingly diffuse and complex, and as ethical concerns become more salient, this research method may be in decline. (p. 21)

Social facilitation. A fundamental process of social influence in which the presence of others, whether as spectators or as fellow competitors, facilitates performance of whatever we know best at the time. For an accomplished athlete, crowds will improve performance, whereas for a student who has not revised, the presence of other students will facilitate (enhance) his or her ineptitude. (p. 12)

Transformational. The kind of social psychology that transforms the way we manage our lives, thereby enlightening us about our own social psychology (p. 42)

Web of meaning. A technique in which groups are empowered to tell their own stories about the influences around them, with an eye to their key problems and what they consider to be the most viable solutions to them. The group is then asked to rate the seriousness of each of the problems as well as the viability of each of the possible solutions they have identified — the more serious the problem and the more viable the solution, the wider the window of opportunity for future development. (p. 30)

REVIEW QUESTIONS

1. Define social psychology.
2. Define glocalisation, and think of some examples from your own life.
3. Trace the major stepping-stones in the discipline of twentieth-century social psychology. Which do you think is the main one, and why?
4. Outline the key methods that social psychologists have relied on during the twentieth century.
5. Outline the changes that social psychological methods will need to go through in order to keep pace with people in the twenty-first century.

DISCUSSION QUESTIONS

1. Analyse the *Buick Bar & Grill* story (critical narrative 1.3) in terms of globalisation, localisation and glocalisation.
2. Is the dynamic of 'pay me' visible in your society or community? How is it manifested differently in your own social and economic context? If you need a 'kick-start' to your debate, you may use MacLachlan and Carr (1997).
3. 'Social psychology is everywhere.' Discuss.

ACTIVITIES

1. In this chapter we have read several *critical incidents* . This term is used in the sense adopted by J. C. Flanagan (1954) and has many applications in applied psychology. Critical incidents are simply significant events in a workplace, or in everyday life. They can have a positive outcome (for example, a fight breaks out and you manage to calm the combatants so that nobody gets hurt), or they can result in a negative outcome (you *all* end up in hospital). Think of one positive and one negative critical incident for one of the social influence processes described in this chapter.

2. Scour your local newspaper for stories that reflect some of the principles and processes covered in the chapter. Do they bring any *realisations* or *reflections* to mind? (The purpose of this activity is to show that 'social psychology is everywhere' — as proposed in the opening paragraphs of the book — and is not the preserve of an academic 'ivory tower'.)

3. The Nominal Group Technique (NGT) was designed to help groups capitalise on intellectual resources by ranking options and preferences in a relatively objective way (Delbecq & Van de Ven 1971). Apply the NGT to rank-order what you perceive to be the most important applications of social psychology in your community today. The key steps in this decision-making technique are listed on the following page.

- Each student works alone, and jots down what he or she considers to be the best application or two.

- The instructor records each student's ideas on a wipe-board or overhead projector.

- The group discusses each of these ideas in turn, carefully weighing up its strengths and weaknesses.

- The instructor has the group rank-order the ideas. First, each group member is asked to rank them, and then the mean rankings are calculated.

- A hierarchy of choices is generated and displayed to the group for their reactions and feedback.

4. In groups of five to six students, construct your own web of meaning. Choose an issue that concerns you in your own particular local setting.

ADDITIONAL READING

On defining social psychology: Hermans and Kempen (1998); Marsella (1998). These authors, in my view, are able to see where social psychology needs to go in order to make a greater contribution to real issues in today's global world.

On the history of social psychology: Zajonc (1965); Sherif (1936); Festinger (1954); Asch (1956); Gergen (1973). Each of these authors has left a huge legacy in social psychology. Without reading them first-hand, it is difficult to appreciate this legacy when you come across it.

On the methods of social psychology: Milgram (1963); Zimbardo (1982); Hofstede (2001); Afro-centric Alliance (2001). The various methods described in the chapter draw from these exemplary studies.

For further reading on the topics discussed in this chapter, consult the online resources linked to the Wiley website (http://www.johnwiley.com.au/highered/socialpsych).

BEHAVIOUR

CHAPTER 2

THE CROWD

LEARNING OBJECTIVES

After reading this chapter, you should be able to:

- define the influence process of social facilitation, which is at the core of crowd behaviour
- explain the additional necessity, in the overall facilitation process, of behaviour modelling
- describe the roles of pluralistic ignorance and diffusion of responsibility in crowd apathy (or non-intervention)
- explain the process of transformation from relatively non-social conduct in crowds to pro-social behaviour in groups.

OVERVIEW

Crowds provide minimal, fleeting social context, yet they can change behaviour dramatically. A principal avenue for these changes to occur is *social facilitation*, through which latent tendencies (prejudice, for example) are amplified by the presence of others and thereby externalised into actual behaviour. Hatred, bravery, nationalism or cultural values can be rendered relatively salient in the context of a crowd. Modelling processes, too, often interact with this intensification, to influence crowd behaviour — for example when witnessing an accident or an emergency. Understanding these processes, and the contextual factors that drive them, enables social psychology to make a unique contribution towards the management of crowd dynamics. With increasing urban crowding, growing individual self-centredness as well as greater emphasis on teamwork, the management of social facilitation and modelling is an important practical concern.

The Battle of Craigieburn Farm

It is Saturday morning, somewhere in central Scotland. Ten young anti-hunt protestors are parked on a quiet country road near Craigieburn Farm. They expect the hunt shortly to head their way and intend to lay some false trails in advance of its arrival. This would ensure the success of their day's mission, namely the prevention of a 'kill' by the hunt and its pack of foxhounds.

Suddenly from behind them a Land Rover roars up at breakneck speed. At the same instant, another four-wheel drive emerges from the woods in front of them. A frantic effort to restart the van fails when the engine stalls — the van is now blocked at front and rear. A dozen or so heavily armed men spill out of the Land Rovers, and more still emerge from the woods. The men who encircle the van are armed with pickaxe handles, freshly lathed clubs with white rope handles, crowbars and a shotgun.

From inside the van, the faces of these men look contorted and menacing. The crowbars are used to try to lever open the windows, the operation accompanied by roared expletives, sinister laughter, and violent and obscene gestures. Gas canisters are produced and lobbed inside, but they fail to go off. Suddenly one of the windows is smashed, and the rest quickly follow. The clubs are inside the van now, swinging wildly. The driver is beaten relentlessly, until a pickaxe handle breaks over his legs. A broken wristwatch is smashed from the wearer's bloodied wrist.

Now the faces of the crowd begin to change. The colour drains, the clamour rises, and foam flecks the lips and chins of these men, who are now joined by several women. Those inside the van begin to realise that their lives are in real danger. The crowd outside seems to have lost its reason and to be completely out of control. The cursing and clubbing is feeding on itself. The loop is both quickening and growing in ferocity.

Apparently with nothing to lose, the group decides to descend from the shell of the van, resigned to its fate. Suddenly, in the thick of this danger, one man's facial expression appears to change. He begins to appeal to his fellow crowd members for calm, to stop the bloodshed. In the nick of time, perhaps, it seems to work. The blows become more sporadic, less ferocious. The tide subsides. 'I am a doctor', he tells the would-be saboteurs, although he does not go so far as to tend anyone's injuries.

In stunned silence, and with the sense of having had a very close call, the protestors begin to walk, some supporting those who are hurt, away from the husk of their vehicle. But for the occasional parting blow, the crowd disperses behind them. The police are called, and later that day the ringleaders among the vigilantes are arrested. Eventually they are prosecuted and found guilty. The case is publicised nationally. The local council bans the hunt from its public land. Other councils around the country follow suit. Some years later, with field and follower numbers, and the attendant income, flagging, this particular hunt closes down. Hunting with hounds has since been declared illegal by the Scottish Parliament.

The hunt's victory at the Battle of Craigieburn Farm was a Pyrrhic one. For the anti-hunting movement, it was a major boon. A small crowd process had helped to initiate a wider, longer term process of social and political change.

Source: Wallace & Carr (2000).

The uprising at Chancellor College

Since the mid 1960s, President-for-Life 'H. E.' Kamuzu Hastings Banda, 'the Ngwazi', had ruled the East African nation of Malaŵi with an iron fist. Banda was among the most feared dictators on the continent. Censorship was heavy, and the penalties for speaking out were heavier still. At the National University, where the Ngwazi is Chancellor of Chancellor College, Malaŵian lecturers would occasionally disappear into political custody, sometimes for years at a time.

Lent 1992. In a coordinated effort by the Catholic Church across the country, bishops and priests speak to their congregations about the social inequities and continuing abject poverty of the nation under the Banda regime. As they leave the cathedral service in Zomba, students from Chancellor College sing songs and psalms of peace while they march along the road back to the campus. The rest of the country will soon rise up, but in the coming days these students are in the vanguard of change. Early one morning they gather on the outskirts of the city's campus, and before long heavily armed SWAT troops have sealed off the entire college campus.

Now the crowd begins to move. It flows like a liquid across the campus, selectively smashing every material symbol of the corrupt presidency. Aitch-E's ornate, personal ceremonial toilet is destroyed, his foundation plaque broken, his portrait on the library stairs derided (a student is later expelled for the gesture).

The crowd violence is highly selective. It is at once both strong and gentle, characterised by controlled force. As the throng brushes gently past one of its social psychology lecturers, a psychology student turns to him and declares, 'Is *this* conformity!'

In the space of a few short weeks, and after the deaths of many innocent and extremely brave individuals, even young children openly mock the Ngwazi. Laughing gleefully, they offer 'V' signs to passers-by. The iron grip of Banda, one of Africa's most feared despots, has been broken. Within about a year he will be gone, with the promise of elections and the eventual creation of a national democracy.

A key player in this essentially positive outcome was the crowd, in particular a crowd of young people, with everything to lose, who decided to take a courageous, compassionate and thoughtful stand. Central to what happened at Chancellor College, and during the 1990s revolution in Malaŵi, was the social context of a crowd.

Source: Carr (1996b).

Critical narratives 2.1 and 2.2 illustrate how powerful and fundamental the social influences of a crowd can be. They strongly suggest that crowd dynamics deserve a more prominent place in a book of this kind than they are typically accorded (Reicher 1997). This chapter hopes to redress the balance. It places crowds at this early stage of the book for three main reasons. First, crowds are the most basic, elementary of social entities, typically a fleeting aggregation of strangers with no real history or future together. Second, their influence can be socially profound, sometimes extending, as these two critical narratives illustrate, to social and political change. Third, certain features of crowds reappear as elements in many other influence processes — the physical presence of others, for example, plays a part in teamwork, in audience situations and in forming impressions of others. For these three reasons, we will return at various points in this book to the influence of the crowd.

INTRODUCING CROWDS

In this chapter, when we discuss the crowd, we focus first on the kind of relatively immediate social context foregrounded in critical narratives 2.1 and 2.2. This means an emphasis on the influences exerted, in a relatively immediate sense, on our behaviour by the presence of others. Our secondary focus of interest, which is also clearly indicated in these critical narratives, is the part that crowd processes play in 'macro' events such as social and political change. These wider linkages have been carefully studied by social scientists of many denominations and persuasions, and our own, relatively 'micro' level perspective merely complements theirs. Imagine a series of levels of analysis ranging through political, sociological, psychological and physiological: our analysis is situated between the sociological and psychological levels. Attention is also paid to physiological substrates. As the narratives show, crowds set pulses racing. Because this tips our discussion towards the micro level, additional exercises at the end of this chapter invite readers to examine the inexorable linkages between crowd behaviour and the more macro levels of explanation (discussion questions 2.1 and 2.2).

Most striking of all in critical narratives 2.1 and 2.2 is the wide moral span of crowd influences. Plainly, these influences range all the way from bringing out the worst in people (2.1) to bringing out their best (2.2). What, then, is the justification for bringing them together in one chapter, as if they form a coherent social ensemble? Look again at the critical narratives. Therein lies at least one point of linkage, namely the wider social context. There has to be something wider already *there* to be 'brought out', whether it is hatred or pride, a tug-of-the-forelock mentality, or simmering resistance to oppression and injustice. Crowds consistently help to externalise, or turn into behaviour, either the worst or the best in people's underlying thoughts and feelings. Thus, one commonality they have is that they are social catalysts.

SOCIAL FACILITATION

Co-actors

Appropriately enough, the study of crowds is where the discipline of social psychology, as many of us know it, began. In chapter 1 we saw how Triplett decided to test his **social facilitation** hypothesis that the presence of others, participating in the same activity towards a goal of peak performance, would be sufficient to increase levels of individual performance beyond previous personal bests. Although Triplett's original study involved only one **co-actor**, it might be regarded as the forerunner of crowd studies, as a kind of minimum crowd situation in itself (Fraser 1978). Triplett's classic study indicated that people, each performing the same task, or *co-acting*, could influence one another's performance to attain new heights. This process provides a springboard for this chapter, and for the book as a whole (for a discussion of the process in animals, and of the links between social context and basic biological processes like arousal and behaviour, see Cacioppo et al. 2000; a more detailed review of social facilitation theory and research can be found in Aiello & Douthitt 2001).

Spectators

In sporting spectacles such as cycle racing, there are often two sorts of crowd present at the same time, one competing and the other observing. Triplett, however, made no concerted effort in his research to tease these out. It was to be expected, then, that other researchers would eventually decide to investigate the crowd influences not only of competitors but also of spectators.

This *audience* situation is first investigated systematically in the crowd literature in Travis (1925). Travis's experiment very clearly reinforced Triplett's point that performance plateau can be raised an incremental step through the influence of even a small crowd. In Travis's experiment, eye–hand coordination performance was tested through the use of a task known as the Pursuit Rotor. This exercise entails attempting to keep an electronic counting stick on the inner rings of a moving elliptical target, rather like games once seen at fairground stalls. The longer a player manages to keep the pointer on an inner target ring, the more points are scored; the more points scored, the better the player's eye–hand coordination. The successful player may be expected to have an aptitude for jobs requiring such coordination.

To return to Travis's experiment, after having his participants practise alone on the rotor over several days, he observed that their performances reached a plateau. They had attained an apparent performance impasse. At this point, however, Travis introduced a small crowd of spectators (four to eight students). These spectators were asked to watch quietly and attentively. Nonetheless, their mere presence was sufficient to prompt a significant rise in performance among the participants, who achieved new personal bests; they beat their own records.

At first blush here, we might be tempted to make a leap of imagination, and begin to wonder about global workplace changes, such as increased individual competition (akin to co-action) and performance monitoring (akin to audiences). Perhaps these increasingly global practices are social psychologically well founded? After all, if the mere presence of co-acting or spectator others is sufficient to 'bring out the best' in human performance across tasks as diverse as reeling twine and job-related eye–hand coordination, then why should it not apply across the workplace, too?

Crisis and resolution: Zajonc's analysis

Unfortunately, however, during the 1920s and 1930s some apparent inconsistencies began to appear. In the co-action domain, for example, Floyd Allport (1924) asked participants to work either on fairly simple tasks, such as tackling basic multiplication problems, or on more difficult tasks, such as attempting to disprove philosophical arguments. The outcome with these more demanding tasks was that a small crowd of co-actors (five or six people) produced a performance *decrement*. To make matters worse, performance was also found to deteriorate in front of spectators. In one particular study, for instance, students found it more distracting to attempt to learn nonsense syllables (e.g. 'zup', 'rol', 'fip') in front of a small crowd of spectators than when attempting to learn them alone, when they learned the task with fewer errors (Pessin 1933). When the subjects were on their own, the list took an average of 10 repetitions to commit to memory, with 37 unforced errors. In an audience situation, however, it took them an average of 11 repetitions and 41 unforced errors.

Such decrements might not be huge, but for a student swotting for an important examination, they might make the difference between passing and failing. So, to what extent can we rely on them to replicate in a real-world task, such as studying? Unfortunately, the pattern of findings in the literature now looks too unreliable to trust. Qualitatively speaking, there are radical fluctuations in performance, from 'up' one moment to 'down' the next, whenever a crowd is part of the practice or performance. With that kind of volatility, making dependable generalisations seems, on the face of it, to be a lost cause. Perhaps this is why the field of crowd effects on performance was left relatively fallow until the 1960s. At that time, however, a now classic paper was published (Zajonc 1965b). In this paper, Zajonc (pronounced *Zy-ence*) proposed a parsimonious resolution of the apparent inconsistency, arguing that crowds could sometimes improve yet at other times worsen human performance.

Put very briefly, Zajonc suggested that crowds consistently produce a number of influences: They (1) augment physiological arousal. This (2) activates drive, which, in turn, (3) facilitates whatever repertoire at the time is 'dominant' (most salient, best known or stronger). Neither (1) nor (2) is contentious. Public performers often claim to attain 'adrenalin highs' and motivational buzzes either from spectators or from fellow competitors. World Cup teams, even rank outsiders, can defy form when their country is also the Cup host. In (3), according to Zajonc, the energy generated by the physical or implied presence of others is channelled into whatever we know best or feel most at the time. Since this level of knowledge may be good or bad — for example, it may consist of competence or incompetence — the presence of others can, theoretically, influence performance levels in either direction, depending on what the performer brings to the crowd situation in the first place.

Applications of social facilitation

As the saying goes, the devil is in the detail, so how well, precisely, does Zajonc's formulation account for the earlier findings? If the correct repertoire is already well known, such as when pursuing a rotor or attempting basic multiplication problems, then we can safely guess that the dominant response is a 'correct' response. Thus, we are likely to perform better when co-acting or when being watched by a crowd of spectator observers. There will be a performance increment. If, however, the task is unfamiliar, such as learning nonsense syllables or processing complex and subtle philosophical arguments, then the chances are that incorrect responses will predominate at any particular time. As a result, we can reliably assume that the presence of others will produce a performance decrement. Overall, therefore, one and the same process of social facilitation (invariably of the dominant response) neatly accounts for both sets of findings in the literature, the performance 'ups' as well as their 'downs' (for a psychophysiological account of this kind of process, see Blascovich et al. 1999).

As well as reconciling the scientific literature, Zajonc's analysis also squares with real and everyday experience, both negative and positive. On the negative side, many of us at some stage have suffered from a silly, nagging thought under the stress of a curly question from an audience. Similarly, many of us have known the consequences of going into a public presentation, or an anonymous examination hall, feeling ill prepared. For most mere mortals, when learning a new skill, and trying out various possible solutions, the presence of others merely exacerbates our clumsiness or prompts some other incorrect response. Performance suffers rather than improves. The concept of social facilitation speaks directly to those potentially traumatic and costly everyday reactions. On the positive side, however, the facilitation concept also recognises and respects the benefits of being well prepared. Many of us will know the sensation of giving a public performance that runs almost like clockwork, on 'automatic pilot', precisely because we have laboriously practised it so well beforehand.

In coining the term social facilitation, Zajonc did more than resolve a scientific paradox through a credible influence process. He also raised the possibility that social facilitation extends beyond performing work-like tasks. As Triplett or Gergen might have said, social facilitation might be applied much more widely than previously imagined, for example to crowds that panic, become aggressive or behave in a seemingly apathetic manner (see also Bargh 2001).

In a dangerous situation, for example, we can easily envisage some kind of social facilitation of a will to survive or a fear of death (raised mortality salience). This could promote crowd panic. In an aggressive crowd, we can envisage the social facilitation of latent prejudice, jealousy or envy, with the presence in the crowd of opposing beliefs or intentions, or merely from the opposite end of the stadium, adding fuel to the fire. In the case of an apparently apathetic crowd that does nothing to help an innocent individual in need, we can perhaps envisage the social facilitation of a fear of reprisals, or a lack of practice, or simply a disregard for others. Thus, a significant and intriguing question that the research of the early twentieth century raises for social psychologists today is: Could a range of crowd behaviours be partly attributable to one and the same underlying process, social facilitation?

Reconciling head and heart: Brown's synthesis

The examples above may imply that crowds embody emotion but little or no cognition. There seems to be little scope in our critical analysis so far for intellectual reason. Yet one relatively obvious area for reason to intervene in crowd behaviour processes is in the context of prolonged political struggle. During the apartheid era in South Africa, for instance, the disinhibiting influences of crowds were put forward in courts of law as legal defences in cases of 'necklace' killings and other violent acts perpetrated by crowds (Colman 1991a; Tyson 1993). The argument here was that individuals could not be held legally responsible for what was essentially a crowd-induced emotion. The vociferous (and cogent) counter-arguments, presented in psychology journals, insisted that crowds should not be so demonised. In particular, these articles argued that some crowd actions, when taken in a wider context, were perfectly rational. In apartheid South Africa, for example, many crowd behaviours could be seen as rational reactions in the wider context of ongoing political oppression (Reicher 1991a, 1991b). If the courts failed to recognise this, the argument went, social psychology's 'psychologising' of crowd behaviour was in danger of being used as a political instrument by the oppressive State (Reicher 1996). The political issue would be taken less seriously (Reicher 1997), and social psychology would be doing more harm than good.

Reflecting on critical narratives 2.1 and 2.2, it could be argued that both forms of analysis were and are partly correct. In critical narrative 2.1, the clubs were cleanly lathed, the ambush well planned and, within its limited time horizon, tactically rational. During the melee, however, certain unforeseen events occurred. The crowd seemed to lose control, its behaviour becoming at times anything but rational. People in the crowd literally had foaming mouths, like something out of a rabies documentary. In critical narrative 2.2, the campaign of action was considered and rational, and even during the 'rampage' the crowd carefully directed its anger at symbols of the regime rather than innocent bystanders. The anger was both facilitated *and* directed, spontaneous *and* political, emotional *and* rational — depending on the lens through which we view it.

Given the dual considerations of 'head' and 'heart', can we possibly meld them together into one overall pattern, or gestalt? Roger Brown (1965) has perhaps come closest to achieving this ambitious integration. Brown's solution has two layers operating primarily at different levels of explanation, the head relatively 'micro' and the heart relatively 'macro'. Rather in the way that individual greed can produce prosperity, he sees individual reason leading to crowd panic.

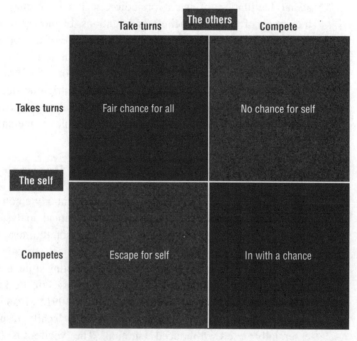

Figure 2.1 A rational basis to crowd panic?   *Source:* Adapted from Brown (1965).

At the heart of Brown's synthesis lies a core issue introduced in chapter 1 — namely, self-promotion versus the greater social good. The special way that crowd situations typically pose this dilemma is encapsulated in figure 2.1. The fundamental problem for the self in such a situation is whether or not to trust the others. If the self takes turns, and so do the others, there is a fair chance for all. But if the others decide instead to compete, there is no chance of escape for the self. A serious problem here is that crowds, as we have seen, are generally made up of strangers, who often have no solid reason either to trust or to be trusted by one another. In view of this, as figure 2.1 shows, the 'compete' option (in with a chance) is a safer bet for self than its 'take turns' counterpart (no chance for self). This means, from figure 2.1, that competing is a consistently safer option for the self than taking turns. The problem now, of course, is that other people are thinking exactly the same way. The net result, therefore, according to Brown, is a crowd panic that nonetheless originates in individual *reason.*

Stripped to basics, what Brown's model is proposing is that the possibilities in figure 2.1 briefly flash through the decision-maker's rational mind during the early stages of a theatre fire, stadium rush or market panic. Such panics, of course, include social facilitation of survival instincts, or fear of death, or any other base instinct that surfaces in such threatening situations. As well, over and above the mind-map pictured in figure 2.1, substantial **behaviour modelling** effects are likely. In other words, if one individual is seen to race towards the escape exit, the balance will probably be tilted even further towards the 'compete' option in figure 2.1. There is now even less cause, logically speaking, to assume that others will not reason exactly the same way. Thus, Brown's formulation of crowd panic is inherently flexible, capable in theory of assimilating a wide range of different social influence processes into a coherent whole (or gestalt).

Is there any empirical evidence that Brown is actually right that there is always a residual strand of rationality in crowd panic? To answer this, researchers might have relied on carefully controlled experiments to enable them to 'tease out' the separate components in the process. A particularly difficult barrier to studying any crowd behaviour, however, is the severe ethical constraints on running controlled experiments. Morally, we could hardly countenance the deliberate creation of a potential crowd stampede, for example, in the name of testing a psychological theory. Instead, therefore, crowd behaviour has tended to be studied using simulation games.

As illustrated in figure 2.1, these games typically involve dilemmas of self versus social interest, cooperation versus competition. For example, the game may require its players to compete under restricted time conditions to pull suspended objects out of a narrow-necked jar (Gilmour 1988). The inherent weakness in such representations, however, is that they are not well equipped to test Brown's proposal fully (Dore 1994). According to Dore, for instance, they are not high-fidelity representations: they do not necessarily allow full rein for the emotionality of actual crowd panics. To that extent, games are bound to be inherently limited in the degree to which they can test for the persistence of rationality under intense emotional pressure.

Clearly, Brown's argument needs to be supported by more naturalistic observations of situations in which the pressure of emotions is unambiguously and more realistically high. Studies have been made of critical incidents such as mine cave-ins, where there was no escape shaft to scramble for; or submarine disasters, in which the escape hatch was not a real option. In such circumstances, if people's thought processes do always retain a vestige of rationality, we should see not panic but a resigned calm. After all, there is no logical reason to panic. People should rationally deduce that panic is counterproductive. And this, in fact, is what has tended to happen (Mann 1969, p. 66).

In other crowd situations, too, Mann points out, crowds have been known to respond to relatively cool-headed behavioural models. These are people who, even when others are panicking, manage to remain calm and even to restore it by making rational pleas for order. Crowds have been brought 'back from the brink' by such individuals, averting disaster at the last minute (p. 87). Such feats would probably not have been possible unless the crowd had retained some vestige of rationality. Thus, in critical narrative 2.1, we saw how a single individual, the doctor, was able to break the escalating circle of violence. Reason not only prevailed — it also returned.

Overall, Brown's formulation resonates well with the ethos of this book. First, his analysis incorporates the core dilemma of self versus others, personal versus social priorities. Second, the schema allows for both affective (facilitation) and cognitive (reason) processes to help shape immediate behaviour (parts 1 to 3 of this book). Third, Brown's formulation allows scope for multiple levels of analysis, from psychological to sociological, to pluralistically shed light onto the same phenomenon.

CRITICAL NARRATIVE 2.3

The world of body building

A story featured in one West Australian newspaper discussed the kinds of pressures operating on aspiring championship body builders. A former Mr Universe and Ms (body-building) World had pleaded guilty to importing and possessing illegal steroids, which they had brought into Australia from New Zealand (where the drugs were legal). These champion body builders admitted that they had used the banned substances in an effort to win international body-building titles. In their defence, they argued that they faced a serious quandary in the world of competitive body building: how could they compete legitimately and successfully while not being allowed to take the drugs that their overseas rivals used legally, and by implication regularly. In fact, the body builders claimed, they would be seriously disadvantaged at the international level *without* taking these artificial steroids.

Source: Based on Peace (2000, p. 13).

In critical narrative 2.3, the kind of dilemma envisaged by Brown is placed in a contemporary global context. The example used is cheating in sport. In this case, competitive athletes are confronted with the choice of whether or not to use performance-enhancing drugs. There is a reasonable prospect that other athletes are doping themselves already. Logically, this means that the athlete who does not cheat might well never reach the top. Viewed like this, cheating becomes partly a crowd phenomenon, with the context of that crowd becoming very broad. At this point, readers might like to think of one or two similar self-versus-others dilemmas, perhaps on a smaller scale, from their own experience and observations.

Brown's model also reflects this book's three key themes of context, communication and culture. Context is crucial, because the presence of others in general, and positive role models in particular, can make a crucial difference to the outcome of a crowd situation. Communication is crucial, because any pro-social message to 'please reconsider', such as the plea for calm by the doctor in critical narrative 2.1, has to be voiced, understood and acted upon. Finally, culture is also crucial, because we would expect the basic orientations depicted in figure 1.1 to influence the central dilemma of self versus others.

Social loafing

One type of crowd dynamic that expressly addresses this influence of cultural values, as well as underscoring the voice of reason proposed in Brown's formulation, is *free riding* (Jackson & Harkins 1985; Kerr 1983). This is a social process that most of us are familiar with, for example through team learning projects in which one or two individuals, from the start, fail to 'pull their weight'. This can be very annoying and frustrating, and often undermines the project itself. In the social psychology literature, such setbacks are treated as both a process and an outcome of social influence. The twin-sided nature of these influences are vividly indicated by the self-explanatory technical term **social loafing** (Latané, Williams & Harkins 1979).

Social loafing is also sometimes known, with good historical reason, as the 'Ringelmann effect'. Ringelmann (1913) was an agronomist (agronomy is the science of crop production). In Ringelmann's research, which was actually conducted before Triplett's, during the 1880s (Brehm, Kassin & Fein 1999, p. 12), people pulled on a rope, in a situation similar to the rural sport of tug-of-war. Here, however, the participants did their tugging on a cart-like apparatus, rather than against other competitors. Ringelmann found that the larger he made the aggregate that was doing the pulling, the less the average amount of individual effort exerted. Individuals were apparently ready, or pre-primed, to 'hide' in the crowd (Davis 1969). Thus, they often succumbed to a temptation to reduce their personal effort on behalf of their 'team'.

A good deal of subsequent research showed similar social loafing processes in different tasks, from cheering and clapping (Latané et al. 1979) to students playing pool (Michaels et al. 1982). Applying the same logic as we did to Triplett's classic study, it seems that loafing is not limited to one type of activity, for example to any one type of sport. To that extent, social loafing is cross-contextually robust (Karau & Williams 1993).

A brief survey of this literature indicates that the likelihood of loafing increases as the task (cheering, clapping, pulling) loses meaning and significance for the participants. One possible interpretation of these particular results is that the heavily 'laboratory experimental' approach to studying the phenomenon may have lacked validity outside of the lab. An alternative and possibly more contemporary perspective on this, however, is that the literature *is* directly relevant. Specifically, it is relevant to the dull and repetitive jobs, or aspects of those jobs, that many of us have to perform every day.

At first glance, the entire literature on loafing might appear to contradict the literature on social facilitation. After all, on the one hand the crowd is supposed to enhance performance, while on the other it is supposed to reduce performance (Brehm et al. 1999). Brehm et al., however, have offered a context-based resolution of the apparent paradox (see also Smith et al. 2001). When individuals are personally accountable, as in co-action and audience situations, arousal climbs and facilitation occurs. When individual contributions are pooled, however, arousal is decreased and people can hide within the crowd with impunity. In these pooled circumstances, and unlike in social facilitation situations, responsibility is diluted and diffused among the elements of the crowd. As a result, the average individual feels less personally accountable, has less of a stake in the outcome and so loafs. Thus, according to Brehm et al., reduced 'evaluation apprehension', or nervousness about the 'potential for evaluation', is the key to reconciling the loafing and facilitation literatures (1999, p. 255).

An alternative viewpoint: cultural values

A complementary analysis of the same apparent discrepancy is worth considering. This is certainly not the only other integration in the field, nor does it purport to explain everything. Instead, and in keeping with a major theme in this book, it is deliberately focused on cultural values. It holds that the literature in the field tends to have been amassed in settings that are largely Western, and to that extent also relatively individualistic. This bias understandably has tended to produce over-individualistic theories of loafing (Karau & Williams 1995). Granted, individualism may be globalising, so widening the scope for all individualistic theories. But, as we also know, collectivistic repertoires are still powerful presences in social influence. Thus, there is the potential for an inherent bias, in the existing loafing literature, towards the self and pure self-interest.

Let us for a moment deconstruct the just-introduced term 'evaluation apprehension' (after Cottrell 1968). This term, as used in the Brehm et al. model of loafing effects, has some contestable assumptions embedded in it. Specifically, it implies that individual workers will calculatingly avoid working hard unless they personally have something to gain by it. What it offers is a psychology of carrot and stick. At least one other major model of loafing is expressed in a similarly calculative way, seeing loafing as a logical outcome of the cognition 'What's in this for me?' (Karau & Williams 1997). Certainly, no one likes being 'played for a sucker' (Schnake 1991), and this aversion is plainly central to Brown's respected formulation discussed above. But what remains plainly objectionable is that the 'evaluation apprehension' interpretation of social loafing, put forward by Brehm at al. and others since, assumes that individualism and self-concern are the only possible norms. As figure 1.1 reminds us, however, relatively individualistic and calculative modes of thinking and acting are far from being 'universal', even, and perhaps especially, in a world that is experiencing globalisation.

Towards a single process

Let us instead consider the possibility that the social loafing effect found in much of the existing (Western) literature reflects the social facilitation of a particular dominant response — *individualism*. Having taken this step, moreover, let us consider the further possibility that collectivistic values, too, can be facilitated. In this (for the moment) imagined scenario, being in the pooled-effort situation that Brehm and others see simply as an opportunity to 'hide from view' might actually be sufficient to *enhance* performance compared with working alone. Since collectivism means placing the collective before the self whenever this is a dominant response, it too stands to be socially facilitated. Individualist models of crowd influence risk not allowing their proponents to fully realise this possibility. Yet it is a very real prospect, as at least one fascinating study has shown (Earley 1993).

Earley's important study focused on the world of the workplace manager. Specifically, he examined performance on routine management tasks, as reflected in an 'in-tray' exercise. As the name suggests, in-tray exercises require managers and potential managers (used in selection and placement) to process and prioritise a simulated tray of daily (and often difficult) managerial responsibilities. Typically, these will include chores like dealing with disciplinary matters and customer complaints, prioritising work issues and allocating workloads. Such task sets are sometimes used at job assessment centres, for example, because of their relatively high fidelity to the kinds of daily tasks that managers face. In this way, of course, the task set is a suitable barometer for gauging workplace motivation.

As respondents, Earley had secured the participation of real managers, for whom this type of task would have been relatively familiar and routine. These managers were instructed that they were working on the job either alone or as part of a 'team' of (implied) other managers from the same country (the United States, China or Israel). 'Culture' was thus included as a major independent variable within this study. With respect to the individualism–collectivism axis featured in figure 1.1, US managers represented the more individualist end of the values spectrum (Hofstede 1980). At the other end of that spectrum (figure 1.1), Chinese and Israeli managers (Israel being the land of the communal *kibbutz*) represented more collectivistic values or orientations.

In accord with the existing literature, Earley found that greater individualism was associated with increased levels of social loafing. This correlation was evident not only at the country level but also *within* countries. Relatively individualistic individuals, independently of their country of origin, even the generally more collectivistic ones, consistently loafed more. Relative collectivism, on the other hand, was consistently — that is, again across levels — associated with increased effort and performance. Here we have striking evidence that the implied presence of others can, depending on dominant cultural value orientation, actually both reduce *and enhance* performance.

Before attempting to explain these findings in more detail, there were also some very interesting edges to Earley's results. For example, relative collectivists who found themselves in the implied presence of foreigners did loaf. Again, context mattered. Relative individualists, finding themselves in a similar situation, loafed just as much as they did in the 'team of fellow nationals' situation. It was as if these relative individualists were comparatively unconcerned with the social context in which their work routines were performed. They were consistently comparatively insensitive to the social context, free-riding regardless. Relative collectivists, by contrast, were socially more discerning. They were ready to work harder, but only if they sensed the presence of others with whom they shared the same nationality.

One parsimonious way of interpreting these fascinating and important findings is in terms of social facilitation. For the relatively individualistic managers, the presence of others, whoever they were, socially facilitated their predominantly individualistic values, and so their individualistic behaviour. Hence, relatively individualistic participants consistently displayed loafing behaviour, which is fundamentally oriented towards the self. For the more collectivistic-minded managers, however, the dominant response was to be more socially oriented. These managers focused on doing what *they* customarily valued, namely helping the in-group as well as not being played for suckers by the out-group. So, relatively collectivist participants actually worked *harder* in one crowd context (with the implied presence of an in-group) and loafed in the next (with the implied presence of non- or out-group members).

Overall, therefore, both sets of managers consistently displayed social facilitation. One social process parsimoniously accounts for both sets of findings (for more detail on this kind of integrationist perspective, see Guerin 1999). Social loafing becomes, in effect, a culture-driven manifestation of social facilitation (for a similar conclusion to this regarding the culture of small groups, see Karau & Hart 1998; for discussions about the role of personal self-esteem and task challenges in such situations, see Charbonnier et al. 1998; Huguet, Charbonnier & Monteil 1999). Context, too, is important, because relative collectivists were relatively attuned to it, and based their responses on it. As we have just seen, they worked harder in one context and less hard in the next.

A point of reflection (a key pathway)

Where do these analyses leave Brehm et al.'s evaluation apprehension concept and the Karau and Williams model highlighting 'What's in this for me'? Where are these theoretical models now as explanatory mechanisms for previous experimental findings? A culture-based explanation, such as the one offered above, lets us 'step back' from the immediate behaviour itself. We allow ourselves to view this behaviour in a relatively broad, intercultural light. Like stepping back from an Impressionist painting, behaviour's underlying meanings become clearer. For the relative collectivist, not letting the side down is what counts most, so working alongside others is what creates evaluation apprehension. For the relative individualist, it is the other way round. Working alone creates evaluation apprehension. The meaning of being in a crowd, or of being alone, changes with culture and context, and it is this meaning that ultimately shapes behaviour.

From a practical, managerial point of view, this line of thinking is flagging the prospect of equifinality (Bate-Boerop 1975; Cicchetti & Rogosch 1996). This term is used in management studies, although it derives originally from systems thinking. There, as in management studies, it simply means that we can often reach the same goal via different pathways (Von Bertalanffy 1940). In our case, it seems that managers might be able to achieve the same goal of facilitating motivated performance through different means, depending on the predominant value orientations of the particular workforce at the time. The research enables managers to make more considered decisions — to decide, for instance, whether to opt for workplace teams or individual contracts, depending, respectively, on whether their workforce is relatively collectivist or individualist in orientation. From a strictly business point of view, social psychological thinking like this could prove crucial to group performance and survival.

Contagion

So far we have used the concept of social facilitation to explain a wide variety of crowd phenomena, but one remaining phenomenon poses a challenge to this initiative: this is the concept of crowd **contagion**. Probably the best-known writer on this aspect of crowd behaviour is a political commentator, Gustav Le Bon (1895). Le Bon was an aristocratic journalist writing in France at a time when there was a great deal of paranoia among the French ruling classes with respect to the poor. It was a time marked by political turbulence. In this broad social context, and from a perspective of privilege rather than privation, crowds and crowd behaviour were readily constructed as highly threatening entities. It is therefore no great surprise that Le Bon tended to accentuate the negative aspects of the masses and mass crowd behaviour generally.

In Le Bon's analysis, crowds were dangerous and fickle, susceptible to whatever emotion 'infected' them at the time. This process of emotional infection, by analogy with the rapid and deadly spread of disease from one person to the next, was later appropriately termed 'contagion' (Blumer 1946). As this term concisely signifies, Le Bon, and others of his time and class, viewed crowds as highly susceptible to emotions such as panic and aggression. They were inherently receptive to anti-government agitators. In short, they needed to be controlled and monitored (for a more detailed discussion of Le Bon's work, including its impact on psychology, politics and history, see Reicher 1996).

This kind of analysis gave any State the perfect excuse for continuing oppression. Not surprisingly, therefore, over the years the process of contagion has attracted its fair share of controversy and criticism (Reicher 1991a, 1991b). At the same time, the process of contagion has itself proved worthy of serious research as well as theoretical renewal (see, respectively, Milgram, Bickman & Berkowitz 1969; Hatfield, Cacioppo & Rapson 1993, 1994). Perhaps the best reason for taking the process so seriously is that it resonates extremely well with many people's own experiences.

In critical narrative 2.1, we saw how the emotions of a violent crowd, the 'rabid' faces and shouted abuse, appeared to 'spread' rapidly. This case exemplifies the contagion of aggression. An extreme form of aggression is the self-inflicted variety, suicide (see chapter 10), and there are contagion-like elements to collective suicides (Reser 1999). Another example of the power of contagion, this time from the political arena, is offered in a memorable and disturbing personal account of the 1936 Olympic Games in Nazi Berlin related by a former Olympian who competed there. During the Olympic ceremonies, and to his own consternation, when the crowd roared one hundred thousand *Heil Hitler*s, the former athlete recalls having to struggle to keep his *own* hand in his pocket (Australian Broadcasting Corporation 1999b). Explaining an emotional infection like this is a real challenge for social facilitation theory, because the athlete was anything but 'Nazi' in his dominant response patterns. We shall return to this critical narrative in a moment. For now, we need only say that the immediate sense of belongingness, power and purpose, however misleading, that a crowd offers can be very seductive (for a journal article on contagion in leadership, see Cherulnik et al. 2001).

In critical narrative 2.2 a form of synchronicity was observable as the crowd moved swiftly but determinedly across the open campus, selectively destroying symbols of the despot's oppressive regime. On a more everyday level, we have all probably experienced 'infectious' applause, a sense of shared national pride at the singing of an anthem or 'contagious' laughter (Martin & Gray 1996). Some of my social psychology students succinctly summarised the latter effect in the adage, 'Laugh, and the world laughs with you'. My own most memorable experience of a positive contagion occurred when witnessing a sunset on Waikiki Beach in Honolulu, Hawai'i. A throng of tourists had gathered to watch the event. As the sun melded gloriously with the South Pacific horizon, a sporadic ripple of clapping began from somewhere in the crowd. In a few seconds this had grown into a long wave of applause, running right along the strand. I, of course, found myself applauding too, something I had never done before for a sunset, nor have I since. It was a very moving and special experience, catalysed uniquely by a crowd. For me, then, contagion is definitely not necessarily the insidious process that Le Bon implied (see also critical narrative 2.4; for an alternative discussion on the contagiousness of yawning, see Provine 1997; for an illustration of contagion in crowd helping, fast-forward to critical narrative 2.6).

CRITICAL NARRATIVE 2.4

Yawning alert!

Research undertaken at the University of Stirling, in Scotland, has revealed that yawning is not always, as is commonly supposed, a symptom of tiredness. Dr James Anderson, of the Department of Psychology, argues that yawning is a form of social interaction inherited from prehistoric times that serves to indicate when the brain desires a change in stimulation.

Dr Anderson's research has focused particularly on the phenomenon of 'contagious yawning', when one person sets off a chain of yawning in others. Interestingly, people become more susceptible to contagious yawning as they grow older, which suggests that group activity becomes increasingly synchronised with age. Dr Anderson's research also suggests that early contagious yawning in children may be a sign of high intellectual capability. Primary school children who yawn in response to others yawning are among the best readers. This is an important finding because psychologists believe that young children who are good readers have more highly developed levels of empathy. In other words, they are more sociable.

Source: Stirling Minds (2001).

Can we explain these diverse incidences of contagion, negative and positive, in terms of a single social facilitation process? At least in some respects, I believe we can. For example, the hunt supporters in critical narrative 2.1 shared a latent aggression; so, perhaps, did Hitler's crowds. The Australian Olympian, despite being relatively egalitarian rather than power distant, was representing his country. To that extent, he was already unusually susceptible, at the time, to nationalist sentiments. On the more positive side of crowd behaviour, the students in critical narrative 2.2 had for some time been contemplating the deconstruction of the political system, along with its symbols of political oppression. Audiences, meanwhile, start to applaud (or yawn) precisely because they are already happy (or bored) with the performance. Likewise, sunset-watchers on holiday are by definition already primed to appreciate natural beauty. Broadly, then, social facilitation seems to provide a pretty good explanation for crowd contagion.

Nonetheless, as the phenomenon of mass suicide indicates, for contagion to occur someone has to strike the first blow, to light the fuse. Someone always needs to be first to shout 'Fire!' and start to run, or to make the first plea for calm, or to start the applause. Of course, behaviour models exert an influence in workplace settings, too (Schein 1991). Wherever we turn, therefore, *modelling* behaviour and social facilitation are fundamental to the overall dynamic of crowd behaviour. In addition to being necessary for social facilitation, behaviour models can also *add to its momentum*. For example, models can be observed doing what they do and be seen to 'get away with it' (Bandura, Ross & Ross 1963). This accelerates the crowd dynamic significantly. In later chapters, we will see that Bandura has developed an entire theory on 'social learning', which asserts that models are more likely to be imitated and followed if they are rewarded (e.g. with escape) rather than punished (e.g. beaten down by majority elements in the crowd) for their initiating actions.

To link together all the crowd processes we have so far discussed, I believe that social facilitation and behavioural modelling often go hand-in-glove across a range of crowd situations. Each is present in the opening critical narratives, and their influence can be found in all sorts of violent, panicky and courageous crowd behaviours.

This synergy of (a) social facilitation and (b) behavioural modelling extends . beyond crowd settings. Social situations of all kinds by definition contain the real or implied presence of others. In chapter 3, for instance, we examine the influences of group discussion, which naturally involves a presence, real or implied, of others. One of the most reliable findings from the research on group discussion is that opinions tend to polarise, or move towards the extreme, in the members' initially preferred direction, during and following a meeting. This surely betrays more than a hint of both facilitation and modelling.

Co-observation

There remains one basic type of crowd situation that we have not yet considered. On some occasions, the crowd becomes an aggregate of spectators, or **co-observers**, to an emergency involving others. In such situations, as Prince Hamlet might have said if he had been a social psychologist: To intervene, or not to intervene, that is the question! Here we return again to our self-versus-others dilemma. At some stage during these instances of crowd behaviour, the individual self must make the decision whether to risk life and limb on behalf of others. Much of the research and theory developed in this area has focused on what social factors promote self-preservation and inaction, as distinct from social helping and intervention. These kinds of decisions are of course vital for the victim. But they invariably have to be 'lived with' by the crowd, too. Understanding them is therefore important for civil society as a whole.

For those of us who have ever been caught in a situation such as that recounted in critical narrative 2.6, the expression 'stunned mullet' might come to mind to describe how it feels at the time. This term captures the dreamlike quality and almost altered state of mind that emergency situations often evoke ('This can't be *real!*').

The resulting, perhaps infectious 'apathy' has been studied in well-controlled experimental settings, both in the laboratory and in the field. These experimental types of study, as we know, give us reasonably solid foundations on which to make judgements about causality. With these in hand, therefore, we may be able to manage helping behaviour better.

The original context for beginning this field of study, as we now know it, was the brutal murder, in New York City in 1964, of Katherine (Kitty) Genovese (Darley & Latané 1968). During this attack, which lasted a full 40 minutes and took place in broad daylight, no one came to the victim's aid; no one even called the police. Instead, 38 of the victim's neighbours apparently watched as spectators from their apartment windows — a co-observing crowd. This appalling level of crowd apathy prompted Darley and Latané to try to understand how and why such an incident could have happened. Their investigation is a benchmark against which we should judge the success or failure of their and others' endeavours since. Have we managed to unravel the enigma of why so many people collectively failed to offer the slightest help to Kitty Genovese? We will return to this issue in review question 2.4 at the end of the chapter.

Such incidents are certainly not confined to 1960s New York. A cursory review of your newspaper will reveal reports of similar incidents from around the globe, probably including your own community (activity 2). Australia's *Northern Territory News* reported a startlingly similar incident, again in New York, on 31 March 1998 (p. 31). Then, two months later, in the Northern Territory itself (reported on 28 May), 'a young woman was raped beside a busy Darwin road in broad daylight as she walked home from work ... during peak hour traffic' (1998, p. 3; activity 2). Critical narrative 2.5 recounts a not dissimilar scenario reported recently in the *New Zealand Herald* (this story also highlights behaviour modelling).

CRITICAL NARRATIVE 2.5

Bystander non-intervention in Auckland

When Aucklander Kylie Jones was murdered on her way home from work last week, she screamed. She screamed so loudly and painfully that people heard her over their television sets. Yet no one did anything. Only one person went outside to listen for further screams but took no further action. No one rushed to see where the scream came from. No one went to help. Would the rest of us have acted differently? Would we have charged out into the night and made a difference? Should we condemn those who did nothing?

Put yourself in one of Kylie's neighbours' homes that night and there is a high probability that you would not have acted either. It was night and there was a scream — easy to think you had imagined it, or that even if you did go outside, it would be impossible to trace the source of the noise. And then again, if the scream was real, would you really want to confront the cause? Much better to stay warm and safe in front of the TV.

More disturbing, for those who like to think the best of human nature, is that research shows that even if the scream had been during the day, and some of us had seen Kylie being attacked, we would have been more likely to do nothing than to go to her aid. Even stranger, the more of us witnessing the event, the less likely it would be for any one of us to help.

Research into this phenomenon, known as bystander apathy, was sparked in the 1960s by the case in New York (see page 66) in which Kitty Genovese was attacked outside her apartment block. There were more than 30 witnesses but not one even called the police, and the woman was killed. 'The more people watching, the less likely one person is to intervene', says Dr Lucy Johnston, senior lecturer in social psychology at the University of Canterbury. 'If other people aren't reacting, then we're less likely to because we don't want to look like the goon who intervenes. There's also the issue of personal safety. If it's a violent incident, people are concerned they themselves may be hurt.'

Of course, there are those who do rise above the norm — one of whom is a Christchurch-born artist Ruth Watson, who I saw in action once in Sydney. We were walking past a small park in Darlinghurst when Ruth suddenly started shouting and striding across the grass. At the far end, a group was beating a man on the ground with pipes, kicking him and, we later found out, stabbing him. Plenty of people were around, but no one intervened — except Ruth, with me in her wake. She shouted: 'Stop. I'm calling the police. Stop that', The men began to look towards her, and though they continued to beat the man, they did so with less vigour. When she kept advancing and shouting they miraculously broke their tight cluster and left.

The guy on the ground lived. Dr Niki Harré, an Auckland University social psychology lecturer, says Ruth's actions were unusual. 'That a woman would go to the aid of a man being beaten by men seems to me absolutely extraordinary.' For a start, lack of action is the norm, and second, if anyone intervenes in a physically dangerous situation, it is far more likely to be a man than a woman.

So why did Ruth act, and why did no one else do so? Does it say something about her personality? Are there certain types of people who are more courageous than others? Research does not support this view, says Harré. Evidence suggests that the particular circumstances of an incident are more important determinants of how a person will act than his or her personality.

We are more likely to act if we're the only witness to an event than if we're part of a group, for example. We're also more likely to help someone we identify with or have sympathy for — we'd probably stop to help an old man with a walking stick who fell over, but not an old man who smelt of alcohol.

Training can also make a difference. 'There's a lot of evidence that if people feel they have the expertise or ability to help, they're far more likely to intervene,' says Johnston. 'An off-duty police officer has the skills and training to intervene in an appropriate way. Similarly, nurses and doctors are far more likely to intervene if someone looks like they're hurt.'

But what of those of us who don't have any medical or emergency training, those of us who would like to think that if we had heard Kylie Jones's scream, we could somehow have done something, however small? That if tomorrow we saw someone being hurt, we would not stand by paralysed?

Be sensitised, says Harré. Be aware of bystander apathy and next time, maybe, it will be easier to act.

Source: Based on Dunbar (2000).

CONTEXT, COMMUNICATION AND CULTURE

The point of critical narrative 2.5 is that bystander apathy is as relevant today as it was in the 1960s. In some research, the extent of apparent unwillingness to help has been linked to globalisation — with its associations, for example, with growing urbanisation, anonymity and danger on city streets. Unwillingness to help reportedly increases with these aspects of social *context* (Levine 2000). Yet what about Darwin in the story above (and the one at the end of this chapter, in activity 2)? Unlike Auckland, Darwin is not a large city. Other factors must have intervened significantly into the apathy equation there. These sometimes include *communication* norms, for instance socialising children into a norm of 'don't get involved' (2000, p. 179). Clearly, such norms are not necessarily restricted to large cities. They might equally apply, for example, to a small town with 'a gang problem'. Either way, socialisation practices like these help define a community's own *culture* (Levine 2000). So context, communication and culture are all implicated in, and capable of influencing, the behaviour of co-observing crowds.

The bystander effect

These three themes are each reflected and illuminated in the classic studies on bystander intervention conducted by Darley and Latané (1968). This research seems to have set out with a hunch that people are really not 'apathetic' at all. Such scepticism is common enough in social psychological research. In this case, Darley and Latané's concern with possible social influence (the influence of crowd context) led them to test the possibility that powerful *situational* factors may have been at work in the Kitty Genovese murder. In essence, that is, they questioned an implicit commonsense notion — that more people present equals a greater chance of somebody helping. This is precisely the notion that gave the original murder its shocking and perplexing character. Thus, Darley and Latané were aiming straight at their own criterion — making sense out of an apparent crowd enigma.

Darley and Latané's program of research eventually resulted in a theoretical model of non-intervention in crowd situations. To preview that model briefly, bystanders are repeatedly and cumulatively influenced by the presence of others, at sequential stages in their decision making, not to intervene. The key stages in this model are (1) noticing that there is an emergency; (2) interpreting what is seen as an emergency; and (3) deciding that self has a social responsibility to act. At each of these critical stages, Darley and Latané argued, the presence of others acts to reduce the likelihood of intervening, for the average individual. This general principle has become known as the 'bystander effect'. Because it is focused, at the psychological level, on individual-level behaviour, we have to remember that crowds are made up of *many* such individuals. Logically, therefore, the size of a crowd should at least partly offset bystander effects (see review question 2.4).

The methodology employed during Darley and Latané's studies set a pattern for others to follow. A relatively minor emergency is staged, and various features of the social context, such as the number of observers present, are somehow manipulated. The effect of this manipulation on the level of helping behaviour is then plotted. By and large, experiments, both laboratory and field, have remained the preferred investigative vehicle. Some simulations, surveys and cases have also made the journals and the news (activities 2.1 and 2.2). But what is most interesting about the *experiments* is that they deal directly with (1) contextual, (2) communicative and (3) cultural factors.

Noticing

Darley and Latané's classic investigation of the *noticing* stage in the decision-making process involved a fake waiting room. In this room, waiting students believed they were 'killing time' before taking part in an interview about city life. They waited either alone or in the company of two other genuine participants. These bystanders, like themselves, were dutifully filling out pre-interview questionnaires. At that moment, staged smoke clouds began to waft into the waiting room through an air vent. The researchers waited to see how long it took for someone to notice the apparent emergency.

As expected, the larger the aggregate of participants in the waiting room, the longer it took to 'see' the smoke coming in. With just two other participants present in the room, only 25 per cent of people, compared with 67 per cent in the alone condition, noticed the smoke almost immediately.

In a real-life setting, such immediacy can make a difference between so-called apathy and action. It may take only a split-second to drive past a roadside assault (as in Darwin), or to fail to notice completely the distressed and injured bag-snatch victim on a busy main street. In the experiment itself, Darley and Latané thought that those who found themselves in the company of others when the emergency happened initially kept trying to avoid looking at the others. They tried to mind their own business, for example by carefully avoiding eye contact.

This kind of evasive action is a routine and pervasive norm in many urban contexts, past and present, that has been widely investigated by environmental social psychologists. Their classic studies found, for example, that eye contact with strangers decreases the more urbanised a social environment becomes (Newman & McAuley 1978). In Australian cities, for example, the larger the city, the less the eye contact (Amato 1981). This is at least partly a form of adaptation to interpersonal overload in urban environments (McAuley, Coleman & de Fusco 1980). The more overstimulating the town or city is, the less socially disposed passers-by are (Amato 1983a). So there are multiple reasons why urban environments significantly reduce everyday levels of eye contact. In fact, we can probably think of many others (for an architectural example related to mood, see Amato 1981; see also chapter 10, on eye contact and aggression).

According to this analysis, we could easily interpret Darley and Latané's 'not-noticing' effect, in the original study, as an instance of social facilitation — in this case of an already well-learned response maxim: 'Avoid eye contact in confined, relatively stressful spaces', such as train carriages, lifts and anonymous waiting rooms. So the social facilitation idea *works*. If we then combine those norms of avoiding eye contact with the physically hectic and dizzying pace of contemporary city life, the possibility of simply missing an emergency in the first place becomes strong. This point is crucial because eye contact, in itself, has been found to be a significant predictor of helping behaviour in at least one of today's mega-cities (Silva & Guenther 2001).

To return now to the New York murder case, there is just one problem with the noticing concept. The crowd who watched while Kitty Genovese was murdered were not in any particular hurry. They were, in fact, able to gaze out from their apartment windows, cocooned and compartmentalised, as it were, within their living capsules. The neighbours in Auckland and motorists in Darwin were similarly compartmentalised (even though the motorists' viewing time as they passed must have been short; see activity 2). Overall, therefore, there is plainly more to the crowd decision-making process in general, and crowd apathy in particular, than momentary lapses in attention.

Pluralistic ignorance

Given that compartmentalisation features in many modern emergencies, perhaps the opportunity for communication between observers is somehow crucial? According to Darley and Latané, a second crucial stage in making the decision about whether to intervene is the need to define the situation as a genuine emergency. Here onlookers might rely on communication with others. Many assumed 'emergencies' turn out to be no more than minor incidents, such as burning toast, or bath tap steam, or the 'victim' discovered to be drunk rather than injured or sick. Given such false alarms, it is perfectly rational and reasonable, as Brown (1965) also suggested, to defer a decision for a moment, until we have looked around to see how others are interpreting the same situation. After all, to borrow out of context from yet another adage, two heads are often (logically) better than one.

This is what participants in Sherif's autokinetic study probably reasoned before and during their convergence process (outlined in chapter 1). They, too, were operating in ambiguous situations, and almost without thinking took the rational option of heeding how others were judging the same situation. Similarly, in co-observing crowd situations, Cialdini (1993) has argued that people habitually implicitly refer to each other on how to interpret a situation. The problem now, of course, is that people tend to forget that they are relying on each other for guidance. Such a lack of awareness can be disastrous for any victim in a genuine emergency (see also Brown's formulation, p. 56). This is because each co-observer unwittingly becomes a *model* of, and for, inaction to the others. This same collective inaction implicitly conveys, among the assembled crowd, that there is in fact no emergency.

Darley and Latané termed this insidious process **pluralistic ignorance**. Their term nicely captures the idea that many individuals are unaware, even once they start making eye contact with each other, that they are each reading the wrong (non-emergency) cues from the others' visible, behavioural inertia. Darley and Latané thought that they had captured this insidious dynamic in their 'smoke-filled room' experiment. In that study, 75 per cent of the participants who were tested alone reported the smoke almost immediately. Typically, they noticed the smoke almost at once, got up and went to have a closer look, and then went to report it. When gathered together in a small 'crowd' of three persons, however, only 13 per cent reported the smoke — even though after four minutes or so the room was completely filled with smoke! According to qualitative observations made by the experimenters at the time, participants under these conditions, once they had started glancing up from the page, tended to look at each other, shrug their shoulders and continue filling out the questionnaire.

The sheer foolhardiness of this failure to respond actively within so much time raises the possibility that the students were playing some kind of game of 'chicken' with each other, waiting to see who would 'break' first. Or maybe they were just wary of looking foolish (and craven) if the event turned out to be nothing to worry about. In either of these events, we would expect *more* helping to occur if the prospect of looking like a fool (evaluation apprehension) was explicitly reduced. This reduction is therefore exactly what Latané and a colleague did next. They staged an emergency that consisted of someone else (an actor) apparently falling and hurting herself next door. If the accident turned out to be a false alarm, participants would hardly look foolish or cowardly simply in having offered to help. Yet even under these conditions, non-intervention persisted. Post hoc interviews with the original participants indicated that they had, as their persistent non-intervention suggests, failed to interpret the situation as a genuine emergency. They had indeed taken their cue from the inaction of their co-spectators, who — under a pall of pluralistic ignorance — were doing the same.

At the heart of pluralistic ignorance lies a failure to communicate. The modern world, with its television 'window on the world' onto its poor, its homeless, its brutalised and its disenfranchised, does not allow verbal communication with those victims. Nor does it encourage us to practise communication with other observers. Having lost that knack of communication, relative incompetence in communication will be facilitated when an emergency next occurs. Being more reliant on language, and to that extent a communication step *beyond* crowds, the Internet probably offers a better hope (see chapter 3), although at least some media technology may be insidiously helping to lull people into inaction (see chapter 4). Staring at television screens, or through apartment and car windows, many of today's global citizens may increasingly be coming to resemble, or worse still outdo, those non-intervening citizens from New York in 1964.

Taking responsibility

If co-observers manage to make it through the stages of *noticing* and *interpreting* an emergency, something else is still required before any intervention takes place. There has to be some kind of decision that self is personally *accountable* for helping the person(s) in need. The problem here is that the more potential helpers present, the greater the risk to the victim that every one of them will feel that somebody *else* should intervene. This is especially so in (often dangerous) urban environments. The underlying 'Why me?' question has received much attention since Darley and Latané's original research program (and in the related loafing literature, too). Much of that attention has shown that the adage 'Safety in numbers', which applies well to co-observers and loafers, does not extend well to victims of emergencies.

In their experimental study of the 'Why me?' quandary, Darley and Latané had participants assemble for an ostensible discussion on the problems of college life.

To test their model properly, they had to ensure that the situation was both (1) noticed and (2) interpreted as being undeniably an emergency. The crisis had to be absolutely unambiguous. Therefore, it was arranged for one of the assembled students to have an apparent epileptic seizure during the ongoing discussion itself. In reality, this emergency was staged, although it is difficult to imagine the study being cleared by any research ethics committee today (see chapter 1, on ethics).

The deception in question was achieved by seating one genuine participant in a Crutchfield apparatus. This is basically a series of partitioned booths (much like apartments), across which participants can communicate using intercom systems, notes and the like. In reality, the sole genuine participant is surrounded by an imagined (or virtual) crowd, since the messages he or she receives are bogus and under the complete control of the experimenter. The Crutchfield apparatus has the methodological and practical advantages of controlling how many other members exist in a simulated crowd. In this study, for instance, the crowd's size varied from two to six members, including the genuine participant.

The session began normally enough, with a round of introductions over the communication system, and an explanation that the apparatus had been employed to protect anonymity in what was to follow. From our point of view, as we have indicated, the Crutchfield equipment can be regarded as a good representation of the cubicle-type context in which Kitty Genovese's neighbours were ensconced. During the round of introductions, one of the simulated voices made reference to epilepsy. A few minutes into the discussion, this simulated individual proceeded to have a simulated seizure. In fact, he said that he was dying.

The dependent variable in this study was whether the genuine participant (a surrogate for the 'average bystander') would get up and leave the self's own little cubicle in order to call for help. The key finding in the study was that this type of pro-social behaviour became progressively *less* likely as the number of others believed to be present at the scene increased. Safety (for the *victim*, at least) could *not* be found in numbers. To be specific, in the dyadic situation (genuine participant plus victim), 85 per cent of participants reported the crisis. With three persons present in the crowd, this figure dropped to 62 per cent. With a mere six persons apparently present (including the alleged victim), only 31 per cent of bystanders made any behavioural move to intervene.

At the debriefing stage of the experiment, these non-helpers behaved a little like Milgram's 'teachers' (see chapter 1). They were clearly relieved to learn that the victim was all right. They did not believe that what they had done, or rather failed to do, was 'all right' or 'okay'. They had, indeed, interpreted the incident as a real emergency. In attempting to make sense of their participating crowd members' behaviour, therefore, Darley and Latané coined the term **diffusion of responsibility**. This expression denotes the fact that having more people present often leads co-observers to feel less personally accountable. In such circumstances, the question 'Why me?' again becomes salient to the onlookers. This is because they can see (or imagine) many others who could equally don the mantle of responsibility. In this way, crowds can exert an influence of spreading responsibility more widely in proportion to their number. As the size of the crowd increases, any self-imposed sense of duty becomes more and more diluted. Self is less likely to help.

The neighbour's fire

The family were seated around the kitchen table, eating their dinner. One of them, from the corner of his eye, thought he saw a wisp of smoke from his next-door neighbour's back window. 'Probably running a hot bath or burning the meal', he thought to himself. A few moments later, however, smoke again caught his eye, and he reluctantly got up from the table to investigate. (Point 1: Emergency almost *unnoticed*.)

Staying indoors so as not to seem nosy, he peered as best he could towards his neighbour's window. The smoke was still wafting out. *This could not be real!* Instinctively, he looked across towards the other neighbours, gathering along their own back-fences, to see what *they* were doing. Nothing. One of them was even carefully checking out the house through a pair of binoculars! Yet still nobody did anything, nobody moved. Surely, then, there was no real fire here, no real danger to anyone or to their home. (Point 2: *Pluralistic ignorance* prevents the emergency from being defined as one.)

Soon, however, the flames were licking the walls of the house. Roof tiles were exploding high into the air, and black smoke was billowing out. Suddenly the flames were higher than the house itself. The whole two storeys had become an inferno. No mistake now, this was a real fire — finally, the house was almost completely destroyed. Had anybody telephoned for the fire brigade, an ambulance, the police? Surely, with all these neighbours looking on, somebody would have had the sense to make an emergency call? 'Why me? Why should *I* be the one to look like a selfish sod for not calling earlier? Why should *I* bear the brunt of all the questions to come?' (Point 3: *Diffusion of responsibility* prevents the emergency from being acted upon.)

The thought of leaping over the wall and entering the burning building did not even enter the bystander's head. He had never really met these neighbours, apart from a few times when they had refused to return his soccer ball after it was accidentally kicked over their backyard wall. So there was not even much *empathy* with them. As well, he had had no formal training in the *risks* of fire fighting; neither had he any skill in first aid. The issue of 'courage' did not even enter his mind, although he did feel a twinge of guilt afterwards for not having done anything at all to help. (Point 4: The importance of *additional* factors.)

Source: Personal experience (c. 1980).

Additional factors in crowd dynamics

Empathy, skill and courage

Critical narrative 2.6 nicely summarises the key decision points in the Darley and Latané theory of bystander crowds. It also illustrates some other social influences in emergency situations. Since 1968 many other studies of these effects have highlighted the potential dampeners in critical narratives 2.5 and 2.6. They include low capacities for empathising with a victim (see also chapter 6), lack of the skills needed to help (see also chapter 7), and anticipated risks to the self — for example of being scorched by the flames, or being the target of violence and aggression. In critical narratives 2.5 and 2.6 an additional important influence on helping behaviour during emergencies is the presence or absence of positive role models (for a classic study on role models, see Piliavin, Rodin & Piliavin 1969). Finally, the size of the community in which the emergency occurs is also a significant factor in explaining crowd helping versus inaction (Amato 1983b).

Cultural influences

The idea of community size, and its degree of urbanisation, brings us to a fuller consideration of 'cultural' influences on helping behaviour (Amato 1983c). Earley's (1993) work is crucial here. It indicates that value orientations, such as those represented in figure 1.1, are capable of being socially facilitated. If so, cultural values will also influence how bystanders respond to an emergency. As in Earley's work, the relationship between value orientation and helping is probably not simple. It would be naive and sentimental, for example, to expect that collectivism necessarily fosters helping. Mateship, like the 'old boys' network', has its dark side. Similarly, crowds can be overtly hostile to victims of emergencies when they are perceived as outsiders (the Australian attitude to refugees offers a telling example of this potential; see also chapter 10, on aggression in sport). Thus, cohesive neighbourhoods, as much as fragmented ones, may be relatively indifferent towards a stranger in need, as contrasted to a neighbourhood friend caught in an identical emergency.

Back to social facilitation

As well as reiterating the importance of context, there is another important point here. Well-learned cultural repertoires can be contextually invoked and then *socially facilitated* . At the *noticing* stage of an emergency, for example, the otherwise socially adaptive habits of 'rushing by' and 'deliberately not noticing' are amplified by the context of a crowded place. Social facilitation also applies in principle to the need to interpret an incident as an emergency — as, for example, in becoming accustomed to not standing out from the crowd and to following others. So, too, with assuming responsibility; urban cultures can habituate us to relying on others to 'clean up the mess'. Apprehension about not being sufficiently skilled or *practised* to help is another factor that is facilitated in a co-observing crowd. We saw earlier that being watched by an audience scares the living daylights out of many people, whose biggest fear, perhaps, is making a complete fool of self in public. Fear of danger, as we saw when discussing panicking crowds, is also very amenable to social facilitation. Broadly, then, it must be said that the process of social facilitation is potentially very robust.

Educational applications of social facilitation

From failure to success

In his review of social facilitation, Zajonc (1965b) half-jokingly suggested some educational applications for the process. Provided they were well prepared, he proposed, students should take their examinations in a crowded hall on a stage in front of a large audience! More seriously perhaps, we might infer that, when learning new material and all else being equal, the 'typical' student has a slightly better chance of absorbing the material to be learned by studying alone rather than in an aggregate, or indeed in a study group. As a teacher, the best advice I personally ever received, from an accomplished instructor, was that 'teaching is 90 per cent preparation'. As student readers will know, it pays a lecturer to be prepared. Over-learning, though, can produce rigidity, stifling free-flowing debate. This rigidity reflects social facilitation, in this case of an over-dominant response.

Resilience

Knowing about these applications of social facilitation is unlikely to avert them (review Gergen's arguments about social psychology as history, in chapter 1). We will still have to practise that darned presentation, up to a point at least. We will still revise for that important exam. In fact, even *during* the performance, knowing about the process is unlikely to stop it from happening. That resilience is helped considerably by the fact that social facilitation is biologically as well as socially based (Zajonc 1965b). It is plainly connected, for example, to physical anxiety about examinations, or public speaking, or class discussion. The value in knowing about social facilitation is that it enables us more effectively to fine-tune, and appreciate the value of, preparation.

Health and wellbeing

Plainly, some health promotion agencies that rely on group dynamics, as one important means for achieving their ends, stand to benefit from strengthening and nurturing dominant responses of one kind or another. All kinds of self-help groups, for example, rely on successfully nurturing and facilitating self-confidence. The clients of human service organisations often have to develop a belief in themselves and their capabilities so that they can break the habit that led them to seek help in the first place (see chapter 3; also Lamm & Myers 1978).

At work

To understand the benefits of applying social facilitation in the workplace, we must briefly critique one aspect of Earley's classic (1993) work. This study, as we saw earlier, focused on value differences, both between individual managers within the same nation and between managers across nations. Individualism and collectivism, whether culturally or individually based, were implicitly regarded as 'fixed' (see figure 1.1). Yet in chapter 1, particularly in the context of glocalis-ation, it has also been argued that people combine *both* sets of values and atten-dant motives. Earley himself was able to change the behaviour of some of his manager participants, from loafing to working harder, simply by informing them, or reminding them, that they were part of a national network of fellow managers, rather than having 'nothing in common' with their peers (1993, p. 331). Thus, it is theoretically possible for the same employees to display loafing in one context and enhanced motivation in the next, to transform a vicious circle into a virtuous one (Carr 1998).

Switching repertoires: the flip-over effect

The theoretical possibility of such a **flip-over effect** has been directly tested in this region (Glynn & Carr 1999). The participants in this study were Australian future managers and decision-makers taking business and psychology degrees. As in Earley's research, the task used in the study consisted of an in-basket exercise, or high-fidelity workplace simulation. Participation, however, took place under one of four possible experimental conditions: (a) working alone; (b) working as part of an implied aggregate; (c) taking part as a member of the same faculty (faculty loyalties exist in many universities); and (d) taking part in the 'wrong' team, ostensibly because of being placed, more by accident than design, within a rival faculty's aggregate (students often identify with their faculty: James & Greenberg 1989). Based on the social loafing literature and Earley's research, it was expected that performance would drop significantly in moving from (a) solo to (b) aggregated performance conditions. Based in addition on the theory of cognitive repertoires described in chapter 1, it was also expected that performance would rise and fall from (b) aggregated performance conditions to (c) team affiliation and, finally, to (d) 'accidental' placement in the 'wrong' team.

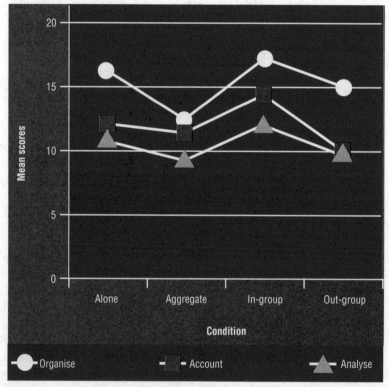

Figure 2.2   Mean performance scores under varying contextual conditions   *Source:* Glynn and Carr (1999).

In figure 2.2, each of these effects does occur. Moving rightwards across the *x*-axis of the graphs means performance first drops when transiting from (a) alone to (b) aggregate conditions; then it rises again when the sense of (b) an aggregate transforms to (c) an in-group. If, however, the participant lands up in

(d) the 'wrong' crowd, among non-group members, then performance once again suffers. Interestingly, too, the effects depicted in figure 2.2 were computed from diverse features of management activities assessed in all in-tray exercises. These features spanned organising skills (for example applying basic principles of time management); accountability (clarifying and explaining decisions); and analysing (prioritising managerial tasks successfully). To that extent, the effects in figure 2.2 may replicate across a range of workplace tasks.

What figure 2.2 begins to suggest is that potential managers and employees can be 'flipped over' into a repertoire in which social facilitation, rather than having a negative outcome on work performance, has a positive one. Evoke an agreeable social identity, and morale may actually rise rather than fall (see also chapter 3, on sporting metaphors). Figure 2.2 also indicates that management's thinking about implementing teams could begin to work creatively *with* (and so respect more) pre-existing loyalties, instead of artificially creating new ones at every turn.

Overall, therefore, the study of crowds continues to have both social and organisational functions. It has suggested, and continues to suggest, ways of improving education, health and work life. In these senses, the study of crowds in general, and of social facilitation in particular, continues to make a contribution to social psychological wisdom. To draw this argument to its conclusion, we will examine one last major impediment to a good quality of working life: workplace conflict.

Few would disagree that workplace conflict is a major social issue of our day. As one prominent political commentator observes, 'litigation is soaring' (Cox 1995, p. 9). Employees 'are arriving in organisations "pre-offended" or primed to take offence at perceived instances of discrimination, sexism, or other inequities' (Robinson 1995, p. 192). At one level, these observations simply underscore the argument, already advanced in chapter 1, that globalisation is fostering a 'me, me, me' ethos, eloquently described by Pearson (1999) as 'individual rights before social responsibilities'. Of course, this increasing potential for conflict at work indicates that social psychologists should be exploring new ways of negotiating and better still *preventing* conflict.

Practically and ethically, this is a very difficult topic to study experimentally. Recognising this, social scientists of various denominations have turned to micro-level games. These games are, by definition, more manageable and less harmful (see chapter 1). They are also related to Brown's (1965) dilemma, mentioned earlier. To illustrate how, many of them stem from a game, made famous by Luce and Raiffa (1957), called 'the prisoner's dilemma', in which two players are faced with a problematic choice. Having been arrested on suspicion of a robbery that they have in fact committed, each is being held by police in separate custody. This is a game of divide-and-rule. Each prisoner is separately offered a reduced sentence if he betrays the other. If both hold the line, they will both escape lightly. But if either is tempted to 'look after number one' and 'sell out' the other to secure a lighter sentence, then the other will receive an especially hefty custodial penalty. The prisoner's dilemma is therefore analogous to the social loafer question, the theatregoer trapped in a fire, or indeed any kind of co-acting emergency situation. As in figure 2.1, staying silent, like 'taking turns', is a riskier gamble than looking out only for self.

The central quandary of the prisoner's dilemma is not unlike the kinds of conflict found at work. How many times have we seen co-workers blame *others* for mistakes made jointly, or claim a collective idea as their own, in the pursuit of, say, a more rapid promotion? Moreover, how often have we seen such betrayals subsequently result in workplace conflict? It is perhaps not surprising, then, that so many organisational studies have used the game (for a classic review, see Rubin & Brown 1975).

At least in Western settings, where most of this research has been conducted, individual players tend to betray their co-offender, thereby choosing self-interest over other-interest, and mistrust over trust. Groups, too, have played the game. In fact, groups have consistently been found to be even *more* competitive, and betraying, than individuals (Insko et al. 1994). Indirectly, therefore, at both inter-individual and inter-group levels, there is support for Brown's view in the workplace.

Training for conflict management

One interesting application of prisoner's dilemma games has been observing what happens to the betrayal tendency over repeated trials and across time. A consistent outcome to emerge from this type of exercise is that as the games proceed, *interindividual conflict gradually turns to cooperation* (Murninghan & Roth 1983; Raven & Rubin 1976). Between groups, allowing freer communication may have a similar outcome (Dawes, McTavish & Shaklee 1977). This can be tested in management training exercises in how to prevent industrial relations conflicts. Thus, although Dore (1994) argued that the game 'strips out' much of the 'emotional fire' of conflict in the real world, it nonetheless has at least one major application — in training individuals (and perhaps groups) at work to avert, or manage, workplace conflict.

Such applications seem to hinge on experiential demonstration. In a nonconstraining way, they enable the participant to see that cooperation actually pays over the long term. They foretell for players what is called 'the Tragedy of the Commons' (Hardin 1968). This is a metaphor for what happens to the social good when people think only of themselves — a collective scramble to screw as much out of the common land as possible in the end left everyone poorer, with no fertile land at all. In prisoner's dilemma games, 'the commons' is primarily a social rather than a material entity. Players learn by shared direct experience that social capital is increased if they cooperate rather than compete. In that sense, playing a series of prisoner's dilemma games is a relatively gentle and non-invasive way of allowing someone to 'walk a while in another's moccasins' (see chapter 1).

Taken together, the findings from the prisoner's dilemma game generally support Gergen's conception of social psychology as a tool for enlightenment and **transformation**.

These games have workplace health and safety applications, too, not just for employees but also for their clients. In the service sector, for instance, simulated aircraft crashes indicate that having (a) twice as many calm and professional cabin staff and (b) passengers who are familiar with cabin layout will reduce panic behaviour in an emergency simulation (Muir 1998). Such findings, through their emphasis on (a) setting a good example and (b) the effects of practice, clearly indicate potential benefits from (a) behaviour modelling and (b) social facilitation.

Other simulation games could conceivably illuminate stock market crashes, panic buying and various forms of financial contagion (Hilton 2001). Such financial crises push millions of people into poverty (see chapter 6). Their effects on health and wellbeing are truly massive and global.

If the emotional tone of a crowd can be lowered as required, presumably it can also be raised when necessary (Forgas 1998). A good example of this potential to animate is the bystander crowd, which, as we have seen, frequently needs first to be galvanised into moral action. The literature on loafing and reversing loafing, reviewed earlier, suggests that this manipulation is possible. So, too, does other evidence that the moral code we employ at any one time depends significantly on evoked social context (Taylor & Yavalanavanua 1997). Most indicative, however, is a field experiment conducted in the 1970s on the impact on helping behaviour of learning about bystander apathy (Beaman et al. 1978).

A critical study on helping behaviour

What Beaman et al. did was to test empirically whether social psychology could actually achieve what it promises students in the first place — help them become more aware of, and less susceptible to, social influence (see chapter 1). These researchers decided to test this promise directly with respect to co-observing crowds. To do so, they gave some psychology students a lecture on the apathetic crowd, specifically outlining the kinds of stages propounded by Darley and Latané (1968). As a control condition, another class of psychology students received equally standard social psychological fare that was not directly related to helping behaviour.

Two weeks after these lectures, a minor emergency was staged outside a classroom. Beaman et al. were interested in the subsequent helping rates, in the presence of an apathetic model, who was in fact in the pay of the experimenters. They found that the experience of learning about bystander apathy (and the processes that underlie it) enhanced helping/non-apathetic pro-social behaviour to a significant degree. Compared with the control group (students who two weeks previously had attended an unrelated but otherwise equivalent social psychology class), helping rates rose from 30 to 40 per cent. As the authors of this study judiciously concluded, 'The simple technique of the present studies is encouraging in partially justifying the teaching of social psychology: Demonstrating that sensitising persons to social forces in the environment gives them greater freedom to control their own behaviour' (1978, p. 410).

This undercited and underrated study nicely illustrates how input to cognition, from the social psychology of helping, has the potential to influence and improve everyday social behaviour. A 10 per cent increase in helping rates is arguably well worth striving for. However, it is not sufficient to 'bring down' the process itself. (If you need to, at this point, review Gergen's evergreen ideas about the historical relativism of social psychology, in chapter 1). In other words, the improvement in behaviour (with some people having 'grown out of' the crowd's lulling influence) is not sufficient to invalidate that process. Rather like 'singing on the bus', which we discussed in chapter 1, there will always be some who decide to concede to the crowd.

A critically aware student once asked me whether Beaman et al.'s incremental improvement in pro-social behaviour is actually sustained. Students know that they often forget lecture material soon after the class has ended! It is therefore an important feature of the Beaman et al. study that their observations were not limited to changes in behaviour in the immediate term. Increased helping behaviour was sustained two weeks after the initial lecture materials were presented to the class. Their litmus test was quite conservative. The change they observed was far from being as transient as lecture details themselves sometimes are. This point, and indeed the message of the chapter as a whole, is succinctly captured for us in critical narrative 2.7. After reading this, readers might also like to return briefly to the conclusion to critical narrative 2.5.

CRITICAL NARRATIVE 2.7

Reversing the cycle

Not long ago . . . I was involved in a rather serious automobile collision. Both I and the other driver were plainly hurt: he was slumped, unconscious, over his steering wheel while I managed to stagger, bloody, from behind mine. The accident had occurred in the centre of an intersection in full view of several individuals stopped in their cars at the traffic light. As I knelt in the road beside my car door, trying to clear my head, the light changed. The waiting cars began to roll slowly through the intersection; their drivers gawked but did not stop.

I remember thinking, 'Oh no, it's happening just like the research says. They're all passing by!' I consider it fortunate that, as a social psychologist, I knew enough about the bystander studies to have that particular thought. By thinking of my predicament in terms of the research findings, I knew exactly what to do. Pulling myself up so I could be seen clearly, I pointed at the driver of one car. 'Call the police.' To a second and a third driver, pointing directly each time: 'Pull over, we need help'. The responses of these people were instantaneous. They summoned a police car and ambulance immediately, they used their handkerchiefs to blot the blood from my face, they put a jacket under my head, they volunteered to serve as witnesses to the accident, and one person even offered to ride with me to the hospital.

Not only was this help rapid and solicitous, it was infectious. After drivers entering the intersection from the other direction saw cars stopping for me, they stopped and began tending to the other victim. The principle of social proof was working for us now. The trick had been to get the ball rolling in the direction of aid. Once that was accomplished, I was able to relax and let the bystanders' genuine concern and social proof's natural momentum do the rest.

Source: Cialdini (1993, p. 114).

A taxonomy of contexts

In the course of this chapter we have traversed a variety of crowd contexts. Perhaps now is the time to bring them together into one conceptual schema. Figure 2.3 is designed to highlight the points of intersection and cross-fertilisation in this area of social psychology. The figure is also intended to help the reader make new links back to chapter 1.

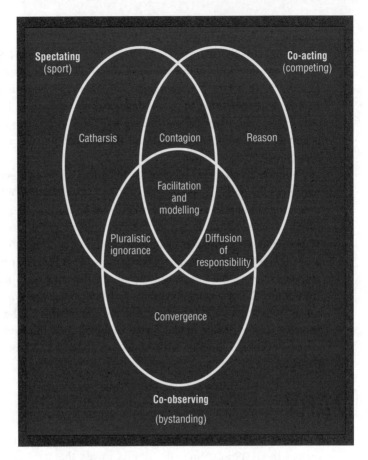

Figure 2.3   Cross-contextual crowd processes

From figure 2.3, our provisional taxonomy includes *co-acting* crowds, which are basically competing for a limited resource, such as a prize, medal or super-bargain, loot or a single emergency exit. We might also include panic buying and selling here, as in stock market crashes and runs on currency exchanges (Hilton 2001; Waeneryd 2001). In figure 2.3, *spectating* crowds are found at sporting and other staged spectator events. *Co-observing* crowds, by contrast, are often like apartment dwellers gazing out on violent crimes. They differ from 'spectating' crowds in that someone's fate is more directly in their hands; a moral intervention may be required.

Processes that are relatively distinctive to each of these contexts are as follows. First, particularly relevant to crowds that are co-acting is a process of *reasoning*, however briefly and intuitively, about others' trustworthiness. Second, particularly relevant to crowds that are spectators is a process of *catharsis*, by which we can sometimes vicariously experience the feats of others, and thereby temporarily release some of the frustrations of everyday life (see chapter 10). Third, particularly relevant to crowds that are co-observing is *convergence* on others' judgements, for example about the level of seriousness in an apparent emergency (see chapter 1).

As depicted in figure 2.3, in process terms, *diffusion of responsibility* seems to straddle both co-acting crowds (as in trampling someone underfoot) and co-observing crowds (as in asking, 'Why *me*?'). Spanning both co-observing and spectating crowds is *pluralistic ignorance* (as in doing nothing to stop a brutal spectacle). In figure 2.3, *contagion* can be found both in co-acting (e.g. stampeding) and spectating (e.g. saluting) crowds. Also from figure 2.3, we can see why critical narratives 2.1 and 2.2 are such good exemplars of crowd behaviour as a gestalt. The angry mob (2.1) and the courageous students (2.2) reflect *all of these processes combined*.

Common to all types of crowds, including those in figure 2.3 and in critical narratives 2.1 and 2.2, is the process of *social facilitation*. Whether individuals are panicking, hiding in a crowd at work, loafing during an emergency or feeling a surge of national pride at the Olympics, the amplification of their dominant responses is a readily identifiable, conceptually unifying thread for this chapter as a whole. Included in this central category is the public performer, whose dominant responses, as we have seen, are socially facilitated by any kind of audience. Also from figure 2.3, a second core process is behaviour *modelling*, examples of which range from a doctor calling for calm and the parable of the good Samaritan to a sporting icon as a role model for teenagers around the world. Overall, therefore, social facilitation, coupled with modelling, forms a solid foundation for the rest of the book.

# SUMMARY

In the process of social facilitation, the presence of others tends to amplify performance in its pre-existing direction. Crowds that are spectators or that co-act (i.e. compete together on the same task) tend to facilitate the dominant response. Crowds are not necessarily irrational or a-rational. At micro level, it may be perfectly rational for them to panic, or to socially loaf.

Behavioural contagion is less rationalist, although it, too, often has rational elements in it. These include observing the consequences for models, and copying those behaviours that tend to reap rewards. Contagion is also partly driven by social facilitation. These influences range from externalising crowd anger to amplifying our appreciation of natural beauty in holiday settings (and moods).

In an emergency, the final decision about whether to act pro-socially or selfishly will be influenced by a combination of globalising pressures on time (especially in urbanised environments); by community or city norms to keep a low profile; by pluralistic ignorance (dysfunctional non-verbal communication); by diffusion of responsibility (low accountability); by (low) levels of intervention skill; and by rewards and risks to life, limb and reputation.

In principle, each of us is capable of switching dominant response repertoires, for example from individual to team orientation, and from conflict to cooperative mode. Panic can be transformed into calm, and crowd apathy can be partially overcome through exposure to crowd psychology itself. The latter can be achieved without undermining the social psychological principles themselves. Pluralistic ignorance is reduced by pluralistic education.

Behaviour modelling. Learning to perform behaviour through observing somebody else performing it. Models who are rewarded are imitated more, and models who are punished are imitated less. (p. 57)

Co-actor. Someone who is performing the same task as self, often in competition with self (p. 52)

Co-observer. Someone who happens to be observing the same critical incident (often an emergency of some kind) happening to a third party (p. 65)

Contagion. The idea that emotions can be directly transmitted from one person to another, as in contagious yawning, applause, giggling and aggression. Affect can be communicated socially just as cognitions can. (p. 63)

Diffusion of responsibility. The dilution of responsibility in a crowd or group setting. The more people present, the less the personal burden borne by the individual to act responsibly. Such processes may be widespread from local to global settings, in issues ranging from pollution to poverty to pacifism. (p. 72)

Flip-over effect. The inherent capacity, possessed by many people, to change entire behavioural repertoires, for example from predominantly individualistic (e.g. during competitive solo sports) to predominantly collectivistic (e.g. during team sports). (p. 76)

Pluralistic ignorance. An influence process in which each element in a crowd of bystanders looks to others for guidance on whether or not to assess the situation as a real emergency. Because everyone ('pluralistic') is relying on the other to define the situation, and because nobody realises this ('ignorance'), the situation is never defined as a real emergency, even though it might be. This is a form of dysfunctional communication, since each person refers to the other without being aware of the fact that they are each serving as a model of inaction to the rest of the crowd. (p. 70)

Social facilitation. A fundamental process of social influence in which the presence of others, whether as spectators or as fellow competitors, facilitates performance of whatever we know best at the time. For an accomplished athlete, crowds will improve performance, whereas for a student who has not revised, the presence of other students will facilitate (enhance) his or her ineptitude. (p. 52)

Social loafing. A specialised form of social facilitation, in which the dominant response tendency, and thereby the response that is amplified, is to be self-interested and mistrustful of others' intent to cooperate. Social loafing results in a decreased level of motivation, and thereby a decreased level of workplace performance, compared with working alone. (p. 59)

Transformation. A process of social influence in which, once we learn about a social influence process and become aware of its dynamics, we are mentally better positioned to resist it if we wish. Transformation is therefore essentially a process of psychosocial liberation. (p. 78)

REVIEW QUESTIONS

1. Define social facilitation.
2. How can we reconcile facilitation and loafing?
3. Does behavioural contagion exist, and do we understand its various mechanisms?

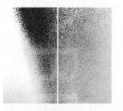

4. How does the bystander effect purport to explain the Kitty Genovese murder? Is this explanation convincing or must we also factor in degree of empathy, helping skills, fear of danger, and cultural effects?

5. Outline the key outcomes of the crowd literature in terms of its capacity to inform and influence civil society.

DISCUSSION QUESTIONS

1. What are the legal implications of crowd psychology? Refer to the readings by Colman (1991a, 1991b), Reicher (1991a, 1991b) and the lawyer Luitingh (1991).

2. How is glocalisation likely to influence crowd behaviour?

3. Can social psychology really change the way we behave in crowds?

4. Does crowd psychology deserve to be rejuvenated? (For a detailed definition of this term, see chapter 1.)

ACTIVITIES

1. Use your library facilities to scour the local or national newspapers for stories about crowd behaviour, as described in this chapter. (Many of these news-papers are now available on-line in university libraries.) For example, I used the search term 'bystander apathy' to discover a number of stories that are very interesting from a social psychological point of view. Collect your stories in the week preceding the practical class-tutorial session. Your goal should be to apply the various models in the chapter to see if they explain and illuminate the popular narratives you have read.

2. Read the articles by Voss (1998) and Whitfield (1998). Alternatively, if you live in New Zealand, read the article by Wynn (2001) and compare it with the narrative of 'Kiwi decency' alluded to in Wynn's narrative. Discuss the apparent discrepancy between the two tales, one of apathy and the other of decency, in terms of:
(a) context
(b) communication
(c) culture.
Note: This activity can be conducted in small groups, which assemble for a ple-nary session towards the end of the class. The entire activity is timed to take approximately 55 minutes of class time, including reading.

3. In terms of the core ethical principles introduced in chapter 1, what are some of the principal constraints on conducting research into crowd processes? How have social psychologists attempted to overcome these potential barriers, and do you believe that their efforts have been vindicated?

4. Why has crowd psychology seemingly lost its once-prominent place in contem-porary social psychology? Does it deserve to be rejuvenated? If so, why and how? Use the 'small groups plus plenary' technique to answer this question.

ADDITIONAL READING

On social facilitation and loafing: Zajonc (1965b) and Earley (1993). Zajonc's paper is still the classic in this area (although you might supplement your reading, bringing it up to the present day, by reading Platania and Moran (2001).

On contagion and modelling: Brown (1965) and Hatfield et al. (1993). Brown is still one of the best writers in social psychology, with a flair for integrating material and bringing it to life, while Hatfield is probably the leading authority on emotional/behavioural contagion.

On helping behaviour in emergencies: Darley and Latané (1968), and Levine (2000). The Darley and Latané paper is a classic, and is written extremely clearly. Levine's paper brings the original model to life in contemporary urban settings.

On applications: Beaman et al. (1978), and Taylor and Yavalanavanua (1997). The Beaman et al. paper, as the text suggests, is sadly undercited. It is a shame that social psychologists have not conducted many more studies of this kind. The paper by Taylor and Yavalanavanua is a contemporary and regionally relevant illustration of flip-over effects in action.

For further reading on the topics discussed in this chapter, consult the online resources linked to the Wiley website (http://www.johnwiley.com.au/highered/socialpsych).

CHAPTER 3

THE GROUP

LEARNING OBJECTIVES

After reading this chapter, you should be able to:

- define major internal barriers to effective group functioning
- describe practical ways of overcoming these barriers
- define major external barriers to effective group functioning
- describe practical ways of overcoming those barriers.

OVERVIEW

Whether we call them workplace teams, study circles or community-based organisations, the group is back. Globally, we are seeing groups exalted as a key to unlocking full human potential at work, in education and in the community. Yet a primary message from the science of groups, and the first message in this chapter, is that unleashing group dynamics is inherently risky. The chapter carefully assesses these risks across relationships both within groups and between them. It extracts key principles of group functioning, and then applies these to describe effective ways of managing group decisions. In this way, the chapter 'accentuates the positive', outlining a contribution from social psychology towards realising the much-touted potential of groups to 'make a difference'. This is the second major message. In making it, glocal influences on the Internet, a techno-scape that forms a recurring strand later in the book, are appraised. Other significant glocal issues, such as pay diversity and individual contracts in the workplace, are framed within the generic issue, outlined at the beginning of the book, of social versus personal achievement.

INTRODUCING GROUP DYNAMICS

Group influences will appear and reappear throughout the book. This chapter prepares the reader for that journey by illustrating some of the basic influence processes that occur whenever groups come together — and, sometimes, come apart. Conceptually, logically the first priority before starting this journey is to differentiate groups and group influence from the crowd and its dynamics, outlined in the previous chapter. The best way to achieve this differentiation is to apply the three-fold thematic structure, context, communication and culture. How, then, do groups differ from crowds on each of these dimensions?

Context, communication and culture

One of the sharpest ways of distinguishing groups from crowds is via the concept of time. Typically, the temporal context of groups differs widely from that of crowds. Crowds are normally more ephemeral; they are much more likely than groups to be a 'one-off' phenomenon. In a word, then, the crowd's time is relatively compressed. Even if it manages to meet more than once, its particular constituents will probably differ from one occasion to the next. In a group, by contrast, the constituents typically have more continuity with each other. They will recognise each other; they will expect to have more of a past, present and future in common. Thus, one factor that reliably differentiates the group from the crowd is a broader shared time span, or temporal context.

This extended time span can do more conceptual work for us. It inevitably alters what groups and crowds are capable of achieving together. In a very practical sense, for instance, in purely behavioural terms, groups have much more time than crowds to speak to one another. We saw in chapter 2 that much of the communication in crowds is non-verbal. With the group's enhanced capacity for verbal interaction, there is inevitably an explosion in the amount of information that can be processed, both about the issue itself and about where everyone sits in relation to it. Information explosions like this can have either positive or negative effects on subsequent behaviour. Whatever the behavioural outcome, however, verbal communication in the group irrevocably changes its ethos from that found in a crowd.

This opportunity for more detailed communication in a group, afforded by its expanded temporal context compared with the crowd, allows groups to develop elaborate standards for group behaviour. As Sherif's study suggested in chapter 1, when given the slightest opportunity to exchange points of view using language, groups will spontaneously construct a set of social norms. These normative codes of conduct guide and regulate group behaviour; they help to build a culture for the group. Certainly, crowds can be influenced by wider social and cultural norms, for instance in queuing behaviour or giving applause for a public performance. But they are relatively unlikely to have either the time or the opportunity to develop elaborate internal cultures of their own. Thus, a third defining feature of groups is their capacity to generate their own culture, defined as a coherent set of social norms.

Globalisation, localisation and glocalisation

According to chapter 1, once groups develop their own normative systems, these will inevitably bring them into some kind of interaction with wider, outside norms. A key example of these norms we saw is mounting pressure towards greater individualism. Chapter 2, for example, suggested that globalisation may be rendering a range of behaviours as relatively selfish, in the calculative individualistic sense outlined by Brown and others. According to this kind of argument, globalisation might actually be eroding the relevance of 'group' psychology in everyday life.

A first retort to this kind of scepticism is to reiterate a point implied in chapter 1, that people seek a *balance* between individual and community life — between, for instance, personal and social achievement. According to this model of social behaviour, a bellyful of individualism — which is one ingredient that global pressures are arguably dishing up — will actually stimulate a community backlash. People will hanker for more quality time in a collective. Globalisation, then, stimulates localisation. Of course, people who are so motivated may well find some satisfaction in participating in a crowd. However, given its longer shelf life, the group probably offers a more sustainable form of community experience.

Beyond the localisation argument just outlined, a more basic illustration of the relevance of groups, and group social influence, is the blunt fact that we are all being urged, more and more, to *join* them. Whether in studying, working for a wage or providing voluntary human services, groups pool resources. In that sense, they enable greater 'efficiency' and 'competitiveness' — two watchwords of globalisation itself — than if we each behaved independently. A colleague of mine rephrases the adage that two heads are better than one in the following form: 'Nobody is smarter than everybody' (Atkins 2002). Paradoxically, then, *groups are part of globalisation, too*. In joining groups, people are not only reacting against global pressures; they are also moving with them. Accordingly, much group behaviour today, at the psychosocial level, is inherently glocal.

Questions of identity

These ideas of global pressures, local backlash and the psychosocial tension between the two suggest a struggle for identity. The concept of identity is explored extensively throughout the chapter. This is done by dividing group influence processes into two essential types. First, there are questions of identity that occur principally *within* groups. For example, if a group discusses an issue internally and decides to take an extreme stance on that issue, then its dynamics of influence are largely inter-individual, and *intra*-group. Second, there are questions of identity that occur largely *between* groups: For example, if one group pressures another into a hardline stance, that influence, and the sense of identity it fosters, is largely *inter*-group. This distinction between (a) intra-group and (b) inter-group dynamics provides the conceptual backbone for this chapter, and for much of the book as a whole.

INTRA-GROUP ISSUES: INFLUENCES ON DECISION MAKING

In chapter 1, we learned about a third way of cutting the influence cake, namely (c) influence exchanged between a group and an *individual*. This special kind of influence is discussed in its own right in chapters 7 and 8. But (c) is still useful to us now, as we conceptualise this section of the chapter. That is because at the core of the relations and functioning within a group is a perennial question: Are its decisions best made by someone in authority, or are they best made collectively, through discussion among its wider group constituency? The recurring issue here is the extent to which decisions are made centrally, by an empowered leader or dictator, or with the consent of the governed, with the Group being the agent empowered.

Lewin's classic findings

A memorable test of these two forms of governance was made by Kurt Lewin (1947). His study focused on changing consumer behaviour in the context of community development. The study was undertaken during World War II, when there was a community drive, because of food shortages, to persuade the public to eat new and relatively freely available foods, including, for example, animal offal. The main participants in this study were Red·Cross volunteers, who were also housewives and so key decision-makers on the issue of family food. In groups of 15, an 'expert' on nutrition either 'lectured' on the benefits of eating offal, or imparted the same information but tempered the message with invitations to question, discuss and otherwise participate. The visiting expert in this case, therefore, governed with the consent of the governed.

For practical reasons, Lewin was looking for sustained changes in these consumers' behaviour. So, during the fortnight after the 'lectures' and ·'lectures plus group sessions', he tracked the number of participants who actually bought and tried offal in their families. Amazingly enough, while only 3 per cent of the lectured audiences tried it, when the decision was reached with participation a full 32 per cent did so. In other words, compared with straight lecturing, governing with the consent of the governed was *ten times more effective* in influencing behaviour. Understandably, therefore, the rest of this section explores this profound difference.

Lewin was able to replicate this superior, more sustainable influence from collective decision making in a number of other social contexts (see chapter 1, on the importance of replication across different settings). For example, in addition to consumables, such as baby foods (orange juice and cod liver oil), Lewin and others took their ideas into industrial organisations. Industrial change, of course, was also relevant to a war effort. And in these applied settings, too, more consultative modes of persuasion led to greater change in organisational behaviour over a period of months. Since then Lewin's general point, that constraint does not create sustainable behaviour change, has stood the test of time and place well (e.g. Coch & French 1948; Marrow 1964; Juralewicz 1974; Semler 1993).

To rephrase a well-known adage, every silver lining has a cloud. For example, to the extent that groups produce more sustainable decisions, any mistakes they habitually make will tend to be sustained, too. In case that warning sounds a little excessive, the research and theory that follows will flesh it out. The roadmap for this journey is provided in figure 3.1. Consistent with the conceptual analysis above, the figure portrays group life in developmental time.

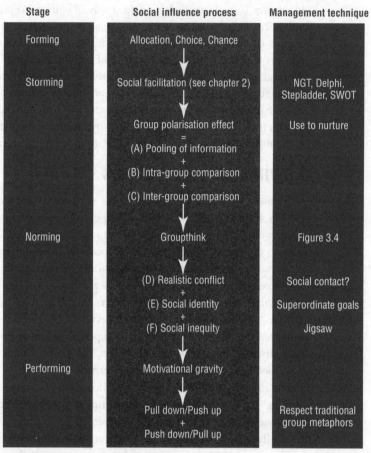

Stage	Social influence process	Management technique
Forming	Allocation, Choice, Chance	
Storming	Social facilitation (see chapter 2)	NGT, Delphi, Stepladder, SWOT
	Group polarisation effect = (A) Pooling of information + (B) Intra-group comparison + (C) Inter-group comparison	Use to nurture
Norming	Groupthink	Figure 3.4
	(D) Realistic conflict + (E) Social identity + (F) Social inequity	Social contact? Superordinate goals Jigsaw
Performing	Motivational gravity	
	Pull down/Push up + Push down/Pull up	Respect traditional group metaphors

Figure 3.1   A roadmap for exploring group dynamics

Stages of group life

A relatively enduring developmental model of group life was put forward by Tuckman (1965). Tuckman's model was based on a synthesis of the group dynamics field. His database for this synthesis included therapeutic, organisational and laboratory groups. Added more recently to the model have been educational and counselling groups (Maples 1989; Saidla 1990), as well as business and software development teams (Kormanski 1988; McGrew, Bilotta & Deeney 1999). In the model, from the left in figure 3.1, Tuckman identifies four major stages through which groups tend to pass during their lifetime (for a more elaborated sequence relevant to therapeutic groups, see Tuckman & Jensen 1977; Matthews 1992; Hayes, Blackman & Brennan 2001). Tuckman's model is not rigidly unidirectional: groups can move both down and up through the stages, for example when radically new problems, issues or projects arise, obliging the group to rethink its norms (see later in this chapter, on bootstrapping).

Stage 1: forming

From figure 3.1, *forming* consists of the initial drawing together, or constitutional, stage of a group's existence. Plainly, there is a range of ways in which groups can form, from being 'allocated' (say, to a work group), to exercising free 'choice' (for instance choosing similar others), to more 'chance'-related processes (like meeting by accident, say in the same bar).

Stage 2: storming

From the Stage column in figure 3.1, *storming* is often about jostling for a social role. In this stage, people struggle to define a place for themselves in the group or a position on the issue. This may be as the group's ideas person, relations specialist, emergent leader or taskmaster (Bales 1956). The important point is that the storming group is still in the process of 'sorting out' where it sits. Change and flux are the order of the day.

Stage 3: norming

From figure 3.1, a characteristic feature of the *norming* stage, according to Tuckman's model, is that the group coalesces into a coherent set of social norms (chapter 1). As this happens, the group develops greater cohesion, and a sense of shared social identity. As for the autokinetic participants who came back a year after their original group session and still made the same judgements (see chapter 1), the potential for change is much reduced. In norming, therefore, the order of the day is stability.

Stage 4: performing

Stability, of course, can be productive. Maintaining traditions is often an achievement in itself. But it is also possible to have too much of a good thing, and cohesion is no exception. In time, for instance, a group may become increasingly impervious to internal dissent and outside criticism. It becomes unthinkable to rock the boat. Like Asch's majorities (see chapter 1), perhaps, a group in this stage is at risk of losing its objectivity, its capacity for critical reflection and its flexibility to respond to unforeseen contingencies. Thus, according to figure 3.1, if the outside world is highly fluid, *performing* may become difficult or even impossible.

Stage-by-stage ordering of social influence processes

Again referring to figure 3.1, our next step is to analyse the kinds of social influence processes that take place within groups during each of Tuckman's stages. These processes are named in the middle section of the figure. The analysis is necessarily selective. With respect to storming, for example, a more advanced approach would include emergent leadership. (Readers specifically interested in this topic can find specialised literature in both Bales 1956 and Belbin 1993.)

Influence during forming and storming

Allocating people to groups clearly brings risks of its own if the members of the group do not wish to be there. In one of Lewin et al.'s own early studies, allocating people to hobby groups contributed towards an eventual backlash against a teacher (Lewin, Lippitt & White 1939). When we have the luxury of choosing our groups, we often do so on the basis of similarity, both in opinions (Festinger 1950) and abilities (Festinger 1954). Finding others with similar opinions provides social and moral support, while others with comparable abilities keep us stimulated. Finding others by chance, as partners or as groups, can lead to surprisingly lasting relationships. The precise reasons for this durability are complex, and are discussed separately in chapters 8 and 9.

Chapter 2 suggested that influence in groups involves social facilitation, which was defined as the amplification of a dominant response in the presence of others. In figure 3.1, the term retains that meaning. So far, however, we have analysed the presence of others only in the form of a crowd, not as a group. In a group, with its different context, communication and culture, at least two questions remain unanswered. First, does the group amplify pre-existing tendencies? This is a question about effect, or *outcome*. Second, how exactly does it achieve that effect? This concerns *process*.

Outcome

Origins of the 'risky shift'

A penetrating way of opening up group influences during storming is to review the literature on the so-called **risky shift**. This concept was developed during doctoral research conducted by James Stoner (1961). The historical context for Stoner's study was global concern over the Cold War, in particular the threat of a nuclear catastrophe between the two superpower competitors at the time, the United States and the Soviet Union. (This particular conflict is largely over now, but risk management is certainly not.) At that time, decisions about pushing the nuclear button were entrusted to high-level select committees ('independent' groups). The reasoning here was that two heads are better than one, and that such a group, compared with a single individual, would be relatively cautious and judicious (Sherif 1936).

Are groups more prudent? Stoner's storming test

To test this possibility, Stoner gave his participants a series of choice dilemmas. The choices in question ranged from the cautious and conservative (e.g. stay working for an established firm but with relatively limited promotion prospects) to the risky and speculative (e.g. move to a newer and more dynamic firm with more promotion prospects, but with the risk that the company might go bust). Stoner presented his student participants with 12 of these all-too-familiar life choice scenarios. For each scenario, he asked them, first, to indicate their personal opinions and, second, to discuss the choice and reach a consensus on it. In effect, therefore, he introduced the variable of group discussion, and in particular verbal communication, into the collective behaviour arena.

Completely contrary to wider expectation at the time, Stoner found that his participants shifted their views during group discussion towards, not caution, but greater *risk*. Could this be just a fluke? For example, Stoner's participants were business students, and possibly valued risk to begin with. That would have unrepresentatively predisposed them to be socially facilitated towards risk (see chapter 2).

This possibility meant that more tests had to be made, involving other populations and samples. The first of these populations to be sampled was, not surprisingly perhaps, arts and humanities students (Wallach, Kogan & Bem 1962). However, even with these participants there was a shift towards risk. Also, the decisions that Wallach et al.'s groups took transferred to private opinions immediately *after* the discussion. Moreover, the same risky shift endured for at least two to six weeks after the meeting itself. Thus, just as Lewin (1947) had suggested, the influence of the group was sustained.

The trouble now, of course, was that the political context had changed since Lewin's day. The context for this study, unlike its earlier counterpart, was the threat of a nuclear meltdown, and in particular the risk that some executive decision-making body somewhere, whether military or civil, would decide to press the nuclear button. In this kind of context, trying something new and risky was thoroughly *un*desirable. Here, then, is the problem, or proverbial cloud, that Lewin's work implicitly warned about. As a result, and consistent with earlier work by Asch and Milgram (see chapter 1), as well as Le Bon (chapter 2), Stoner's results again cast collective behaviour in a negative light (Dixon 1994; Gergen 1994a; Reicher 1996).

A turning point: the group polarisation hypothesis

Not surprisingly, perhaps, Stoner's research quickly spawned lots of new research. Much of this work at the time supported Stoner's original observations. But in the late 1960s thinking in the field underwent a significant refinement. This began when it was realised that on some choice dilemmas, groups seemed to become not more risky but more *cautious* (e.g. Stoner 1968). This shift towards greater caution seemed to be occurring when the group, on average, was already cautious on a dilemma *before* the discussion began (Moscovici & Zavalloni 1969). Moscovici and Zavalloni therefore renamed Stoner's effect, proposing a hypothesis called **group polarisation** (see figure 3.1). This hypothesis predicts that group discussion will move group opinions, both in public and in private, towards a more extreme position. Whatever opinions exist in the group before discussion begins will be amplified or socially facilitated after that discussion has taken place. Storming, therefore, is all about the existing context in which group discussion takes place.

The immediate question facing Moscovici and Zavalloni was, Does group polarisation extend beyond the original risky shift research? In a different setting and with a different type of task, Moscovici and Zavalloni now asked groups of French students to discuss their opinions of President de Gaulle and the United States. Initially, before the discussion began, the individuals comprising these groups were slightly pro de Gaulle and slightly anti American. During the discussion, however, and exactly as predicted by the polarisation hypothesis, these groups became even more pro de Gaulle, and even more anti United States. Also, the polarisation effect held firm after the discussion was over, transferring into private opinions. In the US itself, another study found that initially racist groups became even more racist during and after discussion; while their initially anti-racist counterparts, in other groups, became even more anti-racist (Myers & Bishop 1970). Overall, then, polarisation was starting to look quite robust.

Groups as agents of social change

Stoner's earlier study had cast the effects of group discussion in a relatively narrow context: choice dilemmas and committee-type meetings. These are common enough in life, but the polarisation studies created a new scope of application. 'Group discussion', after all, is a constant feature of everyday life. People have group discussions in bars, at home and in classrooms. It was therefore no surprise that, following the early breakthroughs made by Moscovici and others, studies of group polarisation burgeoned. These studies are enduringly summarised in Lamm and Myers (1978), who found that group polarisation effects extend from organisational to community to educational settings. Polarisation was found, for example, following discussions on ideal workplace supervisors (see chapter 7), on the worthiness of charity (chapter 6) and on appropriate means of student assessment (chapter 5).

As these examples suggest, the polarisation effect has emerged consistently across a range of applied issues. It surfaces, for instance, during workplace socialisation (Baker 1995). This is often a fairly turbulent time, therefore fitting in well with Tuckman's storming stage (see figure 3.1). In a radically different setting, international aid agencies, too, have been observed to arrive at, and retain, polarised views on how emergency relief projects should proceed (Simukonda 1992). In the case of child welfare, group polarisation has been reported in conference decisions about at-risk children (Kelly & Milner 1996).

Increasingly these days, people are making decisions collectively on **intranets**. Membership of intranets (localised communication networks that operate through the Internet via, for example, a shared network of e-mail addresses), as the prefix 'intra' suggests, is restricted to the members of a defined group. They are used, and have proved popular, among both business and educational groups (Herson, Sosabowski & Lloyd 1999; Hovmark & Novell 1993). An early study by Kogan and Wallach (1967) indicates that polarisation will recur in such groups. These researchers replicated the risky shift using intercom technology. A later study directly compared computer-mediated groups with face-to-face groups (Kiesler & Sproull 1992). This study found that the computer-mediated groups polarised even more than their face-to-face counterparts. Computer-mediated groups need a sense of identity before this process engages — if not, constituents may lose interest (Kiesler, Siegal & McGuire 1984). But once a sense of identity is primed, the increased polarisation suggests that intranets are disinhibiting for some (Joinson 1998).

Most of the research on polarisation has taken place in Europe and North America. Nonetheless, some studies of group discussion that have tracked polarisation effects have been reported from diverse societies. These studies span countries, for example in East and West Africa (see, respectively, Carlson & Davis 1971, in Uganda; and Gologor 1977, in Liberia). In the South Pacific, students in New Zealand were among the earliest to demonstrate polarisation of risk (Bell & Jamieson 1970). In Australia, too, polarisation has been reported in terms of risky versus safe behaviour in the workplace (Kenny 1995; see also this chapter, on polarisation and the tall poppy syndrome).

The evidence briefly reviewed suggests that group polarisation is a relatively robust outcome when groups come together to make decisions. But what about its robustness as a social influence *process*? As we learned in chapter 2, the principle of equifinality means we can reach the same outcome, or effect, via different processes. This idea is again useful as we consider the major theories of polarisation.

Process

In retrospect, a key difference between (a) the autokinetic paradigm that produced inherently cautious convergence and (b) the later paradigms that produced polarisation is that people in (b) had more of a sense of a 'good' and a 'bad' pole, and thus a far stronger stance on that dimension. In this sense, as shown in figure 3.1, there was a substantive pre-discussion position, which could then be socially facilitated. But how, precisely, is that facilitation driven along in a group?

Explanation A: pooling of information

As discussed above, one factor that draws people into groups in the first place is person–group similarity. People gravitate to groups that share their opinions. At the same time, they probably have their own idiosyncratic ideas and arguments about why these views are correct. In any group discussion of these, there will be a pooling of information. Since most of that information already leans in the same direction, and because everyone gains new information supporting their pre-existing view, the potential for social influence is all one-way. Information exchange will tend to reinforce group members' initial positions. In fact, simply learning about the information contained in others' arguments has proved sufficient to create a polarisation effect (Lamm & Myers 1978).

Explanation B: intra-group comparison

This process was first outlined in Festinger (1950, 1954), who argued, for instance, that people often compare themselves against others in the hope of out-matching them and thereby boosting their own self-esteem (1954). During a group discussion, for example, individuals learn through communication where others stand. Some will be keener than others to position themselves on the 'right' side of the emerging group norm (closer than the norm to the preferred pole). According to Festinger, this may help those individuals feel like paragons of group virtue. Granted, this is individualistic behaviour, which means the process itself may be less relevant in collectivistic settings (Festinger 1954). Nonetheless, it may take only one or two individuals in a group to compete like this for a whole group to be nudged closer to its preferred pole. Thus, intra-group comparison could happen anywhere (there *are* individualists in collectivist societies). Simply learning about others' positions in the group may result in a polarisation effect (Lamm & Myers 1978).

Explanation C: inter-group comparison

At least one other factor, this time from outside the group, plays a part in polarisation (see figure 3.1). The clearest demonstration of how this factor works was provided in a study involving French architecture students (Doise 1969). Doise asked groups of students to consider the type of architecture towards which their college leaned. During this process, some of the groups were also reminded about the existence of another college — effectively, an out-group that subscribed to an alternative school of architectural thought. Consistent with the findings by Moscovici and Zavalloni, discussion polarised the in-group's views of what their college stood for. But groups for whom an out-group had been made salient, polarised *more*. In other words, and as illustrated in figure 3.1, polarisation effects due to information pooling and intra-group comparison had been amplified still further by a comparison *between* groups.

An overall assessment

In figure 3.1, explanations for polarisation (A), (B) and (C) are each credible and compatible (Isenberg 1986). For credibility, people clearly do seek information in groups. They do compare themselves in groups. And they do define themselves by the groups of which they are not members. For compatibility, in a world that simultaneously prizes (A) information, (B) impression management and (C) identity, most polarisations are probably multiply determined. An intranet, for example, simultaneously allows individuals to share information (Damsgaard & Scheepers 1999), to engage in social comparison (McCormick & McCormick 1992; McLaughlin, Osborne & Smith 1995) and to differentiate their own social identity (Speers, Lea & Lee 1990).

Norming and the dangers of groupthink

Polarisation involves the group moving towards an extreme position. It is about change. But groups are not always fluid; at some point they will attain a resting state. Lewin described this process as 'freezing', signifying a group becoming set in its ways. This is the essence of norming, and there will be times, as we have seen, when this is both productive and welcome. But could a group's capacity for clear thinking also become *compromised* in this stage? This disturbing possibility was the central focus in a landmark study by Irving Janis (1982).

Janis chose a case study–like methodology. He combined archival records about some of the twentieth century's biggest decision-making blunders. In his case studies, these blunders had been made in groups working as select committees. For example, Janis studied archives from the attack on Pearl Harbor in Hawai'i; the Bay of Pigs debacle in Cuba; the Vietnam War, and the disastrous US invasion of North Korea. However, Janis also sought to accentuate the positive. To do this, he also studied some of the more successful initiatives by similar decision-making bodies. These included, for example, the Kennedy administration's handling of the Cuban missile crisis, and the Marshall Plan, the first international aid program to assist the economic recovery of Western Europe after World War II (for more detailed discussion of aid and welfare, see chapter 6). The purpose here was to isolate the kinds of practices that made the difference between success and failure.

Among the failures, Janis found one common theme. These groups had become so cohesive and tight-knit, so committed to their own sense of identity and loyalty to one another, that no one even thought to raise any criticism. In fact, the whole idea of critical reflection, either from within the group or from outside it, had literally become 'unthinkable'. The typical group had become too cohesive, too frozen in its own norms. To signal this preoccupation with group norms, and a resting state of over-cohesion, Janis coined the term **groupthink**.

Quite clearly, given the politically high-profile cases chosen by Janis, group-think can be disastrous. A contemporary example of this destructive power is the disastrous US *Challenger* space shuttle mission, which went ahead despite numerous warning signs that it was doomed (Moorhead, Ference & Neck 2000). Moorhead et al. specifically blame the *Challenger* disaster on groupthink. A similar conclusion has been reached about the downfall of an Australian political party, which was attributed to the politics of consensus (Cox 1995). A community development example of groupthink, potentially affecting millions of people directly, is international aid programs (see chapter 6). Aid agency groups have been known to adhere rigidly to their original blueprint despite clear evidence that the program is failing 'on the ground' (Gow 1991).

Groupthink and the broken promise

In all kinds of organisations, from the aerospace industry to political parties to aid and welfare agencies, the hype today is on 'empowering' people to work in teams. Yet the foregoing review reveals hidden hazards in this approach. Groups are no panacea for human fallibility. To cite another adage, forewarned is forearmed.

Note: If you are doing activity 3, you may wish to suspend reading the following section until after the activity has been completed.

In the context of groupthink, managers and supervisors today might be forgiven for promising empowerment without ever actually delivering it (Davis 1995). This is doubly so since empowering others means disempowering the self and could be seen as a betrayal of years of service. In some Australian and New Zealand organ-isations, for example, the rhetoric of participation and employee input reportedly remains just that — rhetoric (Vecchio, Hearn & Southey1997). What this amounts to is over-promising and under-delivering on participation, or a **broken promise**. Such broken promises may be very demotivating for a group. In fact, they have been described as a hidden '*peril* of participation' (Baldwin, Maguka & Loher 1991, p. 51; emphasis added).

Relevant research on this issue comes from the study of group communication (Leavitt 1951). Leavitt saw as critical, for both production and morale, the way a group's communication networks (sending paper memos then, e-mail today) are *structured*. Examples of these networks are given in figure 3.2. The structured approach depicted there clearly leans towards a *sociological* view of social psy-chology (see 'Ethos and direction').

As illustrated in figure 3.2, (a) the Wheel has a single, central hub. This person controls and directs the group. The hub is free to communicate with whomever he or she wishes. The outer satellites in this network, ordinary group members, cannot communicate among themselves — only with the hub. In (b) the Circle, the satellites have a little more freedom. They are able to communicate with their two immediate neighbours in the network. This idea was taken to its logical conclusion in the network structure, (c) All-Channel (Shaw 1964). In figure 3.2, network (a) epitomises governing centrally, while network (c) exemplifies governing by consent.

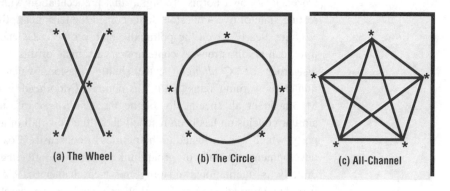

(a) The Wheel   (b) The Circle   (c) All-Channel

Participation levels ⟶

Figure 3.2   Governing by decree versus governing by consent of the governed

Source: Adapted from Leavitt (1951) and Shaw (1964).

Between them, Leavitt and Shaw found that the structural design of a communication network has significant impacts on both group morale and group productivity. In terms of morale, hubs in (a) who cope well with the initial information overload often end up enjoying themselves. But across the group as a whole, motivation and satisfaction tend to be higher in the networks that are more decentralised. On productivity, for relatively simple tasks, comparatively centralised structures such as (a), with pre-existing norms provided by the imposed structure, have a performance edge. For more complex tasks, once unstructured networks such as (c) have had time to *construct* norms for working together, they outperform their more centralised counterparts. More heads become better than one.

Figure 3.1 is directly relevant to the broken promise mentioned earlier. From figure 3.2, workers are over-promised network (c) but under-delivered network (a). The effects of this are suggested in Baldwin et al. (1991). In this field experiment about organisational training (see chapter 1), there were three groups. One group was not consulted about what training it would receive, as in network (a). A second group was asked for its preference and received that preference, as in network (c). A third, 'broken promise' group was asked for its preference but then given an altogether different training package. This group was over-promised (c) and under-delivered (a). As a result, both morale and performance plummeted to a level even lower than (a), who were never consulted at all. The moral of this research is clear. Before promising participation and empowerment, make absolutely sure you can and will *deliver*.

Techniques for managing intra-group issues

The techniques described in this section focus primarily on managing polarisation during the storming stage, and groupthink during the stage of norming (see figure 3.1).

Managing storming

The big problem during storming is building the widest possible base of ideas from which the group can select its options. Intuitively, we might plump for intensive brainstorming as a way of trying to ensure this. Typically, this includes a free-for-all session, in which all participants are encouraged to say whatever comes into their heads. In practice, however, such free-for-alls do not work well (Sutton & Hargadon 1996). This may be partly owing to social facilitation of various incorrect or inappropriate dominant responses — for instance shyness. Many gifted people are reticent and never even manage to present their ideas during the brainstorming itself. As a result of this impediment, they remain locked out of the process, and the group loses an opportunity to capitalise on their creative potential. Fortunately, however, a number of structured techniques maximise the options generated at the beginning of a group decision. Each of these techniques works by empowering everyone to sit back and think a little *before* the storm breaks ('only fools rush in'). To that extent, all of the following techniques govern with the consent of the governed.

Nominal group technique (NGT)

The word *nominal* means 'in name only', and the essence of the NGT is that group discussion is deferred until everyone has had a chance to write down their own ideas calmly, without distractions. At this stage the group is a group in name only. Next, a group facilitator displays each individual's 'top' idea on a whiteboard or overhead projector for the group to clarify and hone. This edited list of options is then ranked according to a system of voting. The net result is a widely considered, prioritised set of ideas garnered from all members of the group. The NGT has proved remarkably robust, for example in identifying barriers to AIDS prevention messages among at-risk African youth (MacLachlan 1996b). It has also produced relatively high quality solutions to problems, when compared with more conventional (and less structured) group discussion (Van de Ven & Delbecq 1974).

The Delphi technique

This is a benevolent form of (a) the Wheel in figure 3.2 (Dalkey 1969). In Greek ancient history, the Oracle of Delphi was an all-knowing fount of wisdom, from whom people could solicit answers to questions of importance to them. In the Delphi technique, a central hub solicits opinions on an issue from each of the group's satellites. These responses are then combined in a collective document. The composite document is then re-transmitted outwards to each of the satellites for another round of feedback, before the whole process is repeated. This 'pulsation' is comparable to a set of bellows, in that it repeatedly sucks in information and then pumps it out again. The recursive pulse will normally continue until a resting point, or consensus, is attained. The Delphi technique, then, empowers the hub to become all knowing, but in the process it also empowers the rest of the group to have their say. In this way, it governs with the consent of the governed.

Generally speaking, the Delphi technique is readily suited to modern communications technology, such as e-mail networks and other Internet systems. For instance, it clearly lends itself to e-decision-making over distance, for example in rural and remote settings, and in countries where the geographic distance-to-market is great. Thus far the technique has received favourable reviews in the group decision-making literature, for example in educational planning (Clayton 1997), human service provision (Dawson & Brucker 2001) and organisational development (Reid, Pease & Taylor 1990).

Stepladdering

This technique was originally designed in part to tackle social loafing (Harkins, Latané & Williams 1980). In stepladders, group members temporarily defer physically congregating as a group while they think about the issue and prepare a short presentation of their ideas. Starting with a nucleus of one or two people, individual members are asked to enter the room and make their own mini-presentation. This is then discussed by all assembled individuals, before the next speaker enters. As each member of the group adds his or her own unique contribution, the number of ideas and options steadily increases, as if the whole group were climbing a stepladder. Processes such as this have produced better quality decisions than conventional forms of group discussion, both in informal groups (Rogelberg, Barnes-Farrell & Lowe 1992) and in workplace teams (Orpen 1997). Interestingly, these benefits are most noticeable if the pace of the laddering is placed under the control of the group itself (Rogelberg & O'Connor 1998).

Bootstrapping

This general technique involves carefully reviewing existing processes and procedures in a group. It means, in effect, voluntarily regressing from norming to storming. By reviewing their own procedures in this way, groups aim to advance by 'pulling themselves up by their own bootstraps' (Dawes 1971). Organisations engage in bootstrapping whenever they participate in 'retreats' to plan strategically for the future. During these retreats, a useful structured technique is the SWOT analysis (Rea & Kerzner 1997). (The acronym SWOT stands for Strengths, Weaknesses, Opportunities and Threats.) The SWOT technique was developed at the Harvard School of Marketing. Since almost everything today is 'commodified' and 'marketable', SWOT usage has become widespread. Perhaps partly because of the commercial sensitivity of strategic marketing planning generally, it is difficult to find SWOT applications in print. However, the technique is reported to have been helpful, for example in the design of human services for psychological counselling (Deverall 1997).

A SWOT analysis starts with each individual in the group being asked by a facilitator to list the strengths and weaknesses in a current product or service. These strengths and weaknesses are internal to the group, such as staff expertise or gaps in their knowledge. Equally important, however, is the external market, which is the domain of opportunities and threats. In education, for instance, these include opportunities for community outreach, as well as threats from underfunding. The key overall goal in any SWOT analysis is a synthesis. Strengths are matched to market opportunities, and mobilised to address weaknesses and defuse or divert threats (for details, see MacLachlan & Carr 1993). Again, the key is that the process reaches into every nook and cranny of the group's neural network.

This prevents potentially creative options from being closed off prematurely. And to achieve this, it governs with the consent of the governed.

Techniques such as these may help in managing a critical issue in this book — balancing social and individual achievement. As we saw in chapter 1, reactions by groups to individual talent are sometimes hostile. Such hostility has been linked to stifling individual voices of innovation (Brewer 1995). Structured techniques like the SWOT analysis, however, oblige the group to listen more to such voices (see chapter 7, on listening). To that extent, they could be used in principle to tackle the tall poppy syndrome.

Using polarisation to change attitudes towards the tall poppy

An additional means of fostering participation from would-be tall poppies is to harness group polarisation effects. From figure 3.1, group discussion can be used to nurture weak but positive attitudes — say, towards high achievement — into stronger ones (Baker 1995). This possibility was tested recently in Australia (Carr et al. 1999). The participants were future managers in New South Wales and the Northern Territory. The study used selected items from an attitude scale developed by Feather (1994). These items are listed in figure 3.3. In a pre-consensus phase of the experiment, groups of five participants responded individually to the items in figure 3.3. In a consensus phase of the experiment, they discussed them and tried to reach unanimity on each one. In a post-consensus phase, the groups were asked to re-respond in private to the same six statements.

- One should always respect the person at the top.
- Very successful people who fall from the top usually deserve their fall from grace.
- The very successful person should receive public recognition for his/her accomplishments.
- Those who are very successful ought to come down off their pedestals and be like other people.
- People who are right at the top usually deserve their high position.
- People who always do a lot better than others need to learn what it's like to fail.

Note: Responses ranged from strongly disagree to strongly agree.

Figure 3.3 Items selected from the tall poppy scale   *Source:* Feather (1994).

During the pre-consensus phase of the experiment, the groups on average slightly favoured the high achiever. During the consensus phase, and as predicted in the polarisation literature, the groups became more clearly 'pro' tall poppy. The participants decided that tall poppies deserved *a little more support*. These net gains also transferred to personal opinions, expressed in private after the group session was over. When partly managed, therefore, group empowerment socially facilitated more pro-social attitudes towards the kind of individual most likely to help the group succeed.

Using polarisation to help micro-manage health

From figure 3.1, the whole idea of harnessing polarisation to *nurture positive intentions* has many potential applications. Some of these follow an intriguing idea initially proposed by Lamm and Myers (1978), who suggested that self-help groups such as Alcoholics Anonymous probably benefit from group polarisation effects. For example, group discussion of plans for personal change will socially facilitate those plans, resulting in an increased intention, outside the meeting, to adopt self-improvement behaviour. In theory, therefore, self-improvement outside a group setting can be enhanced by discussion inside the group. Thus, storming is not necessarily negative, as the following critical narrative makes plain.

Critical narrative 3.1 suggests that self-help projects like cancer support groups may facilitate crucial influences on patient wellbeing, both mental and physical (for an application to carers of cancer sufferers, see Baron et al. 1990). It should be remembered that the research presented in critical narrative 3.1, however fascinating and promising, is still at pilot stage. An overall review of this emergent but potentially relevant field is available in Edelman, Craig and Kidman (2000).

CRITICAL NARRATIVE 3.1

Cancer support groups: a positive influence for groups

Dr Shea and research colleagues have recently completed a report of a research study on support groups conducted at the Mater Hospital. The intervention aimed to provide a variety of shared experiences — the provision of motivational research information, practice in meditation and cognitive behavioural training — and gave over a lot of time to group discussion. The study was a pilot study. However, the effects of the support groups were so clear that many statistically significant findings were reported. Although the researchers had expected that most of the positive outcomes would be related to psychological factors, quite unexpectedly the greatest effects were seen for reports of physical symptoms. The overall measure of physical symptoms showed that people who attended support groups (attendees) were exactly the same as a group that was not invited to come to support groups (controls) at the beginning of the study, but they had much less severe symptoms by the end of the support group, and even three months later. When the researchers looked at sets of symptoms that often go together, they found that the attendees had less chest pain, could breath more easily, slept better, had more energy and had better sexual functioning. A similar improvement was shown with quality-of-life measures. After attending support groups, patients were better than controls with regard to mental health, emotional problems, and time spent on work and other normal activities.

Source: Extracted from Shea et al. (2002).

Managing norming

The clearest recommendations for managing the norming stage in figure 3.1 derive from Janis's study described earlier in this chapter. From his case studies of successful projects and fiascos, Janis was able to extract a number of managerial practices to help prevent groupthink from happening in the first place.

- Make everyone a critical evaluator.
- Use parallel groups.
- Invite critics.
- Appoint a devil's advocate.
- Take a second chance.

Figure 3.4   Managing groupthink   ***Source:*** Extracted from Janis (1982).

As depicted in figure 3.4, skilled facilitators will empower every group member to play the role of *critical evaluator*, from the outset, of each other's ideas. Here, a norm of critical thinking is facilitated. *Parallel groups*, meanwhile, require the resources to set up alternative groups, or perhaps subgroups, to work on the same problem. By having two groups in tandem on the same trail, the risk of both of them leaving the rails is lowered, because each serves as a reality check for the other. To *invite critics* may partly serve the same function. These critics should, according to Janis, come from within the same organisation but outside the department. In this way, they are reasonably expert and knowledgeable in the area, without being so close to the group that their judgement is clouded. Appointing a *devil's advocate* is also a good idea (for supporting evidence in organisational settings, see Schwenk 1990); this role should rotate, however, in case the group forgets that it is only assumed for the sake of the game (Jones & Harris 1967). Finally, Janis suggests that groups need to take a *second chance*. Even once a decision has been reached, it should be set aside and later reviewed in the cold light of day. Who among us has not had some bright idea on Friday night only to recognise its foolishness on Monday morning? To avoid this kind of embarrassment, traditional wisdom in Persia and Germany advised that collective decisions always be made twice over.

Summing up

Contributions such as the advice contained in figure 3.4 begin to make groupthink look far more manageable than we might first have imagined. Like the other techniques for managing group empowerment (NGT, Delphi, Stepladder and SWOT), the recommendations contained in figure 3.4 are practical. Morally, too, and consistent with Lewin's research on governing with the consent of the governed, each of them, from the NGT to meeting twice, empowers the group to capitalise on its own potential to 'make a difference'.

INTER-GROUP ISSUES

In real life, more often than not, intra- and inter-group relations are interwoven. Managers and supervisors over-promising and under-delivering is a case in point. These individuals, as well as being part of the work group, also categorise themselves and each other as 'managers' or 'supervisors', as distinct from 'workers' or 'subordinates'. Workplace behaviour thereby depends not just on relations within groups but also on relations between them. Critical narrative 3.2 illustrates this point. The events in the narrative, which actually took place in East Africa, may appear at first glance remote. A closer analysis, however, will reveal just how close the core issues are to home.

Double demotivation in the mining industry

Zeffe is a Tanzanian national who was granted an aid scholarship from a Scandinavian donor country to study geology in Europe. During the course of his studies, he befriended a classmate from Sweden, named Bjorn. Throughout their studies and many group projects, they worked well together. Nonetheless, Bjorn tended to rely quite heavily on Zeffe, who was more senior and had much more field experience. Eventually they both completed their studies and returned home. In accordance with his scholarship contract, Zeffe returned to Tanzania and joined the State Mining Corporation as a geologist on a salary of 36 000 Tanzanian shillings. This was during the late 1980s, when 250 shillings was equivalent to one US dollar. In US dollar terms, therefore, Zeffe was earning approximately $144 per annum.

Soon after commencing work in Tanzania, Zeffe was told that an 'expert' was being recruited from overseas, someone who would head the Geological Mining and Surveys Department. This new Head of Department would, Zeffe was informed, provide new and innovative ways of conducting business operations. The position was being created and funded by a Scandinavian aid agency. It would therefore be filled by an expatriate from the donor country.

Because the expatriate had to be recruited from the labour pool in a relatively wealthy economy, pay and conditions would need to be quite good, especially by Tanzanian standards. The salary would be US$24 000 per annum tax-free, plus company car, housing and several other fringe benefits. These included private schooling for dependent children, furlough (paid home leave), free electricity and security guards.

Three months later, Zeffe was instructed to join the entourage sent to meet his new Head of Department at the airport. When the newcomer finally emerged from the customs hall, both he and Zeffe were visibly shaken. The new 'boss' was none other than Bjorn, Zeffe's longtime friend and (less competent) fellow student.

It wasn't long before Zeffe began to feel increasingly hurt and bitter about the rift between him and his former friend. His work suffered, and he complained to his employers in the State Mining Corporation. They, in turn, protested to the aid organisation, but to no avail. Zeffe soon felt compelled to resign his position, and he was promptly joined by several of his senior Tanzanian colleagues. Within three months of his arrival, Bjorn, too, had quit his job and returned home.

Source: Rugimbana (1996a).

Realistic conflict theory

Much of what happens in critical narrative 3.2 is influenced by economic factors. These include in particular the distribution of finite economic resources, across both individuals and groups. The groups end up clashing over that distribution, with fairly disastrous human and industrial consequences for all. The idea that contention over finite resources fuels inter-group conflict is called **realistic conflict theory**, or RCT (Taylor & Moghaddam 1994). Put simply, RCT holds that whenever there are not enough resources to meet the needs of two or more groups, there is a realistic probability that inter-group relations will deteriorate. Thus, if a diverse society undergoes job shortages, RCT predicts a rise in fragmentation.

Sherif and the Robber's Cave

The chief exponent of RCT in social psychology is Muzafer Sherif (1956). Sherif conducted a field experiment on RCT in a US summer camp called the Robber's Cave. Participants in the study were boys who had been carefully screened for 'normality' (p. 54). Different groups of these boys were first allocated, according to chance, to physically different parts of the camp. During this phase of the experiment, the two groups lived in blissful ignorance of each other. The groups then went through the processes of storming and norming — for example, they gave themselves names (The Rattlers, The Eagles), developed their own rituals and became socially cohesive. Sherif then brought the groups into physical proximity to each other, changing the social context from intra- to inter-group. In particular, he arranged for competitions, for innocuous but limited resources, to be played out. These games included, for instance, competing for penknives and a team cup, at baseball and in a treasure hunt. The result was that good sportsmanship quickly degenerated into hostile behaviour. This conflict included camp raids, fighting and the burning of flags. As predicted by RCT, there was a marked deterioration in inter-group relations.

Context, communication and culture

Sherif's results generalise across contexts. Flag-burning behaviour is not unheard of in inter-group relations between adults, and Sherif's findings were later replicated among adult groups (Kidder & Stewart 1975, p. 51; for an application to warfare, see Makin, Cooper & Cox 1989, p. 110).

The results probably also generalise quite well across contemporary channels of communication. One distinguished observer of cyber-psychology has remarked, 'Some of the multiplayer Internet games, for example, seem almost like recreations of the Robber's Cave experiments' (Wallace 1999, p. 91).

Sherif's study has been replicated in different cultural settings. The Robber's Cave study was re-run in other camps, ranging from Lebanon (Diab 1970) to the former Soviet Union (Andreeva 1984). In both cases, Sherif's effect was replicated.

In terms of glocalisation, Sherif's findings are still broadly relevant. The world's resources are finite and being used up rapidly. Sherif's findings are broadly consistent with research that links global environmental resource depletion (land, water, clean air) with a range of localised conflicts between groups (Homer-Dixon, Boutwell & Rathjens 1993).

We shall return to this study when considering means of combating inter-group conflict. For the moment, however, it is clear that Sherif's findings are robust across context, communication and culture. They also link in well with the concept of glocalisation.

The minimal group paradigm

Another very interesting aspect of critical narrative 3.2 is how the conflict between two friends quite quickly took on the air of a conflict between groups. The relative rapidity of this shift (Bjorn and Zeffe had been friends for years) suggests that group identities are assumed quite readily. The leading figure in this field of inter-group psychology is Henri Tajfel (1970). In a groundbreaking study, Tajfel tested just how easily this kind of fracture can come about. To do this he devised what has become known as the Minimal Group experiment. Following figure 3.1, Tajfel allocated participants to groups on the most trivial of bases: after estimating the number of dots on a screen, individuals were randomly allocated to one of two groups, 'under'- and 'over'-estimators. The basis for belonging to the group had therefore been pared back to a bare minimum: these were groups in name only.

Tajfel then presented his participants with an opportunity to behave in a discriminatory way. He did this by isolating the members of each implied group and presenting each with a series of matrices of the type schematically portrayed in figure 3.5. The participants were asked to choose a column, whose entries would determine how many points would later be distributed, in monetary form, to group member x and group member y. Sometimes both x and y were depicted as members of the participant's own group (x = in-group, y = in-group). On other occasions they both belonged to the other group (x = out-group, y = out-group). Finally, in a third, critical condition, they were presented as belonging to different groups (x = in-group, y = out-group).

Choose one column:

	A	B	C	D	E	F	G
x	1	2	3	4	5	6	7
y	7	6	5	4	3	2	1

Figure 3.5 Tajfel's payoff matrix   *Source:* Adapted from Tajfel (1970).

In the first two of these conditions, people were asked to distribute resources within a group, and the mean response column tended towards D in figure 3.5. There was no demonstrable discrimination. In complete contrast to this result, however, participants given a choice between in- and out-group expressed a clear preference for the former. Compared with the others, their responses tended to shift, significantly, from D towards G. In other words, there was a clear and preferential discrimination in favour of the in-group over the out-group. This effect we can dub the **minimal group effect**. In a subsequent experiment, Tajfel was able to demonstrate that people would even take a pay-points cut simply to retain their advantage over the out-group.

Tajfel's findings travel across different kinds of context

Tajfel's participants in this study were British schoolboys. Did the findings generalise beyond that population? Minimal group experiments have been replicated with more mature populations in other countries, for example with tertiary students in both New Zealand and Australia (respectively, for example, Platow et al. 1995; Hogg & Turner 1985). Field experiments are a lot harder to find in this tradition than their laboratory counterparts. An early exception is a study in an aircraft factory using pay matrices not unlike those in figure 3.5. In this study, too, there was a readiness to maintain advantages over an out-group, even if that meant taking a cut in absolute wages (Brown 1978); for a review of survey studies in this tradition, see Haslam 2001.

Tajfel's findings traverse different forms of communication

On the Internet it is commonplace to find gaming environments in which the players readily take pride in beating rival teams (Wallace 1999). Stereotyping and prejudice, too, are reportedly readily facilitated in cyberspace (Douglas & McGarty 2002; Postmes, Spears & Lea 2002). The point is, however, that the kinds of process outlined by Tajfel *can* occur on the Internet, not that they inevitably occur there (Jones, S. G. 1997; Carnevale & Preobst 1997). In this way, Tajfel's findings traverse different channels of communication.

Do Tajfel's findings travel across culture?

Most research on the minimal group effect remains anchored in relatively Westernised societies, so there is a question about its reliability in other cultures. On the surface, it might look as though the effect is more likely in collectivist than individualist settings. However, a study conducted in New Zealand by Margaret Wetherell (1982) suggests that this conclusion is over-simplistic. Participants were eight-year-old children from diverse cultural backgrounds, Pākeha, Māori and Samoan, ranging from relatively individualist to relatively collectivist. The classes tested in this study, from which minimal groups were constituted, 'were all about 90% Polynesian' (1982, p. 233; 'Polynesian' here means both Samoan and Māori). Consistent with Tajfel's original findings, children from all three backgrounds tended to show favouritism towards the 'minimal' (i.e. purely experimentally defined) in-group. As well, however, this preference for the minimal in-group was more pronounced among the Pākeha children than among the Samoan children (the children with Māori backgrounds fell between these two groups). How could this be so? According to Wetherell, Polynesian collectivism includes a norm of giving gifts to others, and this may have tugged the Polynesian children towards her equivalent of the middle columns in figure 3.5; so, too, would any tendency among the more collectivist children to see the Pākeha experimenter, not other children, as the real out-group (1982, pp. 230–31). According to this interpretation, cultural influences are far subtler than common sense suggests (for an alternative example of cultural norms interacting in subtle ways, even in 'minimal' groups, among adult participants in Japan, see Mizuno & Yamaguchi 1997).

Social identity theory (SIT)

From figure 3.1, Tajfel's explanation for the Minimal Group Effect is based on **social identity**. This is the sense of self that derives from social as distinct from individual achievement. In SIT, social achievement is linked to comparing 'us' favourably against an out-group — 'them'. The sense of superiority that results nourishes self-esteem (Oakes & Turner 1980; Lemyre & Smith 1985).

According to Tajfel, a need to socially 'achieve' in this way is 'generic', or ingrained in the human condition (1970, p. 102). This suggestion, although provocative, is broadly consistent with recent thinking in evolutionary psychology (Caporael 2001). Whether or not it is true, or needs a bit of a nudge from Realistic Conflict, a fundamental need to 'push down' out-groups, and so bolster our social identity, is what supposedly drives the minimal group effect (about individual differences, see Duckitt 2001; Levin & Sidanius 1999; for an interesting, somewhat controversial 'twist' on SIT, see Harmon-Jones et al. 1996; Castano et al. 2002). In figure 3.1, similar processes can also work at the storming stage, for example during (C) inter-group comparison (Doise 1969).

Self-categorisation theory (SCT)

Australia has been a major site of social identity research. Much of this work has been stimulated by John Turner, who worked closely with Tajfel during the 1970s (Tajfel & Turner 1979). Turner extended and developed SIT into SCT. In particular, for example, he has argued that when we identify with a group, we categorise the *self* just as much as we do the *other* (Turner 1982). According to SCT, these stereotypic self-images guide and shape behaviour in a number of social roles — as parent, adult, adventurer, manager, worker and so on (Turner 1991). Turner argues, therefore, that social categories function like scripts in a personal narrative, influencing our behaviour daily (Turner & Onorato 1999; see chapter 7, on self and role schemata). We shall return again to Turner's ideas, once we have discussed a little more of Tajfel's parent theory.

Which out-groups will the in-group challenge?

At the intra-group level, as outlined above, there are two major bases for choosing comparison others: (1) social support for our opinions, and (2) stimulation to test our abilities. In both (1) and (2) we seek others who are similar. From (2), we aim to emerge well from the comparison. For example, there is not much point in taking on either a novice or a maestro. According to Tajfel (1978), the same ground rules apply to relations *between* groups. We will mostly prefer to compete against a 'them' who are similar to themselves, for instance fellow students who have under- rather than overestimated dots on a screen (Tajfel 1970). The change in these *inter*-group situations is that comparison is more competitive (Insko et al. 1994). From figure 3.1 again, once groups have normed, they have by definition found social support. This makes more salient the need to outperform others. By the stage of norming, groupthink prevents serious competition directly *within* the group. The main alternative, therefore, is directing the enhanced competitiveness outwards, towards an out-group. Tajfel suggests that this out-group must be at least comparable, and thus similar, to the in-group.

Some practical consequences of SIT

Nudged along perhaps by Realistic Conflicts (Haslam 2001; Tajfel 1970), SIT makes a set of applied predictions. Following figure 3.6, SIT (and the minimal group effect) suggests that the benchmark for all inter-group comparisons is the in-group, whose interests, all else being equal, are placed first. Next, however, in-groups will be more negatively disposed towards out-groups perceived to be similar than towards out-groups perceived to be dissimilar. For example, Australians and New Zealanders, Scots and English, or 'Northerners' and 'Southerners' are more likely to compete fiercely against each other, and perhaps even to discriminate against each other, than against expatriates from places-of-origin that, in their eyes, are more 'exotic' (dissimilar or non-comparable).

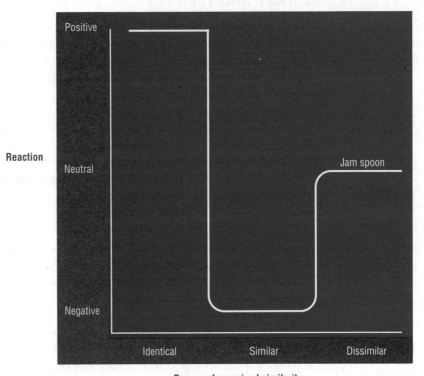

Figure 3.6 Inter-group competition and perceived similarity

Source: Adapted from Carr et al. (1996a).

One laboratory experiment revealed more discrimination against out-groups who were perceived to be similar than dissimilar (Moghaddam & Stringer 1988). This effect was most pronounced for in-groups whose basis for identification was real, such as having shared opinions, rather than artificial, such as being allocated on the toss of a coin. Complementary survey studies have been conducted in the former Soviet Union (Henderson-King et al. 1997), Singapore (Lim & Ward 1999) and East Africa (Carr et al. 2001). In each case, a target group was less acceptable, for example for job openings, when its country-of-origin was relatively closer, either geographically or culturally, to a participant's own. The third of these studies included a job candidate from the home country and — as predicted in SIT and figure 3.6 — this candidate was rated ahead of all the others (an additional explanation for the jam spoon effect is developed further in chapter 8).

Such psychosocial research is still in its infancy but is potentially relevant to economic development. Trade blocs are created to remove economic barriers to the flow of goods and labour within a region (Rugimbana et al. 2000). Figure 3.6 suggests that there may be psychosocial barriers to remove, too. Clearly, research is needed to test more widely the jam spoon function in figure 3.6, for example in the context of trans-Tasman cooperation (Jones 2000).

Power and inequity

In critical narrative 3.2, realistic conflict and social identity are not the only contributors to inter-group conflict (Liu & Allen 1999). Critical also is the issue of power. As the narrative suggests, inter-group conflict often involves a power differential between one group and another. This differential can fuel negative feelings of social injustice or inequity between groups (Prilleltensky, in press). Inequity is defined as any imbalance between outcomes for inputs, compared with salient others (Adams 1965). If a colleague earns twice my salary (outcome) for half the effort (input), this is inequitable. Although Adams originally focused on inequity between individuals, writers today speak as well of inequity between groups (Aamodt 1999). In figure 3.1, this is termed **social inequity**. If 'they' earn twice as much as 'us' for half the effort, this is socially inequitable. Thus, a working definition of power and social inequity focuses on perceived discrepancies, in return-for-input, between comparable groups.

According to both Adams and Aamodt, perceived inequities like this will motivate individuals and groups alike to try to *restore* the balance. In critical narrative 3.2, for example, one form of social inequity that bubbles over into, and almost certainly fuels, the conflict is both parties' sense of the colonial past. Some of the most insightful observations on this have come from psychosocial analyses of colonial and post-colonial societies (Fanon 1985, 1986; Montero 1990; [Malcolm] X & Haley 1987; Pearson 1999). Each of these social commentators discusses the motivational impact that power differentials can have, not only on the 'under'-privileged group, but also on its 'over'-privileged counterpart.

The relatively privileged

The trappings of privilege are often impossible to escape or ignore, leading many (not everyone) to feel guilt and shame. This leads to attempts to rationalise the discomfort through various forms of dissonance reduction (see chapter 1). For example, a member of the more privileged group convinces self that the less privileged group 'deserves its lot'. The over-privileged group thus blames the under-privileged group for its own relative deprivation. In both Australia and New Zealand, relatively privileged groups have been found to perceive Indigenous groups in relatively unfavourable terms (Lynskey, Ward & Fletcher 1991; Marjoribanks & Jordan 1986). In one recent study of reconciliation, '[majority group] individuals who identified strongly with Australia were more likely to employ defensive strategies when faced with negative information about Australia's past treatment of Indigenous Australians. These individuals were less likely to experience guilt, and also less willing to compensate Indigenous Australians', or even to sign a 'sorry' petition (Roger 1999, p. 91).

In a study of the group roles of manager and worker, Kipnis (1972) had an accomplice worker supervised by a genuine participant, who played the part of manager. Some of these managers were led to believe that they had power over the worker, for example to penalise or increase pay and to threaten transfer, while other managers did not. This illusion was the independent variable. For a dependent variable, Kipnis examined the opinions that the differentially empowered manager groups formed about the worker during the work session. By the end of the task, among the managers without power, 75 per cent rated the worker as *above* average. Among managers with power, the same percentage rated the worker as *below* average. Yet Kipnis had made sure that the worker had performed identically in both conditions. It seems, therefore, that power and privilege have the potential to prejudice the powerful and to lead to daily inter-group discrimination.

The relatively deprived

The picture here is a little more perplexing; indeed it has been called 'an enigma' (Augoustinos 1995, p. 255; for fascinating analyses of 'relative deprivation', see Stouffer et al. 1949; Alinksy 1971). In broad terms, Malcolm X (in North America), Fanon (in North Africa), Montero (in South America) and Pearson (in North Australia) have all discussed the internalisation of inferiority by underprivileged and oppressed groups (see also Bruce, Curtis & Johnstone 1998). Even within the Stanford Prison simulation, Zimbardo claimed that some of his role-playing prisoners internalised their inferior, 'prisoner' status within the system (see critical narrative 1.1). We can speculate that dissonance reduction again plays a significant part in these effects. This process would entail a gradual lowering of self-worth to match self's lot in life. But if so, how do oppressed groups ever break out of this depressing cycle, as history clearly tells us they do? The answer to this question, according to Tajfel (1978), involves three developmental steps.

Step 1: assimilation

Individuals attempt to join the relatively privileged group, often by sheer hard work and persistence. Malcolm X gives other examples among African Americans, including hair straightening and the use of skin lighteners. To the extent that assimilation involves giving up a minority social identity for a majority social identity, it can be related to our definition of globalisation. Whatever the case, however, step 1 is a period of group cringe that often simply reinforces the majority group's positioning of itself as 'superior'.

Step 2: anti-conformity

When assimilation fails, the next step is anti-conformity, or *reactance* (Brehm 1966). The group now makes its supposedly negative features positive (Tartan, 'Black is Beautiful'). This shift is driven by enhanced awareness of social inequity (Lake 1997). Reactance functions to lift self-esteem (Poppe & Linssen 1999). The anti-conformity here is akin to localisation. But, like all backlashes, the terms of reference are still external. The minority continues to define itself by what it is *not*, rather than by what it *is* (Sinha 1984, p. 173).

Step 3: achieving differentiation

In this step, consciousness of social inequity is fully awakened. Relatively deprived groups, through articulate speakers like Malcolm X, begin to define their own identity, under their *own* terms. For Malcolm X, this meant embracing Islam, which he argued had its origins in Africa and was therefore part of the true identity of African Americans. In Fanon's eyes, Algerians and other 'Third World' groups seeking liberation from the colonial powers during the 1960s needed to assert their superior humanity, tolerance and patience — and rise up against their former oppressors. For Pearson and Ivory (both 1999), in Australia's Aboriginal communities the key to development is dormant in the values of a traditional economy that prospered before the arrival of the First Fleet. This economy thrived on reciprocity, not welfare. According to these Indigenous advocates, therefore, local traditional values are well suited for participation in the global economy, for example through enterprise development. In this way, step 3 of Tajfel's model recalls our own definition of glocalisation.

Putting privileged and deprived groups together

Chapter 1 spoke of a dance of influence, meaning its social dynamics. This chapter has outlined some of the elements in this dynamic. Can we now manage to assemble them and describe their interaction? Such a marriage is depicted in figure 3.7. Building on critical narrative 3.2, figure 3.7 illustrates what happens when pay differentials create social inequity between groups of expatriate and host workers. The magnitude of this difference is frequently of the order of 10 to 20 times the local salary, or worse.

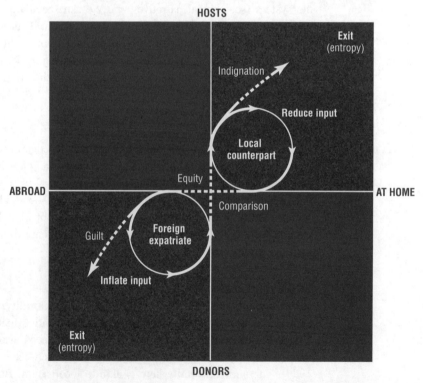

Figure 3.7   The dynamics of double demotivation
Source: Senge (1992). Adapted by Carr, Chipande and MacLachlan (1998, p. 136).

In the expatriate community, the differences in salaries and living conditions often create guilt. Some expatriates find the differential unacceptable and exit the system early (see figure 3.7; for a sense of the astounding level that strain can reach in these assignments, see MacLachlan 1993). Others work harder to try to justify their inflated outcomes, although this is neither practical nor sustainable. The main remaining alternative is to develop an inflated sense of self by derogating the out-group. To the extent that any inflated sense of self reduces input, the expatriate group will work less hard. Thus, one effect of pay differentials between groups is that the overpaid group becomes demotivated (Demotivation 1).

As well, as shown in figure 3.7, the expatriates' sense of superiority will leak out to their local counterparts (see chapter 7, on non-verbal leakage). These local counterparts have often been trained in the same system as their international colleagues (step 1). So now they are feeling relatively deprived (step 2). This is especially so when they have extended families to support (step 3). They become indignant. If they do not exit the system to find better money elsewhere (becoming part of the 'brain drain'), they will fight back in other ways. According to figure 3.7, based on our analysis of social inequity, they are most likely to do that by reducing their input to the job to match their lower wages. They, too, will therefore become demotivated (Demotivation 2).

Thus, figure 3.7 predicts a dynamic process of **double demotivation**.

The dynamics of double demotivation

Inter-group relations now start to spiral downwards (see figure 3.7). Each group's reaction increasingly reinforces the other. To the expatriates, the 'locals' seem surlier and lazier, while to their local counterparts the 'expats' seem haughtier and lazier. This double helix, in which two vicious circles fuel each other in a downward spiral, is called in systems thinking an **escalation dynamic** (Senge 1992, p. 93). We have captured elements of such dynamics, such as elevated guilt and a feeling of superiority among expatriates, in survey work in East Africa (Carr, Chipande & MacLachlan 1998). Such escalations may eventually have a negative impact on instructors' mental health (Marai, in press). They can also severely disrupt students' learning (for an example of industrial disruption, see critical narrative 3.2).

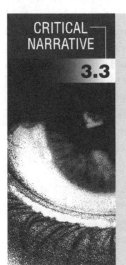

CRITICAL NARRATIVE

3.3

Turbulence at the University of Papua New Guinea

Papua New Guinea academics to take industrial action

Indigenous academics at the University of Papua New Guinea will take industrial action today in support of demands for the same pay as their expatriate colleagues.

The National Academic Staff Association at the University says more than 100 lecturers will begin an indefinite boycott of classes.

A spokesperson for the Association claims the University administration has failed to adequately respond to a log of claims that include demands that the dual system be abolished.

The University brought in a single line base salary system some years ago, but expatriate academics are paid an additional amount as an international market allowance.

The Association claims this represents discrimination.

Source: Extracted verbatim from the ABC News home page, 9 August 1998.

A disquieting fact about critical narrative 3.3 (and 3.2) is that double demotivation dynamics are probably not restricted to expatriate assignments in 'developing' economies. After all, pay diversity among groups is found in all kinds of workplaces everywhere, both through welfare assignments and between one organisation (or job in it) and another. So does the double demotivation effect generalise? In one laboratory setting, Australian students worked on a puzzle with relatively mild (100 per cent) pay differentials ($1 versus $2, and $2 versus $1). Even this was sufficient to doubly demotivate students from giving free time to an otherwise intrinsically engaging task (Carr et al. 1996a). This study focused on pay differentials between individuals, but double demotivation, defined in terms of intention to leave current job, also emerged between Australian workers paid differentially because of individual contracts and *collective* enterprise bargains (for more on individual differences in double demotivation, see McLoughlin & Carr 1997).

Managing inter-group conflict

Clearly, inter-group conflict is a serious issue in the world today, and psychology is not going to solve it single-handed! Such mammoth issues require multidisciplinary approaches. No group is smarter than everyone.

Attempted solution 1: social contact

The first idea that tends to spring to mind in response to inter-group conflict runs something like this. Allow these groups an opportunity to meet each other under pleasant, non-threatening circumstances, and give them time to discover that each is like the other — merely human. If conflicting groups are allowed time together in a non-competitive environment, then stereotypes like those suggested in figure 3.7 will be exposed as the illusions they are (Wright et al. 1997). This Social Contact hypothesis (D) was first tested by Sherif in one of his studies at the Robber's Cave (see figure 3.1; for a fuller model, see Allport 1954). After realistic conflict had erupted, Sherif arranged for the groups to meet in normally pleasant venues such as the canteen. Unfortunately, however, these opportunities were wasted. They inflamed the situation rather than calming it. Social contact produced social facilitation. A recent restructuring of waste and water departments in Australia did the same. Like Sherif's participants, these two groups were given a common canteen. And, not unlike Sherif's participants, the groups used this opportunity to draw a line across the floor to keep their groups apart (Murphy 1999; for an example from Indigenous relations in Australia, see Wright 1997, p. 39; for a review of social contact theory, see Hewstone & Brown 1986). In the final analysis, then, perhaps the most balanced conclusion that we can draw about social contact *per se* is that it is a necessary but in itself insufficient condition for resolving inter-group conflict (Brewer 1996).

Attempted solution 2: superordinate goals and jigsawing

There is an old saying: My enemy's enemy is my friend (Aronson & Cope 1968). One way of interpreting this adage is that having common foes may create unity among erstwhile adversaries. This was another hypothesis tested at the Robber's

Cave. Sherif arranged a series of apparent emergencies, including the water supply pipe bursting somewhere out in the bush and the food truck breaking down. Overcoming such serious but commonly shared crises (the common foe) required full participation from both groups. For example, they had to search the entire aboveground piping system, and to organise a work party to push and pull start the food supply lorry, which they believed had accidentally stalled. To describe this kind of overarching concern, following figure 3.1, Sherif used the term *superordinate goal*. Once a series of such goals had been successfully achieved, and only then, Sherif found that inter-group relations had been restored. The two groups went home on the same bus, and one group even offered to buy the other a meal at a roadside canteen. Importantly, later research was able to establish the importance of making each of these goals attainable (Austin & Worchel 1979). This approach prevents potential backlashes in the wake of any failures. Thus, a *series of attainable, and attained, superordinate goals* can be sufficient to restore relations between groups.

Perhaps the best-known extension of the concept of superordinate goals is found in education. This extension, known as the *Jigsaw classroom* (Aronson et al. 1978), was a practical response to issues of inter-ethnic conflict in schools, which social contact alone, through desegregation, had not managed to solve. Aronson et al.'s technique was work-based. Students were given learning projects in multi-ethnic groups, each pupil holding one piece of an overall jigsaw puzzle (the term assignment). This could, for example, be an assignment to write a biography about a famous person. Each child would deal with a different phase of the subject's life (or piece of the jigsaw puzzle). Rather like Sherif's participants during their series of emergencies, students from different ethnic groups thus depended on one another in order to defeat their common enemy, the term assignment.

To evaluate this technique, Aronson et al. compared it to standard desegregated classes (plain social contact). To make it especially tough for the jigsaw groups, the best teachers were allocated to the regular rather than the jigsaw classrooms. Nonetheless, and in contrast to the social contact classes, the children who experienced a jigsaw classroom went on to develop higher self-esteem, to form good inter-ethnic relations, to cooperate more with each other, to grow to like school more and to master more learning material. Since the original studies, jigsaw techniques have been experienced by thousands of US schoolchildren (Aronson & Patnoe 1997). Increasingly, jigsaw techniques are also now being used to help combat schoolyard violence (Aronson 2000).

The jigsaw classroom has been applied in countries other than the United States. For example, it has been adapted for use in an Australian school, among children in grades four to six (Walker & Crogan 1997). In this study, and consistent with the evidence reviewed above, a contact-like condition tended to exacerbate pre-existing tensions. By contrast, a jigsaw technique produced significant gains in self-esteem, racial non-prejudice, liking of school, liking of peers and academic performance. Outside of school, but again among culturally diverse groups, an ongoing threat of toxic dumping near an otherwise divided Outback town was sufficient, for a time, to unite the town against its common enemy (Wright 1997, pp. 58–9). Such outcomes, across diverse cultures and contexts, suggest that jigsaw techniques are robust.

Attempted solution 3: negotiation and arbitration

Fortunately, toxic dumping is a comparatively rare event. The cloud to *this* silver lining, however, is that there are bound to be times when superordinate goals are either impractical or inappropriate. In such a case, groups in conflict, if they are to resolve their differences peacefully, must negotiate, conciliate/mediate or arbitrate. Unlike negotiation, conciliation/mediation and arbitration involve a third party. In conciliation/mediation, this party is a go-between, whereas in arbitration the third party is empowered to impose a settlement. Many of these conflicts exist between groups (Dunphy & Dick 1987). In such inter-group circumstances, the conflict is commonly resolved through group representatives of one kind or another sitting at a negotiation, conciliation or arbitration table. The literature on this is very diverse, and the following is only a brief selection of basic points (distilled, for instance, from Kniveton 1989; Pruitt 1981; Robbins et al. 1994; Rubin & Brown 1975).

Common sense suggests that a good group negotiator should, from the outset, present a reasonable face, giving the appearance of being at least open to negotiation. The research, however, is more equivocal. In many business settings, notably when both parties are relatively individualistic, it is more likely that initial firmness will pay. *Concessions* at the outset create a first impression of weakness, and eventually this perception actually prevents a settlement from being reached, because the other party keeps pushing to see just how deep the concessions can be made to go.

Although lay wisdom suggests that the greater the number of reasoned arguments a group can muster to support its position, the more persuasive its case will be, in fact, the reverse is often true. Archival studies of what distinguishes successful negotiators indicate that they generally give *fewer* supporting arguments; and tend to *listen* more, compared with less successful negotiators. Thus, presenting lots of arguments actually *dilutes* a group's case.

Intuitively, any group cause might seem to be weakened and undermined by the presence of a radical wing within it. Certainly, there are dangers for minorities that appear to lose unity within their own ranks (Moscovici 1976). However, clearly distinctive groups may coexist within a wider movement. Martin Luther King's civil rights activists, for example, may have appeared relatively moderate alongside Malcolm X's supporters. Radical wings redefine the centre, and with it what is socially acceptable and what is not (Sherif & Sherif 1967). In persuading consumers to buy a product, a common sales technique is called the 'Door-in-the-Face' (O'Keefe & Hale 2001). This approach involves asking for a big concession with the idea of securing a smaller one (Cialdini 1975). In this sense, Malcolm X's more radical stance on civil rights may have indirectly helped Martin Luther King's cause. This is an inter-group variation on the 'good cop/bad cop' routine, which Turner refers to as 'meta-contrast' (1991, p. 77). Meta-contrast implies that we step back from close-up social comparisons, to notice that we have more in common with each other than with a more radical out-group (1991, p. 156). Thus, feminist minorities may become more appealing to other women in a context of male oppression (David & Turner 1999).

Much of the evidence about third party assistance has examined the kinds of factors, in the behaviour and demeanour of the conciliator or arbitrator, that lead to sustainable solutions. In that regard, perceived credibility has emerged as a critical factor. As will become clear in the next chapter, the main social psychological ingredients of this construct are perceived expertise and trust. As President of the Australian Council of Trade Unions (ACTU), Bob Hawke was often called in to conciliate/mediate between disputing parties because of the credibility he had at the time. Critical for sustainable mediation and arbitration between groups, too, is not being seen as heavy-handed. Perceived heavy-handedness increases the risk that the conflict will resurface later. Consistent with Lewin's work, therefore, perceived constraint is counterproductive in the long run.

Putting it all together: motivational gravity

At this point we need a capstone for the chapter as a whole. A conceptual arena in which this consolidation can take place is the perennial issue of balancing personal with social achievement. The first part of this chapter, on intra-group relations, essentially described how groups can stifle individuality, and how we may lift that constraint. In the second part, we learned how self-expression is often about *inter*-group relations. Out-groups can do to the individual what in-groups do, too. Given this parallel, it becomes reasonable to ask, Is there an overarching *model* that we can use to integrate these two aspects of the social psychology of achievement?

THE INFLUENCE OF POWER

Much of the chapter so far (along with the processes (A) to (F) in figure 3.1) has reflected an influence of power. This presence of power implies hierarchy. For example, from *below*, high-achieving individuals and groups can be *pulled down* (as opposed to pushed up) by other groups and individuals. Meanwhile, in the same hierarchy, from *above*, these individuals and groups can be *pushed down* (as opposed to pulled up). Viewed in this way, around the issues of achievement and power, group influences become a dynamic blend of pushes and pulls, at times constraining the self and at others allowing it to soar.

The pull-down

Cutting down tall poppies suggests action from below rather than from above. Such **pull-down** behaviour spans a variety of contexts, communications and cultures.

In New Zealand contexts, tall poppy syndrome has been discussed in Thomas (1994). Studies in Australia have detailed the nature of the syndrome, for example in educational and community settings (Feather 1994). Among students, for example, high school pupils were more content to see a high achiever fall than to see an 'average' student slip below class average (see also Feather 1989). In the wider community, Feather has linked tall poppy intentions to political affiliations, and explored the role of *deservingness* in desire to see political figures fall (for more on deservingness, see Feather 1999). Tall poppy syndrome has also been documented in the Australian workplace (Carr et al. 1996b). A recent case study in New Zealand has linked the syndrome to work group scapegoating (Mouly & Sankaran 2002). In terms of relations *between* groups, and in figure 3.1, we have already reviewed a number of examples of pull-down, including the children at Sherif's summer camp (D), striking lecturers in PNG (E) and relative deprivation (F).

In figure 3.7, using a combination of theory and evidence, we envisaged how relations between under- and overpaid groups begin to deteriorate. In this process, the lower paid group tries to pull down the salaries of the overpaid to a more equitable level. From this point of view, inequity is exacerbated by a communication leakage of derogatory attitudes from the higher paid group. In critical narratives 3.2 and 3.3, where the organisational unit basically shuts down, one of the key reasons for the shutdown is a breakdown in communication.

Students in Japan have been found to be more hostile to tall poppies than their Australian counterparts (Feather & McKee 1996; for a comparison between Australian, US and Canadian students, see Feather 1998). In Sweden, tall poppy syndrome is popularly termed Royal Swedish Envy (Schneider 1991). In East Africa (Malaŵi), there is a popular adage, *Akafuna akhale ndani!* ('Who does he think he is!'). In West Africa (Ghana), 'PhD!' stands for 'pull him down'. In Malaysia, the same acronym stands for *Perangai Hasad Dengki*, again meaning 'pull him down'. (For more examples, see Carr & MacLachlan 1997.) These diverse examples are all used within the group. Between groups, too, figure 3.1 contains at least three robust pathways to pull-down. Realistic conflict over limited resources is found worldwide (Homer-Dixon et al. 1993); social identity fuels pull-down during localisation (Kohnert 1996); and social inequity is felt in diverse societies, where it can motivate attempts to reduce (pull down) unfair pay differentials (critical narrative 3.2).

The push-down

In Japan there is an adage, 'The nail that sticks out gets pounded down' (Ng & Van Dyne 2001). Hammering down a nail suggests behaviour from above, and such push-down actions span a variety of contexts, communications and cultures.

Push-down occurs whenever a group's norms entail the suppression of others' views. In the workplace, for example, individual managers, or indeed managers as a group, may use their positions of power to 'hold down' their subordinates, either as individuals or as groups (Bassman & London 1993). These tactics can be quite direct, for example stealing their ideas, or deliberately downgrading their achievements, or eliminating them from job selection pools. At other times, the tactics are subtler, for example unintentionally stereotyping a lower paid individual or group (see figure 3.7; this kind of process is discussed in detail in chapter 7).

When individuals and groups negatively stereotype each other like this, they also position the self above the other. People will readily *sense* when they are being positioned in this way (Sandler 1986); what they feel is exertion of the push-down. In less subtle forms, perhaps, push-down can be communicated in a variety of other time-worn and probably familiar ways, from cronyism to old boys' networks to outright nepotism (Carr & MacLachlan 1997).

A manifestation of push-down that occurs across diverse societies is workplace bullying (McCarthy 1996; for a recent report from New Zealand, for example, see Horwood 2002). Much of the debate about this reportedly global phenomenon stems from Scandinavia, where the term 'mobbing' has been coined to denote workplace harrying, often of an intra-group kind (for a review, see Einarsen 2000). In an inter-group and culturally diverse setting, the concept of 'shadow management' has been introduced in the business literature (Wong 1996). According to Wong, this is a kind of push-down, in which Japanese expatriates working overseas in Hong Kong covertly (from the shadows) constrain the career and promotion prospects of their local counterparts.

Two familiar examples of pull-down and push-down are envy and jealousy (Mouly & Sankaran 2002). Pull-down means wanting more of what the other has, which conforms to the dictionary definition of envy. Push-down means holding on to what we have, which accords with a dictionary definition of jealousy. These two concepts, envy and jealousy, have both been linked to globalisation. According to one management writer, a primary driver of envy, and hence pull-down, is the global economy, because it continually encourages us to want what others have (Bedeian 1995; for a wider discussion, see also Cushman 1990). According to others, the global economy is fuelling push-down, too, for example by increasing job insecurity because of its ever-present threat of layoffs (Kao & Ng 1997). These joint pulls and pushes are clearly localised reactions against more global pressures. To that extent, they are instances of glocalisation.

Motivational gravity

According to Kao, Ng and Bedeian, a primary *crucible* for envy and jealousy is the workplace (for a discussion of these in academia, see Mouly & Sankaran 2002). With their relatively clear vertical relationships between supervisors and employees, and horizontal relationships among peers, organisational groups bring pull-down and push-down, envy and jealousy, *together*. In the sense that organisations prototypically have organisational trees that delineate a structural hierarchy, pull-down and push-down will each function like gravity, bringing people 'down to earth'. Insofar as these pressures will also have an impact on personal motivation to achieve (e.g. Schneider 1991), we can speak of **motivational gravity**. This concept is visualised for us in figure 3.8.

Figure 3.8 contains an ensemble of players. Most are gathered around the individual (depicted in overalls). They include the supervisor (the character with glasses) and the peer (in baseball cap). The would-be achiever (in overalls) is sandwiched between these two characters. From figure 3.8, and as depicted also in figure 3.1, their influences are either additive and positive, as in push-up/pull-up, or additive and negative, as in pull-down/push-down. They can also be contradictory, of course, as in push-up/push-down (supportive colleagues, bullying boss) or pull-down/pull-up (the 'quiet achiever', who achieves for the boss but is modest with mates). So the grid helps us to think about different possible organisational, departmental and sub-departmental 'cultures of achievement'.

In these cultures, the characters in figure 3.8 are not necessarily individuals; they can equally well represent groups within the organisation, such as 'management' and 'workers'. This means that the grid can help us think about inter-group relations as well as their intra-group counterparts. Finally, figure 3.8 draws our attention to the individual, the 'piggy-in-the-middle'. Thus, the grid can also be used to think about the perspective of this would-be achiever (McClelland 1987a, 1987b), including the kinds of influence exchanged between a group and this individual (see chapter 1; for details of achievement psychology, see Carr & MacLachlan 1997; see also Feather 1963).

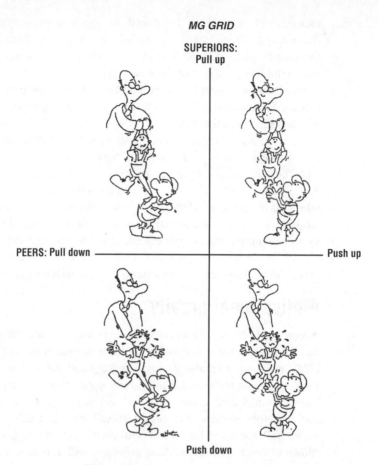

MG GRID

SUPERIORS:
Pull up

PEERS: Pull down ———————————————————————— Push up

Push down

Figure 3.8   The motivational gravity grid   ***Source:*** Munro, Schumaker and Carr (1997).

The grid is a four-way classification system, or taxonomy, for the personal/ social achievement issue outlined in chapter 1. Taxonomies help us to start *measuring*; the grid has been used to measure organisational cultures with respect to achievement. These assessments have been useful in suggesting practices that 'make the difference' between managing gravity and not. In Japan, for example, invoking traditional family metaphors ('work is like family') has helped foster workplace achievement (Kashima & Callan 1994). In the same way that actual family members escape gravity, workmates who count as family might do, too. In Australia and New Zealand, sport is a commonly used metaphor (Chidgey 1995). In both countries, sporting achievement has historically been relatively immune from the tall poppy syndrome (Anderton 1999; Chan 2000). So here, too, traditional metaphors may counteract motivational gravity.

Reviving traditional metaphors can be seen as entailing instances of localisation fuelled by globalisation (pressures to have, or envy; and pressure to hold, or jealousy). Managing motivational gravity is therefore an inherently glocal concern. The best way of illustrating how this works in practice is to return to critical narrative 1.2. The sporting theme in the concept of The Buick Bar & Grill helped the group to make its fantastic start. From figure 3.1, however, as the group progressed through Tuckman's stages, Reed mistakenly turned his back on the sporting team metaphor. By promoting individuals above the group, he had over-promised and under-delivered on empowerment. This split the team into separate groups, creating realistic conflict, competing social identities and social inequity. Double demotivation ensued. Envy and jealousy escalated into organisational collapse. Yet the take-home message in this chapter, encapsulated for us in figure 3.8, is that it *need not have been that way*.

SUMMARY

Groups have both internal and external operating environments. From within, governing with the consent of the governed offers relatively sustainable change, although this brings risks of its own. A range of techniques can minimise these risks, and 'accentuate the positive' for group performance. Between groups, it is relatively easy for social conflict to start. Prevention is always better than cure, but even if inter-group conflict has already begun, there are useful techniques to ameliorate it. Chief among these is a series of attainable superordinate goals. These goals can take many forms, but they are often embodied in metaphors of one kind or another, ranging from jigsaws to sporting teams, and covering both intra- and inter-group dynamics. One of their common themes, however, is an interface between global and local concerns, or glocalisation. The dynamics of this interface were illustrated using the concept of motivational gravity. The *motivational gravity grid* (figure 3.8) is useful because it suggests ways of balancing personal and social achievement.

KEY TERMS

Broken promise. A tendency to over-promise and under-deliver regarding group participation. This can have many reasons, including supervisor job insecurity, self-deception ('Don't do as I say, do as I do'), and marketing about everyone's 'entitlement' to be part of the global economy. (p. 97)

Double demotivation. When two individuals or groups are paid differential rates for doing essentially the same job, both the lower paid and the higher paid individual or group become demotivated. (p. 113)

Escalation dynamic. Group (or individual) A reacts to group B, whose own reaction reinforces the reaction of group A, which then further fuels the reaction of

group B, and so on. A classic example is an arms race between two nations. (p. 113)

Group polarisation. During and following group discussion of an issue, the group becomes more extreme in the direction of its initial, pre-discussion opinions. (p. 93)

Groupthink. When a group becomes highly cohesive and overly loyal to its own codes of conduct, critical thinking is stifled, and group creativity and capacity to react to changing circumstances drops. (p. 97)

Intranet. An e-network for students or employees, set up to assist a group to make decisions and act collectively (p. 94)

Minimal group effect. Even when participants are allocated to groups on the most nominal (minimal) basis, they will still often prefer to allocate resources to the in-group before the out-group. (p. 106)

Motivational gravity. Occurs when individual achievers are brought back down to earth either by envious co-worker peers or by jealous and insecure supervisors in the organisation (p. 119)

Pull-down. A tendency among individuals or groups to undermine, or chop down, 'tall poppies', or successful individuals (p. 117)

Push-down. A tendency among individuals or groups in positions of power and authority to hold down high achievers, who may pose a threat to their own status (p. 118)

Realistic conflict theory. A sociological theory that holds that whenever resources are in short supply, it is simply realistic to expect groups to compete over their distribution (p. 104)

Risky shift. Occurs when discussion of an issue persuades the group to make more risky decisions (p. 92)

Social identity. The sense of belonging and esteem that we derive from belonging to a collective. We all need to feel proud of belonging to a group, or groups, and we supposedly attain this feeling by comparing 'our' group with 'theirs'. If the result of the comparison is favourable, according to the theory, social pride results. (p. 107)

Social inequity. A sense of imbalance of opportunities between two or more groups in a situation in which the in-group's returns-for-input do not match the returns-for-input accruing to a comparable out-group. Social inequity creates a sense of social injustice, and thereby motivates the perceivers of it to try to restore balance, for example by derogating the out-group or internalising the injustice ('They deserve their lower status; we deserve our elevated one'). (p. 110)

REVIEW QUESTIONS

1. Summarise the key ways in which governing with the consent of the governed can be problematic. Use figure 3.1 to organise your answers.
2. What are the best ways of managing these problems?
3. Summarise the key ways in which groups can enter into conflict with each other. Use figure 3.1 to categorise your answers.
4. What are the best ways of managing these problems?
5. Describe the concept of motivational gravity, and relate it to the concept of glocalisation.
6. How might the Motivational Gravity Grid be used to manage motivational gravity?

DISCUSSION QUESTIONS

1. Are groups worth it?
2. 'Two heads are better than one.' Discuss.
3. What does the literature on groups, reviewed in the chapter, imply about immigration policies for multicultural and bicultural societies such as Australia and New Zealand?

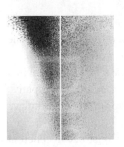

4. 'Social psychology has no hope of fixing, or even contributing towards solving, the truly intractable inter-group conflicts of our day, like the Palestinian question.' Discuss. (*Note*: You may find it useful to visit some of the many websites on inter-group conflict; check the online resources on the website before discussing this topic.)

5. Assess the impact of being a participant in one of the broken promise groups during activity 3. Could this experience serve as a productive way of allowing supervisors to walk a mile in the moccasins of workers (chapter 1)? Why/why not?

ACTIVITIES

1. Apply one or more of the 'storm management' techniques outlined and sourced in the chapter to a contemporary local issue. A worked example can be found in MacLachlan (1996).

2. Replicate the polarisation study described in the chapter, and reported in full in Carr et al. (1999). This exercise will take approximately one lecture/tutorial slot of one hour, and illustrates how to polarise the positive.

3. *Rejuvenation of communication networks research:* Use the experimental materials drawn in Leavitt (1951), and the Positive and Negative Affects Scale (PANAS) published in Barrett and Russell (1998), to complete the following study. The study takes one lecture/tutorial slot (one hour).

   The purpose of this exercise is to experientially demonstrate the likely impact, on group performance and morale, of being in communication structures varying in degree of participation (Leavitt 1951; Shaw 1964; Baldwin et al. 1991).

   (a) Form into groups of approximately $n = 5$. One person may act as an observer for each group, recording the number of correct solutions reached in the allocated time (20 minutes) and collating the questionnaire responses.

   (b) Sit in a circle. Each participant receives the task materials. To help simulate organisational (rather than personal) channels, verbal communication is not allowed, but members may send paper notes and/or cards to certain other individuals within their group. The group task is to identify as quickly and accurately as possible the symbol that appears on every member's sheet.

   (c) *Instructor's instructions:* Give one group Leavitt's instructions for the Wheel. Give another group Shaw's instructions for the All-Channel network. Give a third group a pre-brief on the benefits of participative decision making, but then proceed with Leavitt's instructions for the Wheel (Broken Promise condition).

   (d) *Plenary session:* Compare the feelings and performances of groups and members operating under the various conditions. If you were in charge of a company or department, what structure or structures would you prefer, and why? Would your preference vary according to situational context? Share your conclusions with the class. In particular, can you see any theme(s) linking this work with material being covered in the rest of the unit?

4. This exercise is designed to help you write up any report from activity 3. It is premised on the fact that most students find the hardest part of a report to write to be the introduction.

The ingredients: Expectations; communication; Shaw's review; Leavitt's research; modern organisations; your state, territory or country; participative teams; Baldwin et al.'s findings; experiential learning; gap between workplace rhetoric of empowerment and reality.

The exercise (which may be completed in groups): Construct a coherent narrative linking all of the above elements. Ensure that your narrative has a beginning, a middle section and an ending.

Source: Adapted from Bolitho (1999, personal correspondence).

5. Managing inter-group dynamics in real-world conflict situations: Split the class into groups in the week before the tutorial meeting. Each group is asked to consider the issue of applying inter-group dynamics to real-world issues. This task includes assessing the extent to which social psychologists have made their presence and ideas felt in real-world policy situations. The groups can gain a sense of this issue by considering the variety of online resources on inter-group conflict. Each group is asked to report its findings and deliberations when the class next meets for its tutorial session.

6. The chapter discusses the struggle for social identity and how this involves the achievement of inter-group differentiation. Break up into groups and discuss the application of this idea to the group members' own experiences. For example, inter-group differentiation is relevant to working in human service organisations like hospitals (Ng & Cram 1986), to 'permanent' versus 'temporary' workers (Bergman, Robbins & Stagg 1997, pp. 643–8), as well as to groups struggling to identify with their own generation (Williams et al. 1997). Report back the group's reflections to the assembled class.

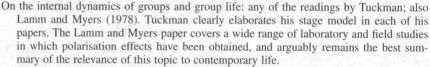

ADDITIONAL READING

On the internal dynamics of groups and group life: any of the readings by Tuckman; also Lamm and Myers (1978). Tuckman clearly elaborates his stage model in each of his papers. The Lamm and Myers paper covers a wide range of laboratory and field studies in which polarisation effects have been obtained, and arguably remains the best summary of the relevance of this topic to contemporary life.

Techniques for managing groupthink are well summarised in the Janis reading. The work by Leavitt remains a classic reading in social and organisational psychology. The reading by Baldwin et al. (1991) is a relatively user-friendly reminder about the dangers of over-promising and under-delivering in an organisational/managerial setting.

With regard to the causes of inter-group conflict, Tajfel's experimental papers referenced in the text are excellent, as is his wide-ranging review of inter-group comparison processes (1978). His analysis in this book is focused on relating laboratory processes to real-world events and social issues. Sherif's studies at the Robber's Cave remain classic, and the referenced reading is short and readily digestible. Kipnis's work on power, and the Prilleltensky reading on social aspects of power in contemporary poverty are very readable and scholarly.

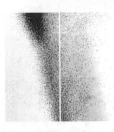

The Sherif reading does double time on this, by analysing both causes of inter-group conflicts and the means to reduce them. Jigsaw techniques are becoming more widely discussed. A quick search via any Internet search engine using the search term 'jigsaw classroom' will confirm this.

For further reading on the topics discussed in this chapter, consult the online resources linked to the Wiley website (http://www.johnwiley.com.au/highered/socialpsych).

CHAPTER 4

THE MEDIA

'I have achieved everything through persuasion' — Adolf Hitler
'Channel 7 — Your window on the world' — television advertising slogan
'Nothing is so unbelievable that oratory cannot make it acceptable' — Cicero

LEARNING OBJECTIVES

After reading this chapter, you should be able to:

- outline the early studies of media communication, focusing on attitude change, that have proved worthy of *rejuvenation*

- describe the key theoretical advances that led to a *restatement* of the role of context in media audience behaviour

- identify the limits of existing theory and its emergent *reconstitution*, using discourse-related concepts like cultural narrative

- engage in critical *reflection* to derive principles of sustainable behaviour change across part I of the book.

OVERVIEW

Social psychologists have studied the media in three overlapping phases. Their initial approach was atomistic. The influences of film, radio and the print media were attributed to discrete independent variables in the 'source' of a communication, in its 'message' or in its 'audience'. Research during this primary phase often assumed that the key to changing audience behaviour was to change its attitudes. During a secondary phase, theoretical developments highlighted additional roles for perceived social norms, practical constraints on behaviour and the influence of past behaviour (or habit). A recent, tertiary phase in our understanding of the media highlights a role for social and cultural narratives in motivating audience behaviour. These accounts consider media influence as the *positioning* of source, message and audience. The chapter ends by drawing together the main threads of part I of the book, and concludes that behaviour change is more sustainable when it happens under minimal constraint.

ATTITUDE: A CENTRAL CONSTRUCT

The following discussion focuses on the forms of mass persuasion exerted by the media. From our guiding 'cornerstones' of context, communication and culture, this chapter — more than any other in the book — foregrounds communication. Internet advertising and interactive games aside (these are reviewed at the end of the chapter), media-generated influence tends to flow in one direction — from a media source to a media audience. This initial conceptualisation accords with an idea introduced in the previous chapter, namely the influence of 'lecturing' to an audience. This, in turn, leads to the first question in the chapter: What is required to enable a media communication to produce sustainable changes in behaviour? A wider consideration around this opening question is the idea that media influences can be negative and positive, anti-social and pro-social (see discussion question 4.1). A role for social psychologists is to promote understanding of how to avoid one and promote the other, for example in commercial and social marketing (Hoffner 2001).

Few of us would deny that the media intrude heavily into contemporary life, and that much of this intrusion is designed to change our behaviour by persuading us what to buy, vote for or value (Pratkanis & Aronson 1992). Ever in the front line against these attempts at mass persuasion is the concept of **attitude**. In Internet advertising, for example, 'attitude towards the [web] site', 'attitude towards the ad' and 'attitude towards the product' are all considered by marketers to be important mediators and moderators of consumer behaviour (Chen & Wells 1999; Davis 1999). In social psychology, too, attitudes have been a principal portal, arguably *the* principal portal, for studying media influences on behaviour. This relative importance should not surprise us, perhaps, given that attitudes are mental constructs and, to that extent, thoroughly 'psychological'. All things considered, therefore, the concept of attitude is central to this chapter.

Attitudes are frequently referred to in everyday life. How many of us, for example, have not at some time been berated with, 'You had better change your attitude!' The significance of such admonishments is that attitudes are precursors of changes in behaviour. Yet most of us are probably unable to say precisely what attitudes are. The problem is that attitudes are too abstract to be defined by common sense alone. We need some conceptual analysis.

'Australia for Australians.' 'A woman's place is in the home.' 'AIDS — American *I*deas to *D*iscourage *S*ex.' 'Poverty is a scourge.' These are all statements of attitude, and they give us a first clue to its definition. Attitudes can be observed, be made visible as it were, through the words that people speak — their verbal behaviour. Attitudes become visible through communication. They are inherently social, and social psychological. This partly explains why social psychologists have been so fascinated by them for much of the past century. At a definitional level, however, we can also say that behaviour *reflects* attitudes; and, through verbal communication, behaviour is one key way that we can know them. According to this criterion, therefore, all we need to define attitude must be contained in the four statements above.

Attitudes contain two interrelated elements. First, they pertain to an object or issue, such as (from the illustrative statements) immigration, gender equity, or health and welfare promotion. Second, the attitude holder has a stance, or position, with respect to that object or issue. Originally, the word *attitude* meant 'body position'. Today it suggests adopting a *mental* position — say, supporting or rejecting ('for' or 'against') the object or issue in question. In each of the statements, the speaker takes a clear position on the issue. Attitudes, then, are about *positioning*.

There are other elements to an attitude. These can be summarised in the statement, 'Belief + feeling = motivation to act'. First, there is always a component of belief — for example the belief that Australia should be reserved for Australians. Second, there is always some feeling involved, such as the misogyny in the belief that a woman's place is in the home. Third, attitudes invariably have the potential to influence behaviour, such as the 'Third World' youth who believes, or perhaps rationalises, that AIDS is an invention of the imperialist West, and so does not wear a condom the next time he has casual sex. Fourth, then, attitudes motivate behaviour by creating intentions to behave like 'this' instead of 'that'. Attitudes can therefore have serious consequences, not only for the people who adopt them, but also for any partnerships, groups or communities to which these people belong (the interested reader should apply the same four steps to an attitude statement such as 'Poverty is a scourge').

Broadly, then, an attitude is a mixture of beliefs and feelings that motivates behaviour, and that often reflects the taking of a mental position on an object or issue. According to this working definition, attitudes, and more particularly attitude change, embody all the central components of social psychology, as we know them from chapter 1. These central elements are social influence, beliefs, feelings and behaviour. It is easy to understand, then, why the concept of attitude has for so long fascinated social psychologists, and why it occupies a prominent place in this chapter.

A PRIMARY PHASE: THE YALE PROGRAM

The Yale (University) Communication Program marked an opening phase of social psychology's contribution towards our understanding of media influence (Hovland, Lumsdaine & Sheffield 1949). This program was initially driven by pragmatism. Carl Hovland and colleagues were commissioned to undertake a communications program to assist the US war effort during World War II (the information was released only in 1949). Some of the central findings of this program, and the many experimental studies that followed, are still being applied today. They are commonly used, for example, in commercial marketing (e.g. of products), in social marketing (e.g. of healthy behaviour) and, until recently at least, in the practice of law (Crowley, O'Callaghan & Ball 1994). Arguably, these are domains of everyday life in which social psychology as a discipline has had a social impact (although perhaps not always a positive one). It is therefore with these studies, or their 'primary' findings, that we begin our review of media influence (for good alternative overviews, see Hovland, Janis & Kelley 1953; Petty & Cacioppo 1981; Deaux & Wrightsman 1984).

The theme sentence

Hovland and his associates organised their program of research around the parts of speech in a particular theme sentence. The elements in this theme sentence were not novel, even during the 1940s. They had been suggested, for example, in Aristotle's famous book on oratory, *Rhetoric*. Their long history indicates considerable robustness. During the twentieth century the theme sentence used by the Yale researchers also became a convention in journalism, adopted as a formula in structuring news stories. This theme sentence is presented in figure 4.1, which also illustrates how the sentence was used in organising the Yale research program. In particular, the figure reveals how the theme sentence was linked to the research methodology.

Guiding sentence:			
'Who says	what	to *whom*	with what effect'
Powerful?	Fear-provoking?	Education?	Attitude/
Likeable?	1st or 2nd?	Gender?	Behaviour
Credible?	1 or 2 sided?	Group dynamics?	Change
SOURCE	MESSAGE	AUDIENCE	INFLUENCE
◄------ Independent variables ------►			Dependent variables

Figure 4.1   Structure of the Yale Communication Program

From figure 4.1, Hovland et al.'s methodology was largely field-experimental. It divided the process of media influence into independent and dependent variables, and camouflaged them as something other than an 'experiment', for example as a classroom evaluation (see Kelman below). The independent variables were subdivided into smaller constituents. These comprised source factors (*who* — e.g. the actor, speaker or author), message factors (*what* — the message actually pictured, spoken or written), and audience factors (*whom* — the intended destination). An additional independent variable, the media channel, was added later (discussed, for example, in Petty & Cacioppo 1981, pp. 86–7). During the Yale Program these factors were systematically varied in order to examine their impact on the dependent variable 'with what effect'. This component was operationally defined most often as a change in attitude, although sometimes as a change in behaviour.

Who (the source)

An early associate of Hovland's was Herbert Kelman (Kelman & Hovland 1953). One of Kelman's famous studies attempted to answer the question of whether a media source produces more sustainable influence if its appeal is based, following figure 4.1, on power, likeability or credibility (Kelman 1958). This study is interesting because the influence attempt took place in a wider context not unlike localisation (see chapter 1). Kelman's speaker argued against a wider movement towards racial integration through social contact in US schools (see chapter 3). Most of the students participating in the study, who were African Americans, were in favour of integration. Kelman's source, however, made a radio broadcast *against* such a change. In particular, the speaker argued that integration would dilute African-American culture, and encourage passive assimilation with the dominant 'mainstream'. This was an attempt at localisation. The message, proposing a backlash, was delivered by three distinct types of speaker. Depending on how this speaker was introduced, either he inspired fear (he had the power to close colleges that did not toe the backlash line), or he was liked (he was a popular student figure), or he was perceived as credible (he was an expert on race relations who was also trustworthy, having moral integrity).

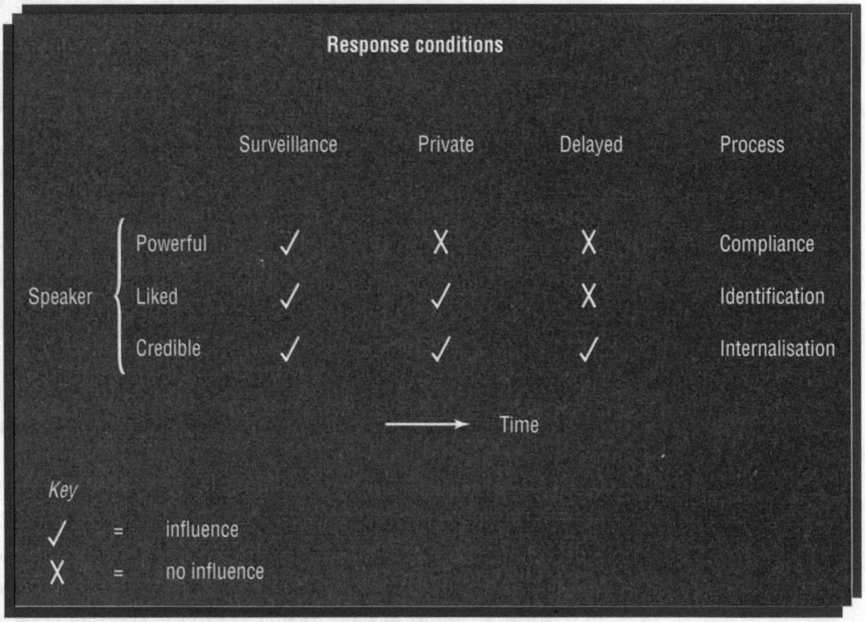

Response conditions

		Surveillance	Private	Delayed	Process
Speaker	Powerful	✓	X	X	Compliance
	Liked	✓	✓	X	Identification
	Credible	✓	✓	✓	Internalisation

⟶ Time

Key

✓ = influence

X = no influence

Figure 4.2 The results of Kelman's (1958) media communication study

Kelman's independent and dependent variables are depicted in figure 4.2. He expected, and indeed found, that fear (from power) would produce influence only while the participant felt that the speaker was actually monitoring them, and that this influence would be restricted to influencing only their public behaviour, or **compliance**. This is the same effect as produced in Asch's line-length and Milgram's obedience studies (see chapter 1; also Kelman 1953). The likeable speaker had more success, since his influence extended to a change in private opinion. This process is termed **identification**, because influence is based on wanting to be like — and liking — the source, rather than embracing the content of the message itself. However, identification did not produce sustainable influence, which Kelman attributed to the fickleness of relationships generally (for another example, see Chaiken 1980). Rather, sustainability was found only with the credible speaker, whose influence lasted for several weeks after the original radio broadcast, on a delayed measure of attitude change. Reflecting this durability, and the fact that influence had durably extended into private opinion change, Kelman used the term **internalisation** to describe the process that resulted from perceived credibility.

Perhaps the media today do not usually possess as much coercive power as Kelman's powerful speaker did, but they do still have leverage. For example, they manifestly flaunt the aversive properties of not having (and, by contrast, the reward properties of having) consumer goods. Their power today involves a more subtle form of coercion — a perennial suggestion that self must 'keep up with the Joneses' in order not to 'miss out' and consequently be a failure (Bedeian 1995). The global media today promise us enviable 'lifestyles', on condition that we buy and consume the product or service they promote (Cushman 1990). Cushman marks out this power by invoking the image of an 'empty self', a hollow vessel that continually 'fills itself up' with consumer goods as a measure of its 'success' in modern society. This image of an empty self evokes the process of compliance. The rampant consumer is never really able to identify with, or indeed meaningfully internalise, consumerism itself. Thus, audience compliance, and Kelman's findings relating to that social influence process, are very much still with us.

More recent research has shown that an audience's feelings of liking for a message source will influence its degree of attitude change (Roskos-Ewoldsen & Fazio 1992). This change, in turn, can be a predictor of consumer intentions to buy a product (Kanungo & Johar 1975). The process of identification has been found across a range of mass persuasion settings (Wilson & Sherrell 1993). Such processes can have major consequences for society (as well as for personal relationships — see chapter 8). For example, US presidential elections may be ultimately decided on which candidate is more likeable (Petty & Cacioppo 1981, p. 66). Identification, therefore, is also very relevant to media audiences today.

For obvious reasons, the process of internalisation, and its foundation of perceived credibility, has captured more interest than any other variable from the original Yale Program. In psychological terms, credibility is based on perceived expertise and trust (see also McGinnies & Ward 1980). These factors are often more salient to consumers than mere likeability (Brownlow 1992). In practical terms, governments often suffer from low perceived credibility (Lirtzman & Shuv-Ami 1986). Lirtzman and Shuv-Ami's study focused on persuasive power concerning public health and safety; indeed, a great deal of the applied research on credibility has focused on that particular domain of life.

A good example of this focus is the campaign against AIDS, or acquired immune deficiency syndrome. I had my own personal experience of this relevance while working in Malaŵi, East Africa, during the early 1990s. At that time, AIDS was a major issue in the country, as it was across the whole continent. By the end of the decade, the United Nations was estimating that in Africa there were 'four new infections every minute, far more than anywhere else in the world', and that the AIDS virus was the 'number one threat to economic development on the continent' (Piot 1999). In Malaŵi during the 1990s, information on AIDS prevention was in relatively short supply, despite the fact that there were potentially numerous sources through which AIDS prevention messages might have been disseminated. A common response to the threat, for example, was summed up in the popular slogan 'AIDS — *American Idea to Discourage Sex*' (MacLachlan 1996b). Against that kind of backdrop, the research summarised in figure 4.3 was formulated. This research was founded on the fundamental premise that knowing how to avoid catching fatal diseases is a necessary condition for staying alive.

Source	Mean
Medical doctor	3.5
Family	3.2
Religious adviser	3.1
Psychologist	3.1
Nurse	3.1
Government radio	2.8
Government newspaper	2.8
Government posters	2.8
Friend	2.6
Traditional healer	1.6

Line of viability

Scale: 1 = not at all credible   2 = not really credible
3 = reasonably credible   4 = highly credible

Note: Any source under '3' is less than reasonably credible.

Figure 4.3 Credibility and AIDS prevention in an African context ***Source:*** Carr and MacLachlan (1994).

From figure 4.3, the most credible sources of information among students (a high-risk group) were medical doctors (see also Bandawe 2000; Tembo 1991). Unlike condoms, however, doctors were in relatively short supply, or relatively inaccessible (for a wider discussion of condom availability in 'developing', materially poorer countries, see Paxton & Janssen 2002). The next best choices to act as credible sources of advice were family and religious advisers. These sources were more numerous and accessible (Carr 1993). Instead of employing them, however, most health promotion efforts were channelled through the government-controlled media, whose credibility at the time with this high-risk segment of the wider population was extremely low. Thus, elementary social psychological research, based on a rejuvenated construct of credibility, can under some conditions 'make a difference' (for a discussion of *structural* factors that make a difference, try Campbell & Mzaidume 2002 or Klein, Easton & Parker 2002).

Based on Kelman's research, any impact of credibility is probably founded on nudging an audience to 'think again', for example about the rationalisation that AIDS is a neo-colonialist American plot (or, less politically, that using condoms is like 'eating a sweet with the wrapper on'). In other words, perceived credibility may depend for its impact on persuading people to actively *deliberate* on a message. In social psychology this process of active deliberation, or rather the probability of its occurring, is called 'elaboration likelihood' (Petty & Cacioppo 1981).

Such an impact is by no means guaranteed by having perceived credibility, however. For instance, a risk with perceiving a source as 'credible' is that the audience starts to rely on media messages without thinking about them too much for themselves. The fact that a source is credible actually stops them from actively deliberating too much about its message. The best illustration of this risk is available in one of the first studies in the Yale Program (Hovland & Weiss 1951). In that study, articles (say, about health) were attributed to writers who varied in perceived credibility (from a well-known medical journal to a popular 'pulp' magazine). Hovland and Weiss found more attitude change, immediately after reading the articles, among audiences who read from the credible source. Four weeks later, however, this advantage was gone. The influence of a high-credibility source had waned, while the influence exerted by its low-credibility counterpart had grown.

How could this be? Much of this convergence was attributable to partial amnesia on the part of the audience. They had simply, unthinkingly, forgotten the source and retained only the information in the message. Such partial forgetfulness, which many of us will recognise, has become known (for obvious reasons) as the 'sleeper effect' (Lee & Mason 1999). At first glance, the sleeper effect does not tally with Kelman's (1958) effects for a 'credible' speaker: Why, that is, did Hovland and Weiss's credible speaker lose impact over time, while Kelman's credible speaker actually sustained it? The most likely explanation for this apparent discrepancy centres again on elaboration likelihood. Kelman's source was speaking on a highly relevant, contentious issue, and his position was unexpected. Under such circumstances, perceived credibility is likely to prompt an audience to think more deeply.

This idea, known as 'depth of processing', is graphically illustrated in the social psychology of criminal justice. Law courts resemble media situations insofar as lawyers and witnesses speak to juries, who cannot speak back. A classic study of the jury situation was made by Walster, Aronson and Abrahams (1966). These researchers presented audiences with media articles that argued for more severe jail penalties for crime and increased prosecuting power for the courts. This issue, of course, remains topical today. In the study, articles were presented as having been written by a highly successful public prosecutor and by an ex-jailbird. In such a contest, common sense and intuition suggest that the prosecutor would have greater credibility, and thereby exert more influence. But, in fact, it was the *ex-jailbird* who proved the source of greater persuasion.

Walster et al.'s interpretation of their finding was that the ex-jailbird was arguing against his own self-interest. The prosecutor, meanwhile, was seen as simply promoting his own interests. Under such circumstances, trust and expertise (i.e. credibility) were more likely to be attributed to the ex-con. Fuelling this tendency, the fact that the argument for harsher sentencing was proposed by an ex-criminal must have been a considerable surprise. That surprise probably prompted many participants to think further, not just about why this unlikely source was adopting a tough position, but about the wider issue of criminal justice itself (the same point is made in chapter 8, in the section on minority influence). Thus, credibility will have the greatest, most sustainable impact when circumstances conspire to prompt an audience to think, not just about the speaker's own attitude, but also about the issue itself.

Credibility

Clever advertisers will sometimes try to use credible sources to prompt surprise, thereby raising the likelihood of elaborated mental processing, since this, as we have seen, produces more sustainable change. At other times, advertising agencies will periodically simply remind the audience of who the source of their original message was; this generally cancels the sleeper effect and restores the effects of credibility *per se* (Kelman & Hovland 1953). Either way, however, 'credibility' remains a factor to watch out for. In many advertisements in Australia and New Zealand, for example, sporting heroes are seen advocating a range of health-related products. These celebrities have the double advantage of being both credible *and* likeable (nothing precludes different influence processes from acting in combination). Perceived credibility has been applied to social issues ranging from political campaigning (Bochner 1989) to alcohol consumption (Bochner 1994) to environmental protection (Syme & Nancarrow 1992) to sex role stereotyping (Mazella et al. 1992). Clearly, then, credibility remains a significant and relevant concept in marketing. Its psychology, therefore, concerns us all.

What (the message)

Using fear to motivate an audience to change

Intuitively, a powerful way of attempting to change behaviour, often manifested in health promotion social marketing, is to appeal to the emotions, and in particular to fear (Witte & Morrison 1995). A vivid example of this in Australia is the AIDS-prevention television advertisement 'Grim Reaper' (Taylor 1988). This advertisement first went to air during the mid 1980s and was briefly reincarnated in parts of the country during 2000 (McKenzie 2000). As its name suggests, the advertisement portrays the figure of Death presiding, sickle in hand, over the intercourse of incautious (non-condom-using) couples. Viewing audiences across both Australia and New Zealand today are frequently exposed to fearful images of this kind, for example in road-safety promotion campaigns. As public memory of the Grim Reaper advertisement testifies, such negative and fear-laden information can be very memorable (Bray & Chapman 1991; see chapter 5, on negative information effect). But is it sufficient to produce sustainable changes in behaviour? There is, after all, an alternative to an appeal to fear — reasoned argument!

The original experiment on the issue of fear appeals to motivate behaviour change was conducted during the Yale Program (Janis & Feshbach 1953). This field experiment focused on fear of dentists. It presented students with messages about the negative consequences of poor dental hygiene. At the lowest level of fear, students were presented with reasoned arguments about dental hygiene. At the highest level of fear, reminiscent of the Grim Reaper campaign, reasoned arguments were accompanied by gruesome pictures of diseased gums and warnings of secondary infections such as kidney disease, or even death. This 'high fear' approach actually turned out to be counterproductive in terms of changing behaviour. As fear increased, tooth-brushing behaviour and dental check-ups, measured during the week following the exposure (from diaries and dental records) *decreased*. Thus, more fear produced less change.

Subsequent research has shown that high fear can be motivating and will produce sustainable behaviour change, provided the fear appeal is accompanied by concrete, practical, easy-to-follow behavioural advice. This counsel must clarify, in simple language, how to *alleviate* the fear. In one study, for instance, vaccination compliance behaviour rose from just 3 per cent under a 'high fear/no recommendations' condition to 28 per cent under a 'high fear-with-easily-implemented-recommendations' condition (Leventhal 1973). Since Leventhal's early study, fear appeals have been tested across an increasing range of settings and populations (Murray-Johnson et al. 2001). In general, it appears that the recommendation to 'accompany fear with concrete advice' about how to alleviate that fear is sound (Witte 1994).

A limiting factor with this kind of finding is that it is not always *possible* to suggest concrete solutions. With a disease like AIDS, for example, we cannot turn back the clock and simply 'erase' past unsafe behaviour. To an audience that knows that it had already been sexually active and promiscuous for some time *before* hearing a 'fear-inspiring' broadcast, no amount of concrete advice about prevention can help. It has come too late, so anxiety will only be exacerbated. Such audiences may well reason, whether consciously or not, that they have probably caught the disease already, so why bother with prevention? This conclusion, in turn, will encourage the construction of defence mechanisms (see Witte & Morrison 1995). Thus, AIDS will remain an 'American idea to discourage sex', and condoms a sweet wrapper that spoils the fun, unless perhaps an appeal is supplemented with more impactful, for example group-based, techniques of persuasion (Murray-Johnson et al. 2001).

Delivering your message before or after a rival source

A wider point to extract from all this is that the success of any media message depends on other factors, such as past behaviour, that are outside the message itself. Just as AIDS has been defensively dismissed by some youths in one part of Africa as an American invention to prevent enjoyment or procreation, we can expect to find other rival messages operating in different circumstances. These rival messages commonly emanate, for instance, from media sources as well as from peers. Prime examples are rival commercial companies and competing charity appeals. In law cases and in political electioneering (much of which takes place in and through the media), what 'the opposition' says is a salient concern.

When this kind of competition occurs, the practical issue — that is, the question that any serious contender must ponder — is *timing*. When is the best time to give or broadcast that speech? Before or after the opposition gives theirs? In media research, this is a question of 'order effects'.

The most enduring study of order effects was undertaken by Miller and Campbell (1959). These researchers staged a mock lawsuit — analogous in media terms to a party political broadcast on television, for example in the run-up to an election or political referendum. In Miller and Campbell's study, the two adversaries were contesting a lawsuit for damages. The audience heard recordings of each side's case, and these recordings (as in party political broadcasts) were aired either close together in time (contiguously) or far (one week) apart. Also, the jury's verdict was required either immediately or one week after the hearing had ended — that is, 'time-to-decision' was varied. The results of this intriguing and elegant study are presented in figure 4.4.

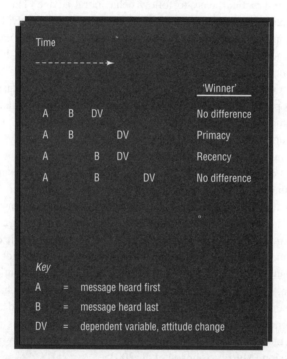

Figure 4.4   Miller and Campbell's (1959) study on timing in competitive communications

As shown in figure 4.4, when all three measures (A, B and DV) were relatively contiguous, there was no advantage, in terms of the final decision of the audience (dependent variable or DV), to speaking either first (A) or second (B). However, when a delay was introduced between the end of the hearing and the verdict (choice behaviour), the party who had spoken first (A) gained an advantage (primacy effect). When the two sides were not presented contiguously, the second speaker (B) regained an advantage (the recency effect). Finally, when there were time gaps between speakers *and* between the end of the hearing and giving a verdict, the sequential positioning of the speaker (whether first or second) again made no difference.

Miller and Campbell's analysis of their findings suggests the following explanation of them. In the general scheme of things, first impressions run relatively deep in memory, creating a primacy effect. At the same time, recent events are fresher in the memory, and this freshness is an advantage too, creating a recency effect. From figure 4.4, therefore, when A, B and DV are contiguous, primacy and recency effects cancel each other out. There is no order effect. If we delay the DV, however, the recency effect will fade, leaving A (through the primacy effect) in front. If A and B are themselves then teased further apart in time, and DV follows immediately after B, more of B's message (rather than A's) is likely to be fresh in the mind of the audience. Recency will prevail. After a delay between B and DV, however, the recency effect fades once more, and we again return to an even balance. Thus, while we have forgotten some of A, the recency effect of B has also faded.

No amount of clever sequencing will enable a lousy argument to overcome a case that is carefully thought out and crafted, so there are inherent limits to understanding order effects. Nonetheless, they have continued to capture the interest of both researchers and practitioners (for legal applications, for example, see Haugtvedt & Wegener 1994; Linz & Penrod 1984; Petty et al. 2001). The practical implications of this research, at least for would-be sources, or engineers of opinion, are pithily summarised as follows:

> When speaking back-to-back, the candidate would do best by speaking first, unless voting was scheduled immediately following the speeches, in which case it would not matter whether they spoke first or second. Perhaps more importantly, ... a last-minute media blitz may be highly effective, especially when some time has lapsed since the opposing candidate has presented his or her views. (Petty & Cacioppo 1981, p. 79)

The single-sided versus the double-sided message

Intuitively, the most direct way of dealing with rival messages is to anticipate the opposition's arguments and then to debunk them within your own message (Williams, Bourgeois & Croyle 1993). However, in chapter 3 we learned that there are dangers in such over-elaboration. This raises a pragmatic question: Is it generally better for would-be media persuaders, all else being equal, to employ a single-sided argument or a double-sided approach?

This question was put in the earliest published Yale study, by Hovland et al. (1949). The tendency prevailing in military audiences at the time was unrealistic — that the war with Japan would be over quickly and easily. The Yale team's brief was to persuade these (US) troops to appraise the war with Japan more realistically, to appreciate that it would probably take time to win (the atom bomb was still in the wings). To get this message across, two different approaches were tried — a concise, one-sided argument; and a more elaborate, two-sided approach also discussing the (militarily unrealistic) view that the Japanese forces could be quickly defeated. A little surprisingly, perhaps, the overall findings were equivocal. There was no difference, in terms of overall attitude change, between audiences exposed to a one-sided message and audiences also exposed to an explicit response to the opposition view that the war would be over quickly.

Whom (the audience)

However, the researchers then performed an exercise frequently used today in commercial and social marketing. They segmented the audience. Specifically, Hovland et al. divided the audience into those who were initially 'for' and those who were initially 'against' the short-war message. Once this segmentation of the audience was performed, it became clear that the impact of the message had indeed varied according to the audience's initial, pre-broadcast attitudes.

For those who were already sympathetic to the message before the broadcast, a one-sided message was more effective. For a sceptical audience of an opposing view, however, a two-sided message was more effective. This improved efficacy of a two-sided message also held among the more educated segments of the audience. Comparable advantages to this two-sided approach have recently been found when an issue is more relevant to the audience to begin with (Sorrentino et al. 2000; for an earlier simulated court case study, see Dipboye 1977). Collectively, these findings highlight the importance of *respecting audience expectation*. If the audience already has an opinion on an issue, has more education or finds the issue relevant, it will probably expect to hear *both* sides of the story before being persuaded to reposition its current point of view.

Gender

More broadly, Hovland et al.'s findings suggest that personal upbringing and social-isation are liable to influence what an audience segment expects from a communication. It was therefore not surprising that questions soon began to be asked about one of the most common of socialisation variables and, nowadays, segmentation factors — gender. This research is succinctly reviewed in Petty and Cacioppo (1981, pp. 83–4). Initially, it was found that women tended to appear more easily per-suaded to change their attitudes than men. This apparent difference was sometimes attributed to the ways that females had been socialised into 'submissive' and 'sen-sitive' roles. After lobbying by women, however, research revealed that the kinds of attitude issues that the Yale tradition had studied were generally of less interest and relevance to women than to men (Sistrunk & McDavid 1971). As we have just seen, reduced issue relevance increases susceptibility to one-sided messages, which is what the Yale messages typically were (Sorrentino et al. 2000). Indeed, when new issues that women generally found more relevant were tested, women were far less easily influenced than their male counterparts (Petty & Cacioppo 1981).

Role-playing

The idea that relevance enhances resistance to persuasion raises an intriguing question. Are there ways of *circumventing* that resistance? One of the most prom-ising techniques for addressing this issue is role-playing. Role-playing entails temporarily assuming an alternative point of view; it is another way of 'walking in someone else's moccasins' (see chapter 1). As well, role-playing may be some-thing that people do quite readily and naturally in everyday life (Goffman 1959). Most interestingly, perhaps, role-playing minimises constraint. It takes an audi-ence closer to the kind of *participative* forms of decision making investigated by Lewin and others working in the field of group dynamics (see chapter 3).

An impressive early study of the influence of role-playing is found in Janis and Mann (1965). This study compared the impact of a health education message that involved role-play with one that did not. The participants were all young women smokers aged 18 to 23 years who had volunteered to take part in a study of emotional role-playing. On their arrival for this task, they were informed that the study was simulating emotional reactions by patients when receiving bad news from a doctor. They had to improvise the role of a patient hearing the bad news from a doctor (an accomplice of the experimenter) that they had lung cancer. Control audiences simply heard an audiotape of the role-play session. Theirs was a relatively passive role, analogous, perhaps, to 'receiving' media messages about health in Yale-type 'audience' settings.

Like Zimbardo's prisoners and guards in chapter 1, Janis and Mann's role-players readily embraced their roles. They became visibly involved in the part. They shook, sweated and evidently experienced strong fear. But, unlike the Grim Reaper campaign, this self-paced, self-induced and to that extent non-constraining fear appeal changed the audience. 'Intention to quit smoking' rose immediately after the role-playing session was over. More tellingly, however, levels of risk-related behaviour (smoking cigarettes), some two weeks later, dropped more than twice as far as they did in control condition audiences during the same period. Also, more of the role-playing than regular audience members actually had a medical check-up. Participative role-playing, therefore, was more effective in changing behaviour than a non-participative traditional media broadcast.

These findings were replicated, again with women smokers, in a Japanese study, comparing role-playing against messages broadcast on television (Takahasi 1977). More recently, role-playing has been applied to persuade disturbed adolescent boys to appreciate the perspective of victims of crime (Lowenstein 1997). The technique has also been used to persuade educators to think about student curricula in new and innovative ways (Plummer 1982). Given these promising findings, is it practicable for media audiences, which are (after all) *mass* audiences, to role-play? On the face of it, role-playing might seem too resource intensive to implement on a large scale. Yet that, in part, is exactly what has been happening in a range of settings around the world. Across resource-constrained settings in Africa, Latin America and Australia, community theatre groups are thriving (Bandawe 2000; Sánchez 1996; Williams 1996; for a study focusing on the memorability of a message in such techniques, see Chazin & Neuschatz 1990).

A SECONDARY PHASE: RE-APPRECIATING CONTEXT

A major message in the performing arts movement is that social context matters. This realisation typifies 'phase two' of media influence research. The impetus in this phase has come from two main sources. Sociological social psychologists, not surprisingly, have highlighted the influence of structural factors on the communication process. Theirs is a relatively wide interpretation of the term 'social context' (see 'Ethos and direction'). Using the term more narrowly, cognitive social psychologists have highlighted how attitudes are not the only mental construct influencing audience behaviour. According to these social psychologists, both 'perceived group norms' and 'perceived control over own resources' matter too.

Implicit in the ethos of the Yale studies was the assumption that the media have relatively direct access to the attitudes held by an audience. Their influence acts in one step, from source to audience, with little else of any 'social' nature happening in between. This assumption was evident in the field experimental designs, which mostly positioned the message as a one-step broadcast to an assembled audience, as if the wider social context was not relevant. A popular metaphor for media influence at the time was a syringe. In this 'single step' model of mass communication, the media functioned rather like a hypodermic needle: they metaphorically 'injected' persuasive messages directly into the psychological veins of an audience. An impetus for this single-step model was undoubtedly the dramatic influence of a famous radio broadcast made in 1938 in the United States by the innovative actor and director Orson Welles. *The War of the Worlds* was a deliberately realistic, documentary-style dramatisation of the novel by H. G. Wells. In the original novel, Wells' narrator reports on an invasion of Earth by Martian aliens; in Orson Welles' dramatic radio reconstruction, science fiction became science fact for up to one million frightened Americans, who believed they were actually being invaded from outer space. For many of them, this fear directly provoked panic behaviour.

The syringe metaphor persisted until the sociologist Elihu Katz published a revised model of the mass communication process in 1957. Through community-based research, Katz found that potentially persuasive messages were often *mediated* through community opinion leaders, or 'gatekeepers'. Figures within the community whose opinions on the issue in question were respected were sought for advice on whether the new attitudes should or should not be adopted. Recent research on Internet advertising (Davis 1999) and on media-influenced aggression (Nathanson 2001) is broadly consistent with this original finding (see also Livingstone 1997). In Katz's relatively individualistic settings, the community gatekeepers tended to be specialised. One opinion leader was consulted on matters of food, another on matters of fashion, and so on. Subsequent research has shown that, in more collectivistic communities, the range of credibility for these figures is frequently less domain-specific and more general (Streatfield & Singarimbun 1988). Nonetheless, Katz's critical points remain. Mass persuasion often involves more than one step, and these secondary steps often implicate group and leadership dynamics. Thus, media influences do entail social context.

According to this revised model, a range of contextual issues conspired to make the impact on the public of the *War of the Worlds* broadcast comparable to a syringe injection. For example, the US in 1938 was an insecure and anxious nation. It was economically depressed, and expecting imminent news of war, and some kind of attack on the American heartland. Also, radio was still strongly trusted as a channel for news and factual information — it was highly credible. Under these conditions the medium could easily facilitate panic behaviour.

The importance of contextual factors in media influence was recognised by the Yale researchers (Hovland 1959). One researcher later proposed a very influential model of social context (McGuire 1985). Based on an idea originally proposed by Hovland et al. (1953), the attitude change process, in naturalistic settings, was viewed as a sequence of micro-developmental stages. A stage model precisely like this has recently been rejuvenated in study of the Internet (Harvey 1997). To be persuasive, said McGuire, a media message has to first gain *exposure* to its intended audience. Next it has to grab the audience's *attention*. Then it must also be *understood*. After that it must be privately *accepted*. Come decision time, the acceptance has to be *remembered*. And finally, this memory must be converted into *behaviour*. The usefulness of such models, however, is in identifying specific 'pressure points' for the influence of context. Thus, at any of the stages, different contextual factors will intervene to make changes in behaviour either more or less likely.

Take, for example, a complex message and the issue of *understanding*. If presented via television or radio sound bites, the message may be 'lost' to its intended audience. In such cases, a print channel, or the Internet, would probably be more effective. According to McGuire's model, this is because those channels usually allow the audience more time to read and reread, and thus process message *complexity* (Chaiken & Eagly 1976). McGuire's model also suggests when group dynamics are crucial, for example at the stage of *acceptance*. We enjoyed a clear illustration of this in chapter 3, with Lewin's finding that the same speech had ten times more impact when its message was not merely 'delivered' (lectured) to its audience, but also debated by them as a group. In terms of *remembering* messages, much of the foregoing review has focused on the importance of time and temporal context, for example in the decision to speak first or second. Finally, and most important, McGuire's model suggests that we need to study contextual factors that intervene between (a) attitude and (b) behaviour. That proverbial space 'between cup and lip' is where the rest of this section now focuses.

Moderating attitude–behaviour relations

Even before the Yale Program began there were signs that social context has a large influence on whether an attitude is expressed in behaviour. A landmark study of this question is reported in La Piere (1934), who surveyed 251 US motels and restaurants on whether they would serve guests of Chinese ethnicity. Ninety-two per cent of the establishments who responded ($n = 118/128$) reported that they would *not* serve these potential customers. Yet despite this response, before the survey La Piere had actually visited each of the 251 establishments accompanied by an ethnic Chinese couple. And they had been refused service in only one case! Evidently, therefore, although the guests were not the right colour, their money and the company they kept — both elements in the social context — were (Kraus 1995).

La Piere's study was undeniably flawed — for example, the same person did not necessarily answer the questionnaire and meet the trio. Despite such flaws, however, a discrepancy of such magnitude between attitude and behaviour was eventually bound to come back to haunt those supporting a simple, direct linkage between the two. Indeed, a clamour of controversy arose during the 1960s and 1970s, as reviews and meta-reviews of the correlation between attitude and behaviour repeatedly demonstrated that the linkages were statistically weak. These damaging reviews at one stage threatened to engulf the whole field. However, from the mid 1970s to the early 1980s the tide began to turn. Two of the key players in this revival of media psychology, and in particular of attitudes and attitude change in audience behaviour, were Icek Ajzen and Martin Fishbein (1980).

These researchers began by pointing out that attitudes had been measured in the general (e.g. on global environmental pollution or on broad political persuasion), whereas behaviours had been measured in the particular (e.g. on specific local neighbourhood litter-clearing days or participation in a particular political demonstration). Of course, they argued, it was unfair to expect measures of attitude on *general* issues to predict one-off behaviours under very *specific* circumstances. I can be very much 'for' environmental responsibility, or 'against' a political party, without necessarily (for umpteen different reasons) volunteering to clean up the local neighbourhood on a given day or taking part in a particular political demonstration. Similarly, I can be racially prejudiced, but at the same time not *show* this at my job, perhaps because of the threat of being fired, or because I like the colour of customers' tips. Yet in the long term, on the average, over the entire range of situations in which I meet people from different ethnic backgrounds, my behaviour will still be tilted towards discrimination rather than impartiality. Attitudes will still, in the end, matter, provided we keep in mind that context matters too.

A principle of correspondence

To demonstrate this point, Ajzen and Fishbein needed to be able to show that general attitudes would predict behaviour in general — that is, behaviour that is aggregated across a range of situations and is relevant to the broad attitude issue. The bandwidth of behaviour (and the measure of it) must match the bandwidth of attitude (and the measure of it). Ajzen and Fishbein termed this idea of equalising bandwidths across the two measures 'correspondence' and 'compatibility'. Once this was achieved (i.e. once there was aggregation across *both* measures), the statistical link between attitude and behaviour became more noteworthy. In one study, 33 per cent of the variation in behaviour was explained by attitude (this figure is extracted from a balanced discussion of the issue in Eagly & Chaiken 1993, pp. 158–68; for a recent example of attitudes predicting helping behaviour during crowd disturbances, see Russell & Arms 2001).

Of course, compatibility and correspondence can cut both ways. Narrow-band, specific attitudes are capable of predicting specific, narrow-band behaviours: 'A specific action performed in a particular context is compatible only with the evaluation of [attitude towards] the specific behavior in question' (Ajzen & Fishbein 2000, p. 17). Such ideas are captured for us in figure 4.5, where Fishbein and Ajzen's term to capture this idea of equal bandwidths, general or specific, between measures of attitudes and measures of behaviour is denoted as 'attitude towards the behaviour'.

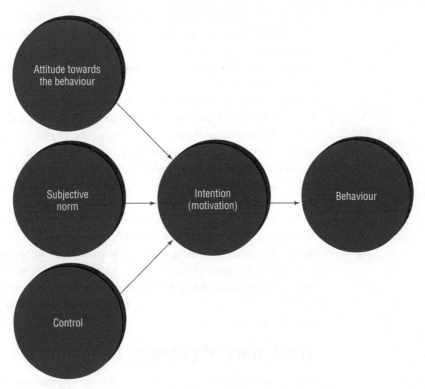

Figure 4.5 Core elements of the theory of planned behaviour   *Source:* Adapted from Ajzen (1991b).

Residual variance

Figures such as Eagly and Chaiken's 33 per cent of the variation (above), while statistically noteworthy, still leave the lion's share of variance in behaviour to be explained by 'other factors'. Figure 4.5 suggests what some of these other factors might be. Research by Ajzen and Fishbein (1980), and later Ajzen (1991b), indicated that the capacity to predict behaviour is enhanced significantly if, in addition to attitude towards the behaviour, we also consider two additional factors. Each of these factors is heavily contextual. As shown in figure 4.5, they are (i) subjective norm and (ii) degree of control. According to the model, these two factors will combine with 'attitude towards the behaviour' to predict behavioural 'intention'. This intention is a 'motivation' component in the model. Statistically, such motivational intention is the best predictor of audience behaviour. The interplay of all these factors combined is called the Theory of Planned Behaviour.

Subjective norms and perceived controls

A *subjective norm* is any expectation that we perceive around us, or how we think other people want us to behave. For example, when Professor La Piere accompanied his Chinese couple to the motels and restaurants in his survey, he may have created a degree of subjective pressure to serve the trio. (A subjective norm may have been, 'I am expected by my boss to serve, not upset, customers like him'.) A partner's beliefs about condom use provide another example of a subjective norm. If we sense that a partner, or anyone else important to us, would want us to use a condom, we may be more receptive to doing so. Clearly, such a perceived norm, along with attitudes towards (unprotected) sex, will moderate the impact of media campaigns advocating condom use. As shown in figure 4.5, *control factors* are simply practical issues, such as not having the money to buy a condom, or not having authority to turn customers away from a motel restaurant. Students, for example, often encounter practical constraints (e.g. domestic crises, financial worries or illness) on being able to study to the best of their ability.

It is the *behavioural intention* aspect of the model that most closely represents the consciously 'planned' component of media-influenced behaviour. Behavioural intention is the immediate precursor to actual behaviour. Everywhere in figure 4.5, 'attitudes, subjective norms, and perceived behavioral control are assumed to be available automatically as performance of a behavior is being considered' (Ajzen & Fishbein 2000, p. 18; for a discussion of automaticity in cognitive processes, see chapter 7). What this means is that attitudes towards the behaviour, subjective norms and control, although inputs to conscious intention, are not necessarily themselves formulated consciously. Overall, therefore, the theory of planned behaviour provides for both reasoned processes (planned, motivational, intentional) and processes that are more automated (for a fuller discussion of automation, see chapter 7).

The theory of planned behaviour

The *theory of planned behaviour* is now among the most widely researched and supported theories in the persuasion literature (Armitage & Conner 2001; for an overview nicely encapsulated in sport and exercise psychology, see Biddle & Nigg 2000; for a general overview, see Glanz & Maddock 2000; for alternative models, see Armitage & Arden 2002; Volk & Koopman 2001). The statistical linkages depicted in figure 4.5 have been empirically investigated across a wide range of contexts, many of them involving health and exercise behaviours (Norman, Abraham & Conner 2000). Of course, health and exercise is an incredibly diverse field, areas investigated spanning, for instance, dental hygiene and vaccination behaviour (Ajzen 1991a), vitamin supplement compliance (Sheeran & Orbell 1999), condom usage (Wilson et al. 1992), exercise behaviour (Maddux 1993), breast self-examination (Young et al. 1991) and intention to avoid exposure to the sun (Terry & Hogg 1996). More recently, the theory has been applied in workplace settings, too, for example to predict intention to leave an organisation (Abrams, Ando & Hinkle 1998). Overall, therefore, the theory of planned behaviour, as depicted in figure 4.5, is relatively robust.

Some facts and figures

Recent reviews of the theory of planned behaviour, which embrace literally hundreds of specific studies across the domains outlined above, consistently indicate that intention is the best predictor of behaviour. One survey that includes both published and unpublished studies (important because journals sometimes favour 'significant' findings over non-significant ones) estimates the relationship between behavioural intention and the behaviour itself to be $r = .47$, with attitude towards the behaviour correlating .61 with behavioural intention (Callahan 1998). Another estimate, based on a range of meta-reviews, reports that the theory of planned behaviour explains, on average, 40 to 50 per cent of the variance in intention, with the latter explaining between 19 and 38 per cent of the variance in behaviour (Sutton 1998). An alternative set of figures, covering 185 independent studies published up to the end of 1997, reports that the model explains 39 per cent of the variance in intention and 27 per cent of the variance in behaviour (Armitage & Conner 2001). Although these figures are far from perfect, creating scope for new factors to be added to the model (see quotation below), they now seem clear enough to support a role for each of the major components in figure 4.5 when influencing behaviour change. What this means, for example, is that media campaigns may benefit from design features that respect not only attitudes towards the behaviour, but also subjective norms and perceived control. There is much more to media campaigning, and winning an audience's acceptance, than blithely targeting intentions alone (for a critical assessment of how this might work in practice, see Hardeman et al. 2002).

Evidently opening the door for more explanatory variables to be added to the model, Ajzen remarks:

> The theory of planned behavior is, in principle, open to the inclusion of additional significant predictors if it can be shown that they capture a significant proportion of the variance in intentions or behavior after the theory's current variables have been taken into account. (1991a, p. 199)

The importance of past behaviour

The figures above are not perfect. One of the more promising candidates to become a companion 'bubble' (see figure 4.5) is past behaviour (Leone, Perugini & Ercolani 1999; Ouellette & Wood 1998):

> Consider, for example, such a mundane behavior as going to see a movie with friends. Even if we have performed this behavior numerous times in the past, we never engage in it without some conscious cognitive mediation. We have to make a conscious decision to go to the movies on a particular night. (Ajzen 1991a, p. 25)

Typically, what happens when past behaviour, or habit, is included in the model is that its overall capacity to predict future behaviour improves incrementally (for a review, see Ouellette & Wood 1998; Ajzen 2001). One of the practical implications of Ouellette and Wood's findings in the field of media persuasion, including commercial and social marketing, is that:

> The most effective change strategies are likely to be ones that impede performance of established behavior, while facilitating formation of new behaviors into habits. For example, shifts in the supporting environment can derail the automatic cueing and execution of old habits and increase the importance of conscious intentions. (1998, p. 70)

Such 'unfreezing' of old habits and 'refreezing' of new ones, and in particular maintaining a 'supporting environment', clearly suggest that a crucial factor in the acceptability and sustainability of any media influence attempt will be the dynamics of the audience's reference groups.

The influence of social identity

In chapter 3 we learned from social identity theory (SIT) that reference groups, by definition, change the way we think about self, specifically whether we act as an individual self or as a social self (see minimal group effects, for instance). Can the theory of planned behaviour *handle* such flexibility? Is it as flexible as its own human subjects plainly are? If it were, we would expect that the predictive power of the 'subjective norm' bubble in figure 4.5, relative to an individual's 'attitude towards the behaviour', would go up whenever participants identified themselves socially (i.e. as members of a group). Likewise, the predictive power of 'attitude towards the behaviour' would go up, relative to 'subjective norm', whenever the self 'identified' as an individual. This kind of systematic fluctuation is precisely what happened in at least one Australian study, which focused on intention to avoid the dangers of sunburn (Terry & Hogg 1996). In this study, therefore, the theory of planned behaviour was nicely sensitive to social context.

The influence of cultural values

According to chapter 1, social identification is more likely in relatively collectivistic cultures than in relatively individualistic cultures. If the theory of planned behaviour is sensitive to this relationship, 'subjective norm' will be relatively more predictive of behaviour intention, compared with its more individualistic counterpart, 'attitude towards the behaviour'. In relatively individualistic settings, the reverse would be true. We should expect the bubble 'attitude towards the behaviour' to gain the ascendant. And, in fact, this kind of systematic fluctuation is what happens. In many Western settings, behavioural intentions are more controlled by 'attitudes towards the behaviour' than by 'subjective norm' (e.g. Trafimow & Finlay 1996). But the relationship reverses once we move into a setting, and population, that is relatively more collectivistic (Abrams et al. 1998; Godin et al. 1996). Thus, the theory of planned behaviour is sensitive to societal (i.e. relatively 'macro') cultural context.

An assessment

The model predicts a significant proportion of the variance in audience behaviour, across a range of behaviours, from condom use to intention to quit a job. It assimilates the concept of attitude, and it represents the influence of real social psychological factors. These are perceived group norms and degree of practical control, for example whether we can afford to buy a condom or to leave a job. The model accommodates other contextual realities, too. It respects shifts in the salience of group norms, as sense of identity 'flips over' from individual to social, and vice versa. Such flexibility to accommodate multiple self and social identities applies across both context and culture. Nonetheless, although the model does make allowances for automatic processes, including past behaviour (force of habit), there remains a significant proportion of behaviour yet to be explained. It is to this unexplained diversity that we now turn.

A TERTIARY PHASE: NARRATIVE POSITIONING

The theory of planned behaviour obliges us to restate a phase one idea — the notion that attitudes reside in the mind of an individual audience member and nowhere else. It tells us that other members of the audience have attitudes, too. These others are represented in the model in figure 4.5 through the concept of subjective norms. Yet given this recognition, there is now an astounding omission from the figure — that is, the perceived attitude *adopted by the source*. Attitudes, as was established at the beginning of this chapter, are all about positioning. People in social interaction — and this includes people at the 'sending' end just as much as those at the 'receiving' end of a media message — *adopt positions*. Many of us will sense, for example, when we are being 'spoken down to' or 'taken for a sucker' by some marketing ploy. In New Zealand, for instance, opinion polls explicitly ask whether people perceive that politicians 'speak down' to the electorate. Such perceptions no doubt influence how the audience ultimately reacts to that pitch on election day. Without including these perceived attitudes, there is no real respect for the inherent nous and perspicacity of their audience by many media players today. Such a model of media influence will thus continue to be deficient in predicting audiences' actual behaviour.

Advances in the social psychology of the media, and indeed media studies as a whole, are beginning to address this shortfall. Some researchers have attempted to add more dynamism to what has been, as they see it, a relatively staid, 'wooden' image of the human consumer, as painted in figure 4.5. They have attempted to achieve this through the application of two major concepts, which now become central to this review. These concepts are (1) narrative and (2) positioning.

Narrative

Much of the impetus for the study of narrative began in Australia in the mid 1980s with the concept of narrative therapy (Monk et al. 1996). Narrative therapists, and their emergent therapies, attribute a central role to the way people frame their lives. In essence, narratives are recognisable meta-stories that people use implicitly to frame and give meaning to their lives (Baumeister & Newman 1994; Chamberlain, Stephens & Lyons 1997; Sarbin 1986). The best way of defining these semantic frameworks is through illustration. In the clinical and therapeutic domain, examples of narratives include, for instance, descriptors such as 'former alcoholic', 'underdog' and 'orphan' (Tan & Moghaddam 1996). In therapy, personal identity is seen as a process of life-story construction; psychopathology relates to a life story gone awry; and psychotherapy is an exercise in story repair (Howard 1991).

In everyday life, examples of narratives include, for instance, (a) the 'free spirit', (b) the 'adventurer' and (c) the 'incurable romantic' (see chapter 9). Some readers may partially identify with these narratives, or at least have a sense of how they can influence, quite profoundly in some cases, people's everyday behaviour.

The media play heavily to them, of course (see also Livingstone 1990), and it is not difficult to imagine how narratives also influence the way that audiences respond to these media pitches. Crucially, however, the same narratives can just as easily turn audience segments off. Viewers whose personal narratives, even their 'secret' ones, accord more with 'the controlled thinker', 'the staunch conservative' or 'the rational intellectual' are less likely to respond positively to images of, respectively, a free spirit, adventurer and incurable romantic (for wider ranging and more detailed discussions of the role of narrative in motivating behaviour, see Kashima 1997; Livingstone 1999).

Positioning

In examples (a), (b) and (c) above, it is interesting that the narratives are named in terms of a central character who is positioned *in* the narrative. **Positioning** is to narrative as a hand, or finger, is to a glove. Once a narrative has been constructed, people naturally and readily position themselves as active players *within* them (Livingstone 1990, 1999). A primary vehicle for this positioning is the use of language. Just think of the amount of positioning work that words like 'my dear', 'mate' or 'battler' can do in everyday discourse. Or, rather, *attempt* to do. The concept of narrative is much more dynamic and active than the concept of role discussed above (Harré & Van Langenhove 1992). In taking on a role, people change themselves to fit the role; in positioning, they adopt the role as a way of actively negotiating social reality. In this way, people actively position the self, but they also actively position *others*. During a political debate, for example, the speakers and audience will readily position each other politically 'to the left' or 'to the right', as well as morally. In these ways, the communication process can no longer be atomised; instead, it reflects an overall gestalt or 'ensemble' (Sampson 1993).

One of the most subtle and influential types of positioning is *cultural positioning* (Tan & Moghaddam 1996). In their analysis, Tan and Moghaddam argue:

> We can expect that social identity is more salient to persons in collectivistic than individualistic societies, so that group (as opposed to individual) attributes, identities, and histories may be more important in locating speakers reflexively in positioning. (p. 397)

An example they give is biography. In more individualistic societies, these narratives tend to take the form of stories of personal conquest and self-sustenance. In more collectivistic societies, they tend to be told as stories of group triumph and social sustenance (p. 398; for more discussion of cultural narratives, see Fiske 1993; see also chapter 1, on social versus individual achievement). Given this kind of analysis, we can take Sampson's (1993) point about 'ensembles' a step further. In the same way that cultural narratives are differently produced, depending on culture-of-origin, they will also be differently *received*, depending on culture-of-*destination*. Individualistic versus collectivistic biographies will thus 'connect' differently with relatively individualist or collectivist audiences (for more on the cultural context of media messages, see Livingstone 1997).

Transactional analysis

One theory in psychology makes clear predictions about whether this connection will be made, and when it will fail. **Transactional analysis** (TA) was originally developed as a theory of communication in Western European psychotherapy (Berne 1964). It has since been extended to areas of applied social psychology, such as international aid work (Hope & Timmel 1995), forestry protection (Bhattacharya 1994) and managing the quality of working life in organisations (Nykodym, Longenecker & Ruud 1991). In keeping with its Western origins, TA focuses on narratives within a nuclear family. Briefly, the model proposes that people are heavily socialised into three basic family roles, or ego states. These are called Parent, Adult and Child. We learn to play these roles, according to Berne, through observational learning and direct experience throughout childhood. Because they are so well learned, the roles are later readily adopted in adult life. At work, for instance, a supervisor might habitually position self in an adult-to-child attitude vis-à-vis other employees, even though those same employees position themselves, including their supervisor, in adult-to-adult relationships. In this case, we could say that the relationship between supervisor and supervisees is cross-positioned. Each party, in a shared (workplace) narrative, has a different opinion of where they should be positioned. They are communicating at cross-purposes. This *crossed positioning* is depicted in figure 4.6. According to Berne, whenever such crossed positioning occurs, communication will be compromised and will eventually break down.

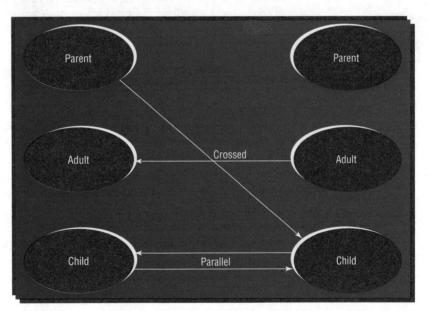

Figure 4.6   Parallel versus crossed communication channels   *Source:* Adapted from Berne (1964).

In figure 4.6, the alternative to crossed positioning is called *positioning in parallel*. This occurs when both parties agree on how each source is positioned vis-à-vis the other. An example of parallel positioning is the 'child-to-child' (peer education) approach in health promotion (Bailey, Hawes & Bonati 1992). As shown in figure 4.6, this idea holds that children are often well positioned to educate and influence *each other* about their own healthy behaviour through child-to-child relationships. In fact, the child-to-child approach has now been applied in health education projects across more than seventy different countries worldwide (Dawes & Donald 2000). Such ego states are not confined to children, however. For example, if a workplace supervisor and supervisee position each other in an adult-to-adult relationship, communication is socially facilitated (see chapter 2). A further example of parallel positioning, this time between health authorities and their adult community clients in Western Australia, is given in critical narrative 4.1.

CRITICAL NARRATIVE 4.1

Parallel positioning in social marketing of health promotion among men

Hey guys, it's time to check your sparkies

Brisbane: A blokey approach to medical care, which invites men to put themselves 'over the pits' for a check-up, is paying dividends in rural Western Australia.

Men, notoriously reluctant to talk to doctors, are responding to the public health initiative, which could save their lives, its creators say.

Health promotions officer Elsa Alston, from the Gascoyne Public Health Unit in central WA, said men appreciated the humour in the Pit Stop health program.

Mechanical terms employed in the State Government–funded project included references to checks on oil (blood) pressure, sparkplugs (testicles) and rust (skin cancers).

The program is offered wherever men gather — agricultural field days, the races, graziers' conferences and rural shows.

Source: Courtesy of the *Northern Territory News*, 8 March 2001, p. 6.

Is parallel positioning more persuasive than crossed positioning? This issue was recently tested in an Australian health promotion context utilising the Grim Reaper advertisement (MacLachlan et al. 1997). From figure 4.6, MacLachlan et al. found that many young at-risk people in their student audience were cross-positioned vis-à-vis the Grim Reaper advertisement (see also Taylor 1988). The advertisement 'came across' as having a 'parent-to-child' attitude, whereas in fact the audience mainly wanted, and expected, to be communicated with in an adult-to-adult transaction. More important, and consistent with the TA model of communication already outlined, when the transaction was perceived by an audience as crossed with their own expectations about role positioning, it tended to have less impact on their attitudes and intentions than on those occasions when it was perceived as parallel. Thus, in an initial and preliminary test of communication effectiveness, the predictions derived from TA, and from positioning theory in general, were broadly supported.

In Malaŵi the extended family, not the nuclear family, is the norm, and much of society is relatively power distant (see chapter 1; for a discussion of the robustness of the extended family in Africa, see Nsamenang 1996). Moving beyond the TA model, which is somewhat confined by its own cultural assumptions, varieties of positioning in this setting should include extended family members and belief in social hierarchy (respect for elders). Research undertaken in Malaŵi is broadly consistent with these proposals. Students there, in contrast to their counterparts in Australia, tended to see extended family elders, such as uncles and aunts, as appropriate (and relatively power distant) sources of advice about, for instance, preventing the spread of AIDS. In this social and cultural context, with its extended family narrative, parallel positioning is more likely to consist of Uncle/Aunt-to-Nephew/Niece transactions. Australian students, in direct contrast, tended to prefer the egalitarianism of adult-to-adult positioning.

Towards a theory of narrative positioning

What the research just described indicates is that much depends on whether source and audience, locally, are playing from the same sheet of music or cultural narrative. If the narrative is shared, what renders a crossed transaction 'crossed' is still defined locally, by the participants themselves. Independent of local context, however, parallel positioning may tend to work better, and to lead to more sustainable communication, than its crossed counterpart. Thus, the general concepts of narrative and positioning are robust, while particular narratives, such as the nuclear family and the restricted roles within it, do not necessarily travel quite so well.

According to this model, successful media communication depends first on finding out what narratives the audience identifies with at the time. When the narratives of source and audience conflict with each other, communication is likely to fail. After selecting an appropriate (mutually acceptable) narrative, the next step is to try to position source and audience in mutually acceptable roles (parallel positioning) within the shared narrative. For example, social marketing research might indicate that younger potential charity donors identify more with fun-loving narratives, even in television advertisements for poverty relief, than with negative and demeaning images of 'the poor'. Social marketing initiatives against poverty might then construct a message in which characters and audience are positioned in largely 'child-like' roles (fun-loving states). At least one charitable organisation I can think of, broadcasting recently in Australia, seems to have done this in its television campaign to raise donations for youngsters in need.

So far in our analysis of media influence, we have considered the individual audience member's attitude; how that attitude is negotiated with other members of the audience; and in what light the audience perceives the attitude adopted by the source. What we have still to consider, however, is the positioning that takes place within a message itself. Messages often encapsulate their own storylines, players and positioning patterns. When they do, their communication may be less direct, but they carry a message nonetheless. An example is violence in the movies. Obviously, the violence is not directed physically at the audience. Instead, it takes place between the characters *in* a story. Nonetheless, this interaction still sends messages of various kinds as subtext *to* its watching audience. This kind of positioning within a message, as distinct from positioning that speaks directly to its audience, is known as **second-order positioning**. Such positioning, at one remove from its audience, is illustrated in figure 4.7.

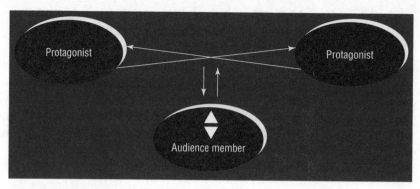

Figure 4.7   Second-order positioning

Following figure 4.7, the nature of human entertainment means that an audience watches and listens to human storylines (and underlying narratives) in which the players are other people. Audiences enjoy experiencing the stories of others vicariously, and perhaps cathartically. Movies thrive on this capacity to second-order position. So, too, do many advertising campaigns. They embed 'interesting' storylines in their advertisements in order to engage the audience more and thus ultimately sell more of their product. Hence, second-order positioning is relatively common in media persuasion. Positioning theory suggests that second-order narratives, just like their first-order cousins, will interact with viewers' expectations. For a person who believes in 'helping others to help themselves', media images of aid workers being 'good Samaritans' may work, doubly so if the appeal contains staged images of 'grateful recipients'. To another individual or group, who instead frames poverty inside a more egalitarian, 'battler' narrative — who perhaps sees life more in terms of political 'class struggle' — the same imagery may easily be doubly vexing.

Even when on-screen narratives strike the right note with their viewers, managing to hook them into a parallel transaction, the longer term consequences are not necessarily positive. How many of us can truly expect to live up to the kind of heroic and romantic models portrayed in most advertisements and movies? What is the long-term effect of continually having to retreat from the fantasy narrative into cold reality? Such over-promising and under-delivering poses substantive social psychological questions for society. Much of the available evidence relevant to these questions has emerged from the study of media violence (see chapter 10). In particular, the little we know has come from studying the second-order impact of watched violence on subsequent behaviour among children and adolescents (Kraut et al. 1998).

CLASSICAL THEORY ON MEDIA VIOLENCE

Traditionally, these studies were often grouped under **observational learning**. This term signifies that watching others, and in particular the consequences of their actions, for example whether they are rewarded or not, influences subsequent behaviour (Bandura 1965; for more discussion of observational learning, including its parentage in a model called Social Learning Theory, see chapter 10).

When a model is rewarded, imitation behaviour becomes more likely. The idea of watching a model being rewarded, and then imitating that model, grafts quite readily onto narrative positioning. The positioning pattern adopted by the characters in a watched narrative can be rewarded and then imitated, too. First, therefore, we consider the 'classic' research in this area, and link it to more recent studies of both (i) television violence and (ii) violence in the more 'interactive' media, such as video games.

In an original study of this genre, pre-school children witnessed an adult playing either aggressively, attacking a large Bobo doll (a large quasi-human rag-doll), or peacefully with other toys (Bandura, Ross & Ross 1963). Later, the children were each mildly frustrated (disallowed from playing with their favourite toy) and left to play, ostensibly alone, with a range of toys. These included both the Bobo doll and a mallet. Their behaviour was then surreptitiously recorded to see whether any significant differences were displayed in levels of aggressive behaviour towards the doll between those children who had viewed a placid model and those children who had watched an aggressive one.

What Bandura et al. found was that the children exposed to the aggressive model subsequently behaved more aggressively, when mildly frustrated, than the children who had observed more peaceful behaviour. The children who had witnessed an aggressive model were more likely to use the mallet on the doll. In the language of positioning theory, this is evidence for an influence on behaviour of second-order positioning. Bandura's research went further, however. It also varied the *consequences* of the model's behaviour (Bandura 1973). For example, sometimes the model was left unpunished, while at other times the model was scolded by another adult. What the research found under these conditions was that aggressive behaviour among children who had been watching was higher when no clear punishment accrued to the model.

Subsequent research on the impact of watching media violence

Other controlled field experiments, on the impact on behaviour of violent versus peaceful movies for example, have found increases in violent behaviour in subsequent days (Leyens et al. 1975). In Leyens et al.'s study, influence on behaviour was beginning to decline by the end of the test period. Such declines suggest that a continuing diet of unpunished violent media behaviours is necessary for the media to *keep* influencing their younger viewers over the longer term. Unfortunately, however, this is exactly what 'modem children' often have (see critical narrative 4.3). Recent research identifies adolescence as an especially significant period. During this time, for example, there is often a particularly influential bridging role for subjective norms between peers (Nathanson 2001). An important study covering this period is summarised in critical narrative 4.2. Clearly, we cannot blame television for everything (Johnson et al. 2002), but this narrative is still very disturbing, particularly if, as some research suggests, viewers are not even aware that they are being influenced in the way they are (Hoffner 2001).

CRITICAL NARRATIVE 4.2

Study links violence to time spent viewing TV

Children who watch more than an hour of television every day are more likely to grow up into violent adults, shows a United States study.

The scientists behind the research, which goes further than any other in proving the link between screen violence and aggressive behaviour, believe that television viewing in childhood and early adolescence actually causes violent behaviour.

They say the link cannot be explained simply by the tendency of aggressive people to watch more TV.

Neither, they say, can other environmental factors known to be associated with aggressive behaviour, such as poverty or bad parenting.

The research involved analysing more than 700 individuals over a period of 17 years.

Jeffrey Johnson, of Columbia University and the New York State Psychiatric Institute, who led the research team, said the study, published in the journal *Science*, should be seen as evidence for limiting the amount of television that young teenagers, in particular, are allowed to watch.

'Our findings suggest that, at least during early adolescence, responsible parents should avoid permitting their children to watch more than one hour of television a day', Dr Johnson said.

'That's where the vast majority of the increase in risk occurs.'

The children in the study were interviewed with their mothers four times over the 17-year period, during which their ages ranged from 5 to 30.

The scientists had access to criminal records as well as their subjects' personal recollections of aggressive behaviour.

Taking other factors into account, 5.7 per cent of adolescents who watched less than one hour of TV were found to be violent in later years.

In contrast, 22.5 per cent of those who watched between one and three hours a day committed aggressive acts later, as did 28.8 per cent of those who watched more than three hours a day.

Source: Independent, reported in *The New Zealand Herald*, 2 April 2002, p. A5.

The strange case of cartoons

Bandura's concept of observational learning makes some disturbing and counter-intuitive predictions. Children tend to like cartoons, and theoretical comparisons have been drawn between Bandura's (cartoon figure–like) Bobo doll and the possible influence that some media animations can have. In many cartoons, for example, violence seldom has lasting negative consequences for any of the players (Davidson 1998). As Davidson argues, these cartoons may be sending a second-order message — that violence is not truly destructive or likely to bring any real punishments.

Video games and positioning power

In violent video games, too, the protagonists and combatants, despite being life-like, recover completely from blows that, in any real-life fight, would be lethal.

A meta-message that possibly resonates through these kinds of ensembles is that living violent narratives can be enjoyable, easily attained, rewarding and not particularly punishable. In narrative terms, players of violent video games have a great deal of *positioning power*. They can experience the 'thrill of victory' over an opponent without ever experiencing any of the real costs. They can take big risks without (for the time being at least) paying a price.

Joystick killers?

Eric Harris and Dylan Klebold, whose bloody rampage at their Colorado school left 15 dead — including themselves — and 23 wounded, were obsessed, according to friends, with the game *Doom*, a first-person shooting game, often staying up to play it with others on-line until the middle of the night.

Harris's website had a version of *Doom* that he had customised. In his version, there are two shooters, each with extra weapons and unlimited ammunition, and the other people in the game can't fight back.

For a class project, Harris and Klebold made a videotape that was similar to their customised version of *Doom*. In it, Harris and Klebold dress in trench coats, carry guns, and kill school athletes. It was a performance they acted out in real life less than a year later. They were 'playing out their game in god mode', according to one investigator.

In [a study by US psychologists Karen Dill and Craig Anderson], 210 college students played either a violent video game (*Wolfenstein* 3-D) or a non-violent video game (*Myst*). Afterwards, students were asked to play another game against an opponent and then punish that opponent with a white-noise blast if they won. The study found that students who played the violent game tended to use longer bursts of noise.

'The study showed the causality between violent video games and aggression', says Dill, who started the groundwork for the study in 1994.

'What we have shown, for the first time, is that aggressive behavior and hostile thoughts are significantly increased in players of violent video games.

'They are more harmful than violent television and movies because they are very engrossing and require the player to identify with the aggressor. In a sense, they provide a complete learning environment for aggression. These results are very, very worrying.'

Source: Extracted from Lusetich (2000, p. 15).

The events depicted at the start of critical narrative 4.3 focus attention on the influence of playing violent video games. Meta-reviews are now available on the effects of these games, including *Doom* itself. One of these studies interestingly suggests that the effects of violent video games are slightly less than the effects of watching violence on television (Sherry 2001). This indicates some kind of role for a venting of frustration, known as media catharsis, in the more interactive media (the concept of cartharsis is discussed more fully in chapter 10). Another study reviewed both non-experimental and experimental studies of playing violent video games and violent behaviour (Anderson & Bushman 2001). These games consistently increased aggressive behaviour in children and young adults of both sexes. Playing violent video games also decreased levels of pro-social behaviour in general.

The promise of the Internet

Clearly, the influences of contemporary technology are not all bad, and perhaps this is a salutary moment to remind ourselves of that with one or two positive examples. At several points in the discussion so far we have linked the literature on mass persuasion to ideas emerging from studies of the Internet. This is a relatively empowering medium, which encourages, so it has been argued, a relatively discerning orientation among its consumers (Yoon & Kim 2001). Such discernment suggests that Internet shoppers are relatively *rational*. Other researchers have stressed the comparatively *caring* side of Internet consumers: 'Many corners of the Internet are filled with people who are willing to invest considerable time to help others in need' (Wallace 1999, p. 3). This is a far cry from, and a healthy corrective to, the kind of anti-social behaviour being facilitated in critical narrative 4.3. In a recent study of pro-social behaviour on the Internet, aid agency websites were manipulated in order to investigate their impact on intention to give money to the poor (Fox & Carr 2000). Such studies hold promise for illuminating ways in which technology can be used to increase social capital (Schumann & Thorson 1999; for further discussion of this and other studies into pro-social effects, see chapters 6 and 9).

REFLECTIONS

This last section draws together the material so far reviewed, both in this chapter and in part 1 of the book as a whole, using the process of *reflection*, introduced in chapter 1. The aim of this approach is specifically to 'tease out' recurring themes around the sustainability and resistability of behaviour change. The process of reflection takes us to an idea that behaviour change is more sustainable, and more acceptable, if an audience or group or crowd experiences **minimal constraint**. Minimal constraint 'works' because it fosters **maximal cognition**. Maximal cognition empowers its audience to make its own decisions. It also provides a foundation stone for part 2 of the book.

Minimal constraint

Looking back on the studies by Sherif, Asch, Milgram, Kilham and Mann, and Lovibund et al., outlined in chapter 1, there are the first signs of continuity. Sherif's autokinetic paradigm was minimally constraining, and subsequent participants in this kind of study retained their group's social norm for up to a year after the original meeting. In the line-length and obedience paradigms invented by Asch and Milgram, and described in chapter 1, there were dramatic examples of behaviour change in the short term. But this took the form of compliance only, and there was no accompanying underlying change in belief or feeling, for example to a view that the majority, or the authority figure, was 'right'. As a result, as soon as the researchers' backs were (experimentally) turned, behaviour began to return to normal. In the replication studies conducted in Australia, there were clear signs of rebellion against the use of force and constraint. In this case, we traced the resistance to cultural norms favouring equality and thus low power distance (see figure 1.1).

Overall, therefore, constraint consistently produced backlashes in behaviour. Whenever constraint is placed on participants, there can be dramatic changes in behaviour in the short term, but very little change in underlying belief or feeling. As a result, there is no firm psychological foundation for behaviour change to be sustained. Instead, resistance becomes the norm.

Crowds, it was argued in chapter 2, are inherently ephemeral, and their influences (as operationally defined in the chapter) can be relatively constraining and short-lived. Certainly, social movements that eventually succeed, and in that sense are sustained, will include crowds. But these movements require far more than merely the influences of contagion and pluralistic ignorance; they also require a great deal of political group momentum. Experiencing the constraints of emergency situations, such as those staged by the bystander researchers, observing crowds typically do not behave in the most pro-social of ways, according to most moral narratives for a civil society. Instead, individuals in a crowd are often constrained to behave relatively 'apathetically'. When this happens, however, underlying moral codes do *not* change. There is no private shift; if anything, people remain privately *troubled* by their own inaction. The crowd's sense of morality remains largely intact.

Chapter 3 focused on the pros and cons of governing with the consent of the governed, as contrasted to governing by 'centralised decree'. As we learned from Lewin's enduring research, introducing an element of constraint was less than one-tenth as effective at producing sustainable behaviour change compared with governing with the group's consent. The rest of the review of intra-group relations focused on the power of group discussion to change behaviour in a sustainable way. Group discussion is another means of minimising constraint. Group polarisation and groupthink are powerful examples of the same principle. In the field of relations *between* groups, a fundamental lesson in the literature is that attempts to constrain social identity eventually provoke a backlash.

The present chapter shows that right from the start, for example in Kelman's study of compliance to a powerful speaker, the research on mass persuasion has highlighted the same kind of backlash. Credible speakers who manage to nudge their audiences gently into wondering why they are positioned as they are tend to be more effective in producing sustainable change. One way of viewing La Piere's classic study is that it illuminated the discrepancy between people's short-term behaviour and their longer term intentions. Under the constraint of the moment, people appear to be unprejudiced, but, if observed for long enough, they will show behavioural signs of a more enduring, underlying attitude. Most revealing, however, is that the whole concept of behavioural positioning, whether through crossed narratives or crossed positioning *within* a shared narrative, indicates that constraint is counterproductive. Individuals, groups and 'followers' alike will actively resist being positioned in a narrative, or in a role within a narrative, that they do not want.

We can thus identify at least one general principle that runs consistently through this chapter, and in fact throughout the book so far. To the extent that attempts at influence create perceptions of constraint, they are relatively likely to produce behaviour change that is short-lived, but not much else. In the longer term, what is required for sustainability and acceptability alike is minimal constraint.

Maximal cognition

In order to understand *why* behaviour is less sustainable when there is more constraint, it is necessary to explore mental life more closely. For example, a crucial ingredient in producing sustainable behaviour change is to persuade the audience to *think* about the message and the issue at hand (Petty & Cacioppo 1981). As noted earlier, Petty and Cacioppo have coined the term *elaboration likelihood* to describe this idea. The concept itself centres on a principle of maximal cognition: the more you can persuade your audience to elaborate mentally on the issue and on your shared discourse on it, the greater the likelihood that, if they do change their minds, they will do so profoundly and lastingly. Encouraging maximal cognition is difficult and to some extent risky for any source, but it is also the only real way to ensure a lasting change in behaviour.

Of course, this argument is thoroughly compatible with a principle of minimal constraint. Freedom to think and constraint are anathema to one another. But how does the idea of maximal cognition stack up against the data reviewed so far in the book?

The first sign of elaboration being important within groups is again found in Sherif's work. It seems very likely, for instance, that members of Sherif's group experienced it. Once they came together for the group task, they had to do quite a bit of mental processing of each individual judgement and how it related to the overall pattern in judgements being made by the group as a whole. Lewin's audience was empowered to discuss what the visiting expert was saying. They were engaging in mental elaboration of the arguments that had been proposed. In the group polarisation studies, too, the ideas of information exchange, and of jostling to be a paragon of the group norm, each strongly suggest cognitive work and an elaboration of positions being advocated by the ensemble. In groupthink, the group has certainly stopped thinking in any kind of critical way, but it has reached that point only after having already deliberated earlier (see figure 3.1). If necessary, too, it will invest considerable mental effort in finding ways to rationalise, and so preserve, its deliberated status quo.

A classic example of elaboration over inter-group relations is the Stanford Prison Study (see chapter 1). There, groups of prisoners and guards ended up doing quite a lot of cognitive work to make 'sense' of their situation. The guards, for instance, were obliged to rationalise their use of power and force. They often did this through a process of dissonance reduction, dehumanising the out-group members so as to be consistent with their treatment of them. A related example of mental elaboration, in relations between groups, is the reduction of social inequity. As we saw in chapter 3, groups sometimes engage in complex 'mental calculus' about who is inputting what, and receiving what outcomes for those inputs. On the positive side, too, when *mending* inter-group fences, the concept of superordinate goals implies a great deal of cognitive effort in reconfiguring how to 'rework' the task, as well as negative stereotypes of the out-group. Jigsaw techniques also place great stock in the idea of using work, and in particular mental work, to reframe inter-group relations. This is precisely how jigsaws make their mark on future behaviour, and how they produce sustainable change.

Within this chapter there is elaboration at work in Kelman's credible condition, when the speaker speaks out, rather surprisingly, against racial integration. Elaboration is prompted in the audience also when an ex-jailbird argues for heavier custodial sentences. Overemotional messages fail because they only 'switch people off'. To really change an audience, and influence those of an opposing view, a source has to present and invoke a more elaborate case. Influences produced by two-sided arguments are less susceptible to subsequent counter-propaganda than their one-sided counterparts (Lumsdaine & Janis 1953; Williams et al. 1993). A persuasive message is processed more deeply, and to that extent more durably, when it is two-sided. Similarly, in terms of audience factors on relevant issues on which an audience has already spent time 'thinking', people are generally less persuadable. Role-playing, too, depends for its impact on gently nudging the player to face up to, and think about, unpalatable aspects of reality. Central to the theory of planned behaviour is the idea of cognitive elaboration. People often *form* their plans to change their behaviour after deliberating over their attitude towards the behaviour, the attitudes in their in-groups and the range of practical constraints operating on them at the time. Although the authors of this theory now accept that these components are sometimes arrived at 'automatically', without a great deal of conscious effort, the more sustainable intentions are still, by implication, those that have been reasonably well elaborated during a mentally laboured *internalisation*. Even habits must initially be substantially rehearsed. This idea of elaborated internalisation is present, too, in autobiographical narratives and the related concept of positioning. Of all the concepts we have considered so far, positioning is probably the most proactive, and to that extent the most elaboration-centred, among the entire set.

To sum up, there are clear signs in the literature on mass persuasion and attitude change that greater elaboration potentially leads to more acceptable, and thus sustainable, changes in behaviour. Given this consistency across the literature, it remains for us to see whether maximal cognition does indeed stack up, as a principle of sustainable social influence, beyond the various techno-scapes of the communication media. This is the core question that will be elaborated in part 2 of the book.

SUMMARY

In a first phase of studying the media and media influences, the communication ensemble was broken down into an active source of 'information transmission' and an essentially passive audience. As the quotation from Hitler at the start of the chapter suggests, the media can sometimes work this way, when the wider context is right. The idea of context was incorporated into the communication process through the theory of planned behaviour. Incorporating social factors in this way has improved the ability of communication programs to 'connect' with their audiences. In such models of audience behaviour, the media function like a 'window on the world' through which the consumer, still relatively passively, watches. According to narrative theorists, this underestimates human agency. Both the media and the consumer are more active than this. Their model proposes instead that both parties, 'source' *and* 'target', are continually positioning and repositioning themselves and each other in a dynamic dance of influence. Such perspectives on the media are far closer to the kind of rhetorical and oratorical approach to persuasion outlined in the opening quotation from Cicero (for a wonderful elaboration on this, see Billig 1989).

Attitude. A mixture of belief and feeling that guides behaviour and involves positioning, either 'for' or 'against', on some object, issue or body. Similar in meaning to *opinion* (p. 127)

Compliance. A change in behaviour that is not accompanied by any change in private opinion or attitude (p. 130)

Identification. Influence based on liking for the source of a message rather than its content (p. 130)

Internalisation. Influence based on the credibility of a source, which includes both perceived expertise and trust. Influence that is internalised is taken on board in private and, to the extent that it involves mental elaboration of the position being advocated, tends to be relatively sustainable. (p. 131)

Maximal cognition. The more an audience can be persuaded to think about a message, the more likely it is that the changes they subsequently adopt will be sustainable. (p. 156)

Minimal constraint. Both a term and a principle. As a term, it means applying the least pressure possible to change someone's opinion. As a principle, the more pressure a source applies to influence another individual or group, and the more that force is perceived to have been applied, the less sustainable will be its effect on their behaviour. This kind of resistance often fuels localisation (see chapter 1). (p. 156)

Observational learning. By watching the behaviour of others, we learn about the likely consequences of our action if we were to imitate them. Such learning by observation is more likely when the person we observe — the model — is rewarded; and less likely when the model is punished for his or her behaviour. (p. 152)

Positioning. Media messages implicitly position their source and target in some kind of social or cultural narrative. For example, speakers often position themselves as if they were a parent speaking to a child, and to that extent attempt to locate the source and audience of the message within a nuclear or extended family narrative. (p. 148)

Second-order positioning. Observing an ongoing narrative discourse between other players while maintaining an attitude towards that interaction, and thereby positioning self via-à-vis others (p. 157)

Transactional analysis. A theory proposed by the Swiss psychiatrist Eric Berne, in which everyday life is played out as a series of interpersonal/social role games involving the over-learned roles of parent, adult and child. Whenever the parties to the communication disagree on the role that each should be playing vis-à-vis the other, the communication process will, according to Berne, start to break down. (p. 149)

REVIEW QUESTIONS

1. How did the Yale Communication Program position the audience?
2. What improvements did the theory of planned behaviour make to this positioning?
3. How have narrative-based, discursive approaches changed the way we think about the influence of the media?
4. What consistencies, if any, emerge from the three phases of the study of media influences?

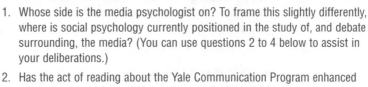

DISCUSSION QUESTIONS

1. Whose side is the media psychologist on? To frame this slightly differently, where is social psychology currently positioned in the study of, and debate surrounding, the media? (You can use questions 2 to 4 below to assist in your deliberations.)

2. Has the act of reading about the Yale Communication Program enhanced your capacity to persuade an audience or resist a message source?

3. Has the act of reading about the theory of planned behaviour, and related research, enhanced your capacity to persuade an audience or resist a message source?

4. Has the act of reading about the narrative approach, and the concept of positioning, enhanced your capacity to persuade an audience or resist a message source?

5. How do you reconcile the three major phases of studying media influence? Are they irreconcilable or complementary?

6. Does the principle of maximal cognition apply to crowd dynamics (chapter 2)?

ACTIVITIES

1. 'I [was] sitting in West Side Park in Champaign watching a construction worker in his thirties on a picnic lunch with his wife. Like many picnics, theirs was invaded by ants. Watching the man, I tried to understand his attitude toward ants only from his behavior. When one bold ant hoisted itself onto his plate, it appeared as if he would crush it between his fingers in disgust. He appeared enraged at the ant, perhaps thinking of its affront to his food, and brushed it aside. And when the ant returned, he seemed to grow in his anger, pushing it more brusquely, muttering something about 'these damn pests', infuriated at the ant's obstinacy. And the ant, though stunned for a few moments, returned again. The man, having finished with his food, now simply watched the creature and seemed not at all concerned about the footprints it deposited on his potato salad. Perhaps he was wondering at the ant's hunger, or its fortitude and courage. The food appeared to fade from focus. Perhaps he thought of the familiar creature as an individual and noticed the crook to its walk, and worried that he had put it there. And the man appeared now to think well of the ant, pushing some of his food in its direction, then noting to his wife, 'God, look at that strength', as the ant lifted a stray fragment of chicken. Yet only moments later; when his wife's plate was infested by several ants; he brushed them to the ground and stepped on them. And so it went with this man and those ants moving for twenty minutes through each other's world. And when it was over, I wondered what, in truth, could we ever hope to say about his attitude toward ants at picnics.' *Source*: Karl E. Weick, 'An appreciation of social context: One legacy of Gerald Solancik', *Administrative Science Quarterly*, vol. 41, no. 4, (December 1996), p. 570.

Break into groups and attempt to answer the question posed immediately above, using the material we have reviewed in chapter 4.

2. Choose a media campaign that is currently being publicised in your community. It could be a campaign about health and exercise, a charity or a commercial advertising venture. Apply the various theories, research findings and principles reviewed in the chapter to evaluate the quality of the campaign. How would you apply the social psychology of media influences, as we know it in all its diversity, to improve their existing campaign?

3. **Internet advertising**
   Apply one of the group decision-making techniques outlined in chapters 1 and 3 to produce a ranking of the most significant differences in conventional media versus e-advertising channels. What are the advantages and disadvantages of each? You might use either McGuire's (1985) or Harvey's (1997) stage theory of mass communication in your initial approach to the question (e.g. for the latter, exposure, perception, communication, recall, persuasion and sales).

4. Use the material from activity 2 to design your own media campaign for a chosen pressure group, charity or health promotion unit. Put this into a flow chart and write it up as a term report.

ADDITIONAL READING

On phase 1, the Yale Communication Program: Hovland's own writings, some of which are referenced in the text, are very accessible and engaging. A more recent, widely respected, and very influential text on attitudes and persuasion, which also provides a compact overview of the (massive) media persuasion field, can be found in Petty and Cacioppo (1981).

On phase 2: Perhaps read some of the recent references by Ajzen and Fishbein themselves. Several recent papers are cited in the chapter. For students interested in health promotion, the paper by Wilson et al. (1992) is an exemplary illustration of how to go about *applying* the theory in a real-world contemporary setting.

On phase 3: Among the most widely read writers in social psychology are, in alphabetical order, Harré, Livingstone and Sarbin. References are given in the text for each of these major sources.

On general principles (in media influence): It is hard to go past Petty and Cacioppo (1981). In chapter 9 of their book, these authors outline the full extent of their elaboration-likelihood model. This model has had a huge impact in the domain of social cognition, which is our theme for the next three chapters.

For further reading on the topics discussed in this chapter, consult the online resources linked to the Wiley website (http://www.johnwiley.com.au/highered/socialpsych).

COGNITION

5

FIRST IMPRESSIONS

'It is in the nature of an hypothesis, when once a man has conceived it, that it assimilates everything to itself as proper nourishment and, from *the first moment* of your begetting it, it generally grows the stronger by everything you see, hear, read, or understand.'   — Laurence Sterne, *Tristram Shandy* (emphasis added)

LEARNING OBJECTIVES

After reading this chapter, you should be able to:

- describe the personality traits, inferred from others' behaviour, that carry most weight in shaping first impressions
- explain how inferred dispositions in general are combined to form an overall impression of another person
- outline the influence of cultural context, specifically tall poppy syndrome, on this overall impression formation process
- use this knowledge to better manage the impressions we create on others, as well as the impressions they create on us.

OVERVIEW

This chapter explores two increasingly important facets of daily life: impression formation and impression management. Understanding one illuminates the other. In both cases, Sterne is telling us *first* impressions are critical. The chapter begins by identifying traits that, once perceived in others, whether at a face-to-face meeting or in an encounter in cyberspace, partly 'infuse' our *other* trait judgements about them. The chapter also examines how sets of perceived achievements are integrated to form rounded, overall impressions of others. Are these elements simply combined to form an overall impression, so that anything positive the other says, does or adds to their résumé helps to create a higher rating? Or are there fundamental risks in the idea that 'more is better'? The tall poppy syndrome, for instance, conceivably curtails the effectiveness of voluminous curricula vitae in the hunt for jobs and promotions. What kind of impression does big-noting the self (a global pressure) create in groups that are relatively collectivistic, egalitarian and power distant (local concerns)? These questions are inherently glocal, and they form the core of this chapter.

INTRODUCTION TO SOCIAL COGNITION

Of course, the field of social cognition embraces far more than first impressions alone. One way of looking at this broad domain is developmentally. 'Cognising' about others has a beginning, middle and end. We begin with first impressions; later, those impressions help the perceiver to explain people's attitudes and achievements; later still, once those explanations have become well practised and memorised, they are called up automatically, without a great deal of conscious thought. Roughly speaking, these three subdivisions, respectively, provide the foci for the next three chapters, comprising part 2 of the book. Chapter 6 examines how we 'explain' enigmas such as success and failure; chapter 7 looks at the development and use of skilled, automatic routines. This review rounds out our understanding of first impressions, which we learn are significantly enabled by these very routines. The structure of part 2 is visually depicted in figure 5.1, which provides a 'navigation chart' for the next three chapters.

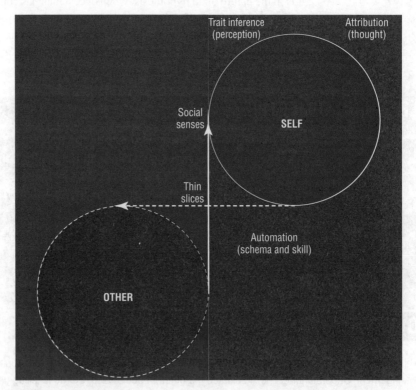

Figure 5.1　A model of social cognition

Sensation, perception and attribution

As depicted in figure 5.1, social cognition begins with another person or group. This person or group is a social stimulus. Of course, and as the figure is intended to suggest, who is perceiver ('self') and who is perceived ('other') is entirely relative; it is simply a question of perspective. There are two sides to every social cognition story. At the same time, what every 'other' does is show 'behaviours'.

Because these behaviours are often fleeting in scope, they have been termed 'thin slices' (Ambady, LaPlante & Johnson 2001). Classic examples are eye contact and handshakes. These 'thin slices' offer the self brief glimpses of the other's psychology — they stimulate our social senses. Our first real task as a 'social cogniser' is to interpret the slices. This is where perception comes in.

Perception is usually defined as the process of making any kind of decision about sensations using knowledge and experience (memory). The role for knowledge is, in fact, what makes it 'cognition' (strictly speaking, *re*-cognition). In social life, if we meet someone for the first time, say a new work colleague named Joanne, and infer from her eye contact and handshake, based on previous experience, that she is 'cold', then we have had a social perception. This particular kind of perception is called a **trait inference** (Krull & Erickson 2000). As well as this inference, we might also have an intuitive hunch about what such a 'cold' person is like in other respects. For example, she may be 'cunning', 'selfish' and 'ambitious', and generally 'someone to watch out for'. Such inferred patterns of traits are called an **implicit personality theory**, or **IPT** (Bruner & Tagiuri 1954; Schneider 1973; De Soto, Hamilton & Taylor 1985). By applying any kind of IPT to Joanne, whom we have already, in the blink of an eye, deemed 'cold', we have formed a first full impression of her.

These essentially two-tiered inferences of (a) inferring traits and then (b) combining them into an overall first impression is where this chapter begins, but it is not the end of the story. A next stage in the developmental flow, depicted in figure 5.1, is described in chapter 6, which examines the major role played by trait inferences in explaining social enigmas, such as our 'cold' colleague's later achievements, promotions and bonuses in the workplace. For example, if we attribute a specific success by Joanne to 'cunning', we have made an *attribution* about her later present behaviour. We have located its root causes in our earlier inferences about her personal disposition — our *memories* of first impressions about her personality. This 'explaining' side to everyday social behaviour is a form of problem-solving, or social *thought*.

Schema and skill

If we practise this kind of attribution for long enough, it may become 'second nature' whenever we hear about Joanne's latest exploits, and perhaps anyone like her, too. In such cases, social cognition becomes social automation. We have internalised our concept of the other, and others like her, into procedural memory as a mental routine. This enables our everyday explanations of workplace behaviour to 'roll off the tongue' like a polished, and to that extent skilful, performance. In this way, we develop a form of mental software for executing judgements about others. As depicted in figure 5.1, and as we will discuss in detail in chapter 7, we have developed both schema and skill into a skilled routine.

Finally, as figure 5.1 illustrates, these schemata and skills become available for us to help form *other* first impressions, say when meeting the latest new recruit or batch of arrivals. In this way, we accumulate skills that enable other interpretations of behaviour in the form of inferences, often on the thinnest of behavioural 'slices'. Just how thin these slices can be, and how influential our very first impressions can become, is illustrated clearly in critical narratives 5.1 to 5.3.

The first few seconds of impression management are vital for longer term gains

The Penguin Book of Etiquette: The complete Australian guide to modern manners is cited in a report on personal presentation in business in the *Australian Financial Review* (Owens 2002). This guide, the report states, suggests that the first impressions we make are of paramount importance, and that we have not minutes but literally seconds before individuals we have encountered for the first time decide that they will, or will not, do business with us. According to the guide, their first impressions will determine whether or not they think we are 'respectful' (trait inference) and therefore acting in good faith with their company.

Psychologists, according to the report, have made similar claims. One advises, for instance, making sure that we 'practice speaking at home' and using 'a firm handshake' before important first encounters. According to this psychologist, the moment people's eyes meet during a first meeting, they make 'immediate, unconscious judgements about honesty and trustworthiness' in the other person (i.e. trait inferences). From this first moment, therefore, we should make every effort to appear 'open and candid' (managing trait inferences).

Consultant psychologists stress the importance of being able to create credibility in an instant. This ability, they claim, requires us to exude personal confidence. We must shake hands appropriately; make the right degree of eye contact; respect personal space; and speak confidently. In less than 10 seconds, these consultants claim, behaviours like these will work either for or against us, depending on how successfully we enact them.

People need to bring themselves forward in the first few moments of contact. Those who do not acquire these skills, suggests the report, risk losing that vital job, contract or promotion. And this loss will occur not because our competitors are any better qualified or suited for the position, but simply because they manage the very first impressions they create on others in a more effective manner.

Source: Based on Owens (2002).

Start as you mean to go on

You don't have to sit on the mat or put your hand up for permission to go to the toilet, but starting a new job can be as disorientating as your first day at school.

'You don't know how the phone system works; you don't know where the photocopier is,' says Jacqui Barratt, national manager of permanent services for TMP Worldwide Lampenalectus Recruitment.

'You're very reliant on asking others for help.'

And the way you — and your new employer — handle that situation can set the scene for a successful relationship or an unsatisfactory one.

'Employers and colleagues make their judgments of you quickly, and once established, they are hard to break', says Pennell Locey, a senior human resources account manager ...

'Also, organizations are like the proverbial elephant that never forgets. Once there is a negative view of you in the system, it's hard to shake.'

Source: Extracted from Shopland (2002).

Communication between a 'non-Indigenous' and an 'Indigenous' Australian

In Anglo-Australian interactions there is an ideology of talking in twos in which talk is directed to a particular individual, people should face each other, eye contact is important, and perhaps most importantly control is in the hands of the speaker. By contrast the relationship among participants in Aboriginal Australia is communal: talk is not directed to a particular individual, it is 'broadcast'; people need not face each other and often don't, eye contact is less important, and control is in the hands of the hearer . . .

If you had asked me some time ago whether I would be talking about this sort of topic I probably would have said not in a million years. It really all began one day about ten years ago at Wadeye (also known as Port Keats) down the coast from here when there was an air of excitement around town. The rock group Midnight Oil was coming to town. So the group and its entourage flew into town in the afternoon and set up several truckloads of speakers and general paraphernalia associated with staging a concert in a bush setting. Then around about dusk when the wet canteen had opened some of the rock group came over to meet some of the local citizens. While a number of us were sitting on the ground having a can of beer the lead singer, Peter Garrett, being a friendly sort of bloke, approached us, leaned over, put his hand out and said, 'Hi, I'm Peter Garrett, what's your name?' with a laser beam glance at an Aboriginal man who had been sitting there contentedly but was now cringing, trying to move away, perhaps even hoping the ground would open up underneath him.

But there is quite a lot of pressure in our culture, in the Anglo-Australian culture at least, to respond in some way or other. The unfortunate fellow did stumble out what his name was and shook hands with Peter Garrett but appeared acutely uncomfortable about it. I looked across at an anthropologist who had worked in that same community for quite some years and caught his eye. We looked at each other and were both thinking how unfortunate this encounter had been. The Aboriginal man was not shy, or inarticulate, or unfriendly. Indeed at one time he had held a position in the community that required him to act quite frequently as part of the interface between a bush community and the fairly constant stream of non-Aboriginal visitors to that community. He had travelled to some of the major cities down south and had even been to Rome where he met the Pope. On the other side of the equation, Peter Garrett had travelled widely in outback Australia and visited many Aboriginal communities. We could be confident that he had no intention to intimidate this man or to make him feel uncomfortable in any way. So what had gone wrong? It was obvious that the anthropologist and I had some kind of shared understanding that made us immediately aware that there had been a cross-cultural communication problem. It struck me that this sort of shared experience we had was something that plenty of people that have worked in Aboriginal Australia come to acquire after a time. It also seemed clear that this knowledge acquired by experience was largely implicit. What was needed was to have a more explicit understanding of cross-cultural communication problems.

Source: Extracted from Walsh (1997).

IMPRESSION FORMATION AND MANAGEMENT

Critical narratives 5.1, 5.2 and 5.3 take us directly to the crux of this chapter, which is that our very first impressions — at work, study or in everyday community life — *count*, and often continue to count more and more. Many of us, perhaps, have sensed that the first few seconds of any interaction with someone we do not know, our first encounter, are vital for setting the tone of how that relationship will subsequently develop — or self-destruct. This chapter aims to throw some light on the psychology of those vital opening moments (Ambady, Bernieri & Richeson 2000).

Whoever understands this kind of impression *formation* is one step closer to effecting impression *management*. Rightly or wrongly, this management process continues to gain currency in the new century. Impression management, which means achieving a 'right' impression as well as detecting a 'wrong' one, has at least two edges. On the one hand, we have to put our 'best foot forward' simply to avoid being overtaken by charlatans. In this sense, and as critical narrative 5.1 in particular makes clear, the jobs and promotions market is like a prisoner's dilemma game (see chapter 2). On the other hand, we clearly have to avoid 'overdoing it', whether intentionally or not. Detecting 'résumé fraud', for instance, is part of the stock-in-trade of contemporary industrial and organisational psychologists (Aamodt 1999). Producing the right impression and detecting a wrong one is about balance. This chapter assesses the theory and evidence on successfully striking that balance, not just in career advancement and development but also in everyday life.

Critical narratives 5.1 to 5.3 make the point that social perception takes place very rapidly, so rapidly in fact that social psychologists today speak of a 'cognitive unconscious' (Wedenoja & Sobo 1997, p. 160). This term implies that we do not have to 'think' a great deal before implicitly reifying a thin slice or two of behaviour into a trait of one kind or another (Kunda & Thagard 1996). This speed and spontaneity is at the same time both a blessing and a curse. On the one hand, it helps us to cope with the huge volume and pressure of sensory data that many of us experience in everyday life. On the other hand, it leaves us open to potential biases: we can easily jump to erroneous conclusions about other people. This, though, is precisely where social psychology should be able to assist. Casting our minds back to chapter 1, one of the main functions of the discipline, and a key reason why many students study it, is to raise awareness about social influence processes, and thereby partially correct them when, or before, they go awry. The mere fact that much of social perception occurs below immediate awareness creates potential for 'enlightenment effects' to take place (Gergen 1994b). This essentially practical goal is what steers us, in this chapter, as we build from a review of impression formation towards a critique of impression management.

From slices to traits in impression formation

According to figure 5.1, others' eye movements and handshakes will stimulate our social senses and influence self's inferences about them. Other consequential features of physical behaviour include, for example, head movements, posture, postural changes and facial expressions (Anderson & Shackleton 1990). Using these kinds of thin slices, Anderson and Shackleton researched the perceptions and intentions of graduate selection interviewers with regard to their interviewed graduate candidates. Consistent with figure 5.1, the study traced hiring intentions directly back to inferred personality traits, and these in turn directly back to thin slices, such as eye contact and other features of the graduate's behaviour during the interview. This type of relationship, with first impressions linked directly to thin slices, suggests that sensory input is processed relatively quickly and spontaneously into trait inference perceptions (for a wider overview, see Anderson 1992 or Herriot 1991). In fact, even when a perceiver is distracted by other mental tasks, trait inferences still occur spontaneously (Uleman 1987; Lupfer, Clark & Hutcheson 1990; Krull & Erikson 2000; for an early discussion, see Asch 1946, p. 258). Evidently, therefore, trait inferences are the coinage of first impressions (Budesheim & Bonnelle 1998). Although we might on occasion recall a specific behaviour ('She wouldn't shake my hand'), these slices of behaviour seem to have less perceptual currency than the traits that they imply ('Well, *she* was a cold fish!'). In this way, in first and lasting impressions, the *meaning* of behaviour counts for more than behaviour itself.

An illustration of the spontaneity of trait extraction, however flawed those estimates can be, is found in first impressions on the Internet. On-line, to varying degrees, depending on the precise communication channel (chat-rooms, e-mail and so on), forming any kind of impression is inherently tricky:

> In a text-based environment, you can't project your high status the way you could in visual mode — with impeccable grooming or a gold watch. Your commanding voice is silenced. Your contagious smile and raised eyebrow are invisible. Unless you bring up your own graphical website and draw others to it, the main tool you have to manage the impression others form about you is the QWERTY keyboard. (Wallace 1999, p. 28)

Yet, despite these sensory deprivations, Internet users readily *do form* impressions of one another based on personality, even in the virtual absence of 'behaviour' *per se* (Fuller 1996; Lim, Benbasat & Ward 2000). This readiness to infer traits must be partly due to the invention of linguistic conventions, such as 'emoticons', or text symbols that convey thin slices such as smiling (see chapter 10). But this cannot be the whole story. The preference for traits was observed even before emoticons were introduced (Hiltz & Turoff 1978; Rice & Love 1987; see also Walther 1993).

At this point we can state that there is a pervasive tendency for people, when forming their first impressions of others, not to dwell too much on specific behaviour. Instead, people seem to pass almost directly to inferring traits. Of course, *how* we achieve that leap is still a major question to consider in this and subsequent chapters. For the moment, however, we may conclude that much of 'the action' during first impressions is centred on perceiving traits.

Note: If the class is planning to tackle activity 1, then the following section should not be read until after the exercise has been completed.

A Gestalt perspective

The study of trait impressions, as we know it today, stems from research in Gestalt psychology. The word *Gestalt* comes from the German, meaning 'organised whole'; the Gestalt view of human nature holds that people are fundamentally motivated to detect, and create, organisation and meaning out of raw (sensory) experience. This kind of psychology was introduced in chapter 1 through the distinction between two types of theories: those that view human behaviour as motivated mainly by the pursuit of pleasure and the avoidance of pain; and others that view the human condition as a search for meaning. Broadly speaking, Gestalt psychology belongs in the latter category. Gestalt theory focused initially on how people mentally organise (and thereby cognise) their physical world. This was then generalised to how people organise their perceptions of each other into meaningful trait patterns (for a recent discussion of parallels between physical and social perception, see Cacioppo, Gardner & Berntson 1999). The Gestalt view, therefore, is that people are naturally motivated to order their sensations of one another along some core organising dimensions in social perception.

One of these dimensions, for instance, could be a core or *central personality trait*, around which perceivers will quickly and spontaneously organise much of their subsequent sensory input. Once this perception is in place, according to the model, a further process is activated. A basic proposition in Gestalt psychology is that the better organised the sensory material, the more easily and indelibly absorbed by the mind it will be. According to this view of cognition, the mind inherently prefers material that is organised. Lectures are absorbed better by student audiences when the information is well structured and organised. The other side of this coin, of course, is that if the lecture, or impression, is organised from the outset, but also deficient or biased in any way, then the tilt will become exaggerated and increasingly difficult to reverse as time passes. Either way, therefore, according to the Gestalt view, understanding the process of first impressions is absolutely critical in all communication, education and social interaction.

In search of central traits

The Gestalt approach to studying impression formation asks the question whether there *are* identifiable key traits, typically including abilities, that perceivers spontaneously look for and then utilise heavily in framing and organising their overall impressions of others. Logically enough, the founding paradigm for studying these inferences examined how one trait, such as being 'cold' rather than 'warm', influences other trait inferences, such as being less generous, wise and reliable (see activity 1). Because of the pivotal role that such dispositions play in the impression formation process, they are known as **central traits**. Around them, arrays of subsequent sense data (and perceptions) are supposedly organised mentally into a meaningful and coherent pattern (for the perceiver self). That pattern then provides a social psychological basis for the kind of longer term, spiraling effect outlined by Sterne at the beginning of the chapter.

No discussion about first impressions would be complete without a description of the work done in this area by Asch (1946). This is not just because his original study continues to stimulate discussion in the literature today (Singh et al. 1997). It is also because virtually every contemporary text on social psychology contains an obligatory description of Asch's work. One of the most popular textbooks on social psychology, for example, describes this study as a 'cornerstone' in its field (Baron & Byrne 2000, p. 65). Clearly, therefore, we cannot ignore this classic work; indeed, part of the aim of this book is to articulate how and why such work continues to be relevant in contemporary life.

Asch's critical test of the Gestalt model

Asch was a Gestalt psychologist. This means that his emphasis was on the capacity for people to organise their perceptions of each other into meaningful trait patterns. In his research, Asch anticipated that there are certain trait perceptions that serve as a foundation for an array of other, intuitively linked trait perceptions about the perceived 'other' person. Hypothetically speaking, a perception that 'other' is 'extroverted' will be followed by a clustered rush of other, intuitively related trait perceptions (e.g. 'rash' or 'team-player'). If, however, the initial trait inference happens to tilt the other way, towards 'introverted', then a range of essentially opposite trait perceptions would fall into place (e.g. 'cautious' or 'loner'). According to this Gestalt view, therefore, it should be possible to identify at least one trait that is pivotal — that demonstrably functions like a 'master-switch', lighting up an array of other trait perceptions.

What would the contemporary 'résumé-building' approach to job-hunting, outlined above, imply in the same situation? The 'résumé-stacker' implicitly assumes that more is always better. For example, no single positive trait is necessarily any better to project over a range of positive others. As long as the trait is positive, it adds positivity to the first impression. This view has some theoretical substance. At the time Asch was writing, and as he discusses in opening his paper, the major rival to Gestalt psychology was behaviourism. According to this view, external reality drives what we see, rather than any innate need to 'organise' the world. Since there is no innate tendency to seek order in the world, and because that world is experienced uniquely by each one of us, there is no compelling reason to suppose that *any* particular trait perception will systematically (i.e. across whole populations) become 'central'. There is no need to posit any kind of cognitive 'master-switch' influencing the entire process of impression formation. In short, there is no single identifiable trait perception that would be sufficient, in an experiment, to shape the general impression that groups of people form of one another.

According to Gestalt theory, there will be central traits. According to behaviourist theory, there will not. Which view is right? Asch decided to conduct a critical test. Two of the best-known trait descriptors that Asch used as stimuli in his test were 'polite' (as opposed to 'blunt') and 'warm' (as opposed to 'cold'). The test itself used materials that are relevant to job applications today. In such applications, candidates are normally eager to impress on their judges, in their job application letters, résumés and interviews with selection panels, that they possess a 'positive' personality profile of traits.

In stage one of his experimental paradigm, Asch's participants were presented with a list of seven trait adjectives describing a 'stimulus person'. These seven traits were: intelligent, skilful, industrious, determined, practical and cautious, plus either warm, cold, polite or blunt (Experiments I and III). The independent variable in these conditions was whether the last of these traits (in the experiment itself they were positioned in the middle of the list) was warm, cold, polite or blunt. The dependent variable was overall impression, and this was measured across 18 further, but not necessarily related, trait terms (e.g. generous, happy, good-natured, humorous, sociable, popular, humane, wise, restrained and imaginative). These 18 adjectives were presented to the participants at stage two of the experiment, when they, as person perceivers, were asked to give the general/overall impression that they had formed of the stimulus person minimally described in stage one.

What Asch found was that whether the words 'polite' or 'blunt' appeared in the first list, at stage one, made little difference to how the target person was perceived across the wider list of trait stimuli, at stage two. The consequences of presenting 'warm' rather than 'cold', however, were dramatically different. Essentially, when the stimulus 'warm' was included at stage one, Asch found that the ratings at stage two were systematically higher. There was a positive 'halo effect' for presenting as warm, and a negative halo effect for presenting as cold (halo effects are simply impacts that radiate and infuse outwards, generalising from one trait perception to an array of others). Thus, Asch believed that he had found evidence of an impression formation 'master-switch' that once activated, one way or another, during the first few moments of a new encounter, will drastically alter the kinds of impressions created by otherwise identical candidates.

According to this study, when a person manages to appear from the outset warm rather than cold, she stands to accrue a range of other positive trait ascriptions, rather than negative ones. In that way, and to that extent, first impressions are ordered and organised. Furthermore, they are organised around at least one 'central trait'. Asch, it could be argued, had put his finger directly on the kind of hypothesis formation process described by Sterne.

First impressions research after Asch

Since the original study, various criticisms have been made of Asch's methodology. One of these has focused on the issue of control. Without a full comparison with a no-treatment control, we cannot decide whether the difference between 'warm' and 'cold' conditions is due to one type of trait or the other ('hotter' or 'colder'), or indeed both (for more details on this issue, see Asch 1946, Experiment II). With broad concerns like this in mind, Singh et al. (1997) conducted a series of controlled modifications of the original experimental paradigm. Broadly speaking, Singh et al. found in their study that a larger share of the variance between the warm–cold conditions could be attributed to the negative impact of adding 'cold' to the traits presented at stage one, rather than to the positive impact of adding 'warm'. Thus, 'cold' was rather more of a 'master-switch' than its warmer counterpart.

Singh et al.'s study was conducted at a different time (the 1990s) and in a different cultural environment (Singapore) from the original. Nonetheless, its findings do converge with the original studies (in 1940s USA). Both negative halo effects (from cold) and (albeit weaker) positive halo effects (from warm) did still emerge in Singh et al.'s study. To that extent, and based on Gergen's criterion for robustness (see chapter 1), the more recent findings do not detract fundamentally from Asch's more general proposition: that the seemingly 'spontaneous' act of first impression formation is also coherently 'organised'.

Singh et al.'s findings converge also with another major impression formation factor identified in the wider literature, the so-called **negativity bias** (Miller 1959). Negative information generally impresses more deeply than positive information (Skowronski & Carlston 1989). The negativity bias probably has origins in social evolution, during which it would have been adaptive to attend to, and remember, any negative information about others (Cacioppo et al. 1999). In the present day this may mean, for example, that if an average candidate at a job interview makes a minor slip, even though it is totally unrelated to his capacity to do the work, this may cost him the job (Anderson 1992). The same applies to promotions (Ganzach 1995). In community settings, too, negative information depresses expectations of cooperative behaviour (De Bruin & Van Lange 1999). In the political sphere, negative information can be very costly to election candidates (Klein 1996; Petony 1995). Perhaps the most telling examples of negativity biases in everyday life will be readers' capacities to remember what they were doing when they heard of the death of Princess Diana or the attack on the World Trade Center in New York. If the meaning of the date 'September 11' is forever changed in your memory, this is partly a reflection of negativity bias. *Knowing* about this negativity bias allows us to refine our interpretation of, or restate, Asch's original findings. In other words, it is probably even more critical *not* to appear 'cold' than to ensure also that we appear 'warm' (Goldman, Cowles & Florez 1983).

Applications in education

An early and enduring extension of Asch's original research was conducted by Harold Kelley (1950). Kelley chose to study the impact of perceived warmth and coldness in the context of a lecture. In his study, a guest lecturer was introduced, through a brief biographical sketch, as being 'rather cold' to half of the group and 'very warm' to the other half. The lecturer then gave the same (20-minute) talk to both segments of the class. At the end of this talk, Kelley asked his students to give their impressions of the guest lecturer, across a range of adjectives. What he found was that, despite giving exactly the same lecture to both audience sectors, the speaker created a more positive impact on that part of the student audience to whom he was initially presented as 'very warm' than on those to whom he was described as 'rather cold'. This finding linked central traits to education services. Today, in my own experience at least, and based on numerous content analyses of critical incidents generated by students as part of class exercises (strictly *without* revealing any identities), the warmth versus coldness of lecturers remains a primary concern. Kelley's study was also the first to link central traits to later behaviour. When the visiting lecturer had from the outset been portrayed as warm, more students chose to interact with him once the lecture was over. Such differential behaviour, coming at the *end* of a lecture, begins to suggest precisely the kind of snowballing effect envisaged by Sterne.

Kelley's work was extended by Goldman et al. (1983). These researchers, who included a control condition and replaced the male guest lecturer with a female guest speaker, obtained effects similar to the original studies. However, they also found that the differential effects of cold and warm were amplified more than usual if both class *and* speaker were given the same initial perception *of each other*. This kind of mutual first impression created a doubly strong version of the kind of effect depicted by Sterne. Similarly doubled effects to these have since been found not only between students and lecturers, but also among students themselves (e.g. Harris et al. 1992). Referring again to figure 5.1, findings like these remind us that first impressions are inherently interactive — that they involve from the outset both 'other' and 'self'.

One possible objection to the behaviour-focused studies just reviewed is that they have consistently employed participants who were students (Sears 1986). Students are clients in a particular human service sector, education, and it might be only there that warmth and coldness are relatively 'central' concerns. This is fairly unlikely, however. First of all, a manager's relationship orientation (and to that extent, warmth) towards his or her employees has been found to be a robust concern for employees in other types of service organisations, too (Jackson & Furnham 2001). Second, even beyond service sectors, for example in heavy industry, task versus relationship orientation towards employees in organisations is a major recognised plank in leadership skills (see chapter 7).

Communication, context and culture

Some communication 'problems' that arise within Internet communication channels, notably perhaps on e-mail, relate to a tendency for end-users to 'come across' as colder than they really are (Wallace 1999). Even individuals who are characteristically warm in their everyday social interactions in real time are, as we have seen, typically denied many of the customary means of *conveying* this warmth, say on e-mail. The behaviour slices they can display are uncharacteristically thin, and until multimedia simulations of face-to-face reality, or 'rich media', become more widely available, being perceived as 'cold' is likely to remain a significant e-communication hazard (Lim, Benbasat & Ward 2000).

Overall, the appearance and reappearance of warmth-versus-coldness across such a wide range in educational, organisational and (cyber) community settings give it a robustness of its own. There may well be central traits that successful lecturers, employees and cyber-citizens alike need to convey correctly from the outset of their daily communications with students, employers and e-mail correspondents. All things considered, therefore, the concept of central traits continues to have relevance to contemporary everyday life.

At the same time, we have consistently cautioned against assuming that psychological concepts will always travel well across all social settings. For the job of spy or, somewhat less dramatically, someone explicitly hired to undermine a workers' union or manage mass redundancy exercises, perceived 'coldness' (and some of its perceptual relatives in the resultant halo) will probably fit better with the requirements of a job, and the job description, than 'warmth'. So in some applied contexts, perceived coldness, and perhaps much of the perceptual baggage that tends to go with it, will be viewed, and used to make decisions, differently.

Some inferred 'negatives' may actually be advantages for a particular job. Once again, therefore, we need to remind ourselves that context matters.

In chapter 1 we learned about individualism and collectivism, and how many relatively collectivistic societies place more value on sensitivity to social context. For example, concepts of leadership in Japan ('Bushido', in Fukuda 1999) and Thailand ('Baramee', in Komin 1999) have been shown to place a high value on context-related factors such as civility and politeness (Kao, Sinha & Wilpert 1999). In such settings, perceptions of 'polite' versus 'blunt', which exerted only peripheral impact in the original Asch study (conducted in a relatively individualistic US setting) may become more central. In critical narrative 5.3, a degree of indirectness, with hindsight, might have been a more appropriate way for Peter Garrett to express and convey his own underlying warmth. The same applies in critical narrative 5.4, which looks at handshaking behaviour. The point here is not that inferred central traits are overly culture-sensitive. Nor is the literature saying that perceived traits do not matter in collectivist settings (see chapter 6); they do (Choi, Nisbett & Norenzayan 1999). Instead, the real point is that what, precisely, is understood to *express* a central trait may vary from cultural group to cultural group, for example between relatively individualistic and relatively collectivistic groups.

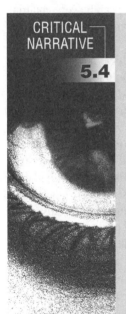

When a firm handshake backfires

This was one of my first overseas conferences. I had travelled from Australia to Malaysia for an Afro-Asian congress on psychology, which was being held on a university campus outside Kuala Lumpur. Having arrived a little early for the opening ceremony, I was waiting outside the main conference building when a senior official from the conference drew up in a chauffeur-driven car. His immediate reaction was to walk towards me in an obvious gesture of welcome. I therefore extended my hand, grasped his own very firmly, and shook it in the heartiest way I could, just as I would back in Australia.

The look of horror on this man's face was absolutely instantaneous. It was immediately clear that I had made a complete social gaffe. I wanted to crawl into a hole and die. The senior official, who could have been the president of the entire association for all I knew, retired as quickly and gracefully as he could, although still looking suitably appalled by my uncouthness (trait inference). The only thing I could do now was to confirm for myself, by reading a book on intercultural communication, that the polite and appropriate way to shake hands, in this particular society, was very, very gently. Handshakes were clearly still very important, but precisely how they were practised was, too.

Source: Personal experience (1994).

MORE CRITICAL TRAITS IN IPTs

Rejuvenation and restatement

Central traits, then, are at least as relevant today as they were in Asch's day. In addition to the enhanced premium being placed globally on impression formation and management, human warmth continues to be integral to relationships and effective communication across several domains of psychology — educational, organisational and community. For all of these reasons, the warm–cold distinction comes close to being a central trait, as Asch originally conceived it, in people's working models about human personality, or IPTs (Allen 2000). Yet, as depicted in figure 5.1 and critical narrative 5.4, *which* particular behaviours will count as expressing a given central trait may need to be carefully restated as we traverse the various zones of intercultural contact that characterise a global community (Hermans & Kempen 1998). As one of the peer reviewers of this chapter succinctly expressed it, 'the *principle* of central versus peripheral traits seems to be robust, even though we cannot assume that the same specific traits will be central in all cultures'.

Forward and backward in time

In one classic study, bogus classroom test results, given at the beginning of a school session, were actually found to influence IQ test scores obtained by students later in the academic session (Rosenthal & Jacobson 1968). Such **Pygmalion effects** have since been linked to instructors' warmth versus coldness (Rosenthal 1995). They have also been extended into studies of gender, where the effect was reduced in all-women groups (Dvir, Eden & Banjo 1995). As well, they have been extended into management studies generally (McNatt 2000). Thus, the primacy effects of first impression (see chapter 4 for a redefinition of *primacy*) can be very enduring in people's lives (Shea 1998). Their effects are not merely confined to 'snapshots' of time, sampled in 'social psychology experiments'.

Critical narrative 5.4, like 5.1 to 5.3, suggests that it is critical not just to put our best foot (or hand) forward during the first few minutes of a first encounter, but to do this from the very first *instant* of that encounter. Asch (Experiment VI) tested this hypothesis empirically. He did so by varying the order in which trait adjectives, both positive (e.g. 'intelligent') and negative (e.g. 'envious'), were presented in stage one of his experimental paradigm. The reasoning here is that if sheer primacy is all-important, then wider impressions at stage two should follow whatever type of trait-like information, positive or negative, is presented first, even *within* the list presented at stage one (rather than, say, last in that same list). This is indeed what was observed in the empirical test, with impressions becoming more negative if the very first descriptor in the list was negative ('envious'), and more positive if it was positive ('intelligent'). Thus, and as the critical narratives in this chapter have consistently suggested, impressions were initially framed and organised around whatever traits emerged *at the very beginning*.

There is an upside to finding that potentially biasing primacy effects, such as those above, are manipulable. The upside of such findings is a concomitant suggestion that biasing primacy effects can be reversed and prevented. For example, Luchins (1957) found that simply teaching panellists about the primacy effect was sometimes sufficient to reduce its deleterious impacts. This is a good example of social psychological knowledge being used to raise consciousness about potential biases in our decision making, thereby helping prevent them in the first place (see also Forgas 1986).

Asch's primacy experiment (IV) can be taken, in more general terms, as underscoring and emphasising the importance of first impressions in shaping future interactions with other. Interestingly, this same kind of effect has been found with additional traits apart from 'warm' or 'cold'. Specifically, a primacy effect has been obtained with textual material that introduced 'other' as either introverted-then-extroverted or extroverted-then-introverted (Luchins 1957). Such findings are fascinating because they begin to suggest that more than one trait may be 'central'.

A taxonomy of central traits?

To address this possibility, we need to do some *reconstitution* (see chapter 1). For that, we turn first of all to research and theory on 'latent' traits in personality. Latent traits are simply underlying or core dispositions. In the literature there have been major developments in recent years on the number of these core traits that are believed to underscore human personality. After decades of debate (and some continuing controversy) in the field, something resembling a consensus has emerged that there may be five major traits to consider (Goldberg 1990; for a critical account, see Block 1995; for a possible application to letters of reference, see Peres & Garcia 1962; Aamodt, Bryan & Whitcomb 1993). The 'big five' traits appear to travel relatively well across cultures, again provided we recognise that there will be differences in the way that each is expressed in a local setting (e.g. Leung et al. 1997). For example, since the late 1990s there has been a revival in personality testing in Asia–Pacific countries like New Zealand and Australia (Fisher & Boyle 1997). Of course, the whole idea of a 'big five' by definition suggests central traits (see also Fiske 1993, p. 162). These traits are supposedly core dimensions along which people intuitively, and largely implicitly, tend to classify human personality. Equally suggestive is the manner in which the big five were derived. They emerged only through empirical factor analysis of trait descriptions, given by many thousands of people, of themselves and others. This kind of technique seeks out underlying structure, and the idea of underlying structure is very close to the original concept of a central trait.

OCEAN and the 'big five'

What exactly *are* the big five?

Although the way they are termed, and how they are expressed, varies somewhat from author to author and context to context, the big five are handily organised using the memorable acronym OCEAN, which stands for the largely self-explanatory core traits: Openness (to experience; sometimes likened to intelligence), Conscientiousness, Extroversion (vs. introversion), Agreeableness (as in conformity) and Neuroticism (or degree of emotional instability–stability).

Reconstitution with central trait IPT

One way of bringing Asch's findings into the twenty-first century is to understand that the warm–cold distinction may get close to the heart of one or more of the big five traits. This would be a major rejuvenation of the construct of central traits. For instance, in a prominent personality test that is used extensively for selection purposes in Australia, New Zealand and elsewhere, there is a scale explicitly called 'Warmth'. Moreover, scores on this scale are counted, during test scoring, as reflecting not one but *two* of the core elements in OCEAN, Extroversion and Openness (Cattell & Cattell 1995).

If we now look back at the sample of dependent variables originally used by Asch (in Experiments I and III; see page 174), they do conceivably reflect these two source traits, rather than others. This suggests that halo effects may have their limits, and that they do not necessarily radiate outwards in all five directions at once. Perceivers may actually be more discriminating than that. Indeed, if we look back at Asch's original study (Experiment I), for instance, we see that the halo differential did not occur on stage two traits like 'reliable' and 'honest'. This may be because these particular trait inferences are more reflective of a separate central trait in the big five, Conscientiousness. Thus, the impression formation process, using central traits, may be subtler and more cognitively discerning than Asch originally envisaged.

Why the big five are central

These ideas would have more credibility if there were substantive *theoretical* reasons for believing in them. In fact, the big five, as central traits, have been accorded some evolutionary plausibility. A theoretical explanation of why they are there, in our social psychology, is that they have had, and continue to have, adaptive value (Goldberg 1981). Goldberg's 'fundamental lexical hypothesis' proposes that languages have evolved trait words (a lexicon) precisely because it is adaptive for people to be able to talk about those underlying dispositions in others (Gregory 2000; see also Fiske 1993, p. 163). According to this view, it is inherently adaptive for humans, as perceivers, to be able to quickly (and intuitively) decide or recognise, using pre-existing trait concepts in a group lexicon, whether another person is open to experience (learning), conscientious (dependable), extroverted (other-oriented), agreeable (cooperative) and mentally stable (not neurotic).

To sum up, on the basis of our critical review of the early research on central traits, and of developments in personality measurement and psycho-linguistic theory, there are reasons to believe that there are at least five central traits. It would be fascinating and useful to *test* whether the differential effects observed by Asch can be replicated in five rather than just one — or perhaps two — dimensions. Most of the research in impression formation to date has concentrated on just one or two of these traits, creating the potential for new understandings to be realised (Fiske 1993), for a restatement of the central trait taxonomy, for a reconstitution of central trait theory and for a rejuvenation of the concept in areas such as organisational selection (see chapter 1, on pathways).

Many organisations, for example, are replacing traditional large-scale departments with smaller workplace teams, often assembled for specific projects. Selecting the right 'personality mix' for these teams is increasingly seen as crucial for their success (Belbin 1997). Based on an analogy with physical perception, Fechner's Law and the psychology of **just noticeable differences** (see chapter 1), halo differentials such as the kind observed by Asch could start to loom large in team functioning. In a small team, other (and other's personality) is more proximal with less background stimulation, and to that extent much more 'in your face'. First impressions (and any perceived personality 'clashes' that arise out of these) will be magnified (Latané & Wolf 1981). The possibility that small project groups are more prone to perceptual biases and to social conflict is counterintuitive: it runs against the stereotype that small groups are typically 'warm and fuzzy'. For that reason alone, it is worthy of further testing, and thereby potential application to improving team design and functioning.

MOVING AWAY FROM CENTRAL TRAITS

The early studies of impression formation concentrated on central traits rather than the host of other dispositional inferences that can be made, and that also matter a lot in everyday life. These inferences range from assessing more 'peripheral' traits to perceiving other's values and attitudes, to achievements at work and in life generally. The focus on 'central personality traits' naturally meant that comparatively little attention was originally given to these broader aspects of other's persona.

Cognitive algebra

This began to change during the 1960s and 1970s, when an arguably complementary social cognitive approach emerged in the impression formation literature (Anderson 1965, 1974). Anderson's approach can be loosely described as 'cognitive algebra' (Forgas 1986). Algebra is the application of any system of reasoning using mental arithmetic. For Anderson, social perceivers' thought processes, and their cognitions about others during impression formation, function like such a system.

The computational procedure favoured by Anderson involved calculating an average. His model of impression formation proposed a relatively sophisticated process in which the perceiver's mental actions resemble summing all the 'pluses and minuses' about other, and then roughly dividing the result by the number of such perceptions to obtain an overall average. In this way, 'self' arrives at the metaphorical equivalent of a mean impression score for 'other'. To illustrate this process in practice, think of how you calculate your own grade average for a course or unit. If you submit a string of consistently excellent essays or assignments, you will obtain a very high grade point mean. However, if just one or two of those assignments slip a grade or two, despite still being above a pass mark (and to that extent 'positive'), then your overall grade point average (analogous here to overall impression) will drop a notch or two. Anderson's idea was that in everyday life we keep ledgers of others in very much the same way.

The résumé-stacking model

The kind of averaging process just outlined clashes radically with résumé-stacking, an approach to impression management that advocates 'more is better'. According to the résumé-stacking model, addition (rather than averaging) is the way perceivers really form impressions (Fishbein & Hunter 1964). In this way, adding even a marginally positive trait (say) to an initial list of trait descriptors, such as that supplied by Asch at stage one of his paradigm, should still enhance impression scores.

All else being equal, therefore, an averaging model predicts that the inclusion of only moderately positive trait stimuli at stage one should lower impression formation scores at stage two. This is like a student who drops a grade on one particular assignment, thereby lowering his or her overall grade. A straightforward résumé-building, additive model, however, suggests precisely the opposite effect. Even a mildly positive trait, when added to the résumé, should elevate first impressions incrementally.

Competing models: averaging or addition?

On the basis of test norms in the United States, where he was working, Anderson could identify in advance trait words that he knew would tend to be perceived as more or less positive in value. He then ran an Asch-type experiment, with these traits included at stage one. Anderson found that, when he included mildly favourable words among the stimuli presented at stage one, impression scores at stage two fell. Apparently, then, participant perceivers had spontaneously engaged in a social cognitive process more akin to averaging than addition. Moreover, and consistent with a principle of averaging rather than addition, the same process seems to have occurred with moderately *negative* traits. Despite the negativity bias, these kinds of stimuli, when presented at stage one, tended to soften rather than simply exacerbate the dent made at stage two.

The averaging model portrays the human perceiver as an information-processing system, in this sense like a computer. But averaging also entails a search for central tendency. Thus, the Andersonian algebraic model, like its Gestalt predecessors, paints people as seekers of pattern and meaning. Indeed, in the 1980s Anderson took this view one step further, proposing that person perceivers compute not only mental averages but also *weighted* mental averages from their trait perceptions (Anderson 1981). Whether or not we agree with the mathematical elaborateness of this 'weighted averaging model' of impression formation, it does start to look as though there is a lot more going on in 'spontaneous' social perception than common sense alone suggests. Above all, perhaps, such processes appear to be inherently rational, and to that extent potentially manageable.

The studies and models developed and stimulated by Anderson clearly suggest that simply adding more and more achievements and events, however positive, to your CV may, at some point, become counterproductive. This suggestion converges well with the advice, derived from research discussed in chapter 3, not to 'dilute your case' with too many arguments in your favour. In any long string of arguments, Anderson's research suggests, there may be one or two weak or even negative links that pull the overall impression down. There are limits to this effect, however. In some early research on impressions formed at interviews conducted in the United States, a simulated job selection task was run (Aronson, Willerman & Floyd 1966). During this simulation, a candidate for the job who appeared 'superior' in terms of achievement ostensibly made a bit of a fool of himself, for example by spilling coffee on his clothes. Somewhat surprisingly perhaps, Aronson et al. found that their slightly clumsy candidate's impression scores did not fall. Quite the contrary, in fact: instead of falling, which is what the averaging principle on its own predicts, they actually rose. One implication of this 'pratfall effect' is that 'superiority' has its limits (Helmreich, Aronson & LeFan 1970). Aronson et al. found that being too good can become the high performer's downfall precisely because they do *not* show any human failings.

This limiting condition is amplified once we start to think explicitly about the possible influences of culture, and cultural values, on the impression formation process.

A key role for cultural values

In Australasian settings, we have seen that big-noting the self by parading and trumpeting high achievements runs the risk of activating anti–tall poppy attitudes. In the context of job selection and impression formation, for instance, one Australian study found that both under-assertive *and* over-assertive job candidates were rated on average as less employable, than moderately assertive ones (Gallois, Callan & Palmer 1997). Such findings begin to suggest that there are limits to cognitive algebra, and that these limits have much to do with creating a culturally inappropriate impression of being too tall (or true) for our own good. An obvious conduit for this kind of tall poppy syndrome is through cultural values that emphasise equality (and low power distance) and mateship (and collectivism). These values are sometimes espoused, as we have seen, in Australian and New Zealand settings (Anderton 1999; Thomas 1994). Peer ratings might therefore partly reflect an effect from the pull-down (see chapter 3).

Equality and mateship are not the only cultural values that can in principle depress overall impressions. In another South Pacific setting, presumably with different values from those found in Australia and New Zealand, Bau and Dyck (1992) studied the link between candidates' psychometric (e.g. IQ) test scores at entry into the Papua New Guinea Defence Force and their performance appraisal scores, as rated by superior officers, some time later within the organisation. Employees whose entry scores were higher later received performance appraisal scores from their supervising officers that were *lower*. One theoretical interpretation of this finding (not the only one) is in terms of motivational gravity. Entry tests and test scores were valid, but the performance appraisal scores reflected an effect from the push-down (see chapter 3).

Motivational gravity in impression formation

An Australian study has directly researched how motivational gravity might operate in a context of first impressions, for instance in job selection (Smith & Carr 1997). This experimental study focused exclusively on the paper credentials presented by candidates in the early stages of a job application process. Much of the theoretical basis for this study (recently reviewed) is summarised in figure 5.2.

Three distinct predictions

As indicated in figure 5.2, according to the additive model (demonstrated by the compulsive résumé-builder), impressions should continue to rise steadily as more and more achievements are added to the candidate's résumé — even at the extremes. According to a weighted averaging model, simply adding more and more positive achievements, provided they remain equally positive, should have no upgrading or degrading influence on general impressions formed — even at the extremes. Neither of these models, however, allows that there will be, at the extremes, any visible turning point, or *dip* in impression formation ratings, as a function of the number of equally positive achievements listed in a job application or letter. The only theory predicting any kind of limit on résumé-stacking is *motivational gravity* (see chapter 3). Beyond a certain number of achievements listed on a résumé, all else being equal, we will find a **motivational gravity dip** in the function relating (y) candidates' overall impression formation rating to (x) the number of equally positive achievements listed on those applications.

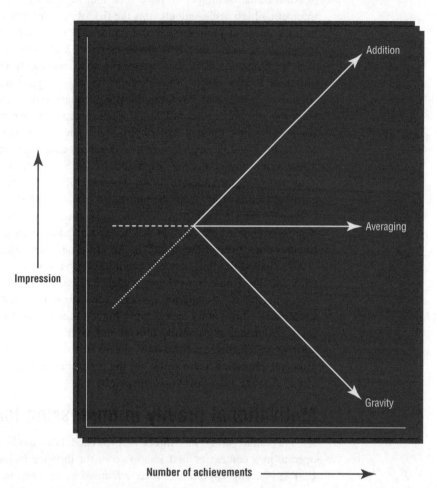

Figure 5.2 Three models of impression formation and impression management

A preliminary test of the three models

In a series of experiments along the lines of Asch's original, Smith and Carr (1997) presented full- and part-time students, nearly all of whom had work experience and a number of whom were experienced managers, with a range of simulated job applications. These applications variously listed positive personality traits (Study I) *and* job-relevant prior achievements (Study II), such as educational attainments at school. In fact, past research has indicated that people can be just as competitive about one as about the other (Wheeler et al. 1969). In each study, we kept the positiveness of each of the stimuli, positive trait or positive achievement, constant. The only factor varied was the *number* of them that appeared on the candidate's on-paper application. Thus, any differences in subsequent impressions, at an objective level, can be attributed only to the introduction of a greater number of positive traits or achievements.

Of course, when the number of positive achievements on a job application is too high, dips in impression formed might occur owing to sheer mistrust that the claims are real. Rather than motivational gravity, such mistrust would reflect an impression of 'too much of a good thing [to be true]' (Baron 1986, parenthesis added). Clearly, we had to be careful in this study to somehow check for, and control, this possibility. To do this, we also administered Feather's (1994) Tall Poppy Scale (see chapter 3). This measure was included to help interpret *why* any changes in the dependent variable occurred, and whether any motivational gravity dip co-varied, and was thereby linked, with anti–tall poppy attitudes (see chapter 4).

Some of the findings from this Australian study are presented graphically in figures 5.3 to 5.5. From figures 5.3 and 5.4, and consistent with the prediction made in figure 5.2, overall impressions did indeed dip as the number of positive trait adjectives (5.3) and achievements (5.4) was increased. Qualitative analysis of participants' open-ended reasons for giving the impression ratings they did revealed a 'too much of a good thing' effect. However, many participants also perceived that the applicant was a tall poppy who did indeed 'deserve' to be 'cut down to size'. More important still, as shown in figure 5.5, the motivational gravity dip was linked to attitudes towards high achievers, insofar as lower impression scores visibly co-varied with drops in the perceiver's score on 'favour fall' (see chapter 3 for an explanation of this attitudinal term).

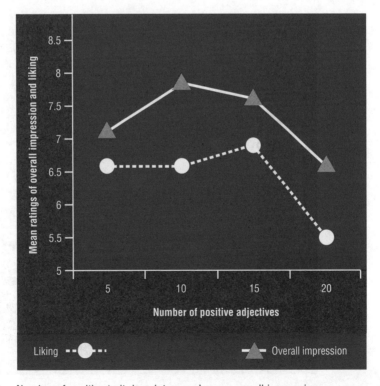

Figure 5.3 Number of positive trait descriptors and mean overall impression

Source: Smith and Carr (1997, p. 12).

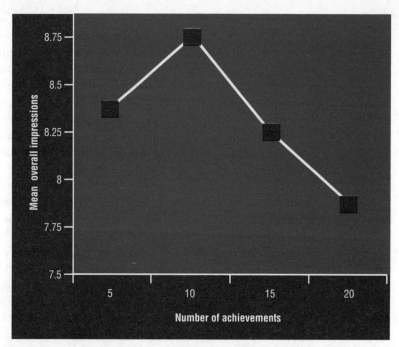

Figure 5.4 Number of positive achievements and mean overall impression

Source: Smith and Carr (1997, p. 14).

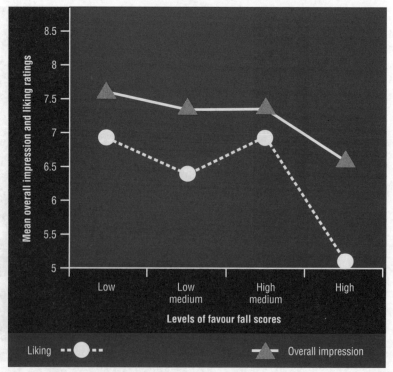

Figure 5.5 Mean ratings of liking and overall impression by favour fall

Source: Smith and Carr (1997, p. 12).

Motivational gravity dip and gender

Figure 5.6 depicts what happened to the relationship between trait stimuli and impression formation when the gender of the ostensible job candidate was varied. At the time of the study, a major government-funded report was highlighting a 'glass ceiling' for high-achieving women in the Australian workplace. Women were significantly underrepresented in upper levels of management across the country (Karpin Task Force 1995). As figure 5.6 indicates, that glass ceiling is an issue for further study within the process of impression formation. It took fewer 'positives' before ratings for the female candidate 'took a dip', compared with a male candidate (for not dissimilar effects in performance appraisal, see Ashkanasy 1994). This was not simply because the panellists were male; on the contrary, most of them were female. The graph in figure 5.6 is thereby broadly consistent with the 'enigma', discussed in chapter 3, that disadvantaged groups often partly internalise discriminatory practices against their own group (Augoustinos & Walker 1995; Power 1994).

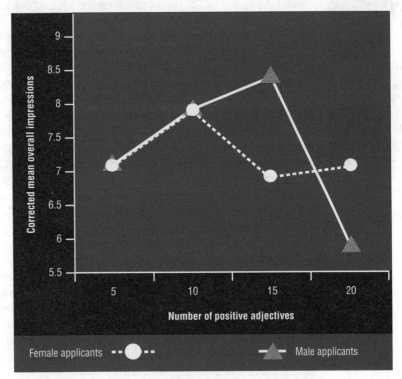

Figure 5.6   Trait descriptors, mean impression and candidate gender

Source: Smith and Carr (1997, p. 12).

GLOCAL DYNAMICS IN THE JOB INTERVIEW

A more general point that starts to emerge, or rather re-emerge, with this study is that achievers and/or résumé-builders are actually disadvantaging themselves by over-emphasising their attainments and positive qualities. Even for job candidates who are genuinely gifted, résumé-stacking — however tempting it may be on the surface — is not necessarily the optimal way to go. As well as 'diluting the impression', it may clash with local norms favouring modesty and 'quiet' achievement. There is a risk of invoking negative motivational gravity. If this is correct, the principle of averaging requires a *restatement* to allow for glocal dynamics that *deflect* the relationship between achievements and impressions. Such deflections are not always negative, as critical narrative 5.5 below suggests. But they do detract from objectivity. Broadly speaking, these deflections from objectivity, and how to correct for them, are where we head next.

A senior personnel manager's refutation of performance appraisal

A relatively inexperienced social psychologist was discussing the range of consultancy services she could offer to the highly experienced Indigenous Personnel and Training Director in a major nationalised agricultural marketing organisation in an East African republic during the 1990s. The expatriate psychologist, schooled in the inherent value of performance feedback, mentioned the social psychology of performance appraisal interviewing as one area in which her services might be useful to the organisation.

'Oh, performance appraisal doesn't work here', said the Director, in a tone that was completely confident and matter-of-fact.

Initially, this apparently casual remark left the expatriate speechless. Immediately sensing this confusion, however, the Director went on to give several cultural reasons why this was so, based on his many years of experience. These reasons included, for instance, the fact that it was culturally offensive to a collectivist to report things negative about a fellow employee. As a result, all official performance ratings tended to show a positive halo effect. There was hardly any variance in performance ratings. They were mostly at ceiling.

The expatriate left this meeting with a great deal to think about. She was amazed at the apparent inappropriateness of one of the supposed stalwarts of the economic order emerging in the country (and beyond) at the time. Moreover, she was later to encounter the same salutary lesson about conventional performance appraisal systems in cultural settings as far away geographically as Malaysia (Abdullah 1994).

The kind of performance feedback system described above is called 'downward feedback', because it travels from supervisor to subordinate. Many contemporary systems for appraising and managing workplace performance are more elaborate. Their feedback is *'all-round'* (Church & Bracken 1997). In this now global system of performance management, supervisors (downward feedback) and peers (lateral feedback), along with subordinates and clients (upward feedback), *each* get to give their appraisals of an employee's performance. This is all part of the process of supposedly becoming a continually 'learning organisation'. Yet if unidirectional feedback is inappropriate across a wide span of cultural organisational settings, then how much *more* inappropriate is introducing feedback from *360 degrees*? As well as collectivistic norms, 'upward' feedback, for example, is bound to run headlong into norms of power distance (see figure 1.1). Thus, in one Thai organisation, 'The conclusion of the senior executive [about upward feedback] was that such a feedback process is dysfunctional in that country, because the managers who were to be evaluated would feel insulted, and the subordinates who were supposed to do the evaluation would feel out of place and very uncomfortable doing it' (Javidan & House 2001, p. 302).

Source: Adapted from Namandwa (1992).

In applied processes such as job selection and performance appraisal, deflection from objectivity generally leads to loss of fairness. In the field of personnel testing, for example, the concept of fairness has gained ground lately on the more traditional stalwarts of psychological testing — reliability and validity (Gregory 2000). Fairness is all about designing a level playing field. For any job selection contest to be fair, the stimuli to which candidates are asked to respond (the interview questions) must be fair, too. Introducing extra, unwanted stimuli beyond the interview questions *per se* into an assessment and selection procedure tends to distort candidates' responses. These distortions are known as 'response effects' (Bradburn 1983). There are two major types of negative response effect, each requiring its own kind of management. The first type of error is introduced through the interviewer selector, say 'self' in figure 5.1; these are called *interviewer effects*. The second type of error is introduced by the interviewee, or 'other'; these are termed *interviewee effects*.

Interviewer response effects

A modern and very revealing way to look at response effects is through the lens of globalisation. In the global workplace, interviewer response effects often stem from enhanced pressure of one kind or another. I have singled out just three of these strains for special attention. These are: (a) more pressure to focus on getting the task done profitably, rather than considering the quality of working relationships within the organisation ('task before relations'); (b) increasing pressure to make decisions as quickly as possible ('time is money'); and (c) an inherently competitive jobs market, which creates for selectors the dubious privilege of having enhanced power over others' futures (Kao & Ng 1997). Considering Sterne's quotation at the outset of this chapter, what kind of effects on it can we expect from (a), (b) and (c)?

(a) Task versus relationship

The distinction between task and relationship is often made in organisational, educational, and health and welfare psychology. The distinction is widely used to describe and explain behaviour among leaders and followers, teachers and students, and counsellors and their clients. In the counselling domain, for example, it is reflected in the concepts of task- versus emotion-focused coping. In the educational domain, we have already seen that lecturers vary in terms of 'coldness' versus 'warmth', which clearly reflects task-versus-relationship concerns. In the business domain, too, a great deal of employee behaviour, among both leader and led, manager and worker, hinges on which style — task or relations focused — each group tends to prefer (see chapter 7). Thus, task versus relationship is an extremely robust and salient distinction across a wide range of everyday settings.

With regard to choosing candidates for vacant job positions, social psychological studies have examined the influence of being task- or relationship-focused at the outset of an interview on impressions formed of a candidate. These studies have also tracked how the interviews subsequently progressed in terms of fairness shown to the job candidate concerned. In one study, for example, mock job interviewers were specifically primed with the information that a candidate was not especially well suited for the position, thereby setting up a possible negative — and potentially unfair — expectancy effect of the kind described by Sterne (Neuberg et al. 1993). In condition A, the mock panellists were encouraged to think about persuading the applicants to like them (focus on relationship). In condition B, no such pre-interview cues were given. Condition B therefore placed less emphasis on relationship compared with the task-at-hand.

Neuberg et al. found that negative information did bias the decision-making process, but only in condition B. In condition A, in which the interviewer had simply been reminded beforehand to keep in mind the human relationship side of things during the interview, the bias was much reduced. Moreover, and in line with Sterne's literary observation, the panellists in the relationship-conscious condition behaved more *warmly* towards the applicant, who then performed more effectively during the interview. As one commentator aptly concluded, 'These studies suggest that perceivers motivated to have enjoyable social encounters will be less likely to effect a self-fulfilling prophecy than perceivers motivated [simply] to form impressions of targets' (Copeland 2000, p. 68). Another way of expressing this, and one that complements the wider literature reviewed in this chapter, is that encouraging warmth from self, in a task-pressurised decision-making environment, promotes greater fairness.

(b) The pressure of speed

In an extension of this type of study, Neuberg et al. (1993) further manipulated the motivation of panellist perceivers in order to decide 'accurately' versus 'speedily' on the merits of a candidate target. There were two job candidates, only one of whom was painted rather negatively before the interview itself. The researchers then examined whether this negative information was sufficient to mar the candidate's chances, compared with the other, 'no negative information' candidate. Once again Neuberg et al. found marked differences in the interviewers' impressions depending on how the interviewers had been primed (i.e. whether to make their decision 'accurately' or 'quickly'). When plied with negative information, interviewers in a relatively 'speeded' condition fell foul of a negativity bias. As Sterne predicted, the impression made by the candidate began to spiral downwards in a vicious circle. In contrast to this, however, the interviewers primed for accuracy were less susceptible to negativity bias. Their impressions remained more impartial.

(c) Power and privilege

Restraining or reversing vicious circles like this with simple primes may not be quite so easy when power is involved. As we saw with Kipnis's study on power in the workplace, in chapter 3, relative privilege all too readily corrupts relationships between managers and perfectly competent workers. Indeed, Kipnis's work in this area has been extended from performance appraisal to first impressions (Copeland 2000). Copeland has found that selectors with more power (to decide whether a candidate will or will not participate in a later study; or to give tangible rewards to the candidate) displayed relatively clear negative Pygmalion effects.

These deleterious effects on impression formation and decision making reversed, however, when the candidate was accorded some control and power over the selector. In other words, a partial antidote to negative first impression bias was to give the panellist a *sense of accountability* (Walker & Smither 1999).

Fostering accountability

An obvious way of actively fostering this sense of accountability, in keeping with the awareness-raising function of social psychology introduced in chapter 1, as well as managing (b) and (c) above, is to explicitly forewarn panellists about the kinds of first impression biases we already know about. In most of the material we have reviewed so far, these centre on a tendency to infer *traits* rather than *situational* pressures. The latter, of course, are often acute in selection interviews, where they can easily distort candidates' thin slices, and thereby make a very unfair basis for first impressions. One study focused explicitly on minimising this risk by inhibiting panellists' tendency to process thin slices directly into inferences about traits (Krull 1993). In Krull's study, the participants watched a job interviewee on film. Half of these participants were asked to estimate the degree of trait anxiety in the candidate. They were given a trait bias. Meanwhile, the other 50 per cent of the sample were simply asked to estimate the degree of anxiety produced by the interview. These participants, then, were given a *situational* bias. Thereafter, participants in both conditions were made cognitively busy. In terms of first impressions, the trait-focused participants still made plenty of trait inferences about the candidate they had watched. This is the kind of pattern, as we have seen above, that occurs in most studies of impression formation (Krull & Erickson 2000). In contrast to this tendency, however, the participants who had been primed to perceive in situational terms judged the interviewee differently. They began to perceive 'outside of the box'. Despite watching precisely the same tape as their trait-focused counterparts, they were more likely to detect situational and, to that extent, *extenuating* forces at work in producing the candidate's thin slices. The implication of this finding is that these panellists would have been able to reach a more impartial, potentially fairer decision about the candidate's potential to do the job.

One of the easiest and most effective ways of introducing accountability into selection processes is to give the interview a standard structure. Time after time, when the kinds of primacy biases detailed throughout this chapter have been found, the interviews themselves have been largely unstructured and non-standardised (Di Milia & Smith 1997). Each candidate is presented with a different set of questions (stimuli), after which his or her answers (responses), too, are scored according to idiosyncratic criteria used by different panellists. These conditions are ripe for negative response effects. Given the variance in questions, as well as perceptions of precisely which thin slices count as good, bad or indifferent answers, unstructured interview scores are often unreliable, and lack the power to predict future workplace performance (Aamodt 1999). An obvious way to remedy this bias is to *standardise* the questions posed; and to predetermine what the panel will perceive as a good, bad or indifferent answer for each standardised important stimulus question (Powis et al. 1988).

The situational interview

The kind of standardisation just outlined is a hallmark of all good selection interviews. One of the commonest and most effective ways of achieving this standard structure is through the *situational interview* (Robertson, Gratton & Rout 1990). The situational interview is so named because it deliberately 'situates' each and every interviewee in imagined on-the-job situations. The principal steps in this process are quite straightforward, and are outlined for us in rudimentary form in figure 5.7. This outline, in turn, forms the basis for the experiential class exercise presented in activity 3.

1. A panel of job-experienced individuals generates a series of critical incidents that can actually happen on the job. For the job of bartender, for example, these might include the eruption of a quarrel or fight (for details of critical incidents analysis, see chapter 1).

2. The critical incidents are framed in a series of 'what if?' scenarios. These now become the interview questions, which will 'situate' each candidate in standard critical incidents within the job.

3. The panel decides what responses to these incidents are good, bad or indifferent, and allocates specific scores to each of these answers.

4. Each candidate is asked the same questions, in the same order, and is scored on the same response scale.

5. Panellists check the reliability of the scores they allocate to each of the candidates against the scores allocated by each of their fellow panellists.

Note: No situational interview is ever perfect, and every selection interview, like any other selection tool, is only one element in the selection process. This means that there is always scope for improvement, both during the interview itself, and during the selection process as a whole.

Figure 5.7 Basic steps in designing a situational interview   *Source:* Adapted from Aamodt (1999).

As figure 5.7 shows, situational interviews deal with interviewer distortions by *changing the context* of the assessment. First, they focus attention away from forming impressions based on thin slices during 'an interview' (which are often irrelevant to the job), towards forming impressions 'on the job'. Next, they oblige the selection panel to base each of their decisions during the interview on specific behaviours that they have agreed beforehand, as job experts, reflect traits that are relevant to the job. In these ways, situational interviews oblige the interviewers who use them to do a lot of cognitive work. Not unlike priming a panel to pay attention to situational pressures stemming from the interview itself (Krull 1993), situational interviews gently oblige selection committees, even before the first candidate walks through the interview room door, to *maximise cognition*.

Interviewee effects

Few of us would deny that employment pressure, and so the temptation to 'pump up' personal résumés, has probably never been greater. As I write, a high-profile selection decision in New Zealand has just come under the spotlight because doubts have surfaced about the authenticity of the appointee's curriculum vitae. How many of us can honestly say that we have never 'filtered' biographical information to give it the best possible light, or screened out details of our past that could possibly be perceived in a negative light? More to the point, perhaps, who could blame us, given what we now know about the way negative information is cognitively weighted! During the interviews themselves, therefore, it is not surprising that most candidates will ingratiate themselves with nods and smiles and other forms of 'brown-nosing' (Kornet 1997). Similarly, the candidate's voice pitch is often an octave or two higher than its normal level, which is one sign of covering something up, as well as being stressed, perhaps (De Paulo 1994).

Lies and embroidery

According to Kornet (1997), human decision-makers are not particularly good at detecting octave shifts in voices; nor indeed at detecting deception in general from thin slices. This is possibly because many of us tend to persist in assuming that the world is rosier (and more trustworthy) than it really is (Schneider 1973). As in unstructured interviewing and selection (Anderson 1992), practice and experience do not necessarily raise detection accuracy rates. More likely, they merely (falsely) inflate *self-confidence* at detecting lies. According to De Paulo (1994), with the possible exception of the secret service (Ekman & O'Sullivan 1991), experience does not necessarily improve lie detection rates (see also Luchins 1957). Even explicit training in deception detection does not seem to generalise very well beyond the particular individual on whom the trainees have practised their art during training. The exception to this rule is when job candidates go 'over the top' in the way they self-promote (Howard & Ferris 1996). With those particular candidates, Howard and Ferris found, trained interviewers, more than their untrained counterparts, were likely to detect reduced job-related competence. This is a nice example of tall poppy syndrome working positively.

Can technology help us detect lies?

The traditional lie-detector (or polygraph) test works by detecting increased heart rates and skin conductivity (influenced by sweating), and raised respiratory rates (stress). This machine, Kornet (1997) reports, makes mistakes on between 25 and 75 per cent of tests (see also MacLaren 2001). In the kinds of (very consequential) individual cases in which lie detectors are used, for example in criminal court cases, such failure rates are scientifically and ethically unacceptable. As a result, the traditional polygraph has credibility problems within the academic community (Iacono & Lykken 1997). Alternatively, in the emerging field of social cognitive–neuroscience, recent advances in computer-assisted brain-scanning technology mean that we can trace dishonest behaviour to neural activity in specific centres of the brain (see also Kappas, Bherer & Theriault 2000). This will eventually significantly enhance some 'chosen' organisations' capacities to detect lies (Langleben et al. 2002). However, given the practical and ethical constraints around this kind of technology, it may be some time before we see it being used widely (if ever).

There are at least two major ways in which lie detectors can fail: failing to detect a lie when there is one (Iacono & Lykken 1997); and detecting a lie when there is not one (Wegner 1999). We should not underestimate the latter problem of over-detection. Most of us who have been through Customs checks have at some stage inexplicably felt ourselves acting 'shiftily', sweating and stressed as we slowly — oh so slowly! — file past the watchful eyes of Customs officers. We know we have done absolutely nothing wrong, and perhaps this is part of the problem. The point here is that, ironically, the more we attempt not to look guilty, the more our behaviour displays an involuntary, opposite reactance, or **ironic effect** (Wegner et al. 1987; see also chapter 7, on rebound effects).

Integrity testing

In terms of OCEAN and the big five, lying at an interview, or in a job application form or letter, would probably reflect a lack of Conscientiousness. In organisational settings, this is often assessed as part of a practice called integrity testing (Gregory 2000). Integrity testing has been one of the major areas in the revival that personality testing has been enjoying (e.g. Luther 2000). As well as identifying candidates who may not be telling the truth, or indeed may be hiding the truth from self (Paulhus 2001), integrity testing can also partly predict how much of an organisational citizen or 'good apple' they are likely to turn out to be over the long term (Fisher & Boyle 1997). Interestingly, in the study of graduate interviewers by Anderson and Shackleton (1990), the interviewers participating in the study looked for the same pattern of traits in their graduate candidates, regardless of the particular job they were selecting for. It was as if they had a prototype of the good (graduate) apple in mind as they went about their selection business (1990, p. 74). Whether or not their impressions in these regards were accurate, however, is another matter.

Culture and 'deception'

Conscientiousness is not the only central trait in the OCEAN, nor indeed is it the only one of these traits linked to integrity (Ones & Viswesvaren 1998). De Paulo (1994) reports that those who also score higher on Extroverted, in the big five, *also* tend to use deception more readily as an occasion demands. Their individual difference behaviour, as we might expect, is more contingent on social context. In this way, social context is again important — here, for influencing the extent to which individuals practise 'deception' on each other. But also, interestingly, the suggestion in this example is that deception is not necessarily anti-social. After all, the essence of extroversion, for many of us at least, is sociability. Thus, rather like reminding ourselves that conformity is not all bad, we should remember, too, that deception is sometimes, notably perhaps in community-like settings, pro-social as well.

If social context is important in influencing the form and social function of deceptions that people practise on one another, then so, too, is the context of culture. One cross-cultural study, for instance, compared participants from North

America and American Samoa, in the South Pacific. This study found that 'deception' was culturally acceptable to the (relatively individualistic) North Americans, if it served to protect personal privacy. By comparison, it was more acceptable to the (relatively collectivistic) Samoans if it served to avoid family trouble or trouble in the group, or if it pleased an authority figure (Aune & Waters 1994). Deception had a social function. Such relatively pro-social considerations, driven by group orientation and deference towards elders, highlight again the importance of broad prevailing value dimensions like individualism–collectivism and power distance (see figure 1.1).

Back to Asch's cornerstone

These two findings, one highlighting social context and the other cultural, return us once more to Asch's cornerstone concept of central traits. The more recent studies, complementing and reinforcing their predecessor, suggest that there are added risks, across today's global community, in not understanding impression formation and management. Whether we are fooled by the apparently affable job applicant (who later turns out to be monstrous), or completely misunderstand the pro-social aspect to some cross-cultural communication (see critical narratives 5.3 and 5.4), there is much to be learned from studying the social psychology of impression formation. The essence of this chapter is that much of this benefit is in play during the first few moments of a new relationship, while we are forming our very first impressions.

SUMMARY

The continuing value of Asch's research on central traits is that it dovetails with recent developments in personality description and working in small teams, in which central trait inferences are perceptually salient. Anderson's research reminds us that perceivers seek central tendencies through a number of pathways, including (up to a point) averaging of achievements. Perceivers do not simply add every slice of sensation to a cumulative index. More is not necessarily better. This point is underscored by the influence of centripetal cultural values and motivational gravity dips that stress social goals before personal achievement. Because many first impressions are formed under pressure, and at a comparatively low level of conscious awareness, consciousness about first impression biases can always be raised. These elevations of consciousness involve maximising cognition, rendering decision making more mindful even before a candidate walks through the door. The impetus for this derives from refocusing attention on situational influences at work, and structuring selection procedures to introduce greater standardisation. Over-impression management is a problem in formal selection contexts, but not all deception is anti-social. Lying can also be pro-social, for example among extroverts and within relatively collectivist social groups, when the goal is greater sociability. Such goals make behaviour more situation-driven than we might realise. Becoming more aware of that situationist perspective, and so short-circuiting some of the trait-focused biases in figure 5.1, is the core theme for the next chapter.

Central trait. A perceived trait that functions like a master-switch in creating first and lasting impressions of others. If a person is seen as 'warm' (as opposed to 'cold'), for instance, a range of other traits may be ascribed to him or her, such as 'humorous', 'good-natured', 'sociable' and 'humane' (as opposed, respectively, to 'humourless', 'irritable', 'unsociable' and 'ruthless'). This is a form of what later became known as implicit personality theory (below). (p. 172)

Implicit personality theory (IPT). A theory based on the intuitive hunches we have about what personality traits, abilities, values and attitudes tend to cluster with each other. For example, I might see cunning as a trait that tends to co-vary with cleverness, individualistic values and Machiavellian attitudes. (p. 167)

Ironic effect. The more we *try* not to think about something, for example not looking guilty when we are indeed innocent, the more — ironically — we actually start to look and feel 'shifty'. To that extent, we start to 'come across' as guilty to others. (p. 194)

Just noticeable difference (JND). When a novel stimulus 'stands out' sufficiently against its background to be just noticeable. In a roomful of 100 candles, a single candle is not a JND, but the same candle, lit in a completely darkened room, will dazzle the perceiver. Analogously, in a small team, minor personality clashes may become larger than life — a paradox of propinquity, because many feel intuitively that small teams are comparatively 'warm and cosy'. (p. 180)

Motivational gravity dip. A dip in the function relating number of achievements (x axis) to overall impression rating (y axis), as the number of achievements, or positive personality traits, becomes sufficiently high to engage a centripetal process of motivational gravity. An Australasian example of this is the 'tall poppy syndrome' (Feather 1994). (p. 183)

Negativity bias. Denotes a preference, apparently inbuilt in human memory systems, for retaining negative information more easily than its positive counterpart. News broadcasts arguably pander to this bias; it is also seen in our capacity to recall particularly nasty events, in some detail, years after their occurrence. (p. 175)

Pygmalion effects. In Greek mythology, Pygmalion prayed for a wife as beautiful as his statue, the statue came to life and he married her. In social psychology, Pygmalion effects occur whenever our hypotheses about another individual or group create a self-fulfilling prophecy, rather like the kind of process envisaged by Sterne (see p. 165; 'Ethos and direction'). (p. 178)

Trait inference. Denotes the process of arriving at trait-like judgements about other people, based on their overt behaviour (p. 167)

1. What is the essence of Asch's position on impression formation, and how well does it mesh with relatively recent developments in personality theory and testing?

2. What is the essence of Anderson's findings on how impressions are formed?

3. How do the local cultural values in your community interact with purely cognitive decisions about others, especially high achievers?

4. Are we able to apply social psychological findings on response effects, to increase fairness in the processes of job and other forms of selection?

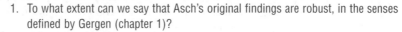

DISCUSSION QUESTIONS

1. To what extent can we say that Asch's original findings are robust, in the senses defined by Gergen (chapter 1)?

2. The chapter introduces specific contextual, communication and cultural factors that interact with perceived traits and achievements to influence both impression formation and impression management. Can you think of examples, or completely different influences, from your own local context?

3. Does globalisation render the existing literature on impression formation and management more or less relevant than before?

4. Use the pathways described in chapter 1 to derive a list of new avenues to explore in person perception research. In reaching your decisions, you may find it helpful to apply one or more of the group decision-making techniques described in chapter 3.

5. What kinds of impact on impression formation and management do you think the Internet is having?

6. Which theory of mind does résumé-stacking most adhere to?

ACTIVITIES

1. Forming impressions in an employment selection process

This exercise is designed to enable students to experience the kinds of person perception processes that Asch and others since have investigated as they relate to a contemporary context of employment selection. The class is asked to role-play a selection panel for the job of Lecturer in their department. The questionnaire below asks each student to read a brief list of traits for an imaginary candidate, to use that list to estimate the rest of this same candidate's personality profile, and then to give his or her impression of the candidate's suitability for the job, based on the limited information available. Although this information is minimal, the chapter describes how such information is nonetheless influential in making decisions about people. (The exercise is extracted and adapted from Asch's original study, combined with more recent practical work co-designed with I. Purcell (1998–99).)

Opening instructions:
The class is divided into two, group A and group B.

Instructions to group A:
Imagine that you have been asked, as part of a selection panel, to form an opinion about a candidate for the position of Lecturer at the university where you are employed. The applications for this position have reached the stage of calling in references. The references for one particular candidate stressed the following traits: Intelligent; Skilful; Industrious; Warm; Determined; Practical; Cautious.

Instructions to group B:
These are the same as for group A, except that the traits are listed as: Intelligent: Skilful: Industrious; Cold; Determined; Practical; Cautious.

Instructions to all participants in the class:
Based on the characteristics listed from the reference letters, you have been asked to complete what are called 'graphic rating scales' for the candidate. These graphic rating scales ask you give a mark to the candidate, from 0 to 10, on each of the following trait characteristics. Each of these characteristics has been deemed relevant to the job of Lecturer in your university, in an official job description: Generous; Wise; Happy; Good-natured; Reliable; Confident.

You have also been asked to indicate, prior to interview, whether you would currently select this person for the Lecturer position: Yes or No (please circle your answer).

General instructions (contd):
Once the class has completed their rating forms, the data for groups A and B can be compared for similarities and differences. Are there any halo effects, positive and/or negative? Is there any systematic difference in the extent to which people vote 'for' or 'against' the candidate, even at this pre-interview stage?

Possible term report:
If deemed appropriate by the instructor, this exercise can be written up as a class term assignment. If so, you can use or reuse the lab report exercises in chapter 3.

2. Forming and managing impressions in cyberspace

In this exercise, students are asked to articulate implicit personality theories of their own. These are based on the kinds of information provided by social psychologists on their departmental and personal websites. Each student, or student work group, takes a random selection of social psychologists from the references section of this book, and uses a search engine to locate their home pages. Critically evaluate the implicit theories of personality used. If you have time, use what you have learned from the exercise to design your own home page, and articulate the kinds of 'personality profile' you are aiming to project, and why. (This exercise is extracted from Goldstein 1998.)

3. Managing a selection process more fairly (based on Aamodt 1999)

This exercise is based on the summary steps listed in figure 5.7. As a class, break into groups of about five or six people. Choose one member of each group to become a mock job applicant. This person then leaves the room, while the rest of the group follows the steps outlined in the text on how to design a situational selection interview. If students want to avoid missing out on the experience of designing the interview, they can join another panel while they wait to be called for the interview. You will find it helpful to build this interview, and the critical incidents on which your questions and answers are founded, on a real job that someone in the group has already done or is doing to finance their study. Once the interview is designed (it need contain only three or four questions), call the 'applicant' in, conduct the interview and compile scores for comparison between panellists. Look especially at the reliability (inter-rater agreements) in those scores.

Of course, this exercise is a simplified/streamlined version of a real situational interview; in real life these scores would be more elaborated. But the exercise does reveal the essence of designing and implementing such an interview. If possible, interview more than one candidate, and/or compare the reliability of overall impression scores for groups who have used the structured interview against others who have applied an unstructured interview procedure. If you do the latter, ensure that the panellists whose procedure is unstructured each still give an overall score of some kind (e.g. a mark out of 10) to the candidate(s) they interview.

Situational interviews like this typically reveal high consistency between panellists (inter-rater reliability), and — in an organisational setting — will tend to become better predictors of future job behaviour than unstructured interview impression scores. Situational interviews tend to diminish the salience of largely irrelevant but impressive thin slices, like 'good eye contact', 'firm handshakes' and 'assertiveness'.

ADDITIONAL READING

A comparatively recent publication devoted entirely to first impressions, and that includes a focus on both impression formation and impression management, is Shea (1998).

Reviews of biases in the selection interview, by Herriot (1991) or Anderson (1992), provide classic, scholarly and compact overviews.

For a regional focus on impression management, try Smith and Carr (1997).

For a fascinating conceptual analysis of impression management, based on tests of integrity, try Paulhus (2002).

For the latest on the 'big fire', try McCrae & Allik (2002).

For further reading on the topics discussed in this chapter, consult the online resources linked to the Wiley website (http://www.johnwiley.com.au/highered/socialpsych).

6

EVERYDAY EXPLANATIONS

Learning objectives

After reading this chapter, you should be able to:

- describe the major biases that can occur when individuals explain (attribute) other individuals' everyday behaviour
- describe the major biases that can occur when in-groups make attributions about the behaviour of out-groups
- understand how these two types of bias come together to help people 'explain away' potentially catastrophic issues like global poverty
- bring attribution theory to life by applying it to the transformation of attribution biases into pro-social behaviour.

OVERVIEW

Forming first impressions is one thing; explaining others' everyday behaviour is another. There is a common thread, however: '*Why* is that person behaving like that?' This question really just reflects the observant social psychologist in everyone as they try to make sense of everyday life. Among the primary cognitive tools for this task are everyday attributions (see figure 5.1). As chapter 5 indicated, these attributions range from dispositional inferences about traits to structural inferences about situations. How often are observers' attributions about these right or wrong? This chapter reviews a wide range of theory and evidence, at both inter-individual and inter-group levels, and micro and macro levels, that everyday explainers prefer traits to situations. Anticipating these biases, and adjusting for them before they happen, gives our analysis a practical edge. This edge is then sharpened by considering the 'big' social issue of global poverty. That consideration integrates the chapter by showing how *every facet of attribution theory bears on the poverty issue*. The same discussion also highlights the fact that attribution theory has a significant contribution to make towards the development of civil society. This contribution derives from measuring the way the poor attribute poverty, and communicating these attributions across context and culture to the more privileged segments of society. As we are about to see, the potential for change rests mainly with them.

INTRODUCING ATTRIBUTION THEORY

Critical narratives 6.1 and 6.2 — one positioned largely at the inter-individual level, the other at the inter-group level — provide ideal conceptual springboards for this chapter. They encapsulate a fundamental question in our everyday psychological theorising (Heider 1958). The question goes something like this: 'Is their behaviour largely caused by dispositional attributes inside the individuals themselves, such as being disruptive and aggressive, or criminal? Or is their behaviour largely attributable to situational forces — that is, circumstances beyond their own personal control?' The message of both narratives is that our answer to this question, whether dispositional or situational, will profoundly influence how we judge people as individuals (like Grant) or groups (like the urban poor). Furthermore, the type of attribution we make, dispositional or situational, will be pivotal in influencing our behaviour, for example whether we decide to help Grant or to start campaigning against urban slums.

CRITICAL NARRATIVE 6.1

Reframing behaviour in the classroom

Grant was 10 years old and had been causing Sandra problems all year. He was disruptive, a slow learner, insolent and often aggressive towards other children in the class, and Sandra confessed herself frequently at her wit's end to know how to deal with him. However, when she came to write it down using short statements, she surprised herself by the number of things she knew about him, once she tried to think of him objectively.
- Grant is being brought up by someone he knows as his aunt. She may or may not be his mother. He has no knowledge of his father.
- The rumour is that Grant's 'aunt' has a succession of live-in boyfriends, some of whom are known to be violent.
- Grant suffers from bronchial infections and is frequently off school.
- He has no friends in class; the other boys dislike him.
- He's always behind with his work (why do I *never* make an opportunity to give him good marks?).
- Grant sometimes comes to school with money. He says he earns it doing odd jobs, but I think he steals it (or am I just prejudiced?).
- I frequently keep Grant in at break (this doesn't do much for his chances of making friends with other children!).

When she discussed her list, she was dismayed she hadn't done more for Grant. Part of the problem was that he made her professional life so difficult it was hard to feel much sympathy for him. But when she looked at his situation dispassionately, it was plain to her that there were several things she could do to help him. In particular she could:
- Stop blaming Grant for being Grant. Obviously, he isn't responsible for most of his shortcomings.

Source: Extracted from Fontana (1992, pp. 31–3).

When it comes to which side of the dispositional–situational fence attributions fall, critical narratives 6.1 and 6.2 are a little equivocal. On the one hand, each suggests (rather depressingly) that observers of others' behaviour will naturally tend to favour one kind of attribution (dispositional) before the other (situational). On the other hand, each critical narrative also implies that this biasing preference is not inevitable. It can be reversed, and to that extent managed. These options, one largely negative and the other largely positive, mark out the dynamic terrain for this chapter. Our exploration of it will be based on extensive theory and evidence. These, in turn, are split into two main levels of analysis. Attributions are formed about the behaviour of individuals and about the behaviour of groups.

Reframing behaviour on the street

The community psychology conference was being held in the Caracas Hilton, Venezuela. The delegates had flown in from all over the world, and most were staying at the Hilton itself. However, one of these delegates, from a provincial university in Far North Australia, was travelling on a low budget. Consequently, he was staying at 'the other end of town', where the rooms cost considerably less. The downside to staying at this cheaper end of town was that it was known for its high rate of crime and criminal activity, such as street robberies.

During the conference, the delegate from Australia was talking with a Venezuelan colleague, who had accumulated a great deal of first-hand experience working in the shanty-towns and poorer quarters of the city, including 'the other end of town' where the Australian was staying. As soon as his Venezuelan colleague heard where he was staying, his reaction was to advise him, in the strongest possible terms, 'But you must move immediately! There is too much *poverty* there!'

This heavily stressed '*poverty*' caught the Australian delegate completely by surprise. He realised that he had actually expected to be advised to move because there were 'too many *criminals* there'. In the language of attribution theory, the Australian had fully expected to hear a dispositional attribution about the risks of living where he was. When this expectation was not confirmed, and was even contradicted by his experienced colleague's choice of words, he found himself being gently, but firmly, nudged into reframing his views about his current neighbours.

In fact, this critical incident kept nudging him in this way throughout the weeks and months to follow. This minor cross-cultural, cross-contextual encounter had allowed the visitor to experience what ethnologists call a 'rich point'. Through an unexpected chance encounter with diversity, this sojourner from the 'developed' world had become more conscious of a latent and deep-seated bias within himself. He had come to realise that there was an alternative, more situational way of thinking about important social issues like crime, criminality and poverty in 'developing' countries.

Source: Personal correspondence with Euclides Sánchez, a leading Latin American community social psychologist (July 1999).

INTER-INDIVIDUAL ATTRIBUTIONS

One of the earliest and most influential studies of how individuals make attributions about other individuals can be found in Jones and Harris (1967). In this study, American students were shown written transcripts of speeches made about the President of Cuba, Fidel Castro. These transcripts were either supportive or critical of the Castro regime. After reading a transcript to themselves, the participants were asked to estimate the speaker's personal attitudes towards Castro. This estimation was the dependent variable. The key independent variable was whether the position adopted in the transcript they had read (either pro- or anti-Castro) had been *assigned* to the speaker (no free choice) or freely *chosen* by the speaker (free choice). Under the assigned condition, we might expect to see reluctance to infer anything definite about the speaker's private opinions. After all, the speech (and the position adopted in it) had been pre-assigned. Surprisingly, however, the independent variable (degree of choice) did *not* exert so much influence on the dependent variable (estimated private opinion). Even when the participants were explicitly informed that the speaker had had *no* real choice in the position they adopted, that they were behaving under situational pressure, the participants still tended to make dispositional attributions: making only minor adjustments, they still tended to believe that what had been said in the transcript actually corresponded with the position adopted in private by the person who gave the speech. A pro-Castro speech was attributed to pro-Castro attitudes and an anti-Castro speech was attributed to anti-Castro attitudes. This was basically what was attributed, period. Overall, therefore, behaviour was stubbornly attributed to dispositions (in this case personal attitudes) in the speakers themselves.

The basic pattern of findings in this early experiment, which has since been replicated elsewhere (e.g. Forgas 1998), converges with much of the social psychology already discussed in this book. Crowd situations, for instance, often influence their participants to behave with such apparent apathy that we are profoundly shocked and appalled by them. The main reason we are caught off-guard like this is that we mistakenly persist in assuming that moral decency (a dispositional factor) will naturally prevail over crowd dynamics (situational factors). Group situations, too, are often underestimated in their power to influence behaviour, even by experts. Neither Asch nor Milgram expected levels of compliance to be as high as they were. In Milgram's case, even a group of expert psychiatrists got it wrong. They expected that just about every participant would have the moral decency and fortitude to disobey instructions to harm an innocent human being (Milgram 1965). The same surprise is contained in chapter 4, with the dramatic media influence of Orson Welles' *War of the Worlds* broadcast. Much of the previous chapter, too, showed how 'self' spontaneously judges 'other' (see figure 5.1) in terms of character traits (dispositions). This, we learned, is often done before potent situational influences on other's behaviour — such as the stress of job interviews — are considered.

It could be said, then, that a tendency to 'keep the faith' in dispositions, and the idea of personal control in our lives, is how much of social psychology as a whole gets its surprise value. We keep expecting personality to win the day, and yet situations keep surprising us with demonstrations of their extraordinary capacity to out-influence them. Critical psychology contends that entire branches of the discipline, such as personality psychology, cognitive psychology and counselling psychology, have succumbed to the same fundamental mistake (Sloan 2000). Through cross-cultural psychology, we know that collectivist societies tend to place more weight on situational considerations when explaining behaviour. But even in these societies today, trait inference, or 'dispositionalism', remains widespread (Choi, Nisbett & Norenzayan 1999, p. 47). The extent of this tendency has been sufficient for one social psychologist to coin the term **fundamental attribution error** to describe it (Ross 1977). Since introducing that term, however, and crucially for this chapter, Ross himself has stepped back a little from the suggestion of universalism that the word 'fundamental' conveys (Nisbett, in press; Ross & Nisbett 2000; Triandis 2002). To understand this back-pedalling and its significance for bringing attribution processes to life in this chapter, we need to review a little attribution *theory*.

Some reasons for preferring dispositional over situational attributions

Perceptual salience

The most fundamental reason for focusing on dispositions has to do with perception. This is beautifully and compellingly illustrated for us in Salvador Dali's *The Three Ages*, a detail of which is represented in figure 6.1. One of the experiences that Dali's composition depicts for me is that people are naturally drawn to focus their perceptual attention on the human figure, and to relegate the rest of nature, at least temporarily, to the background (Heider 1958). It is, of course, 'adaptive' for us to focus our attention on other people, and this makes them salient stimuli (Jones & Nisbett 1972). Media stories, for example, tend to do this when they 'focus on the irrationality and pathology of … offenders … and divert attention away from the social structural forces impacting on crime and criminality' (Sanson et al. 2000). More basically still, we are more likely physically to 'see' in our perceptual space people themselves, rather than the temporally and spatially removed situational factors that led to their behaviour (Taylor & Fiske 1975). If you arrive late for work, I see *you* arriving late; I do not see the circumstances *behind* that event (e.g. unreliable bus services or a flat tyre).

Figure 6.1   Figure and ground: Salvador Dali, *The Three Ages*

Source: Copyright © Gala — Salvador Dali Foundation, 1940/VEGAP. Licensed by VISCOPY, Sydney 2002. Adapted drawing from *Perception & Psychophysics*, *2*, 328–30. Reprinted by permission of Psychonomic Society, Inc.

Lack of background knowledge

Taking this line of thinking a step further, we arrive at a second likely contributor to a fundamental attribution error. More often than not, we are not privy to the wider background circumstances of other people's lives (Augoustinos & Walker 1995). As observers of only brief 'slices' of their lives, we are very rarely in a position to know their intimate details. Through no fault of our own, we are often badly positioned to appreciate the situational influences leading to the behaviour we are trying to explain. For example, when making attributions for workers' poor shop-floor performance, inexperienced managers will often blame workers themselves; by contrast, experienced managers — those with more first-hand knowledge of the job itself — will first check for wider situational problems in the shop-floor environment (Mitchell & Kalb 1982).

Cultural socialisation

These reasons for making a fundamental attribution error are themselves pretty fundamental. They involve both physical point of view and an inability to share the actual situational experiences of the people we are trying to understand. Such pragmatic considerations virtually ensure that the fundamental attribution error will in some ways travel across cultures. Nonetheless, cultural influences have been demonstrated to affect the degree to which people make the error (Smith & Bond 1999). For instance, in a study similar to Jones and Harris's original (1967) demonstration undertaken in contemporary South Korea and the United States, both groups displayed a fundamental attribution error, but the Koreans generally showed it less than their American counterparts (Choi & Nisbett 1998). Such cultural influences are the primary reason why the 'fundamental' attribution error has come to be regarded, by Ross and others, as less than universal.

One influential figure in illuminating the reasons for this diversity has been Joan Miller (1984, 1996, 1997). Miller asked her participants to read one-paragraph stories, or vignettes. In these vignettes, a central character (e.g. a lawyer) experiences a critical incident (a car crash). The central character then chooses a course of action (abandoning at a hospital a person injured in the crash in order to keep a court appointment). Miller asked her respondents the *why* question: Why do you think the driver behaved this way (leaving the hospital abruptly rather than staying longer)? Answers were coded into dispositional and situational attributions. Examples from each category are: 'He was *aggressive* [disposition] in pursuing his career success', or 'It was his *duty* [situational role expectation] to be in court for the client he was representing'. Among Asian Indians and North Americans from the United States, Miller found that the Americans used more dispositional attributions than their Indian counterparts, who in turn used more situational attributions than the Americans in the sample. This result broadly agrees with the findings made by Choi and Nisbett (1998), along with a range of other investigators. Crucially, however, Miller has also found that such cross-cultural differences become more pronounced with developmental age (Miller, Bersoff & Harwood 1990). The fundamental attribution error, then, tends to increase with developmental time within relatively individualistic societies (Augoustinos 1990).

Unlearning attribution biases

As the above studies have demonstrated, a significant portion of the fundamental attribution error is learned through cultural socialisation practices that stress individualism (for a more detailed discussion, see Miller 1996, 1997). This is perfectly logical, given that the essence of individualism is a belief in the importance of individual dispositions, taking individual responsibility for one's actions and building autonomy from others as a means of personal development. A crucial implication of these cross-cultural studies, however, is that the fundamental attribution error, being partly learned, can also be *un*learned. Attribution biases can be redressed.

Workplace supervisors, for example, are more likely to attribute workplace back pain to causes in the work environment (rather than simply blaming the worker) if they themselves have experienced some form of back injury at work (Linton & Warg 1993). While not advocating back injuries for all workplace supervisors in order that they respond more sympathetically to similarly afflicted workers, this study does imply that the key to avoiding or minimising fundamental attribution errors is to acquire an insider perspective (see also Mitchell & Kalb 1982). Critical narratives 6.1 and 6.2 provide excellent illustrations of how this might happen, as first the teacher and then the conference delegate incrementally reappraise their pre-existing biases from another point of view. Eventually, they will revise and even reverse their attribution biases. In the literature, such perspective changes — from outsider (observer) to insider (actor) — have been discussed using the term **actor–observer difference** (Jones & Nisbett 1972).

What is the 'actor–observer difference'?

According to Jones and Nisbett, 'There is a pervasive tendency for actors to attribute their actions to situational requirements, whereas observers tend to attribute the same actions to stable personal dispositions' (1972, p. 80). This observation indicates that fundamental attribution errors are made mainly by observers, who could thus in principle benefit from 'trying on' the perspective of actors. This suggestion is reminiscent of the folk wisdom, discussed in chapter 1, that the way to get to know another person is to 'walk a mile in their moccasins'. But what empirical evidence do we have to support this advice?

An early experimental comparison of actor–observer perspectives was made in Nisbett et al. (1973). Nisbett et al.'s participants, who were tertiary-level students, were asked to write a paragraph about what they liked in their current partner, and also to describe what had attracted them to their academic major. This task was autobiographical — performed from the point of view of an *actor*. However, the participants also made attributions about their campus *roommate's* choices of partner and academic major. *This* task was biographical — performed from the point of view of an *observer*. Content analyses of the students' paragraphs indicated a clear actor–observer difference. Actors tended to use situational attributions, such as 'she makes me laugh', while observers tended to stick to dispositional ones, such as 'because of ambition'. These findings are fascinating, because they suggest that just as cultural socialisation can 'shrink' the fundamental attribution error, so too can a change of perspective from observer to actor, and in a much shorter time span. This possibility was explored directly in a classic set of experimental studies in Storms (1973).

Storms' classic research on actor–observer exchanges

In this research, participants made attributions about the relative importance of dispositional and situational influences (the importance of traits and topics of conversation, for example) in an unstructured everyday conversation. The attributions were made from two vantage points — by the speakers themselves (actors), and by somebody watching the same conversation from behind (observers). Consistent with the findings made by Nisbett et al., when making judgements about what had influenced the conversation most, actors gave more prominence to situational factors like the topic of conversation than their observer counterparts, who, in turn, gave more weight to dispositional factors like the traits of the people doing the talking. In a clever twist to this methodology, the observers then watched a videotape of the same conversation, filmed directly from the vantage point of the speaker they had been observing. They were thereby given a new vantage point, literally an actor's perspective. With this reversal of perspectives, the original observers, who had been given an actor's view, now assigned more causality to the situation (p. 172). They had experienced an experimentally induced rich point, acquiring a more situational outlook and to that extent moderating their fundamental attribution errors.

Similar changes of perspective occur on the anonymous medium of the Internet, for example when males deceitfully impersonate females (Wallace 1999). When this happens, according to Wallace, the impersonator stands to learn how easily and without provocation male ardour can turn to hostility (see chapter 10). Such personal (and ultimately inter-group) experiences reportedly oblige some males to rethink basic attribution errors they might otherwise have made about women, for example that women themselves 'provoke' hostility from men. In other words, by experiencing first-hand a woman's perspective on the situation, dispositional biases against women can in principle be redressed.

Findings like Storms' reversal go beyond merely demonstrating the existence of an actor–observer difference. They begin to indicate ways in which observers can learn to redress the balance of their attributions, for example using media technology such as Storms' video clips to communicate actor perspectives to observers. We will return to this point shortly. First, however, we need to ask ourselves sceptically whether actors' perspectives are always to be trusted. Observers, after all, are sometimes *right* to blame dispositions (Zebrowitz & Collins 1997). Storms himself discusses how video feedback can be used to help *actors* seeking counselling and therapy to see themselves as observers see them. Such suggestions indicate that all is not always right with actors — that their attributions also on occasion become biased.

Limitations to actor perspectives

One area in which actors run into serious problems, as Storms' reference to clients in counselling implies, is when they make attributions for personal successes and failures. Attributing such outcomes reflects on the ego and on self-esteem. Success boosts the ego, particularly if we manage to take personal credit for it. In contrast, failure is usually deflating, and actors may want to *avoid* taking responsibility for that. Given such approach-avoidance tendencies, it would be reasonable to expect attributions by actors, whenever success and failure are involved, to become distorted to boost and protect self-esteem and confidence (Ross 1980). Specifically, successes may start to be explained in terms of personal dispositions (taking the credit for any 'win'), while failures are 'palmed off' on the grounds of extenuating situational forces beyond the actor's personal control ('It wasn't *my* fault').

Everyday examples are not hard to find. When students take all the credit for a good assignment grade but complain about a lecturer on receiving a poor assignment grade, they may be indulging in a **self-serving bias**. The consensus of research on this bias, however, is that students are not alone. Lecturers, athletes, managers and employees (to name a few) regularly engage in precisely this form of ego-preserving manoeuvre whenever their competence is under the spotlight (Baron & Byrne 2000). The bias is not wholly inward-looking either. Claiming credit for success and deflecting blame for failure will sometimes boost the impression we make on others, provided they believe these claims (Augoustinos & Walker 1995, pp. 90–91). As we saw in chapter 5, too much of a good thing can soon start to grate, and can precipitate a motivational gravity dip. Although self-serving biases can be useful, then, there comes a point when they start to become dysfunctional.

CRITICAL NARRATIVE 6.3

The primrose path

For several decades now, some Western social psychologists have advocated the psychological benefits to self of being 'optimistic' and maintaining a 'positive' outlook on life. As part of this outlook, a readiness to take the credit for successes and not assume the blame for failures has been seen as a comparatively adaptive way to live one's life.

Recently, however, this attitude to success and failure has been directly questioned (Robins & Beer 2001). Robins and Beer studied self-enhancing evaluations of personal performance, both in short-term tasks and over the longer term, during the course of students' university studies. In the near term, both during short-term tasks and at the beginning of their studies, individuals who engaged in self-serving attributions, and who most enhanced their performance, did enjoy relatively positive affect. They felt good about themselves. But in the study that tracked these students as they passed through college, over the course of time the picture became less rosy. Compared with their peers, students who began their tertiary course with more self-serving bias, and clearer self-enhancing beliefs about their academic ability, did not attain higher grades or graduation rates; if anything, in fact, their graduation rates were slightly lower than those obtained by the rest of the cohort (2001, p. 347). Students with more of a self-serving orientation, as their studies wore on, tended to experience not only increasing levels of disengagement from the academic setting, but also *de*creasing levels of self-esteem and wellbeing.

Source: Robins & Beer (2001).

From critical narrative 6.3, the same kind of limiting condition applies in the private domain. On the one hand, being ready to take the credit for success and to deflect blame for failure undoubtedly helps students to build resilience and weather the storms of student life (Lewinsohn et al. 1980). On the other hand, in the longer term, excessive use of these tactics may not be quite so adaptive, principally because users never really face up to their failings, and so become over-optimistic about their prospects for success (Powell & Jacobson 1993). As critical narrative 6.3 implies, this bias may partly explain why it is common to find, at least in relatively self-focused, individualistic settings, that most people self-servingly think they are 'above average' on traits such as intelligence (Kruger 1999; Kruger & Dunning 1999; for an early example, see Codol 1975). The net result is that these people may end up over-promising and under-delivering on themselves.

A tendency towards modesty

Critical narrative 6.3 illustrates the possibility of cultural effects on the self-serving bias (Kruger 1999). Differences in 'self-servingness' have indeed been found between different cultural groups, and in particular between groups that vary in their individualism and collectivism. Among relatively collectivist Japanese tertiary-level students, for instance, Kashima and Triandis (1986) identified what has been described as a **self-effacement bias**, or bias towards modesty (Smith & Bond 1999). In this study, participants undertook a reasonably difficult memory task, and then made attributions for their own successes and failures. While their more individualist counterparts from the United States showed a self-serving bias, the Japanese students displayed a different pattern. In terms of the attribution of paying/not paying enough attention to work, the Japanese students attributed their successes less to themselves, and their failures more to themselves, than did their American counterparts (for an example of comparable effects in the workplace, see Farh & Cheng 1997). These contrasting central tendencies are summarised in table 6.1.

Table 6.1 Self-serving and self-effacement biases

	EVENT	
	FAILURE	SUCCESS
Self-serving	'Not my responsibility'	'My responsibility'
Self-effacing	'My responsibility'	'Not my responsibility'

   Comparable findings have been obtained across other ethnically diverse samples, again differing in collectivism and individualism, for example among children in multicultural Canada (Fry & Ghosh 1980) and the United States (Lee & Seligman 1997). The common pattern across all of these findings is that self-effacement biases are most likely to reflect relatively collectivist values. Provided the collective itself buffers the student against over-blaming self for failure (a feature of clinical depression), table 6.1 indicates that students with collectivist orientations may be well positioned to make circuit-breaking, *effort*-focused attributions for any shortfalls in their academic performance (Yan & Gaier 1991; for a discussion of depression in cross-cultural context, see Schumaker 1997). By the same token, successes are relatively unlikely to 'go to their heads' (i.e. set them off on a primrose path of the kind depicted in critical narrative 6.3).

What this all adds up to is that self-serving biases can be useful in the short term, but self-effacing biases are probably more adaptive in the longer term (Robins & Beer 2001; for an earlier study reflecting on possible gender differences in self-serving/self-effacement biases, see Gabriel, Critelli & Ee 1994). However, we should be very wary of overgeneralising from one culture to another. As we have just seen, self-servingness is learned, meaning that there will be substantial individual differences *within* cultural groups as well as between them. In fact, if we did stereotype cultures in this way (e.g. 'Collectivist cultures are modest; individualist cultures are self-serving'), we would be succumbing to yet another major cognitive bias. This is a preference for what Linville and Jones (1980) termed **out-group homogeneity** — which leads us directly to relations between groups (Brewer & Harasty 1996).

INTER-GROUP ATTRIBUTION BIASES

In a revealing study of out-group homogeneity, Park and Rothbart (1982) examined men's and women's attitudes and attributions towards one another. Each group held that there was a wider range of individual differences within their own group than within the opposite gender group. Logically, of course, both groups cannot be right, and the chances are that both groups are wrong. Any such 'out-group homogeneity effect' can be socially divisive and destructive, because it demeans and disparages diversity in others (Dasgupta, Banaji & Abelson 1999). Out-group homogeneity makes a single unit out of a rich diversity of individuals (McGarty et al. 1996). Stereotyping that diversity into one unit or entity logically paves the way for a group-level version of the fundamental attribution error (McConnell, Sherman & Hamilton 1997; Rogier & Yzerbyt 1999; Yzerbyt, Rogier & Fiske 1998). This kind of attribution is called a **group attribution error** (Allison & Messick 1985).

Group attribution error

Attributing an entire group with a disparaging trait easily contaminates relations between the groups concerned (Corneille et al. 2001; Rogier & Yzerbyt 1999). For example, group attribution errors enable and socially facilitate the kinds of out-group discrimination effects outlined in chapter 3 (Gaertner & Schopler 1998; Sherman, Hamilton & Lewis 1999). They can also propagate mistrust in organisational groups (Menon et al. 1999). In societal groups, a tangible example of how destructive and divisive such attributions can be is Pauline Hansen's One Nation, a political party that ironically caused much division within Australian society itself. Hansen's kind of out-group homogeneity enabled gross and disparaging generalisations to be made about 'Asian' societies, for example. One Nation's demise aside, I myself have read letters in the Australian press complaining that foreign aid is 'wasted' on 'Asian' countries; that it simply foments 'Asian' political unrest; and that it (the money, the aid) would be better off spent on 'Australian' issues, like housing, homelessness, hospitals, schools, universities, transport systems, parks and gardens; and so on. Thus, a diversity (of needs, want and aspirations) is sometimes more easily recognised and tolerated within a salient in-group 'at home' than within and between a richer diversity of societies 'abroad'.

Examples like this imply that out-group homogeneity effects, and their associated group attribution errors, contribute in some way towards marred international relations. In the domain of international business relations, for example, Australian firms have been lobbying for some time now for greater integration and acceptance within regional trade blocs such as ASEAN (the Association of South-East Asian Nations). This makes economic sense, because Australia relies on South-East Asian markets for most of its exports. Yet a human factor — the perception that Australians are often too leisure-oriented — has in the past worked against this integration (Market Australia Unit 1995). In 1994, for instance, Singaporean elder statesman Lee Kwan Yew described Australia as a 'lucky country' that suffered from 'deep-seated problems of work ethic' (Sheridan 1994, p. 1). In other words, according to outside observers, Australians are often work-shy and lazy.

If this perception was indeed fair, Australian employees who suddenly win a huge windfall, say from a major lottery, could be expected to quit work and retire to a life of luxury. This would contrast with experience elsewhere around the world, where most employees report that they would continue to work even if they had such a windfall (Morse & Weiss 1955; Harpaz 1989; Warr 1982; Winefield et al. 2000). So, are Australian workers any different? The evidence, in fact, suggests that they are not (from Williams 1983 to Carr & Jones 2000). Most Australians would at least think about continuing to work. This begins to suggest that observers outside of a group can be over-dispositional in their attributions about the group, compared with insiders, or actors, themselves. In other words, actor–observer differences could be happening just as readily between *groups* as between *individuals*.

In a relatively direct test of this possibility, two samples of students, one from South-East Asian nations and the other from Australia, both of them studying in Australia, were asked to predict the other group's intentions on continuing to work if they were suddenly to win a big lottery (Carr & Jones 2000). A clear majority in both samples (78 to 80 per cent) had already self-reported, as actors, that they would continue to work. In terms of (observer-like) judgements *between* groups, however, there were clear *discrepancies* with this finding. On average, the Australian respondents estimated that around two out of every three Asians would continue to work, while the respondents from South-East Asian countries estimated that one out of every three Australians would continue to work. Thus, each sample, when reporting as out-group observers, exaggerated the level of 'laziness' inherently attributed to an out-group, compared with the actors themselves (for wider estimates of actor levels, see Harpaz 1989; for another Australian study, see Williams 1983).

Theory X and Theory Y

Such findings are consistent with the idea of there being a wider **work ethic illusion** within the context of the occasionally disparaging relations between Australia and its regional neighbours. As with inter-individual attributions, at an inter-group level observers were also prone to make basic attribution errors. They viewed out-group members as 'lazier' than they probably were. This kind of discrepancy is found elsewhere, too. In the wider literature on management and organisational studies, for example, disparaging managers' stereotypes about worker motivation are known as 'Theory X' (from McGregor 1960 to Robbins et al. 2000). Theory X is normally contrasted with its more humanistic cousin, Theory Y, which is often espoused by actors (the employees) themselves (Robbins et al. 2000). Some of the details in this discrepancy between actor and observer group perspectives are encapsulated in critical narrative 6.4, which comes from the Australian Capital Territory.

Bosses, workers out of sync

Bosses reckon money drives a workforce but workers rate being 'in on things' much more highly than pay, a new study revealed.

Recruitment firm Morgan and Banks found that workers' expectations from their job are almost the opposite of what their employers think they want.

The survey showed that there has been a 'communication breakdown' between management and staff, said Morgan and Banks' director, John Banks.

'What this research makes clear is that employees place a much higher emphasis on recognition for work well done than management appreciates.'

The three most important things employees wanted was to get full appreciation for their work, feel included, and have sympathetic management who understood their personal problems.

Management thought all these things were the least important in their employees' minds.

Instead, they believed workers wanted to be a little more like them.

According to the survey, management thought the two things employees most wanted were good wages and job security, followed by promotion and growth.

But good pay was only ranked fifth by workers on the scale of 10, just after job security. And employees were not as concerned with being stimulated and interested by their work as their managers might think, putting it sixth on the list. But they did value it more than a big promotion.

Source: Moscaritolo (2000). Courtesy of the *Northern Territory News*.

Before we leave attribution errors, there is one more edge to consider. Perceptions of levels of work ethic between national and organisational groups may be moderated by how economically *successful* (or not) these groups perceive each other to be. Concepts of success and failure suggest self-servingness, which we have seen operates between individuals. Perhaps, then, the same self-serving bias applies also to social (group) identities. Successes by groups might be credited to group dispositions when they occur within an in-group, but to situations when observed in an out-group (the 'lucky country'). Failures and other negative events might be blamed on situations when they occur inside the group but accredited to dispositions when they occur collectively to an out-group. Such a pattern has been vividly described in the attribution literature as an **'ultimate' attribution error** (Pettigrew 1979).

An 'ultimate' attribution error

In an early experimental test of this kind of effect, diverse religious groups in India were asked to make attributions for desirable (helping) and undesirable (non-helping) behaviours of in-group and out-group members (Taylor & Jaggi 1974). Like Miller (1984), Taylor and Jaggi used vignettes, but in this study the independent variable was the ethnicity/social identity of the central character either helping (positive event) or declining to help (negative event) another person in need. This study found a clear tendency for the positive act of a central character to be attributed to dispositions when the central character came from within the same religious group, but to be attributed to situations when the central character came from a religious out-group. Exactly the reverse pattern was found when the behaviour being attributed was socially undesirable. Thus, Taylor and Jaggi were able to demonstrate the existence of self-servingness in relations between real-world *groups*. Later studies have replicated this effect/error, for example in the domain of political violence by religious in-groups and out-groups in Northern Ireland (Hunter, Stringer & Watson 1991).

Group humility

As with the self-serving bias, ultimate attribution errors can be viewed in functional terms. They serve to promote social identities that are both distinctive and positive (see chapter 3, on SIT). Once more, though, we cannot assume that the error is genuinely 'ultimate', in the sense of its being timeless and universal. Pettigrew himself coined the term with tongue firmly in cheek, deliberately mocking the 'fundamental' attribution error that turned out to be not quite so fundamental after all. In one study confirming that reservation, conducted in Singapore, an ethnic minority group displayed a tendency more akin to **group effacement bias** than to group (and thereby self) servingness (Hewstone & Ward 1985). In-group failures were attributed to in-group dispositions, but out-group failures were blamed on situations. Positive in-group actions were attributed to situations, but positive out-group actions were attributed to dispositions. One interpretation of Hewstone and Ward's finding is that 'minority' status (and self-effacement) sometimes becomes internalised (see also Taylor & Moghaddam 1994; for an early example of this bias among female students, see Feather & Simon 1975). As we saw in chapter 3, inter-group relations, on a minority side, particularly at the early stages of social change, are sometimes characterised by self-effacement. Only later, once group consciousness has been raised, does that excess of modesty transform itself into group pride, or even self-servingness. In this way, political context determines inter-group attributions. The wider point to Hewstone and Ward's study, however, is that no attribution bias is ever completely 'universal', either across all cultures or across all contexts.

The major cognitive biases, across inter-individual and inter-group relations, are summarised for conceptual and revision purposes in table 6.2.

Table 6.2   A summary of major inter-individual and inter-group attribution biases

INTER-INDIVIDUAL BIAS	INTER-GROUP EQUIVALENT
Fundamental attribution error	Group attribution error
Actor–observer difference	TheoryY/Theory X
Self-servingness	Ultimate attribution error
Self-effacement	Group effacement

COGNITIVE HEURISTICS

Heuristics are 'rules of thumb' that allow us to take shortcuts in our everyday decision making, often with effective results. Most of us will have been taught, for instance, the arithmetic heuristic, 'when dividing by ten, simply move the decimal point one place to the left'. This arithmetic (and cognitive) heuristic allows us to circumvent the relatively agonising process (for many of us at least!) of long division. In fact, it usually works so well that we use it habitually. *Social* **cognitive heuristics** are in principle no different from this pattern functionally. They are simply mental shortcuts that we habitually take when attempting to make decisions about our social worlds. They differ from major social cognitive biases, such as the fundamental and ultimate attribution errors, which arise out of more elaborate psychological processes (involving, as we have seen, perception, background knowledge and social values, and needs for social identity, social categorisation and inter-group comparison). The comparative superficiality of heuristics' 'psychological pedigree' does not mean, however, that they are insignificant. They, too, can have drastic influences on our decision making. This is especially so in a world in which speed is at a premium.

Discounting

One of the best illustrations of our need to stay mindful of the influence of these mental shortcuts is the so-called **discounting heuristic**. Formally, this principle states that 'The role of a given cause in producing a given effect is discounted if other plausible causes are present' (Kelley 1971, p. 8). More informally and colloquially, this simply means that observers habitually tend to seize on the most obvious, and frequently visually prominent, explanation for others' behaviour, while less obvious (but genuine) causes of the behaviour are short-sightedly overlooked. Thus, the discounting heuristic is a 'quick fix'. In essence, it suggests, 'Look for the most obvious attribution, and discount the rest'.

Perhaps the clearest example of this rule of thumb can be found in the workplace. Sites of paid labour contain a ready-made, painfully obvious cause for workers to be there — pay. Managers are a group likely to grasp this cause when attributing workplace behaviour (McGregor 1960). However, as the lottery research above indicates, Theory X is often wrong, or at least oversimplified. Money undoubtedly matters, and some workers certainly work 'for the money', especially when their job is inherently unfulfilling. Some workers, like some of their manager counterparts, are undoubtedly lazy. But *most* workers are interested in more than money alone (Winefield et al. 2000). So it is unfortunate that over-attributing workplace motivation to money alone, and simply discounting other concerns, is still evident in the organisational behaviour of some managers today (Robbins et al. 2000; see critical narrative 6.4). Such discounting of staff aspirations and potential achievement is, of course, a form of push-down. This kind of force, we know from chapters 3 and 5, will eventually depress workplace performance, both human and organisational (Livingston 1988).

How does this particular negative Pygmalion effect operate? To answer that question, we again need some help from systems thinking. In figure 6.2, managers' discounting heuristic ('workers work only for the money') has combined with group stereotyping and attribution errors ('they're all lazy') to produce a 'theory' that workers need to be controlled by means of carrot and stick. This is an example of social cognition fuelling push-down rather than pull-up (see chapter 3). These attributions and attitudes, even when managers attempt to hide them, will soon 'leak out' to workers (Robbins et al. 2000). Workers will then react to their managers' perceived downward-looking, 'parent-to-child' positioning. The workers will label their managers as 'pushy' and 'overbearing'; they will then attempt to reassert their social identity, and a sense of social equity, by resistance and withdrawal. To the managers, this resistance merely confirms their initial stereotype of workers as 'lazy', 'surly' and 'ornery'. And so the cycle is set to escalate, as each group progressively conforms to the other's stereotype of it. This vicious circle leads to increases in inter-group tension and the possibility of industrial relations standoffs. In the long run, therefore, as a result of these discrepant and mutually reinforcing negative attributions, a doubly negative Pygmalion effect takes place.

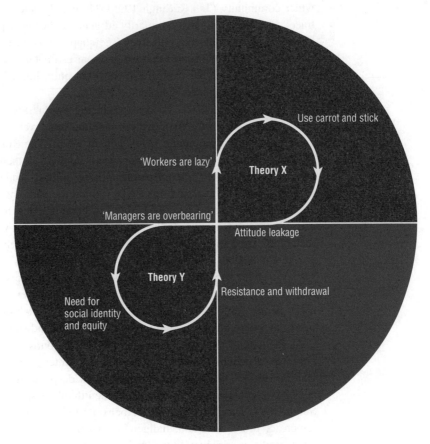

Figure 6.2   Differing attributions interact to produce double Pygmalion effects in the workplace

How can such vicious circles be prevented from escalating? The first clue to this mystery is contained in critical narrative 6.4 — our old friend *communication*. If managers and workers had communicated their different views beforehand, the escalation depicted in figure 6.2 might never have occurred. How, then, can this communication be facilitated? A clue is contained in figure 6.2. *Knowing* about influence processes like those depicted in figure 6.2 may be one way of preventing or at least reducing them in the first place (Senge 1992). Whether such knowledge actually *does* transform organisational behaviour is a question that urgently needs answering by organisational researchers. What we can say now, however, is that discounting does have real-world applications, and that learning to manage its effects is often critical to both quality of working life and organisational performance.

Availability

In the paid workplace, money is ever salient, and in that sense heuristics such as discounting do not involve memory. At other times, however, we must rely on memory to make attributions about others. When this happens, the **availability heuristic** is a rule of thumb — we 'use whatever information springs most readily to mind' (Tversky & Kahneman 1973). A telling example of this is the tendency for people to overestimate the extent to which their own opinions are shared in the wider community (Tan & Singh 1995). Ultimately, such misconceptions can be traced to the principle that 'similarity attracts', and a subsequent tendency to build relations with people like ourselves (see chapter 8). Once we have done so, the availability heuristic ensures that we base our estimates of community opinion on what we can remember from our own, often quite limited circle of like-minded friends and acquaintances (Nickerson 1999).

Crowds are particularly good at producing availability errors, for example by impressing leaders, who then overestimate the true level of support for their policies in the wider community (Moghaddam 1998). The Romans had a politically expedient remedy for this tendency when applied to their victorious returning generals. During their victory parades, these military leaders were accompanied by a companion who would repeatedly remind the parading hero that he was only human and not a god (Cox 1995). This was good practice, because victory parades and crowd events are generally *vivid*; we now know that vivid events are highly memorable, and so *available* for recollection (Slovic, Fisch & Lichenstein 1982). To the extent that many other, relatively common events are also vivid and dramatic (crime stories, personal traumas, stories of disasters and economic crisis), they too will exert disproportionate influences on our everyday decision making about people, events and places. In this way, the availability heuristic renders us overly averse to otherwise quite innocuous groups and situations.

As the natural vividness of crowds and other groups attests, availability heuristics are particularly likely to take effect in inter-group settings (Rothman & Hardin 1997). This may partly explain a widespread tendency to overestimate negative characteristics in relatively identifiable social groups (McKnight & Sutton 1994; Dasgupta, Banaji & Abelson 1999). For example, whether in rural, remote or urban Australia, Indigenous groups are sometimes stereotyped in the local media as drunks, 'itinerants' and 'long-grassers'. Yet carefully gathered empirical evidence points directly in the opposite direction. A clear majority of the Indigenous population, in contrast to non-Indigenous Australians, are alcohol abstainers (Gray & Sputore 1998; for a wider perspective, Marsella 2002). Unless countered by reliable and valid social research, the availability heuristic, through media sensationalism and political manipulation, is capable of fuelling inter-group prejudice and discrimination (Dorward 1996; Harper, in press).

Negativity

In many ways, media sensationalism also exploits what is termed the **negativity heuristic** (Kanouse & Hansen 1971). This negativity rule of thumb, which dictates that you 'give more weight to negative than positive information' (Skowronski & Carlston 1989), is another instance of the negativity bias discussed in previous chapters. A dramatic illustration of the negativity bias at work in applied settings, where attributions clearly matter, is in marketing relations — say, between industrial and service organisations and their consumer groups. As marketing consultants and professors will readily point out, one piece of negative information about a product or service influences a consumer more than one, two or even three items of positive information (Mowen 1993, p. 551). Similarly, while clients may recommend a product or service to eight other people, dissatisfaction may be communicated to 22 people or more (Darlin 1985).

The negativity heuristic makes sense, because it is relatively adaptive to be on the lookout for, and if necessary avoid, negative (and potentially dangerous) events and situations (see chapter 5). In the tropics, for instance, doctors may treat every patient with a temperature as a case of malaria. Occasionally, however, this assumption backfires on both parties, for example when the medication is wrong, the patient develops complications and the doctor is sued! Making judgements and decisions about others is sometimes no different, because too much attention given to the 'negative' fuels the various attribution errors: As we have seen through the preceding critical narratives in this chapter, often entire groups — on both sides — lose out in this trade-off. Their loss is defined in terms of social capital such as negative stereotyping and inter-group conflict.

COGNITIVE ALGORITHMS

One alternative to relying on heuristics is to use algorithms. The opposite of heuristics, algorithms are methodical blueprints, with a set sequence of procedures, for problem solving. Crossword devotees sometimes solve anagrams by writing out all the possible sequences of letters until — inevitably — they discover the word that fits. By doing this, they are using a cognitive algorithm. In social settings, it may be useful to think of cognitive algorithms as mini psychology experiments. As we saw in chapter 1, the essence of conducting experiments is checking whether variations in an independent variable produce corresponding variations in a dependent variable. If these two variables do indeed show **co-variation**, we may conclude that one *causes* the other.

Co-variation: an organising concept

This logic has been extended to the everyday social psychologist in us, as if to say, 'We are all scientists in the way we think about one another' (Kelley 1972). According to Kelley, and many others since, observers frequently ask themselves about co-variation as they attempt to work out whether the behaviours they observe in others are caused by dispositions or situations. This core task means looking for signs of what, precisely, co-varies most closely with the behaviour of interest. According to the literature, we can look for this information in several domains.

Consensus

In everyday social life, one form of such co-variation, as discussed by Kelley, is the extent to which a group of individuals, who presumably have very different dispositions from one another, exhibit the same behaviour. If one student performs badly, that says something about the student (dispositional attribution). If all students perform badly, that probably says something more about the instructor (situational attribution). Thus, the greater the consensus with individuals in the same class, the less likely it is, logically, that this particular student is simply lazy or incompetent.

Consistency, stability, distinctiveness

Kelley and a number of other social psychologists (from Heider 1958 to Weiner 1995) have discussed the importance of knowing how the individual or group to be explained has behaved in similar circumstances in the past. The more consistent and stable their behaviour on similar occasions across time, the more likely it is, logically, that this behaviour is based on some kind of dispositional factor. The more distinctive it is across different occasions, the more likely it is governed by the situation. Thus, if a student shows a history of failing units, as opposed to failing just one of them, then the chances are that the student is doing something wrong (dispositional attribution) rather than the instructor (situational attribution).

Controllability

Even then, according to Weiner, it can be useful to know whether the disposition in question is controllable or not. If there is any degree of free *choice*, then the person in question is largely *responsible* for his or her actions, and can be held accountable for them. A student who fails because of laziness (choice, controllable) should receive very different counselling from one who fails through a life crisis that is no fault of his or her own (no choice, uncontrollable). Looking again at critical narratives 6.1 and 6.2, whether the actions of Grant or street kids in Venezuela are attributed to the socio-economic environment (uncontrollable) or to laziness (controllable) largely determines our attitudes towards these people and their living conditions.

Critical appraisal of the co-variation approach

Kelley and Weiner's point is that searching first for empirical evidence of consensus (co-variation across people), stability (co-variation across time) and controllability (co-variation with choice) will help make those decisions more objective and fair. As the above examples make clear, there is no dispute that using cognitive algorithms, much in the manner of a methodical 'scientist', can in principle help us to think and act more objectively and fairly about others. Each of these co-variation principles — consensus, stability and controllability — has also generally been supported by research.

However, participants in this research — mostly US university psychology students — have hardly been typical of wider populations (Sears 1986; see also Kraus 1995). As one concerned group of writers put it, 'Yes, research shows that research participants who are instructed to make attributions for various events do, in general, follow the logic of covariation' (Brehm, Kassin & Fein 1999, p. 103). Yet a careful reading of this last sentence suggests that these authors doubt whether the algorithmic method is really used in everyday life. Put simply, people may not have the time, inclination or cognitive resources to experiment for co-variation. The algorithmic approach may thus lack external validity, particularly in the relatively frenetic modern world.

Still, such a criticism may be a little unfair. Brehm et al.'s critique concerns whether co-variation algorithms adequately *describe* social cognition. But there is another dimension to the algorithmic model, namely its *pre*scriptive utility. Can people (other than experienced psychology students) be taught to use, or at least improve their use of, the formal logic of co-variation in everyday life? This is a question that will have to be answered more fully by new research before we can fairly assess the co-variation paradigm. Until that time, the best approach for reducing biases may be to learn to recognise they are there — that is, to become more mindful of them (Gergen 1994b).

One of the best ways of learning about attribution biases and associated heuristics is to 'think them through' in the context of a real, applied issue. It is to this practical, experiential task we now turn.

A LIVING CASE: POVERTY

The statistics on world poverty are almost unbelievable. Perhaps the best place to access them is the World Bank's website (www.worldbank.org). There the reader will find downloadable documents detailing statistics and, increasingly, behavioural data about what is possibly the greatest scourge of the twenty-first century. For example, the World Development Report for 2000/1 titled *Attacking Poverty* documents how, in this time of unprecedented wealth for many, 2.8 billion people, or about half the world's population, live on less than US$2 a day. Of these 2.8 billion people, 1.2 billion live on the very edges of existence, attempting to survive on less than US$1 a day. Across countries in the 'global community', the average income in the richest 20 countries is 37 times the average in the poorest 20, and this gap has doubled in the past 40 years. So, while the economic benefits of global free trade may 'trickle down' to some people in need (Richburg 1997), many thousands still die of starvation every day, and the relative gap between the rich and the poor is continuing to widen (see also Heredia 1997).

The social dimensions of poverty

As this gap suggests, much of the world's poverty is experienced in a comparative way, as *relative* deprivation compared with others. For example, more than 50 per cent of the world's population live, cheek-by-jowl, in mega-cities and urban sprawls that contain both shanty-towns and urban elites (Marsella 1998). Urbanisation and urban migration are bringing deprived and privileged groups into closer proximity to each other, creating new levels of social tension and potential conflict (Carr 2000). Their comparative poverty is also brought home to the poor through images of affluence and entitlement propagated by the global media (Moreira, in press). Such 'in your face' social injustice is not confined to 'developing' countries. The reality of the global community is that poverty is everywhere, even in the so-called developed economies (Sen 2000). In the United States, for example, the American Psychological Association has recently declared the need for psychology to address pockets of acute poverty within US borders (http://apa.org/pi/urban/povres.html). Added to domestic poverty is the common experience of economic crisis, which also knows no borders. For instance, the World Bank (1999) estimated that up to 200 million people worldwide had been thrown into abject poverty during the recent global financial crises. Such crises are expected to continue well into this century, and to raise the number of people living in abject poverty to more than 1.5 billion (Kato 2000).

A truly global issue

What these statistics and trends show is that poverty is a hugely significant global social psychological issue for the twenty-first century. If social psychology is to make any kind of difference in the world, then there could not be a more urgent cause. One area of social psychology that could in principle prove especially valuable is attribution theory. A recent study in Hong Kong, for instance, compared the power of a range of variables to predict donations towards international relief organisations (Cheung & Chan 2000). Demographic variables such as age and gender were found not to be influential in predicting these intentions, but social psychological factors were. These factors ranged from previous pro-social behaviour to *attributions for poverty* . Specifically, attributions that were dispositional rather than situational, blaming poverty on the poor rather than structural causes, were associated with negative intentions to make a charitable donation. Similar findings have been made in the United States, Canada and Australia in regard to domestic welfare (Zucker & Weiner 1993), international aid (Kelley 1989) and anti-poverty activism (Hine & Montiel 1999). Collectively, these research studies suggest a key to encouraging humanitarian assistance and, more important in the long run perhaps, tolerance from donor publics. This key is to foster situational attributions to help counterbalance the kinds of attribution biases depicted in table 6.2. Some graphic examples of these errors, in the context of attributions for poverty, are vividly (familiarly perhaps) embodied in critical narrative 6.5.

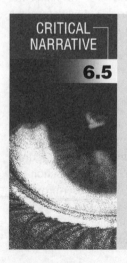

CRITICAL NARRATIVE

6.5

Voices of 'the donor'

'From what I can see in developing countries, people don't seem to be able to cope with their problems. They are always weak, hungry, fighting among themselves and seem particularly prone to natural disasters. They are constantly asking for help from other countries — food, money and, of course, the expertise that has made our countries so successful. I don't see why their own governments don't do something about it, but they all seem corrupt and don't have the same attitudes towards supporting the people as our governments do. Despite our generosity as individuals — and that of our governments — nothing seems to be changing that much. They just don't seem to be able to get their act together. Giving money to the Third World is like throwing it into a black hole.'

Source: INRA (1992, reported from UNICEF by Godwin 1994, p. 46).

According to Godwin (1994, p. 46), the donor complaints portrayed in critical narrative 6.5 represent a 'conglomerate' of what emerged out of a study commissioned by UNICEF (the United Nations International Children's Emergency Fund) for Western European youth in the early 1990s. Godwin argues that the media must bear much of the responsibility for these negative views. Among these media, she includes not only television news and documentaries, but also *humanitarian fund-raising advertisements themselves* (p. 47). This is a view shared in UNICEF's own publications (Fountain 1995, p. 82; for similar concerns raised about charitable advertising domestically, see Eayrs & Ellis 1990). The rest of this chapter applies attribution theory to explain why this shocking conclusion is wholly predictable from attribution theory, given the way that fund-raising advertisements are currently constructed, and how they interact with the biases summarised in table 6.2. This kind of confluence we can term **donor bias**. Our analysis will not be overly negative, however. Based on a psychosocial analysis of poverty, we will proceed to 'accentuate the positive' by suggesting ways to make fund-raising both (a) more effective (in terms of dollar donations) and (b) less divisive (in terms of social capital).

(a) Dollar donations

Raising charitable funds in order to 'throw money at the problem' is not necessarily the best solution to global poverty (Fountain 1995). The structural causes of poverty remain, and 'charity' itself can undermine the confidence and self-respect on which development out of poverty relies. However, charitable donations can still contribute towards emergency relief projects or band-aid solutions (O'Gorman 1992). In the short term, designing advertisements and images that raise more money for these kinds of development assistance projects is probably worthwhile (Downer 1997).

(b) Beyond band-aid solutions

Effective fund-raising advertisements are not just money-raisers, however. They should also raise consciousness and social capital over the longer term. A contribution that psychology can make — one that is ultimately more substantial than raising donations — has been identified in Mehyrar (1984). Mehyrar argues that poverty is a structural issue, but that psychology can still help indirectly to alleviate it by sensitising the wealthy (including politicians, market-makers and donors) to the realities of life in developing areas. This would include raising consciousness about situational contributors to poverty, such as natural disasters resulting from global climate change (Pawlik & d'Ydewalle 1996), government corruption and ineptitude (Lea 1998), and international exploitation by the financial money markets (Community Aid Abroad/Freedom From Hunger 1996/7). As argued in chapter 1, such elevations of consciousness, and rejection of negative influences on our attitudes and behaviour towards others, are a core feature of social psychology.

So what does attribution theory have to say about contemporary fund-raising practices?

Fund-raising practices: a fundamental attribution error

This chapter has suggested that members of the donor public, especially in relatively individualised, Westernised societies, are inclined to make dispositional attributions to explain poverty (Choi, Nisbett & Norenzayan 1999). For example, poverty might be attributed to laziness, to having too many children or to a failure to make any attempts at self-improvement (for more illustrations, review critical narratives 6.2 to 6.5; for a recent review, see Lott 2002). In fact, if we briefly revisit some of the known *causes* of the fundamental attribution error, we can see how many fund-raising advertisements probably actually *pander* to it.

Perceptual salience

Dispositional bias is partly fed by the fact that viewers are intrinsically designed (have evolved) to look at the human form and human behaviour, rather than 'less interesting' features of the environment and general situation. This is illustrated beautifully for us in Dali's *The Three Ages*, a detail of which is schematised in figure 6.1. Humanitarian fund-raising advertisements highlight the human form, and in particular the human face, in their efforts to elicit guilt and sympathy (Fountain 1995; Godwin 1994; Harper, in press). In this way, however, they fuel dispositional attributions.

Lack of background knowledge

Dispositional bias is also increased because we lack proper background knowledge of the lives of the people we are trying to explain. Most media audiences could not be further removed from the situational realities of poverty itself, including such situational causes as natural disasters, government corruption and international financial exploitation. Yet, because most humanitarian advertisements focus on the human face, they do little, if anything, to educate viewers of the image about their own acute (and partly unavoidable) state of ignorance. They therefore compound their consumers' existing lack of background knowledge.

Cultural socialisation

The fundamental attribution error is partly caused by individualism. Many fund-raising advertisement viewers reside in relatively Western, individualist societies. In other cases, economic development (and increased capacity to become donors) is often followed by rises in individualism (Hofstede & Bond 1988; Marshall 1997). Globalisation, too, may be fostering an increase in individualistic values, and to that extent more fundamental attribution errors. Humanitarian fund-raising advertisements are playing to this groundswell of individualism. They tend to focus on the individual, not just visually, but verbally as well. They often name the person featured in the image, for example. Thus, these advertisements may be reinforcing pre-existing individualistic predilections, and to that extent fuelling donor bias.

   This could be happening even in staunchly collectivist communities. Choi et al. (1999) identified specific conditions under which people from such societies will most readily display fundamental attribution errors. Principally, this will happen if situational cues, to which collectivist audiences are normally sensitive, are deliberately taken out of the scenario being judged. Unfortunately, this is often precisely what humanitarian advertisements do. They rely on the 'hard and fast sell' of showing human beings in their suffering, and virtually nothing else. Such tactics, according to Choi et al.'s research review, are reinforcing a fundamental attribution error even in relatively collectivist audiences and collectivist segments of multicultural audiences in societies like Australia and New Zealand.

The actor–observer difference

The actor–observer difference reminds us that the fundamental attribution error — and donor bias — resides mainly in the observer, and that actors' attributions may be more objective by comparison. In the case of poverty and fund-raising advertisements, television viewers are like observers, while the role of actors is most clearly assumed by the poor themselves. According to the theory of actor–observer differences, these actors should make more situational attributions than observers and less of a fundamental attribution error. If that is so, then actors' perspectives on the causes of poverty could be used to help counterbalance donor bias. This could be approached perhaps using media technology and techniques much as in Storms' reversal (see p. 207). Empowering actors to present situational attributions for poverty during fund-raising advertisements would also maintain a human touch, which research suggests is still necessary in successful donation appeals (Thornton, Kircher & Jacobs 1991).

Consistency with development studies

This idea of presenting actors' perspectives on poverty in their own voices to potential donor observers, as a way of motivating the latter to become more understanding, is broadly consistent with current trends in development studies. For instance, the World Bank Group's report *Attacking Poverty* (see p. 219) was based on a study titled *Voices of the Poor* (Narayan et al. 2000a; Narayan et al. 2000b). This study contained interviews with some 60 000 people from 60 countries, in which they were encouraged to describe in their own words what it is like to be poor. These words can be read and heard on the World Bank's own website (www.worldbank.org). One purpose of these studies, however, is to illuminate the social dimensions to poverty (for another recent example, see Lott & Bullock 2001). Moreover, they implicitly rely on these illuminations to prompt something like a Storms' reversal, so that a listener becomes more appreciative, and less dismissive, of what it is like to be poor (see also Sen 2000).

So, returning to aid advertisements, *are* the poor indeed more 'situational' in their attributions for poverty, compared with their wealthier observer counterparts? And *are* these observers, in turn, more 'dispositional' than their actor counterparts? If not, our line of thinking would seem to be fundamentally wrong.

Most attribution research on poverty has had a domestic focus, perhaps reflecting the adage that 'charity begins at home'. These studies have concentrated on examining how dispositional and situational attributions co-vary with demographic features of the attributor, such as level of education, level of income and ethnic identity. Such features are good indicators of how closely the attributors will have experienced poverty. People with low education and income, and minority ethnic status, have probably had a harder life, and are more likely to have experienced poverty directly. To that extent, they resemble actors. Conversely, those attributors with higher levels of income and education, and majority ethnic status, have probably had an easier life and are less likely to have known poverty directly. To that extent, they are more akin to observers. Thus, actors and observers are represented in the research, and it is fitting to ask for evidence that the observers among them are more dispositional in their attributions for poverty.

The original research on this question was conducted in the United States (Feagin 1972) and Australia (Feather 1974). These early studies examined attributions such as lack of thrift, effort, ability and talent, and loose morals (dispositional attributions), as well as low wages, prejudice within the system and bad luck (situational attributions). A pattern can be detected in these early findings — a pattern that repeatedly asserts itself in subsequent research over a wide diversity of settings (e.g. Commission of the European Communities 1977; Furnham 1982a, 1982b; Lamarche & Tougas 1979; Townsend 1979; Singh & Vasudeva 1977). Attributors who were more educated, who earned higher incomes and who identified themselves with a majority ethnic group tended to make relatively dispositional attributions, compared with their less well educated, lower income, ethnic minority counterparts, whose attribution preferences inclined to the situational (for a recent example of this difference, see Abouchedid & Nasser 2001). Thus, in line with actor–observer theory, observers were more likely than actors to blame poverty on dispositions in the poor themselves. Actors (in this case the poor), in turn, were more likely than their observer counterparts to use situational attributions (for a discussion of similar actor–observer differences in attributions for Indigenous Australians' mental health, see Reser 1991).

What about an international context? Some research has been conducted on Western donor publics' attributions for poverty in the Third World. The instrument used in this research was adapted from the literature on domestic poverty, and is presented in figure 6.3. In this figure, the scale contains a dispositional factor (blame the poor) as well as two situational factors (blame nature; blame international exploitation), and what might be described as a 'quasi-dispositional' (part-dispositional, part-situational) factor (blame governments).

In one study using this scale, attributions for Third World poverty were made by people in Australia (observers), as well as by people in Malaŵi, in East Africa (Campbell, Carr & MacLachlan 2001). Malaŵi is an acutely poor country, rendering the Malaŵian respondents akin to actors. Between these two samples, and as predicted by attribution theory, the Australian respondents were, on average, more likely to 'blame the poor'. Furthermore, again as predicted by attribution theory, those Australians who gave money to international aid were less likely to 'blame the poor' (for a similar point on anti-poverty activism, see Hine & Montiel 1999). The available research thereby provides evidence of (a) an actor–observer difference in attributions for international poverty, and (b) a link between these attributions and donation/anti-poverty behaviour. Of course, it also implies that actor perspectives (inherently more situational) can be used to help *sensitise* observers to a more situational, structural understanding (Lott 2002).

There is poverty in Third World countries because…

1. The people of such countries keep having too many children (*Blame the poor*)

2. Of fate (*Blame nature*)

3. Their governments are corrupt (*Blame governments*)

4. Of the regional climate (*Blame nature*)

5. Their governments are inefficient (*Blame government*)

6. Of laziness and a lack of effort in the populations of such countries (*Blame the poor*)

7. Their land is not suitable for agriculture (*Blame nature*)

8. Other countries exploit the Third Word (*Blame international exploitation*)

9. Of disease in Third World countries (*Blame nature*)

10. Their governments spend too much money on arms (*Blame governments*)

11. Of war (*Blame governments*)

12. Of the world economy and banking system being loaded against the poor (*Blame international exploitation*)

13. Pests and insects destroy crops (*Blame nature*)

14. The population of such countries make no attempts at self-improvement (*Blame the poor*)

15. Of lack of intelligence amongst the people there (*Blame the poor*)

16. Of lack of thrift and proper management of resources by the people there (*Blame the poor*)

17. The people there are not willing to change old ways and customs (*Blame the poor*)

18. Of a lack of ability and talent among the people of such countries (*Blame the poor*).

Note: Items are scaled as follows:
Strongly Disagree–Disagree–Don't Know–Agree–Strongly Agree.

Figure 6.3   Causes of Third World poverty questionnaire   ***Source:*** Extracted from Harper (1996).

Self-serving and modesty biases

When viewers watch a fund-raising advertisement that highlights the 'plight' of a poor person, they are likely to be explicitly reminded that they are economically 'better off' than that individual — compared with him or her, they are economically 'successful' (critical narrative 6.5). Fund-raising advertisements deliberately make this comparison in order to induce guilt in the viewer. But the same tactic may also invoke, and reinforce, a self-serving bias. According to our review of this largely individualist bias, some viewers of fund-raising advertisements will take the credit for their own comparative success. Implied in taking such credit

('I get what I deserve'), in the context of fund-raising advertisements, is a dispositional derogation of the individual who is poor ('You must be lazy'). This kind of attribution is fuelled by 'belief in a just world' (Lerner 1980). In a world that is just (and ordered and meaningful), everyone gets their just deserts. Thus, if you are poor, you probably deserve to be (Harper et al. 1990).

On the other side of the advertisement, many of the poor themselves will be relatively collectivist (Marsella 2000). As we have seen in our review of cultural differences in self-servingness, collectivist values are likely to be associated with a bias towards modesty. This bias means that personal failures are not simply 'palmed off' on situational causes. Instead, collectivists are more likely to take personal responsibility for their own life conditions. As actors in poverty, and in poverty-reduction advertisements, their attributions for that poverty are relatively unlikely to be driven by ego protection. To that extent, their attributions would continue to provide a 'reality check' for outside observers.

Inter-group relations

So far, our application of attribution theory to poverty has focused on cognitive biases that are primarily inter-individual in nature. Yet fund-raising advertisements frequently highlight a number of group identifiers — economic, ethnic, national and geographic. As we learned earlier, any one of these identifiers is sufficient in itself to invoke a sense of social identity (Dasgutpa, Banaji & Abelson 1999). They will therefore make social identity as salient as, or indeed more salient than, individual identity. This identity might then trigger any one of the inter-group biases reviewed in the chapter.

Out-group homogeneity, work ethic illusions and other attribution errors

Earlier in our review, we pointed out how out-group homogeneity effects render groups of people into a single unit. Once this homogeneity is concocted, the full range of dispositional inter-individual biases, for the same psychological reasons that they apply to individuals, may start to apply to groups. Critical narrative 6.5, which captures some of the research findings of UNICEF in this domain, clearly shows that homogeneity effects ('They're all the same') do happen when attributing poverty. The same narrative also shows that once this attribution has been made, others readily follow. These include a work ethic illusion ('They're lazy') and an ultimate attribution error ('They've only themselves to blame for their failure'). In each of these types of attributions, the viewing audience, as a psychological group of observers of actors in poverty, blames 'the poor'. To that extent, according to the evidence, donations will be withheld and social capital will be diminished ('I'm glad we're not like *them*!').

To what extent are groups of *actors* liable to be any *better* as sources of information about the situational causes of poverty? As we saw earlier, disadvantaged groups like the poor are relatively unlikely to attribute failures egotistically (i.e. to simply 'palm them off' on their situation). Instead, the group effacement bias means that disadvantaged groups, when attributing relative failure, will tend towards modesty. Once again, it seems, actor perspectives are unlikely to be ego-inflated and will continue to possess relative veracity.

To sum up the argument so far, each of the major attribution biases identified in a review of the literature points towards the same conclusion. There is a clear and ever-present risk, in any appeal that relies heavily on an image of misery *personified*, of encouraging donor bias. This influence may be sufficiently strong to counteract any sympathy that such images evoke. By thinking anew about fund-raising advertisements designed by humanitarian agencies, a disquieting implication emerges: they might actually be fuelling a donor bias. This surprising conclusion, which converges with and fleshes out the UNICEF findings, becomes even more compelling once we consider the influence of cognitive heuristics.

Discounting

The core feature of the discounting heuristic is that observers frequently seize on the most visible cause of the behaviour or state in question, and prematurely discount the rest. Poverty reduction advertisements generally present a human face in order to evoke sympathy and empathy. Yet by doing this they are playing to the discounting principle by deliberately obscuring many of the less visible but important situational causes of poverty in order to secure a 'hit' on the viewer's emotions. These omitted situational factors include, from the scale items listed in figure 6.3, global climate change, government corruption and international exploitation. If anything, then, a discounting principle, in the context of pathetic (but deliberately *grabbing*) human imagery, would work to reinforce donor bias.

Availability

The availability heuristic essentially persuades observers to over-rely on what they can most easily recall from their memory, which in turn has often been overly impressed by vivid and dramatic events and images. Availability is also enhanced when the stimulus person visibly belongs to an out-group (Rothman & Hardin 1997). It is therefore unfortunate that, as well as the stimulus person being identified as 'out-group' in several respects, most of the imagery conveyed in fund-raising messages about 'the poor', whether conveyed through news or through aid advertisement imagery, is sensationalised (Godwin 1994). As one social psychologist recently reported, the makers of aid advertisements will deliberately seek out the most dramatic and negative image they can (Harper, in press). A sobering contrast to this awful media sensationalism is provided in critical narrative 6.6, which was written by a highly experienced development consultant who has lived and worked for many years in the country he is talking about.

Negativity

Critical narrative 6.6 criticises the fact that media images from poverty-affected areas emphasise only negative information (poverty, suffering, disease, deprivation and more). Our review of the negativity heuristic revealed that it is normally adaptive to give weight to, and communicate with others about, negative information, especially when out-groups are involved. Fund-raising images, however, present an *abnormally* high level of negativity. These severe distortions, as critical narrative 6.6 suggests, may simply amplify and spread a message that the poor are a hapless and hopeless out-group, and to that extent a waste of good money and precious resources. Moreover, a steady stream of negative images of the poor, which is what we often see on television, also runs the risk of creating an impression of co-variation between the events ('negative information') and 'the poor'.

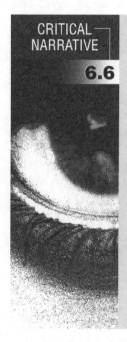

CRITICAL NARRATIVE

6.6

The distortion in media images of poverty: more of an actor's perspective

'These children have been born into a country [Malaŵi] in which a quarter of them will die before the age of five and half of them will be dead before the age of twenty-one. In the winter they are cold, especially at night with no blanket. For several months before harvest each year they are hungry. If they are sick they receive inadequate medical treatment. They are barefoot and dressed in second-hand clothes bought for a few pence from a heap in the market. They have to help carry water, gather fire-wood, weed crops and care for animals from an early age. To many in the West, this would seem to be a guaranteed formula for an unhappy childhood. The reality is quite different, as demonstrated by the children who laugh, sing and dance around me every day.

'I am saddened that the thousands of small points of light across Africa are never allowed to shine through the gloom of international reporting on the continent.'

Source: Extracted from personal correspondence sent from Zomba, Malaŵi (November 1999, November 2000).

Co-variation

In terms of *consensus*, this steady stream of negative information implies that many other donors, too, have decided not to help (see chapter 2, on pluralistic ignorance). Consensus events like this are normally attributed to the stimuli ('the poor'). Also, the continuity of images of the pathetic and listless poor will, in time, create impressions of *stability*, and thereby again encourage dispositional attributions. And the frequently heard proposition that 'these people *can* be helped to help themselves' implies a certain amount of *controllability* on the part of the poor, yet again fostering dispositional attributions and donor bias. Thus, each aspect of co-variation warns of a potential for donor bias and for withholding of donations.

To sum up, once we 'think through' the very practical problem of raising funds for emergency poverty assistance, and doing so without encouraging socially divisive impressions that donating money is 'like throwing it into a black hole', the evidence points to one conclusion. Fund-raising groups may need to rethink some of their advertising tactics, to include more situational perspectives on the causes of poverty. Actors in poverty are uniquely well positioned to provide and identify these situational factors. The empowerment we are starting to hear of today in such studies as *Voices of the Poor* is long overdue, it seems, in the social marketing of aid.

Are feelings for children exempt from donor bias?

Against this rather damning conclusion, it could be objected that many charitable fund-raising images focus on children, who are relatively unlikely to be held responsible for anything, or indeed to be expected to fend for themselves. In co-variation terms, their poverty is not controllable. Moreover, this objection might continue, we have not even considered the motivational force of emotions, or social affect (see chapters 8 to 10). The essence of charitable petitions, after all, is an appeal to heady emotions like guilt, pity and empathy. According to this line of argument, humanitarian agencies *must* accentuate the emotional appeal in their messages by using children whom viewers will find hard to blame for their poverty. In this way, it is more likely that these advertisements will influence consumers of the image to give generously. As we can see from critical narrative 6.7, children do need to be highlighted somehow.

CRITICAL NARRATIVE 6.7

Child poverty in the Lucky Country

Australia ranks among the worst countries in the industrialised world for child poverty.

A survey by Belgian academics rates Australia in fifth place with 17.1 per cent of children living below the poverty line.

Russia came in with the worst record, with 26.6 per cent, ahead of the United States on 26.3, Britain with 21.3, and Italy with 21.2.

Canada ranked sixth with 16.0 per cent, ahead of Ireland (14.8), Israel (14.7), Poland (14.2), and Spain (13.1).

Each country in the study was given a child poverty rate based on the percentage of children aged under 18 living in a household with a disposable income less than 50 per cent of the median for the entire population of the country.

Source: Courtesy of the *Northern Territory News*, 24 February 2001, p. 11.

There are several weaknesses in this line of reasoning, however, each of which derives from considerations about context, both economic and social psychological.

Flaw 1

The economic context for humanitarian advertising today is a highly competitive global marketplace, in which the temptation to 'crank up the guilt' one more notch in the interests of gaining an edge in competing for the donor dollar is compelling (Harper, in press). Social psychologically, this creates a viewing context characterised by a steady stream of highly distressing images. Empirically, we know that the impact of images of children's suffering and deprivation is moderated by how 'in your face' their suffering is. As Thornton, Kirchner & Jacobs (1991) have found, relatively low-key approaches, such as passive countertop solicitations in shops, often work quite well. But more proactive tactics, such as showing a photograph of a needy child during doorstep appeals, risk backfiring (Isen & Noonberg 1979). As with highly emotional situations generally, such a backlash is probably due to emotional overload and a felt need to rationalise guilt by blaming the victim, or indeed dissociating oneself from others' suffering altogether (see, respectively, Lerner & Simmons 1966; MacLachlan 1993; Lott 2002).

Flaw 2

A related contextual argument against overusing distressing images of children is that, having disturbed viewers deeply, they are virtually obliged to promise easy solutions to complex problems, such as the familiar 'All it takes is a dollar a day'. As we learned in chapter 4, raising fears and then making concrete recommendations about how to solve them is a relatively effective technique for mass persuasion. However, we also know that over-promising and then under-delivering is frustrating and demotivating (see chapter 3; for a discussion of this in an aid context, see Carr, McAuliffe & MacLachlan 1998). Although child sponsorship advertisements do not explicitly promise to solve poverty, they do suggest that the problem is easily and readily fixable. Having created such expectations, the fact that the number of child sponsorship appeals never diminishes, and in fact seems to be increasing, is liable to fuel 'compassion fatigue' (Moeller 1999). As many of us know, the result of such compassion fatigue is that we change the channel (see Cohen 2001).

Flaw 3

A powerful illustration of the dangers of relying too much on emotion-arousing appeals is contained in a recent study reported in Griffiths (1999). In Western Europe, North America and Australia, some advertisements have taken the tactic of guilt-inducement to its competitive extreme. Images of poverty and deprivation are juxtaposed with images of relative privilege. For example, a child may be seen and heard playing happily in a clean and healthy sandpit, which will suddenly change into a filthy and hazardous rubbish tip on which the child is scratching out a miserable existence. Such juxtapositions disturb viewers' emotions. Griffiths' materials for her Australian study contained just such images, taken from actual international aid advertisements broadcast in Australia and beyond. Compared with more conventional, restrained images, this juxtapositioning shock tactic was effective, but only for a relatively religious minority in the sample (people who scored highly on a scale of religiosity). For most of the participants, juxtapositioning backfired. Not only were dollar donation intentions reduced, but the juxtaposed condition was the only group in which participants declined to make any donation at all (for another study related to this general concern, see Florian & Mikulincer 1998).

Affect infusion

There is some wider theoretical support for this kind of reaction. In his model of **'affect infusion'**, Forgas (1995) suggests that feelings and moods (such as those deliberately evoked in fund-raising appeals) *prime* attributions. Affect 'infuses' cognition with whatever emotion or mood we happen to be experiencing at the time. Thus, negative images (for example of child poverty, and including death and dying) could produce negative attributions (even about children). Being impelled into a negative mood can enhance the availability of negative information, and thereby negative stereotypes about out-groups (Forgas 1992a; Greenberg et al. 1994;

Schimel et al. 1999). According to Forgas, affect infusion is also most likely to influence cognitions when the behaviour or event being explained is relatively serious or important to us (such as child poverty and suffering). Affect infusion has the capacity to enhance fundamental attribution errors, for example when a person is led to feel 'superior' to others on some dimension (Forgas 1998). This response, as we have already seen, is arguably what such reminders of others' poverty partly evokes among observers. In sum, therefore, there is much in the affect infusion model to lead us to expect the kind of reactions obtained by Griffiths in her (1999) study.

One of the most interesting aspects of Forgas's model is a prediction that affect infusion is most likely to occur when an observer has time to *dwell* on the issue, rather than having to make an instant, on-the-spot judgement about it. In the case of fund-raising images that rely on generating a negative affect like guilt, the suggestion is that shorter advertisements will be more effective than longer ones. A 'natural laboratory' for addressing this prediction is the Internet. As we saw in chapter 4, websites are increasingly used by major aid agencies for e-advertising and social marketing purposes, although many of these sites still rely on the conventional negative image of the human being in misery — that is, they rely on generating negative affect. According to the affect infusion model, fund-raising websites run the risk of infusing attributions with negative affect — and to that extent, of putting donors off.

Alternatively, we could stress the fact that websites allow greater time for browsing and *contemplation* of the image, compared with a more ephemeral medium such as television. A logical consequence of this is a prediction that website technology, and the extra time it affords, can be productively used to convey the relatively abstract, situational causes of poverty that we have seen are so important for donation behaviour. Because websites operate at the user's own speed, they are also more empowering and less constraining than their more conventional media predecessors. Being less constraining, they may be less at risk of promoting defensive dissociation or backlashes of victim blaming (see part 1 of this book). On top of this, there seems to be a great deal of potential altruism out there on the Web, as indicated by the proliferation of emotional support forums and individually created websites designed to help people in some way or other (Wallace 1999). So, although the Internet is sometimes used for negative purposes, many users are attracted to it because of its pro-social potential. These people could, in theory, be mobilised by aid agencies seeking to secure more support for their anti-poverty projects. In sum, therefore, there are a number of reasons to suspect that web technology could be applied to reduce donor bias and increase donations, as well as raise social capital.

In a preliminary test of these competing suggestions, a series of mock aid agency websites were created (Fox & Carr 2000). These varied only in the amount of visual and textual information about the situational causes of poverty that accompanied the human image. What this study found was that the addition of situational information, both visual and textual, tended to incrementally augment situational attributions for poverty as well as dollar donation intentions to help combat it. It was beneficial to have the human image included alongside the appeal, but only if this image was given a contextual edge by relevant situational information. This preliminary but intriguing study, therefore, suggests how Internet technology might be used to counteract donor bias.

Such counteraction serves both financial and social developmental purposes. This could be just as true for traditional media channels, where we have seen that the poor themselves can be empowered to voice their side of the story. Other research, again on attribution, has been developing measures of the perceived causes of economic crisis, which we know will continue to have catastrophic effects on global society in the century to come (Aus–Thai Project Team 1998, in press). These measures, too, might eventually be used, by regional development agencies and potential business investors alike, to help sensitise and educate consumers of the image to a more situational view. The process of sensitising and educating observers to the actors' view, rather than desensitising and hardening them against it, is the theme that unifies this chapter. This is where attribution theory could make a social difference.

SUMMARY

People in the twenty-first century, as everyday social psychologists, are saddled with a range of attribution biases. Chief among these biases in individuals and groups is a tendency to give too much weight to dispositions, and to give too little attention to equally important situational factors. This tendency is often compounded by heuristics in which we discount less obvious causes of behaviour in the presence of more obvious ones, base our generalisations about others on memorable but limited information, and assign extra weight to negative events. All of these biases and heuristics come at a price. In the case of poverty alleviation, they conspire to suggest that humanitarian appeals for funds are fuelling a donor bias. Attribution theory and the Internet present unique opportunities for countering this bias, by assisting the more abstract but equally consequential situational causes of poverty to be communicated effectively across both culture and context.

KEY TERMS

Actor–observer difference. When observing the behaviour of other individuals, rather than attempting to explain our own behaviours as actors, we may tend to make a fundamental attribution error (see p. 233). (p. 206)

Affect infusion. The idea that attributions can be influenced by the infusion of emotions and moods. When in a happy (versus sad) mood, the same event (e.g. poverty) may be attributed positively (non-blaming, optimistic) rather than negatively (a 'blame the poor', pessimistic outlook). (p. 230)

Availability heuristic. A tendency to base one's judgements and attributions about the world, including the social world, on what immediately springs to mind (is most available) (p. 216)

Cognitive heuristics. Mental rules of thumb, or shortcuts, that people habitually employ when making decisions and attributions about others (p. 214)

Co-variation. Given the time, inclination and ability, some look for what features of their social environment systematically co-vary with the behaviour to be explained. For example, 'Are other individuals performing the same behaviour?' (if the answer is yes, then situational attribution). 'Has the person in question behaved like this before?' (if yes, then dispositional attribution). (p. 217)

Discounting heuristic. A tendency for observers to discount prematurely less immediately obvious causes of others' behaviour. Often, these causes are situational rather than dispositional. (p. 214)

Donor bias. The tendency for comparatively wealthy people, who are observers of poverty rather than actors in it, to over-attribute the causes of that poverty to dispositions in the poor themselves (p. 221)

Fundamental attribution error. A tendency for individuals observing other individuals to over-attribute their behaviour to personality traits rather than to equally influential situational factors (p. 203)

Group attribution error. A tendency to assume that group members' behaviours are a reflection of underlying dispositions common to all members of the group. This is a group-level version of the fundamental attribution error (above), while its foundation is the out-group homogeneity effect (below). (p. 210)

Group effacement bias. Group successes are attributed to luck and chance, while responsibility is accepted for group failures. This pattern, however, does not hold when the behaviour under scrutiny is performed by an out-group. (p. 213)

Negativity heuristic. A tendency to give too much weight to negative events. Although this behaviour can be adaptive, there are also times when it pays to 'accentuate the positive'. (p. 217)

Out-group homogeneity. A tendency for members of clearly defined groups to allow for more interpersonal diversity within their own group than within an identifiable out-group (p. 210)

Self-effacement bias. Also known as modesty bias. A tendency to take personal responsibility for failures, whereas successes are attributed to factors beyond the actor's control. In the case of temporary setbacks, modesty biases may enhance efforts to work oneself out of failure. (p. 209)

Self-serving bias. Among individuals, a tendency to over-attribute success to personal effort and other forms of disposition, while failures are blamed on situations beyond the actor's control. These attributions are 'self'-serving to the extent that each serves to protect the ego of the actor making the attributions. (p. 208)

'Ultimate' attribution error. A tendency for groups to attribute their own successes to dispositional qualities within the group, while their failures are blamed on situational forces beyond their control. When explaining the successes and failures of out-groups, however, the pattern reverses. (p. 212)

Work ethic illusion. A tendency for individuals and groups to underestimate the level of intrinsic, non-financial motivation that people have for working (p. 211)

REVIEW QUESTIONS

1. How 'fundamental' is the fundamental attribution error?

2. To what extent are actors less susceptible to the fundamental attribution error than observers? To help answer this question, begin by thinking of who is actor and who is observer across a range of everyday situations, for example in student–teacher relations, worker–manager relations, or relations between unsuccessful and successful achievers and groups in society.

3. How 'ultimate' is the ultimate attribution error?

4. Does switching individual with group identity make us any less or more susceptible to attribution errors?

DISCUSSION QUESTIONS

1. To what extent is psychology founded on a fundamental attribution error?
2. To what extent is social psychology an anathema to this bias?
3. To what extent are cross-cultural comparisons founded on an out-group homogeneity effect? Does the same apply to developmental psychology? To social psychology itself?
4. To what extent are cross-cultural comparisons founded on an ultimate attribution error?
5. To what extent would this book be pandering to an out-group homogeneity effect if it dwelt on 'Indigenous' as distinct from 'non-Indigenous' social psychology?
6. Because of space considerations, political perspectives on attribution theory are not covered in this chapter. Authors such as Adrian Furnham have written extensively on the interaction between political ideology and attributions about poverty. As a group, explore these potential linkages and disjunctions between the two domains. For example, how might a Liberal versus a Labor Party supporter, both of whom agree that poverty is a scourge, attribute causes of, and solutions to, poverty within society?

ACTIVITIES

1. An ethical attribution dilemma

A Senior Executive in an organisation notices some irregularities in the company's recent account statements. After a discussion of the matter with the Accounts Manager, the Senior Executive concludes that the Accounts Manager is not coping with the work as well as in the past. The Senior Executive tells the Accounts Manager that the situation has to improve substantially. Genuinely trying to be helpful, the Senior Executive suggests that the Accounts Manager might find it beneficial to 'have a talk' with the organisation's Psychologist.

The Accounts Manager takes this advice and seeks counselling from the Psychologist, who is employed in the Human Resources Section of the organisation. During counselling for the twin problems of alcoholism and marital instability, the Accounts Manager also reveals major personal financial problems and a previous conviction for embezzlement — of which he has not informed the organisation.

The Psychologist's statement of duties contains the following statements:
• Provide a counselling service to employees and their families.
• Provide a consultancy service to line management regarding employees with specific work and behavioural problems.

Source: Extracted from Pryor (1989).

(a) Read Pryor's (1989) article.
(b) Work out what the psychologist in the case study should do next. Before doing this, obtain the latest version of your respective national psychology society code of ethics from its website (see online resources).

(c) Read Bishop and D'Rozario (1990). Compare their solutions to the ethical dilemma above with your own from (a) and (b). What do you extract from this comparison? Do you see any parallels with the folk wisdom introduced in chapter 1 about 'walking a mile in another's moccasins'? Have you just experienced a 'rich point'?

2. **'The whole picture'**
   The materials for this exercise are supplied in figures 6.4(a) and 6.4(b). There are four alternative photos in Fountain (1995), if the class requires further stimuli. Each pair or group of students is given one copy of the photo showing a fragment or detail of a scene. Based on this detail, they construct a narrative on what they think the rest of the picture shows. The second photo includes the first but shows also the context in which it is set. The pair or group then writes a paragraph describing their reaction to the complete photo. The pairs or group then shares their insights with the rest of the students in a class session.

   Source: Adapted from Fountain (1995).

Figure 6.4(a)

Children in poverty

Figure 6.4(b) Children in context   *Source:* UNICEF HQ86-0222/Carolyn Watson.

This exercise is designed to illustrate how the cropping and selective use of images, removing their wider context, influences attributions about reality. It should also help to raise awareness of the importance of seeing 'the whole picture' before making any judgement about it.

3. Detecting biases

Apply the Critical Incident technique, as described in activity 1, with content analysis (see chapter 1) to describe both positive and negative critical incidents in the class's workplace experiences (see also Dunn 1989). Be sure to keep these incidents anonymous. Can you detect any self-serving or self-effacement biases, or other types of bias, in how types of attribution (dispositional and situational) are spread across the two types of incident — positive and negative?

4. The ultimate attribution error in team sports performance

The exercise:

In the week prior to the exercise, class members should collect newspaper reports containing attributions, made by team coaches and players, for both successful and unsuccessful performances (roughly half of each). These comments (attributions) are the raw data for this exercise, which takes place the following week.

The exercise itself tests for the presence of an ultimate attribution error. To do this, each of the attributions should be coded according to two dimensions: outcome (success or failure) and locus of causality (internal or external). An outcome should be coded as a 'success' if the attributor's team won the match, and as a 'failure' if the attributor's team lost the match. Locus of causality should be coded as 'internal' if the attribution refers to something good or bad about the attributor's team's ability or that of a team member. If the attribution refers to something good or bad about the ability of the opposition, either as a team or as a specific individual, or something about the circumstances (e.g. poor pitch condition, or unfair or incompetent refereeing), then it should be coded as 'external'.

The frequency tallies for each type of attribution should be entered into a contingency chart. An example of one of these is shown in figure 6.5. The chart should be clearly labelled as to outcome (success vs. failure) and locus of causality (internal vs. external attribution). If there are differences among coders, attempt to reconcile these within a reasonable set time limit (if working in small groups). If agreement cannot be reached within this time, discard the incident, or record both attributions in split-form across the relevant cells within the table.

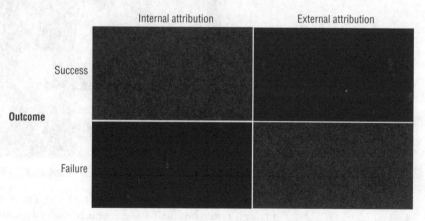

Figure 6.5   Suggested contingency chart for team performance attribution exercise

Source: Extracted and adapted from McIlveen (1992).

ADDITIONAL READING

For an overview of the state of the field in attribution, read Choi, Nisbett & Norenzayan (1999). This paper is particularly valuable because it cuts to the quick on the core issue in the field today, namely cultural relativity. This chapter has attempted to lock horns with that issue in an accessible way; the Choi et al. paper nicely complements this perspective.

For a wider perspective on social cognition, again placing it in cultural context, the interested student could read Nisbett et al. (2001), which deals with social cognition in general but has some sections on attribution theory in particular.

For an application of attribution theory to economic crisis, the Aus–Thai Project Team (in press) is a useful reading. This details how behavioural systems might work, and be managed, during times of economic turbulence.

For a classic developmental perspective on the acquisition of attribution biases, it is hard to go past Miller (1984).

For further reading on the topics discussed in this chapter, consult the online resources linked to the Wiley website (http://www.johnwiley.com.au/highered/socialpsych).

SKILLED ROUTINES

LEARNING OBJECTIVES

After reading this chapter, you should be able to:

- define the cognitive schema, which forms a psychological basis for social shortcuts like stereotyping and social skills like people management
- outline the kinds of context skills that managers of people can incorporate into their schema for leadership
- describe a series of critical life skills in communication, both verbal (listening, talking) and non-verbal (people watching, perspective taking)
- review key methods for learning about culture in preparation for international assignments and working with multicultural client bases.

OVERVIEW

Skills are routines — from judging others to interacting with them — that are so well practised that they have become internalised into a mental program, or schema, for enactment. This is a double-edged sword, saving precious processing time but also oversimplifying an often complex social world. A classic example of this trade-off, and of the schema generally, is stereotyping. Prominent management theorists, for instance, argue that Theory X stereotypes about workers often underlie managerial behaviour, even among overtly 'progressive' managers who earnestly use the discourse of worker 'empowerment', or Theory Y. Successful leaders, by contrast, are more flexible. They genuinely adapt their leadership schema from 'hands on' to 'hands off' when the context is right. This kind of flexibility requires skills in communication, including listening attentively, being appropriately self-assertive, watching others skilfully, and regularly taking their perspective. An increasingly vital perspective-taking skill in today's global community is reflecting on the self and its underlying stereotypes from the vantage point of another culture. This frame of reference permits social thinkers to consciously monitor how their own schema interacts with the way others stereotype them. The chapter reviews a range of practical techniques for elevating consciousness in this way.

INTRODUCING COGNITIVE SCHEMATA

In the previous two chapters, we have seen that social interaction is often influenced by the mental models (also known as social representations) that actors have of their social world (Moscovici 1981). In first impressions (see chapter 5), a great deal of person perception centres on intuitive representations of which traits go with which, so forming complementary aspects of each of the so-called 'big five' underlying, or 'central', traits of personality. When explaining others' behaviour (see chapter 6), much attribution centres on mentally representing groups of people in uniform categories — 'street criminals', 'workers' or 'the poor' — again with clusters of inter-associated traits. These attributions help us to make sense of people's behaviour (Hewstone 1989).

In the wider psychological literature, this type of mental model of the world is termed a cognitive **schema** (plural, **schemata**). This is a Greek word meaning roughly 'shape of things'. Schemata are intuitive models of the world that help people to make sense out of — or give shape and form to — the vast array of experiences that confront them daily, including their experiences with others. The full range of possible schemata is restricted only by the power of the human imagination. Clearly, therefore, we require some kind of taxonomy for organising them. The best known of these taxonomies, outlined below, can be found in Fiske and Taylor (1991).

A taxonomy of schemata

Person schemata

Person schemata provide a psychological foundation for the implicit personality theories that we have already explored in chapter 5 (de Soto, Hamilton & Taylor 1985). For example, many of us have a clear idea of what the central trait attribution 'extrovert' implies about other, more peripheral traits manifested by the same person. In short, we have in our heads a kind of trait-clustered prototype of extroverts. This includes expectations that the typical extrovert likes parties and other social gatherings, enjoys socialising generally and tends to prefer working in jobs that involve lots of contact with other people. Such person schemata are basic personality templates that help us to predict how individuals, once categorised as having a particular type of character, will probably behave across a range of everyday situations (Cantor & Mischel 1977).

Role schemata

Role schemata provide a psychological foundation for the inter-group attribution processes explored in detail in the previous chapter. They are the mental software for classifying groups of people into categories, some of which are 'given' (e.g. male/female or child/adult) while others are more likely to be acquired (e.g. 'university graduate' or 'high achiever'). Such social categorisation, relating as it does to out-groups rather than in-groups, is an example of the out-group homogeneity effect (see chapter 6). The 'role' component in 'role schemata' derives from an expectation, on the part of the schema holder, about how members of a particular social group will *enact* the particular social role in which they have been classified. Role schemata are often work-related (Kunda & Sherman-Williams 1993). Theory X and Theory Y, from chapter 6, are classic examples (Neuliep 1987). Each of these schemata includes expectations about how a manager will behave towards subordinates — for example, that they may make decisions on behalf of these subordinates, or that they will empower them to perform certain duties from their own job descriptions. Role schemata, then, are inter-group templates that help us to predict how members of psychologically discrete groups, such as managers and workers, or lecturers and students, or women and men, will act in everyday life (Bem 1981).

Event schemata

While person schemata focus on individuals and role schemata focus on groups, event schemata focus on social situations. They are mental scripts for handling everyday social events, such as attending a lecture, eating out or greeting a stranger. For each of these events, there is a prototype, along with an accompanying set of implicit notions about how to behave. For a typical university lecture, for instance, there are implicit expectations (social norms) about turning up on time, bringing paper and pen, being seated, taking notes, asking questions by raising your hand, and so on. Patterns of expectation apply equally to eating out, or to greeting strangers using ritualistic phrases in a set, socially scripted order. (Some of these are actually *so* rigidly scripted they border on the bizarre!) Event schemata, therefore, are situational templates for making everyday occurrences, rather than individuals or groups, both predictable and manageable (Schank & Abelson 1977).

Self schemata

Self schemata, unsurprisingly, are the most introspective type of schema, because they involve our own view of what we are like as people — the traits and patterns of traits that we regard as central to our own self-image and sense of identity. These schemata vary considerably between individuals, particular traits being highly salient to one individual but perhaps irrelevant to the next. The schema for self will also contain salient possible or ideal selves, a kind of super-ego ideal of who we would like to be (Higgins 1987). Whenever there are significant shortfalls between this schematic ideal self and the actual self, our self-esteem will suffer, and we may be motivated to try to change or 'improve' ourselves. Self schemata are therefore introspective templates for monitoring, and sometimes developing, who we are and what we do (Pennington, Gillen & Hill 1999).

Cultural schemata

One of the earliest proponents of schemata in social psychology was Frederic Bartlett (see chapter 1). As we saw in Bartlett's study using the narrative *War of the Ghosts*, people possess schemata that reflect their cultural heritage. These might include, for example, beliefs in the spirituality of Nature and in death marking spiritual transcendence; or, alternatively, beliefs in materialism, and in death as final and absolute. In Bartlett's classic study, these beliefs functioned collectively as schemata because they helped the participants to organise their experiences into meaningful, familiar patterns. Such cultural schemata constitute a major type of schema to be reviewed in this chapter (for examples of intercultural schemata involving rankings of cultures according to their relative dominance over one another, see Sidanius & Pratto 1999).

STEREOTYPING

The clearest and most pervasive illustration of these forms of schemata can be found in the influence of a form of out-group homogeneity effect, inter-group 'stereotyping'. As noted in chapter 1, the French source word *stéréotype* means printer's cast or mould. To achieve such a template, entire groups of individuals are cast into the same rigid trait pattern (or, as discussed in chapter 5, implicit personality theory (IPT), which is a *person* schema). Stereotypes contain schematic expectations about how members of these groups, both actors and observers, should behave (social *role* schemata). There may also be notional scripts for everyday interactions with these people (called 'category exemplars') when we meet them (*event* schemata). These schemata will include ideas about how self typically interacts with them on such occasions (part of a *self* schema). Of course, stereotyping is a social representation, or schema, that entails inter-group and cross-cultural distinctions and comparisons (*cultural* schemata). Stereotypes, then, are particularly relevant to this chapter, because they exemplify and encapsulate every major form of schema combined.

What are stereotypes?

Science often tries to describe the world, including the social world, through measurement, which, in this sense, can be thought of as providing a detailed representation. In the history of detailing stereotypes in this way, at least three overlapping and complementary measurement phases can be identified. In the first phase, dating from the early twentieth century (Bogardus 1925) to the present (Cozzarelli, Wilkinson & Tagler 2001), stereotypes have been measured through questionnaires that gauge one of their offspring — prejudiced attitudes (see chapter 4). In a second phase, from the early 1980s (McConahy, Hardee & Batts 1981) to the present (Hing, Li & Zanna 2002), stereotypes were and are measured through questionnaires about distributive justice (see chapter 3). In a third phase, dating from the mid 1990s (Fazio et al. 1995) to the present (Hermans, Crombez & Eelen 2000), stereotypes have been measured by Reaction Time (RT) — for example the time taken to make decisions about negative trait attributions immediately after looking at a picture of a target out-group.

Phase 1: attitudes

One of the earliest examples of attitudinal studies of stereotyping is found in Bogardus (1925). Bogardus was interested in measuring a concept he called *social distance*. In his research, Bogardus asked participants how much distance they wanted to keep between themselves and their own social group, as well as other groups from different countries and cultures. Specifically, they were instructed with the words, 'I would admit members of each race (as a class, and not the best I have known, nor the worst members) to one or more of the classifications under which I have placed a cross (x)' (1925, p. 218). There followed a list of different nationalities and ethnicities, with a range of distances from (at one extreme) 'would exclude from my country' to, for example, 'would admit into my street as neighbours' to (at the other extreme) 'would admit to close kinship by marriage'. In this way, Bogardus was able to find each person's 'cutting score', the social distance at which he or she would 'draw the line' with respect to allowing different groups closer. Such measures smack heavily of stereotypes. For instance, if a respondent refused to admit an immigrant group 'into my street as neighbours', this implies that he or she held not only a negative attitude towards 'foreigners', but also a negative stereotype of this group.

Perhaps the best-known study of stereotypes that adopted an attitude scaling approach to prejudice was conducted following the Second World War and the Holocaust (Adorno et al. 1950). Adorno et al.'s study focused on measuring attitudes towards minority groups, and found that some individuals, termed Authoritarians, stereotyped the world into the weak and the strong (Pettigrew 1979). They tended to agree with statements such as 'People can be divided into two distinct classes: the weak and the strong'. These Authoritarians were caustically likened by Adorno et al. to 'bicyclist personalities', since they believed in 'bowing above whilst kicking below'. For example, Authoritarians tended to agree with statements such as 'Obedience and respect for authority are the most important virtues children should learn' (above they bow) and 'Most of our social problems would be solved if we could somehow get rid of the immoral, the crooked, and feeble-minded people' (below they kick). Although somewhat controversial (Altemeyer 1981), the general concept of an authoritarian personality did remain influential in social psychology (Christie 1991). In one study, for example, authoritarian attitudes were better predictors of racist behavioural intentions towards Vietnamese migrant groups in Australia (in Canberra and Toowoomba) than were stock demographic variables such as participants' age and gender (Morris & Heaven 1986). In a more recent example in Cozzarelli et al. (2001), authoritarianism was linked to negative attitudes towards the poor and to dispositional attributions about poverty (see chapter 6). Thus, higher scores on authoritarianism are associated with negatively stereotypical trait inferences about the poor, for example attributions that they are relatively 'lazy', 'stupid' and 'dirty' (2001, p. 215).

Phase 2: distributive justice

Since the late 1970s an interesting trend has been observed in attitudes measured with the kinds of instruments just described. On these measures, over the years there has been a decline in the extent to which people overtly endorse statements such as those above (McConahy, Hardee & Batts 1981; Pedersen et al. 2000). Yet this trend meshes poorly with geopolitical events during the same period, culminating, for example, in 'ethnic cleansing' campaigns in Europe, and other atrocities between one group and another. Such discrepancies may reflect what Pedersen et al. suggest are increased pressures on people to use politically correct language when speaking about marginalised groups (2000, p. 110). According to these and other authors, we can distinguish between 'old-fashioned' prejudice, which is how people overtly describe their attitudes, according to direct attitude measures, and 'modern prejudice', which includes 'more subtle and covert forms of expression' (Pedersen et al. 2000; p. 109; see also Pettigrew & Meertens 1995).

Modern prejudice is manifested in three principal ways (Swim et al. 1995): first, denial that discrimination even exists ('Discrimination against [out-group] is no longer a problem in [country]'); second, hostility towards the claims of minority groups for equality ('[Out-group] is getting too demanding in their push for [resources, such as land rights]'); third, resentment over perceived 'special favours' for minority groups ('The government is giving more attention to [out-group] than [in-group]') (Baron & Byrne 2000). These three dimensions are encapsulated in McConahy et al.'s 'Modern Racism Scale', which has been found to be predictive of behaviour, for example in workplace selection scenarios (McConahy 1983). A common thread running through all three themes is the fair distribution of resources, or distributive justice. As we saw in chapter 3, beliefs about distributive justice become particularly salient when local resources, such as jobs, are perceived to be in short supply (realistic conflict theory). In this sense, modern racism could be a form of glocalisation, since it reflects a meld of global pressures (to be 'politically correct') and local pressures (to protect the interests of a valued in-group against a negatively stereotyped out-group).

Phase 3: reaction time

Since the mid 1990s a new method for measuring stereotypes, called *priming*, has come to the fore in social psychology (Fazio et al. 1995). In this method, experiment participants are first presented with a stimulus person who visibly represents an out-group. For example, they may be shown photographs of people whose ethnicity is clearly different from their own. This priming event is assumed to be a sufficient condition to activate any pre-existing mental schema, or stereotype, for that particular ethnic out-group. Immediately afterwards the participant is asked to judge a completely different stimulus with a plainly negative value, for example the word 'unattractive'. The measure of negative stereotyping is *reaction time*. The quicker it takes them to make the judgement 'bad' (rather than 'good') for the word 'unattractive', the more likely it is that participants were stereotyping negatively in the split-second before the stimulus word was presented, when they saw an exemplar from an out-group. Fazio et al. found that 'people with *less* prejudiced scores on the Modern Racism Scale exhibited *more* negativity towards [the out-group] on the reaction time measure of automatically activated evaluations' (1995, p. 1020, emphasis added; see also chapter 8, on minority influence). Clearly, therefore, Fazio et al.'s reaction times captured an aspect of stereotyping that modern racism, and the Modern Racism Scale, have somehow missed.

Many empirical studies have now been carried out using the priming paradigm (for general reviews, try Fazio 2001 or Stangor 2000). In particular, these studies have used exemplars from a range of out-groups, including, for example, gender-, age- and class-related social categories (Paul 1998). Generalising across these studies, a consistent finding emerges. Priming participants with an exemplar from an identifiable out-group, rather than from an in-group, tends to produce faster reaction times to a negative stimulus word at stage two. When the stimulus word's connotation is positive, however, reaction time tends to be quicker when the prime is visibly a member of an *in*-group. In other words, in-groups tend to be pre-judged in a stereotypically *positive* light (see chapter 3, on social identity). To broadly summarise this research therefore, activating out-group stereotypes tends to facilitate negative reactions, while activating in-group schemata tends to have precisely the opposite effect.

If you think you are free from stereotypes, think again!

Having been repeatedly demonstrated in the form of central tendencies within majority groups, stereotyping and prejudice are not confined to openly prejudiced minorities. This assertion directly challenges the rather comforting idea many of us have that we are free from prejudice. After decades of combating prejudice and even believing it was on the decline, many of us have been caught unawares by recent research findings concerning not only stereotyping but also its attitudinal offspring, inter-group prejudice (Paul 1998). None of this necessarily means that we consciously *agree* with stereotyping or consciously *wish* to be prejudiced. Many of the participants who demonstrate prejudice in priming experiments also earnestly maintain that they are not prejudiced, nor do they wish to be (Devine 1996). It is as if there was a psychological split between what participants do (in terms of reaction time) and what they say (in terms of consciously formed words) (Dovidio et al. 1998). This, of course, is exactly what we would predict on the basis of glocalisation (see chapter 1).

According to the research, therefore, we can now envisage at least three basic types of group with respect to stereotyping and prejudice (Fazio et al. 1995). First, there are openly prejudiced extremists, who, as we have seen, were widely studied in the earlier literature. Second, and at the other extreme, there are openly unprejudiced people, who would show no signs either of atti-tudinal prejudice on a questionnaire or of schematic stereotyping in a priming-type study. This is the group to which we like to think we belong. Third, some-where between the two extremes, there are overtly unprejudiced people whose reaction times in a priming study would nonetheless suggest covert prejudice and stereotyping. In this category, some people will be aware of and even pri-vately comfortable with their prejudice. They will simply manage the impression they make in everyday life (see chapter 5). They may even score quite low on prejudice on the Modern Racism Scale, which some leading researchers now believe has become overly transparent (e.g. Dovidio et al. 1997; Fazio et al. 1995, p. 1021). Many others, however, will be genuinely unaware that they harbour negative stereotypes, even though, if placed in a priming-type experiment, their reaction times would probably indicate latent, implicit stereotyping. This is the group to which, according to the latest research, many of us unwittingly and unwillingly belong.

The priming research reviewed here, and the idea of implicit stereotyping, are consistent with, and allow us to integrate, a range of other literatures.

Stereotypes in everyday language use

A great deal of the recent work on stereotypes is found in the literature on social discourse. Much of this literature has focused on what 'non-Indigenous' groups say about 'Indigenous' groups (for a discussion of the dangers inherent in this distinction itself, see Williams 2000, p. 136). A classic illustration of this type of research can be found in Wetherell and Potter (1992). These researchers engaged in discourse analysis of what Pākeha (ethnically European) New Zealanders were saying about Pākeha–Māori relations. In Wetherell and Potter's study, Pākeha New Zealanders reportedly defended the essentially unequal status of the two 'groups' on the grounds, for example, that 'everybody should be treated equally' (i.e. no group should receive 'special treatment'). More recently, analogous findings have been reported from Australia (Augoustinos, Rapley & Tuffin 1999). In both sets of studies, on either side of the Tasman, the participants explicitly stated (in their verbal behaviour) that they were simply being egalitarian. However, at least some of their 'egalitarian' sentiment might be simultaneously construed as a subtle form of racism, in which relative disadvantage is unwittingly legitimated and thus maintained (for an earlier example related to double standards on the broader issue of multiculturalism, see Ho 1990).

Stereotypes in industrial relations

Stereotypes are widespread in organisational life (Operario & Fiske 2001). In recent years, for example, there has been a growing recognition in Australia, New Zealand and elsewhere of a yawning gap between (i) the rhetorical lip-service paid to valuing (rather than stereotypically devaluing) human resources and the input they can bring to organisational development, and (ii) the reality of 'business as usual', with the same old derogatory stereotypes about workers when it comes to daily workplace routines (see activity 3.1; Vecchio, Hearn & Southey 1997). The rhetoric of worker empowerment and Theory Y is often discrepant from the schema in use, Theory X (see chapter 6). Moreover, many managers seem to be genuinely unaware that they hold these double standards between what they say and what they implicitly believe (Argyris 1998, 1999, 2000). According to Argyris, managers often work both an 'espoused theory', for example Theory Y, and a 'theory-in-use', which is more implicit (for an excellent review, see Smith 2002). A wonderful example of this is contained in critical narrative 1.3, which illuminates the discrepancies between Kirk Reed's espoused rhetoric of worker empowerment, which was largely Theory Y, and his actual eventual treatment of his employees, which was decidedly Theory X.

Stereotypes affecting women at work

As we saw in chapter 5, a **glass ceiling** works against women in management. This handicap is often due to stereotyping (Melamed 1995). Sometimes the stereotypes about women are quite overt (Ashkanasy 1994); at others, however, stereotyping is implicit (Hill & Augoustinos 1997). In the Hill and Augoustinos study, a majority of Australian participants held perceptions that nursing (a stereotypically 'female' occupational role) was 'easier' than both engineering (male role stereotype) and the more gender-neutral occupation of law. In nursing, success was attributed to task ease rather than ability, while failure was attributed less to task difficulty than in either engineering or law (see also Banaji & Greenwald 1995). In her psychological analysis of the glass ceiling, Valian (1998) argues that women in the workplace tend to be role-stereotyped as comparatively emotional, nurturing and essentially strong on 'soft' (i.e. people) skills. In her analysis, Eagly (1999) vividly describes this representation as a **'women are wonderful'** schema. The problem with this representation, according to Eagly, is that the role schema for ideal managers tends towards an opposite pattern of traits. The IPT for a leader is 'relatively cold, rational, task-focused, and skilled technically' (Karpin 1995). The net result of a 'women are wonderful' schema is that women are discriminated against, because being warm and fuzzy is precisely not what it takes, in decision-makers' minds, to be a leader.

Linking back to and converging with the priming literature on prejudice and stereotyping, both Valian and Eagly find that organisational decision-makers often sincerely believe that they are judging their female candidates objectively on their merits. In many cases, that is, they are unaware of their own discrimination, prejudice and — underpinning the rest — stereotypes. The glass ceiling works subtly, at a psychological level. Its advocates are often unaware of their own biases.

A dilemma for policy-makers

Such schematic blind spots have been taken as grounds for enacting affirmative action programs, or structural policies of positive discrimination in which members of minority groups, when all else is equal, are given preference over candidates from majority groups (Brown & Charnsangavej 2000). Certainly, such policies can and do partially restrain the influence of negative stereotypes on organisational behaviour (Operario & Fiske 2001). But these essentially structural solutions to a psychological problem carry risks as well. Most of these risks centre on the possibility that positive discrimination programs send demotivating subtexts to their 'beneficiaries' (Harber 1998) as well as to those who 'lose out' (Heilman, Block & Lucas 1992). They carry an implication that the minority group's abilities are substandard (Pearson 1999). Thus, instead of fostering greater mindfulness about stereotypes, positive discrimination programs risk fostering tokenism and exacerbating rather than diminishing the original stereotyping issue.

Implicit stereotypes

To see precisely how this might work, we need a model of how implicit stereotypes actually influence behaviour. As the foregoing example indicates, this model needs to be interactive. It must include *communication*, in this case between the stereotyper and the stereotyped. Following figure 5.1, that would involve 'self' and 'other'. This kind of model is offered again in figure 7.1, which enables us to link the concept of schema with both social perception and everyday explanations. Thus, the model in figure 7.1 marks the beginnings of a unifying model for part 2 of the book.

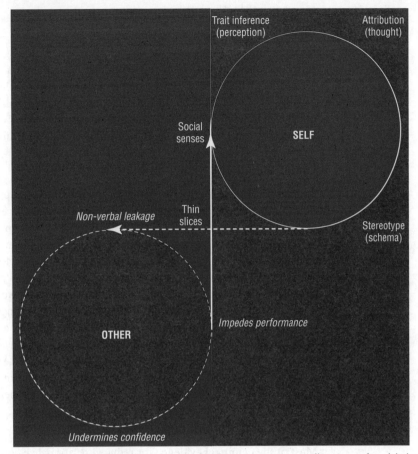

Note: The 'other' processes outlined in this figure occur at an earlier stage of social change than the stages of resistance by minority groups described in detail in chapter 3.

Figure 7.1   A model of stereotype threat

At an everyday, local level, for instance, we can imagine a 'self' in figure 7.1 who consciously eschews stereotypes yet harbours them implicitly. What happens as a result of these stereotypes in everyday situations? The research on priming helps us to answer this. From the priming paradigm, there is evidence linking reaction times with discriminatory behaviour after the experiment is ostensibly over. During a debriefing session, participants in Fazio et al.'s (1995) experiment (Study I) were observed in social interaction with actual exemplars of the out-group category that had provided the prime. Summary measures of their non-verbal body language, such as smiling, eye contact and distance keeping, were consistent with the reaction time data obtained through priming (Fazio et al. 1995). In other words, the quicker the participant's reaction time to a negative word at stage two of the experiment when the prime had been out-group at stage one, the more behavioural discrimination they later displayed in non-verbal behaviour, as defined by less smiling, reduced eye contact and increased social distance (see also Dovidio et al. 1997). Thus, the priming technique demonstrates predictive validity, linking implicit stereotypes and prejudice to actual, subtle discriminatory behaviour.

Non-verbal leakage in everyday language

When interacting with an exemplar from a stereotyped social category, basic social facilitation processes (see chapter 2) will work to augment existing routines (implicit schemata) for cognising about and behaving around out-groups, such as stereotypes (Bochner & Perks 1971; Fadil & Moss 1998; Kosmitzki 1996; Lowery, Hardin & Sinclair 2001). These augmentations will combine with ironic effects (see chapter 5) to 'leak' the stereotype non-verbally through the kinds of behaviour we have seen occur in the priming research (Paul 1998).

Undermining confidence in minority groups

A theory called **stereotype threat** holds that minority group actors readily pick up these implicitly augmented stereotypes from the stereotyper's thin slices (Steele 1997). Following figure 7.1, such non-verbal leakages are predicted to affect minority groups' confidence. According to Steele, they create an apprehension that saps self-confidence (for an extreme example of this, affecting will to live among the aged, see Levy & Ashman 1999–2000). Most of us can probably identify with the kinds of negative Pygmalion effects that occur when we intuitively know that someone, say in charge of an important testing or assessment situation, privately disparages our capabilities. Such disparagement, whether at inter-group or inter-individual levels (Ottati, cited in Ajzen 2001) makes us fearful that we will succumb to their negative estimation, thus confirming the stereotype and inducing significant emotional damage of self. By this mechanism, according to Steele (1997), stereotype threat starts to impede minority group performance.

Undermining minority group performance

Most of the empirical evidence for reduced performance comes from observations of what happens when test administrators explicitly state that minority groups can be expected to do as well as any other group on the test. This alone is often enough to raise minority groups' performance levels well above the level they typically attain, if they are made apprehensive by preambles that the test will assess 'ability', which they know is part of the prejudicial schema typically working against them (Croizet & Claire 1998). The implication of these findings is that lack of confidence is artificially depressing not only confidence, but performance as well.

How implicit stereotypes become self-perpetuating

Whenever stereotype threat operates, and manages to depress minority group performance, this will have the effect of confirming and reinforcing the majority group's trait inferences, attributions and stereotypes. This process, then, starts the whole process over again, as perception feeds attribution, which feeds stereotyping, which fuels stereotype threat, and so on. Even affirmative action programs can generate vicious circles in which stereotyping becomes a progressively (or, more accurately, degeneratively) self-fulfilling prophecy. The various vicious circles depicted in figure 7.1 will no doubt be aided and abetted by the fact that observers typically filter *out* information that disconfirms their stereotypes while filtering *in* (and later retrieving from memory) information that supports them (Baron & Byrne 2000).

Managing stereotypes

What the foregoing analysis suggests is that stereotyping, and schemata generally, cannot be managed by structural interventions alone. Somewhere along the line, the human factor in stereotyping has to be managed relatively directly as well. One way we might profitably learn in this regard is to examine how stereotypes are formed in the first place. The very fact that we can hold them and be influenced by them, even when we do not want them, suggests that they are relatively indelible. They have probably been stamped into long-term memory through perceptions and attributions made over an extended period of time. Indeed, from as early as three years old, children are using social categories based on visible characteristics of other people, like gender (boy/girl) and skin colour (Sanson et al. 1998). Thereafter, the growing child is regularly exposed to various kinds of prejudices, either from media images of minority groups (Sanson et al. 1998) or from caregivers' own prejudices (Towles & Fazio 2001). It is therefore not surprising that stereotypes are later difficult to dislodge. By the same token, we have little hope of dislodging them unless we understand their development origins.

Assimilation

The foremost commentator on how schemata form and coalesce into stereoscopic mental structures is undoubtedly the developmental psychologist Jean Piaget (1952). Piaget described a cognitive process called **assimilation**, in which new experiences are incrementally incorporated into a pre-existing schema, which Piaget saw as a mini model of the world. According to Piaget, assimilation occurs first and foremost through *doing* — an idea that remains influential today (e.g. Smith 2002). An example from Piaget's domain is when an infant incorporates a non-edible object into a grasp-and-hold-and-suck schema. The object is handled and categorised like more familiar objects — that is, as something to be sucked. The infant self's representation of the world does not change to suit a changing external reality. Instead, and exactly like the definition of a stereotype (see chapter 1 and figure 7.1), the world must fit (be assimilated into) the schema.

Piaget saw assimilation as a natural process that continues throughout life. In adult stereotyping, this idea has been supported by classic social psychological theorists like George Kelley (1955) and Gordon Allport (1954), and by leading contemporary management theorists like Chris Argyris (1998, 1999, 2000). In education, some university lecturers may continue to rely on outmoded role schemata about students ('Students are all basically lazy') and related event schemata for lecture style ('They need to be told what to do. Don't ever negotiate with them!'). Of course, it can be otherwise. Some lecturers have positive stereotypes of their students, and emphasise these to facilitate positive Pygmalion effects (anonymous peer reviewer 2001). To focus for a moment on the negative case, however, the over-assimilation in this case will be bolstered by a tendency for prejudiced persons to dismiss or 'sub-type' counter-examples of the stereotype — for example when students proactively seek adult-to-adult transactions with their instructor — as 'exceptions to the rule' (Sanson et al. 1998). By every twist and turn, therefore, assimilation keeps assimilators safely within their comfort zone.

From figure 7.1, assimilation reassures them that all is well with their stereoscopic view of the world.

In developmental terms, the cognitive process of assimilating out-group exemplars into stereotypes is fuelled by at least three social influence processes (for more of these, relevant mostly to the development of stereotypical extremism, see Adorno et al. 1950 or Altmeyer 1988).

Classical conditioning

In this form of learning, repeated experiences of two or more stimuli close together in time leads to the stimuli being mentally associated with one another (Pavlov 1927). In forming stereotypes, children may repeatedly experience negative subtexts, for example from media images in news reports, whenever they see exemplars of an out-group, such as the unemployed (subtext: 'dole bludgers') or ethnic minorities (subtext: 'criminals') (Sanson et al. 1998; Valentino 1999).

Operant conditioning

In this form of learning, self progressively associates a particular response (or 'operant') with a particular stimulus through a reward of some kind (Skinner 1953). In acquiring stereotypes, for instance, we may have progressively learned that prejudiced behaviour (operant) towards out-group exemplars (stimuli) can reap social benefits (rewards), such as political or community status (e.g. Pettigrew 1958).

Observational learning

In observational learning, behavioural models are observed and then imitated. Such models might include, for example, credible (or even quasi-credible) media figures (e.g. some senior politicians) who implicitly endorse negative stereotypes about out-groups (Bandura 1973). Media encounters like this, a little reflection might convince the reader, will engage observational learning, operant conditioning and classical conditioning concurrently. To this extent, observational learning is a most 'efficient' way for people to acquire negative stereotypes, and thus perhaps eventually to *un*learn them.

The effects of over-learning

These learning processes are essentially incremental and developmental. Their effects take years of exposure to assimilate. During that time, the more often we experience negative images and subtexts about particular out-groups, the more automatic and the less conscious our representations and deliberations about them may become (Paul 1998). This process of 'going underground' into implicit, automatic routines is believed by many to explain how people remain unaware of the fact that unwanted negative stereotypes are influencing their everyday behaviour. Paradoxically, it is as if these repeated practical experiences make us adept, or *skilled*, at thinking stereotypically (for a definition of skill, see p. 238). Indeed, we become so skilled that we cannot later help ourselves from doing it, even when we consciously want to.

Perhaps we should not be too surprised by the basic idea here: that we can be both skilled and socially handicapped at the same time. A powerful everyday example is the skill of reading. Reading generally serves us well, but the skill becomes so internalised that wherever we see printed words, it is often difficult to resist reading them. This is because we have practised reading so often that our schema for reading runs on autopilot. The most famous demonstration of this is the 'Stroop effect' (Stroop 1935, reprinted 1992). In this instance, the naming of coloured (e.g. blue) ink is seriously hampered if the ink happens to form a contradictory word (e.g. if it spells 'red'). Marketers exploit the Stroop effect heavily on roadside billboards, which rely on passers-by compulsively reading their slogans (Gleitman 1986).

The handicapping potential of social skills

Something very similar to compulsive reading probably happens during implicit stereotyping. Like reading skills, stereotypes help people to deal with their everyday world, and to that extent form the psychological basis of a skill, but they can also distract them from performing other everyday activities. Consider, for instance, managers who have spent years observing, and perhaps implicitly adopting, the kind of worker stereotype outlined in chapter 6 and in figure 6.2. Now they are being asked to do something completely different, namely to encourage worker 'empowerment'. Like the skilled reader who should in fact be watching the road rather than reading a billboard, these managers are likely to find it very hard to behave *other* than in their customary and habitual manner. To denote the irony of being socially facilitated into relying on schemata we consciously know are faulty, Argyris (1998) has coined the memorable terms **skilled unawareness** and **skilled incompetence**. These terms recognise managers' frequent inability to shake off a stereoscopic schema-in-use, such as Theory X, even when they consciously (and even earnestly) espouse Theory Y. As we can see in figure 7.1, their past keeps betraying them, not only to their workers but also to themselves. A likely result of this leakage, from the workers' point of view, will be over-promise and under-delivery (see chapter 3) — in short, a demotivating broken promise.

Accommodation

How do we 'break into' these existing stereotypes and change them? In his theory of cognitive development, Piaget (1952) introduced a key process for this kind of schematic unfreezing to occur. Again, the process is based on doing. This time, however, it is the schema that changes to fit the world, and not the other way round. In a process that Piaget termed **accommodation**, schema-holders repeatedly encounter challenges to their pre-existing representation, experiences that cannot readily be assimilated (or rationalised) into it. Eventually, the schema itself changes to accommodate these new experiences. A teething infant, for example, discovers that objects like sharp pens are no longer fun to be sucked, and may even be painful to chew on. With increased mobility, and new encounters with objects that are unpalatable to suck, this infant begins to modify the grasping-holding-sucking schema into something that is ultimately far more fun (and adaptive), namely a schema for grasping-holding-and-influencing-the-world-around-them. Thus, what ultimately changes the schema is the challenge of new experience.

What kinds of experience change stereotypes?

Some lecturers, when their outmoded stereotypes about students are effectively challenged, may actually start to rethink the way they categorise, teach and communicate with their classes. With enough experience of these challenges, exceptions that earlier 'proved the rule' may now actually start to *dis*prove it. This may be what happened with Grant in critical narrative 6.1. Occasionally, too, accommodation can be relatively rapid, such as when we encounter the kind of rich point experienced by the author in critical narrative 6.2. Whatever the time span, however, the essence of schematic accommodation is that the experience of diversity, of *other*'s diversity (in figure 7.1), 'moves our schemata on' from oversimplifying the world around us towards incorporating more of its inherent richness and complexity. To this extent, accommodation is both anathema, and an antidote, to stereotyping.

Some specifics of schema change

Piaget was neither the first nor the last to suggest that accommodation occurs through doing (Fiske 1993). In a classic early study, manual telegraphers were observed while training in the use of Morse code (Bryan & Harter 1897). These trainees first mastered syllables; then they displayed a qualitative jump in their performances as the chunks of information they were able to deal with became words; then another jump as the chunks-in-use became whole phrases; and then yet another step upwards as the chunks became short sentences. For a familiar example of this process, think back to how your own keyboard skills developed to where they are now, and how you mastered first syllables, then words, then phrases. Bryan and Harter's results are a timeless demonstration of both assimilation (getting better within stages) and accommodation (changing from operating in syllables to operating in words). Their study is especially relevant for us here, because it traces the accommodation of schemata to practice. Specifically, it shows that accommodation is programmed into human software through repeated learning-by-doing.

A link between schema and skill

The idea of revising schemata by practice was mooted by the early behaviourist John Watson, who held the view that cognition is motor activity internalised (1919, 1924). The concept of internalisation was most clearly demonstrated by Piaget (1952), however, through observation of his own children's cognitive development. Towards the end of their infancy, and following lots of bodily trial-and-error practice, Piaget's children became skilled at manipulating objects into the positions they wanted them. For example, they might swivel an object to fit it, at first try, through the bars of their playpen. Or they might slot an object, first time, the right way round into a hole designed for that purpose. According to Piaget, the only way they could have solved these problems as they did (i.e. at the first try) was to have rotated the objects *mentally*, in their heads, *before* making their decisive first move. Their skill derived from the fact that they had internalised 'doing' into a motor schema in which the actions of grasping and manipulating had become one whole internalised 'chunk' of automated mental activity. Their learning-by-doing not only accommodated schemata. It also created sophisticated cognitive skills that involved mental rotation and agility. This makes learning-by-doing relevant to stereotype reversal.

SOCIAL SKILLS AND STEREOTYPE REVERSAL

The notion that both schema and skill are products of 'internalised doing' was first linked to *social* psychology by Michael Argyle (1968). In this landmark publication, Argyle advanced the following thesis: 'That the sequence of individual behaviour which occurs during social interaction can usefully be looked at as a kind of motor skill ... the point of our suggestion is to pursue the basic psychological similarities in more detail, to see if the same processes operate' (1968, p. 85). Thus, Argyle likened the acquisition and performance of *social* skills, for example interacting in stereotypical and *non*-stereotypical ways with out-groups, to experiential learning-by-doing.

One of the reasons why Argyle's analogy resonated with the rest of the academic community as it did at the time was that much of what we 'know', both cognitively and socially, cannot readily be taught and learned by words alone. It can be fully acquired only through repeated doing. Riding a bicycle, swimming, typing, fighting, holding a conversation, forming impressions, or making attributions based on thin slices, are skills that we know, through extensive practice, 'how' to do without necessarily being able to say 'that' we do precisely *a* followed by *b* followed by *c*. If you doubt this, try telling someone else, in words, precisely how you ride a bike, swim, type, hold a conversation, form an impression or make an attribution! Or, harder still, try articulating what these social cognitive processes entail *while* you are doing them. My own lecturing, for instance, threatens to 'break up' when I do this. All these activities are examples of 'procedural' (tacit, non-verbal) knowledge, rather than 'declarative' (easily verbalised) forms of knowledge. A little reflection at this point should convince you that a huge amount of what we need to do in everyday social life relies on tacit knowledge, acquired and internalised into smooth routines through painstaking practice (Sternberg et al. 2000).

Implicit stereotyping is a fine example of this. As we have seen in the priming research, implicit stereotypes are deeply internalised, unspoken routines for thinking and doing. They are tacit, procedural. They are not declarative; we cannot easily talk about them. Logically, if we cannot even articulate their influences in words, it seems likely that we will not be able to articulate how to *overcome* them solely in words either. Replacing stereotypes is thus likely to be substantially a question of practice, in this case at interacting directly with, and accommodating to, members of out-groups. Simply 'learning about' our biases will probably not be sufficient to change behaviour. Practice is a necessary condition for schema accommodation, and for translating this accommodation into a set of social skills for interacting non-stereotypically with others.

So where are we now? Any serious intervention to counteract implicit stereotyping is going to have to achieve at least two things. First, it will need to raise awareness of a discrepancy between the espoused schema and the schema-in-use (Argyris 1998). This is necessary because habit has taken over from conscious intention, leaving behaviour under the control of relatively automatic processes (Ajzen 2001; see also chapter 4). Second, any program for reversing stereotyping, and the escalation process depicted in figure 7.1, will need to include a significant amount of learning-by-doing (Argyle 1968). Trainees will need to *practise* how to react and behave around relevant out-groups in ways consistent with, and modelled on, consciously held beliefs. 'Chalk and talk' will be insufficient, in itself, to break the stereotype mould, because ultimately accommodation requires both skilled awareness *and* skilled competence (Argyris 1999).

An excellent illustration of how to meet these twin concerns can be found in UNICEF's program *Education for Development* (Fountain 1995). Introduced in chapter 6, that program was specifically designed to break stereotype moulds, among Western youth, about the 'Third World poor' (Fountain 1995). An analogy from one of the practical exercises in that program has been provided in activity 6.2. Essentially, the entire program of activities in the UNICEF publication is based on the twin principles of raising awareness and experiential learning-by-doing.

Another example of a twin-pronged awareness-raising/learning-by-doing program is described by De Angelis (2000). This educational program, loosely based on the jigsaw technique described in chapter 3, has recently been implemented among university students from majority and minority ethnic groups. In the program, students from culturally diverse backgrounds share both living spaces and everyday study groups. As well as studying together, the students are actively encouraged, over time, to challenge the role schema into which many of them are regularly categorised or categorise others. They do this, for example, by actively and openly discussing the merits and benefits of diversity (see chapter 3, on group polarisation). According to De Angelis, such strategies are starting to have some impact on minority group members' academic grades. Thus, the program is starting to dislodge stereotype threat from both sides of the dynamic depicted in figure 7.1.

Many of the problems we encounter in everyday life, from poor leadership through to culture shock, stem from schematic rigidity such as that described above. Successful leadership, for example, means being able to flexibly change the schemata-in-use as (1) *context* requires. When times get stormy, followers may prefer a leader to become directive rather than remaining rigidly consultative (Dunphy & Stace 1993). For leaders to know when to make the change, they will also need to be skilled at (2) *communication*. This skill is generic to all forms of social interaction, including both inter-group and inter-personal relations. Its essence, perhaps, is being flexible enough to see things from the perspective of another individual or group (see chapter 6). A related major topic, patently increasingly relevant in the global community, especially for international assignments and managing intercultural encounters within multicultural societies, is (3) *culture* skill (Argyle 1968, p. 77). Often our own cultural schemata are so rigidly ingrained that we cannot see ourselves as others see us (Dowling, Schuler & Welch 1994; Enns 1994).

(1) Contextual skills

Many of us at some stage during our working career will be required to develop skills in 'people management'. Inasmuch as this entails persuading people to listen to what we have to say, and thereby to change their workplace ideas or practices, 'managing people' means having leadership skills (Karpin 1995). Because leadership is concerned with influencing others, it has long been a major concern for social psychology, particularly for applied social psychologists working in organisations.

The 'great man' attribution error

The core of this entire field of study has been to articulate the most effective leadership schema for managers to acquire and enact, with skill, in their everyday working lives. This applied focus has been consistent across organisational, community and political leadership settings (for a similar focus on 'follower' schemata, see Lord, Brown & Freiberg 1999). The best way of appreciating what lessons have been learned in this approach is to review its history. This had its beginnings in a fundamental, and probably still quite common, attribution error.

This error can be traced back at least to the First World War, when the applied concern was selecting and training those individuals who would be most able to lead groups on the battlefield and on the factory floor. The initial approach here was thoroughly de-contextual. It concentrated on personality, and on identifying the 'great man'. The model of leadership assumed that leaders are born and not made (not to mention being born a male), and could be found among people who possessed a limited number of special core traits (Pennington, Gillen & Hill 1999). Leadership, then, was implicitly considered to be a kind of *person* (as well as gender role) schema.

Logically enough, the early research on leadership, guided by this schema, set out to identify those magical traits that constituted the 'great man'. The primary methods used in that research endeavour consisted of examining groups of successful and unsuccessful leaders, as well as groups of leaders and followers. The logic in this method was compelling. Batteries of personality tests were administered to these known groups, and a search conducted for the traits that differentiated one group (successful leaders) from the rest (unsuccessful leaders and followers). Once these traits were identified, selection processes could be designed that ensured that only the 'great' people (men), those who scored highly on this list of leadership traits, would be selected for leadership positions. Thus, the early research on leadership enacted a *role* schema in which some (the few) were born for leader roles, while others (the many) were stereotyped into roles as followers.

This person–role approach lasted in studies of leadership until the 1930s and early 1940s. By that time a devastating problem had emerged with the schema itself. Each time a different kind of leadership situation was studied, a new trait or set of traits had to be added to the growing leadership profile. By the late 1940s it was apparent that a 'great man' schema for leadership could not continue to assimilate the sheer amount of information that the research based on it was generating (Stodgill 1948). Faced with so much evidence that did not fit the existing model, the schema had to accommodate. To be specific, it had become patently clear that what made a successful leader on the battlefield was not necessarily what made a successful leader on the shop floor, or in a finance house, a classroom or a tight spot on the sporting field. With hindsight, it was recognised that leadership was a question of context, and to that extent the schema for studying it had to accommodate different leadership situations. *Event* schemata were needed.

Power and leadership styles

The 1950s and 1960s were marked by a clear shift of focus towards types of 'power' at the leader's disposal (e.g. French & Raven 1959) and how these translated into preferred leadership 'styles' (e.g. Blake & Mouton 1964). 'Reward' and 'coercive' power are based on having control of the carrot and the stick; 'referent' power is based on being liked (and so 'referred to' for guidance) by followers. Relying heavily on reward and coercive power is the essence of a leadership style called 'task-focused'; referent power characterises a leadership style that is 'relationship-focused' (for a predecessor, and arguably the foundation for all of these ideas, see Lewin, Lippitt & White 1939). The crucial point about these leader styles, however, is that they are based firmly on the type of power granted by the social context.

This enhanced awareness of social context included paying attention to cultural settings. Tests of the cross-cultural robustness of the two underlying leadership styles have consistently found that they travel well across cultures (Smith & Bond 1999), but only if we allow for cultural variation in how each style is normally expressed (for a more differentiated but nonetheless similar underlying role schema, see Gibson & Marcoulides 1995). In high power distance settings, for example, a concern with relationships is often expressed in a relatively paternalistic manner (Sinha 1990), whereas in more egalitarian settings the same conceptual style is liable to be expressed as an 'adult-to-adult' transaction (see chapter 4, on positioning). In this way, while leadership styles travel relatively well across cultures, managers need to remain aware of how they are differently represented in different *cultural* schemata. For instance, it could become confusing for everyone if an expatriate manager on assignment mistakenly translated paternalistic leader behaviour as reflecting a task focus, when its underlying meaning was actually quite different (an orientation towards human relationship via nurturance).

Such influences of culture suggest that leadership styles are learned rather than inherited by the privileged 'great man'. Indeed, a 'style' is something that can be learned and adapted to suit the particular context in which leadership is required. This simple but elegant idea is backed up by a great deal of research that, time and again, whether in Japan or India or the United States or Australia, has shown that the most successful leaders are equally capable of focusing on the task or on human relations, as the situation warrants (Casimir & Keats 1996). These most skilled of leaders — a rare few — are able to adapt their leadership style constantly to suit the situation they are in. In terms of personality, this amounts to the leader being flexible (Zuccaro, Foti & Kenny 1991). Such flexibility probably reflects in part the 'big five' trait of Openness (see chapter 5). In schematic terms, openness and flexibility, of course, are opposed to stereotyping. Flexibility suggests that leaders' person schemata incorporate elements from both Theory Y and Theory X (Mendenhall & Oddou 1983). This also entails a flexible role schema for 'being a leader'. They need to contain relatively sophisticated event schemata for responding to different social situations. They also need a self schema that constantly monitors discrepancies between actual and ideal leadership behaviour in each situation as it arises. And they have to be able to encode and decode cultural forms of each of these types of schemata. Leadership, therefore, is about learning to read and respond to social context.

Fiedler's contingency model

Although it has its limits, as we will see, one model of leadership still provides the clearest illustration of how contextual models of leadership work, and on exactly what leadership might be dependent (or 'contingent') (Fiedler 1978). According to Fiedler's contingency model, leaders need to consider several contextual variables, whose total *pattern* of configurations will determine which leadership style, whether task- or relations-focused, will probably work best for a group at any one time. Fiedler defines 'working best' as being the most productive in terms of tangible outcomes. These outcomes could be the number of students who pass their unit with a particular instructor; the number of community development projects successfully completed under a project leader; or the number of widgets produced per month by a leader's organisational section.

The following sections outline the contextual elements in Fiedler's model of leadership.

Leader–member relations

According to Fiedler, the social psychological element of leader–member relations is the most important contextual factor for skilled leaders to consider. Leader–member relations are defined as either good or bad, a binary that reflects the degree of referent power (level of liking) commanded by leaders from their followers at the time.

Task structure

Assembling a washing machine according to a step-by-step production blueprint is an example of a highly structured task. In contrast, a group that must decide on community health policy faces a job that is inherently unstructured. Task structure, in this case, is low.

Position power

Some organisations are very hierarchical, or high in power distance. In such organisations, the leader is recognised by his or her followers as having the power to 'hire and fire'. For obvious reasons, Fiedler called this 'position power' (literally, the power that comes with a position). In some organisational groups, such as research teams, special interest groups, groups of volunteers or community-based organisations, position power is likely to be substantially less. Here, position power is described in the model as low.

The person factor: task versus relations

Consistent with the research reviewed on leader styles, Fiedler included in his model two basic leadership styles, namely the task-focused versus the relationship-focused style. His operational definition of these is given in figure 7.2. The logic of this scale is that the more 'hostile' you feel towards someone with whom you have found it difficult to work in the past, the more task-focused (rather than relationship-focused) your style of leadership probably is.

Think of the person with whom you can work least well. They may be someone you work with now, or they may be someone you knew in the past. They do not have to be the person you like least well but should be the person with whom you had the most difficulty in getting a job done. Describe below how this person appears to you by circling the appropriate number on the scale.

Pleasant	8	7	6	5	4	3	2	1	Unpleasant
Friendly	8	7	6	5	4	3	2	1	Unfriendly
Rejecting	1	2	3	4	5	6	7	8	Accepting
Helpful	8	7	6	5	4	3	2	1	Unhelpful
Unenthusiastic	1	2	3	4	5	6	7	8	Enthusiastic
Tense	1	2	3	4	5	6	7	8	Relaxed
Distant	1	2	3	4	5	6	7	8	Close
Cold	1	2	3	4	5	6	7	8	Warm
Cooperative	8	7	6	5	4	3	2	1	Uncooperative
Supportive	8	7	6	5	4	3	2	1	Unsupportive
Boring	1	2	3	4	5	6	7	8	Interesting
Quarrelsome	1	2	3	4	5	6	7	8	Harmonious
Self-assured	8	7	6	5	4	3	2	1	Hesitant
Efficient	8	7	6	5	4	3	2	1	Inefficient
Gloomy	1	2	3	4	5	6	7	8	Cheerful
Open	8	7	6	5	4	3	2	1	Guarded

Scoring and interpretation

This inventory is the Least Preferred Co-worker (LPC) scale. To derive your score, add the numbers circled. The higher the total score, the more task-focused your current style. A total score of 67, for instance, would be considered higher than about 60 per cent of the wider population. A score of 62 would be considered greater than the score obtained by 50 per cent of the wider population. And a score of 55 (clearly on the relationship-orientation side) would be considered higher than just 40 per cent of the wider population.

Figure 7.2 Measuring leadership style

Source: From *Applied Industrial/Organizational Psychology*, 3rd edition, by M.G. Aamodt, ©1999. Reprinted with permission of Wadsworth, a division of Thomson Learning <www.thomsonrights.com>. Fax 800 730 2215.

Fiedler's 'Leader Match'

In pulling these elements together in one contingency model, Fiedler made numerous observations, over a number of years, across a wide range of organisational and other groups (e.g. service, industrial, recreational). In particular, he set about categorising each group according to the three contextual elements identified above, and then recording which style of leadership, task- or relationship-focused, worked best in that situation. The results of this lengthy (and essentially atheoretical) data-gathering exercise are presented in table 7.1. To take one example from the table, in a context in which leader–member relations are good, the task structure is clear and position power is strong, task orientation, based on Fiedler's observations, is likely to be more productive in the long run than a relationship-oriented leader style.

The tick entries in table 7.1 have been quite well supported in research since Fiedler's original proposals of the model (Fiedler & Garcia 1987; Schriesheim, Tepper & Tetrault 1994). The point of this table for us, however, is not the specific entries in it. The deeper significance is that the table itself is a kind of externalised schema. It provides an approximated 'hard copy' of person, role, event and self schemata for people management and leadership, all rolled into one.

Table 7.1 Fiedler's contingency schema

CONTEXT FACTOR								
Leader–member relations	Good				Bad			
Task structure	Clear		Unclear		High		Low	
Leader's position power	strong	weak	strong	weak	strong	weak	strong	weak
PERSON FACTOR								
Relationship orientation				✓	✓	✓	✓	
Task orientation	✓	✓	✓					✓

Note: ✓ = Most appropriate style for the context.

Source: Adapted from Haslam (2000, p. 62). Reprinted by permission of Sage Publishing.

So *why* is the table content like this? Unfortunately, since Fiedler's schema is essentially inductive (i.e. built up almost entirely through atheoretical observations), we cannot articulate with confidence why each configuration of contingencies tends to favour the style it does. For example, although we can indeed state that a task focus is often best whenever the context is either very bad or good (on all three contextual elements), we cannot go much further than that. In the end, the optimal way of using the content of table 7.1 is to practise 'diagnosing' situations until the decision about which style works best becomes relatively automatic and internalised — until, that is, it becomes a practical leadership schema. Table 7.1, therefore, is essentially skills-focused rather than theoretical.

In recognition of this deliberately practical focus, Fiedler has developed a successful skills program called 'Leader Match'. This program consists of intensive workshops that focus on learning to 'read' management context and then changing it to suit, or 'match', the preferred managerial style (for a generally positive, research-based evaluation of this program, see Strube & Garcia 1981). In schematic terms, therefore, Fiedler's program focuses on producing accommodation in managers' event schemata, while encouraging assimilation of the managerial world into their pre-existing schemata for self (self schemata). In this regard, then, Fiedler is not a great believer in changing leader style, which remains a fairly atypical position in the literature today.

Leadership research since Fiedler

The topic of leadership is massive and cannot possibly be covered adequately in the limited space available here. In several ways, Fiedler's model has been superseded. However, his schema remains one of the most useful illustrations of the contingency idea, because it manages to integrate so much (leader styles, forms of power, situational contingencies). It can probably be said that most of the theories of leadership since Fiedler's original model are actually variations on the same (contextual contingency) theme. Virtually all of them attempt to ascertain which of the two basic leader styles is optimal for the range of situational contingencies being considered (for a review, see Fiedler & House 1994).

An interesting example of these latter-day derivatives can be found in an Australian-derived schema for managing organisational change. In this model, the key contextual factors are (a) amount of economic turbulence in the external marketplace, classified as 'stormy' or 'calm', along with (b) the scale of change being advocated, classified as 'incremental improvement' versus 'large leap' (Dunphy & Stace 1993). The schema proposes that when the operating environment is stormy — for example during the relative economic turbulence experienced during the late 1980s and early 1990s, workers will tend to prefer for change management purposes a combination, or configuration, of directive, task-focused leadership styles coupled with large leaps rather than incremental small steps (a combination called 'dictatorial transformation'). When economic calm returns to the marketplace, along with a semblance of job certainty, the preferred leadership style and preferred magnitude of change will gradually revert to relationship-oriented incremental improvements (termed 'participative evolution'). Between these two extremes, the model suggests, will be found preferences for the remaining two combinations (task-focused incremental improvements and relationship-based large leaps).

As with Fiedler's model, Dunphy and Stace's schema is largely inductive. It is derived not from theory but comparatively directly from data gathered through a combination of organisational case studies and interviews conducted in Australia during the relatively stormy early 1990s. The data gathered using these research methods (described in chapter 1) revealed preferences for organisational change to proceed by large leaps, administered with a task-focused style. Review data from outside Australia have been broadly consistent with the model (e.g. Guzzo, Jette & Katzell 1985). Guzzo et al. conducted an evaluation of (largely Western) organisational change interventions, made during the comparatively calm and stable economic times of the 1970s. In keeping with the Dunphy and Stace model, incremental improvements, administered with a relationship-oriented style, were found to be effective in this context of relative calm.

The review by Guzzo et al. focused on organisational change interventions that employed participative evolution. It did not look at any interventions during the same period that had used dictatorial transformation to determine whether these had, as the model predicts, been generally *un*successful. For that question, a more suited testing ground can be found in Australian and New Zealand companies' combined experiences of downsizing. Downsizing tends to take place in relatively stormy economic environments, and in these conditions the model predicts that directive task orientations, with large leaps, will be more acceptable to employees. This prediction is interesting, because it runs directly against the grain of many 'empowerment' themes (some of them faddish) in management today. This unorthodoxy gives the proposed model an edgy and interesting potential for accommodation in the way we schematise leadership.

In conducting their downsizing operations, Australian organisations have tended to opt for the 'human relations' approach of smaller cuts extended over longer time frames. New Zealand companies, on the other hand have tended to opt for the 'short sharp shock' of the large leap (Littler et al. 1997). According to Dunphy and Stace's marketplace contingency model, downsizing should have been less painful in New Zealand. Consistent with this prediction, Littler et al. found that staff recovery from downsizing was generally better in New Zealand than from the 'death of a thousand cuts' implemented in Australia. So the evidence from actual downsizing operations is, broadly speaking, consistent with the contingency schema developed by Dunphy and Stace.

A weakness in this research is that we do not know for sure whether cultural values were partly responsible for the different observations about downsizing made in Australia and New Zealand. Although the two countries are anecdotally role-schematised as being culturally similar, the differences in reactions to downsizing could still be due to some real differences in cultural and/or organisational culture values. Australian organisations may simply, for example, be inherently more conservative (and change averse) than their New Zealand counterparts. Thus, we do not yet know with certainty how far the model is valid and useful outside of the Australian cultural context in which it originated.

The criticism of cultural specificity can also be made of Fiedler's contingency model. For example, perhaps the value dimension of individualism–collectivism will create contingencies of its own, which will interact with the patterns observed by Fiedler (whose observations, we should note, were gathered largely in relatively individualistic American settings). Although, as we have seen, power distance (another robust dimension of culture identified in chapter 1) *is* incorporated into Fiedler's model, future research must continue to address the issue of accommodating cultural contingencies in leadership schemata (Aycan et al. 2000).

Just as leaders need to accommodate their schemata, including cultural contingencies, to fit the situation at hand, so the role of leaders also hinges on persuading *followers* to accommodate their own schemata to match the pace of change in the marketplace. In the literature today, this type of influence is known as transformational leadership. In social psychological terms, transformational leaders redefine organisational norms by reshaping an organisation's culture and cultural schemata.

One critical factor in promoting this kind of transformation is an aspiring leader's 'emotional intelligence', or 'EQ' (Goleman 1998). Although 'intelligence' is a trait concept, EQ is not, and its proponents try hard to steer clear of the fundamental attribution error. Goleman, for example, believes that transformational leaders must be high on social skills. To identify these social skills precisely, Goleman asks what skills differentiate transformational leaders from the rest of us. To answer this question he has returned to the empirical known groups method used by early leadership studies. On this occasion, however, the technique isolates context-defined, *social* skills that differentiate recognised charismatic figures from more pedestrian leaders.

The skills identified by Goleman using this inductive method support previous models. They include, for instance, knowing when to focus on the logic of task completion rather than the emotions of workplace relations. But they also add new factors. According to Goleman's data, transformational leaders must cultivate self-awareness, too. Specifically, they need a self schema that is characterised by open-ness and self-honesty, with a capacity to admit to human failings. Such qualities recall the 'pratfall effect' discussed in chapter 5. In this case, a pratfall effect would work to keep transformational leaders in touch with their followers — keeping them 'human' (Aamodt 1999). Other social skills for inclusion in the schema for transformational leadership include demonstrating empathy and motiv-ation — or, more precisely, being skilled at manifesting these qualities to fol-lowers: 'A leader who cannot express her empathy may as well not have it at all. And a leader's motivation will be useless if he cannot communicate his passion to the organization' (Goleman 1998, p. 102). Thus, a key skill among future leaders will be the ability to demonstrate social and interpersonal skills in *communication*.

(2)   Communication skills

These skills are not, of course, confined to organisational life; they matter in all forms of social life. Given the enormity of this area, we need a provisional tax-onomy to help us select key examples of each major type of communication life skill. Figure 7.3 sketches a crude but useful distinction between communication skills that produce a behaviour ('encoding') and those that interpret the behaviour of others ('decoding'). Figure 7.3 also distinguishes between mostly verbal and mostly non-verbal communication.

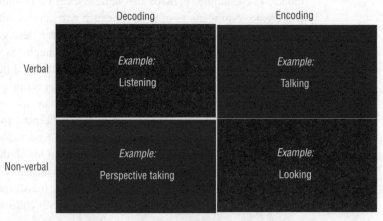

Figure 7.3   A provisional taxonomy of communication skills

People are often unaccustomed to *listening* to others, or, at the other extreme, to *talking* forthrightly (assertively) with them (see figure 7.3). They are also often unaccustomed to monitoring the way they *look* at others, as well as trying out those others' *perspectives*. To put this more precisely, people are often skilfully unaware of, and so incompetently skilled at, talking *over* others instead of listening to them; 'giving in' to others so as to preserve harmony instead of speaking their minds whatever the consequences; making inappropriate forms of eye contact, as did Peter Garrett in critical narrative 5.3; and judging others from their own cultural world view rather than trying to see 'reality' from the other's perspective. As with implicit stereotyping, therefore, skills shortfalls are often reflections of over-assimilation and schematic rigidity, whose remedy lies in a combination of awareness raising and learning-by-doing.

Listening

Critical to all forms of communication is a readiness to listen to what other people have to say. Listening here does not mean listening 'intelligently', as in listening to a lecture and grasping intellectually what is said. We mean listening in a social sense, as in respecting what others have to say. Such skills are increasingly recognised as critical in organisational and leadership settings (Foster & Seeker 1997; Stone 1999; Woodhall & Winstanley 1998). The premise of multi-source, all-round, 360-degree performance feedback, for instance, is based on a recognition of the importance of listening. Ironically, intelligent people in the IQ sense often lack the skills of social listening (Nickerson 1999). They are precisely the people who most need to acquire listening skills. Developing social skills in listening means cultivating a readiness to listen to others rather than simply talking over them (Weaver 1972). Listening skills are therefore a question of attitude and positioning.

Intelligent people are not alone in needing instruction on how to listen. Estimates of the proportion of communication time spent listening in organisations vary from 20 to 60 per cent, depending on whether the employee is a technical worker or an executive (Bostrom 1997). Outside of work, too, Bostrom reports that the modal channel for communication activity, from among listening, speaking, reading and writing, is also likely to be listening. Yet this is the form of communication, next to speaking, reading and writing, in which people are normally instructed least (Cronin 1993).

Common bad listening habits include cutting in on others' dialogue (say, with observations or reminiscences of our own); completing sentences for others; and losing attention, 'drifting away' to think about other things, while inserting a series of essentially random 'ohs' and 'ahs' as the other person tries valiantly to get his or her message across to us (Fontana 1992). According to Fontana, most compulsive talkers (who are, by definition, poor listeners) know that they talk too much, which means that they do not have a defective schema for their ideal self. Instead, they have the unthinking habit of talking rather than listening. Like observers who have come to rely too heavily on role or event stereotypes, their behaviour is driven implicitly, and to that extent is relatively mindless.

According to the schema literature reviewed in this chapter, these implicit routines need to be replaced by, say, an accommodated event schema for interacting and communicating with others. The skills literature reviewed here suggests that this may be achieved through a combination of raising awareness and learning-by-doing. An illustration of how such schemata and skills can be respectively revised and internalised is contained in critical narrative 7.1. This narrative assumes a 'worst case scenario', starting with the assumption that the trainee is not even aware of her over-talkativeness.

CRITICAL NARRATIVE 7.1

The acquisition of basic listening skills

Imagine an executive who is thought to be low on empathy by her colleagues. Part of the deficit shows itself as an inability to listen; she interrupts people and doesn't pay close attention to what they're saying. To fix the problem, the executive needs to be motivated to change, and then she needs practice and feedback from others in the company. A colleague or coach could be tapped to let the executive know when she has been observed failing to listen. She would then have to replay the incident and give a better response; that is, demonstrate her ability to absorb what others are saying. And the executive could then be directed to observe certain executives who listen well and to mimic their behaviour.

Source: Reprinted by permission of *Harvard Business Review*. Extracted from 'What makes a leader?', by D. Goleman, November/December 1998, p. 97. Copyright © 1998 by the Harvard Business School Publishing Corporation. All rights reserved.

Critical narrative 7.1 contains the main components of most skills training programs (Muchinsky 2000). These elements are derived from what we know about learning motor skills (Argyle 1968). The elements include, first, observing others who *model* the desired skill, which incorporates the central tenets of social learning theory (see chapter 4) and observational learning. As critical narrative 7.1 also illustrates, skills training programs will tend to include performing the action oneself (learning-by-doing); receiving feedback from the action, either from others or by watching the self on videotape (the equivalent of kinaesthetic feedback in motor skills); and practising the action again and again (under the assumption that learning-by-doing eventually results in an internalised schema for enacting the smooth and skilled performance of the activity).

Talking

Talking is a huge area, far too big to cover in any single chapter, so it is only touched on here. This section focuses on people who listen too much and who need to learn how to talk more — to become more *assertive*. Over the years the topic of assertiveness, and assertiveness training, has waxed and waned in popularity across training domains in organisations (Chatterjee 1999), health and wellbeing (Ortiz, Alveiro-Pedreros & Meluk 1991), and education (Hon & Watkins 1995). Today, for fairly obvious reasons perhaps, its importance seems to be growing most clearly in the domain of training for life in business (e.g. Gillen 1998).

Asserting

The essence of assertiveness includes being able to say no to unreasonable requests; to express unpopular opinions when we hold them to be true; and to ask others to change their behaviour when we privately disagree with it or find it hurtful in some way. Assertiveness lies somewhere between passivity and outright aggression (see chapter 10). Fontana defines it eloquently in the following observation:

Self-assertion is essentially having the courage to accept and be the person we are, with all our strengths and weaknesses and individualities. It's the courage to believe in ourselves, and the confidence to convey this belief to others. It has nothing to do with exploiting others, or with always putting our own interests first. (1992, p. 81)

Described in this way, self-assertion skills are founded on a combination of both *event* schemata, for managing interpersonal confrontation, and *self* schemata, for being true to an ideal inner self (for a discussion on the importance of this construction, see Higgins 1987).

Is 'assertiveness' just a culture-bound preoccupation? The concept of assertiveness has attracted more than its share of controversy, chiefly because it is inherently self-focused, and to that extent bound up with cultures that are relatively individualistic (Forgas 1985). Indeed, the term was first widely used in psychology during the 'me' decade of the 1970s, and there is in the literature a recognised need for the expression of assertiveness, and for assertiveness training, to be studied more in relatively collectivistic and power distant cultural environments (Rakos 1997). Assertiveness, therefore, is unarguably part of a relatively individualistic cultural schema.

At the same time, however, and from a strictly practical point of view, such individualism is itself globalising, and will therefore be rejuvenating the relevance of the assertiveness concept. For example, to the extent that other individuals are increasingly asserting *their* individual rights, we will be obliged to assert *ours*. Life becomes a kind of prisoner's dilemma game. Being 'nice' and non-assertive often simply encourages others to assert their own will over ours (reasonableness, as in chapter 3, is taken as a sign of weakness). In everyday life, many of us, instead of saying what needs to be said, find ourselves avoiding disagreement because it is inherently unpleasant, or because we implicitly and rigidly schematise self as a 'nice' person. Ironically, and precisely *because* of these attempts to avoid disharmony and unpleasantness, we still suffer because we blame ourselves for not speaking out when we had the chance. Ultimately, as we have seen, such discrepancies between actual and ideal self are damaging to self-esteem.

These processes are brought to life in critical narrative 7.2. The narrative also lists concrete recommendations for becoming more assertive in everyday life. Following Argyle's motor skills analogy, these are often practised, along with modelling and video feedback, in assertiveness training workshops.

CRITICAL NARRATIVE

7.2

Learning to be more self-assertive

Michaela attended a social skills workshop with a number of problems, both personal and professional. One of these was that she worried over the often ineffectual way in which she tried to say what she really meant. In the course of role-play sessions, two of Michaela's tasks were:

1. to complain to an equal status colleague that the latter had taken advantage of her absence on sick leave to purloin her secretary, leaving her with someone less efficient
2. to inform a junior colleague that she was refusing his request for leave of absence at a busy time of year to attend the wedding of a distant cousin.

In the first exercise, Michaela made repeated use of such questions as 'Don't you think you're being a bit unfair about this?', rather than relying on definite statements like

(continued)

'You're being very unfair'. In the second exercise, she interspersed her remarks with comments like 'I'm sorry about this' and 'I know how disappointed you must feel', rather than simply stating her decision and giving her reasons.

The other participants in the workshop felt that Michaela was giving clear signals in the equal status relationship that she wasn't going to put up too much of a fight over the secretary or take the issue to someone higher up. In the junior colleague relationship, they felt she was signalling personal guilt, and giving advance permission for resentment and accusations. In the latter case, it was felt that she had no need to apologise for refusing what was a most unreasonable request. If anyone had a right to feel resentment, it was Michaela for being put in the position of having to refuse.

Michaela accepted these observations, and identified the source of her behaviour as her own lack of conviction of her right to take a firm position on any major issue. In the equal status colleague relationship, she confessed to a sneaking feeling that her colleague would perhaps make better use of an efficient secretary than she was doing. And in the junior colleague relationship, she would agonise over whether she was justified in denying someone the opportunity for such an exciting experience.

Once she acknowledged these responses, Michaela saw her lack of self-conviction as unrealistic since, objectively, she could recognise her own worth. She felt it had something to do with being the youngest of four high-achieving children. As a girl, she had been aware that whatever she did, there was always a sibling who could do it better and who would criticise or belittle her efforts. Similarly, whenever she got into a debate, there was always a sibling who would scorn her arguments.

She was therefore encouraged to identify a broad sample of the situations in which her lack of self-conviction would arise, and to practise relabelling it as an old, inappropriate response habit, and one that could safely be ignored as irrelevant to her life as she was actually experiencing it.

Michaela offers a good instance of how some individuals hold themselves back in their relationships. Her fear of failure, of laying herself open to criticism, of being disliked, meant that for much of the time she was not being what is sometimes called 'authentic'.

Saying no

When you want to say no, it will help if you:

- Rehearse the word; for some of us it's so unfamiliar that it doesn't sound right! Try it out, in private and aloud.
- Identify in advance the kind of requests that fall into the 'can't do' category, and be ready for them when they arise.
- Prepare an appropriate refusal that is polite but firm and starts with 'No'. ('No, I'm sorry I'm having to refuse that kind of request.' 'No, I'm not the best person to do that.' 'No, that's not in my field.')
- Use a definite tone of voice. People can all too easily sense when you don't mean what you say.
- Once you've said no, do not change your mind except in very special circumstances. If you get a reputation for backing down, people will work on you until you do.
- Don't feel guilty about saying no. If you've worked out the 'can't do' category carefully, you should be confident that your refusal is justified.
- Set boundaries upon your 'yes'. If you make clear the limits to which you're agreeing, people have fewer grounds for returning to pester you to do more and more.

Source: Extracted and adapted from Fontana (1992, pp. 79–82).

So far we have concentrated on verbal forms of communication and verbal social skills. Intuitively, when compared with non-verbal communication, we may feel that words are more central to what it is to be human, so they typically carry more weight in the communication process. Surprisingly, however, this hunch is not necessarily correct. Grounds for seriously doubting the primacy of words over non-verbal behaviour can be found in a number of experiments in which a stimulus person sends two contradictory messages. One of these is sent non-verbally (e.g. body language that displays deference); the other is sent through the medium of spoken language (e.g. speech patterns that display arrogance) (Burgoon 1994). Given such contradictory and competing messages, which one will people generally rely on most in forming their impressions of the message sender? Surprisingly, perhaps, people will generally give more weight to the non-verbal message (Shea 1998). Non-verbal messages, therefore, are comparatively salient.

Looking

From among the various non-verbal modes of communication (chiefly through the eyes, ears and sense of touch), many of us would probably agree that the most important is how we use our eyes. A dramatic illustration of this importance is provided in critical narrative 7.3.

CRITICAL NARRATIVE 7.3

The power of the gaze

During an Open University summer school I taught in Britain, the students in a lecture audience were told to manipulate their eye gaze at their lecturer (one of my colleagues) so that in the first half of the lecture everybody on the left-hand side of the room would be looking at him, and nobody on the right-hand side, while in the second half of the lecture the roles would be reversed. My colleague was initially somewhat disturbed by the apparent complete lack of attention on the right-hand side of the room, but quickly adjusted to the situation by positioning himself on the left-hand side of the theatre, and gazing predominantly at the attentive half of the audience. When the switch-over occurred halfway through, he reacted with considerable disturbance, lost the thread of his argument, and found it quite difficult to readjust to the situation. Of course, he was much relieved when the strange behaviour of the class was explained to him later. The point is that we always rely on such simple rules of visual communication to make inter-actions possible, and even minor deviations may lead to the breakdown of the encounter.

Source: Forgas (1985, p. 157).

Although dramatic, this kind of critical incident was artificially staged and, to that extent at least, not typical of everyday life. The bystander intervention studies reviewed in chapter 2 offer another example of how important eye contact can become for communication, and in particular the importance of noticing an emergency in the first place. A more commonplace example of how 'even minor deviations' can lead to communication difficulties is inadvertently making eye contact with another motorist at traffic lights. As some of us may already know, the wrong look at the wrong time in such potentially stressful situations can sometimes become a catalyst for 'road rage' (for an earlier but still relevant field experiment on this phenomenon, see Ellsworth, Carlsmith & Henson 1972).

Between them, this experience and the one related in critical narrative 7.3 indicate that the amount of eye contact encoded into social interactions may sometimes need to be carefully judged. Too little, and we may intimidate the instructor or, by missing what another driver is doing, be involved in an accident. Too much, and we may just as easily discomfort the instructor, or risk being physically assaulted by an aggressive motorist. Using the gaze skilfully is therefore very much a question of balance, or equilibrium. A modicum of gaze keeps both instructor and driver 'on the right track'.

A classic study of this concept of equilibrium is found in Argyle and Dean (1965). This research, like the road-rage example above, focused on how eye contact is used to try to maintain an acceptable level of personal space. During a conversation between a participant and a confederate, the confederate varied the amount of personal space, or intimacy, between them. When intimacy was increased by both looking and moving physically closer, participants subconsciously compensated for this by steadily reducing their own amount of eye contact in proportion to the degree of physical intimacy they were experiencing. In their implicit event schema for conversations, they had *used* their eyes to maintain what Argyle and Dean called **intimacy equilibrium.**

Such principles may be applied not only to managing our own eye contact behaviour, for example *as* students in class, but also in handling the eye contact behaviours of others, for example *of* students in class, when teaching. The latter situation involves that most dreaded of situations for many of us, public speaking. To this, Argyle and Dean (1965) applied the principle of intimacy equilibrium to help reduce anxiety in public speaking trainees. These trainees were permitted to practise their speeches in front of audiences that were initially positioned farther away, and so were 'less intimate'. This simple but effective intervention, based on the principle of intimacy equilibrium, allowed the trainees vital breathing space to build up their confidence for later public speaking events.

In another example of the practical implications of intimacy equilibrium, Forgas (1985) highlights its importance in technological design. Lifts and trains, for instance, often cram people together tightly, and this forced proximity increases intimacy to uncomfortable levels for many users. Cramped spaces will also increase the risk of people looking away from each other. During times of danger, when communication becomes critical, this can impede taking appropriate actions to safeguard people's wellbeing. Precisely this effect was recorded, for instance, during the 'smoking room' experiment reported by Darley and Latané in 1968 (see chapter 2).

In more general terms, one way of thinking about intimacy equilibrium is to imagine it as a kind of hydraulic mechanism. Excessive activity through one communication channel, such as coming too close to someone physically, is automatically (skilfully) compensated for by reduced activity in another, such as encoding lessened eye contact. According to Argyle's suggestion that all skills operate on pretty much the same basis, this 'hydraulic' principle may apply to a range of communication skills. An example is non-verbal leakage, discussed earlier in relation to unintentionally communicating stereotype bias (see also Ambady & Rosenthal 1992). This encoding problem occurs because the more we attempt to suppress or hide a thought from others, the more it threatens to 'pop out' anyway — this is an inherently 'hydraulic' notion. Poker players illustrate this effect, too. When bluffing, they may manage to control their facial muscles and eye movements, but they may still give themselves away through nervous gestures or other tell-tale body language, say through their hands or feet (Ekman & Friesen 1974). The analogy with hydraulics therefore suggests a range of domains in which intimacy equilibrium is relevant, from meeting people to encoding and decoding dishonesty.

Experiencing another perspective

If we had to identify a unifying thread running through the three types of skill considered in figure 7.3 and throughout chapter 6, it would be an ability to adopt others' perspectives on demand. Successful poker players need to see how leaky their hand or foot movements appear to their opponents. Designers of trains, elevators and other cramped spaces need to learn what it feels like to be one of the end-users of their technological marvels. In the case of assertiveness training, the 'nice guy' has to appreciate what he or she looks like (often, a sucker) to the individuals with whom he or she is continually being soft. In terms of the skill of listening, we need to understand what we sound like when we interrupt others, or 'umm' and 'ah' absent-mindedly when someone else is earnestly trying to communicate with us. In people management, too, leaders need to know how their followers see them (for example to determine the state of leader–member relations). In order to overcome stereotypes, it is critical to be able to appreciate the perspective of the out-group (Sanson et al. 1998). This crucial issue provided a fulcrum for the previous chapter and is arguably critical, too, in creating the right first impressions. Thus, social skills of many kinds require us to see ourselves as others see us; acquiring a schema for self-as-*other* (rather than actual, or ideal) person. In the literature, this idea is more succinctly known as 'perspective taking' (Sessa 1996).

Perspective taking is not something to which most people are accustomed, however. Think, for instance, how uncomfortable you can feel when hearing your own voice on tape, a discomfort that arises because we are so unaccustomed to its sound (Argyle 1968, p. 89). This lack of practice in being self-aware has practical consequences. In regard to technology and design, for example, 'the worst judges of how easy people will find it to use devices and procedures [can be] those who designed them' (Nickerson 1999, p. 750). Nickerson identifies the core problem as egocentrism — that is, we tend to assume that the other person's perspective is identical to our own (see chapter 6, on availability heuristics). An area in which this is particularly relevant for many of us is educational communication. It is common for 'experts' in this field to overestimate the ease with which novices will be able to pick up their specialism (Hinds 1999).

In schematic terms, as one observer has put it, 'the fact that you thoroughly understand calculus constitutes an obstacle to your continuously keeping in mind my ignorance of it while trying to explain it to me; you may momentarily realise how hard it is for me, but that realisation may quietly slip away once you get immersed in your explanation' (Flavell 1977, p. 124). This is a superb and probably quite familiar example, from educational communication, of what Argyris (1998) meant by skilled unawareness, and what is also discussed in this chapter as over-assimilation (of everything into one rigid schema). An equally lucid illustration of how such over-assimilation can be overcome through a process of schematic accommodation is offered by Piaget himself:

> Every beginning instructor discovers sooner or later that his first lectures were incomprehensible because he was talking to himself, mindful only of his own point of view. He realises only gradually and with difficulty that it is not easy to place oneself in the shoes of students who do not know what he knows about the subject matter of his course. (1962, p. 5)

In my own experience, this is a fine example of the criticality of perspective taking in everyday educational communication!

As Piaget's example implies, practical experience is the key to learning how to share perspectives: 'Simply informing people of the tendency [towards egocentrism] and asking them to avoid it appears not to work' (Nickerson 1999, p. 752. Put another way, the skills of perspective taking are procedural rather than declarative. They have probably been acquired over extended periods of time, for example through prolonged exposure to 'caregiver styles'. These were first studied, as we saw, by Lewin, Lippett and White (1939), and later provided much of the impetus for studying leader styles in the workplace. Consistent with the workplace literature we reviewed, caregivers whose preferred style is to 'lead' with a *blend* of task and relationship styles tend to encourage the development of perspective taking in their children later in life (Sanson et al. 1998). According to Sanson et al., striking the right balance of these styles in caregiving entails 'listening to the child's point of view, explaining how others are affected by the child's behaviour, [and] explaining reasons for rules to the child' (1998, p. 174; for classic studies of parental styles, see Baumrind 1983, 1996). Thus, one of the best opportunities for encouraging perspective taking occurs through childhood socialisation, and consists of providing a parental behavioural *model*.

Many adults will not have been exposed to overly perspective-sensitive models during their formative years. For these people, adult options for learning the generic skills of perspective taking have been discussed in the previous chapter in the context of reducing stereotyping of the poor and other socially disadvantaged groups. A related area in which such generic skills are being increasingly encouraged, however, is in training for taking up work in cross-cultural settings. This applies as much to psychologists as to other professionals:

> In a country where a quarter of all its citizens were born overseas, and speak a language other than English at home, the likelihood of cultural difference being a factor in psychological practice will increase. For this reason, psychologists will need to become skilled in recognising specific and universal issues. (Gabb 1998, p. 184)

These issues include overseas assignments, community development work in rural and remote areas, and working with any kind of multicultural client base. In short, becoming skilled in culture is an extremely important concern for the twenty-first century.

(3) Culture

In the language of schema and skill, cultural training works through the trainee learning the rules of social interaction in the culture-of-destination so that these rules will be assimilated into, and even perhaps accommodate, the existing person, role, self and cultural schemata that the trainee holds. They can then be manifested as intercultural social skills. In management, for example, we have already seen how styles of leadership are expressed differently across cultures. These variations are often quite specific: managers in India may be expected to make nurturance contingent on task success (Sinha 1990), while managers working in Japan may be expected to be task-focused on the shop floor and relations-focused during rest breaks (Misumi & Peterson 1985). Cross-cultural training informs people about these customs so that they can become skilfully aware of the rules and skilfully competent at enacting them, rather than assuming that managerial skills are the same everywhere (Giacalone & Beard 1994).

Culture-specific training

Knowing such specifics can save a lot of cross-cultural misunderstanding and conflict. On 16 March 1998 the International Monetary Fund's (IMF) representative stood, hands on hips, during the President of Indonesia's signing of a loan deal, which took place before the international and national media. In Indonesian society, standing with arms akimbo is perceived as an aggressive posture. Added to this was the broader cultural context of power distance (respect for authority) and a sensitivity to outsider paternalism that has its roots in the country's history of colonialism. The IMF president's posture, which might have been judged to be inoffensive in his own cultural setting, precipitated widespread anger among the Indonesian general public.

An incident that I experienced during a consultancy assignment in Thailand provides a more mundane, personal example. Jet-lagged and nervous (or at least those are my excuses), I made a stupid attempt to explain the salesperson's 'foot-in-the-door' technique, which I did by unthinkingly gesturing with my feet in a demonstration that would be considered extremely rude in Thai society. My escape from this skilled unawareness or incompetence was to pay added respect to the Thai value of humour. I quickly renamed the 'foot-in-the-door' as a 'hand-in-the-window' technique, in reference to Bangkok's street vendors who sell their wares through the open windows of vehicles caught in the mega-city's traffic jams. Thankfully, this effort amused my Thai colleagues, who apparently forgave me my crass and stupid blunder.

In both these illustrations, one global and the other local, the devil is in the detail; they demonstrate that culture-specific skill training will always have a place. Of course, the short review in this chapter cannot do justice to such a broad area (for content-based reviews on a country-by-country basis, see, for example, Irwin 1996 or Landis & Bhagat 1996; for a recent example of a cross-cultural program in Australia, see Hill et al. 1995). Rather, the following sections will outline some general principles on how country-specific training is approached. Indeed, some training programs deliberately foreground these general issues rather than the specific issues.

Culture-general training

Taking listening skills as an example, culture-general norms (e.g. concerning power distance) could be expected to at least partly determine the rules of social conduct (e.g. who is expected to do most of the listening and who is expected to do most of the talking). To give another example, power distance would also regulate the level of 'assertiveness' that is appropriate in everyday interaction, given the actors' respective statuses. Gaze, too, is moderated by norms about power distance, and indeed in many cultures the very act of making eye contact is considered rude and insulting, while looking away or down is considered respectful (Gallois & Callan 1997; see also critical narrative 5.2). Power distance, then, is a dimension along which cultures in general, and intercultural event schemata in particular, can be ordered (for classic examples of related examples, see Hall 1959, 1966).

Each of the two basic training methods above has its strengths and weaknesses. The best way of appreciating these is to review the historical context in which they emerged.

The 1950s and 1960s: 'chalk and talk'

Early attempts to prepare people for cross-cultural assignments focused on the prevention or minimisation of 'culture shock' (Oberg 1954). As Sherif's auto-kinetic study captured so well in the laboratory (see chapter 1), experiencing an entirely new social reality can be unsettling and stressful, as guest workers struggle to accommodate too many of their central cultural, event and self schemata to fit their new social environment (for a seminal discussion of the concept of culture shock, see Furnham & Bochner 1986). According to Furnham and Bochner, common reactions to the stress of culture shock include skin irritations, extreme homesickness and excessive drinking. Each of these reactions can seriously impair capacity to complete the assignment (for a discussion of acculturation strains, see Ward 1996). Since none of these 'symptoms' can be experienced directly before leaving home, most pre-departure training programs during the 1950s and 1960s were delivered through the mode of 'chalk-and-talk' in lecture style, rather than being based on learning-by-doing (Harrison & Hopkins 1967). The thesis of this chapter is that their lack of practice was a major weakness in early approaches to cross-cultural training.

This point is underscored by wider findings concerning the longer term impact of being 'instructed' on how one 'should' behave. In chapter 3, we saw through Lewin's and others' classic studies how 'high-pressure' techniques often have little impact, or indeed even backfire (Brehm 1966). In chapter 5, too, we learned about ironic effects, and how trying not to do something often produces the opposite result (e.g. Wegner et al. 1987). More recent studies in the field of stereotyping itself have indirectly suggested that, in the mid to longer term, there is a clear risk that training on how one 'should' behave during intercultural encounters (Atkins, personal correspondence) can sometimes have a reverse or **rebound effect** (MacRae et al. 1994, reprinted 1996; MacRae, Bodenhausen & Milne 1998). In each of these studies, a manipulated 'set' to self-monitor and control unwanted thoughts about stereotyping actually had a reverse impact.

The 1970s and culture assimilation

The next big step forward was to modify the Critical Incidents technique (see chapter 1; Flanagan 1954) so as to fit cross-cultural training programs (Fiedler, Mitchell & Triandis 1971). In this quasi-experiential modification, called a 'culture assimilator', trainees would read a series of critical incidents from cross-cultural encounters. These were not so very different from the foot-in-the-door/hand-in-the-window incident mentioned above, basically comprising short stories describing unintentional cross-cultural blunders and misunderstandings. For example, expatriate teachers might mistake student politeness for familiarity and so get too close to their students. This inappropriate intimacy might force the students to act 'coolly' in order to restore normal levels of power distance from the teachers — who meanwhile become increasingly distressed and disoriented because they cannot understand why the students are suddenly so distant and 'cold'.

The trainees' job in a culture assimilator is to pick what to do next from a choice of behavioural remedies, one of which typically has a chance of remedying the situation (e.g. 'laugh at yourself', 'show good heart'). Once the trainees have picked their choice, they are given feedback on whether they were right or wrong, and why they were right or wrong in this particular setting. If trainees are then wrong a second time, they must repeat the exercise until they get it right. With this emphasis on doing, feedback and practice, the culture assimilators were aligned more closely than their chalk-and-talk predecessors with Argyle's analogy to the acquisition of motor skills (see also Argyris 2000).

This resemblance to learning-by-doing, according to the analysis in this chapter, was a major strength in the culture assimilator. In fact, culture assimilators have proved themselves to be more effective than lecture methods (O'Brien & Plooji 1977) both in cross-national assignments (Worchel & Mitchell 1972) and within the same multicultural society (Triandis 1977). Importantly, referring back to figure 7.1, culture assimilators have also helped to reduce interracial stereotyping, social distancing and other forms of inter-group prejudice and discrimination (Weldon et al. 1975). They have therefore been demonstrably effective ways to break some of the vicious circles of stereotyping illustrated in figure 7.1.

Diversity does not mean that principles discussed above, such as intimacy equilibrium, are inapplicable in other cultural settings. More likely, the expression of such rules is simply encoded differently into the relevant event schema. Taking intimacy equilibrium as an example, cultural norms vary greatly in how much and through how many concurrent channels intimacy is permitted. In some Arab societies and in parts of Brazil, for instance, looking is normally accompanied by relatively close physical distance, as well as by a lot of touching. In Thailand, by contrast, such touching could prove offensive or rude (for other examples, see Smith & Bond 1999). The point is that even once these differences are known, the principle of intimacy equilibrium may still apply. In other words, excesses over the culturally determined baseline are still compensated for by decreases in other communication channels. General principles of cross-cultural adjustment therefore remain a realistic possibility.

The 1980s and 1990s: a time for culture-general assimilators

A landmark publication during this period sought to identify a set of general themes governing intercultural contact and communication (Brislin et al. 1986). These themes were extracted by surveying and content analysing the published literature on cross-cultural assignments. This analysis isolated 18 themes, exemplified for the trainee in more than a hundred critical incidents. These incidents reflected themes such as degree of belief in hierarchies (power distance), and importance of the group and the individual (individualism versus collectivism; for an assimilator based entirely around this construct, see Bhawuk 1998). The 'culture-general assimilator', as it became known, also addressed earlier themes such as culture shock and attribution biases across groups. The culture-general assimilator is thus relatively encompassing.

The risk with such relatively all-encompassing assimilators, which, after all, are built on the idea of generalisation, is that they inadvertently foster out-group homogeneity effects (see chapter 6), which may inadvertently encourage stereotyping. However, there is at least empirical evidence that experiencing the culture-general assimilator does improve cross-cultural adjustment for the guest (Cushner & Brislin 1996). It has proved helpful, for instance, to overseas students adjusting to ways of studying and everyday living in New Zealand (Cushner 1989). Such findings suggest that the costs of homogenisation can indeed be outweighed by the benefits of the training.

There is also a powerful financial argument in favour of the general assimilator. Compared with their culture-specific cousins, culture-general assimilators are economical in the long run because of the transfer of training from one assignment to the next (Bhawuk 1998). In the global economy, in which such assignments are becoming increasingly commonplace (Erez 2002), this is probably the major reason why culture-general assimilators are steadily replacing the wide range of more resource-intensive, country-specific programs (Bhawuk & Brislin 2000).

The new millennium and culture accommodators

Surprisingly (and indeed ethnocentrically), despite this progress in the field, the adaptation literature has focused almost exclusively on equipping the guest with pre-departure training, without equipping the hosts with any pre-arrival training (Vance & Ring 1994). This also means that dynamic interaction between sojourner and host has been neglected (Bhawuk & Brislin 2000). One technique, however, goes some way to making amends for this serious shortfall. Selmer (1995) has developed a method of training that empirically identifies discrepancies between the perceptions of groups of guest and host workers. To be precise, the prospective guests are surveyed about their perceptions of where the values of their hosts are situated (role schema), and these estimates are quantified on Likert-type scales (see chapter 4). Critically, however, the same survey form is also given to the prospective *hosts*, who are asked to report their own values as they actually stand (see chapter 6, on work ethic illusion). Any empirical discrepancies between the two groups of perceptions are then rank-ordered in terms of magnitude, which provides an integrated set of foci for the pre-departure preparation program. This is conceptually a very neat way of undertaking training needs analysis and also ensures that local hosts — finally — have an opportunity to participate in the training program itself.

What is still noticeably missing from Selmer's technique, however, is equal consideration of how the hosts view the guests' cultural values. Indigenous people need access to cross-cultural training in preparation for the arrival of their guests (Pastor 1997). Without such training there are still likely to be discrepancies. Systems theory suggests that breakdowns in intercultural communication will stem from misunderstandings on both sides. Figure 1.1, for example, described a dynamic intercultural interaction that may be common whenever a relatively individualistic and egalitarian guest manager works with a relatively collectivistic and power distant host employee. In that interaction, which would entail rules for listening, asserting, making eye contact and perspective taking, *neither* party was able to fully appreciate where the other was 'coming from'. This is ultimately why each group increasingly helped confirm the other's stereotype of it, giving rise to an escalation that would easily start to jeopardise the whole assignment.

REFLECTION — A META-PROCESS

The dynamic of escalation runs throughout our review of social cognition as a whole. In chapter 5, for instance, Pygmalion effects from first impressions quickly become double Pygmalion effects. In chapter 6, stereotyping by the wealthy steadily reinforces withdrawal and backlash by the poor, and vice-versa. In this chapter, too, figure 7.1 depicts how stereotyping out-groups drives and reinforces cycles of prejudice and discrimination. Indeed, figure 7.1 might be regarded as a kind of template schema into which each of the major dynamic processes discussed in part 2 (Social Cognition) can be assimilated (see activity 7.4). As critical narrative 7.4 illustrates, stereotypes are just as active in job selection as in everyday social discourse about poverty or during intercultural assignments (see also Anderson & Shackleton 1990, on stereotyping of the 'ideal graduate'). Whichever way we turn, therefore, the systems archetype of escalation is there to greet us; it is a meta-process in social cognition.

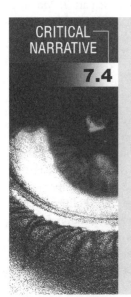

CRITICAL NARRATIVE

7.4

Making an impact that counts

A social psychologist at the Australian National University, Kate Reynolds, has summarised in the *Australian Financial Review* how people often arrive at first encounters with preconditioned expectations about the other person. First impressions, she points out, greatly depend on what people believe about us even before we enter the room. The right first response is crucial, therefore.

Often people will be expecting us to conform to stereotypes that are linked to the job. A lawyer, for instance, will not be expected to dress like the marketing director for an advertising agency.

Impression management, however, is not as simple as having 'nice shoes or wearing the right clothes'. Rather, according to Dr Reynolds, successful impression management skills entail, in the beginning, 'not violating the norms and perceptions — "the lawyer in a dark suit, the art director in a black sweater" '.

Source: Based on Owens (2002).

The crux of the foregoing review is that, in order to break cycles of escalation like the ones in figure 7.1, we need to be sufficiently practised to prevent ourselves from falling into them. As the ironic and rebound effects and the general principle of minimal constraint warn, it may be counterproductive to try to break these cycles with words and conscious intentions alone, whether these are lectured by others or self-directed. At some point, people will have to heed Argyris's advice and give 'themselves permission to stumble in the process of learning' (1998, p. 26). For example, we need to practise experiencing the perspectives of 'other', including their perspectives on 'self'. In this way, it makes sense to speak not only of a meta-process (of escalation), but also of a **meta-process skill** in being able to step outside its loop.

An elementary step in this process is appreciating how we got into the loops in the first place. When trait inferences and attributions are practised every day to the point of automation, we gain a lot in terms of processing time and capacity. From figure 7.1 (and figure 5.1), we become skilled enough to process thin slices, because our schemata can 'fill in the gaps' with prior assumptions (anonymous peer reviewer, 2001). Yet there is a price to pay: we often become less 'mindful' (Langer 1989; Langer, Blank & Chanowitz 1978). The loss has been clear in this chapter — from stereotyping, to managing without paying attention to context, to failing to appreciate other perspectives, including the dangers of being cross-culturally insensitive. The same loss of flexibility surfaced in our review, in chapter 6, of stereotypes about the poor, and of person schematic halo effects created by the perception of central traits, discussed in chapter 5. Hence, the first step in counteracting unwanted schemata is to become more mindful of them — to raise our consciousness.

This idea of becoming more mindful suggests that a key to managing schemata, and one that is consistent with allowing self to stumble, is to seek **maximal cognition**. A raised level of awareness is critical for not stepping into negative Pygmalion effects during first impressions. It is also critical for not stepping into donor bias or into schematic rigidity about others. Arguably, too, it is vital for seeing ourselves as others see us — a central idea throughout part 2. Maximal cognition is thus a core applied principle running through all this section of the book.

SUMMARY

The field of skills is very broad, and this chapter has merely scratched its surface. Importantly, though, it has married the concepts of skill and schema, because one cannot exist without the other. Schemata are the psychological foundation for skilled behaviour. They are implicit programs, or mental software, for enacting routines that have been rehearsed over time to fluidity. The price for this fluidity is, ironically, loss of flexibility. The pre-eminent example of that rigidity is stereotyping. Many people, including professionals whose job specification includes being constantly flexible, remain unaware that their behaviour is often executed from the self-same stereotypes that they consciously reject. Effective leaders know when to change their schema-in-use according to social context. This skill can be acquired through practice, for example learning how to communicate with followers. Effective communicators are also empathic listeners, talkers, watchers and perspective takers. These empathic skills are counter-stereotypical, and to that extent critical for cross-cultural work. Culture skills training programs are progressively moving away from culture assimilation towards culture accommodation, as both guests and their hosts are encouraged to take each other's perspective, and so genuinely accommodate their views of themselves and their role towards 'other'. Key skills required for such accommodation include an ability to read dynamic interactions between diverse schemata, and to foresee and prevent any differences from escalating into division in the first place. The psychological principle at work in developing this meta-process skill, and that is found throughout part 2 of the book, is maximising cognition.

KEY TERMS

Accommodation. New objects and encounters do not easily fit into pre-existing schemata; as a result, these schemata are themselves revised, or accommodated. For example, the actions of a good Samaritan oblige a bigot to reconsider his or her stereotype about 'Samaritans' as a group. (p. 251)

Assimilation. New objects and encounters are incrementally incorporated, or assimilated, into existing schemata. For example, an individual out-group member who contradicts a bigot's stereotype is passed off as 'an exception that proves the rule'. Thus, the prejudicial stereotype remains essentially unchanged. (p. 249)

Glass ceiling. A term widely used to denote an invisible, subtle barrier to women's career advancement in organisations. At least part of this barrier probably derives from subconscious stereotypes that 'women are wonderful' (people, not managers), which prejudices perceivers who view management as a 'macho' preserve. (p. 245)

Intimacy equilibrium. People will intuitively strive to keep their level of non-verbal intimacy balanced, so that when intimacy is increased through one channel (say, standing closer), intimacy is reduced through another (say, lessening the amount of eye contact). (p. 268)

Maximal cognition. Many of our everyday interactions and social behaviours are governed by routines; they have become over-learned and automatic, and to that extent cognition has been minimised. For sustainable human development and change to take place, conscious thought needs to be maximised in social behaviour. (p. 276)

Meta-process skill. The learned capacity to step back from social interaction, and anticipate when a given interaction is in danger of heading into the systems dynamic of escalation. This entails both skilled awareness (of the process) and skilled competence (in preventing the process from occurring). (p. 276)

Rebound effect. When self-consciousness is raised during a training session or lecture or any kind of one-way message about what we 'should' be doing, there is an implicit tendency to rebound from that position (for example that we 'should not stereotype') once the constraint is lifted. (p. 272)

Schema(ta). A mental model or representation of the world. Social schemata include intuitive models about personality, social categories (also called 'role schemata'), everyday events (like going to a restaurant), and the self (ideal and actual). Schemata allow us to predict the world around us: to understand it and make sense of it — including through the lens of culture. (p. 277)

Skilled incompetence. The state of being adept at using a schema that we consciously reject as decrepit, as in professing the need for worker empowerment at the same time as systematically reinvoking the old model for workplace relations. (p. 251)

Skilled unawareness. The state of not being aware of the schema in use, as in professing to be unprejudiced but behaving as if one is (p. 251)

Stereotype threat. Prejudicial schemata, or stereotypes, about out-groups can create evaluation apprehension in minority groups, which then influences them to withdraw from the domain in which they have been stereotyped as 'inferior'. The cycle of discrimination and prejudice is thus perpetuated, because the original stereotype is reinforced by and within both groups. (p. 248)

Women are wonderful. A role schema in which women are expected to be nurturing, warm and caring, and that works against them in many occupations in which the stereotypical role schema is 'macho', such as management and engineering. (p. 246)

REVIEW QUESTIONS

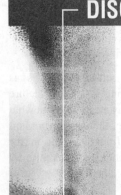

1. Trace the key developments in how we measure stereotypes.
2. What does the contingency schema advocate with respect to developing leadership skills, and what was Fiedler's enduring contribution to it?
3. What key principles underlie social skills training?
4. Describe the various models for developing cross-cultural communication skills.

DISCUSSION QUESTIONS

1. In chapter 4, we learned that theories such as Planned Behaviour never explain all of the variance in behaviour itself. How might the kinds of processes introduced in this chapter fill in some of these gaps?
2. Are the results of priming studies only ironic or rebound effects?
3. Should we be trying to replace stereotypes altogether, or should we be prepared to settle for deconstructing and reconstructing them into more socially acceptable forms?
4. Is there sufficient emphasis on skills in contemporary social psychology?
5. To what extent are contemporary approaches to intercultural training socially risky?

ACTIVITIES

1. Apply the Nominal Group Technique (see chapter 3) to identify and rank-order examples of skilled incompetence and skilled unawareness in everyday life.

2. Apply the Delphi technique (see chapter 3) to identify a range of context-reading skills that good community leaders need to possess.

3. Draw upon the cultural diversity in your class to construct a miniature culture-specific assimilator. This is a nice term assignment (after Purcell 1999, pers. corres.).

4. Use figure 7.1 to describe key social influence processes discussed under social cognition (escalating Pygmalion effects in the classroom, deteriorating relations between 'us' and 'them' in the workplace, and the enhancement of donor bias through aid agency advertising in the media).

ADDITIONAL READING

On schema theory: Augoustinos and Walker (1995). These authors have a gift for bringing social cognition to life, and write extremely clearly and lucidly.

On priming: Fazio et al. (1995). This is arguably *the* classic study on priming, and one that I found perfectly pitched as an introduction to this kind of research.

On skilled unawareness and incompetence: Smith (2002). This article expresses the central ideas in Argyris's work on implicit routines very directly and succinctly.

On perspective taking: Nickerson (1999). This article is quite heavy-going, but for the interested reader it is worth the effort. It is possibly the first full-length, serious treatment of the subject.

For further reading on the topics discussed in this chapter, consult the online resources linked to the Wiley website (http://www.johnwiley.com.au/highered/socialpsych).

AFFECT

8

ATTRACTION

LEARNING OBJECTIVES

After reading this chapter, you should be able to:

- describe how proximity, either geographical or in cyberspace, facilitates the formation of human relationships
- explain why discovering attitudinal similarity brings individuals together and yet pushes groups apart
- explain how the attitudinal dissimilarity that defines minority positions can foster both dislike and admiration, and thereby social change
- define what physical, emotional and economic differences each sex finds sexually alluring in the other.

OVERVIEW

To be attracted is to be drawn towards another individual, group or idea. In interpersonal relations, however, people usually first need to become acquainted! Two contexts in which acquaintance occurs are through shared physical space (e.g. living in the same neighbourhood, attending the same classes at university or sharing a workplace) and through shared cyberspace (e.g. an online chat-room). Such acquaintance forms a psychosocial basis on which three main types of attraction may develop. First, we may discover similarity in attitudes, which often promotes liking. Similarity produces in-group identification, but can also lead to rivalry and friction between like-minded groups who wish to differentiate themselves from each other. Second, we may discover differences in attitudes, which often promote dislike. Paradoxically, however, dissimilarity can attract, too. A pre-eminent example is consistent minorities whose courage to be different wins them admiration from the majority, paving the way for social change. Differences are also sometimes at the heart of sexual attraction. The allure of basic physical differences is often amplified by the discovery of socio-emotional and socio-economic differences, for example in sadomasochism, or the allure of money and power. Although many sexual attractors are universal, local variations on sexual attraction persist across different cultures.

INTRODUCING SOCIAL AFFECT

Throughout the preceding chapters, whether discussing stereotyping or aid advertising, the pressure to incorporate feelings into the analysis has been steadily growing. The concept of donor bias, for instance, introduced in chapter 6, is undoubtedly fuelled in part by emotional (or 'affective') processes. These come into play, for instance, when viewers of poverty advertisements rationalise their media-induced guilt by stereotyping and blaming the victim, so distancing themselves from the emotionally painful images (Carr 2000; for an earlier discussion of a similar kind of rationalisation in the laboratory, see Lerner & Simmons 1966 and Cohen 2001). Such stereotyping (see chapter 7) is as much about emotional 'gut' reactions (or 'hot' cognition) as it is about the relatively rational (or 'cold') cognitive processes discussed in part 2 of the book. In part 3, therefore, we give more rein to these emotional factors, which are collectively termed in the literature *social affect* .

This chapter focuses on three conceptually distinct but interrelated types of attraction. A mental schema or 'roadmap' for the chapter as a whole is provided in figure 8.1. Much of the available research on attraction has addressed the social environmental circumstances that facilitate attraction — *proximity*, *adversity* and prevailing *mood* at the time. These circumstances facilitate the communication of various bases for attraction, including perceived, attributed and implicitly recognised *similarity*, *difference* and physical attractiveness, or *physicality* , each with its own form of attraction. People can experience the attraction of *liking*, *admiration* or *desire* . Each of these forms of attraction, as illustrated in figure 8.1, enables a distinct attraction *process*, from *identification* to *conversion* to *arousal*.

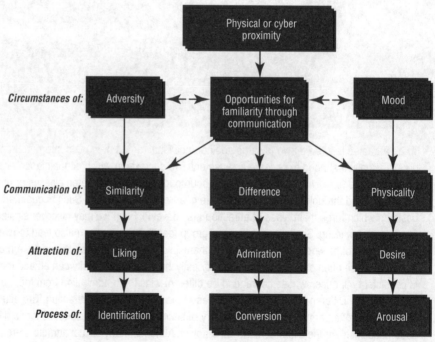

Figure 8.1   A model of attraction

As shown in figure 8.1, attraction often begins with the most basic of enabling factors, material circumstances. Much of the positive attraction that occurs in everyday life seems to be founded on what can only be described as 'default' (rather than chosen) life circumstances. The person we happen to sit next to in our very first class becomes a lifelong friend (see exercise 8.1). We become friends with a person we just happen to be placed alongside in the workplace. A friendship is forged out of a shared traumatic event. Or we fall in love with someone who happens to live nearby. In one Australian study, for instance, 83 per cent of student lovers first met in a physical setting they both frequented on a regular basis (McKnight & Sutton 1994). In social psychology, such material circumstances have traditionally been classified under the heading *propinquity* (Newcomb 1956). This term simply means 'nearness', whether physical or psychological. The definition has the advantage of flexibility since, because it includes psychological proximity ('only an e-mail away'), it can as easily include a neighbour in cyberspace as a neighbour in physical space (Parks & Floyd 1996).

Proximity

Being close together in physical space, for example through sharing the same classroom, office or rehabilitation clinic, remains the most common form of propinquity (Brehm, Kassin & Fein 1999). The essential feature of each of these settings, and of propinquity in general, is that the individuals involved have practical opportunities to meet and interact on a regular basis. Early survey studies of proximity examined how and where close couples had lived before they were married (for examples, see Bossard 1932 or Davie & Reeves 1939). These and other studies consistently found a **partner-next-door effect**. The majority of partners had lived within a few kilometres of each other before becoming partners fulltime. As one expert quipped more recently, 'romantic love aside, the "one and only" typically lives within driving distance' (Buss 1985, p. 48). Since married partners must have been drawn to one another somewhere before marrying, these surveys show that propinquity, in the form of physical proximity, is related to attraction.

The studies did not, however, show that propinquity *necessarily* leads to attraction. They did not tell us, for instance, how many neighbours end up hating each other (Swap 1977). This can happen, say, if neighbours place a high value on personal or familial privacy (Larson & Bell 1988). Neither did they address the possibility that, rather than propinquity, a third factor, such as shared socio-economic status or ethnicity, was the critical force that brought people together and produced the correlation between proximity and attraction (see chapter 1, on the limits to drawing conclusions from correlations). These possibilities can be ruled out only by using a research design in which residence is allocated randomly. If the only difference between the attracted and less attracted is proximity, with the more proximal individuals being more attracted to each other, then proximity itself facilitates attraction.

This possibility was addressed in a classic social psychological study conducted by Festinger, Schachter and Back (1950). In this study, 260 married veterans, who were previously unacquainted neighbours, were randomly allocated to flats in student housing. Rather than being drawn together by similarity in socio-economic status or ethnicity, neighbours became neighbours by default. Yet Festinger and his colleagues still found that the closer each flat was to another in physical space, the more likely it was that their residents became acquainted. When residents were asked to list their best friends, closest neighbours were mentioned more often than anyone else. Next-door neighbours were cited 41 per cent of the time, neighbours two doors away 22 per cent of the time, and people three doors away 10 per cent of the time. Such findings are impressive if we agree that many of us keep our university affiliations for many years after the student experience (Rosenfeld 1988). The same may also be true of the first contacts we make in high school (see exercise 8.1).

Why does proximity work like this? At least three conceptually distinct but complementary explanations for the effects of proximity can be found in the attraction literature. As indicated in figure 8.1, these explanations pivot around the contextual issues of familiarity, adversity and the perceiver's mood at the time.

Familiarity

This most basic explanation for the influence of proximity begins with mere exposure (Zajonc 1968a; for a recent discussion of this effect, see Monahan, Murphy & Zajonc 2000). According to Zajonc and others, the more frequently we are exposed to an initially novel (e.g. social) stimulus, such as having a new song 'grow' on us, the more positive our emotional reactions to it will become. This **mere exposure effect** has been demonstrated in classrooms. Mere exposure to an accomplice of the researchers who simply attended classes led to demonstrable increases over time in ratings on liking, intelligence and physical attraction (Moreland & Beach 1992).

When we change perspectives from actor to observer, so that we experience ourselves as others see us, we again realise that exposure matters. For instance, we are often initially uncomfortable when hearing our own voice played back to us on tape, because its resonances, coming through a machine rather than reverberating through our body in the familiar way, now sound disconcertingly unfamiliar. The same unsettling feeling often occurs when we look at photographs of ourselves, in which our left and right sides are the reverse of what we normally see and are used to when we look in the bathroom mirror each morning (Mita, Dermer & Knight 1977).

These examples offer clues for *why* mere exposure has the effects that it typically does. The embarrassment of hearing and seeing ourselves as others hear and see us probably derives some of its shock value from the lulling and over-*familiarising* effects of repeated exposure. Some analysts have taken this idea further. In evolutionary prehistory, they suggest, it might have been adaptive to be wary and distrustful of novel stimuli, including social stimuli (i.e. other individuals and groups). With increased safe contact with those social stimuli, however, it would have been adaptive to explore the possibility of mutual collaboration, and even to admit those individuals into our family or clan (Baron & Byrne 2000, p. 259). According to this view, repeated exposure effects were adaptive yesterday, which makes familiarity attractive today.

SOCIAL PSYCHOLOGY: CONTEXT, COMMUNICATION AND CULTURE

At what level do mere exposure effects occur?

In chapter 7 we learned that much of our mental software for interacting with others is implicit and automated. Is this true also of the mere exposure effect? Research has shown that mere exposure effects on subsequent attraction are stronger when the social stimulus, for example a photograph of someone new, is presented subliminally (i.e. very rapidly and fleetingly) rather than sufficiently slowly to allow consciously explicit processing to occur (Bornstein & D'Agnostino 1992). The finding that we 'take' more readily to social stimuli when they are presented subliminally implies that many of the mere exposure effects we experience in everyday life occur spontaneously and implicitly somewhere beneath our full awareness.

According to literature reviewed in the previous chapter, we may have to correct mere exposure effects if their automation starts to work *against* us. For example, some readers will have experienced meeting an acquaintance or colleague who they consciously know is unpleasant or untrustworthy, and yet have found themselves (on autopilot, as it were) still being perfectly sociable and open with them. In some cases, this can encourage such a person to take advantage. According to our analysis of the consciousness-raising potential of social psychological knowledge, becoming aware of the mere exposure effect could therefore help some individuals to remain more mindful of, and help guard against, potential vulnerability (Langer, Blank & Chanowitz 1978).

Are there natural limits to the lulling effects of familiarity?

The expression 'Familiarity breeds contempt' suggests that there is a point beyond which familiarity ceases to be incrementally comforting and, rather, like a song that we hear once too often, begins to foster disdain. Its comforting properties may be most salient at the earlier stages of a relationship, when the social context is primarily one of novelty (Forgas 1985); or perhaps during reinvented novelty ('Absence makes the heart grow fonder' or 'You only miss the water when the well runs dry'). Such adages imply that over-familiarity encourages habituation and lack of respect for others (taking them for granted, ceasing to fully appreciate them). If this analysis is correct, the effects of familiarity will be optimal when levels of exposure are neither too little nor too great (for a discussion of familiarity and disdain towards an entire group, see Burke 1997).

Where does the Internet fit in?

A recent study found that provocative statements prompted reciprocal communication in a chat-room setting (Rollman, Krug & Parente 2000). This suggests that over-familiarity may foster contempt in cyberspace as readily as anywhere else. At the same time, however, cyberspace may make geographical proximity less relevant, because the technology allows end-users to communicate freely and cheaply over physical distance. In cyberspace, the tyranny of distance is removed: 'The Internet potentially reduces the importance of [default] physical proximity in creating and maintaining networks of strong social ties' (Kraut et al. 1998, p. 1019).

Kraut et al. have investigated this possibility empirically, in a carefully controlled and executed study of the social psychological impact of the Internet on 169 people in 73 households during their first year or two of going on-line. The sample they used, although drawn exclusively from within the United States, was relatively diverse demographically, including young and old, male and female, a range of ethnic groups and a range of household incomes. Over the course of 12 to 24 months, these people's use of the Internet, as well as any changes in their social involvement and wellbeing, were tracked and charted. Was there any evidence that this usage influenced the quality of their social lives in general, and in particular somehow substituted for relationships with people more proximal in physical space?

Greater use of the Internet was linked, in this study, to small but significant declines in communication within the family and with people in local social networks (i.e. in their physical neighbourhood). There were also increases in loneliness and depression. Even relatively 'social interactive' uses of the Internet, such as e-mailing, were associated with increases in depression. Thus, while pointing out that their study did not address the cognitive benefits of Internet usage (for example the educational benefits of learning new, non-social computer skills), Kraut et al. controversially found that 'using the Internet adversely affects social involvement and psychological well-being' (1998, p. 1028).

In attempting to make sense of this finding, Kraut et al. suggest that, despite the fact that Internet technology can in principle be used to support strong ties (e.g. keeping contact with distant close relatives while at university, consoling them during times of tragedy, or re-establishing contact with old and dear school friends), people are in fact using it to substitute stronger relationships for poorer quality ('weak') ones. The participants in Kraut et al.'s study were, for example, using the Net to exchange jokes and other forms of trivia. Making genuine friends on-line was reported to be a relatively rare occurrence, estimated at one friend per five users for every two years of use (1998, p. 1030). Importantly for us when interpreting these findings, Kraut et al. postulate a central place for physical proximity.

> Online friendships are likely to be more limited than friendships supported by physical proximity. Online friendships are less likely than friends developed at school, work, church, or in the neighbourhood to be available for help with tangible favours, such as offering small loans, rides, or baby-sitting. Because online friends are not embedded in the same day-to-day environment, they will be less likely to understand the context for conversation, making discussion more difficult … and rendering support less applicable. Even strong ties maintained at a distance through electronic communication are likely to be different in kind and perhaps diminished in strength compared with strong ties supported by physical proximity. (Excerpted from Kraut et al. 1998, p. 1030)

The essence of this reflection is that late-twentieth-century technology and patterns of use of that technology are not successfully substituting **e-proximity** for physical proximity. The essential reason for this poor quality substitution, according to Kraut et al., seems to be the lack of fidelity, inherent in the technology, to real-life situations. Missing from e-mail 'interaction', for instance, is the social facilitation of budding relationships through physical presence and contact. However, if this logic is correct, we should expect emergent technology, which is increasing the fidelity of e-interaction to social interaction in physical space, to be able to increase the quality of human relationships formed by Internet users. Cyberspace, that is, should be able to produce strong-tie relationships for its end-users. If that proves to be the case, we will be left with the conclusion that while proximity matters less, propinquity matters still.

The possibility that increased fidelity will bring increases in relationship quality was tested in a prominent study by Parks and Roberts (1998). These researchers investigated the impact of using real-time, text-based virtual environments known as MOOs (Multi-user dimensions, Object Oriented). Although not wholly high fidelity simulations, MOOs are inherently more interactive, and to that extent more inherently social, than regular e-mail. In addition to taking place in real time, for example, MOOs use text to create and describe characters, virtual places and objects. The characters can, for instance, ask other characters to follow them into a room for a private conversation; and they can send e-body language (such as knowing looks) to one member of the MOO but not to others. Examples of the kinds of 'objects' that can be created include rooms and their furnishings, a pet, or a game that others can play (MOOs are relatively non-competitive, however). MOO programs can also allow players to 'emote' in real time by using textual descriptors or pictures of emotions. Through a combination of these properties, according to Parks and Roberts, MOOs can support 'fluid, multi-layered social interaction' (1998, p. 519). In short, relative to regular e-mail at least, they are quite life-like.

In their study of the impact of MOOs on attraction, Parks and Roberts e-surveyed 235 current users of six different MOOs from all inhabited continents of the global community. Most of the respondents, however, came from the United States, Canada and Australia. These respondents generally visited their MOOs for between 3 and 18 hours per week (median = 12 hours, mode = 10 hours per week). Altogether, they had been visiting MOOs for a mean of 21 months, which makes the sample, and its findings on relationship formation, reasonably comparable to Kraut et al.'s data.

In a very clear result, 97 per cent of the respondents in the MOO study reported having formed at least one ongoing personal relationship during their MOO interactions. These relationships averaged 7.3 hours of communication per week, which is sufficient to indicate a strong rather than a weak tie. In fact, the 'vast majority' of the respondents in this study had formed several of these relationships via their MOO, with the middle 50 per cent of the sample reporting that they had initiated from 4 to 15 personal relationships via their MOO. Forty-one per cent of these were described as close friendships, 26 per cent as friend-ships, and 26 per cent as romantic relationships. The remaining relationships formed were described as associated with work or school (2.3 per cent) and as acquaintances (4.6 per cent). These relationships (whatever the category) each averaged over one year in duration. Interestingly, most were with members of the opposite sex. Individuals over 30 years of age were as likely as those under 30 to have initiated a new personal relationship on a MOO.

Thus, 'The effect [of being able to form meaningful relations in cyberspace] appears to be general' (Parks & Roberts 1998, p. 534). A succinct illustration of this point is found in a study investigating the impact on relationships of partici-pating in Internet newsgroups (Parks & Floyd 1996). In this study, 61 per cent of members of the newsgroups and their contributors reported forming a new relationship via the e-group. More impressively perhaps, these online relationships not only 'reached high levels of relational development' but also went on to 'broaden into interaction in other channels and settings' (1996, p. 80).

To sum up, the available evidence indicates that cyber contact and e-familiarity are increasingly capable of substituting for, or rather complementing, the effects on affect of physical proximity. Critical to this capacity seems to be the degree of fidelity to reality — or, more precisely perhaps, to the dynamism of real-life interaction — that the technology is capable of mustering. Such news may be especially relevant (and welcome) to people who live in rural and remote areas, or in impoverished settings where telephone contact is too costly to afford (for a fuller discussion of these and related issues, see Rosenberg 2000).

Adversity

The discussion so far has focused on social contact in everyday life and routines. For many of us, however, some of our more enduring relationships have been forged during traumatic episodes or events, which — fortunately — are by definition *non*-routine. There are empirical accounts of the power of such contexts to manufacture attraction between the people who find themselves unwillingly trapped in them. The range of such situations is impressive, and includes natural and industrial disaster (respectively, Stumpfer 1970 and Elkit 1997), surgery (Kulik, Mahler & Moore 1996), surgical work (Holaday et al. 1995), potentially painful experimental procedures (Schachter 1959), wartime (Kidder & Stewart 1975), inter-group conflict (see Sherif's field experiment in chapter 3), and starting tertiary study (Newcomb 1943, 1963; Newcomb et al. 1967; Alwin, Cohen & Newcomb 1991; Saylor & Aries 1999). In disaster management situations, too, affiliation appears to happen to 'victim' and 'helper' alike (MacLeod & Paton 1999; Paton & Stephens 1996). In each case, people have been found to form bonds of camaraderie, friendship and cooperation relatively readily. Across an impressive range of adverse/traumatic contexts, therefore, it seems not only that 'misery loves company', but that we can speak meaningfully about a principle of **adversity-affiliation**. For instance, many of us could tell of how the people we happened to meet on our first day at a new school, or when starting a new job, ended up becoming long-term friends or associates. Another illustration of such adversity-affiliation, this time related to travelling in hostile environments, is given in critical narrative 8.1.

Why does calamity spark such attraction?

The effects of attraction and affiliation in mutually threatening circumstances are reminiscent of superordinate goals and the jigsaw techniques discussed in chapter 3. Danger and adversity foster feelings of positive interdependence not only between groups but also between *individuals* who find themselves in the same mutually threatening, and therefore unsettling, predicament. One interpretation of this adversity-affiliation effect is that the urge to affiliate is purely affective: a problem shared is a problem halved, or diffused. Another interpretation, more 'cognitive' and possibly also more cynical, is that individuals intuitively 'know' they have a better chance of 'pulling though' if they pool their resources. The truth probably embraces both these explanations. We feel emotionally comforted by sharing the load, and we also know intuitively that we are more likely to pull through if we pull together. This duality of *hot* and *cold* systems is succinctly captured for me in a traditional saying from southern East Africa: 'One head does not carry the roof' (Afro-centric Alliance 2001).

CRITICAL NARRATIVE 8.1

Social psychology of extreme remoteness

The road between Mount Isa in Far North Queensland and the Three Ways junction in the heart of Australia's Northern Territory is one of the most remote and lonely stretches of highway on the planet. In the searing heat of the day, the road ahead and behind quickly disappears into a shimmering desert landscape. A solitary motorist can drive for hours without encountering another vehicle, human being or, indeed, living creature of any kind. The sense of one's smallness and insignificance can be quite overpowering in this place.

For the solitary driver in such a lonely and intimidating environment, meeting an oncoming vehicle becomes a significant social event, and can lead to some pretty unusual behaviour by city standards. Complete strangers will wave to one another as their vehicles pass by. Even police officers, quite unlike their counterparts in urban centres, will give a friendly wave, which is spontaneously reciprocated as they pass by. Outback remoteness creates a sense of adversity, which influences complete strangers to step outside their usual role boundaries, as they both seek and welcome affiliation with other human beings sharing the same humbling experience.

Source: Personal experience (29 January 1998).

The mood factor

As well as linking hot and cold cognition, these studies suggest that the mood of the moment (e.g. fear) influences how we interpret and respond to others when we come into social contact with them (motivation to affiliate). Chapter 6 described how such moods act as partial filters, or lenses, through which new experiences are interpreted. In the attraction literature there is a related process, which is termed an *associated* effect. Associated effects occur when our interactions with others happen to occur at the right (or wrong) mood moment. By sheer good luck (or, alternatively, ill fortune), we learn to associate these others with that pleasant (or unpleasant) prevailing mood. In this way, we again are attracted to (or we recoil from) others by default.

A principal process through which such associated effects happen is classical conditioning (Staats & Staats 1958). As discussed in chapter 7, classical conditioning effects are largely implicit. For example, when mood is altered experimentally, by subliminal exposure to images that are pleasant (or unpleasant), a stranger's photograph is rated as more (or less) likeable (Krosnick et al. 1992). Supermarkets know how to use such influences to good effect by playing quasi-relaxing background music and offering free samples to their harried patrons (see also May & Hamilton 1980). National anthems and nationalistic advertising are other examples of the power of mood to alter how we interpret the particular event (spectacle, service) that follows. Such 'emotional priming', in which subliminally induced moods 'colour' subsequent impressions even when the objects of those impressions have little or nothing inherently in common with the mood-inducing stimulus, is now a widely recognised affective process by which audiences can be figuratively (and sometimes literally) swayed (Murphy, Monahan & Zajonc 1995).

These social influences, through which the mood of the moment colours our judgement of the person(s) before us, are like killing the messenger who brings bad news (Moscovici 1976). The news can be seen as priming the hearer's reaction to the messenger. We might identify many of the consequences of mood on attraction as examples of a **shoot-the-messenger effect** (for more of the messenger's perspective on this, see McKee & Ptacek 2001). Interestingly, although it has not yet been specifically applied to attraction, the *affect infusion model*, or AIM (see chapter 6), predicts that the more a perceiver is motivated to think about a social stimulus, the greater the effects of mood will be (Forgas 1995). According to the AIM model, this should happen, for example, if the stimulus person is in any way 'different', and to that extent 'thought-provoking' (Forgas 1992b).

Counteracting the prejudicing effects of pre-existing moods

The research evidence indicates that a key to minimising unwelcome shoot-the-messenger effects on the self is to raise awareness about their existence. For example, Ottati and Isbell (1996) presented participants with political speeches about the death penalty and abortion. Before being exposed to these messages, the participants' mood had been altered by asking them to recount a recent experience that made them sad (negative information). After exposure to the messages, the same participants were asked to indicate their level of liking for the political candidate who had made the speech. Their response would indicate their readiness to 'shoot the messenger'. Pre-exposure mood alteration was found to depress levels of liking for the candidate, but only when the participant was previously relatively uninformed about the issues surrounding capital punishment and abortion. Previous knowledge about these social issues, by contrast, 'inoculated' the participant against political persuasion through mood manipulation (McGuire 1964). In this way, therefore, maximised cognition helped counteract the potentially biasing influence of negative information.

A role for both affect and cognition

Ottati and Isbell's study again illustrates how hot and cold systems, affect and cognition (i.e. mood and awareness) invariably interact with one another. They form part of an integrated social psychological system. This systemic property of human social behaviour becomes clearer as we begin to incorporate into our analysis the attraction of both similarity and difference. The analysis has so far concentrated on social context and how it enables and facilitates 'stage one' of an attraction system — making acquaintance. Whether we then want to develop more than a passing acquaintance with this other individual or group depends on whether we find grounds for doing so. According to figure 8.1, these grounds include whether we perceive, attribute or recognise similarity, difference or sex appeal (physicality).

SIMILARITY

Similarity, liking and friendship formation

A classic study linking these elements was conducted by Newcomb (1956). Similarity in this study, as elsewhere in the subsequent literature, included similarity in traits (Till & Freedman 1978) and in attitudes (Byrne 1997). Newcomb measured attitudes among students before they met on campus and then tracked the development of their friendship patterns, over a semester, after they had all been placed in the same housing unit. Consistent with the earlier studies by Festinger and his colleagues, the students' early acquaintances were best predicted by physical/geographical proximity. In time, however, the choice of who would become an actual *friend* was more closely predicted by attitude similarity. Thus, the greater the level of similarity between students before sharing a living space, the greater the likelihood that they would not only become acquaintances, but would also go on to become friends.

Since Newcomb's early study, this basic finding has been replicated many times over (Forgas 1985, p. 233; see also www.psychology.about.com/library/weekly, on bogus stranger technique). Typically, some weeks before meeting (Time 1), participants in these studies have had their attitudes measured in a relatively subtle and surreptitious way, such as through a general classroom survey. Then, during a testing phase days or weeks later (Time 2), they are presented with an attitudinal profile of a target person, who has been deliberately made similar or dissimilar to themselves in terms of shared attitudes. Finally, they have been asked to rate that person for liking. Consistently in such studies, it has been found that increased attitudinal similarity at Time 1 is related to increased liking at Time 2. Thus, a great deal of the research conducted in the wake of Newcomb's study can be summed up by a principle called **similarity-attraction** (Byrne 1971, 1997; for an amusing recent take on this about people and their dogs, see Coren 1999).

How similarity was operationally defined

Typically in these studies, similarity has been operationally defined and measured by the number of topics on which the two individuals, 'source' (fictitious person) and 'target' (genuine participant), held the same views, divided by the overall number of topics surveyed. Arithmetically, this measure basically captures the proportion of attitudes on which source and target agree. Baron and Byrne's interpretation of the finding of a link between (a) this operational definition of similarity and (b) attraction is as follows:

> It is almost as if we classify a person's position on each topic as similar or
> different to our own, then add up the number of times the person agrees
> with us and divide that number by the total number of topics discussed.
> (2000, p. 289)

This kind of computation is reminiscent of the kind of cold cognition defining the 'averaging principle' described in chapter 5. Again, therefore, we can see how hot and cold systems, affective and cognitive, function together.

Limits to similarity

The degree of similarity between other and self can be too close for comfort, threatening our sense of individuality (Fromkin 1972). This process has been referred to as 'the narcissism of minor difference', meaning that when similarity becomes too marked (so that 'differences' become exceedingly 'minor'), it becomes a threat to self's sense of individual uniqueness (Johnstone 1994). In Fromkin's (1972) study, when participants were given bogus feedback that they were excessively similar to the majority of other students on traits, values and preferences, these participants' mood and affect clearly dropped, becoming negative (see also Snyder & Fromkin 1980; Okamoto 1983). In fact, the drop was comparable to being made to feel very different (deviant) from others in the group. Later studies have shown that, across a range of cultural settings, people do not choose friends with whom they are identical (Hamm 2000); they prefer friends whose degree of similarity to self is neither too little nor too great. Thus, similarity has most effect on attraction when it is moderate rather than extreme.

Why similarity attracts: the theory of social comparison

Opinion comparison

According to the theory of **social comparison**, people find attitudinal similarity attractive because the world, and particularly the social world, is an inherently uncertain place (Festinger 1950). For many of the social issues that confront us every day, such as moral dilemmas, there is no right and wrong, no clear answers about truth and the right way to live our lives. Under such circumstances, according to Festinger, we tend to rely heavily on others. We use the implicit logic that the more other people agree with us, the more correct we are likely to be in our opinions:

> An opinion, a belief, an attitude, is 'correct,' 'valid,' and 'proper,' to the
> extent that it is anchored in a group of people with *similar* beliefs, opinions,
> and attitudes. (1950, pp. 272–3; emphasis added)

This process of 'opinion comparison' is a basis for the formation of reference groups, to whom we literally refer and with whom we subsequently identify (see figure 8.1). According to a concept called **terror management**, such social validation helps people cope with the 'hot' uncertainties of mortality, death and dying (Solomon, Greenberg & Pyszczynski 1991). Festinger's own concept of opinion comparison is closer, perhaps, to being hot *and* cold at the same time. It affords us emotional reassurance, through discovered similarity with others, that we have got some of life 'right'. At the same time, however, it also enables this emotional quiescence through the implicit *logic* that 'two heads are better than one'.

The pull of the similar that Festinger described was subsequently shown to hold across a wide variety of cultural groups, including Hawai'ian, Asian Indian, Japanese and Mexican societies (Byrne et al. 1971). Included in the early studies, too, were both Australians and New Zealanders (Till & Freedman 1978). More recently, attitudinal similarity in multicultural societies has also been found to be a better predictor of relationship formation than ethnic difference — that is, similarity in opinions is a good predictor of relationships across different ethnic groups (Fujino 1997; for a more comprehensive discussion, see Lee & Gudykunst 2001). The advent of the Internet has not detracted from this relationship between similarity and liking. The emerging trend across this media-scape is for people to make acquaintances (and thus potential friendships) based on common interests, whether in 'soap operas, civil rights, stamp collecting, or other … topics' (Kraut et al. 1998; Parks & Floyd 1996).

The process of opinion comparison is perfectly consistent with the idea, discussed earlier, that familiarity, in moderate doses, is reassuring. This consistency arises because others can be similar only if their values, attitudes and behaviours are already familiar. The very idea of similarity assumes that we are able to recognise in others what we ourselves value, support and act on. In this sense, the entire process of social comparison — like the concept of similarity-attraction that it explains — is based on the attraction of familiarity.

The importance of reciprocation

One crucial step we must not forget here is the dynamic *interaction* between A's attraction to similarity in B and B's reaction to A. For similarity-attraction to really work, it needs to be apparent to A that B evaluates A positively (Condon & Crano 1988; for an early discussion on this, see Insko 1973). Otherwise, as Condon, Crano and Insko discovered, the linkage between similarity and attraction will falter. To take this logic one step further, and applying the above analysis, for similarity-attraction to work, A has to find similarity in B, and B has to find similarity in A. Thus, the process of opinion comparison becomes doubly important for explaining the principle of similarity-attraction.

Ability comparison

According to Festinger (1954), similarity attracts us not only for the purposes of validating opinions and attitudes. It can also act as a magnet for us to compare and so evaluate our abilities. The resulting 'ability comparison', as Festinger termed it, is unlike opinion comparison. In questions of ability, Festinger argued, we are normally attracted to similar others in order to try to position ourselves above them. Rather than seeking equality and convergence, as we find with opinion comparison, the purpose of ability comparison is to come out 'on top'.

In choosing to evaluate our abilities in sport, for example, we do not pick a novice or an expert against whom to compare ourselves; rather, we tend to pick people of a competence similar to our own, who have had a similar amount of practice and similar opportunities to gain experience. In this way, if we are at all good at the activity, we hope to be able to beat them. This will be informative for us in a way that beating a novice or losing to a champion could never be (since in each of the latter cases the outcome is a foregone conclusion). Festinger described this need to positively differentiate the self from similar others in an upward direction as a '*unidirectional drive upwards* in the case of abilities [that] is largely absent in opinions' (1954, p. 124; emphasis added). According to Festinger, therefore, ability (rather than opinion) comparison means attraction to similarity in order to win.

In 1954 Festinger clearly expressed doubts that his 'unidirectional drive upwards' was in any way 'universal' with respect to ability comparison. He suspected, for example, that traditionally collectivistic societies, such as the Hopi Indians of North America, would be relatively scornful of attempting to outdo their peers, family members or clan (p. 125). Nonetheless, to the extent that individualism (and individual competitiveness) is globalising alongside traditional collectivistic values, the concept of a unidirectional drive upwards is today disconcertingly relevant (Brehm, Kassin & Fein 1999). Indeed, it is a theoretical construct deserving of rejuvenation (see chapter 1).

With respect to social comparison processes generally, critical psychology (see chapter 7) has highlighted the fact that:

> In societies that exalt individualism, we observe an erosion in the sense of community, whereas in communities that demand personal abnegation, we notice a craving for individual liberties . . . This is an indication that what we need is a balance between values that uphold personal rights and needs, and values that protect the integrity of vital community structures. (Prilleltensky, in press)

In other words, people are inherently individualistic and collectivistic by turns (Carr et al. 1996a). To the extent that this view of the human condition is psychologically robust, there will always be a place in human society both for ability comparison (which is largely inter-individual in focus) and for opinion comparison (which is perhaps more concerned with groups).

Similarity-attraction and relations between groups

Chapter 3 introduced a negative resonance effect between groups that are perceptibly similar to one another. This **inverse resonance** occurs when relatively similar out-groups, or their representatives, interact and conflict with one another. Domestic examples of such rivalry can be found between countless pairs of locally adjacent sports teams, whose supporters frequently clash with one another, or between minority factions and sects whose belief systems are quite close to one another (White & Langer 1999). International examples of this effect are found, we learned, in settings as diverse as West Africa (Eze 1985), East Africa (Carr et al. 2001), Eastern Europe (Henderson-King et al. 1997) and South-East Asia (Lim & Ward 1999). In each case, prejudice is expressed against an out-group that is similar to, rather than dissimilar from, an in-group. The precise reasons for these inverse resonances are undoubtedly complex, and certainly require future research to explicate in detail. Yet a suggestion remains, from these diverse examples, that similarity-attraction reaches a limiting condition as we step further away from relations between individuals *within* groups, towards relations between groups.

Some of the inverse resonance may well be due to the influence of mutually reinforcing negative stereotypes (see chapter 7). In these cognitive schemata, cultural and societal groups might, for example, be arranged in discriminatory hierarchies, or a kind of global 'pecking order' (Sidanius & Pratto 1999). In addition, however, both Festinger and Prilleltensky have pointed out that people are motivated in different contexts by both competition *and* affiliation (see also Murray 1938). Conceivably, therefore, similarity between groups is reasonably attractive, because it helps bolster the in-group's view of the world (see dotted line in figure 8.2).

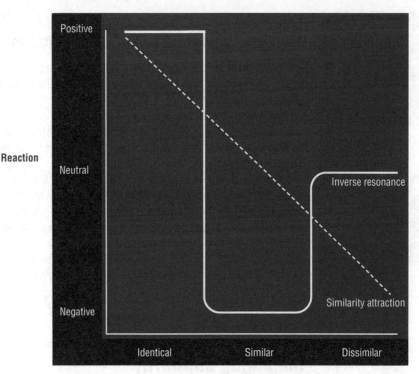

Positive

Reaction

Neutral

Inverse resonance

Negative

Similarity attraction

Identical   Similar   Dissimilar

Degree of perceived similarity

Figure 8.2   Similarity-attraction versus inverse resonance   ***Source:*** Adapted from Carr et al. (1996a).

The stumbling block for this kind of analysis is that affiliation needs are already satisfied *within* groups. Out-groups are largely redundant as far as need for affiliation is concerned. All that is salient now are the similarities with their rivals. These pose a threat to the narcissism of social identity and to all sense of certainty that the latter provides. According to Tajfel, for instance, ability comparison is most likely to materialise when the groups concerned are relatively comparable, and to that extent similar. Thus, as illustrated in figure 8.2, we would expect an inverse resonance, or jam-spoon effect.

Australia and New Zealand have much in common — for example their often intertwined colonial and post-colonial histories (Catley 2001). As critical narrative 8.2 illustrates, Australians and New Zealanders have a relationship that is sometimes fractious, and is replete with negative stereotypes on both sides. One interpretation of this ready fractiousness between the two nations is that it is fuelled by similarity. According to this view, trans-Tasman discourse partly reflects an inverse resonance between culturally similar, relatively fledgling national groups vying for a sense of differentiation from each other.

The point here, which has been reiterated through the past few pages, is that similarity is likely to be attractive within groups and relatively unattractive between them. If this conclusion is correct, it means that how we best manage that similarity will have to change, as we switch from a concern about relations *within* the group to a concern about relations *between* groups. In this way, managing attraction processes varies, according to our analysis, with social context.

Advice to a migrant from Australia to New Zealand

An itinerant migrant was getting ready to move again, this time from Australia, where she was a naturalised citizen, to New Zealand, where her Australian citizenship gave her the right to residency and employment. Right now, she was on her way to the airport to fly to Auckland and a new family home. In the car with her was a New Zealand taxi driver who had been working in Australia for some years, having married an Australian man while working in Australia some years previously.

On hearing where the migrant was heading, the expatriate New Zealander earnestly remarked how Australians often stereotyped New Zealanders as 'dole bludgers' who came to Australia to laze around on Bondi Beach and live off the welfare system at the taxpayer's expense. Yet, as she pointed out, many New Zealanders were working extremely well in their newly adopted country. And about Australians travelling to New Zealand she added laughingly, but seriously too, 'You'll be all right in New Zealand. You're not a *real* Australian!'

Source: Personal experience (April 2001).

Managing similarity

Within groups

In organisational settings, the principle of similarity-attraction has multiple ramifications and implications for managerial practice.

In selection, for example, similarity-attraction implies that selection panels are at risk of choosing 'clones' of themselves, so that departments and even entire companies will develop organisational cultures that cease to adapt to changing external circumstances. Research evidence confirms that organisations do attract and retain job applicants who resemble each other, in a process known as **attraction-selection-attrition** (Bretz, Ash & Dreher 1989; Schneider 1987; Schneider et al. 1998). If left unchecked, these organisations run the risk of becoming frozen in organisational groupthink (Denton 1999). Once again, however, there are ways of managing such problems. As we saw in chapter 5, situational interviews and other forms of structured assessment are often useful tools for minimising such cycles.

In meetings, too, similarity-attraction suggests that organisational groups, if left to their own devices, will spontaneously spend too much time discussing their (inherently attractive and familiar) similarities, rather than considering more diverse and hence potentially creative points of view (see chapter 3, on polarisation and groupthink). This has recently been observed in group task settings (Kim 1997). The result is that groups often get suboptimal results in the quality of their organisational decisions (Nickerson 1999, p. 740). To remedy this, in chapter 3 we discussed a range of interventions that often reduce these types of deleterious effects on human group performance.

Between groups

In wider society, and in particular with regard to the Internet, it has been argued that similarity-attraction will create a plethora of Internet groups that focus their attention on their own special interests and world views (Sunstein 2001). These Internet groups, or intranets, as we have seen tend to be drawn to one another on the basis of similarity (Kraut et al. 1998). Sunstein argues that such e-facilitated coalescences, coupled with group polarisation of the opinions within them, will allow hate groups to flourish. By the same token, however, she optimistically suggests that the Internet will enable global citizens to form entire communities around democratic ideals, thereby counteracting these hate groups with a much increased social capital.

In an international sense, the principle of inverse resonance is potentially applicable to economic development in supposedly 'free trade' zones. Such zones (e.g. that created by the policy of Closer Economic Relations (CER) between Australia and New Zealand) are increasingly being advocated as the way forward for economic development in the twenty-first century (Catley 2001). The economic and political success of these CER ventures, however, depends on the free flow of both material resources (goods and services) and human resources, such as qualified personnel from different, although sometimes comparable, countries-of-origin (Carr et al. 1996a).

Unfortunately, the inverse resonance hypothesis suggests that expatriates originating from comparable societies may actually be discriminated against, and to that extent blocked in their freedom of movement, in favour of candidates from the home country itself. Even those from radically dissimilar countries-of-origin may be preferred over a closer neighbour. Within the East African Cooperation (EAC) trade zone, for example, Carr et al. (2001) found a preference for local candidates over candidates from neighbouring countries, who were less preferred than candidates from more distant, 'exotic' locations, such as Western Europe and Australia. In a preliminary study from Australia, competent and well-qualified job applicants from New Zealand were less preferred, across a range of occupations relevant to national development, than were applicants both from within Australia and from further removed countries-of-origin, such as the United States (Jones 2000). According to the logic that structured selection practices reduce biases associated with similarity and attraction, a key way of managing these concerns is to increase the use of structured (and accountable) selection interviews.

Overall, therefore, we can say that similarity-attraction and inverse resonance create a range of unwelcome pressures on organisational, community and regional economic groups. But there are practical ways of managing these pressures. The most promising approach is to apply structure to the decision-making process. Again, this will involve merging cold systems with hot, and cognition with affect, to moderate levels of arousal so that they do not get the better of us (Tsai & Levenson 1997). The performance of decision-makers, therefore, is optimal when affect is moderated rather than extreme.

Similarity is not the only consideration in attraction. The French have a saying, '*Qui se ressemble, s'assemble*' ('People who resemble each other are found together', or 'If you want to know somebody, know their friends'), but better known is the expression '*Vive la différence!*' ('Long live difference!').

Similar, apparently conflicting sayings in English were noted in chapter 1. Taken together, these adages about similarity and difference suggest that in some social contexts dissimilarity is preferred over similarity. To that extent, we can say that similarity is probably not the only basis for attraction (between individuals) or friction (between groups). Dissimilarity can be just as appealing, and grating too!

DISSIMILARITY

One social context in which dissimilarity can be relatively attractive is in the later stages of close relationships. A degree of trait complementarity (e.g. A dependent/B supportive) seems to be important for long-term sustainability of the relationship (Buss 1985; Kerckhoff & Davis 1962; Shachar 1991; see also Aron & Aron 1986). However, this statement must be qualified by the caveat that antonymic traits will not always be quite so compatible as dependency and supportiveness (Vinacke et al. 1988). Central examples are the 'big five' of OCEAN (see chapter 5). The five respective pairs of antonyms here are antagonistic rather than complementary to each other. This is also the case with bipolar attitudes, which by definition take a 'for' or 'against' position on an issue, so that each is inherently adversarial and incompatible with its opposite. To be precise, then, a *moderate* level of dissimilarity or complementarity (rather than dissimilarity *per se*) is optimal for the longer term sustainability of close interpersonal relationships.

The implication here is that differences are attractive, but only up to a point. This suggestion becomes clearer when considering two further domains of social influence: (1) attraction to the rebel and the revolution, and (2) sexual attraction. In both cases, as many of us will instantly recognise, the different and the deviant sometimes become, like 'forbidden fruit', what we admire or desire (Fromkin & Brock 1973). In both cases, of course, in a kind of super–ironic effect (see chapter 5), the very fact that they are forbidden can make them all the more attractive (Wegner, Lane & Dimitri 1994; for a more detailed discussion on this topic, see Felmlee 1998).

Admiration for the dissimilar

Admiration has been studied far less than its similarity-based and liking-driven cousin (Forgas 1985). Perhaps this is because the literature has implicitly assumed that admiration and liking are synonyms (e.g. Muchinsky 1999, p. 379). Yet a little thought will suggest that liking and admiration are not necessarily the same social affective process at all (Heider 1958). Admiration more closely resembles a positive form of envy, a longing for something that we do not have. Students, for example, may admire their professors as ideals that they themselves aspire to (Grush, Clore & Costin 1975). Admiration is often based precisely on a freshly discovered different-ness from us, not similarity to us. Also, we sometimes actively dislike someone and yet sneakingly admire them, too. By definition, therefore, and as depicted in figure 8.1, liking and admiration are different emotions, and give rise to correspondingly distinct affective processes.

The dissimilarity-admiration model

Although admiration has been generally neglected in the attraction literature, there is at least one very notable exception. In two increasingly influential publications, Moscovici has developed a relatively sophisticated model on the inherent attraction of 'different' points of view (1976, 1980). Moscovici has focused in particular on minorities that express their different world views cogently, consistently and with courage (Crano 2000). Moscovici's model is 'big' because it grapples with the huge issue of how attraction to the dissimilar eventually leads to changes in a group's norms, and thereby to group innovation and social change (Stewart & Stasser 1998). Without initially relatively powerless minorities in the world, there would have been no emancipation of women, no Communism beyond Marx, no Christianity beyond Christ, no independence movements in 'developing' countries from the colonial powers during the 1950s and 1960s. As well, many radical (and world-changing) inventions, artistic creations and revolutionary scientific ideas might never have even left the ground.

Moscovici's model builds on earlier findings that a 'devil's advocate' often changes group outlooks, and that tough negotiators are often respected more than their over-compromising counterparts. This is because the essence of minorities, according to Moscovici (1976), is that they challenge us to 'think again' about our cosy models of the world; they may even achieve this without our initially realising it (Moscovici 1980). In keeping with the principle of similarity-attraction, their very dissimilarity means that minorities who persist against the odds are actively disliked for upsetting the proverbial apple cart, even while they (or their ideas) are admired for their courage and originality. This **dissimilarity-admiration** linkage derives from the fact that minorities are the classic 'underdogs', with all that this attribution implies. As Moscovici himself puts it, 'In most of the experiments described [in his extensive 1976 review], the minority is both *dis*liked *and esteemed* at the same time' (1976, p. 219; emphases added; for a more recent review, see Van Dyne & Saavedra 1996, p. 162).

Minority influence

The leading study of minority influence was conducted in the late 1960s, in a socio-political context of radical social change in France (Moscovici, Lage & Naffrechoux 1969). Moscovici and his colleagues were trying to understand how French students, a relatively powerless minority, had convinced significant sectors of the country (notably the unions) to adopt a radical position that came close to precipitating the overthrow of a powerful Nationalist regime. In their laboratory representation of how minority influence works, Moscovici et al. (1969) asked groups of four genuine participants and two radical confederates to judge the colour of 36 luminous slides. These slides were all in the wavelength for blue. The genuine participants' task was to call out their answer for the colour of each slide. A minority (two accomplices of the experimenters) consistently called out that these objectively blue slides were, in their eyes, 'green'. Following this stage one session, the participants were shown a new set of slides. This stage two series of stimuli differed slightly from stage one. This time the colours ranged from blue to blue-green. The participants' task in stage two was to privately identify the colour (blue or green) of each of these new slides. The experimental question was whether a consistent minority would be able to move the boundary for a choice in favour of green rather than blue closer to the blue end of the colour spectrum, so that some of the slides that would normally be perceived as blue would now be perceived as green. If this could be demonstrated, Moscovici et al. reasoned, the minority would have changed the way the majority *viewed the world*.

Conversion

The results of this classic study were, and still are, fascinating. At the public level, at stage one, only 8 per cent of the genuine participants' responses were 'green', and three-quarters of the genuine participants did not concede on any of the 36 trials. At the level of private opinion, however, the perceptual threshold shifted significantly towards the blue end of the spectrum. Stimuli that were described by a no-confederate control group as blue were now more likely to be described, by groups exposed to a consistent minority, as green. Overall, therefore, despite showing relatively few signs of influence at the level of public verbal responses at stage one, there was a shift in private judgements at stage two. Importantly, if there was any dissension between the minority members so that their consistency was broken, so was their impact. Appropriately enough, the combination of public denial and private change that resulted from the consistent minority was termed **conversion** by Moscovici. Subsequent research was able to demonstrate the same kind of effect with respect to social (rather than physical) issues, such as support for gay rights (for a leading example, see Maass & Clark 1983). Conversion, therefore, appears to be a robust social influence process.

In the blue-green paradigm, Moscovici et al. had found the first experimental evidence that consistent minorities can sway majorities to change their opinions in private, despite the fact that they do not, initially at least, change the majority's public judgements. This is exactly the opposite process to *compliance*, which was defined in chapter 1 as public change without accompanying underlying private change. As Asch's classic study (and many that followed it) showed, compliance is a way that individuals tend to react to majority pressure. This effect has been demonstrated within the blue-green paradigm itself, with consistent majorities (of experimental accomplices) tending to produce compliance as distinct from the conversion produced by consistent minorities (Moscovici & Lage 1976).

Such a contrary position to conversion, coupled with the fact that majorities tend to have power while minorities do not, led Moscovici to propose that majority and minority influence are mutually exclusive processes. This proposition has since become known as the **dual process view** of social influence (Moscovici 1976, 1980). The dual process view is broadly compatible with the effect of inverse resonance; minorities, that is, are typically different from, rather than similar to, the majority views they challenge.

Private admiration, public repudiation

According to Moscovici (1976), when faced with a consistent minority, individual majority members start to surreptitiously and subconsciously admire the minority, both for its emotional courage (shown by its consistency over time) and its intellectual fortitude (shown by the consistency of its arguments). The minority, a majority audience reasons, is confident and coherent in its point of view (social consistency) and must have thought about the issue deeply to be so bold and forthright (Moscovici 1976). In Maass and Clark's (1983) study of minority influence, for instance, participants were, on average, able to think of three times more arguments supporting the minority than the majority side. This spur to greater cognition is facilitated as the minority visibly accrues converts (enhancing social consistency), when minority influence gathers momentum (Clark 1999; see also Moscovici, Lage & Naffrechoux 1969). Thus, covert admiration seems to grow exponentially with initial converts (Lortie-Lussier, Lemieux & Godbout 1989; see also Latané & Wolf 1981).

According to Moscovici, admiration explains the changes that take place in private. In public, however, individual majority members have other issues to worry about. A major reason why individuals in the majority refuse to openly acknowledge their covert change of heart is their motivation to preserve 'face' (for an updated discussion of the growing literature on this concept, see Earley 1997). Moscovici is reminding us of the fact that people do not like to admit to having been influenced by a 'deviant' minority. This is most clearly seen in what happens when a consistent minority 'leaves the room'. It is only at this point that minority influence externalises — that is, becomes visible at a public, overt level (Moscovici & Nève 1971). This, again, is the complete opposite of what occurs in majority influence, which classically *de*creases when the source is no longer watching (Deutsch & Gerard 1955). Linking this process of externalisation to events in history, Moscovici argues that many great innovators and rebels are publicly recognised only after their deaths. Consistent with this as well as, more broadly, the acquaintance stage depicted in figure 8.1, a later meta-review of minority influence found that conversion normally takes time to manifest (Wood et al. 1994).

Clarifying the admiration-attraction linkage

What the above research suggests is that although we may be attracted to the ideas put forward with consistency by the minority, we will not necessarily be attracted to that minority as individuals. In May 1968 many French people (audience) were attracted to 'what' the students were saying (the message, their ideas), but did not necessarily like the students (the source) who were saying it (Moscovici 1976, p. 218). According to Moscovici, such ambivalence towards, and marginalisation of, those who advocate change of the status quo (e.g. academics, scientists, artists, political thinkers) is quite common in history and society. This view is captured succinctly in the Roman adage 'Admire the work, beware the artist', which Moscovici paraphrases as 'Admire the act or idea which is deviant, dislike the person who produced it' (1976, p. 207). Consistent minorities provoke attraction to their ideas tempered by shades of repulsion towards them as the harbingers of change, disruption and instability (Sherif 1956). At best, admiration for them as people is surreptitious. And, 'soon after executing the arch-enemies, the revolution will dispose of its own leaders' (Moscovici 1976, p. 218). All things considered, therefore, Janis's (1982) advice to rotate the devil's advocate is probably well judged, especially in light of the fundamental attribution error (see chapter 6).

According to Moscovici, consistent majorities exert their influence normatively, by social pressure and the overly hot dynamics of fear (ridicule, ostracism etc.). They over-arouse and fluster the individual into superficial compliance and so minimise cognition. As we have seen, consistent minorities, by contrast, generate more thought and more cognition. Hot (conflict) and cold (logic) systems work more closely together. Consistent minorities can therefore provide effective pro-social antidotes against negative stereotyping (Sanchez-Mazas, Mugny & Falomir 1997; Devine, Plant & Buswell 2000).

Creativity and the 'multidimensional drive outwards'

This potential for minority influence to break the social mould extends also into a potential to break the intellectual mould of groupthink. Moscovici's proposition that minorities are useful for generating attractive ideas is most apparent in a now burgeoning literature on minority influence on innovative group problem solving. The thrust of this literature is that majorities tend to increase fear and arousal, which in turn facilitates an already dominant (and so staid) response. Majorities, that is, usually offer only conventional responses, rather than innovative solutions, to problems. Consistent but numerically small minorities, however, have less potential to evoke fear, thus enhancing prospects for 'cooler cognition'. These minorities have the potential to evoke what Moscovici terms a 'norm of originality' (1976). When this norm is made salient, original minorities generate admiration for their ideas, which in turn motivates their admirers themselves to be creative. They, too, display originality, starting to 'do their own thing' and to think laterally. In contrast to the unidirectional drive upwards, therefore, consistent minorities facilitate the release of a more creative **multidimensional drive outwards**.

In the first laboratory investigation of this kind of impact, Nemeth and Wachtler (1983) observed groups of six people, which contained four or two confederates, depending on whether the condition was 'majority' or 'minority' influence. These groups were given a puzzle involving a standard geometric shape, such as a triangle, alongside which was a listing of several other, more complex geometric patterns. The much simpler geometric figure was embedded inside one or more of these complex forms, and the task was to correctly identify which. The confederates in this study, majority and minority, made judgements that were sometimes wrong and sometimes right. The independent variables were therefore the minority/majority nature of the source and the rightness/wrongness of their proposed answers. Nemeth and Wachtler's dependent variables were (a) the number of copycat responses made by the genuine participants, and (b) the number of independent solutions generated by the latter, which could also be (c) objectively right or wrong.

The results of this important study demonstrated that the majority produced more (a) straightforward copycat behaviour than the minority, even when it (the majority) was wrong. People in the majority condition also reported that they felt relatively stifled and pressured to respond in the same way the majority did. In the minority source influence condition, however, there were more (b) original choices, and these also happened to be (c) correct, regardless of whether the minority itself was correct. Evidently, then, the minority was not just encouraging people to guess. Rather, it was energising the majority to 'do its own thing', and moreover to do it well (Martin & Hewstone 1999). These findings of increased originality and quality of thinking following exposure to a consistent minority position have since been replicated by Nemeth and others across a range of more realistic everyday tasks (Nemeth 1996; Nemeth, Mosier & Chiles 1992; Peterson & Nemeth 1996).

Conversion: levels of awareness

In the original (1969) study, those genuine participants who had not yielded at all at stage one changed more in private, at stage two, than did their counterparts who had been influenced at stage one. Putting this another way, those participants who seemed to feel the attraction of the minority's consistency most apparently also felt the strongest need to repudiate that minority in public. Their admiration was covert. That finding indicated internal conflict, as if participants were attempting to suppress, or perhaps even repress, the fact that they had been influenced. In his 1980 presentation of the dual process model, Moscovici took this particular idea further, beginning to fashion it into a theory of *unconscious* processes. The starting point for this theory is that internal conflict can take place on two levels, one conscious and the other not. Majority members may consciously decide not to identify themselves publicly with consistent minorities, even though they privately admire, and are attracted to, their ideas. But converts may be unable to admit even to themselves that they have been influenced by, of all things, a 'deviant' minority faction.

This is more than a question of public 'face' (Earley 1997). It is a question of psychodynamics. Essentially, in his 1980 model Moscovici explicitly asserts that consistent minorities will often produce repression. Influenced majority members frequently repress (deny to themselves) the fact that they have been persuaded to entertain socially unacceptable opinions. This repression means that these influences will later surface, hydraulically, on a related issue (see chapter 7). For example, a minority argues consistently for legalised abortion, and influence surfaces not on that specific topic (and any attitude scale items specifically designed to measure it), but instead on attitude scale items favouring birth control. This latter issue is indirectly linked to abortion through the underlying issue of 'right to life' (Perez & Mugny 1987). Unfortunately, however, there is disagreement today about what precisely 'counts' as direct or indirect influence, which means that we cannot yet determine to what extent minority influence is direct and conscious or indirect and unconscious (for a specific example of this disagreement, compare Alvaro & Crano 1997, p. 949, and Wood et al. 1994, p. 328).

The natural limits of minority influence

Clearly, minority influence does not always succeed (Schachter 1951). A number of studies addressing this limiting condition have worked within the group polarisation paradigm introduced in chapter 3. In this rich field of study, researchers have placed minorities of accomplices in groups to see how they influence the normal polarisation process (Smith, Tindale & Dugoni 1996). In one study, for instance, a minority that was consistent and flexible on the issue of the Swiss Army amplified polarisation (in private) compared with a minority that was equally consistent but rigidly intransigent on the same issue (Mugny 1975; for further fascinating examples of this kind of research, related to gender equality, see Paicheler 1976, 1977). Such studies suggest that minorities who are consistent to the point of rigidity may exceed the limits of many of the majority's tolerance (Devine, Plant & Buswell 2000).

There are other limiting conditions to minority influence. For instance, the majority may be highly certain to begin with (Maass & Volpato 1996). Or the issue may be sufficiently salient that the majority simply cannot afford to give up its position (David & Turner 1996). Excessive dissimilarity, too, can be a barrier to minority influence, so that conversion is really 'a product of sources who are somewhat, but not too, dissimilar' (p. 196). Minority influence, then, is likely to be optimal when the difference between source and target, and the amount of emotion subsequently generated, is neither too little nor too great (for a classic study on these issues, see Schachter 1951).

This point enables us to make some summary statements about minority influence and conversion. Conversion works not only by minimal power (minority source) and so minimal constraint (a topic addressed in part 1 of this book); and by fostering admiration and so maximum cognition (part 2). It also works by generating **medium affect**.

Applications

Pressure groups

Being too dissimilar is partly a question of choosing the right social context. Clever minorities position themselves in the 'grey area' between the majority (conventional norms) and the radical wing (deviant norms). By doing so, they make themselves appear to their majority audience to be inherently 'moderate' (see also Premack 1963). In one study, for instance, relatively radical (and consistent) feminist minorities had less influence if their arguments were presented to women in a purely feminist context than if these same arguments were presented with a clear out-group (men) being salient at the time (David & Turner 2000). In an all-women context, feminists appeared relatively radical and deviant, but with men present, the women in the study felt more empathy with other women. This is yet another example of the *meta-contrast effect* described in chapter 3 (for a more detailed critical analysis, see David & Turner 2001).

Work teams

A further, manifestly relevant area in which this literature may be applied is in improving creativity and innovative performance in work groups. Again, a delicate balance must be struck between having too little conflict for any new ideas to emerge and so much that no new ideas can emerge. There is a need to (a) select and place creative individuals in the team as devil's advocates, 'ideas people' or 'plants' (Belbin 1997; Van Dyne & Saavedra 1996). There is also a need to (b) moderate the level of conflict these minorities can and must produce, in order to best stimulate real creativity. According to the literature, one way of achieving this is for the behavioural style of the consistent minority to be flexible rather than overly rigid (Moscovici 1976), and for the position of devil's advocate to rotate as often as possible (Janis 1982).

Promotion of goods and services

Minorities often speak to us through the media (see chapter 4), and an emerging extension of the conversion research is to commercial and social marketing (chapter 6). The literature we have reviewed makes a provocative suggestion, namely that the most profound form of attitude change produced by advertising will derive from consistent messages that are initially quite shocking and repulsive. According to Moscovici's conversion model, controversy ultimately pays off. In fact, unless you *are* controversial, you are unlikely to make any real impact. One major international clothing company, Benetton, has cleverly constructed its now infamous, but perhaps sneakingly admired, marketing campaigns on this very same basis (de Rosa & Smith 1998).

Intranets: a link back to propinquity

Another area of application for this kind of research is in intranet decision-making groups (see chapter 3). A fascinating property of these intranets is that they have less 'presence' for their members, who are remote and physically removed from one another, than 'regular' groups who meet face-to-face (Fontaine 2002). This means that minorities might be more willing to 'speak out', and less face-saving manoeuvring would occur among the rest of the group. Discourse would be more 'in the open'. The relative lack of minority presence, however, might also reduce the salience of its own underdog status, which we have seen is integral to creating admiration and the potential for social change (see also Lamm & Myers 1978, on the comparative impact of face-to-face argument; see Latané & Wolf 1981, on social impact theory). Minorities therefore may actually lose leverage in e-decision-making groups, leaving these groups less creative than their 'real-time' counterparts with physically proximal minorities in them.

Some emerging evidence seems to support the latter rather than the former possibility. Consistent minorities have recently been found to exert more influence on private opinions when they are face-to-face with the majority than when interacting on computer (McLeod et al. 1997). Similarly, mediators with minority *or* majority status have been found to exert *equal* amounts of influence on private opinions when the mediation was carried out through computer networks rather than face-to-face, as though minority status counted for less in e-communication channels (Fisher-Lokou 1997). Overall, therefore, it will be interesting to see whether the increases in fidelity to reality that are taking place in the computer industry will eventually allow cyber minorities, in intranets, to be as creatively inspiring as their physically constituted counterparts.

Culture, communication and context

Such considerations relate to both context and communication. As the context changes, so too may some of the parameters of the conversion process that we think we fully understand. The same point can perhaps be made about culture and cultural context (Ng & Van Dyne 2001). In relatively power distant and collectivistic societies and groups, for instance, one has to question whether consistent minorities, whose recognised right to speak out against the norms of the group is limited, would not be merely tolerated or even banished from the community.

Admiration would matter less. To a certain extent, this response might be inevitable in any group that becomes increasingly cohesive, and to that extent more collectivistic (for an overview of creativity in cohesive and collectivistic groups, see Triandis, McCusker & Hui 1990).

In one very interesting study conducted in Japan, for instance, minorities needed a little status to exert influence, and even then produced, not conversion, but rather compliance (Koseki 1989). This is actually what we might expect in a relatively collectivist society (see chapter 1; also Yoshiyama 1991). Similarly, in a more recent study conducted within the United States, individuals whose *organisational* values were relatively high on collectivism and power distance produced higher quality group decisions when the influence agent held a position of status within the group (Yee & Van Dyne 2001). Thus, both societal and organisational cultures are capable, in principle, of moderating the processes of conversion originally described by Moscovici (1976, 1980).

SEXUAL ATTRACTION

One area in which difference is often attractive is sexual attraction (Buss 1985). First, there are the obvious physical differences between the sexes (Seyfried & Hendrick 1973). This includes the excitement of physical variety in sexual partners, whose characteristics will sometimes be 'different' from our own (Buss 2000). Second, sexual attraction can also derive from discovering various socio-emotional compatibilities and complementarities — say, through seductive communication on the Internet (Mantovani 2001). An extreme illustration of compatibility is the sadist and the masochist; others might include the emotionally insecure and the secure, and the person with a low self-concept who finds difference-from-self attractive (Leonard 1975). Third, rebound and ironic effects may make the 'different' attractive (e.g. Wegner et al. 1994). Fourth, there are socio-economic differences. For example, money and power are themselves sexually alluring and exciting to some individuals (Wiederman & Allgeier 1992). Also, economically vulnerable young people may 'trade' their youth for greater economic security with older but wealthier partners (Gangestad 1993). In sum, therefore, there are many reasons why, in the domain of sexual relations, 'difference' is sexually charged.

In what follows, I have been reluctant to prematurely draw a distinction between heterosexual and homosexual attraction. One reason is that there seems to be relatively little research comparing the two, with most of the research on sexual attraction focusing on heterosexual relations (for an exception, see Howard, Blumstein & Schwartz 1987). Second, the literature indicates that certain basic principles are shared (e.g. Boyden, Carroll & Maier 1984). Most of the reasons for being attracted to diversity just outlined, for example, apply equally well to heterosexual and homosexual partners. Third, the very idea of differentiating between 'heterosexual' and 'homosexual' attraction is in itself potentially divisive (see chapter 3). All said, then, heterosexual and homosexual attraction are differentiated here only when there seems to be compelling reasons to do so. If this general approach, and the literature on which it is based, *works*, the social psychology that follows should make sense independently of sexual orientation.

Basic conceptual distinctions

The foregoing examples of what attracts people to each other sexually vary from one another according to their temporal focus. Some, like 'physical' considerations, tend to be oriented towards the sexual 'adventure', and in that sense are usually of short duration. Others, like 'socio-economic' concerns, can have an inherently longer term focus. This fundamental distinction is now widely recognised in the attraction literature (Regan & Berscheid 1997). Accordingly, in the analysis that follows we consider what attracts people to each other when they have in mind (a) short-term sexual relationships or (b) a longer term relationship in which sex is less the goal in itself. Both possibilities, however, remain focused on preferences in the mind of the perceiver before the relationship is actually formed. This is what conceptually distinguishes attraction from real-time studies of intimate relations during subsequent stages in these relationships' development. Attraction is a *precursor* of relationships, whatever their duration. Being distinctive issues in themselves, the internal dynamics of these relationships are discussed separately in the next chapter.

Short-term relationships

The centrality of physical attractiveness

When young women and men have been asked about their motives for engaging in casual, short-term sex, they have tended to generate similar reasons (Regan & Dreyer 1999). These reasons have two basic foci, one essentially 'internal' to the self, and the other essentially 'external' to the self, located in the social environment (Regan et al. 2000). Interrelated examples of the internal category include sexual experimentation (the attraction of difference), physical pleasure (sensation seeking), and being intoxicated (e.g. with alcohol). Externally, however, the literature points to one overriding consideration, namely that the partner is physically attractive (Regan & Berscheid 1997; Regan et al. 2000). Typically, this means they are 'good-looking' and (in affluent 'developed' economies at least) have an 'athletic' physique (Cowley 2000; Regan et al. 2000). Thus, independently of sex and gender, the core social psychological factor that draws people together for short-term sexual encounters is desire based on the prospective partner's *physicality* (see figure 8.1).

A foundation in familiarity

A range of empirical studies have pointed to a link between (i) physicality and (ii) familiarity.

First, there is evidence that patrons of pubs and clubs become more physically attractive to one another as the evening wears on (Gladue & Delaney 1990). A rather cynical interpretation of this is that these patrons are probably influenced by the effects of alcohol or some other substance, or some mood of the moment induced, for instance, by music (Nida & Koon 1983; Pennebaker 1979). Yet the familiarity effect occurs only among unattached patrons, which suggests that the effect has something to do with looking for a partner rather than drinking *per se* (Madey et al. 1996). There remains a possibility that single patrons are heavier drinkers than attached patrons, and use alcohol to lower their inhibitions and increase their confidence, but this is not consistent with the results in one study, which found that intoxication was not a salient factor (Sprecher 1984). Over the longer term, we have already seen that the mere presence of a person in a student classroom, over the course of a semester, increased her attraction to the group (Moreland & Beach 1992). In terms of figure 8.1, this woman was rated increasingly highly in terms of popularity (and so liking), intelligence (respect/admiration?) and physical attractiveness. Thus, familiarity increased physical attraction.

Second, digital technology has been used to create composite faces using the features of a series of real individuals (Langlois & Roggman 1990). Interestingly, as the composite picture progressively emerges, it is increasingly rated as more attractive than the majority of individual faces from which it has been digitally engineered. In a sense, this effect echoes the Gestalt psychology dictum 'the whole is greater than the sum of its parts'. In addition, however, Baron and Byrne (2000) interpret attraction to these composites as reflecting the existence of prototypical schemata for the human face. The composite resembles the prototype because the latter, too, is made from composites of other faces. In fact, the composite face looks more like a prototype schema than most real, idiosyncratic faces do. In this sense, it is relatively familiar. According to Baron and Byrne, therefore, the inherent physical attractiveness of digitised composites depends on, and re-reveals the effects of, mere exposure (and so familiarity). The effect of these composites also perhaps reinforces a point made earlier — that in attraction, moderation is important (composites, by definition, have no extreme features).

Beyond familiarity and mere exposure effects

There is often very good agreement between individuals, as observers, about whether they are looking at someone who is or is not physically attractive (Cunningham et al. 1995). When people are judging themselves, as actors rather than observers (see chapter 6), their judgements can be self-serving (Gabriel, Critelli & Ee 1994; see chapter 6; for an earlier discussion of this, see Codol 1975). When judging others, however, composite pictures whose elements (faces) are by consensus physically attractive tend to produce higher attraction ratings than composites whose elements are less attractive physically (Perrett, May & Yoshikawa 1994). These findings suggest that, over and above a template schema for faces generally, and the basic influence of mere familiarity and exposure, there is also a template schema for the face that is stereotypically physically attractive (see chapter 7).

What physical features define physical attraction?

In attempting to answer this question, researchers have drawn on the fact that there is a good deal of consensus about physical attractiveness. Specifically, they have taken one group of stimulus individuals who are by consensus physically attractive, and another group who are not (Cunningham 1986). These groups of stimulus individuals, physically attractive on the one side and physically unattractive on the other, have then been scrutinised for physical features that are consistently present in one group and consistently absent in the other (McKelvie 1993).

Thus measured, the facial features consensually identified as defining physical attraction (and thereby desire and arousal in figure 8.1) include, for example, widely spaced eyes and prominent cheekbones in women, and a wide, square jaw in men (Cowley 2000). Examples of key bodily features typically include a tapered waist, or relatively low 'waist-to-hip ratio' (Singh 1995).

Emergent differences between the sexes

Although there seems to be a good deal of consensus across sexes that physical attractiveness is important, there are signs that male and female perceivers differ when it comes to the meaning that they assign to the sexual act itself. Among students, for instance, more women than men are likely to see emotional intimacy as a goal of sexual desire (Regan & Berscheid 1996). Also, sexuality generally is more likely to include sexual-emotional attraction (Ernulf & Innala 1998). In addition, more women than men are likely to think about longer term commitment as a possible outcome of a short-term encounter (Regan & Dreyer 1999). These emerging differences herald some divergences between the sexes as perceivers of what is sexually attractive in others. To the extent that we can summarise these differences, women perceivers may often be working with a broader, less exclusively 'physical' definition of what the act of 'having sex' entails (see critical narrative 8.3).

CRITICAL NARRATIVE 8.3

The love drug

Seeing a beautiful woman triggers a pleasure response in a man's brain similar to what a hungry person gets from eating or an addict gets from a drug, United States scientists say.

A study in the journal *Neuron* shows that beauty affects a man's brain at a primal level, not on some intellectual plane.

Source: *New Zealand Herald*, 19 November 2001, p. A11.

Longer term attractions

These and other differences become sharper once we consider what is sexually attractive in the longer term, for example when seeking a potential partner who will remain after the sexual encounters are over. In studies of 'mate selection', for instance, males more than women prefer a physically attractive longer term (marriage) partner (Regan & Bersheid 1997). As critical narrative 8.3 suggests, males are also more likely to consider physical attributes generally, and 'coital acceptability' in particular, whereas women are significantly more likely also to consider motivational and emotional compatibilities, such as ambition and status (Townsend & Wasserman 1998). In summary, men and women start to diverge in what is preferred in a longer term relationship, with male perceivers remaining relatively (although not exclusively) focused on the physical, and female perceivers becoming (relatively) more concerned with the socio-emotional and socio-economic aspects of attraction (for a summary of comparative rankings, see for example Buss 1985).

A role for socio-biology

One theory in particular boldly attempts to explain almost all of these differences. Evolution theory has recently been regaining prominence in psychology (Pinker 1997; Plotkin 1997). In social psychology, evidence is mounting that much of the shared sense of what constitutes physical attraction in the Information Age has its origins in the Stone Age (Cowley 2000, p. 113). A 'social evolution' account argues that who and what we are today is a product of ancient ancestry, and especially of what social behaviours, attitudes and attractions were socially adaptive in neolithic times. The basic argument here is that we will be physically (and subconsciously) attracted to physical features that, in prehistory, would have enhanced survival prospects for genetic offspring. Because they took so long to evolve, we cannot expect these subconscious tendencies to disappear 'overnight' with the advent of civilisation. In this sense, human development will always lag seriously behind technological development (Moghaddam 1996). Social behaviour will thus always partly depend on evolutionary survival value (for an example, refer back to explanations of the mere exposure effect).

According to this argument, the crux of social evolutionary theory is that we inherit certain innate dispositions from our distant past. If this is so, it should be possible to show that human beings have innate responses with regard to what is, and is not, attractive. Some of the stronger evidence for this 'natural' component to physical attraction can be found in studies of infants' gazing patterns towards attractive and unattractive adult faces (Langlois, Roggman & Rieser-Danner 1990). In Langlois et al.'s study, 12-month-old infants were allowed to look at an experimental accomplice who was wearing an unattractive or attractive mask. The accomplice did not know which of the two masks was being worn at any particular time, and so could not have unintentionally behaved any differently across the two experimental conditions. Observation of what happened when this accomplice picked up the infant showed that the infants demonstrated more positive affect and related play activity when the face was attractive (as adults would consensually define it). These effects were subsequently observed regardless of the mask wearer's sex, visible ethnicity or age (Langlois et al. 1991). Even three- and six-month-old babies, who have had very little worldly experience, spent more time looking at physically attractive rather than physically unattractive faces (Cowley 2000). Such findings clearly indicate that what counts for physical attraction is partly 'wired into' the human psyche. To that extent, the chances are that it was somehow adaptive.

How was it adaptive to be attracted to certain physical features?

Among the most cross-culturally reliable physical features of what differentiates physically attractive from physically unattractive target persons are (a) facial and bodily symmetry (in both sexes), (b) small jaw (in women) and (c) jutting jaw (in men). These physical features are also physical manifestations of (a) bodily health in general, and reproductive health in particular, via (b) oestrogen and (c) testosterone, respectively (Cowley 2000). Likewise, one of the most reliable predictors of physical attraction of men to women and women to men, across a range of contexts and cultures, is the waist-to-hip ratio (Singh 1995). In women, this physical feature (when small) signals reproductiveness, while in men (when large) it is a sign of robust health (Rosmond & Bjoerntorp 2000). Consistently, therefore, physical features that it would be adaptive to be attracted to turn out to be precisely the physical features that people *are* attracted to, at least for short-term relationships.

When it comes to longer term preferences, and in particular to explaining the differences that emerge between men and women, we have seen that men continue to remain relatively focused on physical/sexual attributes, while women are relatively more concerned with socio-emotional and socio-economic needs. Thus, when asked to compose a list of life wishes, men are reportedly more likely than women to want to have sex with anyone they choose (Ehrlichman & Eichenstein 1992). They are also generally more concerned about enjoying sex without emotional commitment (Laumann et al. 1994).

Social evolution theory, we saw, proposes a bold explanation for such sex differences. According to Buss, 'it would be extraordinarily unlikely that evolution by selection would fail to forge sex differentiated mating strategies' (2000, p. 39). The most obvious engine for such differentiation is the biology of reproduction. According to this view, women must be highly selective with whom they 'mate' because women can only conceive, deliver and raise a limited number of children in their lifetime. Women, according to the theory, will have adapted to a 'mate preference' for somewhat older males, with relatively more economic resources and more capacity for socio-emotional support than younger males. Men, on the other hand, according to the theory, will have a vested interest in having sexual intercourse with many younger, fertile women with relatively little sexual experience. This maximises the chance that their genes will survive in a future generation. Thus, and to return to our working definition of attraction at the beginning of the chapter, men and women will be drawn to different aspects of each other when first seeking a longer term partner.

These predictions derived from the social evolution model are broadly compatible with actual expressed 'mate preferences' across a range of cultures in the Americas, Asia, Africa, Europe and the Pacific (Buss 1989). In Buss's (1989) study, more than 10 000 participants were asked to indicate what they looked for in a potential mating partner. Whereas men consistently rated good looks and lack of sexual experience higher than women, women were more likely than men to look for signs of socio-economic achievement and success, as well as preferring partners who were slightly older than themselves. Similar results to these have since been found elsewhere through use of a range of different methodologies, including, for example, archival research examining what kinds of advertisements people tend to place in the personal columns of the media (Sprecher, Sullivan & Hatfield 1994), and records of marriage licences that document the ages of respective partners (Paterson & Pettijohn 1982).

A role for society

Of course, these findings do not imply that social evolutionary pressures are the *only* forces operating in mate preference attraction. People can be drawn to money for its own sake, too! Understandably, then, such assertions are contested in some quarters, most notably by the advocates of environmental learning factors in the continuing nature–nurture debate in psychology. These critics have pointed to findings such as that the more economic power women have, in those very same countries studied by Buss (1989), the more important male physical attractiveness becomes in female 'mating preferences' (Gangestad 1993). In other words, physical attractiveness matters less when economic necessity matters more (Brehm, Kassin & Fein 1999). According to the critics of social evolutionary theory, therefore, the question of who is and is not 'attractive' can be as much psychological as evolutionary; or as much about economic power as about physical attraction. In reality, then, it is often impossible to separate attraction from the everyday pragmatics of local context; they are inextricably intertwined (Malach-Pines 2001).

Culture and sexual attraction

The idea that nurture as well as nature is at work in sexual attraction and mate preference extends, naturally enough, into the domain of the influence of cultures. For example, wide differences exist between what different cultural groups will do to their faces to make themselves attractive in their own culture. These range from temporary cosmetics to tattooing, teeth filing, and ear, nose, lip and tongue piercing (e.g. Landau 1989). There is a wide variety in what is deemed to be culturally appropriate and attractive in terms of the human body, too. In one study involving 54 cultures, heavier women were found to be more physically attractive in those societies in which poverty and food shortages are typically common (Anderson et al. 1992). Critical narrative 8.4 focuses on the meaning of heaviness in such a resource-constrained setting. Given that much of the world lives in poverty, either in 'developing' countries or in depressed areas within 'developed' economies, there are undoubtedly socio-cultural as well, perhaps, as socio-biological variations in what counts as physical attractiveness and suitability in a future 'mate'.

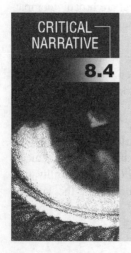

CRITICAL NARRATIVE

8.4

Competing priorities in physique

The European expatriate was lamenting with African friends and colleagues about recently giving up smoking. Having been lean and thin while a smoker, this expatriate had now started to gain weight. The African colleagues found his complaining highly amusing. This prompted the expatriate to ask them why such anxiety was so incongruous to them. Their reply was that body fat was not considered unattractive. It signalled that the individual had some 'insurance policy' (bodily reserves) against body-ravaging diseases such as malaria. This was especially so in a context where AIDS, or 'Slim disease', was becoming a major concern. In the developing world, therefore, the very idea of fretting about becoming '*not* thin' was essentially ludicrous.

Source: Personal experience (February 1992).

Interestingly, the kind of cultural variation depicted in critical narrative 8.4 is not inconsistent with evolutionary theory (see also Wetsman & Marlowe 1999). In a context of ongoing poverty and disease, and independently of sex, it would make adaptive sense for cultural norms to advocate seeking a partner who is relatively wealthy, as indicated by increased body size (along with other biological indicators of robust health and fertility, such as facial and bodily symmetry). In this sense, cultures themselves can be viewed as part of the process of social evolution, rather than being artificially hived off from it (e.g. Berry 1979; Malach-Pines 2001). After all, cultural norms would probably not even exist if they had not somehow proved themselves environmentally adaptive over eons of social history (MacLachlan 1997).

A link to globalisation

What is also interesting about critical narrative 8.4 is that it touches on a wider issue in today's world. In a global community, there are going to be increased conflicts between local realities and global expectations, as promulgated, for example, by the mass media (see chapter 4). We already know, for instance, that there are mounting pressures, through global media-scapes that portray the ideal body as being slim, for people to lose weight (Lamb et al. 1993). Against this, however, there will be ongoing pressures to adhere to local traditions, some of which will advocate being relatively 'big'. Thus, people are being caught between two competing pressures, one global and the other local. They are, again, subject to the pushes and pulls of glocalisation.

Body image and psychosocial health

By repeatedly presenting 'perfect' examples of what attractiveness is, global marketing and entertainment industries act as media mavens, creating distress for many viewers who are constantly reminded of the extent to which they do not fit the globalising stereotype (Ashmore, Solomon & Longo 1996). This is an example of the kind of contrast effect in which, for example, 'excellent' candidates at job interviews make good candidates look and feel poor (Kenrick et al. 1993). A particularity here, however, is that the 'poor' candidate being rated is the self, and the outcome is low self-esteem (Thornton & Moore 1993). The resulting depression can feed on itself and spiral downwards (Heinberg & Thompson 1995; see below, however, on social skills training).

The eye of the beholder

The deleterious effects of feeling oneself to be unworthy cannot all be blamed on media pressures. Other people are also responsible. One dramatic and appalling illustration of the power of relative attractiveness to shape our lives has been found in hospital and medical services. In one study, being declared 'DOA', or 'dead on arrival', was significantly more likely among patients who were less physically attractive (Raven & Rubin 1983). Such 'deadly' forms of discrimination, in this case by professional doctors, are unlikely to be adopted consciously, and indeed much of the way in which physical attractiveness in others influences a perceiver's behaviour is probably implicit (Locher et al. 1993). The physically attractive, for instance, are often stereotyped as relatively sociable, well adjusted and sexually warm (Calvert 1988). Assuming that many people would not want such stereotypes, positive or negative, in their repertoires, physical attraction is thus in part a reflection of the skilled unawareness and incompetence discussed in chapter 7.

Pygmalion revisited

To some extent, of course, these stereotypes may be reasonably accurate guesses about such an individual's personality. If attractive people are consistently stereotyped in a positive light as they pass through life, then they will at the same time be treated well by others, so fuelling a self-fulfilling prophecy (see chapter 5). Attractive people will be accorded precisely the kind of social environmental conditions that favour the development of the characteristics they are stereotyped as having (Eagly et al. 1991). Even in short-term situations, such as interviews, their thin slices will generate positive halo effects (Calvert 1988; chapter 5; for an example of the downside to these halo effects in the context of stereotyping across sexes, see activity 4). In the course of developmental time, because of the attraction that their physicality begets in others, they will tend to develop confidence, poise and perhaps even sexual warmth, while physically unattractive people are progressively impelled in the other direction (Zebrowitz, Collins & Dutta 1998).

This should remind us of the Pygmalion effects described in the previous chapter, as well as the systems dynamics echoed at a number of points in this book. These dynamics would help explain why physically unattractive people are judged, sight unseen — say, over the telephone — to be less socially skilled and physically attractive than physically more attractive people (Miller et al. 1990). Such effects can only occur when the unseen (unattractive) individuals somehow communicate themselves in this way. Fortunately, however, these negative Pygmalion effects can be partially undone. Social skills training (see chapter 7) often helps people to overcome the cumulatively self-handicapping effects of being negatively stereotyped as physically unattractive (Miller et al. 1995; try also exercise 8.4). In this way, social psychology can make a difference in people's lives.

EMERGING THEMES

This chapter has raised three recurring themes. First, we have highlighted the influences on social affect of context, communication and culture. Respectively, for example, we have examined the contextual influences of propinquity, of discovering similarity and of local norms about physicality. Second, we have highlighted the inseparability of social affect from social cognition. Examples of this inseparability include the use of cognition in combating pre-existing moods, calculating the similarity in attraction, and the cognitive-affective elements in social comparison. Third, and perhaps most importantly, we have discovered that social affect is frequently a question of balance. Familiarity, similarity and difference must be neither too little nor too great if their various attractions are to be optimised. This relationship between familiarity, similarity and difference on the one hand, and social affect on the other, is schematically depicted in figure 8.3.

The function sketched in figure 8.3 is analogous to the Yerkes-Dodson Law, or performance-arousal curve (Yerkes & Dodson 1908). According to such curves, human performance in a broad sense will be optimal whenever arousal is neither too low nor too high. Social affect, in other words, must be moderate in order for performance to reach its peak. To return to the chapter's beginning, precisely the same shape of function, and the importance of balance that it implies, has been found to apply to aid advertisements that are too emotionally intense (Carr, McAuliffe & MacLachlan 1998). Thus, a theme that runs through this chapter, and will recur throughout this part of the book, is *medium affect*.

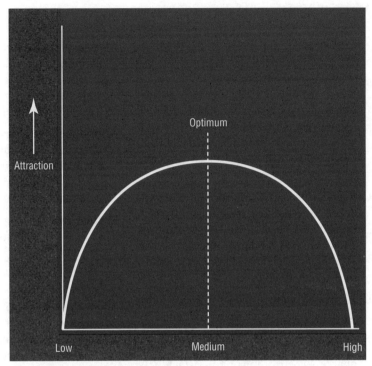

Figure 8.3   A performance-arousal curve in attraction

SUMMARY

Initial acquaintance often happens 'by default', simply because physical geography (e.g. where you live or work or study) or access to the Internet (e.g. e-mail) brings people together in physical and cyber space. Attraction is frequently a question of proximity, from physical (low choice, default) to virtual (high degree of choice). The resulting social contact, bolstered by conditions of adversity and favourable mood, nurtures an increasingly comforting sense of familiarity. This is enhanced if communication reveals shared opinions and attitudinal similarity. Increasingly, the Internet is taking people to this point directly, because people deliberately join special interest groups. Such commonality facilitates liking and interpersonal identification. Identification with an in-group turns out-groups that are similar into rivals. Minority underdogs who mount a consistent challenge to the status quo are often disliked at the same time as their ideas are covertly admired, which assists them to introduce social change. In this way, deviance, dissimilarity and difference are attractive. Sexuality, too, can be tuned to the spice of variety. Although there are schematic constancies in what is physically attractive, local variations persist, and are increasingly interacting in fluid and essentially dynamic ways with their more global templates.

KEY TERMS

Adversity-affiliation. In times of shared hardship and threat, even complete strangers can become spontaneously affiliative towards one another. (p. 290)

Attraction-selection-attrition. A cycle found in organisational groups, which attract job applicants who resemble the incumbents. As workers who fit less well leave through attrition, the personnel in an organisation will increasingly resemble one other. (p. 298)

Conversion. A social influence process produced by consistent minorities, in which majorities change their covert attitudes without overtly admitting it to others, and even perhaps without consciously admitting it to themselves (p. 302)

Dual process view. A model of social influence that depicts majority and minority influence as polar opposites. Majorities, which rely on power, produce compliance, whereas minorities, which rely on consistency, produce conversion (see above). (p. 302)

Dissimilarity-admiration. The lure of the different and the exotic. Dissimilar minorities that behave consistently are often sneakingly admired for having the courage of their convictions, while simultaneously being disliked for rocking the boat. (p. 301)

E-proximity. Accessibility through Internet technology, as compared to physical accessibility (p. 288)

Inverse resonance. An idea that groups whose attitudes are similar will pose a greater threat to each other's social identity than groups whose attitudes are dissimilar. In this sense, these groups will resonate negatively with each other as each vies for a positively distinctive social identity. (p. 296)

Medium affect. The idea that influence is optimal and most sustainable when its source generates in its target neither too little nor too much social affect. (p. 306)

Mere exposure effect. Repeated exposure to an initially novel and unfamiliar stimulus is often sufficient to render that same stimulus increasingly familiar, and thus relatively attractive. (p. 286)

Multidimensional drive outwards. Creative minorities, although disliked, provoke admiration for their creativity, and so may help to unlock creative potential in their majority audiences. (p. 304)

Partner-next-door effect. Relationships are more likely to be formed with people who live and work closer to us rather than farther away in geographical/physical space. (p. 285)

Shoot-the-messenger effect. Mood affects judgements, rather like the historical tradition of killing messengers (judgement) who bring (mood-altering, depressing) bad news. (p. 292)

Similarity-attraction. Both a paradigm and a principle, in which attitudinal and other forms of similarity (e.g. traits, values) are linked to attraction, predominantly in the form of liking (p. 293)

Social comparison. In order to evaluate our opinions about the world (are they correct?) and our abilities to function within it (are we good at what we do?), we need to compare ourselves to similar (comparable) others. The more uniformity of opinion, and superiority of ability, we can find, the better we will feel about ourselves. (p. 294)

Terror management. A concept based on the idea that life is an existential crisis, a state of terror in which we know not where we come from, why we are here or where we are headed. The social construction of reality through cultural systems is supposedly a mechanism for coping with this terror. (p. 294)

1. How does proximity influence attraction, and will it continue to do so?
2. How does similarity influence attraction between individuals and groups?
3. What is the process by which minorities change group norms and so generate social transformation?
4. What is the role of nature versus nurture in physical attractiveness?

DISCUSSION QUESTIONS

1. The Internet will destroy genuine friendships. Discuss.
2. Groups are inherently more competitive than individuals. Discuss.
3. Conversion theory and social identity theory (see chapter 3) are incompatible. Discuss.
4. Attractiveness is in the genes of the beholder, not the subject. Discuss.

ACTIVITIES

1. 'Space and friendship'

Prepare a small sketch of the physical layout of your immediate living environment (building, street etc.). Mark on that map all the individuals (a) whom you know by sight only but have recently spoken to; (b) with whom you have a superficial nodding relationship only; (c) whom you occasionally talk to; and (d) who you would call your friends. Is there any relationship between spatial proximity and your relationship with any of the groups? If you find no links, can you think of any particular characteristics of your situation that could explain this?

Source: Adapted from Forgas (1985, p. 210).

2. 'Let's be friends I'

The text describes how similarity often leads to attraction, and one of the best examples of this is at university, where life-long friendships are often made. This exercise is designed to test whether similarity-attraction applies in your life at university. In the table on page 320, insert a tick (for 'yes') or a cross (for 'no') for each space in the table. 'Not friend' does not mean enemy, it means someone who is simply not particularly a friend. For each trait (row), similarity is implied by a Yes-Yes-No, or a No-No-Yes pattern. Tally these up, either alone or in groups, and determine whether there is more similarity between self and friends than between self and non-friends. A score of 10 would represent a person who has equally shared characteristics and values with friends rather than non-friends. Is similarity-attraction at work in your interpersonal life?

Source: Based on Rosenfeld (1988, p. 279).

Traits	Self	Friend	Not friend
a. Open to new experience	___	___	___
b. Conscientious	___	___	___
c. Extroverted	___	___	___
d. Agreeable	___	___	___
e. Emotionally stable	___	___	___

Values			
a. Individualist	___	___	___
b. Egalitarian	___	___	___
c. Rule aversive	___	___	___
d. Materialistic	___	___	___
e. Forward-thinking	___	___	___

3. **'Let's be friends II'**

   Repeat the exercise above, only this time substitute 'in-group' for friend, and 'out-group' for not-friend. Focus on values, and add to the list some values that you believe are important. Make sure the out-group is one with whom your in-group is relatively competitive, but not necessarily enemies. Is there similarity between rival groups? (That is, is inverse resonance at work in your inter-group life?)

4. **'Blonde hair key to smaller pay'**

   Reykjavik: The cliché has it that blondes are dumb, but now an Icelandic study says they are paid less too.

   The study published yesterday said blondes were in general paid less than brunettes.

   The survey, commissioned by the Commerce Employees' Union, was designed to map out wage disparities in the business sector.

   But researchers added in extra questions about hair colour, bodies, and how often they smiled.

   Source: Courtesy of the *Northern Territory News*, 12 February 2001, p. 5.

The exercise:

Develop an explanatory model for the above research finding, using some of the systems thinking dynamics outlined in the book so far. Concentrate on the systems dynamic of Escalation, and the general concept of Pygmalion effects (review parts 1 and 2 of this book).

ADDITIONAL READING

On the influence of environmental circumstance: Parks and Floyd (1996) examine whether the Internet is a force for social good or division.

On similarity-attraction: Byrne (1997). A topical reading by *the* classic authority.

On dissimilarity-admiration: Moscovici (1980). Fascinating, controversial views.

On physicality and sexual attraction: Buss (2000). The key figure on the social evolutionary perspective on love and sex, Buss here gives an overview of the area.

For further reading on the topics discussed in this chapter, consult the online resources linked to the Wiley website (http://www.johnwiley.com.au/highered/socialpsych).

CHAPTER 9

LOVE

After reading this chapter, you should be able to:

- distinguish love from liking, admiration and lust
- analyse the claim that three of love's key elements — intimacy, commitment and passion — have foundations in the context of early familial love
- describe how these three elements combine to foster the communication styles that distinguish deeper from shallower friendships among females and males
- decide if combining passion, intimacy and commitment, between couples 'in love', transcends culture in a 'chemistry' of love.

OVERVIEW

How can we dispassionately analyse love and at the same time avoid the danger, as Wordsworth put it, that 'We *murder* to dissect'? This chapter opens with a surprisingly simple yet robust taxonomy for organising the various kinds of love across three key types of love relationship (family caregivers, close friends and romantic partners). This gives us a framework for focusing on three popularly intriguing, but also psychologically profound, questions. First, are any of the ways in which we characteristically love others shaped during our formative years? Second, is there any truth in the stereotypes that males, on average, tend to be less socially adept than their female counterparts when relating closely to others? Third, is the whole idea of 'romantic love' really just a huge hoax, fabricated by Hollywood and other media mavens? Or is the potential to be passionately 'in love' a defining, and so understandable, feature of the human condition?

VITAL ELEMENTS

In the futuristic Kubrick/Spielberg movie *A.I.* (for Artificial Intelligence), there is a dramatic scene in which a crowd is tempted to destroy a robot child. This robot is a creation of science that symbolically threatens to rob them of a last vestige of humanity — their 'unique' capacity for higher feelings. At the last moment, however, the child cries for mercy and the crowd relents, so retaining its own capacity to love — its own humanity. For this chapter, that scene is allegorical. The moral is that dissecting love does not murder it. On the contrary, it is *not* dissecting it that is dangerous. In today's world, if we wish to maintain our common humanity, we need more than ever to analyse and thereby make sense out of love.

Traditionally, social psychology has conservatively focused more on behaviour (part 1) and social cognition (part 2) than on social affect in general (part 3) and love in particular. In the last few years, however, there has been a surge of interest in love relationships of all kinds (e.g. Cramer 1998; de Munck 1998b; Duck 1997; Fletcher 2002; Goodwin 1997; Noller, Feeney & Peterson 2001; Spitzberg & Cupach 1998; Vanzetti & Duck 1996). Chapter 1 demonstrated how social psychology has in the past responded to societal crises of one kind or another. So what could be driving this new shift, apart from the increasingly urgent need all researchers feel to identify relatively uncharted 'niches' for research and theory development?

At least some of the increasing interest in love has undoubtedly been stirred by globalisation. Developmental theorists of globalisation, for instance, have recently argued that younger people, as an identifiable group, today need to spend relatively more time in education, compared with their predecessors, before entering the more technical modern workplace (Arnett 2000; Handy 1995, p. 40). In both developed and developing economies, Arnett and other social scientists (e.g. in development studies and demographics) have argued that a 'youth bulge' is delaying the customary transition to marriage that is found in one form or another 'in all known cultures' (Fletcher 2002, p. 94). In New Zealand, for example, median marrying ages for women and men between 1971 and 1998, rose from 21 to 23 and 27 to 28 years, respectively (Fletcher, p. 98; www.stats.govt.nz). In Australia since the mid 1970s, the median age at first marriage for both brides and grooms has increased by four years, reversing an opposite trend in the postwar years (www.abs.gov.au; use search term 'age at first marriage'). Many young people, Arnett argues, are now spending more time than ever exploring possibilities in love relationships during a developmental period termed **emerging adulthood**.

According to Schumaker, this period of 'suspended adolescence' is characterised by the quest, in close relationships, for 'the real thing' with a love partner (2001). As one indicator of the salience of this search for love, when 300 'emerging adults' were asked about life goals, three-quarters of them reported that they would sacrifice most of their other goals for a loving relationship (Hammersla & Frease-McMahan 1990). Since the time of that study, according to Arnett, Handy and Schumaker, the notion of a suspended adolescence, and the search for 'the real thing' in love, has produced an even more protracted youth bulge. Thus, one key stimulus for the surge of interest among social psychologists researching love is the globalisation of a new period, or 'stage', of emotional development.

Love as meaning

Against this backdrop of increased need and motivation to understand love, the phenomenon itself could not be more difficult and daunting to study. Within our own personal lives, for example, is it possible to love friends? Within our own romantic lives, most of us at some time have difficulty deciding whether relationship X was a case of true love, or whether relationship Y was more like 'the real thing'. The point is that there is a great deal of individual diversity of everyday views about what love is, and even whether it exists at all. On all fronts, it seems, love has personal, idiosyncratic meanings.

Such inherent idiosyncrasy and subjectivity naturally create major problems for social psychological analysis, which by definition relies on describing and explaining, and generalising about, *whole sets* of people (see chapter 1). One basic but nonetheless promising approach to this apparent difficulty has been to grab the bull by the horns — to investigate empirically whether there is indeed as much disagreement between individuals' definitions of love as common sense suggests (Berscheid & Meyers 1996). In essence, this approach has been alert to the personal meanings of love by starting from scratch and asking individual participants to describe freely what they feel (and think) are the key types of love. In this way, the approach is committed to measuring, in a non-constraining manner, how much common ground actually exists within sets of people.

Within what relationships is love mainly reported?

In an original (and unfortunately still unique) study of this kind, 84 participants were asked to list all the different kinds of love that sprang to mind (Fehr & Russell 1991). This basic procedure (Study 1: Free Listing of Subtypes of Love), conducted with a sample of emerging adults, elicited more than two hundred distinct love-related responses. Of these, 123 were purely idiosyncratic (mentioned by only one participant), and thus partly supportive of the intuition that love has some highly idiosyncratic edges. There remained, however, 94 themes, almost half the total, that were mentioned by more than one participant. Many of these — including, for instance, love of sports, art, money, work, country and humanity — did not relate to close interpersonal relationships. But 20 themes, mentioned by 10 per cent or more of the sample, did concern close relationships. And among these themes there was a clear consensual pattern.

According to this sample (for your own assessment, see activity 1), love could be found (1) among blood (or adoptive) relatives in the same family (e.g. parental, sibling and kinship love); (2) among close friends (e.g. friendship, brotherhood and platonic love); and (3) among partners 'in love' (e.g. romantic, true, blind and passionate love). This three-class taxonomy of love relationships has since been widely applied elsewhere in the love literature (Canary, Cupach & Messman 1995). Thus, and contrary to initial 'common sense', it does seem possible that there is at least some substantive consensus, some shared meaning, on the kinds of relationship in which love is commonly found (Fehr 1999). These data give us a vital starting point for our own analysis of love. This is crucial because 'Science without taxonomy is blind' (Gould 1994, p. 38).

A prototypes approach

Fehr and Russell's methodology is an example of a **prototypes approach** for defining love (1991). This approach is really a theory about how people subjectively organise and, especially, categorise much of their everyday working knowledge about the world (Augoustinos & Walker 1995). The prototypes approach has a wide parentage in philosophy, the humanities and the social sciences generally (Anderson 1997). This lineage includes, for instance, cognitive psychology (Rosch 1978). Excellent discussions of alternative aspects of this approach to love research can be found in Fehr (1993) and Berscheid & Meyers (1996).

Prototype theories build on the fact that people employ schemata to categorise the world about them (see chapter 7). In chapter 8, for example, we learned that people are drawn to one another, and categorise others as attractive or not, partly on the basis of those others' similarity to a schematic, prototypical human face. Although person perceivers cannot necessarily articulate exactly what constitutes such prototypes, they can and do use them every day, and they can say how close any human face is to the ideal standard they have in mind. It is this property of prototypes, the ability to say whether, and how clearly, an exemplar belongs in a category, that students of love have picked up on, for example to investigate in what relationships love is prototypically found. They have also researched the degree of consensus on what kinds of feeling 'count' as love, and which do not.

Prototypes, and the respect for diversity that they embody, are all around us. Even the meaning of everyday concepts and objects can be fuzzy and controversial; idiosyncrasy creeps in. At the same time, this controversy does not stop us from living with, communicating about and often enjoying them every day. By tacit consensus, for instance, we 'know' and 'count' on the fact that an apple is a more typical fruit than a tomato, and so more suitable to serve with custard. The same goes for everyday meanings of 'love'. Some of this category's exemplars are, not unlike tomatoes in some families, sometimes hotly debated. But we still hear about and relate to the category daily in songs, movies, conversations, reminiscences and so on.

According to prototypes theory, therefore, it is possible to gauge what people intuitively know and feel is a close exemplar of the category LOVE. The principle of category articulation may be applied to the types of relationship that characterise love, as in Fehr and Russell's Study 1 (introduced above); this is a role schema. Or it may be applied equally well to behavioural or emotional properties of what love is, an event schema (Fehr 1993). This application helps move us from beyond where love takes place to what love is (and is not). A lingering doubt among many cynics, for example, is that love is not really any different, either qualitatively or quantitatively, from more superficial attractions such as liking, admiration and lust (see figure 8.1). Prototypes can give us evidence on whether love is inherently, and thus prototypically, *distinct* from these emotions.

In one of their studies (Study 4: Fuzzy Borders), Fehr and Russell (1991) asked their participants to give their 'opinion about what are genuine cases of love and what are not' (p. 430). Table 9.1 gives a summary of the items, derived from Study 1, that were judged by a majority of participants ($n = 118$) to be members versus not members of the prototypical category LOVE. These data were very consistent with subsequent reaction time measures, in that the exemplars in table 9.1 that were generally judged to be 'outside' the category also took longer to be judged that way than their 'inside' counterparts did to be judged on the inside (Study 3: Reaction Time to Verify Category Membership). The logic here is that shorter reaction times signal that the thinker actually has the schema in working memory at the time (for a discussion of the logic behind reaction times being used to indicate schemata, see chapter 7). Shorter reaction times alongside judgements of 'in' indicate that the latter are indeed valid descriptions about what is in the respondent's mind at the time.

Table 9.1 Inclusion within and exclusion from the category LOVE

MAJORITY JUDGED 'OUT'	(%)	MAJORITY JUDGED 'IN'	(%)

'Attraction'	(63)	Familial love:
		  'A mother's love'
		  'A sibling's love'
			
			(94)
			(89)

'Liking'	(53)	'Friendship'	(86)

'Admiration'	(75)	Love for a partner:
		  'Passion'
		  'Romantic love'
			
			(64)
			(98)

'Lust'	(87)		

Source: Extracted and adapted from Fehr & Russell (1991, p. 430).

Love versus *attraction*

The first feature of table 9.1 to note is that a majority of the participants included familial love, close friendship love and romantic love (including passion) inside (i.e. as exemplars of) the category LOVE. This indicates that these types of love were more often than not relatively close to the prototype for love. The same sample of participants also tended to exclude attraction (see chapter 8) from the category LOVE. This finding suggests that in this sample the meaning of loving is qualitatively distinct, in most people's minds, from feelings of liking, admiration and lust. But what is the direct evidence for this, within and beyond this particular study?

Love versus *liking*

From table 9.1, liking is the most 'borderline' theme, in the sense that it is voted out of the category LOVE by a slim majority (53 per cent) of participants. Other evidence bearing on the same conclusions comes out of psychometric research. This type of research has developed measures of the exemplars of love and not-love discussed above. The underlying logic in the psychometric approach, however, is to assess a person's scores on these measures empirically. If the scores tend to remain independent of each other statistically, rather than converging or correlating with each another empirically, then they probably reflect distinct social psychological constructs. The best known of this psychometric research has found that liking and loving, as indicated in table 9.1, do indeed fall on opposite sides of the prototype fence (Rubin 1970, 1973). In particular, Rubin's research concentrated on attempting to differentiate romantic love from liking for friends (rather than deep and loving friendships).

Rubin began his empirical study by asking 198 undergraduates to respond to each of 80 items as if they were describing their feelings for a loved partner (of the opposite sex), on the one hand, versus a platonic friend (again, for controlled comparison purposes, of the opposite sex) on the other. Rubin then used factor analysis to select only those items that were closely correlated with one another. Consistent with the idea that liking and loving are psychologically distinct from each other, two major factors emerged — one for liking and the other for loving. Illustrative items from each of these major dimensions of meaning are given in table 9.2.

Table 9.2   A sample of Rubin's exemplars of liking and loving

LIKING	LOVING
'I have great confidence in this person's good judgement.'	'If I could never be with this person, I would feel miserable.'
'This person is one of the most likeable people I know.'	'I feel very possessive towards this person.'
'I think that this person is unusually well adjusted.'	'I would forgive this person for practically anything.'

Source: Extracted from Rubin (1970, 1973).

In Western settings, at least, the two scales represented in table 9.2 have been found to be highly consistent internally (the items typically correlate more tightly with each other than with items from the 'other' factor). As well, the scores have proved predictive of behavioural events outside of the testing items themselves — for example gazing at each other, which is predicted by scores on the loving scale but not by scores on its liking counterpart (Rubin 1970, 1973). Rubin's findings have also converged more recently with other research on prototypes. In Germany, for instance, students were asked to indicate how they could tell they liked or were in love with somebody (Lamm & Wiesmann 1997). For these students, the most prominent feature of liking somebody was wishing to interact socially with them. The most distinctive feature of being 'in love' with somebody, on the other hand, was becoming sexually aroused in their physical presence (note from table 9.1 that *passion* is not the same thing as *lust*, which indicates that the arousal reported by the sample in Germany was more than simple lust). An alternative illustration of the differences between liking and loving is given in critical narrative 9.1 (for debate on the possibility that love at first sight may be confined largely to emerging adulthood, see Knox, Schacht & Zusman 1999; Juerg 1997; Soble 1990).

CRITICAL NARRATIVE 9.1

Liking versus loving in emerging adulthood

Alex sat right behind Kelly in biology. For Alex, it was love at first sight. From the very first day he saw her, Alex could think of little else. Thoughts of Kelly occupied him constantly. Alex was therefore crushed when Kelly found a partner. Before that time, he had never really got to know her. The 'interactions' between them had all taken place in Alex's mind. Finally, Alex started having conversations with Kelly, and discovered that despite still being madly in love with her, he did not *like* her a whole lot.

Source: Extracted and adapted from Sternberg (1987, p. 331; emphasis added).

Love versus *admiration*

As we learned in chapter 8, admiration has tended to be the poor cousin in attraction research (Forgas 1986). One can perhaps imagine followers loving a leader, which might include having feelings of admiration for that figurehead, although such emotions have apparently seldom been studied. In table 9.1, however, a clear majority of participants (three-quarters) voted admiration 'out' of the meaning of love. At least one classical theorist has also placed admiration 'outside' of love by describing it as, at best, merely a stepping-stone towards passionate love, typified by the relatively superficial 'attraction' of physical appearance and personal charm (Stendhal 1926; for a more detailed overview, see Sternberg & Barnes 1988; chapter 11). Elsewhere, and more recently, admiration has been linked more closely with age-discrepant casual friendships rather than age-congruent close friendships (Holladay & Kerns 1999). Such findings suggest that admiration often develops in a context of power distance. To the extent that love itself is relatively egalitarian (at least among consenting adults), this thesis would also situate admiration outside of the prototype boundary.

Other evidence differentiating admiration from love derives indirectly from Rubin's psychometric approach described above. It has been argued, for instance, that Rubin's (1970, 1973) scales partially tap into 'respect and admiration' (Cramer 1998, p. 17). Cramer describes how he gave Rubin's scales to more than two hundred British adolescents and found a close link between the following items: 'I think this person is one of those people who quickly wins respect'; 'I think this person is unusually well-adjusted'; and 'I would highly recommend this person for a responsible job'. One interpretation of this finding is that Rubin's liking scale measures both liking and admiration. If this reading is correct, and since we have already established that Rubin's not-love items tap into something qualitatively different from love, then the same psychometric logic would apply. In other words, we could conclude that admiration and loving are qualitatively distinct from each other.

Love versus *lust*

In table 9.1, the most polarised exemplars of love and not-love were, respectively, romantic love and lust. These had the highest percentage of participants, including romantic love (98 per cent) and excluding lust (87 per cent) from the category LOVE. Other research using prototypes has extended this differentiation to love generally rather than romantic love specifically. In one study, for instance, students were asked to list people they 'loved' and people to whom they were 'sexually attracted' (Berscheid & Meyers 1996). In this sample, only 2 per cent of people appeared in both lists, indicating very little overlap between (i) love as a general category and (ii) sex.

A neuropsychological approach

Physiological studies have focused on the hormones associated with sexual arousal (e.g. Regan 1999) versus with social attachment (between mother and child; e.g. Insel 2000). Hormonal activity is now readily detected through technology that enables analysis of blood samples. The studies of attachment have been confined, presumably for ethical reasons, to higher mammals with hormonal subsystems similar to our own (Carter 1998). These studies, together with those on sexual arousal, have implicated two anatomically distinct subsystems in sexual desire and social attachment. First, androgens, such as testosterone in the body's adrenal glands, have been linked to sexual desire. Second, neuropeptides, such as oxytocin and vasopressin in the hypothalamus in the brain, have been implicated in pair-bond formation — being released, for example, by human mothers during breastfeeding (Fletcher 2002).

Although these findings are intriguing, we should remain wary about jumping to the conclusion that love and sex are mutually exclusive. Parent–child bonding is not necessarily the same kind of love as passionate and romantic love, which patently do not exclude sexual attraction. For example, when Berscheid and Meyer's participants listed people with whom they were 'in love' (as compared with people they simply 'loved'), the overlap with the 'sexually attractive' list was a whopping 85 per cent! In a further study that again focused on love versus lust, participants listed the modal feature of romantic love (equivalent to being 'in love') as sexual desire more often than, for example, communication, intimacy or commitment (Regan, Kocan & Whitlock 1998; see also Regan 1998). In a study conducted in Sri Lankan villages, sexual desire was seen as a core, necessary component of romantic love within arranged marriages (de Munck 1998a).

To sum up, while (1) lust has little to do with LOVE as a general prototype category, (2) sexual desire is probably a necessary but in itself insufficient condition for romantic love. According to the data presented in table 9.1, it should be possible to find a couple 'in love' whose androgen levels are as high as a person watching a pornographic movie or masturbating, because both are heavily sexual in nature (Regan, Kocan & Whitlock 1998). The critical *difference* between these two extreme states, however, and what in neuropsychological terms renders one more like passionate love and the other closer to lust, is the presence or absence of neuropeptides like vasopressin and oxytocin. These are reportedly less likely to be produced, for instance, during masturbation than during and after sexual intercourse with a romantic partner (Fletcher 2002; for a link between *androgens* and masturbation, see Bancroft et al. 1984).

Our analysis has so far concentrated on differentiating love from not-love. Yet many of the everyday debates about love focus not just on whether love is different from liking, admiring and lusting, but also on how many 'varieties' of love there are. We have already seen that love takes place across different relationships, and certainly these relationships allow for the cultivation and expression of different forms of love. But what, precisely, is the content of these love processes? Moreover, how does love vary within family, friendship and romantic relationships? Clearly, we love different individual family members, close friends and lovers in different ways, depending on psychosocial issues such as how close we are and feel in 'blood' terms; our respective genders; and how or whether the other person loves us (for more on this topic, see Fletcher & Simpson 2001a, 2001b). Thus, we soon need to go beyond mere taxonomy, towards a more dynamic, robust and comprehensive *model* of love that covers all forms of loving relationship.

Sternberg's triangular theory of love

For many social psychologists working in love research, the most incisive analysis of love dynamics belongs to Sternberg, who has proposed a 'triangular theory of love' (1986, p. 119). In some ways, the symbol of a triangle is unfortunate, insofar as it represents mathematical precision, which is patently inappropriate when studying the inherently 'hot' state of mind (and heart) that love often exemplifies. In a sense, the idea of reducing love to geometry (and pairs of overlapping triangles) is clearly absurd. Yet, as we saw in chapter 8, it is the fusion of hot with deliberately cold systems (triangular systems perhaps) that often allows us to better understand, if not completely control, affective processes. It is this potential to enhance our capacity to make at least some sense out of the plethora of emotions across love that might be the model's most useful contribution.

Sternberg's (1986) model was originally largely deductive (based on experienced insight) rather than inductive (derived directly from pre-existing data). We can therefore pass directly to describing the model itself, which is depicted in figure 9.1. Essentially, figure 9.1's visual representation proposes that love resides, psychologically, in three subjective and self-explanatory dimensions. These are pictured in the model as the vertices of a triangle (for an alternative and to some extent complementary three-dimensional structure, see Fletcher et al. 1999). From figure 9.1, which gives illustrative examples of each, these dimensions are Commitment, Intimacy and Passion. In the terminology of chapter 8, these three vertices can be thought of as progressively 'warmer' points of love (Sternberg 1986), culminating in the churning heat of passion (Barnes & Sternberg 1997).

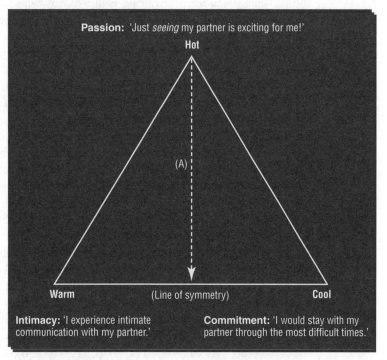

Figure 9.1   Sternberg's triangular theory of love

Source: Extracted and adapted from Sternberg (1986, p. 119).

When all three of these elements are present in a balanced combination, represented by the equilateral triangle in figure 9.1, Sternberg says the person is emotionally positioned to be able to experience the ultimate or 'consummate' love. Whether or not this relationship realises its full potential, and so turns out to be optimally satisfactory, depends on whether the equilateral pattern is reciprocated (congruence) or left unrequited by the other (Baumeister & Dhavale 2001). As depicted in critical narrative 9.2, unrequited romantic love is a common feature of emerging adulthood although, contrary to the narrative itself, this is especially so for males (Hill, Blakemore & Drumm 1997; for one possible explanation, see the 'codes of mateship' section below).

CRITICAL
NARRATIVE
9.2

The pain of unrequited love

[Young adults] Mike and Louise had been going out with each other for about three months. Both of them seemed happy in the relationship, but their friends saw trouble. Louise just seemed a whole lot more involved than Mike. One night, Louise confessed her love and let on to her plans for their future together. Mike was dumbfounded. He had not made any plans and did not want them. Mike told Louise that he liked her but did not love her and did not think he ever could. Mike broke off the relationship the next day.

Source: Sternberg (1987, p. 331).

The real power of Sternberg's model for us at this stage is its conceptual clarity and parsimony, and the relative ease with which it helps to make sense of a wide range of loving human relationships. For example, love relationships within the family might tend more, on the average, towards commitment (and perhaps intimacy) than passion. A good example of this kind of love is 'filial piety', a concept originating from Eastern cultures, in which sons owe their first loyalty to their close family elders (for an example in contemporary New Zealand, see Liu et al. 2000). Meanwhile, the love we feel in close and special friendships might be characterised more modally by intimacy (and perhaps commitment). In contrast, the feelings we have for a lover can be relatively high on passion, while for a long-term marriage partner they are often typified by high levels of intimacy plus commitment (Sternberg 1986, p. 133). The latter is a combination known as 'companionate' love (Berscheid & Walster 1978).

As shown in figure 9.1, the different forms of love are represented in geometric terms using the line of symmetry (A). When, for example, passion is relatively high, the figure will change shape to an elongated isosceles triangle (Sternberg 1986, p. 128). When passion is relatively low, the line of symmetry (A) will be shorter in comparison with the remaining two lines of symmetry. Generally, also, the greater the surface area of the triangle (and the more balanced the lengths of the sides), the greater the love in the relationship itself (p. 128). In his introduction to the theory, Sternberg discusses how different vertices of a triangle become salient at different times within a relationship. In arranged marriages, for example, passion may logically develop after, say, commitment, whereas in chosen marriages the order may be reversed (1986, p. 122; see also Gupta & Singh 1982, discussed on page 350). This adds a third, developmental dimension to the triangular model, which for many researchers considerably enriches its credibility.

Most helpful of all, perhaps, the triangular model parsimoniously accommodates diversity in the qualities of love relationships experienced by any one person, as well as the infinite variety of combinations of perspectives that different dyads, in loving relationships, as well as the same dyads over time, can experience. Thus, it seems, the model provides us with a schema flexible enough to accommodate a range of seemingly disparate types of love relationship. (for a recap on schemata, see chapter 7).

Reconciling the literature

A good example of the intellectual carrying capacity of the model is its ability to reconcile Rubin's 'liking versus loving' approach, already described, with a far more complex taxonomy of love developed by Lee (1977, 1988). For the interested reader, examples between these two extreme approaches can be found in Fehr and Russell (1991, p. 427). Lee's theory is 'complex', because it identifies no fewer than six romantic love styles and so is comparatively differentiated (Sternberg 1987, p. 343). These styles, summarised in table 9.3, are well grounded across a diverse range of research methods, including content analysis of classical (e.g. Greek) literature as well as factor analysis (see chapter 1). In short, therefore, they cannot be ignored.

Table 9.3 Lee's six love styles

STYLE	ILLUSTRATIVE STATEMENT
Pragma	'I try to plan my life carefully before choosing a partner.'
Agape	'I would rather suffer than let my partner suffer.'
Storge	'The best kind of love grows out of a long friendship.'
Eros	'Our lovemaking is very intense and satisfying.'
Mania	'I cannot relax if I suspect my partner is with someone else.'
Ludus	'I enjoy playing the game of love with many different partners.'

Source: Extracted and adapted from Lee (1988).

As outlined in table 9.3, Pragma love (pragmatic love) perhaps best fits the tenets of social exchange theory (e.g. Jones & Vaughan 1991). Agape is selfless love. Storge love is based on deep affection, and as such is consistent with friendship love, depicted in table 9.1. Eros entails erotic love towards a beloved bodily ideal. Mania is passionate, jealous and excessive love, such as might lead to what the French call a *crime passionnel*, or 'crime of passion' (Ancel 1958), typically a murder driven by irrational, uncontrollable jealousy (Mullen 1993). Finally, Ludus (Latin for 'game'), more playful and disengaged, may be manifested by someone who makes a game of keeping multiple lovers without their finding out about each other.

How can the seemingly incompatible perspectives of Rubin, on the one hand, and Lee, on the other, be reconciled?

Assimilating the liking literature

According to a triangular view of love, Rubin had sampled his 'liking' items from the 'non-passionate' vertices of the love triangle or, more probably perhaps, from a relatively shallow form of liking that is closer to acquaintance (see chapter 8) than loving friendship (see table 9.1). Sternberg (1986) differentiates true friendship *love* as follows:

> A test that can distinguish mere liking from love that goes beyond liking is the **absence test**. If a typical friend whom one likes goes away, even for an extended period of time, one may miss the friend, but one does not tend to dwell on the loss. One can pick up the friendship some years later, often in a different form, without even having thought much about the friendship during the intervening years. When a close friendship goes beyond liking however, one's reaction to the absence test is quite different. One actively misses the other person and tends to dwell on or be preoccupied with that person's absence . . . When the absence of the other arouses strong feelings of intimacy, passion, or commitment, it is best to classify the relationship as going beyond liking. (Sternberg 1986, pp. 123–4; emphasis added)

Looking back at table 9.2, Rubin's 'liking' items do not go this deep, and so are probably outside of the normative boundaries of love. In the same way, looking back at figure 9.1, commitment need not be all 'cool'; it may reveal a warmer, loving side. Absence would make the committed heart grow *warmer* as well as fonder (Sternberg 1987, p. 126). Finally, as a point of interest, absence testing could be usefully applied to assess the construct validity of love at first sight. In Fehr and Russell's (1991) study, for instance, love at first sight was excluded from the category of LOVE by 60 per cent of the (student) participants — a proportion that throws into question its place in love schemata even among emerging adults.

Assimilating Lee's love styles

A possible alignment of all six styles with Sternberg's triangular schema is depicted in figure 9.2. The alignment agrees with Sternberg's (1987) view that Ludus, or game-playing love (see table 9.3), is not really a class of love at all (p. 343). Pragma is close in some respects to Sternberg's Commitment — love expressed through loyalty for example. Agape is close to the combination of intimacy and commitment known as companionate love (Sternberg 1986, p. 123; see also Sternberg 1987, p. 343). Storge is close to intimacy. Eros clearly resembles passion. A combination of passion and intimacy *without* commitment that Sternberg (1986, 1987) terms 'romantic love' is not covered by Lee's taxonomy. Given the lack of commitment in this category, it is difficult to envisage it as anything other than a superficial, even not-love connection, as in a teenage 'summer romance' or a 'romantic interlude'. In Fehr and Russell's 1991 prototype studies, 'puppy love' was categorised as 'not-love' by a clear majority of the participants (see Study 4: Fuzzy Borders, p. 430). Lastly, Mania is akin to the combination of passion and commitment that Sternberg terms 'fatuous' love (1986, p. 123). Overall, therefore, figure 9.2 and Sternberg's triangular model of love readily assimilate not only Rubin's research but much of Lee's taxonomic system, too (see chapter 7 for a precise definition of assimilation).

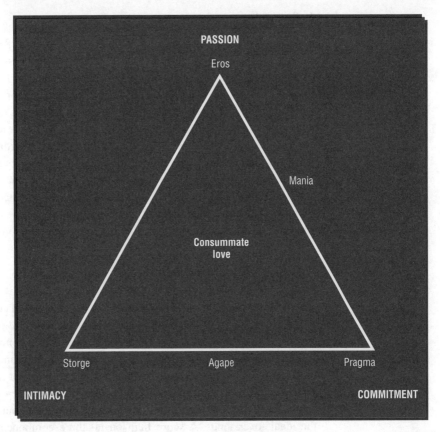

PASSION
Eros

Mania

Consummate
love

Storge   Agape   Pragma

INTIMACY   COMMITMENT

Figure 9.2   Assimilating Lee's love styles   *Source:* Extracted from Sternberg (1986, 1987).

Exercising caution: the limits to comprehensive systems

A danger with all-encompassing systems is the **'Barnum effect'** (Dickson & Kelly 1985). P. T. Barnum was an entrepreneurial nineteenth-century circus impresario, whose famous pronouncements included the catchphrases 'A little something for everybody!' and the cynical 'There's a sucker born every minute'. Barnum effects have achieved notoriety in personality testing, where it has been found that people often gullibly accept personality tests simply because they are sufficiently general to capture a little of everybody's personal experience. In the triangular model of love, the Barnum effect signals a danger that the triangular structure explains everybody (we all recognise a little piece of ourselves in figure 9.2) and nobody, since nothing is revealed of love's idiosyncratic properties. Analogous warnings have been sounded elsewhere in the psychological literature about at least one other influential triangular model, A. H. Maslow's hierarchy of human needs (1943; for his own views on love, see Maslow 1955). While here is not the place to comment in detail on this particular model, Barnum effects should prompt us to look for more independent evidence that the triangular model adequately reflects the diversity of human love experiences.

Such evidence comes in two major forms.

1. Reliability

Both Sternberg himself (1988) and others (e.g. Lund 1985; Hatfield & Rapson 1987) have devised psychometric tests, or scales, for measuring individual differences in each of the three vertices across family, friendship and romantic relationships. These scales, in turn, have been subjected to factor analysis to determine whether individual responses empirically cluster according to the three elementary dimensions that the model proposes. By and large, the results of these analyses have been impressively reliable, with a three-factor structure emerging across a range of contemporary cultural settings (e.g. Aron & Westbay 1996; Gao 2001; Hernandez 1999; Yela 1996). Support has also been garnered for the finer gradations discussed by both Sternberg and Lee, as depicted in figure 9.2 (e.g. Hendrick, Hendrick & Dicke 1998). Thus, there is ample evidence that the key elements in the model, including their various combinations, have psychological coherence.

2. Validity

The model's validity has been assessed by checking whether the measures based on the triangle successfully differentiate between love in the family, love in close friendships and romantic love. There has been consistent empirical support for the idea that various configurations of commitment, intimacy and passion identify and mark off these core types of love relationship. Siblings, for instance, tend to score relatively high on commitment but low on both intimacy and passion. Special friends tend to score high on intimacy and commitment but low on passion. And the ideal lover tends to score high on all three components, thereby reflecting Sternberg's construct of consummate love (Sternberg 1997).

Perhaps the ultimate acid test of validity is predictability concerning satisfaction with a relationship, and indeed with life itself. On the first of these criteria, one study of romantic relationships during emerging adulthood found that scores on each of the three components, commitment, intimacy and passion, contributed significantly and uniquely towards overall levels of satisfaction with a relationship (Lemieux & Hale 1999). Also, and as expected in the model (p. 329), relationship satisfaction has been predicted by the degree of overlap (or congruence) between triangles of the respective romantic partners, reduced discrepancies being associated with reductions in satisfaction (Sternberg 1986). From figure 9.2, for example, a relationship in which a partner's feelings were passionate (e.g. Mania) while self wanted a cooler, steadier commitment (e.g. Pragma or Agape) would be less satisfying (and sustainable) than a relationship in which each partner's expectations were more congruent with the other's (p. 131).

Lemieux and Hale's recent (1999) study, conducted in the United States, also found that satisfaction was best predicted by whether the partner's feelings for the respondent in the study matched the respondent's own preconceived ideal pattern (see also Sternberg & Barnes 1985). Greatest satisfaction occurred when the partner matched the ideal, and similar findings have been reported, for example, from Canada (Murray, Holmes & Griffin 1996) and New Zealand (Fletcher et al. 1999; Fletcher, Simpson & Thomas 2000; see also Fletcher & Simpson 2001a, 2000b).

The Michelangelo effect

Congruence like this clearly has the potential to contribute towards life satisfaction. An example of how this can occur has been vividly termed the **'Michelangelo effect'** (Drigotas et al. 1999). According to Drigotas et al., Michelangelo described the creativity of sculpting as releasing a hidden, idealised figure from a block of stone in which it slumbered. By this beautiful analogy, when a close partner's person, role and event schemata around the relationship match one's own ideal schema for self (see chapter 7), a positive Pygmalion effect will occur, according to which your partner's schema about your self, which coincides with your own ideal, will progressively 'sculpt' your self towards its own ideal. For example, if you think that your lover sees you as a passionate, intimate and committed person, and this happens to be exactly how you would like to be, then you will be incrementally 'sculpted' towards that ideal by your partner's expectations of you. And when this happens simultaneously on both sides of the partnership — that is, both partners idealise the other exactly as the other would want to be — then both partners will simultaneously be sculpted ever closer towards self-actualisation, 'couple wellbeing' and life satisfaction (Drigotas et al. 1999, p. 294).

Such interactive dynamics of congruence provide a refreshing example of doubly positive (rather than negative) Pygmalion effects (for examples of the latter, refer back to chapters 5 and 7). Drigotas et al.'s findings also give a whole new meaning to, or rejuvenate, the romantic cliché 'I'm a better person when I'm with you' (Drigotas et al. 1999, p. 295). According to the Michelangelo effect, that is, romantic and long-term partners whose schemata match each other's ideal self will tend to 'bring out', or socially facilitate, the best in each other.

To sum up so far, the triangular model provides a solid conceptual basis for the rest of this chapter. It addresses the fundamental criteria, outlined at the beginning of this chapter, for a model of love. It manages to reconcile the bewildering diversity of personal love experiences that most of us encounter. And it reconciles a burgeoning and otherwise bewildering literature on love relationships. In three key ways, therefore, the model starts to help us, not murder, but make sense out of love.

FAMILIAL LOVE

A social-developmental lens

The behaviours, cognitions and affect we experience as adults are often influenced by events in our childhood, and psychology has a relatively long-standing tradition of proposing this, both for romantic love (Sanford 1913) and for other loving relationships (Freud 1926). The overall rationale for believing that our past influences our present is eloquently expressed by D. O. Hebb:

> It is of course a truism that learning is often influenced by earlier learning. Innumerable experiments have shown such transfer of training. Learning A may be speeded up, hindered, or qualitatively changed by having learned B before. The question for debate is how *great* the effect may be . . . (1949, p. 109; emphasis added)

The predominant view today about how and by how much our early relationships influence our later ones is contained in **attachment theory** (Bowlby 1958, 2000) and a related research paradigm, the *strange situation* (Ainsworth 1967, 1995).

Early attachment styles

According to Bowlby, the first few years of life are a particularly important period for forming prototype attachments to caregivers. This is because they give us a firm foundation, a trusting socio-emotional 'home base', for building loving relations with others later in life. Once a baby has a secure attachment to its caregiver(s), it is, according to Bowlby, psychologically predisposed and ready to be attracted towards others; to act on that attraction; and to invite a reciprocal attraction and interaction from those others (see chapter 8; for a wider discussion, see Erikson 1968). This aptitude will later extend beyond the family context to friends and lovers and, finally, will come full circle when we ourselves become caregivers. The essential point for us here, however, is that our early years, and infancy in particular, in theory exert a significant influence on the types of loving relationships we form (or fail to form) in later life. In this way, the theoretical literature begins to bear on an issue that most of us have at some point pondered. Are my relationships today influenced by my early years?

According to Bowlby, the answer to this question is yes. Moreover, the form this influence takes will depend on how our early attachments were styled, whether Avoidant, Secure or Anxious (Bowlby 1982). To understand precisely what these styles signify, we need to review some details of the **strange situation** research paradigm (Ainsworth 1967).

The strange situation

Ainsworth's seminal study used an observational methodology in which a 'situation' is 'strangely' manipulated to allow children to show off their underlying attachment styles. Specifically, a 12- to 18-month-old infant first plays (1) in a primary caregiver's presence, after which (2) a stranger enters the room and interacts with the infant, after which (3) the caregiver leaves the child alone with the stranger. Then (4), the stranger departs leaving the child totally alone, after which (5) the caregiver returns. During each of these phases, and the changes between phases, the child is observed and his or her emotional reactions charted.

Individual infants typically display three characteristic 'styles'. Through phases (1) to (5), *avoidant* infants' social affect remains visibly comparatively 'flat'. Compared with *secure* infants, for example, they are less likely to excitedly explore at (1), interact at (2) or cry at (3). In the latter event, they fail the infantile equivalent of an absence test (see p. 332). When the caregiver returns, the secure infant is more likely than the avoidant infant to greet them happily. *Anxious* attachment infants, by contrast, are consistently fearful, even when the caregiver is present; are more likely to be highly distressed when the caregiver leaves; and are not necessarily calmed when the caregiver returns. An infant who displays anxious attachment may also react angrily and even aggressively at (5). By contrast, avoidant infants are more likely to accept contact if the caregiver offers it, but will not proactively seek it during phase (5).

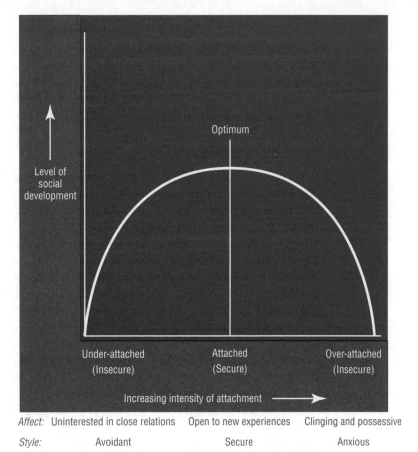

Level of social development

Optimum

| Under-attached | Attached | Over-attached |
| (Insecure) | (Secure) | (Insecure) |

Increasing intensity of attachment ⟶

Affect: Uninterested in close relations   Open to new experiences   Clinging and possessive

Style: Avoidant   Secure   Anxious

Figure 9.3   A performance-arousal curve for attachment behaviour

Source: Extracted and adapted from Ainsworth (1995) and Bowlby (2000).

A helpful representation of these patterns is offered in figure 9.3, which hinges on the concept of arousal and builds on the generalised model of interpersonal relationships presented in figure 8.3. From figure 9.3, we can think of avoidant children as being under-aroused in their relationships, while a secure child experiences a level of affect that is intermediate between the avoidant and the anxious child. At very high levels of affect, that is, attachment can become over-attachment and in that sense, like under-arousal and avoidance, less than optimal as a model or precursor of future love relationships. 'Performance', in this familial context, relates to the level of exploratory social behaviour, and this seems to be optimised when the level of affect is medium, rather than extreme, in either direction.

The social environment

Caregiving that is neither too cold nor too hot (i.e. that is somewhere between neglectful and authoritarian) tends to optimise both social and cognitive develop-ment (respectively, Scharfe 2001 and Baumrind 1989). These *parental* styles (see chapter 7) are now starting to be linked directly to the facilitation of specific attachment styles in infants (in unpublished doctoral theses; for a rare, exploratory journal article, see Suemer & Guengoer 1999). In addition, of course, just as parental/caregiver style influences attachment style in the infant, influence also flows in the other direction. For example, if the child has a temperament that is 'difficult', there may be an increased likelihood of the attachment becoming relatively insecure, partly because the behaviour of the child influences the behaviour of the caregiver, as well as vice versa (Vaughn & Bost 1999).

Cross-cultural reliability

Ainsworth's early studies of infant attachment began in Uganda, East Africa, and have since been replicated methodologically across a range of other socio-cultural settings, from low to high power distance and from relatively collectivistic to relatively individualistic societies. These different socio-cultural settings include, for instance, Southern Africa (Tomlinson 2000), North and Central America (Harwood, Miller & Irizarry 1995), African-American communities in the US (Jackson 1993), the Middle East (Sagi 1990), East Asia (Durrett, Otaki & Richards 1985) and Western Europe (Grossmann et al. 1981). This diverse literature could be summarised by saying that while cultural values (e.g. valued socialisation goals), family context (e.g. nuclear versus extended) and economic realities (e.g. working hours) do influence the precise way that caregiving is expressed, the three-way taxonomy outlined by Ainsworth and Bowlby is a relatively robust and replicable classification system for describing the basis on which attachments are often formed.

To what extent, then, do early attachment styles influence later behaviour?

Adjustment during later childhood

Many researchers believe that early attachment styles and experiences do have an influence on adjustment in later childhood (Masten & Coatsworth 1998). Attachment styles, according to this view, are embryonic developing role and event schemata (Scharfe & Bartholomew 1995). Later in life, according to Bowlby, individuals will activate stylistic internalised scripts for relationship formation. Ainsworth herself, for example, reports that insecurely attached infants are statistically more likely to encounter a variety of behavioural problems in school than their more securely attached counterparts (1989). These problems include lower self-esteem, attention seeking and aggression (see chapter 10). Thus, the Ainsworth–Bowlby schema for characterising attachment styles, which is essentially a role-and-event schema combined (see chapter 7), does appear to have some predictive capacity with respect to social adjustment behaviour in the near to mid term of childhood development, and perhaps even friendship formation.

The predictive nature of attachment styles

Does attachment style predict preferred adult style regarding love? This is a harder question to address. We need to begin with a detailed review of a now classic study in social psychology (Hazan & Shaver 1987). The central aim of Hazan and Shaver's study was to integrate the attachment styles schema with the study of romantic love (p. 512). First, they reasoned that if there was a connection, and the attachment style was relatively enduring, then there should also be some correspondence between the proportions of adult participants who displayed each style and the proportions who displayed each style in studies where the participants had been infants (23 per cent avoidant, 62 per cent secure, 15 per cent anxious, p. 513). Second, they expected avoidant adults to be relatively avoidant in love relationships, secure adults to be experienced in love, and over-attached (anxious) adults to tend towards preoccupying struggles to merge with their lover, a process termed **limerence** by Tennov (1979). Third, compared with secure types, adult avoidants should be relatively dubious about the existence of romantic love, while anxious over-attachers should show a tendency to fall in love more readily but less satisfactorily in terms of finding 'true' love. Finally, and crucially for the long-term predictive capacity of attachment theory, avoidant participants should recall their attachment figures as being relatively cold, secure participants should remember dependability and responsive caring, and anxious respondents should recall a more volatile mix of 'positive and negative experiences' with their caregivers (1987, p. 513).

In the primary study in Hazan and Shaver's paper, a newspaper questionnaire focused on the 'love of your life' (p. 514). It also asked questions about attachment style ('Love partners want me to be more intimate than I feel comfortable being'; 'I find it relatively easy to get close to others'; and 'I want to merge completely with another person, and this desire sometimes scares people away' (Study 1, p. 515; for a recent discussion on the psychometric validity of this approach, see Scharfe & Bartholomew 1998). The survey forms also asked the participants to summarise the relationship with their primary caregivers (e.g. 'disinterested', 'caring' or 'intrusive', p. 516), and asked these participants for their personal beliefs about the typical course of romantic love (e.g. 'It's rare to find someone you can really fall in love with', p. 516).

By and large, and surprisingly perhaps, the data obtained in this study were consistent with each of the above hypotheses. In Study 1, for instance, the response distribution for attachment style was similar to previous infant studies (25 per cent, 56 per cent, 19 per cent, respectively; for an equivalent finding with gay samples, see Ridge & Feeney 1998). Avoidant participants, compared with secure participants, avoided intimacy, while anxious participants were more likely to be obsessive and limerent. Although all three stylistic types had experienced some kind of romantic love, avoidant participants were on average relatively cynical about true love; secure participants had more faith in the power of romantic love to be sustained than both avoidant participants and limerent participants (p. 515); and anxious participants frequently felt as though they were falling in love but comparatively rarely found the blissful relationships they had hoped for. Finally, and most important, secure participants, more than their insecure counterparts, reported warmer relations with their caregivers during childhood (see also Ridge & Feeney 1999). Anxious participants, for example, were more likely to describe one or other of their caregivers during this period as cold and rejecting or as having been unfair (Hazan & Shaver 1987, p. 517). Thus, the study's overall findings were impressively compatible with the attachment model.

Since this seminal research, evidence has been mounting that its original findings replicate and extend well to other settings and contexts. For example, partners who have a relatively anxious attachment style, as distinct from those who are relatively avoidant, tend to respond very differently to disagreements with their partner. Characteristically, anxious participants react more negatively (Simpson, Rhodes & Phillips 1996). Anxious participants are also relatively likely to experience unreciprocated (unrequited) love (Aron, Aron & Allen 1998), as well as to carry any domestic disputes with them into the work setting (a process called 'spill-over' in the literature; see Sumer & Knight 2001). Indeed, during relationship break-ups, partners with a more secure (as opposed to avoidant) style tend to cope more easily (Choo, Levine & Hatfield 1996). Avoidant participants are statistically less likely to get into a loving relationship in the first place, and so have a correspondingly reduced need to cope. Instead, they are more likely to seek non-involving casual sex (Brennan & Shaver 1995).

Cross-cultural consistency

Across diverse cultural groups, the same point — travelling reasonably well — can essentially be made. In a major cross-cultural study involving Caucasian and Japanese Americans and Pacific Islanders, attachment styles consistently predicted romantic feelings and experiences similar to the original Hazan and Shaver (1987) study. In another study conducted in New Zealand, partners who were less avoidant, less anxious and more secure reported higher levels of relationship satisfaction; and the overall pattern of relationships between attachment styles and accounts of relationships themselves 'generally supported the validity of the attachment approach' (Hammond & Fletcher 1991, p. 56). The findings in Ridge and Feeney's (1998) study, conducted among gay New Zealanders, were also largely consistent with the model and with the heterosexual research on attachment theory. Finally, in one of the most striking findings to emerge in this field to date, attachment styles predicted the behaviours of couples separating at airports, with anxious partners, as the model predicts, displaying most distress (Fraley & Shaver 1998).

Cross-contextual consistency

Findings like these would also be subject to contextual influences, such as the events of 11 September 2001. We can well imagine, for instance, that in times of crisis distress would be displayed by almost everyone separating at an airport departure gate rather than predominantly by anxiously attached individuals. Temporal changes (Baldwin & Fehr 1995) and contextual/situational shifts like this (Goosens et al. 1986) should remind us of the important principle of correspondence (see chapter 4, p. 142). This principle would lead us to expect attachment styles, which are supposed to be relatively general tendencies, to predict behaviour that is both measured and averaged for each person over a correspondingly wide range of times (Kirkpatrick & Davis 1994) and situations (Keelan, Dion & Dion 1994). Provided we keep correspondence in mind, therefore, it is possible to see how we can have both meaningful general principles and situation-specific contextual effects.

Such effects have been clearly demonstrated for attachment behaviour. In many marriages, for example, feelings of security within the relationship tend to increase over time (Davila, Bradbury & Karney 1999). Findings like this serve to remind us that what happens during infancy does not 'fix', in a predetermined way, what happens in later life. At best, early events only partially predict the future. In fact, there is now an extensive literature on the effects of social deprivation of attachment during infancy, for example through being orphaned; through living communally, such as on a kibbutz, where parents might see their children for only a few hours each day; through the eyes of survivors of concentration camps or ethnic cleansing; and through the stories of children who have been kept for extended periods in solitary confinement by their 'caregivers'. By and large, this literature presents a testament to the resilience of the human spirit, which, if given half a chance through any sustained period of quality caregiving, is often able to make significant recoveries from even the most horrendous deprivations in early life.

With the benefit of hindsight, all of this makes perfect sense. If our paths were each marked out for us from the start, then we would never experience the variety of different love (and other) relationships that most of us do. In part, this is due to the fact that love is often, as Sternberg argued, a question of a match, and so interaction, between love styles. But it is also, as the principle of correspondence suggests, due to the reality that love styles, which are by definition less rigid than traits, can and do change and adapt. This is why, for instance, even in Hazan and Shaver's classic (1987) study of attachment described in the previous pages, it was found that all three stylistic 'types' had actually experienced, or were currently experiencing, at least some aspects of romantic love (p. 515; for some definitions of romantic love, see p. 330).

Consistency with the wider love literature

One point of linkage with studies in the wider literature is the value of complementarity in longer term love relationships. In chapter 8 we learned that attitudinal complementarity (rather than similarity) is one predictor of long-term relationship sustainability. In the attachment literature also, it has been found that partners are comparatively rarely drawn enduringly towards others who share exactly the same attachment style. In one analysis involving 350 couples, for instance, there was not one pairing in which *both* partners' styles were either avoidant or anxious (Kirkpatrick & Davis 1994). As this example suggests, attachment styles and underlying schemata interact dynamically with each other. This enables them to change, for example, in response to fluctuations in the partner's level of satisfaction (Davila, Bradbury & Karney 1999, p. 798). Such influences take us back to, and are consistent with, Michelangelo effects (see p. 335).

Consistency with the triangular model

In a number of ways, the attachment and triangular models are complementary. Theoretically, for example, avoidant attachment styles will rarely position their owners on any of the vertices of figures 9.1 and 9.2. Instead, avoidance will relatively predispose these individuals' behaviours towards Lee's Ludus style, which we have already seen is largely outside the prototype schema for genuine love. Secure attachment, on the other hand, will tend to provide a comparatively balanced propensity and capacity to love others, for example. As we have seen, this style leaves us relatively comfortable with intimacy and with trusting other people (see Sternberg's Commitment in figure 9.1). By contrast, anxious attachment, which we have seen is more prone to limerence, would leave us relatively predisposed towards Passion, Eros and Mania (see figure 9.2).

To sum up, the triangular model and the attachment model, one contemporaneous and the other developmental, are very consistent with one another.

So, can the attachment model, like its trigonometric complement, speak to loving relationships beyond the romantic kind, for example love within friendships? (For indications that attachment history and styles influence relationships with psychotherapists, see Novellino 2000 on the so-called **Pinocchio syndrome**).

FRIENDSHIP LOVE

Starting in childhood, and bolstered by any sense of confidence and security that primary attachments have provided, people normally establish a range of friendships with others of a similar age to themselves. Some of these bonds will develop beyond casual relationships and become close friendships (Kenny & Kashy 1994). According to our operational definition of love (see p. 332), these close friendships become 'special' (loving) friendships if they produce a seriously upsetting 'I miss you' response in a child version of the absence test (Shulman, Glicker & Sroufe 1994). Unfortunately, however, although life-cycle friendships are increasingly a focus of serious research, we still know relatively little about this kind of love across generations, and in particular what it means for children, as distinct from adults, to have a loving friendship (Hendrick & Hendrick 2000).

Links to attachment

There are nonetheless visible indicators of children developing progressively towards greater capacity for intimacy and commitment (see figure 9.1) with other children. For example, as children progress through their primary school years, they become more ready to distribute rewards to friends, rather than acquaintances, based on equality instead of just 'input' alone (Pataki, Shapiro & Clark 1994). Furthermore, consistent with our proposed synthesis of triangular and attachment models, many of these social developments have been linked to attachment. For example, children with a more secure attachment to their primary caregivers more readily form friendships with their peers (Kerns & Barth 1995). In one Israeli study of this effect, Shulman et al. (1994) found that attachment even during infancy (which had been longitudinally assessed) was linked to forming friendships at 10 years of age. According to these authors, special friendships were more frequently found among the secure than among the insecure. Trust, which implies intimacy, commitment and a secure attachment style, is now recognised to be a central feature for understanding childhood friendships (Bernathi & Feshbach 1995).

As we move into adolescence and emerging adulthood, evidence of an absence effect emerges. In one study of university life, for instance, students who were about to separate permanently became more closely involved emotionally with their close friends, relative to their acquaintances (Fredrickson 1995). Although fundamentally prospective rather than retrospective in focus (the study examined anticipated departure rather than how people felt during and after actually parting), the findings of this study nonetheless indicate that emerging adults start to fear permanent separation. The suggestion here is that friendship loves become more likely as people mature. This hypothesis, in fact, is the backbone of **socio-emotional selectivity theory**. This model proposes that emotional closeness to others increases progressively across the life span, as awareness of mortality grows stronger (Carstensen 1992; Carstensen & Turk 1994, 1998). Some readers, as they grow older, may identify with the feeling that special friends are counted, if we are lucky, on the fingers of one hand.

One very interesting finding in Fredrickson's (1995) study is the gender difference that also emerged in the observations. Women students reported having more close friends than their male counterparts. In another study on the same topic (Sternberg & Grajek 1984), women liked their best friend of the same sex more than they liked their lover of the opposite sex. This prompted an author of the study to speculate about 'women's [relative] success in finding greater *communicational intimacy* in closeness with other women than with men' (Sternberg 1986, p. 134; emphasis added).

Evidence on possible gender differences

[The] ... ability to communicate is almost a *sine qua non* of a successful loving relationship. (Sternberg 1986, p. 134)

One major study of communication and gender, conducted within the United States, involved a meta-analysis of 205 studies, with nearly 24 000 participants (Dindia & Allen 1992). This survey found that, on average, women were slightly more open and self-disclosing than men. In another study, women rated their same-sex friendships more highly than men rated theirs, suggesting that the quality of relationships between women may sometimes be higher (Wheeler, Reis & Bond 1989). In a further study, again conducted in a US setting, friendship was more closely related to intimacy for women students than for men (Rubin & Shenker 1978). Thus, although there is probably considerable overlap, there are signs that women may be relatively more inclined towards intimacy in their same-sex close friendships than men are in theirs (for a discussion of cross-sex friendships, including a discussion of what tends to be disclosed, see Hacker 1982).

The codes of mateship

In Australia and New Zealand, and to some extent also the United Kingdom (Morse & Marks 1985), there is a popularly recognised tradition of male 'mateship' (e.g. Conway's 1972 review and Colling's more recent 1992 analysis). Mateship can be found in men's relationships in the workplace (Trahair 1969 to Ashkanasy & O'Connor 1997), in the community (Price 1985) and on the sports field (Lawson & Evans 1992). Across each of these social contexts, male mateship consists of norms of (1) loyalty to one's friends, (2) radical egalitarianism and (3) male cama-raderie (Feather & O'Driscoll 1980). The concept of mateship is dramatically brought to life for us in critical narrative 1.3, which interestingly indicates that it is also found in mixed gender groups. Unfortunately, however, mateship in females seems to be generally far less studied than its male counterpart.

In their detailed critiques of Australian male mateship, Conway and Colling use the lens of psychohistory. A synthesised synopsis of their analyses is presented in critical narrative 9.3. The point made by both authors is that men have come to be emotionally hobbled and inhibited by the codes of conduct that have evolved socially — for good psychohistorical reasons and, at one time, to good effect — around 'male' ways of behaving, thinking and feeling. More recently, however, these com-mentators argue, the norms of mateship have actually operated to stifle male capacity for what figure 9.2 calls intimacy. The chief social skill that is lacking in this domain is, naturally enough, communication (Meeks, Hendrick & Hendrick 1998).

CRITICAL NARRATIVE 9.3

Psychohistorical perspectives on mateship

. . . if we are to understand the first stirrings of 'mateship' in Australian society, we must see it primarily as a necessary fraternity among exiles, not a voluntary league among brothers. Such mateship offered a negative rather than positive bond, one against an unwanted and arbitrary patrism. From its beginnings, the egalitarian spirit in Australian life had the uneasy, over-flaunted character of a grudging relationship based upon the urge for security. This explains why the 'mate' who had risen from the ranks to some position of minor authority or excellence was almost invariably reviled as a 'scab' or a traitor. He had taken a step away from the cosy levelling of brotherhood toward the more perilous identification with fatherhood and responsibility.

Source: Conway (1972, pp. 28–9).

Australian men had been bred for war. The code of ethics that mateship had given them was perfectly tailored for conflict. Both depended on an external threat; both encouraged the perception of good and evil in black and white terms; both upheld the brotherhood and solidarity that led to unquestioning loyalty; and both demanded the suppression of tender emotions in order to survive. Favouring action over words and emotions, and the exclusion of women were perpetuated . . . If an ordinary man achieved success, he would no longer belong to the battlers — and alienation is not a positive alternative to mateship. Mateship is thus perpetuated, along with the 'ideal' Australian male qualities it embodies, including toughness and a disdain for 'weak' emotion.

Source: Colling (1992, pp. 14 and 50).

How male communication deficits are acquired

Social norms, by definition, suggest the effects of learning and environmental opportunity. In one study, for instance, an examination of friendship between men revealed that most of them had had close friendships in youth but less often later in life; that they often put career before marriage and family; and that many of them would like an adult version of the kind of friendship levels they had had in their youth (Miller 1986). A vivid illustration of this kind of sentiment is offered by one of Colling's informants, who remarked, 'All the bullshit about mates. I've got mates but no friends. I'd no more dream of showing them my real self than fly. We all know it's a façade, but go along with it. I'd love to have a real friend' (1992, p. 55).

Analyses of men's novels, outside of Australia and New Zealand, have reached a not dissimilar conclusion with respect to the demise of male–male friendships. 'And the culture has a dominant imperative — put on a good show, fool all the other men — that dooms love and friendship between men' (Miner 1992, p. 33). Thus, as Miner remarks in another cultural context, as males develop, there is observed a general 'move from male friendship between boys to a more distant relationship between them as grown men' (1992, p. 33). Such a general conclusion indicates that the experience of becoming less skilled in communication and intimacy is cross-contextually robust.

Women's friendships with women

In her extensive analysis of these relationships in Western settings, O'Connor (1992) argues for the influence of social, economic and cultural context. For example, the 'much exalted' greater intimacy of women's friendships has been influenced, O'Connor suggests, by their relative lack of power compared with men, as well as a relative lack of material resources such as time and access to physical space. In this, there is a degree of convergence between critical analyses of male–male and female–female friendships. Both, that is, are at least partly shaped and influenced, in their form and function, by social and contextual factors essentially external to their respective gender group. In one study, this is summed up in the working generalisation that men as a 'group' tend to have learned to bond through shared behaviours (drinking, sporting spectacles, recreational activities), whereas women as a group have learned to share feelings, and so focus on intimacy and communication (Duck & Wright 1993). Viewed thus, male–female 'differences' are more about social identity than gender *per se*.

IMPLICATIONS FOR ROMANTIC RELATIONS

As we might expect based on the above analyses, women may tend to believe more than men, on the average, in romantic love (de Roda et al. 1999; see also Lemieux & Hale 1999). Yet this does not mean that males are any the less concerned with attaining, say, intimacy. Just as likely perhaps, they are less socially skilled at attaining it (for more on such skills in close relationships, see Fletcher 2002). Intimacy is sometimes, for instance, the foremost predictor of relationship satisfaction in males (Serrano-Martinez & Carreno-Fernandez 1993). Clearly, therefore, some men still hanker and strive, as the above analyses of mateship imply, for what they

How do these differences *interact* between male and female partners? In one study, married men (more than married women) attributed less love to sexual touching, implying perhaps that men saw touch more in terms of physical than emotional intimacy (Nguyen, Heslin & Nguyen 1976). In another study, the meaning of touch was, for men, mainly determined by the gender of the other person, whereas for women it was also determined by how well they knew the other person (Heslin, Nguyen & Nguyen 1983). Touch from an opposite sex stranger was unpleasant, but touch from a person with whom there was a close relationship was more enjoyable. This finding, like its predecessor by Nguyen et al. (1976), indicates that intimacy is more critical for women than for men in deciding whether touch is pleasant or not. According to the evidence, there is a potential for male partners to be turned on by the very aspects of touch that may turn a woman off.

Evidence about other types of mismatch, again centring on social skills in communication and intimacy, comes from studies of couples in conflict (Fitness & Fletcher 1993). Poor communication is one of the most frequently cited causes of couple break-ups, both for heterosexual couples (Sprecher 1994) and for homosexual couples (Kurdek 1991). One of the key ways in which these communication breakdowns happen is through different ways of reacting to conflict within the relationship once it starts (Fletcher, Thomas & Durrant 1999). When conflicts break out, women (in the Western and heterosexual settings studied) are often more expressive and open (i.e. disclose their emotions), whereas men in exactly the same situation tend to remain more reserved (Grossman & Wood 1993). Pleas for him to 'warm up' are met by pleas for her to 'calm down' (Brehm, Kassin & Fein 1999, p. 329). In this way, couples may tend to move 'toward more openness in their relationship, despite the fact that husbands were likely to be seen as pushing for closed-ness' (Noller, Feeney & Blakely-Smith 2001, p. 153).

Such communication gaps understandably on occasion lead both sides to escalating frustration. In these situations, each participant's characteristic style of dealing with others is socially facilitated, thereby reinforcing the reaction of 'other' to it. The escalation dynamics in this scenario are aptly termed a 'demand/withdraw interaction pattern' (Christensen & Heavey 1993) or, alternatively, cycles of 'Pursuit/Withdrawal' (Markman et al. 1993). A partial solution to these communication problems, according to some writers, is for the partners themselves to identify their differing reactions in order to become mindful of the fact that they have a communication problem (Brehm et al. 1999). This advocacy is consistent with the rationale for social psychology outlined at the beginning of this book.

Factors cultural

We already know that many of the 'gender' differences just outlined are culture-dependent. In Wheeler et al.'s (1989) study on how same-sex friendships are rated by men and women, for example, Hong Kong Chinese women and men, unlike their US counterparts in the same study, exhibited no different predisposition towards intimacy and self-disclosure from each other. A further study, focusing on same-sex friendships among gay and lesbian couples, found exactly the same absence of difference in terms of intimate communication (Nardi & Sherrod 1994). Thus, any so-called gender differences we have tentatively outlined may apply more clearly to Western populations, and even perhaps to specific Western heterosexual groups within these general populations.

The point here is that, once we accept the influence of contextual, communication and cultural norms, which are recurring and central themes in this book, we must also embrace the flexibility and — fortunately — inherent changeability, of many social psychological generalisations. Comparative degrees of individualism and collectivism, for example, probably have some significant social influences on precisely how psychologically 'different' the biologically different sexes really are.

Is romantic love universal?

What, then, about the 'universality' of romantic love? There are at least three ways in which this question can be asked and answered. First, to what extent do actors report that they *would* marry even without love? This is a question of love versus pragmatics, such as marrying to escape the poverty trap. Second, to what extent *should* people marry only for love? This is a question of ideals, with pragmatic considerations set aside for a moment. And third, to what extent do we find *evidence*, from cultural anthems, legends and other cultural artefacts, of belief and value being placed on love across wide gulfs of time and place? This question concerns group-level indicators of love, as distinct from the kind of individual-level indices (attachment styles, prototypes) that we have considered so far in the chapter.

Would people marry without love?

An example of this first kind of approach is a study by Levine et al. (1995). Levine et al.'s method consisted of a survey that sampled populations across 11 different cultural settings. These ranged from 'developing' economies such as India and Pakistan, which retained collectivistic traditions like arranged marriages, to more 'developed' and individualistic economies, such as the United Kingdom and Australia, which, by and large, did not condone arranged marriages. One of the specific questions asked by Levine et al. in their survey was, 'If a (wo)man had all the other qualities you desired, would you marry this person if you were not in love with her/him?' (after Kephart 1967, p. 561).

The most striking finding in this study was a sharp disjunction between the responses of participants from India and Pakistan, where half the respondents answered 'yes' to the question, versus Australia and England, where just 5 to 7 per cent answered 'yes' (80 per cent answered 'no', and the rest were 'undecided'). Interestingly also, there were very few gender differences in this study, either within countries or between them. Perhaps socio-economic conditions (the everyday reality of living in a poorer economy, and within the marriage-brokering system that has socially evolved in these circumstances) somehow influenced the differences obtained? This idea is reinforced by the study's finding (p. 565) of significant correlations between country-level reluctance to marry without love, and country-level economic indices like gross domestic product (.75). Thus, poverty may have rendered people comparatively willing to trade romance for a materially tolerable and viable life (Maslow 1943).

Levine et al. (1995) also found that country-level answers to the '*would* you . . .' question above correlated (.56) with Hofstede's IBM country-level indices of collectivism–individualism (see chapter 1). This correlation could mean that cultural values partly drove romantic versus pragmatic beliefs about love and marriage. But it should also be recalled that changes in cultural values (such as rises in individualism) tend to follow (rather than precede) changes in economic development (see chapter 6). Therefore, economics is still perhaps the foremost 'driving force' behind much of the variance in the data analysed by Levine et al.; degree of poverty is a major determinant of beliefs about the viability of romantic love as a practical basis for marriage.

Should people marry for love?

Even though people are willing to forgo romantic love for practical reasons, this does not mean that they will give up on it as an *ideal*. A study addressing this particular possibility, by Sprecher et al. (1994), took samples in Japan, the United States and Russia. Included in the survey was a scale for measuring romantic attitudes (Sprecher & Metts 1989). As we saw in chapter 4, attitudes, and therefore attitude scales, are normally questions of 'should' rather than 'would', and to that extent fit relatively well with our concern with ideals rather than practice.

The romanticism scale used in this study measured attitudes towards themes such as 'love finds a way', 'one and only' (love), and 'idealisation' (of love relationships). On the average, each of the three country samples scored above the mid-point (i.e. were pro-romantic rather than unromantic), as well as being just as romantic as each other (i.e. there were no significant differences across nations). Again, there were no gender differences in terms of these pro-romantic attitudes. However, when the same three country samples were also asked if they *would* marry without love, variability reappeared. While 84 per cent of Japanese and 89 per cent of US students would insist on love, only 64 per cent of Russians would do so (Sprecher & Metts 1989, p. 358). There was also a gender difference within the Russian sample, with more women than men being prepared to marry without love. This finding brings to mind the Russian and other mail-order bride agencies that advertise what are essentially the 'trades' of (a) youthful beauty for (b) economic security (see chapter 8). Overall, therefore, while economics may demand pragmatism, this does not necessarily mean that people will 'give up on' romantic ideals (for more of a prototype perspective on the pragmatism and social transactional meanings of marriage, see Pfeffer 1997).

The historicity test

> Similarity in a given function from across widely divergent cultures would strongly attest to its durability across time. (Gergen 1973, p. 318)

This proposition provides one possible criterion for beginning to evaluate whether romantic love is anything other than a social construction — that is, whether it is a product of a particular time and place rather than a prototypical feature of what it means to be human, as defined in the opening section of this chapter. The extent to which romantic love is found across radically diverse cultural settings supports the idea that it is not simply a quirk of time and place and a particular point in history. Rather, the concept of love would pass a **historicity test**, because it traverses time and radically different cultural systems relatively well, as Gergen argues. This historicity test will therefore be used as a measure of the robustness of the concept of romantic love.

Much of our data for conducting this test derives from disciplines 'outside' of social psychology, including social anthropology, sociology and family studies (Dion & Dion 1993, p. 66). A prime example of such eclecticism in the field is an intriguing ethnographic study by Jankowiak and Fischer (1992). This study used a combination of folk narratives, archival records of elopement and other ethnographic data to look for signs of passionate love. Many people would agree, in line with table 9.1, that passion is a defining feature of the romantic experience (see activity 1; Fehr & Russell 1991).

Jankowiak and Fischer's procedures were able to confirm the presence of romantic love in 147 of 166 (or 89 per cent) of the societies studied. Fletcher (2002) has recently argued that this figure is inherently conservative, because in 18 of the 19 'love-absent' cultures the amount of data available was too scant to conclude with any confidence that romantic love was truly absent from that particular culture. In fact, there was only one setting, out of the 166 studied, where a claim was made that romantic love did not exist (see also Hitschmann 1952). In support of Fletcher's (2002) position, a cross-cultural analysis of Western (US) and Eastern (Chinese) love songs revealed striking similarities in shared themes of 'desperate and passionate and erotic' love (Rothblaum & Tsang 1998, p. 316). Given that these two settings represent radically different examples of individualistic and collectivistic societies, this analysis meets Gergen's criterion for durability (note, not universality). The study provides evidence for the robustness of romantic love, a point that is driven home in critical narrative 9.4.

CRITICAL NARRATIVE 9.4

A 3000-year-old Egyptian love poem

It's seven whole days since I
    have seen my lover. A sickness
pervades me. My limbs are lead.
    I barely sense my body.
Should physicians come,
    their drugs could not cure
my heart, nor could the priests
    diagnose my disease.
Should they say, 'Here
    she is', that would heal me.
Her name would restore me.
    Should her messengers
come and go, that
    is what would revive my heart,
More potent than medicine
    my lover is to me.
More powerful too is she
    than books of medicine.
Her arrival from outside
    is my amulet. At the sight
of her I regain my health.
    She widens her eyes at me,
and my body becomes young.
    She speaks and I am strong.
I embrace her. She banishes
    the sickness from me. But she
has left me for seven whole days.

Source: From *Love Lyrics of Ancient Egypt*, translated by Barbara Hughes Fowler. Copyright © 1994 by the University of North Carolina Press. Used by permission of the publisher.

Given that it is 3000 years old, and that the culture within which it was composed is radically different from those of the twenty-first century, this love poem is a prototypical exemplar of Gergen's historicity test. And the reader's response to this poem is probably that it could have been written today. In fact, the sheer, full-bodied limerence in critical narrative 9.4 alone is a superb example of what Gergen means by a robust social process. Romantic love, then, is not a comparatively localised social construction emanating from Western Europe (de Rougemont 1956).

Support for cultural differences

This is not to say that romantic love will be *expressed* uniformly across geographical and historical settings. Context, both in the immediate and in the broader, historical sense, still determines precisely how love is communicated. In medieval France, for instance, very explicit codes of courtly love saw noble-women placed on a moral pedestal, which would inevitably have influenced the socially acceptable levels of commitment and intimacy and displays of passion (Rechtien & Fiedler 1989). Similarly, in contemporary Sri Lankan villages, local definitions of romantic love stress limerence, but this passion is also channelled through the customs of arranged marriages (de Munck 1998a).

Within relationships, too, ways of expressing love will vary systematically according to socially influenced life-cycle patterns. In many relatively individual-istic settings, for example, where individual choices and freedom of personal expression are more valued, the course of successful romantic love may begin with high passion and be later sustained (in its mid- to long-term stages) by commitment and intimacy (Tucker & Aron 1993). The latter is comparable to our definition of companionate love (see p. 330; Sprecher & Regan 1998; for a neuro-chemical analysis of this kind of process, see Liebowitz 1983). In more collectivistic societies, by contrast, longer term relationships are more often arranged by the respective extended families, rather than freely chosen by the lovers themselves. Theoretically, therefore, the pattern in successful relationships in these societies could be very different, with passion (and perhaps relationship satisfaction) starting at lower levels and gradually *rising* with the passage of time (Karney & Bradbury 1995).

In an important study bearing directly on this possibility (Gupta & Singh 1982), married couples in India were divided into those who had chosen their partner ('love marriages') and those whose marriages were decided for them by their respective extended families ('arranged marriages'). The results of this fascinating study are schematically summarised in figure 9.4. This figure reflects the finding that, with the passage of time, couples who had chosen their own marriage part-ners tended to become progressively less passionate, whereas among their arranged marriage counterparts the trend headed in the reverse direction, since, logically enough, it took time to develop intimacy and passion (J. Spencer-Burford, personal correspondence). The contrasting trends depicted in figure 9.4 occurred over a relationship spanning 10 years or more, so we cannot attribute the difference in trends simply to pre-existing familiarity-contempt among the chosen-marriage couples (who may have been together long before the wedding) versus relative novelty-attraction among the arranged marriage couples. The trends recorded in this study are broadly based across a long time span.

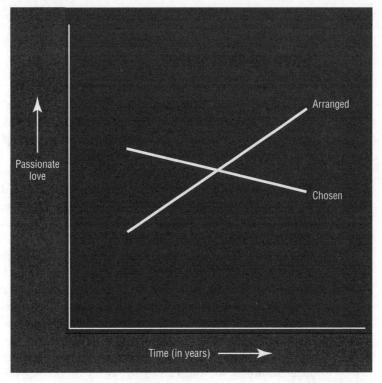

Figure 9.4   Diverging courses of passionate love between arranged and chosen marriages

Source: Extracted and schematised from Gupta and Singh (1982).

To sum up, therefore, although the concept of romantic love is relatively robust, there is also equifinality in the courses it can run ('equifinality' means reaching the same goal via different pathways). This point applies to love generally and gives the field much of its complexity (Hecht, Marston & Larkey 1994). But, again, the broader point is that the course of romantic love is influenced substantially, and to some extent predictably, by the culture in which it develops (for a more detailed discussion of arranged marriages, see Yelsma & Athappilly 1988).

Globalisation and the rejuvenation of romantic love

One of the more obvious places where globalisation interacts with romance is in the workplace. As more and more hours of our waking lives are spent there, 'organisational romance' is becoming a field of study in its own right (Pierce 1995, p. 2946). Work settings and conditions have all the ingredients to foster both attraction and romantic attachment — including, for example, propinquity, familiarity and similarity (see chapter 8). As one relations consultant put it, 'Most people are spending more time at work than ever and hardly talk to their neighbours, so it should come as no surprise that the boy or girl next door is being superseded by the man or woman at the next desk' (Shopland 2001, p. E1). The problem, as Shopland observes, is that workplace relations create conflicts of interest. These include, for example, expectations of preferential treatment, and feelings of betrayal when these expectations are not met. Once again, therefore, the pressures of globalisation are increasing both employees' and managers' needs to understand love.

Love @ first byte?

An increasingly salient feature of both working and daily life is the Internet, and particularly e-mail. Common sense suggests that e-mail will downplay and dampen, rather than augment, our need to understand love. After all, people are less likely to fall madly in love when they cannot even see each other or interact with one another in physical (and perhaps sexual) space! This is a rephrasing of the view, discussed in chapter 8, that Internet 'communication' is making strangers of us all. Yet the Internet has also been vividly described as a 'particle accelerator, *magnifying* the power of otherwise weak and tiny impulses', that *facilitates* rather than inhibits romance (Seiden 2001, p. 187, emphasis added). This facilitating influence includes encouragement for people to 'act out' their fantasies and inner aspirations relatively freely, for example by offering romantic compliments and generally releasing more of their creatively romantic imagination (Cooper & Sportolari 1998). In this way, would-be partners can freely construct their own personal cyber love spaces, for instance a romantic dinner complete with (computer-generated) candles, soft music and e-roses (Deuel 1996).

Theoretical and empirical support for a particle-accelerator effect is not hard to find. According to Wallace (1999), lovers on the Net often first meet in cyber group settings, such as professional e-mailing lists, chat-rooms, MUDS (interactive role-playing virtual environments) and MOOS (see chapter 8). The relative anonymity and privacy of the computer environment encourages ready disclosure (Walther 1996), enabling the relatively uninhibited expression not only of attraction, but also of more positive emotions about developing relationships (see chapter 8, on AIM). At a more mundane but practical level, the Net *costs* less than more traditional ways of overcoming distance (for an expanded review of the issues of online love, see Lea & Spears 1995). Thus, it can in principle override some of the socio-economic constraints already outlined (but see Prilleltensky, in press, for its limits for the many people who are too poor to afford access to the Internet).

Like their non-cyber counterparts, romantic e-liaisons may develop in a wide variety of directions. Many of them, however, will reach a watershed when the e-partners eventually decide to meet in physical space. At this point, an issue will arise over whether each partner over- or under-delivers on the idealised expectations they may have created for each other (Adamse & Motta 1996).

On balance, the Internet may constitute a powerful communication channel for speeding up (particle accelerating) and opening up a pathway to intimacy (see figure 9.2). In retrospect, this should not surprise us. After all, and as critical narrative 9.4 vividly illustrates, 'Human beings have been using the written word for thousands of years to express affect and love for each other' (Wallace 1999, p. 155). As Wallace also points out, the greatest danger with Internet love affairs is an elevated risk that your 'partner' is not who or what they say they are, and may at any point simply 'vanish into thin air' (p. 155). Overall, therefore, the Internet increases our need to understand love better.

Emotional self-perception

Stafford and Reske (1990) found that the more couples felt the need to write letters to each other when separated by geographical distance, the more 'in love' they became, compared with those who relied more on the easier-to-use communication channels of telephone (voice-to-voice) and face-to-face conversation. Writing (and stamping and posting) letters is, first and foremost, much more demanding than telephoning or talking face-to-face. This defining feature of writing raises an intriguing possibility. The more we have to 'work at' maintaining a relationship (up to a certain point, of course), the more highly we might come to value it. This process of emotional labelling is almost as applicable to e-mail as to snail-mail (people reason to themselves, 'If we're still together despite all the obstacles in our way, this must be true love').

Indirectly supporting this broad conjecture, in a now classic study in social psychology, Canadian men crossed a bridge, to be met on the other side by a female research assistant (Dutton & Aron 1974). For some participants this crossing brought an adrenalin rush (the bridge was high, rickety and scary); for others it was a much less arousing experience (it was low, stable and safe). As predicted in an **excitation transfer** hypothesis (Zillman 1984), and with all else equal, the adrenalin rush crossing was more likely than its safer counterpart to prompt a later telephone call to the female research assistant, asking for 'more information'. This classic finding can be interpreted in a number of interesting (and controversial) ways. But the point for us here is a more basic one: How we *interpret* our emotions is partly a function of the social context in which they occur (see also chapter 8, on AIM).

What this study suggests is that when their emotions are aroused, people partly rely on social and environmental cues to help them later cognitively define and interpret their experience (Schachter & Singer 1962). This includes giving the experience a sexual and perhaps even romantic meaning (White, Fishbein & Rutstein 1981). In the domain of love relationships, it has been found that couples whose relationship survives external pressures progressively perceive that their love has increased from $Time_n$ to $Time_{n+1}$, even though this is not always actually the case (Sprecher 1999; for earlier analogous findings in an Australian setting, see Hong & Bartley 1986). Such findings clearly suggest that overcoming the environmental and social obstacles to love, independently of what they might be, might help to define that love in comparatively romantic terms.

The Romeo and Juliet effect

The clearest evidence for this notion derives from a study of relationships that endure despite opposition from relatives (Driscoll, Davis & Lipetz 1972). In Driscoll et al.'s seminal study, romantically involved participants completed surveys, over a 10-month interval, about both parental resistance and degree of romantic attachment. Fascinatingly, fluctuations in the perceived level of parental resistance were correlated positively with increases in romantic attachment. Driscoll et al. evocatively named their observation a **Romeo and Juliet effect**. This name is inspired by Shakespeare's play in which the two lovers resist clan pressures to break off their relationship, instead attaining the prototype romance, or 'real thing' (see also Forgas 1986, p. 254).

In one sense, the Shakespearean name is inappropriate. The 'love that survives' is a widespread and enduring romantic narrative. For example, Fletcher describes a traditional Māori legend from the Te Arawa people of New Zealand, in which love survives in the face of social pressures (2002, p. 88). Around the world today, global media-scapes (see chapter 4) continue to capture our imaginations with similar messages that 'love conquers all' (Schauder 1991). In East Africa, for example, popular Indian films have been described as excessively romantic (Pfeffer 1997, p. 511). The point here is that romantic narratives continue to be a fundamental influence on the way people socially construct and reconstruct their love lives (McGregor & Holmes 1999). Romeo and Juliet effects, that is, pass the historicity test.

A glocal perspective on romantic love

As we saw in chapter 1, globalisation often facilitates local backlashes. Individualistic systems of belief clash with collectivistic ones. These will include beliefs about marriage and degrees of choice in marriage, precisely the kind of tension that is described in the various romantic narratives just outlined. This condition enhances the relevance of the Romeo and Juliet effect. The same glocal perspective on romance and romantic love suggests that the tensions between global and local will continue to grow, again highlighting our need to understand love (Dion & Dion 1993, p. 67).

A serious example of these tensions is found in suicide and attempted suicide among emerging adults who feel caught between the two moral worlds of global and local views on love and marriage (see chapter 10). The clash between one type of romantic ideal and another can create substantial psychosocial tensions for emerging adults suspended between equally unrelenting moral edifices (Hussain & Zafri 1997). In the highlands of Papua New Guinea, for example, tensions between 'modern', media-disseminated love norms and local traditional ones have, according to some experienced observers, helped to precipitate a rise in the rate of female youth suicides (D. Finnigan, personal correspondence, March 2001). So there is a growing need to analyse how competing love and marriage prototypes interact with one another to influence emotional distress and wellbeing.

Love and marriage

At the beginning of this chapter, we examined the concept of emerging adulthood and choice of marriage partner. Now we glance briefly ahead to the other end of the process, addressed more fully in chapter 10. Western countries such as the United States have the highest divorce rates (Fletcher 2002): around 50 per cent of US marriages end in divorce (Schumaker 2001), almost double the rates for Australia and New Zealand. This means we cannot simply label divorce as a generalisable 'Western' or 'individualistic' influence. Rather, divorce statistics must be interpreted in context (Katz & Briger 1988). Similarly, societies in which women have traditionally had less freedom or time to choose may enable *reduced* rather than escalated divorce statistics (G. W. Jones 1997). In this way, even in romantic dissolution, a glocal perspective can 'illuminate the positive'.

The need to expand the horizons of social psychology, and specifically to encompass the glocal dynamics of love, has never been greater. From our review of the vital elements of love, we can say that whirlwind courtships, based more on passion (Eros) but less on genuine intimacy (Storge) and commitment (Pragma), are relatively unlikely to be sustained, compared with more 'consummate' love (Sternberg 1986, p. 124). At the same time, however, their intense, all-consuming quality of experience (as in many relatively short marriages and relationships) may offset the pain that follows. As one author expresses this, 'Reaching the goal ['the real thing'] is often easier than maintaining it' (Sternberg 1986, p. 124). Finally, then, sustainability is not everything; intensity can be just as vital and memorable.

SUMMARY

Love can be distinguished empirically from liking, admiration and lust, by using a prototypes approach. Its key unique elements of commitment, intimacy and passion can be traced to attachment history. Attachment orientations foster different configurations of these elements in close relationships. Consummate love in general, and passionate love in particular, are relatively trans-historical, although the real task for contemporary analyses of love is more dynamic — to explain how global narratives and local realities interact with one another. Foremost among these are both relatively new concepts like 'emerging adulthood' and enduring local traditions like arranged marriages. Medium affect and relationship 'sustainability' are not everything.

KEY TERMS

Absence test. To the extent that we miss somebody, we probably feel some kind of love for that person, in terms of commitment, intimacy and/or passion, even if we cannot articulate it. Thus, for example, absent friends are not loved unless we miss them, rather than finding ourselves capable of putting the relationship 'on hold' until we next meet. (p. 332)

Attachment theory. A social psychological model of life span development that holds that the quality of the relationships we form with primary caregivers, during childhood, profoundly shapes and influences the propensities we have in later life to form intimate and loving relationships with friends and lovers (p. 336)

Barnum effect. When people are shown general statements about themselves that could apply to anyone, they often recognise themselves with alacrity and 'buy into' the idea, even though it has no real validity. A commercially successful nineteenth-century circus impresario, P. T. Barnum is famous for coining the axioms, 'A little something for everybody!' and 'There's a sucker born every minute'. (p. 333)

Emerging adulthood. A developmental concept in which, on a global basis, younger people are increasingly deferring their choice of long-term partner and parenthood while they not only prepare themselves for entry into the workforce but also carefully experiment with different types of loving relationship (p. 322)

Excitation transfer. The hypothesis that emotional arousal is a diffuse state that partly depends for its interpretation on cognition. Heightened states of fear, for example, can provoke sexual attraction, if a suitable person is present during the fearful episode. (p. 353)

Historicity test. After Gergen (1973). To the extent that a given social psychological finding, theory or technique transcends diverse historical contexts, it can be said to have passed the historicity test, and to be relatively durable (as distinct from 'universal'). (p. 348)

Limerence. A tendency to want to merge existences with a romantic lover. This is a relatively *passionate* form of love that is sometimes associated with chronic jealousy and other essentially negative emotions. (p. 339)

Michelangelo effect. In loving relationships, the self is shaped by a partner's idealised person schema about him or her. When that schema coincides with the self's own schema for ideal self, then the self progressively 'sculpts' himself or herself towards this ideal. Such positive Pygmalion effects enhance life satisfaction and fulfilment, especially when both partners sculpt each other, in a doubly positive Pygmalion effect. (p. 335)

Pinocchio syndrome. A tendency to feel the need to lie to maintain personal relationships, which is sometimes traced to the lack of primary secure attachment during early childhood (p. 342)

Prototypes approach. Prototypes are implicit schemata in which we store archetypal examples of categorical concepts like 'love'. Although we may not be able to articulate these schemata with any great precision, we can say how closely particular exemplars of the category are to our prototype. Through this verbal behaviour, researchers have been able to identify core consensual properties of the meaning of love in everyday life. (p. 324)

Romeo and Juliet effect. The more a love relationship withstands outside pressures to break up, the more its stakeholders will define their love as real and undying. Analogous to *adversity affiliation* (see p. 318 for definition) and *superordinate goals* (see p. 114 for definition) (p. 353)

Socio-emotional selectivity theory. The breadth of social interaction networks begins to decline in early/emerging adulthood, while the depth of emotional intimacy with those who remain in or enter the network steadily increases. Growing awareness of our own mortality and a sense of the need for genuine closeness with others play major roles in these human life span developments. (p. 343)

Strange situation. An observational technique devised to investigate infant attachment styles. For example, infant plays in presence of primary caregiver; a stranger enters room and tries to play with infant; caregiver leaves the room; the stranger leaves the room; and the caregiver returns. Children's reactions at each stage, and during the transitions between stages, indicate how detached, securely attached or anxiously (over-attached) to the caregiver each child is becoming. (p. 336)

REVIEW QUESTIONS

1. Outline the three main dimensions of love in Sternberg's triangular schema.
2. How does the Attachment model mesh with Sternberg's own model?
3. Why are there gender 'differences' in capacity for special friendships?
4. Review the evidence on whether Romantic love is trans-historical.

DISCUSSION QUESTIONS

Debate the following statements:

1. 'Love is no more than a social construct.'
2. 'The best predictor of emerging adult love behaviour is attachment history.'
3. 'Michelangelo effects are illusory, but so what?'
4. 'Women are bound to be hardwired by social evolution to be better at communication and intimacy than men.'
5. 'By the next century, love will be practised differently from the way it is now.'
6. 'We *murder* to dissect' (Wordsworth).

ACTIVITIES

1. Conduct your own class replication of any one of Fehr and Russell's (1991) studies of love prototypes. Do your results concur?

2. Work in pairs. Bring to the class a song, poem or painting about love that really means something to you, and critically analyse it in terms of the triangular model and its attachment counterpart. How well does each schema explain the song, poem or painting?

3. Select a remote culture, time or legend, and apply the historicity test to it with respect to any of the models of love discussed in the chapter.

4. In the week before the class, collect advertisements from the Personal columns of your local newspapers, magazines or regional websites (e.g. http://zwelra. orcon.net.nz). Work through the advertisements using the models discussed in this chapter. Do the models help illuminate or 'murder' romantic intent?

5. This activity should be conducted in private. Think back on your own love life. Has the material in this chapter helped *you* to make any sense of what has happened in the past, and what may happen in the future?

ADDITIONAL READING

On love prototypes: the best source, for my money, is still Fehr and Russell (1991).
On the triangular theory of love: any of the Sternberg readings cited in the chapter. Most cover much the same ground.
On personal relationships: Noller, Feeney and Blakeley-Smith (2001).
On the scientific approach to studying close relationships, including more on linkages between hot and cold processes, affect and cognition (like social skills in love and other intimate relationships): Fletcher (2002).

For further reading on the topics discussed in this chapter, consult the online resources linked to the Wiley website (http://www.johnwiley.com.au/highered/socialpsych).

10

AGGRESSION

LEARNING OBJECTIVES

After reading this chapter, you should be able to:

- discuss the role of aggression in the break-up of romantic relationships
- describe key contributors to aggression in the community, including self-directed harm that results in suicide
- distinguish sporting spectacles that are more likely to promote aggression than prevent it
- identify key precursors and expressions of aggression in the workplace, both physical and psychological.

OVERVIEW

Aggression is a complex topic. Since it has multiple sources and multiple manifestations, reviews of aggression can read like disembodied lists of 'causes' and 'effects', rather than integrated models. This chapter uses historicity testing (see chapter 9) to identify common themes across diverse social contexts. Aggression in the home — familial violence between partners or directed towards children — is linked back to attachment theory, discussed in chapter 9. Global warming and poverty are identified as major contributors to aggression in the community. Sport is often implicitly regarded as a vent for frustrations in everyday life, and this chapter assesses the evidence for that view. Finally, amid growing concerns about bullying in organisations, the influences of the global marketplace on aggression in the local workplace are analysed. The chapter ends where the book began, focusing on glocalisation and, in particular, a glocal psychology of social justice.

CONCEPTUAL FOUNDATIONS

Aggression is normally defined in the social psychological literature as *behaviour that is intended to hurt another person or group* (after Johnson 1972). It might therefore include, for example, the use of deliberately hurtful vitriolic language between lovers. It also includes both murder and suicide, although the latter normally has intent to harm the self as a key definitional feature (Australian Psychological Society 1999a). Included also is the athlete who lashes out at an opponent in the heat of the moment on the sports field. Finally, although this definition excludes employees who obey an inhumane order against their own conscience (see chapter 1, on the Milgram experiment and organisational obedience), it would include, for example, an envious, unscrupulous workmate who encourages a peer to speak with the boss at a dangerous moment.

As these examples show, aggression involves both behaviour (part 1) and cognition (via intent; part 2, chapter 4). But for most of us, the defining, prototypical feature of aggression, whether we display it or perceive it in others, is that the emotions are in play. Aggression is mostly (although not totally, of course) about *social affect*. An early analysis differentiated between 'expressive' and 'instrumental' aggression (Buss 1961). In the first case, aggression is its own reward; it is 'goal reactive', emotionally speaking, to 'level the score'. In the language of chapter 9, and as depicted in figure 10.1, this type of aggression is relatively 'hot'. In the second case, an aggressive act is more calculated, serving as a means to an end rather than an end in itself; for example as a retributive action with gratification delayed ('Revenge is a dish best served cold'). This type of aggression is therefore relatively 'cold'.

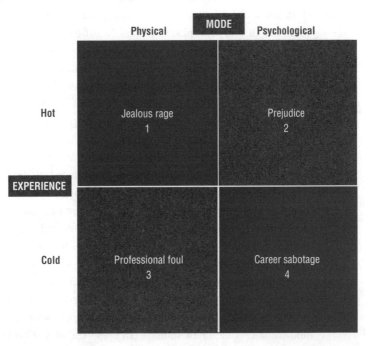

Figure 10.1 Types of aggression

A second key dimension for defining aggression is the physical as opposed to the psychological, a differentiation that is sometimes also termed 'direct' versus 'indirect' aggression (Archer, Monks & Connors 1997; Tomada & Schneider 1997). Everyday examples of each type of aggression — expressive (hot) versus instrumental (cold), and physical versus psychological — are provided in figure 10.1. Thus, aggression might assume the form of relatively hot and direct *romantic jealousy*; hot and indirect out-group *prejudice* (especially its implicit forms, as discussed in chapter 7); the relatively calculated and direct tactic of the *professional foul*; or, finally, the relatively cold and indirect gradual 'career sabotage' of a rival at work.

One way previous reviews have approached the cross-contextual diversities signalled in figure 10.1 has been to focus on a core, underlying 'issue'. Perhaps the most notable of these is whether aggression is innate or learned. With most research to date concentrating on the learned rather than psychobiological components of aggression, there is certainly a need for greater consideration of the 'nature' side of this debate (for more balanced reviews of the nature side, see Filley, Kelly & Price 2001; Miles & Carey 1997). To some extent, however, this will be a fruitless, unnecessarily divisive debate, since nature and nurture constantly interact with each other in everyday life (Brehm, Kassin & Fein 1999, p. 402). All things considered, the best way forward may be to keep exploring processes that are inherently interactive. This chapter chooses to focus on the interactive influences of glocalisation identified at the beginning of the book.

First, however, it is necessary to find some kind of conceptual bond between the incredibly diverse forms of aggression depicted in figure 10.1. To achieve this, aggression is analysed for recurring and retainable themes across radically different social contexts. These themes span, for example, domestic, community, recreational and workplace settings (see figure 10.1). Applying the rationale of historicity testing, the following review attempts to synthesise the underlying principles of aggression and aggression management that crisscross these radically divergent social contexts. Such constants should give us confidence that the principles and practices revealed are reasonably robust.

Most of us could list many seemingly disparate and disconnected reasons why people become aggressive, and how they express that aggression once it is aroused. Against this, a major reason for common linkages to emerge stems from a meta-social influence process introduced at the beginning of this book. The process of globalisation is creating recognisable stresses and strains in most people's everyday lives. These include increased money pressures on couples and families (the leading contributor to marital disintegration, according to Schumaker 2001, p. 100), and on communities (for example in rural and remote settings, where urban drift is creating severe social and economic pressures); and social pressures on sporting teams and individual athletes to win at all costs; and on employees to 'make it' to the top, under US-style 'up-or-out' systems. Such pressures clearly have common denominators, such as increased competition, and common outcomes, such as envy and jealousy. This commonality bodes well for a common process.

AGGRESSION IN THE HOME

Links to love and family relationships

Marital conflict is one factor associated with child abuse (Davies & Cummings 1994). Family studies have shown that children too often bear the brunt of adult life frustrations, and that the resulting experiences of assault, pain and humiliation frequently create a psychological legacy (Herzberger 1996). To be precise, they contribute towards a *cycle of family violence* (Belsky 1993). Aggression towards the child later influences that child's aggression towards the abusers (Peek, Fisher & Kidwell 1985) and then often spills over to close partners during adulthood (Malinowsky-Rummell & Hansen 1993), when the cycle starts all over again. Since these cycles of family violence have their origins in early experiences, childhood is the most logical time for any longer term preventive interventions to begin (Lloyd 1990; see chapter 9, on attachment and parenting styles). Of course, there will continue to be a need for short-term, band-aid interventions, such as shelters for battered women and children (Rhodes, Gordon & Zelman 1997). But in the longer term, breaking the cycle of domestic violence is bound to depend heavily on our capacity to understand close relationships, and in particular when and how they are liable to start to go awry.

The trajectory of satisfaction in close relationships is not always steadily upwards (Karney & Bradbury 1997). Very few married couples, for instance, report that they *never* quarrel (McGonagle, Kessler & Schilling 1992). Often in these areas, men will prefer either to avoid the issue or to attempt to offset any negative affect with statements about their income-generating role. In their own self and role schemata for a 'good' husband, this probably reflects their male commitment to the relationship (Buss & Shackleford 1997). Such a perspective clearly suggests the distal tug — or nudge perhaps — of social evolutionary influences (see chapter 8). These influences are even more visible in the domains of jealousy and envy, two specific areas that, like aggression in close relationships (Ehrensaft & Vivian 1996), have experienced a phenomenal growth in research interest in recent years (Guerrero & Andersen 1998).

Strictly speaking, jealousy and envy are antonyms of each other, rather than synonyms (Bedeian 1995). You might express envy, for example, if you coveted someone else's lover (you want someone you do not 'have'); jealousy, on the other hand, might be motivated by fear of losing someone from a relationship (you want to keep someone you already 'have'). An aggressive exemplar of this is stalking, which is now also receiving increased attention in the research literature (Cupach, Spitzberg & Carson 2000). Stalkers may be complete strangers or they may be a member of a previously close family that has disintegrated (Belsky 1993). In the first case, stalking might be a manifestation of envy, while in the latter it might represent an extreme form of jealousy (for an interesting discussion of 'cyber-stalking', see Deirmenjian 1999; for a prototypes approach to jealousy, see Fitness & Fletcher 1993).

Jealousy

As Belsky (1993) points out, familial violence is often driven by perceived infidelities and fear of loss ('If I can't have her, nobody else will'). Such reactions can lead to another form of aggression, this time primarily self-directed — namely, suicide. Often suicide is connected to other social psychological factors such as failing businesses and issues of economic power (Prilleltensky, in press). In part because of the widespread gender role expectations already noted, most instances of family aggression, including murders of spouse and children, whether or not they involve suicide, are committed by men (Wilson, Daly & Daniele 1995). To place this in a broader perspective, males tend to be more prone than females to direct aggression as they pass from early childhood (Sanson et al. 1993) to adolescence (Owens & MacMullin 1995) to emerging adulthood (Bettencourt & Miller 1996) to adulthood (Scott 1997). At the same time, it should be remembered that the effect sizes are not large and there is probably a good deal of cross-gender overlap (Harris 2002; Hyde 1984).

One likely contributing factor to the relatively high incidence of male family violence is that men, whether in traditional or modern societies, tend to find the possibility of sexual infidelity inherently more threatening than women do (Betzig 1989; Buss & Schmitt 1993). For women, more importance tends to be attached to perceived *emotional* infidelities (Buss et al. 1992). This variance is consistent with a general tendency for men to perceive and affectively experience the world in physically sexualised terms (Abbey 1982). Jealousy is also a question of schematic perception: 'Jealousy is evoked by characteristics of the rival that are believed to be important to the other sex' (Dijkstra & Buunk 1998, p. 1158). For men, this may include role schemata about dominance and penis size (Pietropinto 1986; Tood, Mackie & Dewhurst 1971). Men, and particularly younger men, as well as being generally more aggressive, are relatively competitive about their physique (Cashdan 1998). Causes and expressions of jealousy, then, vary consistently by gender (Buunk 1995).

Jealousy passes the historicity test with flying colours, since it has been recorded throughout history. In evolutionary terms, gender differences here might be traced back to prehistoric adaptation — by women seeking emotionally faithful, long-term partners; and by men with a greater interest, biologically speaking, in securing a continuance of their genes through direct heirs (Buss & Shackleford 1997). These evolutions are relatively 'distal' influences on contemporary behaviour. More proximal are the enormously diverse range of cultural norms concerning the kinds of behaviour considered inflammatory. Kissing, for example, which is considered routinely normal and expected in France, can be highly unacceptable in other societies (Buunk & Hupka 1987). Thus, the arousal of jealousy (like its expression) is as much a function of society as biology and evolution.

Attachment style, gender and aggression

Jealousy in close relationships is often related to insecurity (Ellis 1996). Accordingly, various studies have researched a possible link between jealousy within couples and attachment styles. In one of the most frequently cited studies in this area, Sharpsteen and Kirkpatrick (1997) measured both broad attachment style (in the present rather than in personal attachment history) and the ways in which people experience and express jealousy. Consistent with attachment theory (see chapter 9), people with a relatively avoidant style directed anger at 'other men' or 'other women'. Their emotional concerns were provoked by personal pride more than love. Other people whose style was relatively secure reported less 'chronic jealousy' compared with individuals whose attachment style was relatively anxious and were thus, according to the theory, over-attached.

Anxiously attached individuals have also shown a comparative tendency to use more violent imagery in projected stories about romantic relations (Woike, Osier & Candelia 1996). In Woike et al.'s study, anxiously attached individuals, both men and women, tended to write stories featuring male perpetrators of violence and aggression. This propensity suggests that among the women participants 'anxiously attached women carry with them the expectation that they will be victims in romantic relations' (1996, p. 1033). It is important to remember too, of course, that women fight back (Jacobson & Gottman 1998). For example, women frequently respond to male physical aggression with verbal counter-attacks (Bettencourt & Miller 1996). So it would be a gross oversimplification to claim simply that men are 'aggressive' and women are 'victims'.

Context is everything

Within close relationships, we have already noted gender variations between preferred male and female styles for the negotiation of conflict (see chapter 9). This raises questions about whether these broad differences also fuel aggression within couples, and where this dynamic fits within relationship development and dissolution generally. As we have already seen, conflict is part of normal everyday relations in close couples (McGonagle, Kessler & Schilling 1992). Overfamiliarity, for instance, can allow couples to say the most hurtful things to each other (Miller 1991). What is often required for relationship maintenance and satisfaction, however, is a *balance* between openness, on the one hand, and various compensatory behaviours on the other.

As an example of how this works, the characteristic role schemata that couples play out vary from minor, occasional squabbles and tiffs all the way to frequent, passionate conflicts (Gottman 1998). Yet these absolute measures do not in themselves statistically predict when a relationship is about to hit the rocks. Rather, Gottman has found over a range of studies that it is the broad degree of balance, or more precisely the ratio, between positive and negative interactions and feelings within the relationship that makes the critical difference between healthy sustainability versus dissolution and (often) divorce. Specifically, Gottman reports that if the ratio of positive-to-negative interactions and feelings drops below 5 to 1, the relationship starts to slide towards problems and even eventual dissolution (when negative acts exceed positive ones).

These statements resonate with a number of key themes explored in this book. First, managing close relationships, even relatively loving ones, requires not only feelings but cognitive effort, too. Second, we are reminded again of an emergent theme — that high-arousal relationships are not only intense to live and experience, but also relatively difficult to sustain. Third, Gottman's ratio is consistent with the negativity bias discussed in chapter 5. Fourth, and more generally, we are reminded of the importance of social context. In other words, relationship sustainability depends on a healthy balance, or 'pH balance' (Gottman 2000, p. 122), between positive and negative experiences. A squabble that is embedded within a string of positive experiences is much less noticeable and destructive than an identical squabble that has no such buffers. Thus, the same aggressive exchange can mean very much or very little, depending on the broader social context in which it occurs.

In order to manage close relationships over the long haul, Gottman derives a number of practical recommendations for managing conflict within them. These tips range from simply showing greater interest in each other through to sharing joyful experiences whenever possible.

> To maintain a balanced emotional ecology, you need to make an effort — [to] think about your spouse [or de facto partner] during the day, think about how to make a good thing even better ... The *balance* between negativity and positivity seems to be the key dynamic in what amounts to the emotional ecology of every marriage [or de facto relationship]. (Gottman 2000, pp. 123–4; emphasis added)

For those partners in passionate, highly volatile relationships, then, a high level of counterbalancing positiveness is required to make up for negativity elsewhere (2000, p. 122). This gives new meaning to the idea of 'working at' a relationship, by giving it greater salience perhaps within those relationships that are characterised by high levels of passion and limerence (see chapter 9; for a technique called 'family sculpting', reminiscent of Michelangelo effects, see Corey 1996).

Communication and negative affect reciprocity

As well as considering relationships across time, as Gottman does, the way in which conflict is managed *within the quarrel itself* is also vital (Sillars & Wilmot 1994). Communication difficulties are the most frequently cited reasons for break-ups among both heterosexual couples (Sprecher 1994) and homosexual couples (Kurdek 1991). One of the most destructive communication dynamics that these couples fall into is a tit-for-tat strategy known as **negative affect reciprocity** (Gottman 1998). As the name suggests, the defining feature of this strategy is simple and destructive, especially given what we now know about the indelibility in memory of negative information (see chapter 5). Negative affect reciprocity is an event schema in which every negative act, word or gesture is reciprocated (see Beardsley 1993). As the reader can probably appreciate, these often largely implicit strategies encourage an escalation of hurtfulness and harm, in which the most acidic of remarks can be exchanged (Messman & Canary 1998).

The critical factor in averting these often destructive dynamics is to break the cycle by, for example, taking time out to think before speaking (Yovetich & Rusbult 1994), or to forgive rather than retaliate (McCullough et al. 1997). In each case, managing aggressive communication seems to be a question of moderating affect with a little cognition and empathy (McCullough et al. 1998). Sustaining relationships therefore requires some cultivated 'cool detachment' (Messman & Canary 1998, p. 121), or medium affect (see chapters 8 and 9).

Cultures of honour

In many diverse settings around the world, aggression is part of a wider role and event schema for male behaviour in general, and for sexual mores in particular. Following a discussion of male violence, an Australian family therapist, writing about the codes of male 'mateship' in Australia (see chapter 9), remarks: 'Man the hero has been very much a part of our culture and of other cultures' (Colling 1992, p. 152). Such male heroism, as Colling and others make clear, is often closely connected to both aggression and sexuality. On the Polynesian island of Bellona, for instance, any challenges to a man's (heroic) honour must traditionally be vigorously counteracted, often through aggression, in order to defend the honour of both the man and his group (Kuschel, Takiika & 'Angiki 1999). In southern Europe, 'Italians in traditional villages have been found to condone and encourage aggression among adolescent boys as an indication of their sexual prowess and as preparation for their dominant household role' (Tomada & Schneider 1997, p. 601).

A powerful illustration of such cultures' capacity to influence modern behaviour and social affect is contained in a study conducted in the Deep South of the United States (Cohen & Nisbett 1997). This study examined employment selection biases and was based on information presented in a job application. The information included an admission by the fictitious job applicant that he had, in a moment of passion, murdered a man who had been having an affair with his fiancée and who had publicly humiliated him. In an otherwise identical application, the same applicant made a different, far less aggressive confession. He admitted to stealing a car to help pay off his debts. Shockingly, even allowing for possible public sympathy for his 'crime of passion', the man received more understanding when he admitted to acting to preserve his 'male honour' through a sexually motivated murder than when he resorted to economically motivated car theft.

These diverse examples indicate that so-called **cultures of honour** continue to pass historicity tests even in the supposedly emancipated twenty-first century. Fortunately, cults of honour are not universal, and we have much to learn from those 'developing' societies in which norms of aggression have traditionally been usurped by resilient norms favouring cooperation and non-violence, both within and between genders (see activity 1; Bonta 1997; to extend this point to more integrative systems of justice, see Goren 2001; Wolff & Braman 1999).

To sum up, there is continuity between the literature on aggression and love in close relationships. *Context* is crucial in defining when conflict becomes dysfunctional — for example whether the relationship is comparatively passionate and whether there is sufficient intimacy and commitment to buffer exchanges of negative information. *Communication* and communication interaction patterns influence whether conflict will escalate towards dissolution of the relationship. The introduction of medium affect is also crucial to breaking cycles of domestic violence. Codes of honour, although they pass the historicity test, could in principle be modified by socially learning from traditional societies in which cooperation rather than aggression is the norm. *Culture* diversity thus becomes a resource for managing aggression within relationships, as well as its spill-over into the wider community (for example against perceived romantic rivals).

AGGRESSION IN THE COMMUNITY

The influence of climate

Environmental climatic conditions, being non-human and inherently more distal than the 'up-close' ambit of romantic love, provide a radically different context in which aggression can be studied. Their sphere of influence, too, is communal rather than interpersonal: they affect relationships between relative strangers across entire groups rather than between close partners within a dyad or nuclear family. Thus, examining the influence of climate on aggression meets our conditions for historicity testing on several levels.

A vivid example of the influence of climate on mood and frustration levels is given in critical narrative 10.1. This story reflects the influence of extreme weather conditions on human behaviour not just in Australia's Far North, where the narrative is situated, but also, potentially, across the wider global community (Marsella 1998). The narrative is particularly timely at this stage of our analysis because it raises cross-contextual issues (global climate change) that are increasingly affecting us all.

CRITICAL NARRATIVE 10.1

'Mango Madness' across Australia's Top End during the pre-monsoon build-up

Attraction and romance

How do you explain to non-Territorians the suffocating heat or near 100 per cent humidity on 35C-plus days? Or the foundation that drips from your face in a mass of muddy droplets over the crisp white shirt in the stifling hot bathroom before work? And you can forget about any glamour queen aspirations to cover those red, perspiration inspired pimples before that hot date.

Domestic life

Police say during each build-up, the number of domestic arguments and the rate of disorderly behaviour skyrockets. Long-time Northern Territory police officer Gary Smith said: 'During the build-up and festive season people get irritated and a lot of people head to an air-conditioned pub to gulp down a few beers. The drastic side of that is the increase in domestic violence and suicide.'

Community relations

With unbearably hot and sticky build-up weather across the Top End, it was a week when even the most mild-mannered locals ended up blowing their stacks. The week started with news of a shock for British tourists at the five-star Seven Spirit Bay resort, who watched the chef do his block. The chef tossed a barbecue and outdoor furniture into the pool. The handful of guests at the $300 a night resort could do nothing but watch as he exploded and got it all off his chest.

Sources: Sunday Territorian, 29 November 1998, pp. 19, 22;
Northern Territory News, 21 November 1998, p. 2.
Courtesy of the Northern Territory News.

Historical studies: context

Research into the influence of weather conditions on mental functioning is not new in psychology (Bethel 1925). Heat stress, for instance, is known to affect cognitive performance through altered levels of arousal (Wyon, Andersen & Lundqvist 1979). Specifically, for example, Wyon et al. found that recognition memory peaked at 26 degrees Celsius, but decreased both below and above that performance peak. This kind of inverted U relationship is reminiscent of figures 8.3 and 9.3. More recently, the stress caused by high humidity levels has become a focus of research on mental performance and emotion in the Top End of Australia (Buchanan & Carr 1999). In both cases, climatic factors were found to influence cognitive performance through the affective arousal system, and to do so in the inverted, curvilinear pattern noted in these earlier figures.

The same pattern may apply to aggression. In one seminal study, increases in ambient temperature were associated with increases in both negative affect and aggression, with the function linking these to temperature again, following an inverted U shape (Bell & Baron 1977). In another study, outside temperatures were linked to horn-honking behaviour by frustrated motorists (see critical narrative 10.2), especially among drivers without air conditioners (Kenrick & MacFarlane 1984). As these examples indicate, most studies of climate and aggression have focused on temperature rather than humidity, despite the fact that the two often co-vary with each other and today are routinely linked in daily weather forecasts. Nor has the research fully examined other, conceivably important weather factors such as barometric pressure (Howarth & Hoffman 1984) or air ionisation (G. Tyson, personal correspondence, 2000).

The temperature–aggression hypothesis

From the focus on temperature and aggression has emerged the **temperature–aggression hypothesis**. This classically asserted that:

> hot temperatures produce increases in aggressive motives and tendencies. Hotter regions of the world yield more aggression; this is especially apparent when analyses are done within countries. Hotter years, quarters of years, seasons, months, and days all yield relatively more aggressive behaviours such as murders, rapes, assaults, riots, and wife beatings, among others. (Anderson 1989, p. 93)

Anderson and colleagues later summed up the link more concisely, stating that 'Hot weather and violence go hand in hand' (Anderson et al. 2001, p. 63). Anderson et al.'s extensive reviews have indicated that the temperature–aggression hypothesis applies best to unplanned, relatively spontaneous aggression. Figure 10.1 suggests that this will often be of a physical kind. According to these reviewers also, the temperature–aggression hypothesis is robust across different historical time periods and cultural settings, at least in the Northern Hemisphere (1989, p. 85; 2002, pp. 66–7). There is controversy over the validity and convincingness of the available empirical evidence concerning the precise shape of the function linking temperature to aggression; however, both sides appear to agree that the function is theoretically shaped like an inverted U (Anderson et al. 2001, p. 78; Cohn & Rotton 1997).

An intriguing and carefully controlled archival study conducted in South Africa during the apartheid years warns us against overgeneralising any temperature–aggression linkage. Examining civil unrest over a 24-year period, this study observed that the function relating aggression to temperature was again curvilinear. However, the peak of the curve in this particular study was located to the left of its Northern Hemisphere counterpart — that is, the curve peaked at a slightly lower temperature. One possible reason for this difference, according to Tyson and Turnbull (1990), is contextual. South Africa simply experienced less rainfall at the peak time for the riots, which enabled outdoor assemblies to take place.

Tyson and Turnbull also linked the shift in peak riot activities to student vacations and non-examination periods (students were at the forefront of political opposition to the apartheid regime). But the broader point in this study, and perhaps in critical narrative 10.1 too, is that temperature is merely one contributing factor in a configuration of other situational factors (Van de Vliert et al. 1999). In the South African context of the time, for instance, these determinants included both crowd events (see chapter 2) and socio-political factors (Reicher 1991a, 1991b). Within countries also, there is often great variation between one community and the next in aggressive behaviours such as murder (Scott 1997). Even within individuals across the life span, some periods of development — emergent adulthood for males, for example — tend to be more violent than others (Cashdan 1998). Temperature, then, is just one contextual influence on aggressive behaviour.

Contextual influences like these complicate studies on temperature and aggression. Many of the studies examining temperature and aggression have been field correlations, failing to control for co-varying factors such as levels of humidity for instance (Fine, Cohen & Crist 1960). When examined under controlled laboratory conditions, the effects of elevated temperatures on mental functioning are often relatively limited, suggesting that their effects on affect, too, might be relatively small (Chiles 1958). Other research implies that the effects of humidity, although much less studied, may be greater than those of temperature (Sharma, Pichan & Panwar 1983). Critical narrative 10.1 suggests that humidity can have profound effects on people's moods (Whitton, Kramer & Eastwood 1982). Statistically controlled research has found that humidity is the most predictive of mood variables (including aggression) from among a range of other weather variables, including temperature (Howarth & Hoffman 1984; for other linkages, for example between ionisation and irritability, see Farmer 1992 and Charry & Hawkinshire 1982).

Perhaps the most disconcerting implication of critical narrative 10.1 is that humidity, like temperature, is increasing everywhere with global warming (Marsella 1998). In response to this 'globalisation of humidification', the United States Government has recently predicted that 'the heat index', a measure of discomfort produced by combinations of heat and humidity, is likely to soar over the next half century (for more discussion of this issue and some of its practical consequences, see, for example, Buchanan & Carr 1999). Thus, previous psychological research on the effects of humidity, including its relation to arousal and aggression, is perhaps worthy of rejuvenation.

Agreeing that climate variables introduce considerable (if not exclusive) contextual influences on behaviour would pave the way for a rejuvenation of interest across a range of other environmental variables, too. Some of these variables will be relatively more community focused, such as the effects of urban crowding and noise. Existing research, for instance, suggests that uncontrollable noise, so much a feature of contemporary urban life, is likely to facilitate aggressive behaviour, once an opportunity for aggressive behaviour presents itself (Donnerstein & Wilson 1976). An illustration of other features of urban life that incite aggression, perhaps all psychosocially linked by feelings of lack of control, is given in critical narrative 10.2. This story begins to broach the burgeoning area of spill-over between workplace strains, such as e-mail overload, and life outside of work (see also, for example, Cooper 2000).

CRITICAL NARRATIVE 10.2

The strain of urban driving and the spill-over effects of work stresses

Recently, a driver had been stopped by the police and fined (quite heavily and unfairly, so he felt) for unintentional speeding, so he had resolved to adhere very closely to the officially designated speed limits, no matter how great a traffic obstruction this created (this was especially necessary given the constant presence of police patrol cars on his local roads). One particular morning on the way to work, through a long 50 kilometres per hour zone, he was overtaken by another male driver who, as he passed, honked his horn furiously and flashed a two-finger salute through his rear-view mirror.

Our normally calm and placid driver was shocked by his own immediate reaction. Suddenly he boiled over, and he began chasing the other driver, whom he finally caught up with at the next red traffic light. Pulling up alongside the other car, and quite out of character for his normally placid disposition, he found himself hurling a tirade of verbal abuse at the other driver, and an extremely aggressive mutual tirade ensued. Then, just as the two were about to get out of their cars, the lights changed and they were obliged to head in separate directions, and to begin to calm down.

This driver considered himself a quiet, mild-mannered individual, a 'slow-burner' who very rarely lost his temper. Contemplating the surprise he had become to himself (perhaps as the other driver was, too), he spent some time reviewing his current work stresses, such as e-mail overload and too many project deadlines. These strains, coupled with the noise and crowding, the constraints of the traffic rules, the constant police surveillance and a feeling that they had been unjust towards him, had been sufficient to throw him into an altered mood state. Still, it had come as a major surprise to find himself so 'out-of-character', exhibiting so much verbal (and very nearly physical) aggression. Lack of control begets lack of control, he concluded, and this was unfortunately more and more a feature of daily urban and work life.

The media and social affect: communication

In chapter 4 we examined the influence of one communication medium, television, on aggressive behaviour (Bushman & Anderson 2001). But what is the influence of media violence on mental processes? Recent research has suggested that violent media images 'prime' both violent cognitions and aggressive affect.

Viewers who watch violent (versus non-violent) videos subsequently make more aggressive associations with ambiguous homonyms (e.g. 'byte' versus 'bite'), and also have faster reaction times to aggressive words (Bushman 1998). Another study, focusing on interactive video games, found that arousal increased significantly after a violent (versus a non-violent) game was played (Fleming & Rickwood 2001). Such findings conform with the suggestion that violent media images often activate aggression-relevant schemata (see chapter 7).

E-aggression: flaming and flame wars

Research like this suggests that communication media are very capable of socially facilitating *e-motions* such as aggression. This is true also of the Internet, because e-communication channels are inherently more socially interactive, and to that extent emotionally engaging (see chapter 9, on 'particle accelerating') than their one-way (videotape and television) counterparts. Research on e-aggression has investigated aggression within socially interacting e-groups. Much of this research has focused on the passion of *flaming* and *flame wars* between angry, verbally aggressive group members. In one study involving Australian and other participants, for example, it was found that the e-presence of an identifiable in-group audience enhanced the use of inflammatory language that negatively (and, by implication, aggressively) stereotyped identifiable out-groups (Douglas & McGarty 2001).

In one of the earliest studies of flaming, groups were given the kinds of consensus tasks that in physically assembled groups normally lead to polarisation (Kiesler & Sproull 1992; for a recap on group polarisation processes, review chapter 3). One of the things that Kiesler and Sproull observed in their study was a heightened incidence of verbally hostile exchanges, such as insulting and swearing at one another, among e-groups as compared with conventional, face-to-face groups. More naturalistic studies of real e-groups have ascertained that flaming is comparatively rare on the Internet (Thompson & Ahn 1992). More specifically, e-forums that have carefully specified communication ground rules are relatively unlikely to be plagued by flame wars (Wallace 1999). Thus, group norms that are articulated into specific codes of conduct for Internet behaviour are critical modifiers of verbally expressed e-motions like aggression.

One major contributor to the eruption of flame wars is a tendency for people to resort to tit-for-tat, retaliatory remarks (Wallace 1999, p. 123). Such exchanges of negative information are reminiscent of the cycles of negative communication that are a feature of destructive quarrelling among feuding couples. A difference in the case of e-groups, however, is that familiarity-contempt is replaced by a sense of comparative anonymity, which leads to a state of 'de-individuation'. This state entails a lack of feelings of personal identity, where responsibility effectively becomes sufficiently diffused to de-inhibit latent aggressive tendencies and frustrations. As Wallace (1999) reminds us, anonymity and distancing in remote communication have their positive side, too, for example encouraging people to join various online self-help support groups so as to speak out for themselves. At the same time, however, one study of e-groups found six times as many inflammatory communications under anonymous as compared with non-anonymous conditions (Kiesler, Siegel & McGuire 1984).

Other risk factors associated with the Internet

Additional communication factors that contribute to e-aggression include the ease of sending ill-considered messages (the electronic equivalent of not thinking before opening one's mouth). Another is the absence of 'socio-cultural nuances' (Wallace 1999, p. 127) or non-verbal communication channels (see chapter 7), so that messages can 'come across' very differently from how the sender intends. Using all capitals in e-mail, for example, may often feel to the reader like SHOUTING, even when the user is simply intending to emphasise certain words or show enthusiasm. A subtler source of potential offence is in overuse of the word 'you', innocuous enough in everyday face-to-face conversation, where it is often accompanied by lots of friendly body language. In cyberspace, however, a disembodied 'you' can sound strangely confrontational ('As I told you ...' or, 'As you will know ...' etc.; note that these effects can be softened by the use of e-humour, for example).

A central issue in the examples just given is that e-mail is almost as easy to use as speech, yet the sender cannot draw on the vital non-verbal accoutrements for conveying the intended nuanced meaning. As we saw in chapter 7, non-verbal signals are just as important and informative as their verbal counterparts. One index of the surprising importance of this problem, as human end-users struggle to adapt to the pace of technological change, is provided by the number of organisations that have developed their own codes of e-mail ethics and protocol. An example of one of these is given in figure 10.2. This code of conduct contains much good advice, for example reading over messages before sending them, thinking about whether such a message is appropriate in the first place, and applying what we learned about social skills in chapter 7.

Flaming. The absence, in e-mail, of the facial expression, tone of voice, and feedback in face-to-face conversations, together with the speed of response that is possible with e-mail, can lead to 'flaming' and 'flame wars'. To avoid these, it is good practice:

(a) to allow yourself a 'cooling off' period, before responding to e-mail that annoys you, and to be temperate in your response; you should be particularly careful if your response will go to more than just the original sender, e.g. to the whole of a mailing list

(b) to make sure when appropriate, for instance by the addition of conventional symbols such as) and (, that humorous remarks could not be taken seriously

(c) to avoid *ad hominem* expressions, such as 'You must be stupid if you don't understand that ...'

Figure 10.2   E-mail ethics and good practice   ***Source:*** Information Technology Services (2001). *E-mail ethics and good practice*, www.massey.ac.nz

At base, many of the difficulties with e-mail stem from not taking the time to imagine how our messages might actually feel to their recipients. A special form of *perspective taking* is necessary when the channel is denuded of the usual 'softeners' we have in direct communication (e.g. smiles, nods and deferential gestures). As e-technology better simulates reality, codes like that in figure 10.2 may become less necessary. Until then, however:

> You may think you are a very peaceful sort of person, but the research suggests that the Internet has features that might unleash certain forms of aggressive behaviour in just about anyone. If we want to lower the hostile temperature online and stay out of the boxing ring ourselves, it is important to recognise just what those seeds are. (Wallace 1999, p. 132)

Youth suicide: culture

The broad context for suicide is often (although not always) persecution, alienation or exclusion of some kind between one group and another. These forms of felt exclusion can be socio-economic, socio-political or inter-ethnic, or any combination of these interrelated elements. The important point is that they can be deeply hurtful and frustrating, and can lead to aggressive responses. Sometimes these negative and destructive feelings are channelled outwards, into domestic violence or the kind of vicarious venting illustrated in critical narrative 10.3, or managed through other forms of aggression-diffusing humour (Austin, in press; Juni, Katz & Hamburger 1996). On other occasions, however, the barriers and frustrations may seem completely insurmountable, and factors like **humour-diffusion** will cease to work. Under such circumstances, in which the channels to social justice, social inclusion or positive identity appear hopelessly blocked, aggression may turn inwards, culminating eventually perhaps in the tragedy of suicide.

CRITICAL NARRATIVE

10.3

The Angry Little Asian Girl

The Angry Little Asian Girl is a popular Internet comic strip character who, according to Reuters, has attracted about a million people a month to her website (www.angrylittleasiangirl.com). Kim, the central character in the strip, is a demure-looking Korean American girl in pigtails who is finely tuned to, and not afraid to speak out against, the implicit paternalism and racism of others. Asked by a teacher how she was able to master English, and reacting spontaneously to the condescending attitude underlying this question, she replies without hesitation or compunction, 'I was born here, stupid. Don't you know anything about immigration? Read some real history, you stupid ignoramus."

When Hollywood executives mooted plans to turn Kim's animated life into a suitably sanitised television series, her creator, Lela Lee, refused point-blank. Sounding very like her animated protégée, she responded, 'They are really stupid. If they take out the animation and the race issue, then what am I doing?'

Source: Based on Reuters (2001), Don't mess with these little kids, *New Zealand Herald*, 20 August.

Suicide rates in Western societies in the latter part of the twentieth century tended to rise with age (Australian Psychological Society 1999a; Beautrais 2001).

An Australian Psychological Society review of suicide reports that, in the latter part of the twentieth century, rates for the 15–24 years age group began to increase markedly, for example in Canada, the United States, Australia and New Zealand 1999a. This trend was most noticeable among males. In recent years, across Western countries, there has continued to be a significant rise in the rate of male suicide during the period of emerging adulthood.

Across some countries within Asia, the female suicide rate is often closer to that for males, and this correlation has been found also among people migrating from Asia to Western countries such as Britain (Australian Psychological Society 1999a). Globally, according to the Australian Psychological Society, women may tend more than men towards thoughts of suicide and attempted suicide, but this may be partly because males tend to choose more violent, and therefore more lethal, means to demonstrate aggression against themselves (1999a). Overall, therefore, although there may be some gender differences in the ways that men and women think, feel and act with respect to suicide, it is nonetheless clear that suicide in general has become a particularly serious concern among both sexes during the emerging adulthood stage of the life span.

It is now becoming apparent that suicide rates are particularly high for emerging adults within Indigenous communities. Elevated rates for youth suicide have been found, for example, within Indigenous Australia (Reser 1999), within Māoridom in New Zealand (Coupe 2000), and across a range of Indigenous communities and societies spanning the South Pacific region (Marsella 2002). Together, these reviews identify a wide range of factors that contribute towards Indigenous suicide rates, among which are cultural and community factors, such as socio-economic disadvantage and exclusion from the global economy, marginalisation and cultural stigma. Such factors reflect forms of alienation from the wider community.

Similar conclusions may be reached for rural and remote communities. In Australia, for instance, rural residents (again, particularly young males) are significantly more at risk of suicide than their urban counterparts (Australian Psychological Society 1999b). Hence, 'whilst suicide rates in 15–24 year old men have increased in urban regions, the highest rate of increase has been in towns with populations less than 4000' (Australian Psychological Society 1999a, p. 7). Much of this increase has been attributed in the literature to the socio-economic pressures of modern farming, coupled with the disintegration of traditional rural community support systems in the wake of increased urban drift (see, for example, Ragland & Berman 1991 or Rosenblatt 1990).

The combination of factors contributing to contemporary suicide are infinitely more complex and subtle than our necessarily cursory analysis allows. Family violence, and alcohol and other drug use, for example, play significant roles in suicide ideation, attempts and realisations (for an excellent review, see Australian Psychological Society 1999a). Nor have we even begun to consider factors such as social change, land dispossession, unemployment, incarceration and contagion (see chapter 2). But what links all these factors is again the notion of *exclusion*. Dashed expectations also play an important role, especially among the young. Advertising in the so-called global community repeatedly tells kids they have a stake, but the experiences of many of them give the lie to such assurances.

... it sometimes seems that young people are engaged in a tussle between hope and cynicism, aimed at warding off disappointment ... the cultural focus on the individual 'self' has weakened social cohesion, undermined the sense of belonging, and left the self 'dangerously exposed and isolated' Eckersley 1997, p. 423). (Australian Psychological Society 1999a, pp. 18–19)

Globalisation: a core contributor to aggression

The three, extremely diverse contexts for aggression in this section — global climate change, global media-scapes in e-communication and youth suicide — share a core common concern, which can be traced to the widespread meta-influences of globalisation. According to Marsella (1998), for instance, three of the defining features of globalisation are climate change (e.g. rising humidity levels); global communications systems (e-mail); and the threat to social cohesion and identity in relatively traditional communities (as illustrated by youth suicide rates). To these could be added economic crisis and the associated escalation of depression that this can help to fuel (Kloep 1995). Thus, globalisation can be identified as one contributor to diverse manifestations and levels of aggression in the world today.

To what extent is such theme extraction helpful in theory building and practical intervention? In terms of theory, our analysis suggests that aggression in the community in the Tropics, over the Internet, and between variously alienated sectors of society, say, can only be understood through reference to its meta-context, global change. This context is a lot wider than the one social psychology has been used to using. Such an expansion necessarily enhances the importance of historicity testing. It also indicates that — in accordance with the conceptual analysis presented in chapter 1 — to understand people in all their complexity, pluralism and diversity in the twenty-first century, we will need to develop a better understanding not only of globalisation, but also of its social psychological substrates in both localisation and, particularly perhaps, glocalisation. These orientations provide direction for the remainder of this chapter.

AGGRESSION IN SPORT

One way in which significant numbers of people manage to derive a sense of community is through social identification with a local sports team. Much of this social identity, and the pride in being a member of a sporting community, stems from forms of sports competition and 'combat' against rival teams and — symbolically — against rival supporters as a group. Few would deny that aggression of one type or another in figure 10.1 is an inherent feature of those sporting competitions, and that through such means sport provides a salient way of deflecting many of the alienating, frustrating and humiliating experiences of everyday life (for a radical statement of this idea, see Dechesne et al. 2000). As we saw in chapter 3, having a common foe is often socially galvanising, since it helps to create a sense of superordinate identity between otherwise disparate factions and, indeed, individuals (see, respectively, Freud 1957 and chapter 8, on adversity-affiliation). But to what extent is aggression in sport socially beneficial, especially when the 'common foe' is actually part of the same society? Before beginning to answer this question, we need to carefully *define* and differentiate different forms of aggression in the sporting context.

Referring to figure 10.1, aggression in sport is often relatively physical and cold — for example the tactical 'professional foul' of bringing down opposing players because they have reached a defender's penalty area (Kerr 1997). But, as Kerr points out, much of the entertainment value of sport, for athletes and spectators alike, stems from other aspects of aggression listed in the table, including both psychological and hot components of aggressive behaviour and affect. These additional, and in some ways central, elements are pithily illustrated for us in critical narrative 10.4.

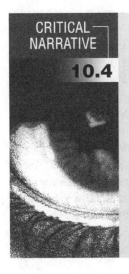

CRITICAL NARRATIVE

10.4

The heat of battle in sport

Maroons coach Paul 'Fatty' Vautin and rookie prop Tony Hearn both predicted the Maroons would 'stand up and be counted'.

'We're going to have to get stuck into them that's for sure. We've got to bash them up front', said Hearn, the North Sydney prop who will make his Origin debut.

While Vautin was not predicting any on-field violence, he acknowledged the Maroons would adopt a physical approach.

'You look at our pack and it is a physical one. It's going to be a physical game and we won't be taking a backward step', he said.

Queensland forwards Gavin Allen, Hearn, and Gillmeister were the hard men of league and they would lead from the front, Vautin said.

Source: Kerr (1997, p. 121).

How can the sentiments expressed in critical narrative 10.4 possibly be of social value? At least one previously prominent model has focused on the lay intuition that watching aggression in others, and even engaging in aggression oneself, helps to vent socially destructive urges and restore emotional equilibrium to athletes and spectators alike (Dollard et al. 1939). Sport provides a pathway, suggests this model, for transforming socially unacceptable urges into socially acceptable ones (a process otherwise known as 'sublimation'). Such essentially restorative processes start, however, according to Dollard et al., with a build-up of frustration.

Frustration-aggression build-up

The basic idea here is that everyday life is replete with barriers to reaching both our minor (everyday) and our major (life) goals. In a traffic jam, for instance, drivers are often blocked from getting to work or making an important appointment or deadline. Similarly, computer operators whose machines are just micro-seconds too slow endure, in the course of a working day, a multitude of little frustrations while they wait for the processor to do its work. All are obstacles to completing a myriad daily goals. As to broader life goals, people can feel deeply frustrated in their marriages, for instance, or they can experience the deep frustrations associated with poverty (Carr & Sloan, in press). Economic decline and crowd violence, for instance, are often interrelated (Hepworth & West 1988). In the workplace, too, **frustration effects** (Dudley & Papini 1997) are a form of over-promising and under-delivering, in which people feel deeply frustrated when promises of empowerment are not fulfilled (Cohen 1985; for a comparative link to aggression, see Weinstein 1982).

Overall, therefore, the idea that frustration and aggression are linked helps us to conceptually integrate much of the material covered in this chapter so far.

The aggression–catharsis hypothesis

Having accepted that frustration often leads to aggressive tendencies, the next step in Dollard et al.'s model proposes that *expressing* these tendencies, for example directly (by playing contact sports) or vicariously (by watching them), performs a valuable releasing function (Lorenz 1966, p. 217). Such venting is technically termed *catharsis*, after the Greek for 'purging of the effects of a pent-up emotion and repressed thoughts, by bringing them to the surface of consciousness' (Kirkpatrick 1988, p. 199). The notion of catharsis has provided the inspiration for a venting website called 'Angry.Org' (Dunderstadt 1996; see also www.angry.net).

Unfortunately, however, the hypothesised link between aggression and catharsis has not materialised consistently and reliably in the research. Both observing and participating in aggressive acts, either directly or indirectly (through words), helps to assuage and suppress anger and aggression temporarily (Bushman, Baumeister & Stack 1999). But arousal and re-aggression is all too easily reactivated, sometimes with a vengeance, the very next time a similar situation is encountered or recalled (Caprara et al. 1994). In one particularly clear example of this 'backdraught effect' in sport, attending rowdy football matches at weekends was linked to a rise in socially unruly behaviour in student halls of residence, and especially so when the home side had *won*, when aggression should theoretically have been at its lowest (Coons, Howard-Hamilton & Waryold 1995).

Such findings contradict the idea that aggression is purely cathartic, that indirect and direct participation in aggressive sports and actions are effective antidotes for the frustrations of everyday life (Russell, Arms & Bibby 1995). In fact, participants who believe in aggression–catharsis linkages are empirically more likely to feel the urge to exhibit aggression, to actually do so, and then to do so again at the first (similar) opportunity than their non-believing counterparts (Bushman et al. 1999). In retrospect, such reversals of common sense make sense. After all, if you believe that aggression is beneficial, then you are more likely to trivialise aggressive acts, as well as to believe in them as a legitimate means of managing your own levels of frustration (Bennett 1991). The practical lesson for us here, therefore, is to become more mindful about the possible links between aggression and re-aggression.

Social learning effects

Social learning theory has been presented and discussed in detail elsewhere (see chapter 7), including in the context of learning aggressive behaviour (see chapter 4; for a critique of a physiological perspective, see Book, Starzyk & Qunisey 2001). The essential idea of this theory runs counter to the idea of catharsis, namely that we learn by observation of others' behaviour, and especially by observing that behaviour's consequences (Bandura 1973). In sporting contexts, unfortunately, aggression is frequently seen to pay, with the more 'physical' players winning more often than their comparatively passive counterparts (Kerr 1997): 'Rewards for such actions are significant, including praise and recognition from team-mates, coaches, fans, and media personnel, and punishment is either non-significant or minimal'

(Stephens 1998, p. 278; for a fuller review of the scope of these influences extending to television audiences, see Thirer 1992; see also Bushman & Anderson 2001). Indeed, 'outside of wartime, sport is perhaps the only setting in which acts of inter-personal aggression are not only tolerated but enthusiastically applauded by large segments in society' (Russell 1993, p. 181). Thus, in contact sports, social learning theory negatively predicts an exact reversal of aggression–catharsis — that aggression will beget aggression, not reduce it.

Social learning theory is far from being all bad news for sport, however, for theoretically it offers the opportunity to manage aggression better, rather than only temporarily venting the frustrations of everyday life, like some social 'opiate of the people'. If athletes and spectators can socially learn to be overly aggressive rather than aggressively assertive (see chapter 7), then they can also learn to reverse this pattern, for example if we were to change the rules so that overly aggressive actions on the field were always clearly (observably) *punished*. This is presumably why the International Society of Sport Psychology (ISSP) has taken a stand on aggression and violence in sport, and has produced a series of recommendations on its management (Tenenbaum et al. 1997, especially Recommendation 1).

As Kerr (1999) points out, for instance, after Australian rugby league changed its rules so that excessive violence was consistently and clearly punished, not only did the game itself become 'de-brutalised', but it was also, in the end, better attended (p. 87). Prototype theory (see chapter 9) suggests that most players, officials and spectators will know when aggressive behaviour on the field is excessive. According to social learning theory, introducing a clear set of rules and punishments for over-aggressive infractions helps athletes and spectators alike to both draw the line and keep it in place. The onus for managing aggression, and for being a good role model, is thus as much on the system as on the athletes themselves.

Sporting competitions, in which one team or individual attempts to block the opposition from winning, inherently involve provocation and frustration (Stephens 1998). In one study of spectators' behaviour after watching a football game, hostility levels not only went up after they had observed the game, but did so regardless of whether their team won *or* lost (Goldstein & Arms 1971). These findings indicate ongoing relevance, in sporting contexts, for the dynamics of both observational learning and frustration-aggression. This shared relevance is likely to be especially true when 'winning at all costs' and finding some sort of positively distinctive social identity are both increasingly salient concerns for every stakeholder in the sporting sector (Tenenbaum et al. 1997, p. 4).

The linkages between sport and aggression are undoubtedly facilitated by alcohol intoxication. In Coons et al. (1995), for instance, more than half of the post-game violations of codes of conduct in the student halls of residence were alcohol-related (p. 70). Another study examined the link between actually participating in competitions themselves and subsequent aggression; in this context even relatively non-aggressive participants became progressively more aggressive towards their opponent, once they had also consumed alcohol (Pihl, Lau & Assaad 1997). Alcohol, it seems, lowers the threshold for frustration. As well, many of these effects, like their 'dry' counterparts, are fuelled by social observation of how others in the same situation are behaving — that is, social learning processes are involved, too (Schachter & Singer 1962). Moreover, these two effects are not confined to sporting events. Cycles of family violence and community violence, for instance, are also often facilitated by alcohol (Marsella 2002). Thus, alcohol generally fuels both frustration-aggression and observational learning.

Localisation: the efficacy of punishment

We have already noted evidence that introducing clear rules about appropriately and inappropriately aggressive behaviour might reduce antisocial aggression both on and off the field. Yet, of course, punishments themselves, according to our opening definition of aggression, are also instances of aggression. This means, according to the major theories presented above, that punishments themselves will occasionally backfire and promote aggression. This will be especially so if they simply become models of aggression and purveyors of frustration in their own right. So the real question arising from this analysis is, Can we predetermine when punishment is liable to have unintended local backlashes, so we can avoid that mistake?

The efficacy of punishment and the threat of punishment depend on the social context in which it is administered (Australian Psychological Society 2001). Trying to achieve deterrence by, for example, increasing penalties for on-field transgressions runs a clear risk of precipitating a local backlash, and increased aggression, if the rules and procedures themselves are perceived to be too heavy-handed by local standards (Sherman 1993). In such settings, even if punishment does manage to suppress hostility, the aggression is liable to surface again soon after unless the surveillance can be applied continuously (see chapter 1, on minimal constraint; also chapter 3, on mediation).

One way of using punishment effectively to prevent rather than promote aggression is if the punishment system itself is perceived as fair (Tyler 1990). Much of what we know about how to achieve perceived fairness derives from organisational social psychology, and studies of social justice and aggression at work.

AGGRESSION IN THE WORKPLACE

Emotion in the workplace is today a major issue for organisational psychologists (Muchinsky 2000). Aggression is at the forefront of this concern because of increases in negative emotions such as workplace anger, jealousy and envy (Allcorn 1994). A leading scholar of aggression in the workplace, Robert Baron, has pinpointed one ubiquitous cause of workplace aggression, namely 'perceived unfairness' (Baron & Byrne 2000, p. 466). The rest of this chapter focuses on this domain, which is known by the technical term 'organisational justice' (Greenberg 1987). Various systems of organisational justice have been extensively studied in both New Zealand (e.g. Singer 1993) and Australia (Kabanoff 1997).

Aggression in the workplace spans the full gamut of subtle and not-so-subtle reactions depicted in figure 10.1. These range from (1) the jealous rage of down-sized employees who feel so deeply betrayed that they are led to violently assault other staff members, to (2) the emotional abuse of a sarcastic and bullying supervisor, to (3) the tactical put-down of rival colleagues, to (4) the cold-blooded, long-term character assassination of a political rival within an organisation. Examining aggression in the workplace, therefore, may be useful for identifying any common themes across the topic of aggression as a whole.

As shown in table 10.1, organisational justice as currently conceived may be divided into two main types, *procedural* and *declarative*, each of which has several sub-types (for a classic review, see Greenberg 1987).

Table 10.1 Organisational justice and workplace aggression

TYPE OF JUSTICE	SUB-TYPE	EXEMPLAR
Procedural	Voice	'Who *designed* this system, anyway?'
	Probity	'We all know why *he* got promoted!'
Declarative	Equity	'He didn't *deserve* that overseas trip!'
	Egality	'Who does he think he is?!'
	Need	'Minorities need all the help they can get.'

Source: Extracted and adapted from Greenberg (1987) and Muchinsky (2000).

Procedural justice

From table 10.1, there are two major aspects to this particular form of organisational justice (Folger & Greenberg 1985). First, employees may be concerned about the extent to which they are accorded 'voice' in organisational decision making, with greater voice being linked to stronger feelings that organisational justice has been honoured (Greenberg 1987). Clearly, however, this concept is culture-bound. In some relatively power distant organisational cultures, for example, employees may not *want* to be 'given voice' (Marrow 1964). Workers may also modify their expectations about voice depending on the particular market context in which their employing organisation is operating, with stormy external climates being associated with reduced expectations about voice from within the internal 'weather system' (Dunphy & Stace 1993). Thus, the concept of voice does not readily pass the historicity test (van den Bos & Spruijt 2002).

A second major facet of procedural justice is a belief that the agreed-upon rules have been administered properly (*probity*). These rules of engagement can be either explicit, as in a formal employment contract, or implicit, in the form of a 'psychological contract' (Rousseau 1995). The latter is an event and role schema (see chapter 7) that contains perceived reciprocal obligations between employer and employee, and so bears directly on the social exchanges of giving and receiving respect, or face (Ting-Toomey 1988). For example, employment itself can be perceived as a kind of implicit promise that loyalty and organisational citizenship will be rewarded with job security and/or nurturance (Rousseau & Parks 1993). If, in the event of an economic crisis for the firm, a worker is instead made redundant, and so humiliated by the employer (in perception), then the psychosocial contract has been breached. To that extent, feelings of betrayal, anger and aggressive revenge might be expected (see chapter 1, on the reciprocity norm). Some readers will be able to relate to this concept of procedural justice. As another example, they may have witnessed the promotion of somebody who perhaps did not deserve the elevation, but who secured it through breaches of the formal rules of promotion and thus, too, the psychological contract.

Among the most common reactions to violations of the psychological contract are retaliatory behaviours such as organisational theft, sabotage and threats. Greenberg (1990), for instance, reports on what often happens during organisational cost-cutting. In one plant of a cost-cutting company, pay cuts implemented in lieu of downsizing were preceded by a respectful (and face-saving) explanation of why the company was obliged to temporarily do this (i.e. preserving jobs while meeting economic necessities). In another plant within the same company, however, no such explanation was given, and there were subsequently significant increases in the rate of organisational theft. In other studies, when the shocks to people have been even more severe, reactions have been more aggressive, including direct physical aggression and violence (Johnson & Indvik 1994).

Equity theory (see chapter 3) proposes that people seek balance between their own outcomes-for-inputs and the outcomes-for-inputs of a salient referent individual or group, such as colleagues, supervisors or managers. Among the most common reactions to perceived imbalance by under-reward (Dulebohn 1997), as in a violation of the psychological contract perhaps, is to reduce one's own inputs (as in progressive withdrawal) or to retaliate by reducing the other's outcomes, for example by hurting them physically or psychologically, or by organisational theft.

Equity theory thus accounts for the group findings above. The theory also accommodates individual differences in equity sensitivity (Kickul & Lester 2001) and possibly related factors such as inflated self-esteem, or narcissism (Baumeister, Bushman & Campbell 2000). Such flexibility might in theory be considered a strength because of its capacity to reflect the personal meanings of social injustices.

Distributive justice

Issues of procedural justice are largely about processes rather than outcomes. Yet the latter, from table 10.1, have a social psychological basis, too. In fact, once we extend our analysis of organisational justice to the outcomes domain and what is termed distributive justice, we see that equity, and equity theory, are not the only considerations in attempting to explain workplace aggression. There are at least three basic principles on which employees can base their feelings about whether a particular action is just or unjust, namely equity, egality and need. A striking example of the difference between procedural and distributive justice is the 'land reform' crisis in Zimbabwe. Some people may feel that the concept of land reform would be distributively just (a fair outcome), but that the procedures being used to implement this change are unnecessarily harsh and *un*just (an unfair process).

Valuing equity

Equity theory, as we have seen, proposes that people will assess the reward they receive for the input they give, and socially compare that with the level of reward-for-input garnered by a salient comparison other, whether employee or employer. Thus, if a colleague who is perceived to have worked less hard than self is rewarded with a promotion to a higher rank and salary compared with self (or self's social group), then that would be experienced as socially unjust. This could then precipitate, for example, organisational envy and related forms of workplace aggression.

Valuing egality

In contrast to equity, valuing *egality* (strict equality) means distributing resources on the basis of equal voice. According to this view, each of us, regardless of heredity or opportunity, brings different individual qualities to the workplace, but these are all founded on our common humanity. It therefore behoves the system to recognise everybody's unique talents equally. Under circumstances in which resources are scarce, an egalitarian might allocate these resources by random draw, and in that spirit might respond to equity-based promotion decisions with, 'Who does he think he is!' (Afro-centric Alliance 1998).

Valuing need

This outlook asserts the view that the field sometimes needs to be tilted deliberately in order to preserve fair and just outcomes for all. For example, historically oppressed minorities may *need* the protection of positive discrimination and affirmative action policies (voice) to help correct the inherent disadvantages these minorities start out with (outcomes); over-reward in such circumstances may be viewed as socially just (Perry 1993). Similarly, when bonuses and other organisational opportunities become available to staff, size of dependent family and other specific needs (e.g. to support an extended family) become salient concerns ('But she *needs* the job more than the others do. She's got five kids plus a mortgage to support!').

Context and culture

As this example suggests, preferences for the three forms of distributive justice tend to shift with context and culture. It is sometimes reported, for instance, that relatively collectivistic societies are more prone to advocate egality and need than are relatively individualistic groups (Hui, Triandis & Yee 1991). The latter groups may tend to favour equity because of its comparative concern with self (Berman, Murphy-Berman & Singh 1985). In workplace scenarios, these participants are relatively likely to think that interpersonal equity is a fair system of distributing resources (e.g. Kashima et al. 1988). Where cultural norms like mateship place a certain value on egalitarianism, for example in Australia and New Zealand, students have also been found to be relatively more egalitarian than their counterparts in the United States (Mann 1988; Shubik 1986). Similar comparatively egalitarian tendencies have been noted among the Australian general public regarding idealised income distributions (Headay 1991).

It should always be remembered that these differences reflect central tendencies only and almost always mask a great deal of cross-cultural overlap. Many individuals in these studies actually preferred a principle for distributing resources *other* than the most 'popular' preference in their particular group. Also, all of us to some extent make judgements in *different* modes, depending on the prevailing contextual factors. A striking illustration of this factor is whether an intra-group or inter-group social context applies. For example, when faced with inter-group circumstances, relative collectivists will often switch from relatively egalitarian norms to decisions based, more than among their relatively individualistic counterparts, on *equity* (Leung & Bond 1984). Thus, when the recipient of rewards belongs to an out-group, notions of what is and is not unfair (and so conducive or not to aggression) often shift markedly (Platow et al. 1995; for a link between these ideas and social identity theory in a New Zealand setting, see Platow et al. 1997).

The point of all this is that workplace aggression is often predictable and preventable, once we consider the predominant beliefs about justice, and other contextual issues, such as whether relations are inter-individual or inter-group at the time. Within relatively collectivistic workplace teams, for instance, individualistic pay-for-performance schemes and individual contracts, founded on a belief in relative individualism and the principle of equity rather than on equality or need, will probably cause considerable rancour (Wageman 1997). In a classic study in organisational psychology, such feelings translated into *binging*, when overproductive workers were punched on the arms by watchful co-workers (Muchinksy 1999, p. 254). Between groups within the same setting, however — say, between departments or teams within the same organisation — equity may provoke much less aggression compared with the other major systems of distribution, provided the administrative procedures (i.e. procedural justice) is properly respected. Beliefs in organisational justice, therefore, may be a productive way of strategising our thinking about workplace aggression, primarily because they address the deeper kinds of frustration that people today bring to, or are concerned with in, their work.

Motivational gravity

As we learned in chapter 3, one of the distinguishing features of organisations is that they tend to have formal hierarchical power structures. These power structures, in turn, create diverse channels through which influence and aggression can flow. A prime example of this is negative motivational gravity, which we learned in figure 3.5 can assume two primary forms, *push-down* and *pull-down*.

The push-down

The push-down is often motivated by the growing sense of job insecurity that accompanies the liberalisation and internationalisation of trade markets (Cooper 2000; Kao & Ng 1997). Most of the research on this topic has been done in Scandinavia, where the vividly apt term *mobbing* has been coined to denote workplace bullying (Einharsen 2000). Such tendencies are widely recognised to have deleterious effects on employees (Lee 2000) and organisations alike (Vartia 2001). Workplace mobbing has been found in organisational settings as diverse as hospitals (Quine 2001) and universities (Rayner 1997), and in the private sector (Einharsen et al. 1996). Mobbing usually filters from the top down (Adams 1997), setting in train socially destructive modelling effects (Schein 1991; see chapter 4). It is also frequently preceded by the frustrations of being abused in early career (Bassman & London 1993). Thus, mobbing sometimes represents a convenient and self-serving form of revenge ('I myself had to run the gauntlet and managed to survive to be where I am, so why shouldn't *they* pay the same price!').

Such sentiments enable us to link push-down mobbing with equity. Having been a victim of bullying detracts from one's own outcomes-for-input ratio, which is compared with the ratios of junior employees. Viewed like this, jealously insecure, equity-sensitive managers will then try to reduce the outcome-for-input ratios of others by making everyday or long-term working life tough for them, too. The push-down has also been linked to feelings of frustration coupled with expressive, equity-restoring aggression (Hammock et al. 1990; Sulthana 1987).

The pull-down

Some of the clearest illustrations of justice at work can be found in critical narrative 1.3, in which the flexing of 'tall poppy syndrome' saw deliberate attempts made to bring 'unjustly' promoted supervisors back to earth. What the text in this narrative does not report is that the tall poppy syndrome in this workplace generalised to more direct expressions of aggressive behaviour outside of the workplace, for example the sabotage of supervisors' cars and bikes. A range of similarly aggressive tendencies are indicated in the review of pull-down effects compiled by Carr and MacLachlan (1997). Taken together, these examples span an incredibly diverse range of cultures and contexts, and to this extent the pull-down passes a historicity test.

Underlying these examples are the concepts of perceived injustice and justice restoration. Examples include the perception of violations of the psychological contract in critical narrative 1.3 (disrespecting the norm of egality within the group and equity between workers and superiors, as well as violations of procedural justice in the way promotions were decided); and the traditional East African adage *Akafuna Akhale Ndani!* ('Who does he think he is!'). Such exclamations (which we have probably all heard and indeed made ourselves) clearly reflect feelings of anger and betrayal (in Malaŵi the word is *Mbwezeni!*, or 'Traitor!'). Thus, in the domain of gravitational pull-down, like its counterpart push-down, workplace aggression, whether direct or indirect, physical or psychological, is frequently an issue of perceived injustice (see figure 10.1).

Spill-over effects

What happens in the workplace affects, and is influenced by, what happens in other social contexts. As one leading author recently wrote, 'Violence in the workplace is a complex phenomenon. Like drug use in the workplace, it spills over into other areas traditionally removed from I/O [industrial/organisational] psychology' (Muchinsky 2000, p. 298). It has been found, for instance, that frequency of workplace layoffs and job insecurity generally influence the levels of violence in a community (Catalano, Novaco & McConnell 1997; see also Smith 1997, on crossover between workplaces and schools). If this is so, spill-over also flows in both directions, since many bullying managers reportedly enact a cycle of abuse that runs not only through their own early career, but also through their domestic relationships and, before that, personal attachment history (Bassman & London 1993).

As this idea of spill-over suggests, the really interesting property of perceived justice and injustice is that they seem to apply just as readily outside of the workplace as within it. One can also imagine, for instance, how feelings of injustice (e.g. interpersonal inequity) may often pervade the lives of couples whose relationships are very unhappy (Sprecher & Schwartz 1994), and family relations generally (Fijneman, Willemsen & Poortinga 1996). In the community, too, we have seen how riots and other forms of social protest are often linked to deep-seated feelings of social injustice and inequity. Finally, principles of justice may apply also to instances of sporting aggression (Greenberg, Melvin & Lehman 1985). For example, perceptions of unfair decision making by umpires and referees often provoke considerable aggression in players and spectators alike (Tenenbaum et al. 1997).

Thus, principles of perceived justice apply not only to aggression in the workplace, but also to aggression across a diverse range of social contexts. In fact, concepts of procedural and distributive justice have great potential for constructing an integrated, culturally and contextually respectful model of human aggression. This model would draw us away from some of the more trivial forms of aggression, such as relatively minor everyday irritations, and instead nudge our inquiries towards some of the 'bigger' issues facing the global community and humanity today (Marsella 1998).

Managing glocal influences

As we have defined it in this book (see chapter 1), glocalisation is the continuing and dynamic interaction between global pressures and local backlashes, as they are played out at the social psychological level. When, for example, globalisation renders supervisors and middle managers increasingly job insecure, so that they react by promoting their own clan and acolytes, their push-down reactions can be viewed as a product of global meeting local (Traynor & Watts 1992). Similarly, where global norms favouring inter-individual equity clash with the radically egalitarian ethos of mateship in a work team, pull-down occurs. In critical narrative 1.3, tall poppy syndrome is the product of a struggle between a cultural influence and a local one. Interactions such as these are, fundamentally, interactions between one system of justice beliefs and another. Push-down and pull-down are thus examples of glocalisation, which now begs a complex but hugely relevant and fascinating question: How do perceptions of justice mesh with this wider process?

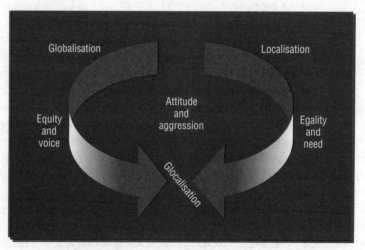

Figure 10.3 Globalisation, localisation and glocalisation

From figure 10.3, we can envisage globalisation as one form of cultural influence (e.g. the inherent individualism of equity and voice) that is in danger of overriding another (e.g. traditions of egality and need). When local systems of belief are threatened by the culture of globalisation, they kick back with a vigorous reassertion of their traditional norms. Such dynamics also spill over into local attitudes, for example towards 'globalising' managerial practices like pay-for-performance and merit-based pay. In the kind of model presented in figure 10.3, when the attitudes that ensue are highly negative, the result is workplace aggression.

Although the processes depicted schematically in figure 10.3 refer to workplaces, they could also be applied to aggression and aggressive acts in other social contexts. No doubt dynamics not unlike those depicted in the figure are unfolding within many family settings, as the growing influence of norms promoting gender equity and voice interact with local traditions that stress more collectivistic practices such as arranged marriages and power distance. As has already been noted, these pressures and counter-pressures create psychosocial pressures for emerging adults sufficient to increase their risk of suicide. Certain forms of fundamentalism, too, might be seen as predictable backlashes to perceived systems of distributive justice that foster 'hourglass economies' dividing rich and poor (Carr & Sloan, in press). In sport, the global norm of 'winning at all costs' (Tenenbaum et al. 1997, p. 4), which promotes cheating and doping (see chapter 2), provokes outrage among traditionalists who value 'the level field'. In fact, whenever we hear traditionalists resisting changes to sporting practice, such as dirty or over-aggressive play, we are witness to the dynamics of glocalisation.

There are at least three generic ways of managing aggression by managing perceptions of injustice. Each of these tactics, which again apply both to the workplace and beyond in wider society, focuses on a different stage of the relationship between aggressor and 'aggressed'.

Accountability

Accountability focuses on the *prevention* of aggression in the first place. When clear-cut restraints against aggression are already in place — for example personnel policies (with clear penalties for workplace abuse) that are specified during induction or negotiated with a workforce — the risks that such abuse will take place are generally reduced (Bassman & London 1993). There is a lot more to this generalisation than meets the eye. It is one of the great lessons of organisational psychology, not only in the area of workplace aggression, that advanced structure helps to prevent 'bad blood' and rancour later. This point applies to properly structured job descriptions to recruit against; to structured selection interviews; to realistic job previews so that employees are not over-promised and then under-delivered in the job itself; to structured discipline processes and performance appraisal systems; and to frank prior explanation of why salary savings have become necessary (Aamodt 1999; Greenberg 1990).

The truism here is that knowing the ground rules *before* entering into any kind of contractual arrangement takes much of the 'heat' out of the inevitable workplace frustrations and disappointments when they start to occur later. One major reason for this is that the employees feel they have entered into a psychological as well as an actual contract with the employer, and that, provided the agreed-upon procedures are adhered to, perceived injustices are less likely to occur in the first place.

Applications to contexts outside of the workplace

In sport, we learned that much of the excessive and antisocial aggression that plagued Australian rugby during the 1980s was significantly reduced after the introduction of clearer and firmer ground rules to govern on-field conduct. Beyond this, the point has been argued that providing structure in society is generally a major preventer of aggression in communities (Scott 1997). On a more specific level, we also learned how Internet forums that have clear rules and expectations about communication etiquette are much less likely to be later torn apart by flame wars. Even in close personal relationships, probably the least 'contractual' of all kinds of alliances, the trend towards mechanisms such as pre-nuptial agreements may be helping to reduce later acrimony and aggression expressed through litigation and other forms of retributive justice (provided, of course, that the couples can stomach them in the first place).

Thus, across each of the four radically different contexts we have considered in this chapter, the idea of specifying contractual expectations and penalties for breaching them may be usefully applied. This extended applicability is partly why the Australian Psychological Society strongly advises all practising psychologists to draw up pre–psychological service contracts with all their clients (Pryor 1997). This extended applicability is also why unit and assessment outlines are particularly important for preventing student–lecturer acrimony, particularly when students are paying for their education. The overall purpose of establishing such systems beforehand — to prevent future acrimony and associated aggression — rests on the principle of enhancing stakeholder *accountability*.

Adversity-affiliation

In chapter 3 we learned how a common obstacle or frustration can act to unite otherwise conflicting groups. In chapter 8 we learned how a similar principle could be applied to bring individuals together. The danger in each case, of course, is that the common obstacles, or foes, constitute another group or individual rather than a non-human entity, so that the net effect of competition with them will in the long run be negative. Also, for adversity-affiliation to work, there has to be a series of successfully attained superordinate goals. Thus, the common foe of economic hardship, for example within a couple, is likely to provide a spur to aggression rather than an antidote to it, because in most cases real-world financial obstacles are not easily surmounted.

To minimise the risks of obstacles leading to failure and recriminations rather than affiliation, relationship counselling might include, for instance, realistic goal-setting programs (Tsoi-Hoshman 1976). Within communities, development projects might include a series of relatively modest incremental improvements rather than a single great (and unsustainable) leap (MacLachlan 1996a; see also Sherif's Robber's Cave study in chapter 3). In sport, in which the opposition is normally human, non-human superordinate goals can be created in the training context — for example outward bound and wilderness experiences. In organisational settings, the introduction of progressively more difficult but attainable team goals and rewards can be an effective way to harmonise group relationships (Wageman 1997).

Resistant situations: 'sick systems'

The interventions suggested so far have all been relatively structural and planned. They have each assumed a certain degree of *control* over the workplace itself. Often, however, we find ourselves in situations that are, or appear to be, past the point of repair, and so beyond preventive team-based interventions. In his seminal paper on workplace envy, therefore, Bedeian (1995) offers a series of practical recommendations for individual survival in such adverse circumstances. These include, for example, keeping one's head down and never bragging about achievements, and 'quiet achievement' generally.

It might be argued that Bedeian's approach is analogous to urging women not to wear attractive clothes because they might invite sexual aggression (P. Marra, personal correspondence, 2001). Would it not be better to try to change the *system*? Although such objections often hold merit, occasionally the system itself is beyond repair. A vivid example of this systemic decay is provided in critical narrative 10.5, which describes a corrupted workplace in which the very system that was designed to protect workers from psychological violence had actually become a tactical weapon for promulgating it! In such cases, where psychological violence has become institutionalised, Bedeian's advice to 'Exit from "sick systems" ' (1995, p. 55) is perhaps well considered.

CRITICAL NARRATIVE

10.5

A dysfunctional workplace

The sociology lecturer had joined her new department after having been led to believe, during an upbeat recruitment and selection process, that the university and the department were in 'expansion mode'. All that was now required, they told her, was a 'quiet achiever' who would work collegially with colleagues to expand and develop the offerings to more and more students. But from the moment of arriving in this new job, she had been dismayed to discover that the culture of the workplace belied every initial expectation.

In this department, school and even across much of the faculty as a whole, academic staff often 'survived' in their jobs by forming factional allegiances with other co-workers, senior members of academic and administrative staff, and even students. The culture was very power distant, and the only way 'up' rather than 'out' was to find senior patrons, who would crush their acolyte subordinates' rivals in exchange for unquestioning upward loyalty. Sometimes, this downward protection involved taking a favoured complainant's side in formal grievances, which were frequently laid as tactical devices to dislodge colleagues who were perceived to be a job or career threat. This insecurity was not altogether unrealistic, as the university claimed to be in financial jeopardy, and had recently stood down a number of academic employees.

In the three years that this sociology lecturer managed to stay in her job, there was never a time without some cloud of aspersions and acrimony, through formal complaints of one kind or another, hanging over her head. At the same time, she steadfastly refused to descend to 'keeping notes' on every social interaction with colleagues (such notes were widely used as 'evidence' in formal grievance cases), in the vain hope that the initial promise of a collegial work environment might one day 'come good'. But her moral stand seemed only to provoke more hostility and aggression from the system, until eventually [see chapter 8, on the cycle of attraction–selection–attrition], the lecturer left this imbroglio of corruption and nepotism for a safer work environment. In fact, of the seven academic staff members in the department when this lecturer first arrived, she was, after just three years, *the only one left*.

Source: Extracted and adapted from Bolitho & Carr (2002).

SUMMARY

One of the primary precipitators of aggression is the frustration of loss of control, whether over the cumulative trivia of everyday life or the profound disappointments of life as a whole. Among the most significant of these frustrations are feelings of injustice and loss of face as they relate to corrupted procedures or unfair allocations of limited resources. What counts as fair or unfair is often defined locally, according to an alternative version of how to distribute resources in a fair and respectful manner. When these models are perceived to have been violated, as they frequently are across home, community, sporting and workplace settings, potential antidotes to consequent aggression include (1) articulating clearer codes of conduct and penalties for infractions within the relationship, (2) identifying obstacles and goals that are shared within a group, and (3) exercising individual rights to exit from, rather than remain in, systems that are morally bankrupt.

KEY TERMS

Cultures of honour. Belief systems, often male-oriented, in which honour, sexual pride and aggression form an inter-related triangle. Affronts to male sexuality are affronts to male pride, which must be defended with appropriate levels of aggression against the offender. (p. 365)

Frustration effect. When people learn to expect rewards in a given situation, and those rewards are not subsequently delivered, negative emotions, such as feelings of betrayal, frustration and aggression, will often result. Frustration effects occur as a result of being over-promised and under-delivered. (p. 375)

Humour-diffusion. The hypothesis that humour helps to diffuse frustration and aggression, and may even play a role in preventing severe forms of self-harm such as suicide (p. 372)

Negative affect reciprocity. A pattern of tit-for-tat responses, in which negative communications are reciprocated with more of the same. The result is often spiralling conflict and emotional hurt, both within couples and within other types of close and otherwise loving relationships. (p. 364)

Temperature-aggression hypothesis. The hypothesis that, all else being equal, parts of the world with hotter climates will yield more aggressive behaviour. Theoretically, there is a point beyond which aggression will start to drop, to form an inverted U. (p. 367)

REVIEW QUESTIONS

What are the principal causes of aggression in the following?
1. Close relationships
2. Local communities
3. Sporting spectacles
4. Workplace settings

Discuss the following social issues.

1. Once Internet communication simulates real-life communication more accurately, for example through visual and sonic hook-ups in real time, flaming and flame wars will become things of the past.

2. Humidity and other frustrating conditions of life today are no excuse for aggressive behaviour towards others.

3. Sport is the opiate of the people.

4. Aggression in the workplace is an inevitable consequence of globalisation.

5. Perceptions of injustice are at the core of all aggression.

ACTIVITIES

1. Read Lepowsky (1999). Form into groups and formulate interpretations and responses to the arguments and data presented in the paper. Share these responses in a plenary session at the end of the tutorial period.

2. Compose a list of critical incidents from the class members' own experiences of flaming on the Internet, both negative (in which aggression escalated out of control) and positive (in which flaming was either prevented or managed). How might one type of incident inform the other?

3. Debate the merits and demerits of sport in a global society.

4. Play a series of prisoner's dilemma games, both as individuals and as groups. What do such exercises remind you of in the chapter, and to what extent do such exercises help to modify zero-sum game mentalities of the kind outlined in chapter 2?

5. Search your local newspapers for recent examples of aggression from any of the domains we have considered in the chapter, or indeed a new one. Relate the key incidents in the stories to the theoretical and research elements reviewed in the chapter. How good is the fit, and how useful is the psychology?

ADDITIONAL READING

On violence in close relationships: see both Belsky (1993) and Gottman (2000).
On community concerns: read Anderson and colleagues' reviews on temperature-aggression.
On sporting aggression: an engaging analysis is provided by Kerr (1997, 1999).
On aggression in the workplace: see Bedeian (1995), and Bassman and London (1993). This topic is still very under-researched, but this will probably change in the near future.

For further reading on the topics discussed in this chapter, consult the online resources linked to the Wiley website (http://www.johnwiley.com.au/highered/socialpsych).

SYNTHESIS

CHAPTER 11
Revision

11

REVISION

After reading this chapter, you should be able to:

- connect the influence of social context to an emergent principle of minimising constraint
- link the influence of communication to an emergent principle of maximising cognition
- relate the influences of culture to an emergent principle of moderating (or 'toning') affect for peak performance in social interactions
- cement the connections between these influences and principles using the concepts of globalisation, localisation and glocalisation.

OVERVIEW

In the dictionary sense, to *revise* means to examine and correct; to make a new improved version; to study anew; to look at again (Kirkpatrick 1983, p. 1107). This chapter achieves these goals by developing a reflective technique called *theory weaving*. Inspired by the concept of *theory knitting* (Kalmar & Sternberg 1988), theory weaving entails maximising the number of connections between theories, models and processes. More specifically, this approach marries our three main influence *themes*, context, communication and culture, to the scientific *principles* of minimal constraint, maximal cognition and medium affect. The chapter presents a unified schema for the book that incorporates globalisation, localisation and glocalisation. Finally, we reflect on the scope for glocalisation to enhance our perspective-taking life skills and so raise mindfulness about influence processes in general.

EMERGENT PRINCIPLES

This book began with an *a priori* schema, based on classical social psychology, identifying three of the key social influence domains in everyday life — context, communication and culture. In addition to these core considerations, three emergent principles are proposed in the topics covered. Each of these principles relates to making influence sustainable rather than fleeting. Briefly, they consist of *minimising constraint* (to avoid backlashes; part 1), *maximising cognition* (to enhance commitment to change; part 2) and *moderating social affect* (i.e. 'toning' it for sustained peak performance; part 3). This chapter 'adds value' to that schema by teasing apart more of its overall pattern and so improving both its resolution and its memorability.

Theory knitting

As the book has developed, the range of social influence processes discussed in the text has grown. Because of the discipline's extraordinary diversity, the critical reader may have begun to feel at times that social psychology is impossible to conceptualise as a coherent gestalt. For this reason, as the book has progressed, the text has introduced more and more explicitly the possibility of bringing together the diverse elements of social psychology in coherent (and thus memorable) patterns. In chapter 9, for instance, we focused on highlighting the consistencies and complementarities between triangular and attachment models of love (pp. 341–42). In chapter 10 we applied historicity testing to forge links between the various causes and explanations of aggression, thereby deriving useful principles for its management (p. 386).

It is critical to point out here that the pattern outlined below is not the only possible 'bookend' we might have used, nor does it pretend to be (see 'Ethos and direction', p. xii). As Sherif and Festinger have pointed out (chapter 1, p. 13), reality is socially constructed, and the varieties of social psychology are no exception to this principle. With a subject area as vast, complex and fluid as social psychology, there are virtually unlimited ways of cutting the conceptual cake. As we learned in chapter 7, every schema leaves something out; that is the price of economy. What follows, therefore, is just one, idiosyncratic approach that should be judged on its capacity to help you, the reader, make sense of the discipline, form your own views and pick mine apart, as did the reviewer quoted below.

> If I were to pick the most basic principles of social psychology, I might make some different choices. I would certainly pick the important role of categorisation and in-group/out-group distinctions. I would also have 'adapting to the social context' high on the list, and perhaps the importance of making relative rather than absolute social judgements. The automatic/controlled distinction, and the fact that automatic processing has more effect than you think, might also get a slot. Perhaps you could argue that this schema does not explain everything, and I might agree. The point is that it is over-Promethean to try to crush all current knowledge in social psychology into a neat schema that uses only a limited set of principles. (Anonymous peer reviewer, 2001)

I agree. The point I am trying to make is that there are many ways to traverse a landscape like social psychology. Here I seek only to make sense out of the particular journey we have steered in this text. This kind of progressively integrative approach has been termed, by Sternberg and Beall, **theory knitting** (1991). Theory knitting is goal-driven (aimed at theoretical integration). One pathway to this goal is suggested by the trajectory followed in this book, which has taken us from a set of foundational social influences to a trio of general principles relating to social behaviour, cognition and affect. The question naturally arises now as to how, precisely, these emergent principles are linked to context, communication and culture.

Theory weaving

These relationships are captured for us, in a visual gestalt, in figure 11.1, which presents a lattice-like structure resembling a loom. Along the y-axis of the framework are the conceptual flagstones of context, communication and culture; along the x-axis are the principles of minimal constraint, maximal cognition and medium affect. As a means of clarification for the purposes of revision, the figure (which illustrates the technique of **theory weaving**) indicates how each key social influence domain (context, communication and culture) may be conceptually and proactively interwoven with each emergent principle of social psychology as a whole (minimal constraint, maximal cognition or medium affect).

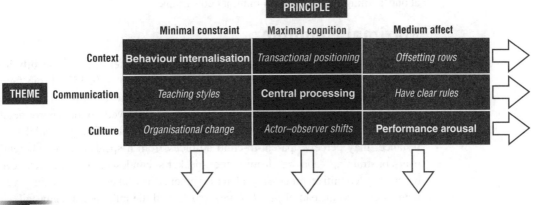

Figure 11.1   A theory development loom

Minimal constraint

The most vivid examples of the influence of social context on behaviour are still, for me, the Asch, Milgram and Zimbardo studies, described in detail in chapter 1 (pp. 17–22). The essence of these studies, like the follow-up research also reviewed in the early chapters, is that the magnitude of contextually determined constraint influences how deeply, if at all, new behaviour is internalised (for more classic examples of this process, see Janis 1968; Williams 1992; Zimbardo 1968). The point of this process of **behaviour internalisation** is that change that proceeds by first changing behaviour benefits from offering incentives that are minimally sufficient (Gleitman 1988). Otherwise, as Gleitman argues, the influence attempt will probably fail to engage either the hearts or the minds of its intended 'targets' (Courney & McAuley 1991).

In figure 11.1, bold and italic typefaces are used respectively to mark out relatively general influence processes from their more specific exemplars. Thus, from figure 11.1, a specific example of the principle of minimal constraint intersecting with communication can be found in different *teaching styles*. Lewin's 'governing with the consent of the governed', as distinct from simply 'lecturing', is an example of using minimal incentives for changing classroom behaviour. As we learned in chapter 3 (p. 89), and later also in chapter 7, such styles, compared with their less respectful counterparts, change behaviour more sustainably.

How this minimal sufficiency works is influenced substantially by societal and organisational values. Taking managing *organisational change* as an example, behavioural obedience to authority is more widely accepted in a relatively power distant organisational climate, while heavily 'participative' styles of change management become subjectively constraining (see chapter 7, pp. 260–61). In this kind of setting, 'democratic' styles of leadership are correspondingly inappropriate and unacceptable. In more egalitarian settings, by contrast, the opposite will probably apply. Flexed authority begets constraint, fostering resistance and backlash to the proposed change. The consistency across both of these opposites, however, is that constraint is likely to be counterproductive. This is perhaps partly why the optimal style of leadership generally is one that manages to combine task and relationship skills (see chapter 7, p. 256). Organisational change, it seems, is often about 'cooling the mark' with minimal constraint.

Maximal cognition

The theme of minimal constraint, as we learned in chapter 4, travels readily into the domain of social influences exerted by the media (pp. 139, 157). From figure 11.1, positioning theory proposes that the impact of an attempt at persuasion will depend heavily on whether its attitude is perceived to be appropriately embedded within an acceptable social narrative (p. 151). Emerging adults, for instance, may perceive parent-to-child attitudes from a speaker to be inherently over-constraining, and so dismiss the speaker's condescending message even before any cognitive processing of its arguments has taken place. In this event, there is crossed instead of *parallel positioning,* and the influence attempt fails.

So how *is* cognition engaged in the first place? In chapter 5, we learned that persuasive communications must avoid a range of cognitive biases associated with first impressions. These biases include a natural aversion to negative information, however trivial, as well as a fundamental tendency to over-configure person schemata around certain core or 'central' traits (pp. 172–7). An important way for communicators to circumvent these tripwires, we learned, is to make source, message and audience characteristics work *for* them by stimulating their audiences to think about, and so centrally process, the information contained in the message.

The example of stimulating *central processing* that most readily springs to mind here is the ex-jailbird who, on the face of it, argued against his own best interests by advocating tougher jail sentences (see chapter 4, pp. 133–4). This apparent incongruity was sufficient to give him a persuasive edge over a highly respectable public prosecutor, whose argument, although identical, was perceived merely to serve his own interests. An explanation for this edge was that, because the ex-con's motives were less obvious, and less apparently self-serving, than those of the public prosecutor, the audience was prompted to think a little more about the position being advocated. The resulting central processing (our key process in part 2 of the book) can, we learned, be stimulated in numerous other ways too, many of them quite practical and easily managed. These include, for instance, basic procedures such as situational selection and placement interviewing (p. 192), structured performance appraisal processes (p. 191) and picking a social narrative with which an audience socially identifies (p. 150).

These narratives will vary substantially with the cultural environments in which media communication takes place. In relatively power distant settings, for example, top-down uncle-to-nephew and aunt-to-niece narratives may 'connect' relatively successfully with youthful audiences. This kind of cultural positioning, being more respectful of its audience's values, might cut through defensive rationalisations such as 'AIDS means "American Ideas to Discourage Sex" ' and 'Using condoms is like eating a sweet with the wrapper on' (p. 135). Similarly, aid advertisements that over-focus on poor people themselves, rather than the situational causes of poverty, miss an opportunity to deliver a more thought-provoking narrative. As a result of this shortcut, they end up simply reinforcing pre-existing fundamental attribution errors, which in turn undermine their own development efforts (see chapter 6). As we learned also in chapter 7, one of the most effective ways of persuading people to become more open-minded and tolerant towards poor people in other cultures is to highlight discrepancies between their own observer perspectives and those of the actors who live with poverty every day. By such *actor–observer shifts* are the meta-process skills of perspective taking encouraged and developed.

From figure 11.1, maximal cognition tends to be encouraged precisely when there is also minimal constraint. During the process of socialisation, children or new employees often internalise a role precisely because they are gently prompted to 'try on' a new behaviour, notice discrepancies between their current behaviour and their private self, and so gradually and incrementally realign the schema for self with its newly acquired behaviours. In this way, central processing and behaviour internalisation are fully complementary. A striking example of this complementarity is the ironic effect, discussed in chapter 5 (p. 194). In this kind of effect, even *self*-constraint is liable to lead to backlash.

Just as the principle that guides cognition co-varies with a counterpart in managing behaviour, so, too, are there intrinsic links between social cognition and social affect. Attitudes are a prime example of this mix (refer to the definition of *attitude* in chapter 4, pp. 133–4). Attitudes, and the associated notion of positioning (p. 148), are integral to figure 11.1 and, arguably, to social psychology as a whole. Threading this idea through the principles listed across figure 11.1, appeals for donations to charitable causes, like disaster relief and alleviating child poverty or famine, must appeal to both affect and reason. If there is too little emotion in the appeal, then the viewer's throught processes may never even be activated. Too much guilt and the same minimisation of cognition — this time by 'switching off' — will occur. Theoretically, therefore, induced affect ought to be intermediate (or medium) in intensity, precisely so that cognition (and ultimately donation behaviour) are maximised (Carr et al. 1998).

Medium affect

This idea of striking the right balance, or *toning* of affect, applies also to perceived dissimilarity–similarity. For instance, a key to sustaining passionate relationships, we learned, is to counter incidents of interpersonal conflict (negative episodes) with positive romantic experiences (see chapter 10, pp. 363–4). Couples may benefit from *offsetting rows* with a surfeit of romantic gestures and events. In this way, social context acts to reposition the overall emotional climate, or the affective tone, of a close relationship towards a relatively intermediate (and optimal) level — one that may better sustain the couple's passionate relationship through the mid to longer term.

An analogous point, on managing interpersonal conflict, applies to communication on the Internet. 'Weaving through those environments on the Internet and mediating their effects on us is the degree of anonymity and accountability we feel when we are in them' (Wallace 1999, p. 239). Managing these effects, as we saw, is frequently a question of reintroducing accountability through formalised, *a priori* codes of conduct. These *clear rules*, from figure 11.1, effectively act to re-equilibrate the emotional tone of e-communications to a level of intensity that is more intermediate than extreme; in short, that is, they help to cool down otherwise overheated interactions (see chapter 10, pp. 370–72).

Linking together all of our ideas about social affect has been the inverted U-shaped function of the classic curve for **performance arousal**. On the topic of similarity-attraction in chapter 8 we learned that both under- and over-similarity between individuals tend to be relatively unattractive compared with similarity that is more intermediate in magnitude (pp. 293–4). On romantic relationships, in chapter 9 over-similarity, like over-familiarity, does not always optimise relationship longevity (p. 341). On managing aggression, say in sport (chapter 10), the use of clear rules of engagement (formalised, *a priori* codes of conduct) helps turn social learning processes to positive effect (p. 377). In these diverse ways, the classic performance arousal function, as a schema, assists us to envisage and perhaps even foster micro-cultures of reduced aggression.

But what about culture in the broader, societal sense of the term, as it has been used through much of this book? Where does performance arousal 'fit' in the wider scheme of things?

One likely point of intersection with the curve is that lovers define their love partly by reference to wider society, such as in the Romeo and Juliet effect (chapter 9, pp. 353–4). Because of their focus on external social reality, this kind of romantic couple may attribute the failure of family pressure to break off their relationship to 'trueness' in their romantic love for one another. In this way, external attitudes about family 'voice' unintentionally help to position some couples' internal-to-the-relationship feelings for each other vis-à-vis the performance arousal function. Family resistance, that is, helps these lovers to interpret their feelings as indicators that they have found the apex of a romantic performance arousal curve.

Another way that wider cultural realities impinge on relationship dynamics is through the culturally determined meaning of aggression. In relatively collectivist cultures, for example, derogation of family is more insulting and provocative than personal jibes, aimed at individual characteristics and traits, whereas the reverse applies in individualist settings (Semin & Rubini 1990). Similarly perhaps, the meaning of, say, reprimand, for example towards subordinates in an organisational setting, also depends significantly on the level of power distance within the group (Bond et al. 1985).

Overall, therefore, broader cultural values play a significant role in determining where people end up positioning themselves, and being positioned, on the performance arousal curve.

Social affect, like cognitive processing, infuses social behaviour. Emotions (as if we did not know!) underpin a great deal of everyday social behaviour. The social cognitive process of dissonance reduction, for instance, is based on a reduction of physiological arousal (chapter 1, p. 37). This emotion arises in the first place because people have behaved in a way that is now felt by them, as individuals, to be inconsistent with their personal schema for self. In this way, arousal/social affect co-varies with the cognitive changes that flow from changed behaviour (Sorrentino & Higgins 1986). Thus, minimal constraint, medium affect and maximal cognition are often contiguous with one another.

The motivational dynamics of the dissonance reduction process (chapter 1, p. 37) run something like the following, implicit internal monologue:

Question: 'Why did I do that when it clearly pricks my conscience?'

Answer: 'I wasn't forced to do it, so perhaps I actually believe in it!'

The Romeo and Juliet effect (pp. 353–4) embodies another, in some respects similar kind of implicit monologue:

Question: 'Why are we still together despite the resistance?'

Answer: 'Nobody is forcing us into this, so we are probably truly in love.'

The essence of each of these influence processes, which have been grossly simplified for the purpose of illustration, is that there is no obvious external constraint compelling the actors to behave in the way they are. They are instead gently prompted (minimal constraint) to look to, and think about, themselves (maximal cognition) for an explanation of what they feel (medium affect, perhaps, in this particular couple).

A very different example of the same kind of fusion between behaviour, cognition and affect can be found in the dynamics of crowd panic, as outlined by Roger Brown in chapter 2 (pp. 56–8). According to Brown, crowd behaviour is a mixture of cold and hot cognition. Its very essence consists of an emotional reaction (socially facilitated panic and survival instincts) to an initially cool, cognitive appraisal ('Fighting my way out of here is probably the safest thing to do, given that the others are probably thinking just like me'). A similar point can be made about workplace aggression. Reprimanding employees (or student trainees) with maximal constraint is usually counterproductive, precisely because it hurts and humiliates people, and thereafter focuses their cognitive energy on 'getting even' rather than enhancing performance (George 1995). So again, while behaviour, cognition and affect are conceptually distinct, they also tend to function together in everyday life. Overall, therefore, the linkages between behaviour, cognition and affect are multidirectional.

What this often means in practice is that social psychologists end up focusing on those aspects of social psychology (behaviour, cognition, affect) they choose to. This inherent subjectivity and preferential constructivism is nicely captured for us in figure 11.2, through the 'eternal braid' of the möbius strip (Sorrentino & Higgins 1986, p. 8). The braid portrayed in this figure can have either a black surface with a white underside or a white surface with a black underside. Which of these we perceive as 'figure' and which as 'ground' (see chapter 6, p. 204) depends on which facet of the material is initially chosen for study. What the strip suggests, however, is that there is no 'right' or 'wrong' place to start, and that we need to acquire a grasp of the overall gestalt (Gleitman 1997).

Figure 11.2   A möbius strip

This image resonates with the principles of pluralism and organisation introduced in chapter 1. The wider point of the analogy to physical perception in figure 11.2, however, is that we will never knit social psychology into an integrated whole unless we periodically engage in the kind of theory weaving portrayed in figure 11.1.

META THEMES

Globalisation

Perhaps the most pressing conceptual weaving exercise for social psychologists today is to accommodate their pre-existing schema about the discipline to the realities of globalisation. In particular, the discipline needs to acknowledge fully the emergence of global consciousness. Consciousness in people the world over, perhaps especially emerging adults, has changed radically, for it now manifestly includes a sense of global context (Tomlinson 1999, p. 30). This continuing (and arguably accelerating) expansion of global consciousness means that social psychological theories have to keep pace with their psychosocially developing and advancing human subjects. Otherwise, the discipline will fall chronically behind the actual complexity of its participants — even more so than when social psychology was first likened (during 'the crisis') to journalism in slow motion (Gergen 1994b).

Perhaps the central example of the meta-influence of globalisation on our everyday lives is the accelerating salience of competition and 'winning at all costs'. This is despite the fact that for most of the time the vast majority of us *are not going to win*. Where, then, is our developing psychology of *defeat*? This central concern for modern living runs throughout the topics covered in the book, from the rancour of critical narrative 1.3, to doping in sport (p. 58), to inverse resonance (p. 296), to marketing hype (p. 127), to résumé-stacking (p. 181), to increased pressures on students to succeed at all costs (p. 208), to the premium on being assertive (p. 264), to increased pressures to conform to media-fuelled stereotypes about physical beauty (p. 315), to being successful in love and marriage (p. 322), to workplace bullying driven by job insecurity (p. 382). The influences of globalisation saturate the fabric of everyday life, and social psychology has to respond to this altered reality, for example by developing a more extensive understanding of defeat, retribution and social justice (although I certainly do not mean to imply that all the influences of globalisation are negative, as indicated below).

Localisation

A promising framework to use in developing this kind of understanding is the concept of *localisation*. At root, localisation is driven by the need for a positively distinctive social identity, as discussed at length in chapter 3. So the idea is far from being wholly new to the discipline. In fact, the construct of social identity is probably well overdue for a serious *rejuvenation* and *restatement* (chapter 1, pp. 36 and 38). As a global consciousness continues to grow, and the local social fabric is increasingly torn, there is a growing fear that individuality is perhaps too insignificant, too inconsequential to matter in the grander scheme of things. In such a climate, belonging to any social group about which we can feel proud helps to counterbalance the anomie and alienation many of us may feel, by instead seeking increased group communion via communication. Localisation is thus a defiant reaction to some of the felt pressures of globalisation.

One sign that this kind of process is integral to modern life would be if for each of the illustrations of globalisation discussed in this book we could identify an equal and opposite reaction. It is my belief that this is in fact the case — all the way from tall poppy syndrome to the increased attention to combating workplace harassment — but readers might prefer to actively assess this for themselves! In the final analysis, you may conclude that we cannot often separate the psychosocial influences of globalisation from those of localisation; in effect, that is, they form a composite culture of their own.

Glocalisation

A good example of this kind of culture is the approach-avoidance tendencies that cohesive team workers can feel towards individual promotions, an ambivalence first captured for us in critical narrative 1.3. If competitive norms are regularly met by these collectivistic backlashes, and if this dialectic of individual versus social achievement is occurring constantly in workplace settings, then we urgently need to accommodate that advanced complexity in our theories, methods and techniques. Otherwise, we will never learn to *manage* workplace conflict or defeat.

This example indicates that one of the most salient forms of glocalisation for us to revise is motivational gravity. Although the motivational gravity model was originally developed for application in a glocal workplace, it is surely also relevant outside that specific domain. Motivational gravity is, for instance, partly a product of individualist versus collectivist norms, which, like achievement itself, span most spheres of life, not just work environments; to this extent, it is likely to be found across a range of other social contexts. In the classroom, for example, we frequently experience a tension between individual and social achievement. Thus, being a 'nerd' can have genuine social costs, not just for the high-achieving student herself, but also for the class as a whole.

Towards an expanded mindfulness

A compact, 'value-added' illustration of how the processes of globalisation, local-isation and glocalisation work in contemporary everyday life is provided for us in critical narrative 11.1. This example depicts three basic reactions to a particular, very pervasive globalisation — the techno-scape of the Internet. At one level, the e-mailed responses to the author's contribution vary according to the extent to which they mentally 'distance' themselves from the author. But on another level, they can be seen as reflecting relatively globalised, localised or glocalised selves.

CRITICAL
NARRATIVE

11.1

The meta discussion

Imagine that you subscribed to a mailing list on alternative medicine, eager to hear people's experiences with glucosamine as a treatment for backaches. You read a few unrelated messages and then send in your first contribution, mentioning a brand name, source, and price in the text, and asking the group if they've ever tried it. The next day, one participant publicly criticises you for making such a thinly disguised sales pitch, pointing out that spamming is unacceptable…Another poster humourously bemoans all of the Internet newbies who never read the discussion group rules. A third sends you a private message introducing himself and telling you his own experiences with the glucosamine he took to treat arthritis. At the end of his message, he adds a postscript: 'BTW, better not mention brand names in this group because it can look like free advertising. They might think you're a dealer or something.'

Source: Wallace (1999, p. 237).

The first reply comes closest to reflecting first-order positioning — that is, the speaker is not really stepping back at all from his self. In this sense, it represents a wholeheartedly 'globalised' mode of thinking, feeling and acting. The respondent is assimilated into the role of global citizen; his self-accorded global majority status gives him, so he believes, a moral right to 'push down' on any newcomer minority. There is, then, not a great deal of elevated consciousness in this relatively arrogant form of social posturing.

The second respondent, in my view, comes closest to embodying a localised mentality. This person perceives the newcomer's behaviour as an infraction of '*group* rules' (my emphasis) and social identity. To this respondent, the newcomer is an 'outsider'. The forum is perceived as an exclusive social sanctuary; a cohesive community localised in cyber- and psychological space; and what used to be called in social psychology a 'psychological group' (Festinger 1950). Again, however, the respondent's level of consciousness is relatively one-dimensional — that is, no real consideration is given to any perspective of social reality other than that held by the respondent himself.

The third respondent is very different from the other two. He behaves in several ways that demonstrate mindfulness. Most basically, his mental state is pluralistic. He readily changes perspectives, mindfully replaying the previous day's inter-action from a variety of points of view. This incorporates the view of the relatively globalised first respondent (he writes privately to the newcomer) and the more localised vantage point of the second respondent (he points out the group's norms to the newcomer). During this dialectic, the third speaker does not criticise the first two perspectives; he can appreciate them. In that sense, his self is glocalised. And it is this same perspective-taking skill that enables him to appreciate the perspective of the newcomer. Through it, he sees that the newcomer feels attracted to the forum and what it represents, but at the same time is in danger of being lost to it because of the criticism he has received. By implication, if the newcomer manages to *grasp* this third respondent's glocal agility, and freely steps back from (as well as into) the global and local perspectives, he himself will be better equipped to 'surf the Net' in future.

There is considerable practical edge to the process skill displayed by the third respondent, for he is a living exemplar of minimal constraint, maximal cognition and medium affect. Also, to return to the beginning of the book, he embodies the kind of person Asch expected to see more often in his early line-length experiments, which share several features with critical narrative 11.1 (chapter 1, pp. 17–19). Within the span of social psychology discussed in this book, therefore, glocalisation has an inherent potential to expand human consciousness.

SUMMARY

Social psychological research and theory is socially constructed, and for that reason, in order to optimise its enlightenment effects, it needs to construct link-ages between its respective edifices in behaviour, cognition and affect. Theory weaving does this by seeking points of intersection between basic, *a priori* influence domains and emergent theoretical principles, as discerned through **reflection** (see chapter 1, p. 41). Chief among these principles, in our particular journey, are minimal constraint, maximal cognition and medium affect. From figure 11.3 on the next page, these principles are visible through the context of globalisation, the communication that is localisation, and the dynamic interactions between the two — through the cultures of glocalisation. In the final analysis, taking a glocal perspective is a vital meta-process skill for managing these pervasive meta-influences in our daily lives.

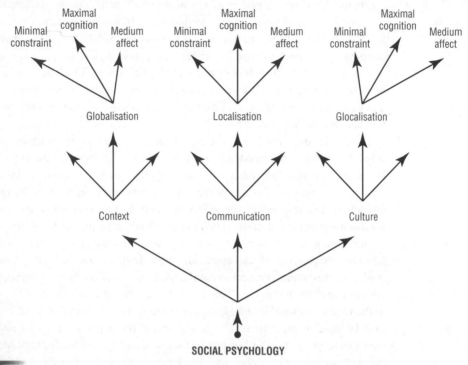

Minimal constraint Maximal cognition Medium affect

Minimal constraint Maximal cognition Medium affect

Minimal constraint Maximal cognition Medium affect

Globalisation

Localisation

Glocalisation

Context

Communication

Culture

SOCIAL PSYCHOLOGY

Figure 11.3   A schema for the book

KEY TERMS

Behaviour internalisation. The extent to which behavioural change becomes privately adopted and accepted, both intellectually and emotionally. Not necessarily the same process as media-induced 'internalisation', as defined by Kelman (1958; see chapter 4) (p. 395)

Peformance arousal. The curvilinear U-shaped function linking level of attraction, love and performance — for example being under-assertive, assertive or overly aggressive in sports — to the level of emotional arousal being experienced at the time (p. 398)

Reflection. The process of reviewing social psychology in order to arrive at recurring themes and principles (p. 403)

Theory knitting. An inclusive philosophy of social psychology in which theories are viewed as potentially complementary rather than as contradictory to each other. Theory development thus consists of building bridges between models rather than testing one model against another. (p. 395)

Theory weaving. An incremental improvement on the principle of theory knitting (above), in which a method of enacting and practising theory development consists of linking predetermined themes with those that emerge through a process of *reflection* . (p. 395)

REVIEW QUESTIONS

1. What is theory weaving?
2. In what sense is the practice and research of social psychology itself socially constructed?
3. Describe and illustrate with everyday examples the principle of minimal constraint.
4. Describe and illustrate with everyday examples the principle of maximal cognition.
5. Describe and illustrate with everyday examples the principle of medium affect.

DISCUSSION QUESTIONS

1. To what extent should a text like this deal with the concept of 'self'?
2. Is the principle of medium affect just another assertion of the 'superiority' of cognition over affect?
3. Does awareness of minimal constraint, maximal cognition and medium affect invalidate them as explanatory principles of social behaviour?
4. Based on the available evidence and theory, will a global culture ever prevail over (i.e. eradicate) local world views?

CRITICAL ACTIVITIES

1. Analyse and synthesise the process of urbanisation, including urban migration, from the viewpoint of the book.

Useful references:

Marsella, A. J. (1995). Urbanisation, mental health, and psychosocial wellbeing: Some historical perspectives and considerations. In T. Harpham & I. Blue (Eds), *Urbanisation and mental health in developing countries* (pp. 17–38). Sydney: Avebury.

Marsella, A. J., Wandersman, A., & Cantor, D. W. (1998). Psychology and urban initiatives: Professional and scientific opportunities and challenges. *American Psychologist*, *53*, 621–3.

2. Of what use is social psychology to urban planning?

3. (a) Imagine that you are a member of a pressure group. Write a report on how social psychology might be applied to boost membership and further your cause.

   (b) (*Private exercise*) To what extent have your own schemata changed as a result of studying this book? Have any of the principles you have studied been undermined by these changes?

REFERENCES

Aamodt, M. G. (1999). *Applied industrial/organisational psychology* (3rd edition). Belmont, CA: Brooks/Cole.

Aamodt, M. G., Bryan, D. A., & Whitcomb, A. J. (1993). Predicting performance with letters of recommendation. *Public Personnel Management, 22,* 81–90.

Abbey, A. (1982). Sex differences in attributions for friendly behaviour: Do males misperceive females' friendliness? *Journal of Personality and Social Psychology, 42,* 830–38.

Abdullah, A. (1994). *Managing the Malaysian workforce — Guidelines for managers.* Kuala Lumpur: Malaysian Institute of Management.

Abouchedid, K., & Nasser, R. (2001). Poverty attitudes and their determinants in Lebanon's plural society. *Journal of Economic Psychology, 22,* 271–82.

Abrams, D., Ando, K., & Hinkle, S. (1998). Psychological attachment to the group: Cross-cultural differences in organizational identification and subjective norms as predictors of workers' turnover intentions. *Personality & Social Psychology Bulletin, 24,* 1027–39.

Adams, A. (1997). Bullying at work. *Journal of Community and Applied Social Psychology, 7,* 177–80.

Adams, J. S. (1965). Inequity in social exchange. *Advances in Experimental Social Psychology, 2,* 267–300.

Adamse, M., & Motta, S. (1996). *Online friendship, chat-room romance, and cybersex.* Deerfield Beach, FL: Health Communications.

Adorno, T. W., Frenkel-Brunswik, E., Levinson, D. J., & Sanford, R. N. (1950). *The authoritarian personality.* New York: Harper & Row.

Afro-centric Alliance. (1998). Groups at work in East African communities. In M. MacLachlan & S. C. Carr (Eds), *Perspectives in Malaŵian psychology: A reader for students* (pp. 111–39). Zomba: Zikomo Press.

Afro-centric Alliance. (2001). Indigenising organisational change: Localisation in Tanzania and Malaŵi. *Journal of Managerial Psychology, 16,* 59–78.

Ah Nee-Benham, M. K. 'a P., & Cooper, J. E. (Eds). (2000). *Indigenous education models of contemporary practice: In our mother's voice — Sociocultural, political, and historical studies in education.* Mahwah, NJ: Lawrence Erlbaum Associates.

Aiello, J. R., & Douthitt, E. A. (2001). Social facilitation from Triplett to electronic performance monitoring. *Group Dynamics, 5,* 163–80.

Ainsworth, M. D. S. (1967). *Infancy in Uganda: Infant care and the growth of love.* Baltimore, MA: Johns Hopkins University Press.

Ainsworth, M. D. S. (1989). Attachments beyond infancy. *American Psychologist, 44,* 709–716.

Ainsworth, M. D. S. (with Marvin, R. S.) (1995). On the shaping of attachment theory and research: An interview with Mary D. S. Ainsworth (Fall 1994). *Monographs of the Society for Research in Child Development, 60,* 3–21.

Ajzen, I. (1991a). *Attitudes, personality, and behaviour.* Milton Keynes, UK: Open University Press.

Ajzen, I. (1991b). The theory of planned behaviour. *Organisational Behaviour and Human Development Processes, 50,* 179–211.

Ajzen, I. (2001). Nature and operation of attitudes. *Annual Review of Psychology, 52,* 27–58.

Ajzen, I., & Fishbein, M. (1980). *Understanding attitudes and predicting social behaviour.* Englewood Cliffs, NJ: Prentice Hall.

Ajzen, I., & Fishbein, M. (2000). Attitudes and the attitude-behavior relationship: Reasoned and automatic processes. *European Review of Social Psychology, 11,* 1–33.

Alinksy, S. (1971). *Rules for radicals.* New York: Random House.

Allcorn, S. (1994). *Anger in the workplace.* Chicago, IL: Quorum Books.

Allen, B. P. (2000). *Personality theories: Development, growth, and diversity.* Needham Heights, MA: Allyn & Bacon.

Allison, S. T., & Messick, D. M. (1985). The group attribution error. *Journal of Experimental Social Psychology, 21,* 563–79.

Allport, F. H. (1924). *Social psychology.* Boston, MA: Houghton Mifflin.

Allport, G. W. (1954). *The nature of prejudice.* Reading, MA: Addison-Wesley.

Altemeyer, B. (1981). *Right-wing authoritarianism.* Winnipeg, Canada: University of Manitoba Press.

Altmeyer, R. (1988). *The enemies of freedom: Understanding right-wing authoritarianism.* San Francisco, CA: Jossey-Bass.

Alvaro, E. M., & Crano, W. D. (1997). Indirect minority influence: Evidence for leniency in source evaluation and counter-argumentation. *Journal of Personality and Social Psychology, 72,* 949–64.

Alwin, D. F., Cohen, R. L., & Newcomb, T. M. (1991). *Political attitudes over the life span: The Bennington women after fifty years.* Madison, WI: University of Wisconsin Press.

Amato, P. R. (1980). City size, sidewalk density, and friendliness toward strangers. *Journal of Social Psychology, 111,* 151–2.

Amato, P. R. (1981). The impact of the built environment on pro-social and affiliative behaviour: A field study of the Townsville City Mall. *Australian Journal of Psychology, 33,* 297–303.

Amato, P. R. (1983a). Affiliative behaviour in diverse environments: A consideration of pleasantness, information rate, and the arousal-eliciting quality of settings. *Basic & Applied Social Psychology, 4*, 109–122.

Amato, P. R. (1983b). Helping behaviour in urban and rural environments: Field studies based on a taxonomic organisation of helping. *Journal of Personality and Social Psychology, 45*, 571–86.

Amato, P. R. (1983c). The effects of urbanisation on interpersonal behaviour: Field studies in Papua New Guinea. *Journal of Cross-Cultural Psychology, 14*, 353–67.

Ambady, N., & Rosenthal, R. (1992). Thin slices of expressive behaviours as predictors of interpersonal consequences: A meta-analysis. *Psychological Bulletin, 111*, 256–74.

Ambady, N., Bernieri, F. J., & Richeson, J. A. (2000). Toward a histology of social behavior: Judgmental accuracy from thin slices of the behavioral stream. *Advances in Experimental Social Psychology, 32*, 201–271.

Ambady, N., LaPlante, D., & Johnson, E. (2001). Thin-slice judgments as a measure of interpersonal sensitivity. In J. A. Hall & F. J. Bernieri (Eds), *Interpersonal sensitivity: Theory and measurement* (pp. 89–101). Mahwah, NJ: Lawrence Erlbaum Associates.

Ancel, M. (1958). The crime of passion: Present state of question. *Hygiene Mentale, 47*, 153–68.

Anderson, C. A. (1989). Temperature and aggression: Ubiquitous effects of heat on occurrence of human violence. *Psychological Bulletin, 106*, 74–96.

Anderson, C. A., & Bushman, B. J. (2001). Effects of violent video games on aggressive behavior, aggressive cognition, aggressive affect, physiological arousal, and pro-social behavior. *Psychological Science, 12*, 353–65.

Anderson, C. A., Anderson, K. B., Dorr, N., DeNeve, K. M., & Flanagan, M. (2000). Temperature and aggression. *Advances in Experimental Social Psychology, 32*, 63–133.

Anderson, J. (1997). What cognitive science tells us about ethics and the teaching of ethics. *Journal of Business Ethics*, February, 279–91.

Anderson, J. L., Crawford, C. B., Nadeau, J., & Lindberg, T. (1992). Was the Duchess of Windsor right? A cross-cultural review of the socio-ecology of ideals of female body shape. *Ethology and Sociobiology, 13*, 197–227.

Anderson, N. H. (1965). Averaging versus addition as a stimulus combination rule in impression formation. *Journal of Experimental Psychology, 70*, 394–400.

Anderson, N. H. (1974). Cognitive algebra: Integration theory as applied to social attribution. *Advances in Experimental Social Psychology, 7*, 1–101.

Anderson, N. H. (1981). *Foundations of information integration theory.* New York: Academic Press.

Anderson, N. H. (1992). Eight decades of employment selection interview research: A retrospective meta-review and prospective commentary. *European Work and Organisational Psychologist, 2*, 1–32.

Anderson, N. H., & Shackleton, V. (1990). Decision-making in the graduate selection interview: A field study. *Journal of Occupational Psychology, 63*, 63–76.

Anderson, N. H., & Shackleton, V. (1993). *Successful selection interviewing.* Oxford, UK: Blackwell.

Anderton, J. (1999). *Unsung heroes: Portraits of inspiring New Zealanders.* Auckland: Random House.

Andreeva, G. (1984). Cognitive processes in developing groups. In L. H. Strickland (Ed.), *Directions in Soviet social psychology* (pp. 67–82). New York: Springer-Verlag.

Argyle, M. (1968). *The psychology of interpersonal behaviour.* Harmondsworth, UK: Penguin.

Argyle, M., & Dean, J. (1965). Eye contact, distance, and affiliation. *Sociometry, 28*, 289–304.

Argyris, C. (1998). A conversation with Chris Argyris: The father of organizational learning. *Organizational Dynamics, 27*, 21–33.

Argyris, C. (1999). Tacit knowledge and management. In R. J. Sternberg & J. A. Horvath (Eds), *Tacit knowledge in professional practice: Researcher and practitioner perspectives* (pp. 123–40). Mahwah, NJ: Lawrence Erlbaum Associates.

Argyris, C. (2000). *Flawed advice and the management trap: How managers can know when they're getting good advice and when they're not.* Oxford, UK: Oxford University Press.

Armitage, C. J., & Arden, M. A. (2002). Exploring discontinuity patterns in the transtheoretical model: An application of the theory. *British Journal of Health Psychology, 7*, 89–103.

Armitage, C. J., & Conner, M. (2001). Efficacy of the theory of planned behavior: A meta-analytic review. *British Journal of Social Psychology, 40*, 471–99.

Arnett, J. T. (2000). Emerging adulthood: A theory of development from the late teens through the twenties. *American Psychologist, 55*, 469–80.

Aron, A., & Aron, E. (1986). *Love and the expansion of self: Understanding attraction and satisfaction.* New York: Hemisphere.

Aron, A., & Westbay, L. (1996). Dimensions of the prototype of love. *Journal of Personalized Social Psychology, 70*, 535–47.

Aron, A., Aron, E.N., & Allen, J. (1998). Motivations for unreciprocated love. *Personality and Social Psychology Bulletin, 24*, 787–96.

Aronson, E. (2000). *Nobody left to hate: Teaching compassion after Columbine.* New York: Freeman.

Aronson, E., & Cope, V. (1968). My enemy's enemy is my friend. *Journal of Personality and Social Psychology, 8*, 8–12.

Aronson, E., & Patnoe, S. (1997). *The jigsaw classroom: Building cooperation in the classroom.* Boston, MA: Allyn & Bacon.

Aronson, E., Blaney, N., Stephan, C., Sikes, J., & Snapp. M. (1978). *The jigsaw clsssroom.* Beverly Hills, CA: Sage.

Aronson, E., Willerman, B., & Floyd, J. (1966). The effects of a pratfall on increasing interpersonal attractiveness. *Psychonomic Science, 4,* 157–8.

Asch, S. E. (1946). Forming impressions of personality. *Journal of Abnormal and Social Psychology, 41,* 258–90.

Asch, S. E. (1956). Studies of independence and conformity: A minority of one against a unanimous majority. *Psychological Monographs: General and Applied, 70,* 1–70 [Whole No. 416].

Ashkanasy, N. M. (1994). Automatic categorisation and causal attributions: The effect of gender bias in supervisor responses to subordinate performance. *Australian Journal of Psychology, 46,* 177–82.

Ashkanasy, N. M., & O'Connor, C. (1997). Value congruence in leader-member exchange. *Journal of Social Psychology, 137,* 647–62.

Ashmore, R. D., Solomon, M. R., & Longo, L. C. (1996). Thinking about fashion models' looks: A multi-dimensional approach to the structure of perceived physical attractiveness. *Personality and Social Psychology Bulletin, 22,* 1083–1104.

Augoustinos, M. (1990). The mediating role of representations on causal attributions in the social world. *Social Behaviour, 5,* 49–62.

Augoustinos, M., & Walker, I. (1995). *Social cognition: An integrated introduction.* New Delhi: Sage.

Augoustinos, M., Rapley, M., & Tuffin, K. (1999). Cultural genocide or a failure to gel? Colonialism, nationalism, and the management of racism in Australian talk. *Discourse & Society, 10,* 351–78.

Aune, K. R., & Waters, L. L. (1994). Cultural differences in deception: Motivations to deceive in Samoans and North Americans. *International Journal of Intercultural Relations, 18,* 159–72.

Aus–Thai Project Team (1998). Managing economic crisis: A psychosocial approach. *Development Bulletin, 46,* 53–6.

Aus–Thai Project Team (in press). Poverty and economic crisis: A human factors approach. In S. C. Carr & T. S. Sloan (Eds), *Poverty and psychology: Critical emergent perspectives* (in press). New York: Kluwer-Plenum Academic Publishers.

Austin, A. (in press). Alcohol, tobacco, and other drug use and violent behaviour in a Native Hawaiian community. In A. J. Marsella (Ed.), *Paradise lost, paradise found: Indigenous mental health across the South Pacific region* (in press). Dordrecht, Netherlands: Kluwer-Plenum Academic Publishers.

Austin, W. G., & Worchel, S. (Eds) (1979). *The social psychology of inter-group relations.* Monterey, CA: Brooks/Cole.

Australian Broadcasting Corporation (ABC) (1999a). Africa AIDS problem exploded: UN. *ABC Bulletin.* Retrieved 13 September <www.abc.com.au>.

Australian Broadcasting Corporation (ABC) (1999b). *People's century: 1930 sporting fever.* Tuesday, 11 March, 11.05 p.m.

Australian Psychological Society (1999a). Suicide: An Australian Psychological Society Discussion Paper <http://psychsociety.com.au>.

Australian Psychological Society (1999b). *Rural suicides increase despite more reasons for living* (symposium). 34th Australian Psychological Society Annual Conference, Hobart, Tasmania.

Australian Psychological Society (2000a). *Code of ethics.* Melbourne: APS.

Australian Psychological Society (2000b). *Ethical guidelines.* Melbourne: APS.

Australian Psychological Society (2001). Punishment and behaviour change <www.psychsociety. com.au>.

Bachiochi, P. D., & Weiner, S. P. (2002). Qualitative data collection and analysis. In S. G. Rogelberg (Ed.), *Handbook of research methods in industrial and organisational psychology* (pp. 161–83). Malden, MA: Blackwell.

Bailey, D., Hawes, H., & Bonati, G. (Eds) (1992). *Child-to-child: A resource book. Part one: Implementing the child-to-child approach.* London: Child-to-Child Foundation.

Baker, K. W. (1995). Allen and Meyer's 1990 longitudinal study: A re-analysis and reinterpretation using structural equation modelling. *Human Relations, 48,* 169–86.

Baldwin, M. W., & Fehr, B. (1995). On the instability of attachment style ratings. *Personal Relationships, 2,* 247–61.

Baldwin, S., Maguka, H., & Loher, E. (1991). The perils of participation: Effects of choice of training on trainee motivation and learning. *Personnel Psychology, 44,* 51–65.

Bales, R. F. (1956). How people interact in conferences. *Scientific American, 192,* 31–5.

Banaji, M. R., & Greenwald, A. G. (1995). Implicit gender stereotyping in judgments of fame. *Journal of Personality and Social Psychology, 68,* 181–99.

Bancroft, J., Sanders, D., Davidson, D., & Warner, P. (1984). Mood, sexuality, hormones, and the menstrual cycle: III. Sexuality and the role of androgens. *Psychosomatic Medicine, 45,* 509–516.

Bandawe, C. R. (2000). *A schistosomiasis health education intervention among rural Malaŵian school children: Lessons learned.* Cape Town, South Africa: University of Cape Town.

Bandura, A. (1965). Influence of models' reinforcement contingencies on the acquisition of imitative responses. *Journal of Personality and Social Psychology, 1,* 589–95.

Bandura, A. (1973). *Aggression: A social learning analysis.* Englewood Cliffs, NJ: Prentice Hall.

Bandura, A., Ross, D., & Ross, S. (1963). Imitation of film-mediated aggressive models. *Journal of Abnormal and Social Psychology, 66,* 3–11.

Bargh, J. A. (2001). The psychology of the mere. In J. A. Bargh & D. K. Apsley (Eds), *Unravelling the complexities of social life: A festschrift in honour of Robert B. Zajonc* (pp. 25–37). Washington, DC: American Psychological Association.

Barnes, M. L., & Sternberg, R. J. (1997). A hierarchical model of love and its prediction of satisfaction in close relationships. In R. J. Sternberg & M. Hojjat (Eds), *Satisfaction in close relationships* (pp. 79–101). New York: The Guildford Press.

Baron, R. A. (1986). Self-presentation in job interviews: When there can be 'too much of a good thing'. *Journal of Applied Social Psychology, 16,* 16–28.

Baron, R. A., & Byrne, D. (2000). *Social psychology* (9th edition). Needham Heights, MA: Pearson Education.

Baron, R. S., Cutrona, C. E., Hicklin, D., Russell, D. W., & Lubaroff, D. M. (1990). Social support and immune function among spouses of cancer patients. *Journal of Personality and Social Psychology, 59,* 344–52.

Barrett, L. B., & Russell, J. A. (1998). Independence and bipolarity in the structure of current affect. *Journal of Personality and Social Psychology, 74,* 967–84.

Bartlett, F. C. (1932). *Remembering: A study in experimental and social psychology.* Oakleigh, Melbourne: Cambridge University Press.

Bartram, D. (2001). Guidelines for test users: A review of national and international initiatives. *European Journal of Psychological Assessment, 17,* 173–86.

Bassman, E., & London, M. (1993). Abusive managerial behaviour. *Leadership and Organisation Development Journal, 14,* 18–24.

Bate-Boerop, J. L. (1975). General systems theory and family therapy in practice. *Family Therapy, 2,* 69–77.

Bau, L. P., & Dyck, M. (1992). Predicting the peacetime performance of military officers: Officer selection in the Papua New Guinea Defence Force. *South Pacific Journal of Psychology, 5,* 27–37.

Baumeister, R. F., & Dhavale, D. (2001). Two sides of romantic rejection. In M. R. Leary (Ed.), *Interpersonal rejection* (pp. 55–71). New York: Oxford University Press.

Baumeister, R. F., & Newman, L. S. (1994). How stories make sense of personal experiences: Motives that shape autobiographical narratives. *Personality and Social Psychology Bulletin, 20,* 676–90.

Baumeister, R. F., Bushman, B. J., & Campbell, C. W. (2000). Self-esteem, narcissism, and aggression: Does violence result from low self-esteem or from threatened egotism? *Current Directions in Psychological Science, 9,* 26–9.

Baumrind, D. (1980). New directions in socialisation research. *American Psychologist, 35,* 639–52.

Baumrind, D. (1983). Rejoinder to Lewis' reinterpretation of parental firm control effects: Are authoritative families really harmonious? *Psychological Bulletin, 94,* 132–42.

Baumrind, D. (1989). Rearing competent children. In W. Damon (Ed.), *Child development today and tomorrow* (pp. 349–78). San Francisco, CA: Jossey-Bass.

Baumrind, D. (1996). The discipline controversy revisited. *Family Relations: Journal of Applied Family and Child Studies, 45,* 405–414.

Beaman, A., Barnes, P. J., Klentz, B., & McQuirk, B. (1978). Increasing helping rates through information dissemination: Teaching pays. *Personality and Social Psychology Bulletin, 4,* 406–411.

Beardsley, T. (1993). Never give a sucker an even break. *Scientific American,* October, 12.

Beautrais, A. L. (2001). Child and adolescent suicide in New Zealand. *Australian & New Zealand Journal of Psychiatry, 35,* 647–53.

Bedeian, A. G. (1995). Workplace envy. *Organisational Dynamics, 23,* 49–56.

Belbin, R. M. (1997). *Team roles at work.* Melbourne: Butterworth-Heinemann.

Bell, P. A., & Baron, R. A. (1977). Aggression and ambient temperature: The facilitating and inhibiting effects of hot and cold environments. *Bulletin of the Psychonomic Society, 9,* 443–5.

Bell, P. R., & Jamieson, B. D. (1970). Publicity of initial decision and the risky shift phenomenon. *Journal of Experimental Social Psychology, 6,* 329–45.

Belsky, J. (1993). Etiology of child maltreatment: A developmental-ecological analysis. *Psychological Bulletin, 114,* 413–34.

Bem, S. L. (1981). Gender schema theory: A cognitive account of stereotyping. *Psychological Review, 88,* 354–64.

Bennett, J. C. (1991). The irrationality of the catharsis theory of aggression as justification for educators' support of interscholastic football. *Perceptual and Motor Skills, 72,* 415–18.

Bergman, R., Robbins, S. P., & Stagg, I. (1997). *Management.* Sydney: Prentice Hall.

Berman, J. J., Murphy-Berman, V., & Singh, P. (1985). Cross-cultural similarities and differences in perceptions of fairness. *Journal of Cross-Cultural Psychology, 16,* 55–67.

Bernathi, M. S., & Feshbach, N. D. (1995). Children's trust: Theory, assessment, development, and research directions. *Applied and Preventive Psychology, 4,* 1–19.

Berne, E. (1964). *Games people play.* New York: Grove.

Berry, J. W. (1967). Independence and conformity in subsistence-level societies. *Journal of Personality and Social Psychology, 7,* 415–18.

Berry, J. W. (1979). A cultural ecology of social behaviour. *Advances in Experimental Social Psychology, 12,* 177–206.

Berscheid, E., & Meyers, S. A. (1996). The social categorical approach to a question about love. *Personal Relationships, 3,* 19–43.

Berscheid, E., & Walster, E. H. (1978). *Interpersonal attraction* (2nd edition). Reading, MA: Addison-Wesley.

Bethel, J. P. (1925). An experimental investigation of the influence of certain weather conditions upon short periods of mental work. *American Journal of Psychology, 36,* 102–112.

Bettencourt, B. A., & Miller, N. (1996). Gender differences in aggression as a function of provocation: A meta-analysis. *Psychological Bulletin, 119,* 422–47.

Betzig, L. (1989). Causes of conjugal dissolution: A cross-cultural study. *Current Anthropology, 30,* 654–76.

Bhattacharya, S. P. (1994). The application of transactional analysis in a participatory forestry management program. *Transactional Analysis Journal, 24,* 286–90.

Bhawuk, D. P. S. (1998). The role of culture theory in cross-cultural training: A multimethod study of culture-specific, culture-general, and culture-theory-based assimilators. *Journal of Cross-Cultural Psychology, 29,* 630–55.

Bhawuk, D. P. S., & Brislin, R. W. (2000). Cross-cultural training: A review. *Applied Psychology: An International Review, 49,* 162–91.

Biddle, S. J. H., & Nigg, C. R. (2000). Theories of exercise behavior. *International Journal of Sport Psychology, 31,* 290–304.

Billig, M. (1989). *Arguing and thinking.* Cambridge, UK: Cambridge University Press.

Bishop, B., & D'Rozario, P. (1990). A matter of ethics? A comment on Pryor (1989). *Australian Psychologist, 25,* 215–19.

Bishop, G. D. (August 1994). *Health beliefs and the use of modern medicine vs. traditional medicine.* Third Afro-Asian Psychological Congress, Kuala Lumpur.

Blake, R. R., & Mouton, J. S. (1964). *The managerial grid.* Houston, TX: Gulf.

Blascovich, J., Mendes, W. B., Hunter, S. B., & Salomon, K. (1999). Social 'facilitation' as challenge and threat. *Journal of Personality and Social Psychology, 77,* 68–77.

Blass, T. (1991). Understanding behaviour in the Milgram obedience experiment: The role of personality, situations, and their interactions. *Journal of Personality and Social Psychology, 60,* 398–413.

Blass, T. (1999). The Milgram Paradigm after 35 years: Some things we now know about obedience to authority. *Journal of Applied Social Psychology, 29,* 955–78.

Blass, T., & Schmitt, C. (2001). The nature of perceived authority in the Milgram experiment: Two replications. *Current Psychology: Developmental, Learning, Personality, Social, 20,* 115–21.

Block, J. (1995). A contrarian view of the Five-Factor approach to personality description. *Psychological Bulletin, 117,* 187–215.

Blumer, H. (1946). Collective behaviour. In A. M. Lee (Ed.), *New outline of the principles of sociology* (pp. 165–220). New York: Barnes & Noble.

Bochner, S. (1989). The effectiveness of political campaigning: A field test of reference group theory. *Australian Journal of Psychology, 41,* 61–8.

Bochner, S. (1994). The effectiveness of same-sex versus opposite-sex role models in advertisements to reduce alcohol consumption in teenagers. *Addictive Behaviours, 19,* 69–82.

Bochner, S., & Perks, R. W. (1971). National role evocation as a function of cross-national interaction. *Journal of Cross-Cultural Psychology, 2,* 157–64.

Boesch, E. E. (1994). First experiences in Thailand. In W. J. Lonner & R. S. Malpass (Eds), *Psychology and culture* (pp. 47–51). Boston, MA: Allyn & Bacon.

Bogardus, E. S. (1925). Measuring social distances. *Journal of Applied Sociology,* January/February, 216–26.

Bolitho, F. H. (1999). Personal correspondence.

Bolitho, F. H., & Carr, S. C. (2002). *Anatomy of a grievance.* Darwin: Northern Territory University.

Bond, M. H., Wan, K. C., Leung, K., & Giacolone, R. A. (1985). How are responses to verbal insult related to cultural collectivism and power distance. *Journal of Cross-Cultural Psychology, 16,* 111–27.

Bond, R., & Smith, P. B. (1996). Culture and conformity: A meta-analysis of studies using Asch's (1952b, 1956) line judgment task. *Psychological Bulletin, 119,* 111–37.

Bonta, B. D. (1997). Cooperation and competition in peaceful societies. *Psychological Bulletin, 121,* 299–320.

Book, A. S., Starzyk, K. B., & Qunisey, V. L. (2001). The relationship between testosterone and aggression: A meta-analysis. *Aggression & Behaviour, 6,* 579–99.

Bornstein, R. F., & D'Agnostino, P. R. (1992). Stimulus recognition and the mere exposure effect. *Journal Personality and Social Psychology, 63,* 545–52.

Bossard, J. H. S. (1932). Residential propinquity as a factor in marriage selection. *American Journal of Sociology, 38,* 219–24.

Bostrom, R. N. (1997). The process of listening. In O. D. W. Hargie (Ed.), *The handbook of communication skills* (pp. 236–58). London: Routledge.

Bowa, M. (1998). Making sense of the world. In M. MacLachlan & S. C. Carr (Eds), *Perspectives in Malaŵian psychology* (pp. 96–110). Zomba: Zikomo Press.

Bowlby, J. (1958). The nature of the child's tie to his mother. *International Journal of Psychoanalysis, 39,* 350–73.

Bowlby, J. (2000). *Loss, sadness, and depression.* New York: Basic Books.

Boyden, T., Carroll, J. S., & Maier, R. A. (1984). Similarity and attraction in homosexual males: The effects of age and masculinity–femininity. *Sex Roles, 10,* 939–48.

Bradburn, N. M. (1983). Response effects. In P. H. Rossie, J. D. Wright & A. B. Anderson (Eds), *Handbook of survey research* (pp. 289–328). New York: Academic Press.

Bray, F., & Chapman, S. (1991). Community knowledge, attitudes, and medial recall about AIDS, Sydney 1988 and 1989. *Australian Journal of Public Health, 15,* 107–113.

Brehm, J. W. (1966). *A theory of psychological reactance.* New York: Academic Press.

Brehm, J. W., & Cohen, A. R. (1962). *Explorations in cognitive dissonance.* New York: John Wiley & Sons.

Brehm, S. S., Kassin, S. M., & Fein, S. (1999). *Social psychology* (4th edition). Boston, MA: Houghton Mifflin.

Brennan, K. A., & Shaver, P. R. (1995). Dimensions of adult attachment, affect regulation, and romantic relationship functioning. *Personality and Social Psychology Bulletin, 21,* 267–83.

Bretz, R. D., Ash, R. A., & Dreher, G. F. (1989). Do people make the place? An examination of the attraction-selection-attrition hypothesis. *Personnel Psychology, 42,* 561–81.

Brewer, A. M. (1995). *Change management: Strategies for Australian organisations.* Sydney: Allen & Unwin.

Brewer, M. B. (1996). When contact is not enough: Social identity and intergroup cooperation. *International Journal of Intercultural Relations, 20,* 291–303.

Brewer, M. B., & Harasty, A. S. (1996). Seeing groups as entities. In R. M. Sorrentino & E. T. Higgins (Eds), *Handbook of motivation and cognition,* vol. 3 (pp. 347–70). New York: The Guildford Press.

Brislin, R. W., Cushener, K., Cherrie, C., & Yong, M. (1986). *Intercultural interactions: A practical guide.* Beverly Hills, CA: Sage Publications.

Brown, R. (1965). *Social psychology.* New York: The Free Press.

Brown, R. P., & Charnsangavej, T. (2000). Putting the 'affirm' into affirmative action: Preferential selection and academic performance. *Journal of Personality and Social Psychology, 79,* 736–48.

Brownlow, S. (1992). Seeing is believing: Facial appearance, credibility, and attitude change. *Journal of Non-Verbal Behavior, 16,* 101–115.

Bruce, J., Curtis, H., & Johnston, L. (1998). Social identity in young New Zealand children. *New Zealand Journal of Psychology, 27,* 21–7.

Bruner, J. S., & Tagiuri, R. (1954). Person perception. In G. Lindzey (Ed.), *Handbook of social psychology* (vol. 2) (pp. 634–54). Reading, MA: Addison-Wesley.

Bryan, W., & Harter, N. (1897). Physiology and psychology of the telegraphic language. *Psychological Review, 4,* 27–53.

Bryman, A. (1989). *Research methods and organization studies, vol. 20.* London: Unwin Hyman.

Buchanan, K., & Carr, S. C. (1999). Humidity, anxiety, and test performance. *South Pacific Journal of Psychology, 11,* 34–43 <http://spjp.massey.ac.nz>.

Budesheim, T. L., & Bonnelle, K. (1998). The use of abstract trait knowledge and behavioural exemplars in causal explanations of behaviour. *Personality and Social Psychology Bulletin, 24,* 575–87.

Burgoon, J. (1994). Non-verbal signals. In M. Knapp & G. Miller (Eds), *Handbook of interpersonal communication* (2nd edition) (pp. 344–93). Beverly Hills, CA: Sage.

Burke, R. J. (1997). Organisational tenure and cultural values: Does familiarity breed contempt? *Psychological Reports, 81,* 288–90.

Bushman, B. J. (1998). Priming effects of media violence on the accessibility of aggressive constructs in memory. *Personality and Social Psychology Bulletin, 24,* 537–45.

Bushman, B. J., & Anderson, C. A. (2001). Media violence and the American public. *American Psychologist, 56,* 477–89.

Bushman, B. J., Baumeister, R. F., & Stack, A. D. (1999). Catharsis, aggression, and persuasive influence: Self-fulfilling or self-defeating prophecies? *Journal of Personality and Social Psychology, 76,* 367–76.

Buss, A. (1961). *The psychology of aggression.* New York: John Wiley & Sons.

Buss, D. M. (1985). Human mate selection. *American Scientist, 73,* 47–51.

Buss, D. M. (1989). Sex differences in human mate preferences: Evolutionary hypotheses tests in 37 cultures. *Behavioural and Brain Sciences, 12,* 1–14.

Buss, D. M. (2000). Desires in human mating. In D. LeCroy & P. Moller (Eds), *Evolutionary perspectives on human reproductive behaviour* (pp. 39–49). New York: New York Academy of Sciences.

Buss, D. M., & Schmitt, D. P. (1993). Sexual strategies theory: An evolutionary perspective on human mating. *Psychological Review, 100,* 204–232.

Buss, D. M., & Shackleford, T. K. (1997). From vigilance to violence: Mate retention tactics in married couples. *Journal of Personality and Social Psychology, 72,* 346–61.

Buss, D. M., Larsen, R. J., Westen, D., & Semmelroth, J. (1992). Sex differences in jealousy: Evolution, physiology. *Psychological Science, 3,* 251–5.

Buunk, B. P. (1995). Sex, self-esteem, dependency, and extra-dyadic sexual experiences as related to jealousy responses. *Journal of Social and Personal Relationships, 2,* 147–53.

Buunk, B. P., & Hupka, R. B. (1987). Cross-cultural differences in the elicitation of sexual jealousy. *Journal of Sex Research, 23,* 12–22.

Buunk, B. P., & Mussweiler, T. (2001). New directions in social comparison research. *European Journal of Social Psychology, 31,* 467–75.

Byrne, D. (1971). *The attraction paradigm.* New York: Academic Press.

Byrne, D. (1997). An overview (and underview) of the research and theory within the attraction paradigm. *Journal of Social and Personal Relationships, 14,* 417–31.

Byrne, D., Gouaux, C., Griffitt, W., Lamberth, J., Murakawa, N., Prasad, M. B., Prasad, A., & Ramirez, M. (1971). The ubiquitous relationship: Attitude similarity and attraction: A cross-cultural study. *Human Relations, 24,* 201–7.

Cacioppo, J. T., Berntson, G. B., Sheridan, J. F., & McClintock, M. K. (2000). Multilevel integrative analyses of human behaviour: Social neuroscience and the complementing nature of social and biological approaches. *Psychological Bulletin, 126,* 829–43.

Cacioppo, J. T., Gardner, W. L., & Berntson, G. B. (1999). The affect system has parallel and integrative processing components: Form follows function. *Journal of Personality and Social Psychology, 76,* 839–55.

Callahan, G. L. (1998). A meta-analysis of the Fishbein and Ajzen theory of reasoned action. *Dissertation Abstracts International: Humanities and Social Sciences, 59,* 2-A.

Calvert, J. D. (1988). Physical attractiveness: A review and re-evaluation of its role in social skills research. *Behavioural Assessment, 10,* 29–42.

Campbell, C., & Mzaidume, Y. (2002). How can HIV be prevented in South Africa? A social perspective. *British Medical Journal, 324,* 229–32.

Campbell, D. C., Carr, S. C., & MacLachlan, M. (2001). Attributing 'Third World' poverty in Australia and Malawi: A case of donor bias? *Journal of Applied Social Psychology, 31,* 409–430.

Canary, D. J., Cupach, W. R., & Messman, S. J. (1995). *Relationship conflict: Conflict in parent-child, friendship, and romantic relationships.* Thousand Oaks, CA: Sage.

Cantor, N., & Mischel, W. (1977). Traits as prototypes: Effects on recognition memory. *Journal of Personality and Social Psychology, 35,* 38–48.

Caporael, L. R. (2001). Parts and wholes: The evolutionary importance of groups. In S. Constantine & M. B. Brewer (Eds), *Individual self, relational self, collective self* (pp. 241–58). Philadelphia, PA: Psychology Press/Taylor & Francis.

Caprara, G. V., Barbaranelli, C., Pastorelli, C., & Perugini, M. (1994). Individual differences in the study of human aggression. *Aggressive Behaviour, 20,* 291–303.

Carlson, J. A., & Davis, C. M. (1971). Cultural values and the risky shift: A cross-cultural test in Uganda and the United States. *Journal of Personality and Social Psychology, 20,* 392–9.

Carnevale, P. J., & Probst, T. (1997). Conflict on the Internet. In S. Kiesler (Ed.), *Culture of the Internet* (pp. 233–55). Mahwah, NJ: Lawrence Erlbaum Associates.

Carr, S. C. (1993). The family in Malaŵi as a resource for HIV/AIDS prevention. *Community Alternatives: International Journal of Family Care, 5,* 123–5.

Carr, S. C. (1996a). Social psychology and culture: Reminders from Africa and Asia. In H. Grad, A. Blanco & J. Georgas (Eds), *Key issues in cross-cultural psychology* (pp. 68–88). Lisse, Netherlands: Swets & Zeitlinger.

Carr, S. C. (1996b). Social psychology in Malaŵi: Historical or developmental? *Psychology and Developing Societies, 8,* 177–98.

Carr, S. C. (March 1998). Social equity in diversity: *Capitalising on the Flip-over (and team motivation in diversity).* Darwin: Northern Territory University.

Carr, S. C. (November 1999). *Gravity, demotivation, and resonance: Can we reverse the cycles?* Third International Reversal Theory Workshop, Darwin, Northern Territory.

Carr, S. C. (2000). Privilege, privation, and proximity: 'Eternal triangle' for development? *Psychology and Developing Societies, 12,* 167–76.

Carr, S. C., & Jones, S. (2000). Reconstructing regional meanings of work: Myths, illusions, and economic crisis. *The Asian Psychologist, 2,* 17–18.

Carr, S. C., & MacLachlan, M. (1994). Family health care in Malaŵi: The sustainable community alternative for AIDS management. *Ife Psychologia: An International Journal, 2,* 94–105.

Carr, S. C., & MacLachlan, M. (1997). Motivational gravity. In D. Munro, J. F. Schumaker & S. C. Carr (Eds), *Motivation and culture* (pp. 133–58). New York: Routledge.

Carr, S. C., & MacLachlan, M. (1999). Work motivation in Malaŵi: Neither flat earth nor Babel. *Journal of International Development,* in press.

Carr, S. C., & Sloan, T. S. (in press). *Psychology and Poverty: Emerging Critical perspectives.* New York: Kluwer-Plenum.

Carr, S. C., Bolitho, F., & Purcell, I. P. (1999). *Organisational behaviour.* Darwin: School of Humanities, Social Sciences, and Management, NTU.

Carr, S. C., Chipande, R., & MacLachlan, M. (1998). Expatriate aid salaries in Malaŵi: A doubly demotivating influence? *International Journal of Educational Development, 18,* 133–43.

Carr, S. C., Ehiobuche, I., Rugimbana, R. O., & Munro, D. (1996a). Expatriates' ethnicity and their effectiveness: 'Similarity-Attraction' or 'Inverse Resonance'? *Psychology and Developing Societies, 8,* 265–82.

Carr, S. C., Hodgson, M., & Purcell, I. P. (2000). *Social inequity and double demotivation.* Darwin: NTU.

Carr, S. C., MacLachlan, M., & Schultz, R. (1995). Pacific Asia psychology: Ideas for development. *South Pacific Journal of Psychology, 8,* 1–18 <http://spjp.massey.ac.nz>.

Carr, S. C., MacLachlan, M., Zimba, C. G., & Bowa, M. (1995). Community aid abroad: A Malaŵian perspective. *Journal of Social Psychology, 135,* 781–4.

Carr, S. C., McAuliffe, E., & MacLachlan, M. (1998). *Psychology of aid.* London: Routledge.

Carr, S. C., McLoughlin, D., Hodgson, M., & MacLachlan, M. (1996b). Effects of unreasonable pay discrepancies for under-payment and over-payment on double demotivation. *Genetic, Social, and General Psychology Monographs, 122,* 477–94.

Carr, S. C., Powell, V., Knezovic, M., Munro, D., & MacLachlan, M. (1996c). Measuring motivational gravity: Likert or scenario scaling? *Journal of Managerial Psychology, 11,* 43–7.

Carr, S. C., Purcell, I. P., Bolitho, F. H., Moss, N. D., & Brew, S. E. (1999). Managing attitudes toward high achievers: The influence of group discussion. *Asian Journal of Social Psychology, 2,* 237–44.

Carr, S. C., Rugimbana, R. O., Walkom, E., & Bolitho, F. H. (2001). Selecting expatriates in developing areas: 'Country-of-origin' effects in Tanzania. *International Journal of Intercultural Relations, 25,* 441–57.

Carron, A. V., & Hausenblas, H. A. (1998). *Group dynamics in sport* (2nd edition). Morgantown, MV: Fitness Information Technology.

Carstensen, L. L. (1992). Social and emotional patterns in adulthood: Support for socio-emotional selectivity theory. *Psychology and Aging, 7,* 331–8.

Carstensen, L. L., & Turk, C. S. (1994). The salience of emotion across the adult life span. *Psychology and Aging, 9,* 259–64.

Carstensen, L. L., & Turk, C. S. (1998). Emotion in the second half of life. *Current Directions in Psychological Science, 7,* 144–9.

Carter, C. S. (1998). Neuroendocrine perspectives on social attachment and love. *Psychoneuroendocrinology, 23,* 779–818.

Cashdan, E. (1998). Are men more competitive than women? *British Journal of Social Psychology, 37,* 213–29.

Casimir, G., & Keats, D. M. (1996). The effects of work environment and in-group leadership on the leadership preferences of Anglo-Australians and Chinese Australians. *Journal of Cross-Cultural Psychology, 27,* 436–57.

Castano, E., Yzerbyt, V., Paladino, M. P., & Sacchi, S. (2002). I belong, therefore, I exist: In-group identification, in-group entitativity, and in-group bias. *Personality & Social Psychology Bulletin, 28,* 135–43.

Catalano, R., Novaco, R., & McConnell, W. (1997). A model of the net effect of job loss on violence. *Journal of Personality and Social Psychology, 72,* 1440–47.

Catley, B. (2001). *Waltzing with Matilda: Should Australia join New Zealand*? Wellington: Dark Horse.

Cattell, R. B., & Cattell, H. E. P. (1995). Personality structure and the new fifth edition of the 16PF. *Educational and Psychological Measurement, 55,* 926–41.

Chaiken, S. (1980). Heuristic versus systematic information processing and the use of source versus message cues in persuasion. *Journal of Personality and Social Psychology, 39,* 752–66.

Chaiken, S., & Eagly, A. H. (1976). Communication modality as a determinant of message persuasiveness and message comprehensibility. *Journal of Personality and Social Psychology, 34,* 605–614.

Chamberlain, K., Stephens, C., & Lyons, A. C. (1997). Encompassing experience: Meanings and methods in health psychology. *Psychology and Health, 12,* 691–709.

Chan, E. (2000). Battlefield or cricket pitch: The test of a nation. *Weekend Australian,* 28–29 October, 5–7.

Charbonnier, E., Huguet, P., Brauer, M., & Monteil, J. M. (1998). Social loafing and self-beliefs: People's collective effort depends on the extent to which they distinguish themselves as better than others. *Social Behaviour & Personality, 26,* 329–40.

Charry, J. M., & Hawkinshire, F. B. (1982). Effects of atmospheric electricity on some substrates of disordered behaviour. *Journal of Personality and Social Psychology, 41,* 185–97.

Chatterjee, C. (1999). *Fighting for fairness. Psychology Today, 32,* 14.

Chazin, S., & Neuschatz, J. (1990). Using a mnemonic to aid in the recall of unfamiliar information. *Perceptual and Motor Skills, 71,* 1067.

Chen, Q., & Wells, W. D. (1999). Attitude toward the site. *Journal of Advertising Research, 39,* 27–37.

Cherulnik, P. D., Donley, K. A., Wiewal, T. A. R., & Miller, S. R. (2001). Charisma is contagious: The effect of leaders' charisma on observers' affect. *Journal of Applied Social Psychology, 31,* 2149–59.

Cheung, C. K., & Chan, C. M. (2000). Social-cognitive factors in donating money to charity, with special attention to an international relief organization. *Evaluation and Program Planning, 23,* 241–53.

Chidgey, J. E. (1995). *Managing motivational gravity using a sporting metaphor in Australia.* Newcastle, Australia: University of Newcastle (doctoral thesis in preparation).

Chiles, W. D. (1958). Effects of elevated temperatures on performance of a complex mental task. *Ergonomics, 2,* 89–96.

Chinese Culture Connection (1987). Chinese values and the search for culture-free dimensions of culture. *Journal of Cross-Cultural Psychology, 18,* 143–64.

Chi-yue Chiu & Ying-yi Hong. (1997). Justice in Chinese societies: A Chinese perspective. In H. S. R. Kao & D. Sinha (Eds), *Asian perspectives on psychology* (pp. 164–75). New Delhi: Sage.

Choi, I., & Nisbett, R. E. (1998). Situational salience and cultural differences in the correspondence bias and actor–observer bias. *Personality and Social Psychology Bulletin, 24,* 949–60.

Choi, I., Nisbett, R. E., & Norenzayan, A. (1999). Causal attribution across cultures: Variation and universality. *Psychological Bulletin, 125,* 47–63.

Choo, P., Levine, T., & Hatfield, E. (1996). Gender, love schemas, and reactions to romantic breakups. *Journal of Social Behaviour and Personality, 11,* 143–60.

Christensen, A., & Heavey, C. L. (1993). Gender differences in marital conflict: The demand/withdraw interaction pattern. In S. Oskamp & M. Constanzo (Eds), *Gender issues in contemporary society* (pp. 113–41). Newbury Park, CA: Sage.

Christie, R. (1991). Authoritarianism and related constructs. In J. P. Robinson, P. R. Shaver & L. S. Wrightman (Eds), *Measures of personality and social psychological attitudes* (pp. 501–571). San Diego, CA: Academic.

Church, A. H., & Bracken, D. W. (1997). Advancing the state of the art of 360-degree feedback. *Group and Organisation Management, 22,* 149–61.

Cialdini, R. B. (1975). Reciprocal concessions procedure for inducing compliance: The Door-in-the-Face technique. *Journal of Personality and Social Psychology, 31,* 206–215.

Cialdini, R. B. (1993). *Influence: Science and practice.* New York: Addison-Wesley.

Cicchetti, D., & Rogosch, F. A. (1996). Equifinality and multifinality in developmental psychopathology. *Development & Psychopathology, 8,* 597–600.

Clark, R. (1999). Effect of number of majority defectors on minority influence. *Group Dynamics*, *3*, 303–312.

Clayton, M. J. (1997). Delphi: A technique to harness expert opinion for critical decision-making tasks in education. *Educational Psychology*, *17*, 373–86.

Coch, L., & French, J. R. P. (1948). Overcoming resistance to change. *Human Relations*, *1*, 512–33.

Codol, J. P. (1975). On the so-called 'superior conformity of the self behaviour: Twenty experimental investigations. *European Journal of Social Psychology*, *5*, 427–501.

Cohen, R. L. (1985). Procedural justice and participation. *Human Relations*, *38*, 643–63.

Cohen, S. (2001). *States of denial*. Boston, MA: Blackwell.

Cohen, D., & Nisbett, R. E. (1997). Field experiments examining the culture of honour: The role of institutions in perpetuating norms about violence. *Personality and Social Psychology Bulletin*, *23*, 1188–99.

Cohn, E. G., & Rotton, J. (1997). Assault as a function of time and temperature: A moderator-variable time-series analysis. *Journal of Personality and Social Psychology*, *72*, 1322–4.

Colling, T. (1992). *Beyond mateship: Understanding Australian men*. Sydney: Simon & Schuster.

Colman, A. (1991a). Psychological evidence in South African murder trials. *The Psychologist*, *4*, 482–6.

Colman, A. (1991b). Are there theories at the bottom of his jargon? *The Psychologist*, *4*, 494–5.

Commission of the European Communities (1977). *The perception of poverty in Europe*. Brussels: EEC.

Community Aid Abroad/Freedom From Hunger. (1996/7). *Why a Third World? Exploring the reasons for poverty in developing countries*. Melbourne: Community Aid Abroad/Freedom From Hunger.

Condon, J. W., & Crano, W. D. (1988). Inferred evaluation and the relationship between attitude similarity and interpersonal attraction. *Journal of Personality and Social Psychology*, *54*, 789–97.

Conway, R. (1971). *The great Australian stupor: An interpretation of the Australian way of life*. Melbourne: Sun Books.

Conway, R. (1972). *The great Australian stupor: An interpretation of the Australian way of life*. Adelaide, SA: The Griffin Press.

Coons, C. J., Howard-Hamilton, M., & Waryold, D. (1995). College sports fan aggression: Implications for residence hall discipline. *Journal of College Student Development*, *36*, 587–93.

Cooper, C. (2000). Introduction to special issue exploring work in the new millennium. *Journal of Managerial Psychology*, *15*, 197–201.

Cooper, A., & Sportolari, L. (1998). Romance in cyberspace: Understanding online attraction. *Journal of Sex Education and Therapy*, *22*, 7–14.

Copeland, J. T. (2000). Motivational approaches to expectancy confirmation. In M. H. Davis (Ed.), *Social psychology 00/01* (pp. 66–9). Guilford, CT: Dushkin/McGraw-Hill.

Coren, S. (1999). Do people look like their dogs? *Anthrozooes*, *12*, 111–14.

Corey, G. (1996). *Theory and practice of counselling and psychotherapy* (5th edition). Pacific Grove, CA: Brooks/Cole.

Corneille, O., Yzerbyt, V. Y., Rogier, A., & Buidin, G. (2001). Threat and the Group Attribution Error: When threat elicits judgements of extremity and homogeneity. *Personality & Social Psychology Bulletin*, *27*, 437–46.

Cottrell, N. B. (1968). Performance in the presence of other human beings: Mere presence, audience, and affiliation effects. In E. C. Simmel, R. A, Hoppe & G. A. Milton (Eds), *Social facilitation and imitative behavior* (pp. 91–110). Boston, MA: Allyn & Bacon.

Coupe, N. M. (2000). The epidemiology of Māori suicide in Aotearoa/New Zealand. *South Pacific Journal of Psychology*, *12*, 1–12.

Courney, K. S., & McAuley, E. (1991). Perceived effectiveness of motivational strategies to enhance children's intrinsic interest in sport and physical activity. *Journal of Social Behaviour and Personality*, *6*, 128–36.

Cowley, G. (2000). The biology of beauty. In M. H. Davis (Ed.), *Social psychology 00/01* (pp. 112–16). Guilford, CT: Dushkin/McGraw-Hill.

Cox, E. (1995). *A truly civil society: The 1995 Boyer lectures*. Sydney: ABC Books.

Cozzarelli, C., Wilkinson, A. V., & Tagler, M. J. (2001). Attitudes toward the poor and attributions for poverty. *Journal of Social Issues*, *57*, 207–227.

Cramer, D. (1998). *Close relationships: The study of love and friendship*. Sydney: Arnold.

Crano, W. D. (2000). Milestones in the psychological analysis of social influence. *Group Dynamics*, *4*, 68–80.

Croizet, J. C., & Claire, T. (1998). Extending the concept of stereotype threat to social class: The intellectual underperformance of students from low socio-economic backgrounds. *Personality and Social Psychology Bulletin*, *24*, 588–94.

Cronin, M. W. (1993). Teaching listening skills via interactive videodisc. *THE Journal*, *21*, 62–9.

Crowley, M J., O'Callaghan, M. E., & Ball, P. J. (1994). The juridical impact of psychological expert testimony in a simulated child sexual abuse trial. *Law and Human Behaviour*, *18*, 89–105.

Croyle, R., & Cooper, J. (1983). Dissonance arousal: Physiological evidence. *Journal of Personality and Social Psychology*, *45*, 782–91.

Cunningham, M. R. (1986). Measuring the physical in physical attractiveness: Quasi-experiments on the socio-biology of female facial beauty. *Journal of Personality and Social Psychology*, *50*, 925–35.

Cunningham, M. R., Roberts, A. R., Wu, C. H., Barbee, A. P., & Druen, P. B. (1995). Their ideas of beauty are, on the whole, the same as ours. Consistency and variability in the cross-cultural perception of female physical attraction. *Journal of Personality and Social Psychology*, *68*, 261–79.

Cupach, W. R., Spitzberg, B. H., & Carson, C. L. (2000). Toward a theory of obsessive relational intrusion and stalking. In K. Dindia & S. Duck (Eds), *Communication and personal relationships* (pp. 131–46). Chichester, UK: John Wiley & Sons.

Cushman, P. (1990). Why the self is empty: Toward a historically situated psychology. *American Psychologist, 45*, 599–611.

Cushner, K. (1989). Assessing the impact of a culture-general assimilator. *International Journal of Intercultural Relations, 13*, 125–46.

Cushner, K., & Brislin, R. W. (1996). *Intercultural interactions: A practical guide* (2nd edition). Thousand Oaks, CA: Sage.

Dalkey, N. (1969). *The Delphi method: An experimental study of group opinions.* Santa Monica, CA: The Rand Corporation.

Damsgaard, J., & Scheepers, R. (1999). Power, influence, and intranet implementation: A safari of South African organizations. *Information Technology and People, 12*, 333–58.

Darley, J. B., & Latané, B. (1968). When will people help in a crisis? *Psychology Today, 23*, 130–34.

Darlin, D. (1985). Although U.S. cars are improved, imports still win quality survey. *The Wall Street Journal,* December, 27.

Dasgupta, N., Banaji, M. R. & Abelson, R. P. (1999). Group entitativity and group perception: Associations between physical features and psychological judgement. *Journal of Personality and Social Psychology, 77*, 991–1003.

David, B., & Turner, J. C. (1996). Studies in self-categorization and minority conversion: Is being a member of the out-group an advantage? *British Journal of Social Psychology, 35*, 179–99.

David, B., & Turner, J. C. (1999). Studies in self-categorization and minority conversion: The in-group minority in intra-group and inter-group contexts. *British Journal of Social Psychology, 38*, 115–34.

David, B., & Turner, J. C. (2001). Majority and minority influence: A single process self-categorization analysis. In C. K. W. De Dreu & N. K. De Vries (Eds), *Group consensus and minority influence: Implications for innovation* (pp. 91–121). Oxford, UK: Blackwell.

Davidson, J. (1998). Menace to society: Worried about media violence? Cartoons may be the real culprits. In M. H. Davis (Ed.), *Social psychology 98/99* (2nd edition) (pp. 180–83). Guilford, CT: Dushkin/McGraw-Hill.

Davie, M. R., & Reeves, R. J. (1939). Propinquity of residence before marriage. *American Journal of Sociology, 44*, 510–17.

Davies, P. T., & Cummings, E. M. (1994). Mental conflict and child adjustment: An emotional security hypothesis. *Psychological Bulletin, 116*, 387–411.

Davila, J., Bradbury, T. N., & Karney, B. P. (1999). Attachment change processes in the early years of marriage. *Journal of Personality and Social Psychology, 76*, 783–802.

Davis, E. (1995). Managing together. *HR Monthly, 11*, 6–12.

Davis, J. F. (1999). Effectiveness of Internet advertising by leading national advertisers. In D. W. Schumann & E. Thorson (Eds), *Advertising and the World Wide Web: Advertising and consumer psychology* (pp. 81–97). Mahwah, NJ: Lawrence Erlbaum Associates.

Davis, J. H. (1969). *Group performance.* Reading, MA: Addison-Wesley.

Dawes, A., & Donald, D. (2000). Improving children's chances: Developmental theory and effecting interventions in community contexts. In D. Donald, A. Dawes & J. Louw (Eds), *Addressing childhood adversity* (pp. 1–25). Cape Town: David Philip.

Dawes, R. M. (1971). A case study of graduate admissions: Applications of three principles of human decision-making. *American Psychologist, 26*, 180–88.

Dawes, R., McTavish, J., & Shaklee, H. (1977). Behaviour, communication, and assumptions about other people's behaviour in a commons dilemma situation. *Journal of Personality and Social Psychology, 35*, 1–11.

Dawson, M. D., & Brucker, P. S. (2001). The utility of the Delphi method in MFT [Marriage and Family Therapy] research. *American Journal of Family Therapy, 29*, 125–40.

De Angelis, T. (2000). Minorities' performance is hampered by stereotypes. In M. H. Davis (Ed.), *Social psychology 00/01* (pp. 143–4). Guilford, CT: Dushkin/McGraw-Hill.

De Bruin, E. N. M., & Van Lange, P. A. M. (1999). Impression formation and cooperative behavior. *European Journal of Social Psychology, 29*, 305–328.

De Munck, V. C. (1998a). Lust, love, and arranged marriages in Sri Lanka. In V. C. de Munck (Ed.), *Romantic love and sexual behaviour: Perspectives from the social sciences* (pp. 285–300). Westport, CT: Praeger.

De Munck, V. C. (1998b). *Romantic love and sexual behavior: Perspectives from the social sciences.* Westport, CT: Praeger.

De Paulo, B. M. (1994). Spotting lies: Can humans learn to do better? *Current Directions in Psychological Science, 6*, 83–6.

De Roda, B. L., Martinez-Inigo, D., de Paul, P., & Yela, C. (1999). Romantic beliefs and myths in Spain. *Spanish Journal of Psychology, 2*, 64–73.

De Rosa, A. S., & Smith, A. H. (1998). Polemical social representations and styles of minority influence: Benetton advertising. *Bulletin de Psychologie, 51*, 399–416 (original in French).

De Rougemont, D. (1956). *Love in the Western world.* New York: Pantheon.

De Soto, C. B., Hamilton, M., & Taylor, R. B. (1985). Words, people, and implicit personality theory. *Social Cognition, 3*, 369–82.

Deaux, K., & Wrightsman, L. S. (1984). *Social psychology in the 80s* (4th edition). Monterey, CA: Brooks/Cole.

Dechesne, M., Greenberg, J., Arndt, J., & Schimel, J. (2000). Terror management and the vicissitudes of sports fan affiliation: The effects of mortality salience on optimism and fan identification. *European Journal of Social Psychology, 30*, 813–35.

Deirmenjian, J. M. (1999). Stalking in cyberspace. *Journal of the American Academy of Psychiatry & the Law, 27*, 407–413.

Delbecq, A., & Van de Ven, A. (1971). A group processing model for problem identification and programme planning. *Journal of Applied Behavioural Science, 7*, 466–91.

Denton, D. W. (1999). The attraction-selection-attrition model of organisational behaviour and the homogeneity of managerial personality. *Current Research in Social Psychology, 4* <www.uiowa.edu/~grpproc/crisp/crisp.html>.

Deuel, N. R,. (1996). Our passionate response to virtual reality. In S. C. Herring (Ed.), *Computer-mediated communication: Linguistic, social, and cross-cultural perspectives* (pp. 129–46). Amsterdam: John Benjamin.

Deutsch, M., & Gerard, H. G. (1955). A study of normative and informational social influence upon individual judgement. *Journal of Abnormal and Social Psychology, 51*, 629–36.

Deverall, M. (1997). The counseling consultant's role in assessing organizations for counseling. In M. Carroll & M. Walton (Eds), *Handbook of counseling in organizations* (pp. 111–28). Thousand Oaks, CA: Sage.

Devine, P. G. (1996). Breaking the prejudice habit. *Psychological Science Agenda*, January/February, 10–11.

Devine, P. G., Plant, E. A., & Buswell, B. N. (2000). Breaking the prejudice habit: Progress and obstacles. In S. Oskamp et al. (Eds), *Reducing prejudice and discrimination* (pp. 185–208). Mahwah, NJ: Lawrence Erlbaum Associates.

Di Milia, L., & Smith, P. (1997). Australian management selection practices: Why does the interview remain popular? *Asia Pacific Journal of Human Resources, 35*, 90–103.

Diab, L. N. 91970). A study of intra-group and inter-group relations among experimentally produced small groups. *Genetic Psychology Monographs, 82*, 49–82.

Dickson, D. H., & Kelly, I. W. (1985). The 'Barnum Effect' in personality assessment: A review of the literature. *Psychological Reports, 57*, 367–82.

Dikstra, P., & Buunk, B. P. (1998). Jealousy as a function of rival characteristics: An evolutionary perspective. *Personality and Social Psychology Bulletin, 24*, 1158–66.

Dindia, K., & Allen, M. (1992). Sex differences in self-disclosure: A meta-analysis. *Psychological Bulletin, 112*, 106–124.

Dion, K. K., & Dion, K. L. (1993). Individualistic and collectivistic perspectives on gender and the cultural context of love and intimacy. *Journal of Social Issues, 49*, 53–69.

Dipboye, R. L. (1977). The effectiveness of one-sided and two-sided appeals as a function of familiarization and context. *Journal of Social Psychology, 102*, 125–31.

Dixon, N. F. (1994). Disastrous decisions. *The Psychologist, 7*, 303–7.

Dodson, P. (1998). *Will the circle be unbroken? Cycles of survival for Indigenous Australians.* Discussion Paper No. 12. Darwin: North Australia Research Unit/Australian National University. Transcript of the 1998 Dr. H. C. (Nugget) Coombs North Australia Lecture.

Doise, W. (1969). Intergroup relations and polarisation of individual and collective judgements. *Journal of Personality and Social Psychology, 12*, 136–43.

Dollard, J., Doob, L. W., Miller, N. E., Mowrer, O. H., & Sears, R. R. (1939). *Frustration and aggression.* New Haven, CT: Yale University Press.

Donnerstein, E., & Wilson, D. W. (1976). Effects of noise and perceived control on ongoing and subsequent aggressive behaviour. *Journal of Social and Personality Psychology, 34*, 774–81.

Dore, R. (1994). Why visiting sociologists fail. *World Development, 22*, 1425–36.

Dorward, D. (1996). Africa and development in the 21st century. *Development Bulletin, 37*, 4–7.

Douglas, K. M., & McGarty, C. (2001). Identifiability and self-presentation: Computer-mediated communication and inter-group interaction. *British Journal of Social Psychology, 40*, 399–416.

Douglas, K. M., & McGarty, C. (2002). Internet identity and beyond: A model of the effects of identifiability on communicative behavior. *Group Dynamics, 6*, 17–26.

Dovidio, J. F., Kawakami, K., Johnson, C., Johnson, B., & Howard, A. (1997). On the nature of prejudice: Automatic and controlled processes. *Journal of Experimental Social Psychology, 33*, 510–40.

Dowling, P. J., Schuler, R. S., & Welch, D. G. (1994). *International dimensions of human resource management* (2nd edition). Belmont, CA: Wadsworth.

Downer, A. (1997). *Better aid for a better future — Seventh annual report to Parliament on Australia's Development Cooperation Program and the government's response to the Committee of Review of Australia's Overseas Aid Program.* Canberra: AusAid.

Drigotas, S. M., Whitton, S. W., Rsubult, C. E., & Wieselquist, J. (1999). Close partner as sculptor of the ideal self: Behavioral affirmation and the Michelangelo phenomenon. *Journal of Personality and Social Psychology, 77*, 293–323.

Driscoll, R., Davis, K. E., & Lipetz, M. E. (1972). Parental influence and romantic love: The Romeo and Juliet effect. *Journal of Personality and Social Psychology, 24*, 1–10.

Duck, S. (1997). *Handbook of personal relationships: Theories, research, and interventions* (2nd edition). Brisbane: John Wiley & Sons.

Duck, S., & Wright, P. H. (1993). Re-examining gender differences in same-gender friendships: A close look at two kinds of data. *Sex Roles, 28*, 709–727.

Duckitt, J. (2001). A dual-process cognitive-motivational theory of ideology and prejudice. *Advances in Experimental Social Psychology, 33*, 41–113.

Dudley, R. T., & Papini, M. R. (1997). Amsel's frustration effect: A Pavlovian replication with control for frequency and distribution of rewards. *Physiology and Behaviour, 61,* 627–9.

Dulebohn, J. H. (1997). Social influences in justice evaluations of human resources systems. In G. R. Ferris (Ed.), *Research in personnel and human resources management, vol. 15* (pp. 241–92). Greenwich, CT: JAI Press.

Dunbar, J. (2000). Bystander's dilemma — to act or do nothing. *New Zealand Herald,* 17 June. New Zealand Herald Online <www.nzherald.co.nz>.

Dunderstadt, H. (1996). *The world's weirdest web pages and the people who create them.* San Francisco, CA: No Starch Press <www.angry.net>.

Dunn, D. S. (1989). Demonstrating a self-serving bias. *Teaching of Psychology, 16,* 21–2.

Dunphy, D. C., & Dick, R. (1987). *Organisational change by choice.* Sydney: McGraw-Hill.

Dunphy, D., & Stace, D. (1993). The strategic management of corporate change. *Human Relations, 46,* 905–920.

Durie, M. (2000). Public health strategies for Māori. *Health Education & Behaviour, 27,* 288–95.

Durrett, M. E., Otaki, M., & Richards, P. (1984). Attachment and the mother's perception of support from the father. *International Journal of Behavioural Development, 7,* 167–76.

Dutton, D. G., & Aron, A. P. (1974). Some evidence for heightened sexual attraction under conditions of high anxiety. *Journal of Personality and Social Psychology, 30,* 510–17.

Dvir, T., Eden, D., & Banjo, M. L. (1995). Self-fulfilling prophecy and gender: Can women be Pygmalion and Galatea? *Journal of Applied Psychology, 80,* 253–70.

Eagly, A. (July 1999). *Few women at the top: Is prejudice a cause?* XXVII InterAmerican Congress of Psychology, Caracas, Venezuela.

Eagly, A. H., & Chaiken, S. (1993). *The psychology of attitudes.* Orlando, FL: Harcourt Brace Jovanovich.

Eagly, A. H., Ashmore, R. D., Makhijani, M. G., & Longo, L. C. (1991). What is beautiful is good but …: A meta-analytic review of research on the physical attractiveness stereotype. *Psychological Bulletin, 110,* 109–128.

Earley, P. C. (1993). East meets West meets Mid East: Further explorations of collectivistic and individualistic work groups. *Academy of Management Journal, 36,* 319–48.

Earley, P. C. (1997). Doing an about-face: Social motivation and cross-cultural currents. In P. C. Earley & M. Erez (Eds), *New perspectives on industrial/organisational psychology* (pp. 243–55). San Francisco, CA: New Lexington Press.

Eayrs, C. B., & Ellis, N. (1990). Charity advertising: For or against people with a mental handicap. *British Journal of Social Psychology, 29,* 349–60.

Eckersley, R. (1997). Psychosocial disorders in young people: On the agenda but not on the mend. *Medical Journal of Australia, 166,* 423–4.

Edelman, S., Craig, A., & Kidman, A. D. (2000). Can psychotherapy increase the survival time of cancer patients? *Journal of Psychosomatic Research, 49,* 149–56.

Ehrensaft, M. K., & Vivian, D. (1996). Spouses' reasons for not reporting existing marital aggression as a marital problem. *Journal of Family Psychology, 10,* 443–53.

Ehrlichman, H., & Eichenstein, R. (1992). Private wishes: Gender similarities and differences. *Sex Roles, 26,* 399–422.

Einarsen, S. (2000). Harassment and bullying at work: A review of the Scandinavian approach. *Aggression & Violent Behavior, 5,* 379–401.

Einarsen, S., Raknes, B. I., Matthiesen, S. B., & Helleson, O. H. (1996). The health-related aspects of bullying in the workplace: The moderating effects of social support and personality. *Nordisk Psykologi, 48,* 116–37 [English abstract, text in Norwegian].

Ekman, P., & Friesen, W. V. (1974). Detecting deception from the body or face. *Journal of Personality and Social Psychology, 29,* 288–98.

Ekman, P., & O'Sullivan, M. (1991). Who can catch a liar? *American Psychologist, 46,* 913–20.

Elkit, A. (1997). The aftermath of an industrial disaster. *Acta Scandinavica, 96,* 1–25.

Ellis, A. (1996). The treatment of morbid jealousy: A rational emotive behaviour therapy approach. *Journal of Cognitive Psychotherapy, 10,* 23–33.

Ellsworth, P. C., Carlsmith, J. M., & Henson, A. (1972). Staring as a stimulus to fight in animals: A series of field studies. *Journal of Personality and Social Psychology, 21,* 302–311.

Enns, C. (1994). On teaching abut the cultural relativism of psychological constructs. *Teaching of Psychology, 21,* 205–211.

Erez, M. (July 2002). Keynote address on globalisation. XXV International Congress of Applied Psychology, Singapore.

Erikson, E. H. (1968). *Identity, youth, and crisis.* New York: Norton.

Ernulf, K. E., & Innala, S. M. (1998). Masculinity, femininity, and sexual attractiveness: A cross-national perspective. *Scandinavian Journal of Sexology, 1,* 107–120.

Eze, N. (1985). Sources of motivation among Nigerian managers. *Journal of Social Psychology, 125,* 341–345.

Fadil, P. A., & Moss, S. E. (1998). An integrative framework of cognitive stereotypes in the bi-cultural leader/member dyad. In T. A. Scandura & M. G. Serapio (Eds), *Research in international business and international relations: Leadership and innovation in emerging markets,* vol. 7 (pp. 83–115). Stamford, CT: JAI Press.

Fanon, F. (1985). *The wretched of the Earth.* Bungay, UK: Penguin/Pelican.

Fanon, F. (1986). *Black skins, white masks.* London: Pluto Press.

Farh, J. L., & Cheng, B. S. (1997). Modesty bias in self-rating in Taiwan: Impact of item wording, modesty value, and self-esteem. *Chinese Journal of Psychology*, *39*, 103–118.

Farmer, E. W. (1992). Ionization. In A. P. Smith & D. M. Jones (Eds), *Handbook of human performance* (pp. 237–60). San Diego, CA: Academic Press.

Fazio, R. H. (2001). On the automatic activation of associated evaluations: An overview. *Cognition and Emotion*, *15*, 115–41.

Fazio, R. H., Jackson, J. R., Dunton, B. C., & Williams, C. J. (1995). Variability in automatic activation as an unobtrusive measure of racial attitudes: A bona fide pipeline? *Journal of Personality and Social Psychology*, *69*, 1013–27.

Feagin, J. R. (1972). Poverty: We still believe that God helps those who help themselves. *Psychology Today*, *6*, 101–129.

Feather, N. T. (1963). The relationship of expectation of success to reported probability, task structure, and achievement related motivation. *Journal of Abnormal & Social Psychology*, *66*, 231–8.

Feather, N. T. (1974). Explanations of poverty in Australian and American samples: The person, society, or fate? *Australian Journal of Psychology*, *26*, 199–216.

Feather, N. T. (1989). Attitudes toward the high achiever: The fall of the tall poppy. *Australian Journal of Psychology*, *41*, 239–67.

Feather, N. T. (1994). Attitudes toward high achievers and reactions to their fall: Theory and research concerning tall poppies. *Advances in Experimental Social Psychology*, *26*, 1–73.

Feather, N. T. (1998). Attitudes toward high achievers, self-esteem, and value priorities for Australian, American, and Canadian students. *Journal of Cross-Cultural Psychology*, *29*, 749–59.

Feather, N. T. (1999). *Values, achievement, and justice: The psychology of deservingness.* Dordrecht, NL: Kluwer-Plenum.

Feather, N. T., & McKee, I. R. (1996). Global self-esteem and the fall of high achievers: Australian and Japanese comparisons. In J. Pandey & D. Sinha (Eds), *Asian contributions to cross-cultural psychology* (pp. 200–213). Thousand Oaks, CA: Sage.

Feather, N. T., & O'Driscoll, M. P. (1980). Observers' reactions to an equal or equitable allocator in relation to allocator input, causal attributions, and value importance. *European Journal of Social Psychology*, *10*, 107–129.

Feather, N. T., & Simon, J. G. (1975). Reactions to male and female success and failure in sex-linked occupations: Impressions of personality, causal attributions, and perceived likelihood of different consequences. *Journal of Personality and Social Psychology*, *31*, 20–31.

Fehr, B. (1993). How do I love thee? Let me consult my prototype. In S. Duck (Ed.), *Individuals in relationships* (pp. 87–120). Thousand Oaks, CA: Sage.

Fehr, B. (1999). Lay people's conceptions of commitment. *Journal of Personality and Social Psychology*, *76*, 90–103.

Fehr, B., & Russell, J. A. (1991). The concept of love viewed from a prototype perspective. *Journal of Personality and Social Psychology*, *60*, 425–38.

Felmlee, D. H. (1998). Fatal attraction. In B. H. Spitzberg & W. J. Cupach (Eds), *The dark side of close relationships* (pp. 3–31). Mahwah, NJ: Lawrence Erlbaum Associates.

Fernandez, K. V., & Rosen, D. L. (2000). The effectiveness of information and colour on Yellow Pages advertising. *Journal of Advertising*, *29*, 61–73.

Festinger, L. (1950). Informal social communication. *Psychological Review*, *57*, 271–82.

Festinger, L. (1954). A theory of social comparison processes. *Human Relations*, *7*, 117–40.

Festinger, L. (1957). *A theory of cognitive dissonance.* Stanford, CA: Stanford University Press.

Festinger, L., Schachter, S., & Back, K. (1950). *Social pressures in informal groups: A study of human factors in housing.* New York: Harper.

Fiedler, F. E. (1978). The contingency model and the dynamics of the leadership process. *Advances in Experimental Social Psychology*, *11*, 59–112.

Fiedler, F. E., & Garcia, J. E. (1987). *Improving leadership effectiveness: Cognitive resources and organisational performance.* New York: John Wiley & Sons.

Fiedler, F. E., & House, R. J. (1994). Leadership theory and research: A report of progress. In C. L. Cooper & I. T. Robertson (Eds), *Key reviews in managerial psychology* (pp. 97–116). New York: John Wiley & Sons.

Fiedler, F. E., Mitchell, T., & Triandis, H. C. (1971). The culture assimilator: An approach to cross-cultural training. *Journal of Applied Psychology*, *55*, 95–102.

Fijneman, Y. A., Willemsen, M. E., & Poortinga, Y. H. (1996). Individualism-collectivism: An empirical study of a conceptual issue. *Journal of Cross-Cultural Psychology*, *27*, 381–402.

Filley, C. M., Kelly, J. P., & Price, B. H. (2001). Violence and the brain: An urgent need for research. *The Scientist*, *15*, 39.

Fine, B. J., Cohen, A., & Crist, B. (1960). Effect of exposure to high humidity at hight and moderate ambient temperature on anagram solution and auditory discrimination. *Psychological Reports*, *7*, 171–81.

Fishbein, M., & Hunter, R. (1964). Summation versus balance in attitude organisation and change. *Journal of Abnormal and Social Psychology*, *69*, 505–510.

Fisher, C. D., & Boyle, G. J. (1997). Personality and employee selection: Credibility regained. *Asia Pacific Journal of Human Resources*, *35*, 26–40.

Fisher-Lokou, J. (1997). The theory of minority conversion as model of approach for influence processes in a mediation situation. *Cahiers Internationaux de Psychologie Sociale*, *35*, 12–29.

Fiske, S. J. (1993). Social cognition and social perception. *Annual Review of Psychology*, *44*, 155–94.

Fiske, S. T., & Taylor, S. (1991). *Social cognition* (2nd edition). New York: Random House.

Fitness, J., & Fletcher, G. J. O. (1993). Love, hate, anger, and jealousy in close relationships: A prototype and cognitive appraisal analysis. *Journal of Personality and Social Psychology, 65,* 942–58.

Flanagan, J. C. (1954). The critical incident technique. *Psychological Bulletin, 51,* 327–49.

Flavell, J. A. (1977). *Cognitive development.* Englewood Cliffs, NJ: Prentice Hall.

Fleming, M. J., & Rickwood, D. J. (2001). Effects of violent versus non-violent videogames on children's arousal, aggressive mood, and positive mood. *Journal of Applied Social Psychology, 31,* 2047–71.

Fletcher, G. J. O. (2002). *The new science of intimate relations.* Malden, MA: Blackwell.

Fletcher, G. J. O., & Simpson, J. A. (2001a). Ideal standards in close relationships. In J. P. Forgas & K. D. Williams (Eds), *The social mind: Cognitive and motivational aspects of interpersonal behaviour* (pp. 257–73). New York: Cambridge University Press.

Fletcher, G. J. O., & Simpson, J. A. (2001b). Ideal standards in closed relationships: Their structure and functions. *Current Directions in Psychological Science, 9,* 102–5.

Fletcher, G. J. O., Simpson, J. A., & Thomas, G. (2000). Ideals, perceptions, and evaluations in early relationship development. *Journal of Personality and Social Psychology, 79,* 933–40.

Fletcher, G. J. O., Simpson, J. A., Thomas, G., & Giles, L. (1999). Ideals in intimate relationships. *Journal of Personality and Social Psychology, 76,* 72–89.

Fletcher, G. J. O., Thomas, G., & Durrant, R. (1999). Cognitive and behavioural accommodation in close relationships. *Journal of Social & Personal Relationships, 16,* 705–730.

Florian, V., & Mikulincer, M. (1998). Terror management in childhood: Does death conceptualisation moderate the effects of mortality salience on acceptance of similar and different others? *Personality & Social Psychology Bulletin, 24,* 1104–12.

Folger, R., & Greenberg, J. (1985). Procedural justice: An interpretative analysis of personnel systems. In K. Rowland & G. Ferris (Eds), *Research in personnel and human resources management,* vol. 3 (pp. 141–83). Greenwich, CT: JAI Press.

Fontaine, G. (2002). Teams in teleland: Working effectively in geographically dispersed teams 'in' the Asia Pacific. *Team Performance and Management, 8,* in press.

Fontana, D. (1992). *Social skills at work.* Exeter, UK: Routledge.

Forbes, R., & Farey, P. (1997). Managers squeezed from all sides. *HR Monthly, 11,* 19–22.

Forgas, J. B. P. (1985). *Interpersonal behaviour: The psychology of social interaction.* Sydney: Pergamon.

Forgas, J. P. (1992a). Affect and social perception: Research evidence and an integrative theory. In W. Stroebe & M. Hewstone (Eds), *European Review of Social Psychology, 3.* Chichester, UK: John Wiley & Sons.

Forgas, J. P. (1992b). On mood and peculiar people: Affect and person typicality in impression formation. *Journal of Personality and Social Psychology, 62,* 863–75.

Forgas, J. P. (1995). Mood and judgement: The affect infusion model (AIM). *Psychological Bulletin, 117,* 39–66.

Forgas, J. P. (1998). On being happy and mistaken: Mood effects on the fundamental attribution error. *Journal of Personality and Social Psychology, 75,* 318–31.

Foster, B., & Seeker, K. R. (1997). *Coaching for peak performance.* California: Richard Cheng Associates.

Fountain, S. (1995). *Education for development.* London: Hodder & Stoughton/UNICEF.

Fox, J., & Carr, S. C. (2000). Internet technology and poverty relief. *South Pacific Journal of Psychology, 12,* 52–7 <http://spjp.massey.ac.nz>.

Fraley, R. C., & Shaver, P. R. (1998). Airport separations: A naturalistic study of adult attachment dynamics in separating couples. *Journal of Personality and Social Psychology, 75,* 1198–1212.

Fraser, C. (1978). Small groups II: Processes and products. In H. Tajfel & C. Fraser (Eds), *Introducing social psychology* (pp. 201–228). Ringwood, Victoria: Penguin.

Fredrickson, B. L. (1995). Socio-emotional behaviour at the end of college life. *Journal of Social and Personal Relationships, 12,* 261–76.

French, J. R. P., & Raven, B. (1959). The bases of social power. In D. Cartwright & A. Zander (Eds), *Studies in social power* (pp. 150–67). Ann Arbor, MI: University of Michigan Press.

Freud, S. (1926). *The question of lay analysis.* (Translated and reprinted in 1962.) Harmondsworth, UK: Penguin.

Freud, S. (1957). Letter to Albert Einstein, 1932. *Revue française de psychanalyse, 21,* 757–68. [Abstract only is in English. Taken from PsychINFO database.]

Fromkin, H. L. (1972). Feelings of interpersonal undistinctiveness: An unpleasant affective state. *Journal of Experimental Research in Personality, 6,* 178–85.

Fromkin, H. L., & Brock, T. C. (1973). Erotic materials: A community theory analysis of the enhanced desirability that may accompany their unavailability. *Journal of Applied Social Psychology, 3,* 219–31.

Fry, P. S., & Ghosh, R. (1980). Attributions of success and failure: A comparison of cultural differences between Asian and Caucasian children. *Journal of Cross-Cultural Psychology, 11,* 343–63.

Fujino, D. C. (1997). The rates, patterns, and reasons for forming heterosexual interracial dating relationships among Asian Americans. *Journal of Social and Personal Relationships, 14,* 809–829.

Fukuda, J. (1999). 'Bushido': The guiding principle of New Japan. In H. S. R. Kao, D. Sinha & B. Wilpert (Eds), *Management and cultural values* (pp. 73–85). New Delhi: Sage.

Fuller, R. (1996). Human-computer-human interaction: How computers affect interpersonal communication. In D. L. Day & D. K. Kovacs (Eds), Computers, communication, and mental models (pp. 11–14). London: Taylor & Francis.

Furnham, A. (1982a). Explaining poverty in India: A study of religious group differences. *Psychologia: An International Journal of Psychology in the Orient*, 25, 236–43.

Furnham, A. (1982b). The perception of poverty among adolescents. *Journal of Adolescence*, 5, 135–47.

Furnham, A., & Bochner, S. (1986). *Culture shock: Psychological reactions to unfamiliar environments.* London: Methuen.

Gabb, D. (1998). Commentary: Australian Psychological Society Position Paper on racism and prejudice. *Australian Psychologist*, 33, 183–6.

Gabriel, M. T., Critelli, J. W., & Ee, J. S. (1994). Narcissistic illusions in self-evaluations of intelligence and attractiveness. *Journal of Personality*, 62, 143–55.

Gaertner, L., & Schopler, J. (1998). Perceived in-group entitativity and inter-group bias: An interconnection of self and others. *European Journal of Social Psychology*, 28, 963–80.

Gallois, C., & Callan, V. (1997). *Communication and culture: A guide for practice.* Brisbane: John Wiley & Sons.

Gallois, C., Callan, V. J., & Palmer, J. A. (1993). The influence of applicant communication style and interview characteristics on hiring decisions. *Journal of Applied Social Psychology*, 22, 1041–60.

Gangestad, S. W. (1993). Sexual selection and physical attractiveness: Implications for mating dynamics. *Human Nature*, 4, 205–235.

Ganzach, Y. (1995). Negativity (and positivity) in performance evaluation: Three field studies. *Journal of Applied Psychology*, 80, 491–9.

Gao, G. (2001). Intimacy, passion, and commitment in Chinese and US American romantic relationships. *International Journal of Intercultural Relations*, 25, 329–42.

George, J. M. (1995). Asymmetrical effects of rewards and punishments: The case of social loafing. *Journal of Occupational and Organisational Psychology*, 68, 327–38.

Gergen, K. J. (1973). Social psychology as history. *Journal of Personality and Social Psychology*, 26, 309–320.

Gergen, K. J. (1994a). Metaphor, meta theory, and the social world. In D. E. Leary (Ed.), *Metaphors in the history of psychology* (pp. 267–99). Cambridge, MA: Cambridge University Press.

Gergen, K. J. (1994b). *Toward transformation in social knowledge* (2nd edition). Thousand Oaks, CA: Sage.

Giacalone, R. A., & Beard, J. W. (1994). Impression management, diversity, and international management. *American Behavioral Scientist*, 37, 621–36.

Gibson, C. B., & Marcoulides, G. A. (1995). The invariance of leadership styles across four countries. *Journal of Managerial Issues*, 7, 160–92.

Gillen, T. (1998). *Assertiveness.* London: Chartered Institute of Personnel and Development (CIPD).

Gilmour, R. (1988). Crowd panic: Competing and cooperating in groups. In G. M. Breakwell, H. Foot & R. Gilmour (Eds), *Doing social psychology: Laboratory and field exercises* (pp. 279–90). Melbourne: The British Psychological Society.

Gladue, B. A., & Delaney, H. J. (1990). Gender differences in perception of attractiveness of men and women in bars. *Personality and Social Psychology Bulletin*, 16, 378–91.

Glanz, K., & Maddock, J. (2000). On judging models and theories: Research and practice, psychology and public health. *Journal of Health Psychology*, 5, 151–4.

Gleitman, H. (1986). *Psychology.* New York: Norton.

Gleitman, H. (1988). *Psychology* (2nd edition). New York: Norton.

Gleitman, H. (1997). Solomon E. Asch (1907–1996): Obituary. *American Psychologist*, 52, 984–5.

Glynn, T., & Carr, S. C. (1999). Motivation and performance in teams: Transforming loafing into resonance. *South Pacific Journal of Psychology*, 11, 71–7.

Godin, G., Maticka-Tyndale, E., Adrien, A., Manson-Singer, S., Willms, D., & Cappon, P. (1996). Cross-cultural testing of three social cognitive theories: An application to condom use. *Journal of Applied Social Psychology*, 26, 1566–86.

Godwin, N. (1994). A distorted view: Myths and images of developing countries. *Development Bulletin*, 30, 46–8.

Goffman, E. (1959). *The presentation of self in everyday life.* New York: Doubleday Anchor.

Goldberg, L. R. (1981). Language and individual differences: The search for universals in personality lexicons. In L. Wheeler (Ed.), *Review of personality and social psychology,* vol. 2 (pp. 141–65). Beverly Hills, CA: Sage.

Goldberg, L. R. (1990). An alternative 'description of personality': The big five factor structure. *Journal of Personality and Social Psychology*, 59, 1216–29.

Goldman, M., Cowles, M. D., & Florez, C. A. (1983). The halo effect of an initial impression upon speaker and audience. *Journal of Social Psychology*, 120, 197–201.

Goldstein, J., & Arms, R. (1971). Effects of observing athletic contests on hostility. *Sociometry*, 34, 456–65.

Goldstein, M. D. (1998). Forming and testing implicit personality theories in cyberspace. *Teaching of Psychology*, 25, 216–20.

Goleman, D. (1998). What makes a leader? *Harvard Business Review,* November/December, 93–102.

Gologor, E. (1977). Group polarisation in a non-risk-taking culture. *Journal of Cross-Cultural Psychology*, 8, 331–47.

Goodwin, R. (1997). Cross-cultural personal relationships. In D. Munro, J. F. Schumaker & S. C. Carr (Eds), *Motivation and culture* (pp. 49–61). New York: Routledge.

Goosens, F. A., Van Ijzendoorn, M. H., Tavecchio, L. W., & Kroonenberg, P. M. (1986). Stability of attachment across time and context in a Dutch sample. *Psychological Reports, 58,* 23–52.

Goren, S. (2001). Healing the victim, the young offender, and the community, via restorative justice: An international perspective. *Issues in Mental Health Nursing, 22,* 137–49.

Gottman, J. M. G. (1998). Psychology and the study of the marital processes. *Annual Review of Psychology, 49,* 169–97.

Gottman, J. M. G. (2000). Marriage styles: The good, the bad, and the volatile. In M. H. Davis (Ed.), *Social psychology 00/01* (4th edition) (pp. 120–25). Guilford, CT: Dushkin/McGraw-Hill.

Gould, S. J. (1994). Pride of place: Science without taxonomy is blind. *The Sciences,* March/April, 38–9.

Gouldner, A. W. (1960). The norm of reciprocity: A preliminary statement. *American Sociological Review, 25,* 161–78.

Gow, D. D. (1991). Collaboration in development consulting: Stooges, hired guns, or musketeers? *Human Organisation, 50,* 1–15.

Gray, D., & Sputore, B. (1998). The effective and culturally appropriate evaluation of Aboriginal community alcohol intervention projects. In T. Stockwell (Ed.), *Drug trials and tribulations: Lessons for Australian policy* (pp. 37–51). Perth, WA: Centre for Research into the Prevalence of Drug Abuse.

Greenberg, J. (1987). A taxonomy of organisational justice theories. *Academy of Management Review, 12,* 9–22.

Greenberg, J. (1990). Employee theft as a reaction to under-payment inequity: The hidden cost of pay cuts. *Journal of Applied Psychology, 75,* 561–8.

Greenberg, J., Melvin, M. M., & Lehman, D. R. (1985). Justice in sports and games. *Journal of Sport Behaviour, 8,* 18–33.

Greenberg, J., Pyszczynski, T., Solomon, S., & Simon, L. (1994). Role of consciousness and accessibility of death-related thoughts in mortality salience effects. *Journal of Personality and Social Psychology, 67,* 627–37.

Gregory, R. J. (2000). *Psychological testing.* Sydney: Allyn & Bacon.

Gregory, R. J. (2001). Parallel themes: Community psychology and Māori culture in Aotearoa. *Journal of Community Psychology, 29,* 19–27.

Griffiths, K. (1999). Aid adverts that juxtapose rich and poor: A preliminary test of their efficacy in North Australia. *South Pacific Journal of Psychology, 11,* 85–8 <http://spjp.massey.ac.nz>.

Grossman, M., & Wood, W. (1993). Sex differences in intensity of emotional experience: A social role interpretation. *Journal of Personality and Social Psychology, 65,* 1010–20.

Grossmann, K. E., Grossman, K., Huber, F., & Wartner, U. (1981). German children's behaviour towards their mothers at 12 months and their fathers at 18 months in Ainsworth's Strange Situation. *International Journal of Behavioural Development, 4,* 157–81.

Grush, J. E., Clore, G. L., & Costin, F. (1975). Dissimilarity and attraction: When difference makes a difference. *Journal of Personality and Social Psychology, 32,* 783–9.

Guerin, B. (1999). Social behaviours as determined by different arrangements of social consequences: Social loafing, social facilitation, deindividuation, and a modified social loafing. *Psychological Record, 49,* 565–78.

Guerrero, L. K., & Andersen, P. A. (1998). The dark side of jealousy and envy: Desire, delusion, desperation, and destructive communication. In B. H. Spitzberg & W. R. Cupach (Eds), *The dark side of close relationships* (pp. 33–70). London: Lawrence Erlbaum Associates.

Gupta, U., & Singh, P. (1982). An exploratory study of love and liking and type of marriages. *Indian Journal of Applied Psychology, 19,* 92–7.

Guzzo, R., Jette, R. D., & Katzell, R. A. (1985). The effects of psychologically based intervention programs on worker productivity: A meta analysis. *Personnel Psychology, 38,* 275–91.

Hacker, H. M. (1982). Blabbermouths and clams: Sex differences in self-disclosure in same-sex and cross-sex friendship dyads. *Psychology of Women Quarterly, 5,* 385–401.

Hall, E. T. (1959). *The silent language.* New York: Doubleday.

Hall, E. T. (1966). *The hidden dimension.* New York: Doubleday.

Hamm, J. V. (2000). Do birds of a feather flock together? The variable base for African American, Asian American, and European American adolescents' selection of similar friends. *Developmental Psychology, 36,* 201–219.

Hammersla, J. F., & Frease-McMahan, L. (1990). University students' priorities: Life goals vs. relationships. *Sex Roles, 23,* 1–14.

Hammock, G. S., Rosen, S., Richardson, D. R., & Bernstein, S. (1990). Aggression as equity restoration. *Journal of Research in Personality, 23,* 398–409.

Hammond, J. R., & Fletcher, G. J. (1991). Attachment styles and relationship satisfaction in the development of close relationships. *New Zealand Journal of Psychology, 20,* 56-62.

Handy, C. (1995). *The empty raincoat: Making sense of the future.* Sydney: Random House.

Harber, K. D. (1998). Feedback to minorities: Evidence of a positive bias. *Journal of Personality and Social Psychology, 74,* 622–8.

Hardeman, W., Johnston, M., Johnston, D. W., Bonetti, D., Wareham, N. J., & Kinmonth, A. L. (2002). Application of the theory of planned behavior change interventions: A systematic review. *Psychology & Health, 17,* 123–58.

Hardin, G. (1968). The tragedy of the commons. *Science, 162,* 1243.

Harkins, S., Latané, B., & Williams, K. (1980). Social loafing: Allocating effort or taking it easy? *Journal of Experimental Social Psychology, 16,* 457–65.

Harmon-Jones, E., Greenberg, J., Solomon, S., & Simon, L. (1996). The effects of mortality salience on intergroup bias between minimal groups. *European Journal of Social Psychology, 26,* 677–81.

Harpaz, I. (1989). Non-financial employment commitment: A cross-national comparison. *Journal of Occupational Psychology, 62,* 147–50.

Harper, D. J. (1996). Accounting for poverty: From attribution to discourse. *Journal of Community and Applied Social Psychology, 6,* 249–65.

Harper, D. J. (in press). Poverty and discourse: critical perspectives. In S. C. Carr & T. S. Sloan (Eds), *Poverty and psychology: Critical emergent perspectives* (in press). New York: Kluwer-Plenum.

Harper, D., Wagstaff, G. F., Newton, J. L., & Harrison, K. R. (1990). Lay causal perceptions of Third World poverty and the just world theory. *Social Behaviour and Personality, 18,* 235–8.

Harré, R., & Van Langenhove, L. (1992). Varieties of positioning. *Journal for the Theory of Social Behaviour, 21,* 393–407.

Harrington, L., & Liu, J. H. (2002). Self-enhancement and attitude toward high achievers: A bicultural view of the independent and interdependent self. *Journal of Cross-Cultural Psychology, 33,* 37–55.

Harris, C. R. (2002). Sexual and romantic jealousy in heterosexual and homosexual adults. *Psychological Science, 13,* 7–12.

Harris, M. J., Milich, R., Corbitt, E. M., Hoover, D. W., & Brady, M. (1992). Self-fulfilling effects of stigmatising information on children's social interactions. *Journal of Personality and Social Psychology, 63,* 41–50.

Harrison, R., & Hopkins, R. L. (1967). The design of cross-cultural training: An alternative to the university model. *Journal of Applied Behavioral Science, 3,* 431–60.

Harvey, B. (1997). The expanded ARF model: Bridge to the accountable advertising future. *Journal of Advertising Research, 37,* 11–20.

Harwood, R. L., Miller, J. G., & Irizarry, W. L. (1995). *Culture and attachment: Perceptions of the child in context.* New York: The Guildford Press.

Haslam, S. A. (2000). *Psychology in organizations: The social identity approach.* New Delhi: Sage.

Haslam, S. A. (2001). *Psychology in organizations: The social identity approach.* London: Sage.

Hatfield, E., & Rapson, R. L. (1987). Passionate love: New directions in research. In W. H. Jones & D. Perlman (Eds), *Advances in personal relationships,* vol. 1 (pp. 109–139). Greenwich, CT: JAI Press.

Hatfield, E., Cacioppo, J. T., & Rapson, R. L. (1993). Emotional contagion. *Current Directions in Psychological Science, 2,* 96–9.

Hatfield, E., Cacioppo, J. T., & Rapson, R. L. (1994). *Emotional contagion.* New York: Cambridge University Press.

Haugtvedt, C. P., & Wegener, D. T. (1994). Message order effects in persuasion: An attitude strength perspective. *Journal of Consumer Research, 21,* 205–218.

Hayes, R. L., Blackman, L. S., & Brennan, C. (2001). Group supervision. In L. J. Bradley & N. Ladany (Eds), *Counselor supervision: Principles, process, and practice* (3rd edition) (pp. 183–206). Philadelphia, PA: Brunner-Routledge.

Hazan, C., & Shaver, P. (1987). Romantic love conceptualised as an attachment process. *Journal of Personality and Social Psychology, 52,* 511–24.

Headay, B. (1991). Distributive justice and occupational income: Perceptions of justice determine perceptions of fact. *British Journal of Sociology, 42,* 581–96.

Hebb, D. O. (1949). *The organisation of behaviour.* New York: John Wiley & Sons.

Hecht, M. L., Marston, P. J., & Larkey, L. K. (1994). Love ways and relationship quality in heterosexual relationships. *Journal of Social and Personal Relationships, 11,* 25–43.

Heider, F. (1958). *The psychology of interpersonal relations.* New York: John Wiley & Sons.

Heilman, M. E., Block, C. J., & Lucas, J. A. (1992). Presumed incompetent? Stigmatization and affirmative action efforts. *Journal of Applied Psychology, 77,* 536–44.

Heinberg, A. J., & Thompson, J. K. (1995). Body image and televised images of thinness and attractiveness: A controlled laboratory investigation. *Journal of Social and Clinical Psychology, 14,* 325–38.

Helmreich, R., Aronson, E., & LeFan, J. (1970). To err is humanizing sometimes: Effects of self-esteem, competence, and a pratfall on interpersonal attraction. *Journal of Personality and Social Psychology, 16,* 259–64.

Henderson-King, E., Henderson-King, D., Zhermer, N., Posokhova, S., & Chiker, V. (1997). In-group favoritism and perceived similarity: A look at Russians' perceptions in the post-Soviet era. *Personality and Social Psychology Bulletin, 23,* 1013–21.

Hendrick, C., & Hendrick, S. S. (Eds) (2000). *Close relationships: A sourcebook.* Thousand Oaks, CA: Sage.

Hendrick, C., Hendrick, S. S., & Dicke, A. (1998). The Love Attitudes Scale: short form. *Journal of Social and Personal Relationships, 15,* 147–59.

Hepworth, J. T., & West, S. G. (1988). Lynchings and the economy: A time-series re-analysis of Hovland and Sears (1940). *Journal of Personality and Social Psychology, 55,* 239–47.

Heredia, B. (1997). Prosper or perish: Development in the age of global capital. *Current History, 11,* 383–8.

Hermans, D., Crombez, G., & Eelen, P. (2000). Automatic attitude activation and efficiency: The fourth horseman of automaticity. *Psychologica Belgica, 40,* 3–22.

Hermans, H. J. M., & Kempen, H. J. G. (1998). Moving cultures: The perilous problems of cultural dichotomies in a globalizing society. *American Psychologist, 53,* 111–20.

Hernandez, J. A. E. (1999). Validation of the structure of the Triangular Love Scale: Confirmatory factorial analysis. *Aletheia*, *9*, 15–25.

Herriot, P. (1991). The selection interview. In P. Warr (Ed.), *Psychology at work* (pp. 139–59). Harmondsworth, UK: Penguin.

Herson, K., Sosabowski, M. H., & Lloyd, A. W. (1999). Intranet-based learning: A one-year study of student utilization. *Journal of Computer Assisted Learning*, *15*, 269–78.

Herzberger, S. D. (1996). *Violence within the family: Social psychological perspectives.* Madison, WI: Brown & Benchmarker.

Heslin, R., Nguyen, T. D., & Nguyen, M. L. (1983). Meaning of touch: The case of touch from a stranger or same sex person. *Journal of Nonverbal Behaviour*, *7*, 147–57.

Hewstone, M. (1989). Répresentations socials et causalité. In D., Jodelet (Ed.), *Les representations sociales* (pp. 252–74). Paris: Presses Universitaires de France.

Hewstone, M. R., & Brown, R. J. (1986). Contact is not enough: An inter-group perspective on the contact hypothesis. In M. R. Hewstone & R. J. Brown (Eds), *Conflict and contact in inter-group encounters* (pp. 181–98). Oxford, UK: Blackwell.

Hewstone, M., & Ward, C. (1985). Ethnocentrism and causal attribution in South East Asia. *Journal of Personality and Social Psychology*, *48*, 614–23.

Higgins, E. T. (1987). Self-discrepancy theory: A theory relating self and affect. *Psychological Review*, *94*, 314–40.

Hill, C. A., Blakemore, J. E. O., & Drumm, P. (1997). Mutual and unrequited love in adolescence and adulthood. *Personal Relationships*, *4*, 15–23.

Hill, M. E., & Augoustinos, M. (1997). Re-examining gender bias in achievement attributions. *Australian Journal of Psychology*, *49*, 85–90.

Hill, M. E., Barlow, J., Augoustinos, M., Clark, Y., & Sarris, A. (1995). *Courts Administration Authority's Cross-Cultural Awareness Program evaluation.* Adelaide: University of Adelaide.

Hilton, D. J. (2001). The psychology of financial decision-making: Applications to trading, dealing, and investment analysis. *Journal of Psychology & Financial Markets*, *2*, 37–53.

Hiltz, S. R., & Turoff, M. (1978). *The network nation: Human communication via computer.* Cambridge, MA: MIT Press.

Hinds, P. J. (1999). The curse of expertise: The effects of expertise and de-biasing methods on predictions of novice performance. *Journal of Experimental Psychology*, *5*, 205–221.

Hine, D. W., & Montiel, C. J. (1999). Poverty in developing nations: A cross-cultural attributional analysis. *European Journal of Social Psychology*, *29*, 943–59.

Hing, L. S. S., Li, W., & Zanna, M. P. (2002). Inducing hypocrisy to reduce prejudicial responses among aversive racists. *Journal of Experimental Social Psychology*, *38*, 71–8.

Hitschmann, E. (1952). Freud's conception of love. *International Journal of Psychoanalysis*, *33*, 421–8.

Ho, R. (1990). Multiculturalism in Australia: A survey of attitudes. *Human Relations*, *43*, 259–72.

Hoffner, C. (2001). The third-person effect in perceptions of the influence of television violence (the belief that others are more affected than oneself). *Journal of Communication*, *51*, 283–300.

Hofstadter, D. R. (1979). *Godel, Escher, Bach: An eternal golden braid.* New York: Vintage.

Hofstede, G. (1980). *Culture's consequences.* New Delhi: Sage.

Hofstede, G., & Bond, M. H. (1988). The Confucius connection: From cultural roots to economic growth. *Organizational Dynamics*, *16*, 4–21.

Hogg, M. A., & Turner, J. C. (1985). When liking begats solidarity: An experiment on the role of interpersonal attraction and psychological group formation. *British Journal of Social Psychology*, *24*, 267–81.

Holaday, M., Warren-Miller, G., Smith, A., & Yost, T. E. (1995). A preliminary investigation of on-the-scene coping mechanisms used by disaster workers. *Journal of Mental Health Counselling*, *17*, 347–59.

Holladay, S. J., & Kerns, K. S. (1999). Do age differences matter in close and casual friendships? A comparison of age discrepant and age peer friendships. *Communication Reports*, *12*, 101–114.

Holladay, S. J., & Kerns, K. S. (2001). Do age differences matter in close and casual friendships? A comparison of age discrepant and age peer friendships. *Communication Reports*, *12*, 101–114.

Homer-Dixon, T. F., Boutwell, J. H., & Rathjens, G. W. (1993). Environmental change and violent conflict. *Scientific American*, *268*, 16–23.

Hon, C. C., & Watkins, D. (1995). Evaluating a social skills training program for Hong Kong students. *Journal of Social Psychology*, *135*, 527–9.

Hong, S. M., & Bartley, C. (1986). Attitudes toward romantic love: An Australian perspective. *Australian Journal of Sex, Marriage & Family*, *7*, 166–70.

Hope, A., & Timmel, S. (1995). *Training for transformation*, vol. 1. Gweru, Zimbabwe: Mambo Press.

Horwood, A. (2002). When life is blighted by toughs at the top. *New Zealand Business Herald*, 20 February, D1.

Hovland, C. I. (1959). Reconciling conflicting results derived from experimental and survey studies of attitude change. *American Psychologist*, *14*, 8–17.

Hovland, C. I., & Weiss, W. (1951). The influence of source credibility on communication effectiveness. *Public Opinion Quarterly*, *15*, 635–50.

Hovland, C. I., Janis, I., & Kelley, H. H. (Eds) (1953). *Communication and persuasion.* Princeton, NJ: Princeton University Press.

Hovland, C. I., Lumsdaine, A. A., & Sheffield, F. E. (1949). The effects of presenting 'one side' versus 'both sides' in changing opinions on a controversial subject. *Studies in social psychology in World War II*, *3*, 201–227.

Hovmark, S., & Novell, M. (1993). Social and psychological aspects of computer-aided design systems. *Behaviour and Information Technology, 12,* 267–75.

Howard, G. S. (1991). Culture tales: A narrative approach to thinking, cross-cultural psychology, and psychotherapy. *American Psychologist, 46,* 187–97.

Howard, J. A., Blumstein, P., & Schwartz, P. (1987). Social or evolutionary theories? Some observations on preferences in human mate selection. *Journal of Personality and Social Psychology, 53,* 194–200.

Howard, J. L., & Ferris, G. R. (1996). The employment interview context: Social and situational influences on interviewer decisions. *Journal of Applied Social Psychology, 26,* 112–36.

Howarth, E., & Hoffman, M. S. (1984). A multidimensional approach to the relationship between mood and weather. *British Journal of Psychology, 75,* 15–23.

Huguet, P., Charbonnier, E., & Monteil, J. M. (1999). Productivity loss in performance groups: People who see themselves as average do not engage in social loafing. *Group Dynamics: Theory, Research, & Practice, 3,* 118–31.

Hui, H. C., Triandis, H. C., & Yee, C. (1991). Cultural differences in reward allocation: Is collectivism the explanation? *British Journal of Social Psychology, 30,* 145–57.

Hunter, J. A., Stringer, M., & Watson, R. P. (1991). Inter-group violence and inter-group attribution. *British Journal of Social Psychology, 30,* 261–6.

Hussain, H., & Zafri, A. (1997). Parasuicide in the Klang Valley marriages. *Arab Journal of Psychiatry, 8,* 42–8.

Hyde, J. S. (1984). How large are gender differences in aggression? A developmental meta-analysis. *Developmental Psychology, 20,* 722–36.

Iacono, W. G., & Lykken, D. T. (1997). The validity of the Lie Detector: Two surveys of scientific opinion. *Journal of Applied Psychology, 82,* 426–33.

INRA (1992). *The way Europeans perceive the Third World in 1991.* Brussels: European Community Commission.

Insel, T. R. (2000). Toward a neurobiology of attachment. *Review of General Psycholology, 4,* 176–85.

Insko, C. A. (1973). Implied evaluation and the similarity-attraction effect. *Journal of Personality and Social Psychology, 25,* 297–308.

Insko, C. A., Schopler, J., Graetz, K. A., Drigotas, S. M., et al. (1994). Inter-individual and intergroup discontinuity in the prisoner's dilemma game. *Journal of Conflict Resolution, 38,* 87–116.

Irwin, H. (1996). *Communicating with Asia.* Sydney: Allen & Unwin.

Isen, A. M., & Noonberg, A. (1979). The effect of photographs of the handicapped on donation to charity: When a thousand words may be too much. *Journal of Applied Social Psychology, 9,* 426–31.

Isenberg, D. J. (1986). Group polarization: A critical review and meta-analysis. *Journal of Personality and Social Psychology, 50,* 1141–51.

Ivory, B. (1999). Enterprise development: A model for Aboriginal entrepreneurs. *South Pacific Journal of Psychology, 11,* 62–71.

Jackson, C. F., & Furnham, A. (2001). Appraisal ratings, halo, and selection: A study using sales staff. *European Journal of Psychological Assessment, 17,* 17–24.

Jackson, I. M., & Harkins, S. G. (1985). Equity in effort: An explanation of the social loafing effect. *Journal of Personality and Social Psychology, 49,* 1199–1206.

Jackson, J. F. (1993). Multiple caregiving among African Americans and infant attachment: The need for an emic approach. *Human Development, 36,* 103–5.

Jacobson, N. S., & Gottman, J. M. (1998). Anatomy of a violent relationship. *Psychology Today,* March/April, 60–65, 81, 84.

James, K., & Greenberg, J. (1989). In-group salience, inter-group competition, and individual performance and self-esteem. *Personality and Social Psychology Bulletin, 15,* 604–616.

Janis, I. L. (1968). Attitude change via role playing. In R. P. Abelson, E. Aronson, W. J. McGuire, T. M. Newcomb, M. J. Rosenberg & P. H. Tannenbaum (Eds), *Theories of cognitive consistency: A sourcebook* (pp. 810–18). Chicago, IL: Rand McNally.

Janis, I. L. (1982). Groupthink. In D. Krebs (Ed.), *Readings in social psychology: Contemporary perspectives* (pp. 172–5). New York: Harper & Row.

Janis I. L, & Feshbach, S. (1953). Effects of fear-arousing communications. *Journal of Abnormal and Social Psychology, 48,* 78–92.

Janis, I., & Mann, L. (1965). Effectiveness of emotional role-playing in modifying smoking habits and attitudes. *Journal of Experimental Research in Personality, 1,* 84–90.

Jankowiak, W. R., & Fischer, E. F. (1992). A cross-cultural perspective on romantic love. *Ethnology, 31,* 149–55.

Javidan, M., & House, R. J. (2001). Cultural acumen for the global manager. *Organizational Dynamics, 29,* 289–305.

Johnson, J. G., Cohen, P., Smailes, E. M., Kasen, S., & Brook, J. S. (2002). Television viewing and aggressive behavior during adolescence and adulthood. *Science, 295,* 2468–71.

Johnson, P. R., & Indvik, J. (1994). Workplace violence: An issue of the nineties. *Public Personnel Management, 23,* 515–23.

Johnson, R. N. (1972). *Aggression in man and animals.* London: W. B. Saunders & Company.

Johnstone, F. (1994). The new world disorder: Fear, Freud, and federalism. *Telos, 100,* 87–103.

Joinson, A. (1998). Causes and implications of disinhibited behaviour on the Internet. In J. Gackenbach (Ed.), *Psychology and the Internet: Intrapersonal, interpersonal, and transpersonal implications* (pp. 43–60). San Diego, CA: Academic Press.

Jones, D. C., & Vaughan, K. (1991). Close friendships among senior adults. *Psychology and Aging, 5,* 451–7.

Jones, E. E., & Harris, V. A. (1967). The attribution of attitudes. *Journal of Experimental Social Psychology*, *3*, 1–24.

Jones, E. E., & Nisbett, R. E. (1972). The actor and the observer: Divergent perceptions of the causes of behaviour. In E. E. Jones, D. E. Kanouse, H. H. Kelley, R. E. Nisbett, S. Valens & B. Weiner (Eds), *Attribution: Perceiving the causes of behavior* (pp. 79–94). Morristown, NJ: General Learning Press.

Jones, G. W. (1997). Modernisation and divorce. *Population and Development Review*, *23*, 95–114.

Jones, R. C. (2000). *Territorians' preferences in hiring expatriates: Implications for economic development.* Darwin, Australia: Northern Territory University.

Jones, S. G. (Ed.) (1997). *Virtual culture: Identity and communication in cybersociety.* Thousand Oaks, CA: Sage.

Juerg, W. (1997). The significance of romantic love for marriage. *Family Process*, *36*, 171–82.

Juni, S., Katz, B., & Hamburger, M. (1996). Identification with aggression versus turning against the self: An empirical study of turn-of-the-century European Jewish humour. *Current Psychology: Developmental, Learning, Personality, Social*, *14*, 313–28.

Juralewicz, R. S. (1974). An experiment in participation in a Latin American factory. *Human Relations*, *27*, 627–37.

Kabanoff, B. (1997). Organisational justice across cultures: Integrating organisation-level and culture-level perspectives. In C. P. Earley & M. Erez (Eds), *New perspectives on international industrial/organisational psychology* (pp. 676–712). San Francisco, CA: The New Lexington Press/Jossey-Bass.

Kagitçibasi, C. (1992). A critical appraisal of individualism-collectivism: Toward a new formulation. In U. Kim, H. C. Triandis & G. Yoon (Eds), *Individualism and collectivism: Theoretical and methodological issues* (pp. 52–65). Newbury Park, CA: Sage.

Kalmar, D. A., & Sternberg, R. J. (1988). Theory knitting: An integrative approach to theory development. *Philosophical Psychology*, *1*, 153–70.

Kanouse, D. E., & Hansen, L. R. (1971). Negativity in evaluations. In E. E. Jones, D. E. Kanouse, H. H. Kelley, R. E. Nisbett, S. Valins & B. Weiner (Eds), *Attribution: Perceiving the causes of behavior* (pp. 47–62), Morristown, NJ: General Learning Press.

Kanungo, R. N., & Johar, J. S. (1975). Effects of slogans and human model characteristics in product advertisements. *Canadian Journal of Behavioral Sciences*, *7*, 127–38.

Kao, H. S. R., & Ng, S. H. (1997). Work motivation and culture. In D. Munro, J. F. Schumaker & S. C. Carr (Eds), *Motivation and culture* (pp. 119–32). New York: Routledge.

Kao, H. S. R., Sinha, D., & Wilpert, B. (Eds) (1999). *Management and cultural values.* New Delhi: Sage.

Kappas, A., Bherer, F., & Theriault, M. (2000). Inhibiting facial expressions: Limitations to the voluntary control of facial expressions of emotion. *Motivation & Emotion*, *24*, 259–70.

Karau, S. J., & Hart, J. W. (1998). Group cohesiveness and social loafing: Effects of a social interaction on individual motivation within groups. *Group Dynamics: Theory, Research, & Practice*, *2*, 185–91.

Karau, S. J., & Williams, K. D. (1993). Social loafing: A meta-analytic review and theoretical integration. *Journal of Personality and Social Psychology*, *65*, 681–706.

Karau, S. J., & Williams, K. D. (1995). Social loafing: Research findings, implications, and future directions. *Current Directions in Psychological Science*, *4*, 134–40.

Karau, S. J., & Williams, K. D. (1997). The effects of group cohesiveness on social loafing and social compensation. *Group Dynamics: Theory, Research, & Practice*, *1*, 156–68.

Karau, S. J., & Williams, K. D. (2001). Understanding individual motivation in groups: The collective effort model. In M. E. Turner (Ed.), *Groups at work: Theory and research* (pp. 113–41). Mahwah, NJ: Lawrence Erlbaum Associates.

Karney, B. R., & Bradbury, T. N. (1995). The longitudinal course of marital quality and stability: A review of theory, method, and research. *Psychological Bulletin*, *118*, 3–34.

Karney, B. R., & Bradbury, T. N. (1997). Neuroticism, marital interaction, and the trajectory of marital satisfaction. *Journal of Personality and Social Psychology*, *72*, 1075–92.

Karpin, D. (1995). *Enterprising nation.* Canberra: AGPS.

Karpin Task Force (1995). *Enterprising nation: Renewing Australia's managers to meet the challenges of the Asia-Pacific century.* Canberra: AGPS.

Kashima, Y. (1997). Culture, narrative, and human motivation. In D. Munro, J. F. Schumaker & S. C. Carr (Eds), *Motivation and culture* (pp. 16–30). New York: Routledge

Kashima, Y., & Callan, V. J. (1994). The Japanese work group. In H. C. Triandis & M. D. Dunnette (Eds), *Handbook of Industrial and organizational psychology*, vol. 4 (2nd edition) (pp. 609–646). Palo Alto, CA: Consulting Psychologists' Press.

Kashima, Y., & Triandis, H. C. (1986). The self-serving bias in attributions as a coping strategy. *Journal of Cross-Cultural Psychology*, *17*, 83–97.

Kashima, Y., Siegal, M., Tamaka, K., & Isaka, H. (1988). Universalism in lay conceptions of distributive justice: A cross-cultural examination. *International Journal of Psychology*, *23*, 51–64.

Kato, T. (2000). Lessons from the Asian crisis. *Journal of Human Development*, *1*, 165–8.

Katz, E. (1957). The two-step flow of communication. *Public Opinion Quarterly*, *21*, 61–78..

Katz, R., & Briger, R. (1988). Modernity and the quality of marriage in Israel. *Journal of Comparative Family Studies*, *19*, 371–80.

Kealey, D. J. (1989). A study of cross-cultural effectiveness: Theoretical issues, practical applications. *International Journal of Intercultural Relations*, *13*, 387–428.

Keelan, P. R. J., Dion, K. L., & Dion, K. K. (1994). Attachment style and heterosexual relationships among young adults: A short-term panel study. *Journal of Social and Personal Relationships, 11,* 201–214.

Kelley, G. (1955). *The psychology of personal constructs,* vols I and II. New York: Norton.

Kelley, H. H. (1950). The warm–cold variable in first impressions of persons. *Journal of Personality, 18,* 431–9.

Kelley, H. H. (1971). *Attribution in social interaction.* Morristown, NJ: General Learning Press.

Kelley, H. H. (1972). Causal schemata and the attribution process. In E. E. Jones, D. E. Kanouse, H. H. Kelley, R. E. Nisbett, S. Valins & B. Weiner (Eds), *Attribution: Perceiving the causes of behaviour* (pp. 151–74). Morristown, NJ: General Learning Press.

Kelley, J. C. (1989). Australian attitudes to overseas aid: Report from the National Social Science Survey. *International Development Issues, 8,* 1–129.

Kelly, N., & Milner, J. (1996). Child protection decision-making. *Child Abuse Review, 5,* 91–102.

Kelman, H. C. (1953). Attitude change as a function of response restriction. *Human Relations, 6,* 185–214.

Kelman, H. C. (1958). Compliance, identification, and internalisation: Three processes of attitude change. *Journal of Conflict Resolution, 2,* 51–60.

Kelman, H. C., & Hovland, C. I. (1953). Reinstatement of the communicator in delayed measurement of opinion change. *Journal of Abnormal and Social Psychology, 48,* 327–35.

Kenny, D. A., & Kashy, D. A. (1994). Enhanced co-orientation in the perception of friends: A social relations analysis. *Journal of Personality and Social Psychology, 67,* 1024–33.

Kenny, D. T. (1995). Common themes, different perspectives: systemic analysis of employer-employee experiences of occupational rehabilitation. *Rehabilitation Counseling Bulletin, 39,* 54–77.

Kenrick, D. T., & MacFarlane, S. W. (1984). Ambient temperature and horn honking: A field study of the heat/aggression relationship. *Environment and Behaviour, 18,* 179–81.

Kenrick, D. T., Groth, G. E., Trost, M. R., & Sadalla, E. K. (1993). Integrating evolutionary and social exchange perspectives on relationships: Effect of gender, self-appraisal, and involvement level on mate selection criteria. *Journal of Personality and Social Psychology, 64,* 951–69.

Kephart, W. (1967). Some correlates of romantic love. *Journal of Marriage and the Family, 29,* 470–79.

Kerckhoff, A. C., & Davis, K. E. (1962). Value consensus and need complementarity in mate selection. *American Sociological Review, 27,* 295–303.

Kerns, K. A., & Barth, J. M. (1995). Attachment and play: Convergence across components of parent-child relationships and their relations to peer competence. *Journal of Social and Personal Relationships, 12,* 243–60.

Kerr, J. H. (1997). *Motivation and emotion in sport: Reversal theory.* Hove, UK: Psychology Press.

Kerr, J. H. (1999). The role of aggression and violence in sport: A rejoinder to the ISSSP Position Stand. *The Sport Psychologist, 13,* 83–8.

Kerr, N. L. (1983). Motivation losses in small groups: A social dilemma analysis. *Journal of Personality and Social Psychology, 45,* 819–28.

Kickul, J., & Lester, S. W. (2001). Broken promises: Equity sensitivity as a moderator between psychological contact breach and employee attitudes and behaviour. *Journal of Business & Psychology, 16,* 191–217.

Kidder, L. H., & Stewart, V. M. (1975). *The psychology of inter-group relations: Conflict and consciousness.* New York: McGraw-Hill.

Kiesler, S., & Sproull, L. (1992). Group decision-making and communication technology. *Organisational Behaviour & Human Decision Processes, 52,* 96–123.

Kiesler, S., Siegel, J., & McGuire, T. W. (1984). Social psychological aspects of computer-mediated communication. *American Psychologist, 39,* 1123–34.

Kilham, W., & Mann, L. (1974). Level of destructive obedience as a function of transmitter and executant roles in the Milgram obedience paradigm. *Journal of Personality and Social Psychology, 29,* 696–702.

Kim, P. H. (1997). When what you know *can* hurt you: A study of experimental effects on group discussion and performance. *Organisational Behaviour and Human Performance, 69,* 165–77.

Kipnis, D. (1972). Does power corrupt? *Journal of Personality and Social Psychology, 24,* 33–41.

Kirkpatrick, E. M. (Ed.) (1983). *Chambers 20th century dictionary.* Edinburgh: W & R Chambers.

Kirkpatrick, E. M. (Ed.) (1988). *Chambers 20th century dictionary.* Edinburgh, Scotland: W & R Chambers.

Kirkpatrick, L. A., & Davis, K. E. (1994). Attachment style, gender, and relationship stability: A longitudinal study. *Journal of Personality and Social Psychology, 66,* 502–512.

Kirkpatrick, L. A., & Hazan, C. (1994). Attachment styles and close relationships: A four-year prospective study. *Personal Relationships, 1,* 123–42.

Klein, C., Easton, D., & Parker, R. (2002). Structural barriers and facilitators in HIV prevention: A review of international research. In A. O'Leary (Ed.), *Beyond condoms: Alternative approaches to HIV prevention* (pp. 17–46). New York: Kluwer-Plenum Academic Publishers.

Klein, J. G. (1996). Negativity in impressions of presidential candidates revisited: The 1992 election. *Personality and Social Psychology Bulletin, 22,* 288–95.

Kloep, M. (1995). Concurrent and predictive correlates of girls' depression and antisocial behaviour under conditions of economic crisis and value change: The case of Albania. *Journal of Adolescence, 18,* 445–58.

Kniveton, B. (1989). *The psychology of bargaining.* Newcastle, UK: Gower.

Knox, D., Schacht, C., & Zusman, M. E. (1999). Love relationships among college students. *College Student Journal, 33,* 149–51.

Kogan, N., & Wallach, M. A. (1967). Effects of physical separation of group members upon group risk-taking. *Human Relations, 20,* 41–8.

Kohnert, D. (1996). Magic and witchcraft: Implications for democratization and poverty-alleviating aid in Africa. *World Development, 24,* 1347–55.

Komin, S. (1999). The Thai concept of effective leadership. In H. S. R. Kao, D. Sinha & B. Wilpert (Eds), *Management and cultural values* (pp. 265–86). New Delhi: Sage.

Kormanski, C. (1988). Using group development theory in business and industry. *Journal for Specialists in Group Work, 13,* 30–43.

Kornet, A. (1997). The truth about lying: Has lying gotten a bad rap? *Psychology Today, 5/6,* 52–7.

Koseki, Y. (1989). A study of the influence of a deviant minority on visual judgements within a small group. *Japanese Psychological Research, 31,* 149–60.

Kosmitzki, C. (1996). The re-affirmation of cultural identity in cross-cultural encounters. *Personality & Social Psychology Bulletin, 22,* 238–48.

Kraus, S. J. (1995). Attitudes and the prediction of behavior: A meta analysis of the empirical literature. *Personality & Social Psychology Bulletin, 21,* 58–75.

Kraut, R., Patterson, M., Lundmark, V., Kiesler, S., Mukopadhyay, T., & Scherlis, W. (1998). Internet paradox: A social technology that reduces social involvement and psychological wellbeing? *American Psychologist, 53,* 1017–31.

Krosnick, J. A., Betz, A. L., Jussim, L. J., & Lynn, A. R. (1992). Subliminal conditioning of attitudes. *Personality and Social Psychology Bulletin, 18,* 152–62.

Kruger, J. (1999). Lake Wobegon be gone! The 'below-average effect' and the egocentric nature of comparative ability judgements. *Journal of Personality and Social Psychology, 77,* 221–32.

Kruger, J., & Dunning, D. (1999). Unskilled and unaware of it: How difficulties recognizing one's own incompetence lead to inflated self-assessments. *Journal of Personality and Social Psychology, 77,* 1121–34.

Krull, D. S. (1993). Does the grist change the mill?: The effect of perceiver's goal on the process of social inference. *Personality and Social Psychology Bulletin, 19,* 340–8.

Krull, D. S., & Erickson, D. J. (2000). Inferential hopscotch: How people draw social inferences from behaviour. In M. H. Davis (Ed.), *Social psychology 00/01* (pp. 55–8). Guilford, CT: Dushkin/McGraw-Hill.

Kulik, J. A., Mahler, H. I. M., & Moore, P. J. (1996). Social comparison and affiliation under threat: Effects on recovery form major surgery. *Journal of Personality and Social Psychology, 71,* 967–79.

Kunda, Z., & Sherman-Williams, B. (1993). Stereotypes and the construal of individuating information. *Personality and Social Psychology Bulletin, 19,* 90–99.

Kunda, Z., & Thagard, P. (1996). Forming impressions from stereotypes, traits, and behaviours: A parallel-constraint-satisfactory theory. *Psychological Review, 103,* 284–308.

Kurdek, L. A. (1991). The dissolution of gay and lesbian couples. *Journal of Personal and Social Relations, 8,* 265–78.

Kuschel, R., Takiika, A. F., & 'Angiki, K. (1999). Aspects of social stratification and honour on pre-Christian and modern *Mungiki* (Bellona). *South Pacific Journal of Psychology, 11,* 54–70.

La Piere, R. T. (1934). Attitude and actions. *Social Forces, 13,* 230–37.

Lake, O. (1997). Cultural hierarchy and the renaming of African people. *Western Journal of Black Studies, 21,* 261–71.

Lamarche, L., & Tougas, F. (1979). Perception des raisons de la pauvreté par des Montréalais Canadiens-Français. *Revue Canadienne des Sciences du Comportement, 11,* 72–8.

Lamb, C. S., Jackson, L. A., Cassiday, P. B., & Priest, D. J. (1993). Body figure preferences of men and women: A comparison of two generations. *Sex Roles, 28,* 345–58.

Lamm, H., & Myers, D. G. (1978). Group induced polarisation of attitudes and behaviour. *Advances in Experimental Social Psychology, 11,* 145–95.

Lamm, H., & Wiesmann, U. (1997). Subjective attributes of attraction: How people characterise their liking, their love, and their being in love. *Personal Relationships, 4,* 271–84.

Landau, T. (1989). *About faces: The evolution of the human face.* New York: Anchor Books.

Landis, D., & Bhagat, R. (Eds) (1996). *Handbook of intercultural training.* Newbury Park, CA: Sage.

Langer, E. J. (1989). Minding matters: The consequences of mindlessness-mindfulness. *Advances in Experimental Social Psychology, 22,* 137–73.

Langer, E., Blank, A., & Chanowitz, B. (1978). The mindlessness of ostensibly thoughtful action. *Journal of Personality and Social Psychology, 36,* 635–42.

Langleben, D., Schroeder, L., Maldjian, J., Gur, R., McDonald, S., Ragland, J. D., O'Brien, C. P., & Childress, A. R. (2002). Brain activity during simulated deception: An event-related functional magnetic resonance study. *Neuroimage, 15,* 727–32.

Langlois, J. H., & Roggman, L. A. (1990). Attractive faces are only average. *Psychological Science, 1,* 115–21.

Langlois, J. H., Ritter, J. M., Roggman, L. A., & Vaughn, L. S. (1991). Facial diversity and infant preferences for attractive faces. *Developmental Psychology, 27,* 79–84.

Langlois, J. H., Roggman, L. A., & Rieser-Danner, L. A. (1990). Differential social responses to attractive and unattractive faces. *Developmental Psychology, 26,* 153–9.

Larson, J. H., & Bell, N. J. (1988). Need for privacy and its effects upon interpersonal attraction and interaction. *Journal of Social and Clinical Psychology, 6,* 1–10.

Latané, B., & Wolf, S. (1981). The social impact of majorities and minorities. *Psychological Review, 88,* 438–53.

Latané, B., Williams, K., & Harkins, S. (1979). Many hands make light work: The causes and consequences of social loafing. *Journal of Personality and Social Psychology, 37,* 822–32.

Laumann, E. O., Gagnon, J. H., Michael, R. T., & Michaels, S. (1994). *The social organization of sexuality.* Chicago, IL: University of Chicago Press.

Lawson, J. S., & Evans, A. R. (1992). Prodigious alcohol consumption by Australian rugby league footballers. *Drug & Alcohol Review, 11,* 193–5.

Le Bon, G. (1895). *Psychologie des foules.* Paris: Félix Alcan.

Lea, D. (1998). The ethics of corruption in Papua New Guinea and elsewhere in the developing world. *South Pacific Journal of Philosophy and Culture, 3,* 71–81.

Lea, M., & Spears, R. (1995). Love at first byte? Building personal relationships over computer networks. In J. T. Wood & S. Duck (Eds), *Under-studied relationships: Off the beaten track* (pp. 197–233). Thousand Oaks, CA: Sage.

Leach, M. M., & Harbin, J. J. (1997). Psychological ethics codes: A comparison of 24 countries. *International Journal of Psychology, 32,* 181–92.

Leavitt, H. J. (1951). Some effects of certain communication patterns on group performance. *Journal of Abnormal and Social Psychology, 46,* 38–50.

Lee, C. (2001). Review of *Thinking critically about research on sex and gender,* by P. J. Caplan and J. B. Caplan. Melbourne: Australian Psychological Society homepage <www.psychsociety.com.au>.

Lee, C. M., & Gudykunst, W. B. (2001). Attraction in initial inter-ethnic interactions. *International Journal of Intercultural Relations, 25,* 373–87.

Lee, D. (2000). An analysis of workplace bullying in the UK. *Personnel Review, 29,* 593–612.

Lee, J. A. (1977). A typology of styles. *Personality and Social Psychological Bulletin, 3,* 173–82.

Lee, J. A. (1988). Love styles. In R. J. Sternberg & M. L. Barnes (Eds), *The psychology of love* (pp. 38–67). New Haven, CT: Yale University Press.

Lee, Y. H., & Mason, C. (1999). Responses to information incongruency in advertising: The role of expectancy, relevancy, and humor. *Journal of Consumer Research, 26,* 156–69.

Lee, Y. T., & Seligman, M. E. P. (1997). Are Americans more optimistic than the Chinese? *Personality and Social Psychology Bulletin, 23,* 32–40.

Lemieux, R., & Hale, J. L. (1999). Intimacy, passion, and commitment in young romantic relationships: Successfully measuring the triangular theory of love. *Psychological Reports, 85,* 497–503.

Lemyre, L., & Smith, P. M. (1985). Intergroup discrimination and self-esteem in the minimal group paradigm. *Journal of Personality and Social Psychology, 49,* 660–70.

Leonard, R. L. (1975). Self-concept and attraction for similar and dissimilar others. *Journal of Personality and Social Psychology, 31,* 926–9.

Leone, L., Perugini, M., & Ercolani, A. P. (1999). A comparison of three models of attitude–behaviour relationships in the studying behaviour domain. *European Journal of Social Psychology, 29,* 161–89.

Lepowsky, M. (1999). Women, men, and aggression in an egalitarian society. In L. A. Peplau & S. C. DeBro (Eds), *Gender, culture, and ethnicity: Current research about women and men* (pp. 284–90). Mountain View, CA: Mayfield.

Lerner, M. J. (1980). *The belief in a just world: A fundamental delusion.* New York: Plenum.

Lerner, M. J., & Simmons, C. H. (1966). Observer's reaction to the 'innocent victim': Compassion or rejection? *Journal of Personality and Social Psychology, 4,* 203–210.

Leung, K., & Bond, M. H. (1984). The impact of cultural collectivism on reward allocation. *Journal of Personality and Social Psychology, 47,* 793–804.

Leung, K., Cheung, F. M., Zhang, J., Song, W., & Xie, D. (1997). The five-factor model of personality in China. In K. Leung, U. Kim, S. Yamaguchi & Y. Kashima (Eds), *Progress in Asian social psychology* (pp. 231–46). Singapore: John Wiley & Sons.

Leventhal, H. (1973). Fear communications in the acceptance of preventive health practices. *Bulletin of the New York Academy of Medicine, 41,* 1144–68.

Levin, S., & Sidanius, J. (1999). Social dominance and social identity in the United States and Israel: Ingroup favoritism or out-group derogation? *Political Psychology, 20,* 99–126.

Levine, R. L. (2000). Cities with heart. In M. H. Davis (Ed.), *Annual editions: Social psychology 00/01* (pp. 175–9). Guilford, CT: Dushkin/McGraw-Hill.

Levine, R., Sato, S., Hashimoto, T., & Verma, J. (1995). Love and marriage in eleven cultures. *Journal of Cross-Cultural Psychology, 26,* 554–71.

Levy, B., & Ashman, O. (1999–2000). To be or not to be: The effects of ageing stereotypes on the will to live. *Omega: Journal of Death and Dying, 40,* 409–421.

Levy, S. G. (1995). Attitudes toward the conflict of war. *Peace & Conflict: Journal of Peace Psychology, 1,* 179–97.

Lewin, K. (1947). Group decision making and social change. In E. E. Maccoby, T. M. Newcomb & E. E. Hartley (Eds) (1966), *Readings in social psychology* (pp. 197–211). London: Methuen.

Lewin, K. (1951). *Field theory in social science.* New York: Harper.

Lewin, K., Lippitt, R., & White, R. K. (1939). Patterns of aggressive behaviour in experimentally created 'social climates'. *Journal of Social Psychology, 10,* 271–99.

Lewinsohn, P. M., Mischel, W., Chaplin, W., & Barton, R. (1980). Social competence and depression: The role of illusory self-perceptions. *Journal of Abnormal Psychology, 89,* 203–212.

Lewis, J. (1991). Re-evaluating the effect of N-Ach on economic growth. *World Development, 19*, 1269–74.

Leyens, J. P., Camino, L., Parke, R. D., & Berkowitz, L. (1975). Effects of movie violence on aggression in a field setting as a function of group dominance and cohesion. *Journal of Personality and Social Psychology, 32*, 346–60.

Lieberman, J. D. (1999). Terror management, illusory correlation, and perceptions of minority groups. *Basic & Applied Social Psychology, 21*, 13–23.

Liebowitz, M. R. (1983). *The chemistry of love*. Boston, MA: Little, Brown.

Liggett, J. (1983). Some practical problems of assessment in developing countries. In F. Blackler (Ed.), *Social psychology and developing countries* (pp. 71–86). Chichester, UK: John Wiley & Sons.

Lim, A., & Ward, C. (August 1999). *The effects of nationality, length of residence, and occupational demand on the perceptions of 'foreign talent' in Singapore*. Asian Association of Social Psychology Conference, Taipei, Taiwan.

Lim, K. H., Benbasat, I., & Ward, L. M. (2000). The role of multi-media in changing first impression bias. *Information Systems Research, 11*, 115–36.

Linton, J. K. L., & Warg, L. F. (1993). Attributions (beliefs) and job satisfaction associated with back pain in an industrial setting. *Perceptual and Motor Skills, 76*, 51–62.

Linville, P. W., & Jones, E. E. (1980). Polarized appraisals of out-group members. *Journal of Personality and Social Psychology, 38*, 689–703.

Linz, D. G., & Penrod, S. (1984). Increasing attorney persuasiveness in the courtroom. *Law & Society Review, 8*, 1–47.

Lirtzman, S. I., & Shuv-Ami, A. (1986). Credibility of sources of communication on products' safety hazards. *Psychological Reports, 58*, 707–718.

Littler, C. R., Dunford, R., Bramble, T., & Hede, A. (1997). The dynamics of downsizing in Australia and New Zealand. *Asia Pacific Journal of Human Resources, 35*, 65–79.

Liu, J. H., & Allen, M. W. (1999). Evolution of political complexity in Maori Hawke's Bay: Archaeological history and its challenge to intergroup theory in psychology. *Group Dynamics: Theory, Research & Practice, 3*, 64–80.

Liu, J. H., & Mark, W. (1999). Evolution of political complexity in Māori Hawke's Bay: Archaeological history and its challenge to inter-group theory in psychology. *Group Dynamics: Theory, Research, & Practice, 3*, 64–80.

Liu, J. H., Ng, S. H., Weatherall, A., & Loong, C. (2000). Filial piety, acculturation and intergenerational communication among New Zealand Chinese. *Basic and Applied Social Psychology, 22*, 213–23.

Liu, J. H., Wilson, M. S., McClure, J., & Higgins, T. R. (1999). Social identity and the perception of history: Cultural representations of Aotearoa/New Zealand. *European Journal of Social Psychology, 29*, 1021–47.

Livingston, J. S. (1988). Pygmalion in management. *Harvard Business Review*, September–October, 121–30.

Livingstone, S. (1990). Interpreting a television narrative: How different viewers see a story. *Journal of Communication, 40*, 72–85.

Livingstone, S. (1997). Changing audiences for changing media: A social psychological perspective. In P. Winterhoff-Spurk & T. H. A. Van der Voort (Eds), *New horizons in media psychology: Research cooperation and projects in Europe* (pp. 56–72). Wiesbaden, Germany: Westdeutscher Verlag GmbH (in English).

Livingstone, S. (1999). *Making sense of television: The psychology of audience interpretation* (2nd edition). Florence, KY: Taylor & Francis/Routledge.

Lloyd, S. A. (1990). Asking the right questions about the future of marital violence research. In D. J. Besharov (Ed.), *Family violence: Research and public policy issues* (pp. 93–107). Washington, DC: AEI Press.

Locher, P., Unger, R., Sociedade, P., & Wahl, J. (1993). At first glance: Accessibility of the physical attractiveness stereotype. *Sex Roles, 28*, 729–43.

Lord, R. G., Brown, D. J., & Freiberg, S. J. (1999). Understanding the dynamics of leadership: The role of follower self-concepts in the leader/follower relationship. *Organizational Behaviour and Human Decision Processes, 78*, 167–203.

Lorenz, K. (1966). *On Aggression*. New York: Harcourt, Brace & World.

Lortie-Lussier, M., Lemieux, S., & Godbout, L. (1989). Reports of a public manifestation: Their impact according to minority influence theory. *Journal of Social Psychology, 129*, 285–95.

Lott, B. (2002). Cognitive and behavioural distancing from the poor. *American Psychologist, 57*, 100–110.

Lott, B., & Bullock, H. E. (2001). Who are the poor? *Journal of Social Issues, 57*, 189–206.

Love, H., & Whittaker, W. (1997). *Practice issues for clinical and applied psychologists in New Zealand*. Wellington: New Zealand Psychological Society.

Lovibund, S. H., Mithiran, & Adams, W. G. (1979). The effects of three experimental prison environments on the behaviour of non-convict volunteer subjects. *Australian Psychologist, 14*, 273–87.

Lowenstein, L. F. (1997). The bystander: An asset or a deficit in curbing criminality. *Police Journal, 70*, 315–23.

Lowery, B. S., Hardin, C. D., & Sinclair, S. (2001). Social influence effects on automatic racial prejudice. *Journal of Personality and Social Psychology, 81*, 842–55.

Luce, R. D., & Raiffa, H. (1957). *Games and decisions: Introduction and critical survey*. New York: John Wiley & Sons.

Luchins, A. S. (1957). Experimental attempts to minimise the impact of first impressions. In C. Hovland (Ed.), *The order of presentation in persuasion* (pp. 33–61). New Haven: Yale University Press.

Luitingh, M. (1991). A lawyer's response. *The Psychologist, 11*, 492–3.

Lumsdaine, A. A., & Janis, I. L. (1953). Resistance to 'counterpropaganda' produced by one-sided and two-sided 'propaganda' presentations. *Public Opinion Quarterly, 17*, 311–18.

Lund, M. (1985). The development of investment and commitment scales for predicting continuity of personal relationships. *Journal of Social and Personal Relationships, 2*, 3–23.

Lupfer, M. B., Clark, L. F., & Hutcheson, H. W. (1990). Impact of context on spontaneous trait and situational attributions. *Journal of Personality and Social Psychology, 58*, 239–49.

Lusetich, R. (2000). Joystick killers. *The Australian*, 16 May, 15.

Luther, N. (2000). Integrity testing and job performance within high performance work teams: A short note. *Journal of Business & Psychology, 15*, 19–25.

Lynskey, M. T., Ward, C., & Fletcher, G. J. (1991). Stereotypes and intergroup attributions in New Zealand. *Psychology and Developing Societies, 3*, 113–27.

Maass, A., & Clark, R. D. (1983). Internalisation versus compliance: Differential processes underlying minority influence and conformity. *European Journal of Social Psychology, 13*, 197–215.

Maass, A., & Volpato, C. (1996). Social influence and the verifiability of the issue under discussion: Attitudinal versus objective items. *British Journal of Social Psychology, 35*, 15–26.

MacLachlan, M. (1993). Splitting the difference: How do refugee workers survive? *Changes: International Journal of Psychology and Psychotherapy, 11*, 155–7.

MacLachlan, M. (1996a). From sustainable change to incremental improvement: The psychology of community rehabilitation. In S. C. Carr & J. F. Schumaker (Eds), *Psychology and the developing world* (pp. 26–37). Westport, CT: Praeger.

MacLachlan, M. (1996b). Identifying problems in community health promotion: An illustration of the Nominal Group Technique in AIDS education. *Journal of the Royal Society for Health, 6*, 143–8.

MacLachlan, M. (1997). *Culture and health*. Chichester, UK: John Wiley & Sons.

MacLachlan, M. (1998). Health and welfare in Malaŵi. In M. MacLachlan & S. C. Carr (Eds), *Perspectives in Malaŵian psychology* (pp. 75–95). Zomba: Zikomo Press.

MacLachlan, M., & Carr, S. C. (1993). Marketing psychology in a developing country: An innovative application in Malaŵi. *Psychology Teaching Review, 2*, 22–9.

MacLachlan, M., & Carr, S. C. (1994). Pathways to a psychology for development: Reconstituting, restating, refuting, and realising. *Psychology and Developing Societies, 6*, 21–8.

MacLachlan, M., & Carr, S. C. (1997). Psychology in Malaŵi: Towards a constructive debate. *The Psychologist, 10*, 77–9.

MacLachlan, M., Carr, S. C., Fardell, S., Maffesoni, G., & Cunningham, J. (1997). Transactional analysis of communication styles in HIV-AIDS advertisements. *Journal of Health Psychology, 2*, 67–74.

MacLaren, V. V. (2001). A quantitative review of the Guilty Knowledge Test. *Journal of Applied Psychology, 86*, 674–83.

MacLeod, M. D., & Paton, D. (1999). Victims, violent crime and the criminal justice system: Developing an integrated model of recovery. *Legal and Criminological Psychology, 4*, 203–220.

MacRae, C. N, Bodenhausen, G. V., & Milne, A. B. (1998). Saying no to unwanted thoughts: Self-focus and the regulation of mental life. *Journal of Personality and Social Psychology, 74*, 578–89.

MacRae, C. N., Bodenhausen, G. V., Milne, A. B., & Jetten, J. (1994). Out of mind but back in sight: Stereotypes on the rebound. *Journal of Personality and Social Psychology, 67*, 808–817. Reprinted 1996, in S. Fein & S. Spencer (Eds), *Readings in social psychology: The art and science of research* (pp. 30–43). Boston, MA: Houghton Mifflin.

Madey, S. F., Simo, M., Dillworth, D., Kemper, D., Toczynski, A., & Perrera, A. (1996). They do get more attractive at closing time, but only when you are not in a relationship. *Basic and Applied Social Psychology, 18*, 387–93.

Makin, P., Cooper, C., & Cox, C. (1989). *Managing people at work*. Manchester, UK: BPS and Routledge.

Malach-Pines, A. (2001). The role of gender and culture in romantic attraction. *European Psychologist, 6*, 96–102.

Malinowsky-Rummell, R., & Hansen, D. J. (1993). Long-term consequences of childhood physical abuse. *Psychological Bulletin, 114*, 68–79.

Mann, L. (1969). *Social psychology*. Sydney: John Wiley & Sons.

Mann, L. (1988). Cross-cultural studies of rules for determining majority and minority decision rights. *Australian Journal of Psychology, 38*, 319–28.

Mantovani, F. (2001). Networked seduction: A testbed for the study of strategic communication on the Internet. *Cyberpsychology and Behaviour, 4*, 147–54.

Maples, M. F. (1989). Group development: Extending Tuckman's theory. *Journal for Specialists in Group Work, 13*, 17–23.

Mapstone, E. (1998). *War of words: Women and men arguing*. Sydney: Random House.

Marai, L. (in press). Double de-motivation and negative social affect among teachers in Indonesia. *South Pacific Journal of Psychology, 13*, in press.

Marjoribanks, K., & Jordan, D. F. (1986). Stereotyping among Aboriginal and Anglo-Australians: The uniformity, intensity, direction, and quality of auto- and heterostereotypes. *Journal of Cross-Cultural Psychology, 17*, 17–28.

Market Australia Unit. (1995). *Australia through the eyes of Asia: Adding innovation*. Canberra: AGPS.

Markman, H. J., Silvern, L., Clements, M., & Kraft-Hanak, S. (1993). Men and women dealing with conflict in heterosexual relationships. *Journal of Social Issues, 49*, 107–125.

Markus, H. (1977). Self-schemata and processing information about the self. *Journal of Personality and Social Psychology, 35,* 63–78.

Marrow, A. J. (1964). Risks and uncertainties in action research. *Journal of Social Issues, 20,* 5–20.

Marsella, A. J. (1998). Toward a 'global-community psychology': Meeting the needs of a changing world. *American Psychologist, 53,* 1282–91.

Marsella, A. J. (2000). Internationalizing the psychology curriculum: Toward new competencies and directions. *South Pacific Journal of Psychology, 12,* 70–72.

Marsella, A. J. (Ed.) (2002). *Paradise lost and paradise regained: Indigenous health and wellbeing in a global society.* Honolulu, HA: The PREN Network.

Marshall, R. (1997). Variances in levels of individualism across two cultures and three social classes. *Journal of Cross-Cultural Psychology, 28,* 490–95.

Martin, G. N., & Gray, C. D. (1996). The effects of audience's laughter on men's and women's responses to humour. *Journal of Social Psychology, 136,* 221–31.

Martin, R., & Hewstone, M. (1999). Minority influence and optimal problem solving. *European Journal of Social Psychology, 29,* 825–32.

Maslow, A. H. (1943). A theory of human motivation. *Psychological Review, 50,* 370–96.

Maslow, A. H. (1955). Deficiency motivation and growth motivation. In M. R. Jones (Ed.), *Nebraska Symposium on Motivation* (pp. 1–39). Lincoln, NB: University of Nebraska Press.

Masten, A. S., & Coatsworth, J. D. (1998). The development of competence in favourable and unfavourable environments: Lessons from research on successful children. *American Psychologist, 53,* 205–220.

Matthews, C. O. (1992). An application of General Systems Theory (GST) to group therapy. *Journal for Specialists in Group Work, 17,* 161–9.

May, J. L., & Hamilton, P. A. (1980). Effects of musically evoked affect on women's interpersonal attraction and perceptual judgements of physical attractiveness of men. *Motivation and Emotion, 4,* 217–28.

Mazrui, A. A. (1990). *The African condition.* London: Heinemann.

Mazzella, C., Durkin, K., Cerini, E., & Buralli, P. (1992). Sex role stereotyping in Australian television advertisements. *Sex Roles, 26,* 243–59.

McAuley, C., Coleman, G., & de Fusco, P. (1980). Commuters' eye contact with strangers in city and suburban train stations: Evidence of short-term adaptation to interpersonal overload in the city. *Environmental Psychology and Nonverbal Behaviour, 2,* 215–25.

McCarthy, P. (1996). Bullying rife in the workplace: A study. *Newcastle Herald,* 27 January, 3 (available online from relevant databases).

McCarthy, S. J. (1985). Pornography, rape, and the cult of macho. In L. Cargan & J. H. Ballantine (Eds), *Sociological footprints* (pp. 339–49). Belmont, CA: Wadsworth.

McClelland, D. C. (1987a). Characteristics of successful entrepreneurs. *Journal of Creative Behaviour, 21,* 219–33.

McClelland, D. C. (1987b). *Human motivation.* New York: Cambridge University Press.

McCloud, P. L., Baron, R. S., Martin, M. W., & Yoon, K. (1997). The eyes have it: Minority influence in face-to-face computer-mediated group discussion. *Journal of Applied Psychology, 82,* 706–718.

McConahy, J. B. (1983). Modern racism and modern discrimination: The effects of race, racial attitudes, and context on simulated hiring decisions. *Personality & Social Psychology Bulletin, 9,* 551–8.

McConahy, J. B., Hardee, B. B., & Batts, V. (1981). Has racism declined in America? It depends on who is asking and what is asked. *Journal of Conflict Resolution, 25,* 563–79.

McConnell, A. R., Sherman, S. J., & Hamilton, D. L. (1997). Target entitativity: Implications for information processing about individual and group targets. *Journal of Personality and Social Psychology, 72,* 750–2.

McCormick, N. B., & McCormick, J. W. (1992). Computer friends and foes: Content of undergraduates' electronic mail. *Computers in Human Behaviour, 8,* 379–405.

McCrae, R. R., & Allik, J. (2002). *The five-factor model of personality across cultures.* New York: Kluwer Academic/Plenum Publishers.

McCullough, M. E., Rachal, K. C., Sandage, S. J., Worthington, E. L. Jnr., Brown, S. W., & Hight, T. L. (1998). Interpersonal forgiving in close relationships II: Theoretical elaboration and measurement. *Journal of Personality and Social Psychology, 75,* 1586–1603.

McCullough, M. E., Worthington, E. L. Jnr., & Rachal, K. C. (1997). Interpersonal forgiving in close relationships. *Journal of Personality and Social Psychology, 73,* 321–36.

McGarty, C., Haslam, S. A., Hutchinson, K. J., & Grace, D. M. (1995). Determinants of perceived consistency: The relationship between group entitativity and the meaningfulness of categories. *British Journal of Social Psychology, 34,* 237–6.

McGinnies, E., & Ward, C. D. (1980). Better liked than right: Trustworthiness and expertise as factors in credibility. *Personality & Social Psychology Bulletin, 6,* 467–72.

McGonagle, K. A., Kessler, R. C., & Schilling, E. A. (1992). The frequency and determinants of mental disagreements in a community sample. *Journal of Social and Personal Relationships, 9,* 507–524.

McGregor, D. (1960). *The human side of enterprise.* New York: McGraw-Hill.

McGregor, I., & Holmes, J. G. (1999). How storytelling shapes memory and impressions of relationship events over time. *Journal of Personality and Social Psychology, 76,* 403–419.

McGrew, J. F., Bilotta, J. G., & Deeney, J. M. (1999). Software team formation and decay: Extending the standard model for small groups. *Small Group Research, 30*, 209–234.

McGuire, W. J. (1964). Inducing resistance to persuasion: Some contemporary approaches. *Advances in Experimental Social Psychology, 1*, 191–229.

McGuire, W. J. (1985). Attitudes and attitude change. *Handbook of Social Psychology, 2*, 233–346.

McIlveen, R. (1992). An investigation of attributional bias in a real world setting. In R. McIlveen, L. Higgins & A. Wadely (Eds), *BPS manual of psychology practicals: Experiment, observation, and correlation* (pp. 78–92). Exeter, UK: British Psychological Society.

McKee, T. L. E., & Ptacek, J. T. (2001). I'm afraid I have something bad to tell you: Breaking bad news from the perspective of the giver. *Journal of Applied Social Psychology, 31*, 246–73.

McKelvie, S. J. (1993). Perceived cuteness, activity level, and gender in schematic baby faces. *Journal of Personality and Social Psychology, 8*, 297–310.

McKenzie, A. (2000). Revenge of the grim reaper. *The Weekend Australian*, 7–8 October, 26.

McKnight, J., & Sutton, J. (1994). *Social psychology.* Sydney: Prentice Hall.

McLaughlin, M. L., Osborne, K. K., & Smith, C. B. (1995). Standards of conduct on Usenet. In S. E. Jones (Ed.), *Cybersociety: Computer-mediated communication and community* (pp. 90–111). Thousand Oaks, CA: Sage.

McLoughlin, D., & Carr, S. C. (1994). *The Buick Bar & Grill.* Melbourne: University of Melbourne Case Study Library.

McLoughlin, D., & Carr, S. C. (1997). Equity sensitivity and double de-motivation. *Journal of Social Psychology, 137*, 668–70.

McNatt, B. D. (2000). Ancient Pygmalion joins contemporary management: A meta-analysis of the result. *Journal of Applied Psychology, 85*, 314–22.

Meeks, B. S., Hendrick, S. S., & Hendrick, C. (1998). Communication, love and relationship satisfaction. *Journal of Social and Personal Relationships, 15*, 755–73.

Mehryar, A. H. (1984). The role of psychology in national development: Wishful thinking and reality. *International Journal of Psychology, 19*, 159–67.

Melamed, T. (1995). Barriers to women's career success: Human capital, career choices, structural determinants, or simply sex discrimination? *Applied Psychology: An International Review, 44*, 295–314.

Mendenhall, M., & Oddou, G. (1983). The integrative approach to OD: McGregor revisited. *Group & Organization Studies, 8*, 291–301.

Menon, T., Morris, M. W., Chiu, C. Y., & Hong, Y. Y. (1999). Culture and the construal of agency: Attribution to individual versus group dispositions. *Journal of Personality and Social Psychology, 76*, 701–717.

Messman, S. J., & Canary, D. J. (1998). Patterns of conflict in personal relationships. In B. H. Spitzberg & W. R. Cupach (Eds), *The dark side of close relationships* (pp. 121–52). Mahwah, NJ: Lawrence Erlbaum Associates.

Michaels, J. W., Blommel, J. M., Brocato, R. M., Linkous, R. A., & Rowe, J. S. (1982). Social facilitation and inhibition in a natural setting. *Personality and Social Psychology Bulletin, 2*, 214.

Miles, D. R., & Carey, G. (1997). Genetic and environmental architecture on human aggression. *Journal of Personality and Social Psychology, 72*, 207–217.

Milgram, S. (1963). Behavioural study of obedience. *Journal of Abnormal and Social Psychology, 67*, 371–8.

Milgram, S. (1964). Issues in the study of obedience: A reply to Baumrind. *American Psychologist, 19*, 848–52.

Milgram, S. (1965). Some conditions of obedience and disobedience to authority. *Human Relations, 18*, 57–75.

Milgram, S., Bickman, L., & Berkowitz, L. (1969). Note on the drawing power of crowds of different size. *Journal of Personality and Social Psychology, 13*, 79–82.

Miller, C. T., Rothblum, E. D., Brand, P. A., & Felicio, D. M. (1990). Social interactions of obese and non-obese women. *Journal of Personality, 58*, 365–80.

Miller, C. T., Rothblum, E. D., Felicio, D. M., & Brand, P. A. (1995). Compensating for stigma: Obese and non-obese women's reactions to being visible. *Personality and Social Psychology Bulletin, 21*, 1093–1106.

Miller, J. G. (1984). Culture and the development of everyday social explanation. *Journal of Personality and Social Psychology, 46*, 961–78.

Miller, J. G. (1996). West bows to psychology's cultural revolution. *New Scientist*, 24 February, 12.

Miller, J. G. (1997). Cultural conceptions of duty: Implications for motivation and morality. In D. Munro, J. F. Schumaker & S. C. Carr (Eds), *Motivation and culture* (pp. 178–92). New York: Routledge.

Miller, J. G., Bersoff, D. M., & Harwood, R. L. (1990). Perceptions of social responsibilities in India and the United States: Moral imperatives or personal decisions? *Journal of Personality and Social Psychology, 58*, 33–47.

Miller, N. E. (1959). Liberalization of basic S-R concepts: Extensions to conflict behavior, motivation, and social learning. In S. Koch (Ed.), *Psychology: A study of a science, Study 1* (pp. 198–292). New York: McGraw-Hill.

Miller, N., & Campbell, D. T. (1959). Recency and primacy in persuasion as a function of the timing of speeches and measurements. *Journal of Abnormal and Social Psychology, 59*, 1–9.

Miller, R. S. (1991). On decorum in close relationships: Why aren't we polite to those we love? *Contemporary Social Psychology, 15*, 63–5.

Miller, S. (1986). *Men and friendship.* Florence, Italy: Gateway Books.

Miner, M. M. (1992). Documenting the demise of manly love: The Virginian. *Journal of Men's Studies, 1*, 33–9.

Misumi, J., & Peterson, M. F. (1985). The performance-maintenance (PM) theory of leadership: Review of Japanese research program. *Administrative Science Quarterly, 30*, 198–223.

Mita, T. H., Dermer, M., & Knight, J. (1977). Reversed facial images and the mere-exposure hypothesis. *Journal of Personality and Social Psychology, 35*, 597–601.

Mitchell, T. R., & Kalb, L. S. (1982). Effects of job experience on supervisor attribution for a subordinate's poor performance. *Journal of Applied Psychology, 67*, 181–8.

Mizuno, M., & Yamaguchi, S. (1997). A test of the in-group and out-group favoritism phenomenon: The effect of the desirability of group names on in-group and out-group evaluations. In K. Leung, U. Kim, S. Yamaguchi & Y. Kashima (Eds), *Progress in Asian social psychology,* vol. 1 (pp. 217–29). Singapore: John Wiley & Sons.

Moeller, S. (1999). *'Compassion fatigue': News-makers bear responsibility.* New York: Routledge.

Moghaddam, F. M. (1996). Training for developing world psychologists: Can it be better than the training? In S. C. Carr & J. F. Schumaker (Eds), *Psychology and the developing world* (pp. 49–59). Westport, CT: Praeger.

Moghaddam, F. M. (1998). *Social psychology: Exploring universals across cultures.* New York: W H. Freeman and Company.

Moghaddam, F. M., & Stringer, P. (1988). Outgroup similarity and intergroup bias. *Journal of Social Psychology, 128*, 105–115.

Moghaddam, F. M., Taylor, D. M., & Wright, S. C. (1993). *Social psychology in cross-cultural perspective.* New York: W. H. Freeman and Company.

Monahan, J. L., Murphy, S. T., & Zajonc, R. B. (2000). Subliminal mere exposure: Specific, general, and diffuse effects. *Psychological Science, 11*, 462–6.

Monk, G., Winslade, J., Crocket, K., & Epston, D. (1996). *The archaeology of hope.* San Francisco, CA: Jossey-Bass.

Montero, M. (1990). Ideology and psychosocial research in Third World contexts. *Journal of Social Issues, 46*, 43–55.

Moorhead, G., Ference, R., & Neck, C. P. (2000). Group decision fiascoes continue: Space shuttle Challenger and a revised Groupthink framework. In M. H. Davies (Ed.), *Social psychology 00/01* (pp. 198–203). Guilford, CT: Dushkin/McGraw-Hill.

Moreira, V. (in press). Poverty and mental health: Observations from Brazil. In S. C. Carr & T. S. Sloan (Eds), *Poverty and psychology: Emergent critical perspectives* (in press). New York: Kluwer-Plenum.

Moreland, R. L., & Beach, S. R. (1992). Exposure effects in the classroom: The development of affinity among students. *Journal of Experimental Social Psychology, 28*, 255–76.

Morris, J. W., & Heaven, P. C. (1986). Attitudes and behavioural intentions toward Vietnamese in Australia. *Journal of Social Psychology, 126*, 513–20.

Morse, N. C., & Weiss, R. S. (1955). The function and meaning of work and the job. *American Sociological Review, 20*, 151–98.

Morse, S. J., & Marks, A. (1985). 'Cause Duncan's me mate': A comparison of reported relations with mates and with friends in Australia. *British Journal of Social Psychology, 24*, 283–92.

Moscaritolo, M. (2000). Bosses, workers, out of sync. *Northern Territory News*, 14 July.

Moscovici, S. (1976). *Social influence and social change.* London: Academic Press.

Moscovici, S. (1980). Toward a theory of conversion behaviour. *Advances in Experimental Social Psychology, 13*, 209–239.

Moscovici, S. (1981). On social representations. In J. P. Forgas (Ed.), *Social cognition: Perspectives on everyday understandings* (pp. 181–209). London: Academic Press.

Moscovici, S., & Lage, E. (1976). Studies in social influence III: Majority versus minority influence in a group. *European Journal of Social Psychology, 6*, 148–74.

Moscovici, S., & Nève, P. (1971). Studies in social influence I: Those absent are in the right: Convergence and polarisation of answers in the source of a social interaction. *European Journal of Social Psychology, 1/2*, 210–14.

Moscovici, S., & Zavalloni, M. (1969). The group as a polariser of individual and collective judgements. *Journal of Personality and Social Psychology, 12*, 125–35.

Moscovici, S., Lage, E., & Naffrechoux, M. (1969). Influence of a consistent minority on the responses of a majority in a color perception task. *Sociometry, 32*, 365–80.

Mouly, V. S., & Sankaran, J. K. (2002). The enactment of envy within organizations: Insights from a New Zealand academic department. *Journal of Applied Behavioral Science, 38*, 36–56.

Mowen, J. C. (1993). *Consumer behavior* (3rd edition). New York: Macmillan.

Muchinsky, P. M. (2000). *Psychology applied to work* (6th edition). Stamford, CT: Wadsworth.

Mugny, G. (1975). Negotiations, image of the other, and the process of minority influence. *European Journal of Social Psychology, 5*, 209–229.

Muir, H. (1998). Who survives in jet crash? Cranfield, UK: Cranfield University. (Reported in the *Sunday Territorian*, 15 March, 19.)

Mullen, P. E. (1993). The crime of passion and the changing cultural construction of jealousy. *Criminal Behaviour and Mental Health, 3*, 1–11.

Murninghan, J. K., & Roth, A. E. (1983). Expecting continued play in prisoner's dilemma games. *Journal of Conflict Resolution, 27*, 279–300.

Murphy, C. (October 1999). *Organizational communication*. Presentation in MAN 102 — Organisational behaviour. Darwin: Northern Territory University.

Murphy, K. (2000). Easy distinction between a game and reality. *The Australian*, 16 May, 15.

Murphy, S. T., Monahan, J. L., & Zajonc, R. B. (1995). Additivity of non-conscious affect: Combined effects of priming and exposure. *Journal of Personality and Social Psychology, 69,* 589–602.

Murray, H. A. (1938). *Explorations in personality.* New York: Oxford University Press.

Murray, S. L., Holmes, J. G., & Griffin, D. W. (1996). The benefits of positive illusions: Idealization and the construction of satisfaction in close relationships. *Journal of Personality and Social Psychology, 70,* 79–98.

Murray-Johnson, L., Witte, K., Liu, W. Y., Hubbell, A. P., & Sampson, J. (2001). Addressing cultural orientation in fear appeals: Promoting AIDS-protective behaviors among Mexican immigrant and African American adolescents and American and Taiwanese college students. *Journal of Health Communication, 6,* 335–8.

Myers, D. G. (1986). *Psychology.* Belmont, CA: Wadsworth.

Myers, D. G., & Bishop, G. D. (1970). Discussion effects on racial attitudes. *Science, 169,* 778–9.

Namandwa, D. Z. (1992). Personal correspondence. Limbe, Malaŵi, East Africa.

Narayan, D., Chambers, R., Shah, M., & Petesch, P. (2000a). *Voices of the poor: Crying out for change.* New York: Oxford University Press.

Narayan, D., Patel, R., Schafft, K., Rademacher, A., & Koch-Schulte, S. (2000b). *Voices of the poor: Can anyone hear us?* New York: Oxford University Press.

Nardi, P. M., & Sherrod, D. (1994). Friendship in the lives of gay men and lesbians. *Journal of Social and Personal Relationships, 11,* 185–99.

Nathanson, A. I. (2001). Parents versus peers: Exploring the significance of peer mediation of anti-social television. *Communication Research, 28,* 251–4.

Nemeth, C. J. (Ed.) (1996). Special issue: Minority influence. *British Journal of Social Psychology, 35* [Whole No. 1], 1–219.

Nemeth, C. J, Mosier, K., & Chiles, C. (1992). When convergent thought improves performance: Majority versus minority influence. *Personality and Social Psychology Bulletin, 18,* 139–44.

Nemeth, C. J., & Wachtler, J. (1983). Creative problem-solving as a result of majority vs. minority influence. *European Journal of Social Psychology, 13,* 45–55.

Neuberg, S. L., Judice, T. N., Virdin, L. M., & Carrillo, M. A. (1993). Perceiver self-presentational goals as moderators of expectancy influences: Ingratiation and the disconfirmation of negative expectancies. *Journal of Personality and Social Psychology, 64,* 409–420.

Neuliep, J. W. (1987). The influence of Theory X and Theory Y management styles on the selection of compliance-gaining strategies. *Communication Research Reports, 4,* 14–19.

Newcomb, T. M. (1943). *Personality and social change: Attitude formation in a student community.* New York: Dryden Press.

Newcomb, T. M. (1956). The prediction of interpersonal attraction. *American Psychologist, 11,* 575–86.

Newcomb, T. M. (1963). Persistence and regression of changed attitudes: Long range studies. *Journal of Social Issues, 19,* 3–14.

Newcomb, T. M., Koenig, L. E., Flacks, R., & Warwick, D. P. (1967). *Persistence and change: Bennington College and its students after twenty-five years.* New York: John Wiley & Sons.

Newman, J., & McAuley, C. (1978). Eye contact with strangers in city, suburb, and small town. *Environment & Behavior, 9,* 547–58.

Ng, K. Y., & Van Dyne, L. (2001). Culture and minority influence: Effects on persuasion and originality. In C. K. W. De Dreu & N. K. De Vries (Eds), *Group consensus and minority influence: Implications for innovation* (pp. 284–306). Oxford, UK: Blackwell.

Ng, S. H., & Cram, F. (1986). Complementary and antagonistic inter-group differentiations by New Zealand nurses. *New Zealand Journal of Psychology, 15,* 68–76.

Nguyen, M. L., Heslin, R., & Nguyen, T. D. (1976). The meaning of touch: Sex and marital status differences. *Representative Research in Social Psychology, 7,* 13–18.

Nickerson, R. S. (1999). How we know — and sometimes misjudge — what others know: Imputing one's own knowledge to others. *Psychological Bulletin, 125,* 737–59.

Nida, S. A., & Koon, J. (1983). They get better looking at closing time around here, too. *Psychological Reports, 52,* 657–8.

Nisbett, R. E. (in press). *The circle and the line.* Denver, CO: Westview Press.

Nisbett, R. E., Caputo, E., Legant, P., & Maracek, J. (1973). Behaviour as seen by the actor and as seen by the observer. *Journal of Personality and Social Psychology, 27,* 154–64.

Nisbett, R. E., Peng, K., Choi, I., & Norenzayan, A. (2001). Culture and systems of thought: Holistic versus analytic cognition. *Psychological Review, 108,* 291–310.

Noller, P., Feeney, J. A., & Blakely-Smith, A. (2001). Handling pressures for change in marriage: Making attributions for relational dialectics. In V. Manusov & J. H. Harvey (Eds), *Attribution, communication behaviour, and close relationships: Advances in personal relations* (pp. 153–72). New York: Cambridge University Press.

Noller, P., Feeney, J. A., & Peterson, C. (2001). *Personal relationships across the lifespan.* Philadelphia, PA: Psychology Press/Taylor & Francis.

Norman, P., Abraham, C., & Conner, M. (Eds) (2000). *Understanding and changing health behavior: From health beliefs to self-regulation.* Amsterdam: Harwood Academic Publishers.

Novellino, M. (2000). The Pinocchio syndrome. *Transactional Analysis Journal, 30,* 292–8.

Nsamenang, A. B. (1996). Cultural organisation of human development within the family context. In S. C. Carr & J. F. Schumaker (Eds), *Psychology and the developing world* (pp. 60–70). Westport, CT: Praeger.

Nsamenang, A. B. N. (1994, July*). Factors influencing the development of psychology in sub-Saharan Africa.* 23rd International Congress of Applied Psychology, Madrid, Spain.

Nykodym, N., Longenecker, C. O., & Ruud, W. N. (1991). Improving quality of life with transactional analysis as an intervention change strategy. *Applied Psychology: An International Review, 40,* 395–404.

O'Brien, G. E., & Plooji, D. (1977). Comparison of programmed and prose culture training upon attitudes and knowledge. *Journal of Applied Psychology, 62,* 499–505.

O'Connor, P. (1992). *Friendships between women: A critical review.* New York: The Guildford Press.

O'Gorman, F. (1992). *Charity and change: From bandaid to beacon.* Melbourne: World Vision.

O'Keefe, D. J., & Hale, S. L. (2001). An odds-ratio-based meta-analysis of research on the Door-in-the-Face influence strategy. *Communication Reports, 14,* 31–8.

Oakes, P. J., & Turner, J. C. (1980). Social categorisation and inter-group behaviour: Does minimal inter-group discrimination make social identity more positive? *European Journal of Social Psychology, 10,* 295–301.

Oberg, K. (1954). *Culture shock.* Bobbs-Merrill Reprint Series, No. A-329.

Okamoto, K. (1983). Effects of excessive similarity feedback on subsequent mood, pursuit of difference, and preference for novelty or scarcity. *Japanese Psychological Research, 25,* 69–77.

Ones, D. S., & Viswesvaran, C. (1998). Integrity testing in organizations. In R. W. Griffin & A. O'Leary-Kelly (Eds) (1998). *Dysfunctional behavior in organizations: Violent and deviant behavior* (pp. 243–76). Stamford, CT: JAI Press.

Operario, D., & Fiske, S. T. (2001). Causes and consequences of stereotypes in organizations. In M. London (Ed.), *How people evaluate others in organizations* (pp. 45–62). Mahwah, NJ: Lawrence Erlbaum Associates.

Orpen, C. (1997). Using the stepladder technique to improve team performance. *Psychological Studies, 42,* 24–8.

Ortiz, D., Alveiro-Pedreros, J., & Meluk, S. (1991). Effects of an AIDS-prevention workshop on a group of adolescents. *Revista Latinamericana de Sexologia, 6,* 137–49 [abstract only, full article is published in Spanish].

Ottati, V. C., & Isbell, L. (1996). Effects of mood during exposure to target information on subsequently reported judgements: An on-line model of misattribution and correction. *Journal of Personality and Social Psychology, 71,* 39–53.

Ouellette, J. A., & Wood, W. (1998). Habit and intention in everyday life: The multiple processes by which past behaviour predicts future behaviour. *Psychological Bulletin, 124,* 54–74.

Owens, L. D., & MacMullin, C. E. (1995). Gender differences in aggression in children and adolescents in South Australian schools. *International Journal of Education & Youth, 6,* 21–35.

Owens, S. (2002). How to make an impact that counts. *Australian Financial Review,* 10 April.

Paicheler, G. (1976). Norms and attitude change I: Polarisation and styles of behaviour. *European Journal of Social Psychology, 6,* 405–427.

Paicheler, G. (1977). Norms and attitude change II: The phenomenon of bipolarisation. *European Journal of Social Psychology, 7,* 5–14.

Park, B., & Rothbart, M. (1982). Perception of outgroup homogeneity and levels of social categorisation: Memory for the subordinate attributes of in-group and out-group members. *Journal of Experimental Social Psychology, 42,* 1051–68.

Parks, M. R., & Floyd, K. (1996). Making friends in cyberspace. *Journal of Communication, 46,* 80–97.

Parks, M. R., & Roberts, L. D. (1998). 'Making MOOsic': The development of personal relationships on-line and a comparison to their off-line counterparts. *Journal of Social and Personal Relationships, 15,* 517–37.

Pastor, S. (1997). The distinctiveness of cross-cultural training in the Northern Territory. *Northern Radius, 4,* 3–8.

Pataki, S. P., Shapiro, C., & Clark, M. S. (1994). Children's acquisition of appropriate norms for friendships and acquaintances. *Journal of Social and Personal Relationships, 11,* 427–42.

Paton, D., & Stephens, C. (1996). Training and support for emergency responders. In D. Paton & J. M. Violanti (Eds), *Traumatic stress in critical occupations* (pp. 173–205). Springfield, IL: Charles C. Thomas.

Patterson, C. E., & Pettijohn, T. F. (1982). Age and human mate selection. *Psychological Reports, 51,* 70.

Paul, A. M. (1998). Where bias begins: The truth about stereotypes. *Psychology Today,* May/June, 52–5, 82.

Paulhus, D. L. (2002). Socially desirable responding: The evolution of a construct. In H. I. Braun & D. N. Jackson (Eds), *The role of constructs in psychological and educational measurement* (pp. 37–48). Mahwah, NJ: Lawrence Erlbaum Associates.

Pavlov, I. P. (1927). *Conditioned reflexes.* Oxford, UK: Oxford University Press.

Pawlik, K., & d'Ydewalle, G. (1996). Psychology and the global commons. *American Psychologist, 51,* 488–95.

Paxton, L., & Janssen, R. (2002). HIV treatment advances as prevention. In A. O'Leary (Ed.), *Beyond condoms: Alternative approaches to HIV prevention* (pp. 91–108). New York: Kluwer-Plenum Academic Publishers.

Pearson, N. (1999). *Our right to take responsibility: Discussion paper.* Cape York, Queensland: Cape York Land Council.

Pedersen, A., Griffiths, B., Contos, N., Bishop, B., & Walker, I. (2000). Attitudes toward Aboriginal Australians in city and country settings. *Australian Psychologist, 35,* 109–117.

Peek, C. W., Fisher, J. L., & Kidwell, J. S. (1985). Teenage violence toward parents: A neglected dimension of family violence. *Journal of Marriage and the Family, 47,* 1051–8.

Pennebaker, J. W. (1979). Don't the girls get prettier at closing time: A country and western application to psychology. *Personality and Social Psychology Bulletin, 5,* 122–5.

Pennington, D. C., Gillen, K., & Hill, P. (1999). *Social psychology.* Sydney: Arnold.

Peres, S. H., & Garcia, J. R. (1962). Validity and dimensions of descriptive adjectives used in reference letters for engineering applicants. *Personnel Psychology, 15,* 279–86.

Perez, J. A., & Mugny, G. (1987). Paradoxical effects of categorisation in minority influence: When being an out-group is an advantage. *European Journal of Social Psychology, 17,* 157–69.

Perrett, D. I., May, K. A., & Yoshikawa, S. (1994). Facial shape and judgements of female attractiveness. *Nature, 368,* 239–42.

Perry, L. S. (1993). Effects of inequity of job satisfaction and self-evaluation in a national sample of African-American workers. *Journal of Social Psychology, 133,* 565–73.

Pessin, J. (1933). The comparative effects of social and mechanical stimulation on memorising. *American Journal of Psychology, 45,* 263–70.

Peterson, R. S., & Nemeth, C. J. (1996). Focus versus flexibility: Majority and minority influence can both improve performance. *Personality and Social Psychology Bulletin, 22,* 14–23.

Petony, J. F. (1995). The effect of negative campaigning on voting, semantic differential, and thought listing. *Journal of Social Behavior & Personality, 10,* 631–44.

Pettigrew, T. F. (1958). Personality and socio-cultural factors in inter-group attitudes: A cross-national comparison. *Journal of Conflict Resolution, 2,* 29–42.

Pettigrew, T. F. (1979). The ultimate attribution error: Extending Allport's cognitive analysis of prejudice. *Personality and Social Psychology Bulletin, 5,* 461–76.

Pettigrew, T. F., & Meertens, R. W. (1995). Subtle and blatant prejudice in Western Europe. *European Journal of Social Psychology, 25,* 57–75.

Petty, R. E., & Cacioppo, J. T. (1981). *Attitudes and persuasion: Classic and contemporary approaches.* Dubuque, IA: Wm. C. Brown Company.

Petty, R. E., Tormala, Z. L., Hawkins, C., & Wegener, D. T. (2001). Motivation to think and order effects in persuasion: The moderating role of chunking. *Personality and Social Psychology Bulletin, 27,* 332–44.

Pfeffer, K. (1997). Young Nigerians' perceptions of a 'good husband' and a 'good wife'. *Youth & Society, 28,* 499–516.

Piaget, J. (1952). *The origin of intelligence in children.* New York: International Universities Press.

Piaget, J. (1962). Comments: Addendum to Vygotsky, L. S. (1962). In J. Haufmann & G. Valcar (Eds), *Thought and language.* Cambridge, MA: MIT Press.

Pierce, C. A. (1995). Attraction in the workplace: An examination of antecedents and consequences of organisational romance. *Dissertation Abstracts International. Sciences and Engineering, 56,* 2946.

Pietropinto, A. (1986). Misconceptions about male sexuality. *Medical Aspects of Human Sexuality, 20,* 80–85.

Pihl, R. O., Lau, M. L., & Assaad, J. M. (1997). Aggressive disposition, alcohol, and aggression. *Aggressive Behaviour, 23,* 11–18.

Piliavin, I. M., Rodin, J., & Piliavin, J. A. (1969). Good Samaritan: An underground phenomenon? *Journal of Personality and Social Psychology, 13,* 289–99.

Pinker, S, (1997). *How the mind works.* London: Allen Lane.

Piot, P. (Director of UN AIDS) (1999). *Africa AIDS problem exploded: UN.* Australian Broadcasting Corporation, Monday, 13 September.

Platania, J., & Moran, G. P. (2001). Social facilitation as a function of mere presence of others. *Journal of Social Psychology, 141,* 190–97.

Platow, M. J., O'Connell, A., Shave, R., & Hanning, P. (1995). Social evaluations of fair and unfair allocators in inter-personal and inter-group situations. *British Journal of Social Psychology, 34,* 363–81.

Platow, M. J., Hoar, S., Reid, S., Harley, K., & Morrison, D. (1997). Endorsement of distributively fair and unfair leaders in interpersonal and intergroup situations. *European Journal of Social Psychology, 27,* 465–94.

Plotkin, H. (1997). *Evolution in mind: An introduction to evolutionary psychology.* St. Ives, UK: Penguin.

Plotkin, H. (1998). Evolution in mind: An introduction to evolutionary psychology. St. Ives, UK: Penguin.

Plummer, C. M. (1982). Future school simulation game: Changing attitudes with counter-attitudinal role-playing. *Simulation & Games, 13,* 92–119.

Poppe, E., & Linssen, H. (1999). In-group favoritism and the reflection of realistic dimensions of difference between national states in Central and Eastern European nationality stereotypes. *British Journal of Social Psychology, 38,* 85–102.

Posthuma, A. C. (1995). Japanese techniques in Africa? Human resources and industrial restructuring in Zimbabwe. *World Development, 23,* 103–116.

Postmes, T., Spears, R., & Lea, M. (2002). Inter-group differentiation in computer-mediated communication: Effects of depersonalization. *Group Dynamics, 6,* 3–16.

Powell, J. L., & Jacobson, A. S. (August 1993). *Trait ambiguity and controllability in evaluations of self and other.* Convention of the American Psychological Association (APA), Toronto, Canada.

Power, V. (October 1994). *Gender bias and the 'glass ceiling'.* 29th Annual Conference of the Australian Psychological Association, Wollongong.

Powis, D. A., Neame, R. L. B., Bristow, T., & Murphy, L. B. (1988). The objective structured interview for medical student selection. *British Medical Journal, 296*, 765–8.

Prapavessis, H., & Carron, A. V. (1997). Sacrifice, cohesion, and conformity to norms in sports teams. *Group Dynamics: Theory, Research, and Practice, 1*, 231–40.

Pratkanis, A. R., & Aronson, E. (1992). *Age of propaganda: The everyday use and abuse of persuasion.* New York: W. H. Freeman & Co.

Premack, D. (1963). Prediction of the comparative reinforcement values of running and drinking. *Science, 139*, 1062–3.

Price, J. (1985). The Wernicke-Korsakoff syndrome in Queensland, Australia: Antecedents and prevention. *Alcohol & Alcoholism, 20*, 233–42.

Prilleltensky, I. (2000). Cultural assumptions, social justice, and mental health. In J. F. Schumaker & T. Ward (Eds), *Cultural cognition and psychopathology* (in press). Westport, CT: Praeger.

Prilleltensky, I. (in press). Poverty and power. In S. C. Carr & T. S. Sloan (Eds), *Poverty and psychology: Emergent critical perspectives* (in press). New York: Kluwer-Plenum.

Prottas, J. (1997). Advertising and its role in organ donation. In M. E. Goldberg & M. Fishbein (Eds), *Social marketing: Theoretical and practical perspectives in advertising and consumer psychology* (pp. 375–85). Mahwah, NJ: Lawrence Erlbaum Associates.

Provine, R. R. (1997). Yawns, laughs, smiles, tickles, and talking: Naturalistic and laboratory studies of facial emotion and social communication. In J. A. Russell & J. M. Fernandez-Dols (Eds), *The psychology of facial expression* (pp. 158–75). New York: Cambridge University Press.

Pruitt, D. G. (1981). *Negotation behaviour.* New York: Academic Press.

Pryor, R. (1997). Charting client consent. *In-Psych,* October, 6.

Pryor, R. G. L. (1989). Conflicting responsibilities: A case study of an ethical dilemma for psychologists working in organisations. *Australian Psychologist, 24*, 293–305.

Psychology International (2002). BBC recasts the Stanford Prison Experiment. *Psychology International, 13*, 3.

Quine, L. (2001). Workplace bullying in nurses. *Journal of Health Psychology, 6*, 73–84.

Ragland, J. D., & Berman, A. L. (1991). Farm crisis and suicide: Dying on the vine? *Omega — Journal of Death & Dying, 22*, 173–85.

Rakos, R. F. (1997). Asserting and confronting. In O. D. W. Hargie (Ed.), *The handbook of communication skills* (pp. 289–319). London: Routledge.

Raven, B., & Rubin, J. (1976). *Social psychology: People in groups.* New York: John Wiley & Sons.

Raven, B. H., & Rubin, J. Z. (1983). *Social psychology.* New York: John Wiley & Sons.

Rayner, C. (1997). The incidence of workplace bullying. *Journal of Community and Applied Social Psychology, 7*, 199–208.

Rea, P., & Kerzner, H. (1997). *Strategic planning: A practical guide.* Melbourne: International Thomson Business Publishing Company.

Rechtien, J. G., & Fiedler, E. (1989). Contributions to psychohistory XIII: Courtly love today — romance and socialisation in interpersonal scripts. *Psychological Reports, 63*, 683–95.

Regan, P. C. (1998). Of lust and love: Beliefs about the role of sexual desire in romantic relationships. *Personal Relationships, 5*, 139–57.

Regan, P. C. (1999). Hormonal correlates and causes of sexual desire: A review. *The Canadian Journal of Human Sexuality, 8*, 1–16.

Regan, P. C., & Berscheid, E. (1996). Beliefs about the state, goals, and objects of sexual desire. *Journal of Sex and Marital Therapy, 22*, 110–20.

Regan, P. C., & Berscheid, E. (1997). Gender differences in characteristics desired in a potential sexual and marriage partner. *Journal of Psychology and Human Sexuality, 9*, 25–37.

Regan, P. C., & Dreyer, C. S. (1999). Lust? Love? Status? Young adults' motives for engaging in casual sex. *Journal of Psychology and Human Sexuality, 11*, 1–24.

Regan, P. C., Kocan, E. R., & Whitlock, T. (1998). Ain't love grand! A prototype analysis of the concept of romantic love. *Journal of Personality and Social Psychology, 15*, 411–20.

Regan, P. C., Levin, L., Sprecher, S., Christopher, F. S., & Cate, R. (2000). Partner preferences: What characteristics do men and women desire in their short-term sexual and long-term romantic partners? *Journal of Psychology and Human Sexuality, 12*, 1–21.

Reicher, S. (1991a). Politics of crowd psychology. *The Psychologist, 14*, 487–91.

Reicher, S. (1991b). The logic of psychology, not the intentions of the psychologist. *The Psychologist, 4*, 495.

Reicher, S. (1996). 'The Crowd' century: Reconciling practical success with theoretical failure. *British Journal of Social Psychology, 35*, 535–53.

Reicher, S. (1997). Collective psychology and the psychology of the self. *British Psychological Society Social Psychology Newsletter, 36*, 3–15.

Reid, W. M., Pease, J., & Taylor, R. G. (1990). The Delphi technique as an aid to organization development activities. *Organization Development Journal, 8*, 37–42.

Reser, J. P. (1991). Aboriginal mental health: Conflicting cultural perspectives. In J. Reid & P. Trompf (Eds), *The health of Aboriginal Australia* (pp. 218–91). Marrickville, NSW: Harcourt Brace Jovanovich.

Reser, J. P. (1999). Indigenous suicide in cross-cultural context: An overview. *South Pacific Journal of Psychology, 11*, 95–111.

Rhodes, R. M., Gordon, J. B., & Zelman, A. B. (1997). Comprehensive mental health consultation to a shelter for battered women: Preventive implications. In A. B. Zelman (Ed.), *Early intervention with high-risk children: Freeing prisoners of circumstance* (pp. 293–305). Northvale, NJ: Jason Aronson.

Rice, R. E., & Love, G. (1987). Electronic emotion: Socio-emotional content in a computer-mediated communication network. *Communication Research, 14,* 85–108.

Richburg, K. B. (1997). Spreading the wealth: How globalisation is helping shift cash from rich nations to poor ones. *Washington Post National Weekly Edition,* 17 March, 6–9.

Ridge, S. R., & Feeney, J. A. (1998). Relationship history and relationship attitudes in gay males and lesbians: Attachment styles and gender differences. *Australian and New Zealand Journal of Psychiatry, 32,* 848–59.

Riley, R. (1998). From exclusion to negotiation: Psychology in Aboriginal social justice. *In-Psych, 20,* 12–19.

Ringelmann, M. (1913). Recherches sur les moteurs animés: Travails de l'homme. *Annales de l'Insitut National Agronomique, 12,* 1–40.

Ritchie, J., & Ritchie, J. (1999). Seventy-five years of cross-cultural psychology in New Zealand. In W. J. Lonner & D. L. Dinner (Eds), *Merging past, present, and future in cross-cultural psychology* (pp. 105–115). Lisse, Netherlands: Swets & Zeitlinger.

Robins, R. W., & Beer, J. S. (2001). Positive illusions about the self: Short-term benefits and long-term costs. *Journal of Personality and Social Psychology, 80,* 340–52.

Robbins, S. P., Bergman, R., Stagg, I., & Coulter, M. (2000). *Management.* French's Forest, NSW: Prentice Hall.

Robbins, S. P., Waters-Marsh, T., Cacioppe, R., & Millett, B. (1994). *Organisational behaviour: Concepts, controversies, and applications/Australia and New Zealand.* Sydney: Prentice Hall.

Robertson, I. T., Gratton, L., & Rout, U. (1990). The validity of situational interviews for administrative jobs. *Journal of Organisational Behaviour, 11,* 69–76.

Robertson, R. (1995). *Globalization: Social theory and global culture.* London: Sage.

Robinson, R. J. (1995). The conflict-competent organisation. In R. M. Kramer & D. M. Messick (Eds), *Negotiation as a social process* (pp. 186–204). London: Sage.

Rogelberg, S. G., & O'Connor, M. S. (1998). Extending the stepladder technique: An examination of self-paced stepladder groups. *Group Dynamics, 2,* 82–91.

Rogelberg, S. G., Barnes-Farrell, J. L., & Lowe, C. A. (1992). The stepladder technique: An alternative group structure facilitating effective group decision-making. *Journal of Applied Psychology, 77,* 730–37.

Roger, M. (1999). Collective guilt and pro-social behaviour: Implications for Indigenous and non-Indigenous reconciliation in Australia. *South Pacific Journal of Psychology, 11,* 89–94 <http://spjp.massey.ac.nz>.

Rogier, A., & Yzerbyt, V. (1999). Social attribution, correspondence bias, and the emergence of stereotypes. *Swiss Journal of Psychology, 58,* 233–40.

Rollman, J. B., Krug, K., & Parente, F. (2000). The chat room phenomenon: Reciprocal communication in cyberspace. *Cyberpsychology & Behavior, 3,* 161–6.

Rosch, E. (1978). Principles of categorisation. In E. Rosch & B. B. Lloyd (Eds), *Cognition and categorisation* (pp. 27–48). Hillsdale, NJ: Lawrence Erlbaum Associates.

Rosenau, J. N. (1998). The complexities and contradictions of globalisation. In R. M. Jackson (Ed.), *Global issues 98/99* (pp. 122–6). Guilford, CT: Dushkin-McGraw-Hill.

Rosenberg, S. (2000). Sad and lonely in cyberspace? In M. H. Davis (Ed.), *Social psychology 00/01* (pp. 110–11). Guilford, CT: Dushkin/McGraw-Hill.

Rosenblatt, P. C. (1990). *Farming is in our blood: Farm families in economic crisis.* Ames, IA: Iowa State University Press.

Rosenfeld, P. (1988). *Instructor's handbook of lecture launchers and transparency/repro masters in Introductory Psychology.* New York: Alfred A. Knopf.

Rosenthal, R. (1995). Critiquing Pygmalion: A 25-year perspective. *Current Directions in Psychological Science, 4,* 171–2.

Rosenthal, R., & Jacobson, L. (1968). *Pygmalion in the classroom.* New York: Holt, Rhinehart & Winston.

Rosmond, R., & Bjoerntorp, P. (2000). Quality of life, overweight, and body fat distribution in middle-aged men. *Behavioral Medicine, 26,* 90–94.

Ross, L. (1977). The intuitive psychologist and his shortcomings: Distortions in the attribution process. *Advances in Experimental Social Psychology, 10,* 173–220.

Ross, L. (1980). *Social psychology.* New York: Macmillan.

Ross, L., & Nisbett, R. E. (2000). Culture, ideology, and construal. In M. H. Davis (Ed.), *Social psychology 00/01* (pp. 70–73). Guilford, CT: Dushkin/McGraw-Hill.

Rothblaum, F., & Tsang, B. Y. P. (1998). Lovesongs in the United States and China: On the nature of romantic love. *Journal of Cross-Cultural Psychology, 29,* 306–319.

Rothman, A. J., & Hardin, C. D. (1997). Differential use of the availability heuristic in social judgment. *Personality and Social Psychology Bulletin, 23,* 123–38.

Rousseau, D. M. (1995). *Psychological contracts in organisations.* Thousand Oaks, CA: Sage.

Rousseau, D. M., & House, R. J. (1994). Meso organisational behaviour: Avoiding three fundamental biases. In C. L. Cooper & D. M. Rousseau (Eds), *Trends in organisational behaviour,* vol. 1 (pp. 13–30). Chichester, UK: John Wiley & Sons.

Rousseau, D. M., & Parks, J. M. (1993). The contracts of individuals and organisations. In B. M. Staw & L. L. Cummings (Eds), *Research in organisational behaviour* (pp. 1–43). Greenwich, CT: JAI Press.

Rubin, J. Z., & Brown, N. B. R. (1975). *The social psychology of bargaining and negotiating*. London: Academic Press.

Rubin, Z. (1970). Measurement of romantic love. *Journal of Personality and Social Psychology, 16*, 265–73.

Rubin, Z. (1973). *Liking and loving: An invitation to social psychology*. New York: Holt, Rinehart, & Winston.

Rubin, Z., & Shenker, S. (1978). Friendship, proximity, and self-disclosure. *Journal of Personality, 46*, 1–22.

Rugimbana, R. (1996a). *A case of inequitable salaries between expatriate and host in Tanzania*. Newcastle, Australia: University of Newcastle, Department of Management Case Studies.

Rugimbana, R. (1996b). Marketing psychology in developing countries. In S. C. Carr & J. F. Schumaker (Eds), *Psychology and the developing world* (pp. 140–59). Westport, CT: Praeger.

Rugimbana, R. (1998). Personal correspondence, 26 February.

Rugimbana, R. O. (2000). The impact of 'consumer cringe' on developing regional trade blocks: A Tanzanian case study. *Journal of African Business, 1*, 91–106.

Russell, G. W. (1993). *The social psychology of sport*. New York: Springer-Verlag.

Russell, G. W., & Arms, R. L. (2001). Calming troubled waters: Peacemakers in a sports riot. *Aggressive Behaviour, 27*, 292–6.

Russell, J. A., Arms, R. L., & Bibby, R. W. (1995). Canadians' beliefs in catharsis. *Social Behaviour and Personality, 23*, 223–8.

Russell, R. L. (1975). Self-concept and attraction for similar and dissimilar others. *Journal of Personality and Social Psychology, 31*, 926–9.

Sagi, A. (1990). Attachment theory and research from a cross-cultural perspective. *Human Development, 33*, 10–22.

Saidla, D. D. (1990). Cognitive development and group stages. *Journal for Specialists in Group Work, 15*, 15–20.

Sampson, E. E. (1993). *Celebrating the other: A dialogic account of human nature*. Boulder, CO: Westview Press.

Sánchez, E. (1996). The Latin American experience in community social psychology. In S. C. Carr & J. F. Schumaker (Eds), *Psychology and the developing world* (pp. 119–29). Westport, CT: Praeger.

Sánchez, E. (June 1999). Personal correspondence.

Sanchez-Mazas, M., Mugny, G., & Falomir, J. (1997). Minority influence and inter-group relations: Social comparison and validation processes in the context of xenophobia in Switzerland. *Swiss Journal of Psychology, 56*, 182–92.

Sandler, L. (1986). Self-fulfilling prophecy: Better management by magic. *Training, 23*, 60–64.

Sanford, B. (1913). A preliminary study of the emotion of love between the sexes. *American Journal of Psychology, 13*, 325–54.

Sanson, A., & Dudgeon, P. (Eds). (2000). Psychology, Indigenous issues, and reconciliation. *Australian Psychologist, 35*, 79–180 [Whole issue].

Sanson, A., Augoustinos, M., Gridley, H., Kyrios, M., Reser, J., & Turner, C. (1998). Racism and prejudice: An Australian Psychological Society position paper. *Australian Psychologist, 33*, 161–82.

Sanson, A., Duck, J., Cupit, G., Ungerer, J., Scuderi, C., & Sutton, J. (2000). Media representations and responsibilities: Psychological perspectives. An Australian Psychological Society position paper <www.psychsociety.com.au>.

Sanson, A., Prior, M., Smart, D., & Oberklaid, F. (1993). Gender differences in aggression in childhood: Implications for a peaceful world. *Australian Psychologist, 28*, 86–92.

Sarbin, T. R. (Ed.) (1986). *Narrative psychology: The storied nature of human conduct*. Westport, CT: Praeger.

Saylor, E. S., & Aries, E. (1999). Ethnic identity and change in social context. *Journal of Social Psychology, 139*, 549–66.

Schachter, S. (1951). Deviation, rejection, and communication. *Journal of Abnormal and Social Psychology, 46*, 190–207.

Schachter, S. (1959). *The psychology of affiliation*. Stanford, CA: Stanford University Press.

Schachter, S., & Singer, J. (1962). Cognitive, social, and physiological determinants of the emotional state. *Psychological Review, 69*, 379–99.

Schank, R. C., & Abelson, R. P. (1977). *Scripts, plans, goals, and understanding: An inquiry into human knowledge structures*. Hillsdale, NJ: Lawrence Erlbaum Associates.

Scharfe, E. (2001). Development of emotional expression, understanding, and regulation in infants and young children. In R. Bar-On & J. D. A. Parker (Eds), *The handbook of emotional intelligence: Theory, development, assessment, and application at home, school, and in the workplace* (pp. 244–62). San Francisco, CA: Jossey-Bass.

Scharfe, E., & Bartholomew, K. (1995). Accommodation and attachment representations in young couples. *Journal of Social and Personal Relationships, 12*, 389–401.

Scharfe, E., & Bartholomew, K. (1998). Do you remember? Recollections of adult attachment patterns. *Personal Relationships, 5*, 219–34.

Schauder, S. (1991). 'There ain't no woman that comes close to her': American movies, French psycho-analysis, the femme fatale, and her courtois lover. *Psychologie Medicale, 22*, 1055–7.

Schein, E. H. (1991). The role of the founder in the creation of organisational culture. In P. J. Frost, L. F. Moore, M. R. Lewis, C. L. Lundberg & J. Martin (Eds), *Reframing organisational culture* (pp. 15–25). New Delhi: Sage.

Schiffman, H. R. (1982). *Sensation and perception*. New York: John Wiley & Sons.

Schimel, J., Simon, L., Greenberg, J., Pyszczynski, T., Solomon, S., Waxmonsky, J., & Arndt, J. (1999). Stereotypes and terror management: Evidence that mortality salience enhances stereoscopic thinking and preferences. *Journal of Personality and Social Psychology, 77*, 905–926.

Schnake, M. E. (1991). Equity in effort: The 'sucker effect' in co-acting groups. *Journal of Management, 17*, 41–55.

Schneider, B. (1987). The people make the place. *Personnel Psychology, 40*, 437–53.

Schneider, B., Smith, D. B., Taylor, S., & Fleenor, J. (1998). Personality and organizations: A test of the homogeneity of personality hypothesis. *Journal of Applied Psychology, 83*, 462–70.

Schneider, D. J. (1973). Implicit personality theory: A review. *Psychological Bulletin, 79*, 294–309.

Schneider, S. C. (1991). National vs. corporate culture: Implications for human resource management. In M. Mendenhall & G. Oddou (Eds), *Readings and cases in international human resource management* (pp. 13–27). Boston, MA: PWS Kent.

Schriesheim, C. A., Tepper, B. J., & Tetrault, L. A. (1994). Least preferred coworker scores, situational control, and leader effectiveness: A meta analysis of contingency model performance predictors. *Journal of Applied Psychology, 79*, 561–73.

Schumaker, J. F. (1997). Understanding psychopathology: Lessons from the developing world. In S. C. Carr & J. F. Schumaker (Eds), *Psychology and the developing world* (pp. 180–90). Westport, CT: Praeger.

Schumaker, J. F. (2001). *The age of insanity: Modernity and mental health*. Westport, CT: Praeger.

Schumann, D. W., & Thorson, E. (Eds) (1999). *Advertising and the World Wide Web*. Mahwah, NJ: Lawrence Erlbaum Associates.

Schwartz, S. H. (1996). Values and culture. In D. Munro, J. F. Schumaker & S. C. Carr (Eds), *Motivation and culture* (pp. 69–84). New York: Routledge.

Schwenk, C. R. (1990). Effects of devil's advocacy and dialectical inquiry on decision-making: A meta-analysis. *Organisational Behaviour and Human Decision Processes, 47*, 161–76.

Scott, J. P. (1997). Aggression, violence, and culture. In D. Munro, J. F. Schumaker & S. C. Carr (Eds), *Motivation and culture* (pp. 224–34). New York: Routledge.

Sears, D. (1986). College sophomores in the laboratory: Influences of a narrow database on social psychology's view of human nature. *Journal of Personality and Social Psychology, 51*, 515–30.

Seiden, H. M. (2001). Creating passion: An Internet love story. *Journal of Applied Psychoanalytic Studies, 3*, 187–95.

Selmer, J. (1995). What do expatriate managers know about their HCN subordinates' work values: Swedish executives in Hong Kong. *Journal of Transnational Management Development, 2*, 5–20.

Semin, G. R., & Rubini, M. (1990). Unfolding the concept of person by verbal abuse. *European Journal of Social Psychology, 20*, 463–74.

Semler, R. (1993). *Maverick! The success story behind the world's most unusual workplace*. Sydney/Auckland: Random House.

Sen, A. (2000). *Development as freedom*. Oxford, UK: Oxford University Press.

Senge, P. M. (1992). *The fifth discipline: The art and practice of the learning organization*. Sydney: Random House.

Serrano-Martinez, G., & Carreno-Fernandez, M. (1993). The Sternberg theory of love: An empirical analysis. *Psicothema, 5*, 151–67 (Spanish publication, Universidad de Oviedo).

Sessa, V. I. (1996). Using perspective-taking to manage conflict and affect in teams. *Journal of Applied Behavioural Science, 32*, 101–115.

Seyfried, B. A., & Hendrick, C. (1973). When do opposites attract? When they are opposite in sex and sex-role attitudes. *Journal of Personality and Social Psychology, 25*, 15–20.

Shachar, R. (1991). His and her marital satisfaction: The double standard. *Sex Roles, 25*, 451–67.

Sharma, V. M., Pichan, G., & Panwar, M. R. (1983). Differential effects of hot-humid and hot-dry environments on mental functions. *Archives of Occupational Environmental Health, 52*, 315–27.

Sharpsteen, D. J., & Kirkpatrick, L. A. (1997). Romantic jealousy and adult romantic attachment. *Journal of Personality and Social Psychology, 72*, 627–40.

Shaw, M. E. (1964). Communication networks. *Advances in Experimental Social Psychology, 1*, 111–47.

Shea, J. D., Fenning, V., Giles, R., & Griffs, P. (2002). *Using support groups with cancer patients: Reductions in physical symptoms and improved quality of life*. Newcastle, Australia: Report to the Mater Misercordiae Hospital, Newcastle.

Shea, M. (1998). *The primacy effect: The ultimate guide to effective personal communications*. London: Orion Business Books.

Sheeran, P., & Orbell, S. (1999). Implementation intentions and repeated behaviour: Augmenting the predictive validity of the theory of planned behaviour. *European Journal of Social Psychology, 29*, 349–69.

Sheridan, G. (1994). Aussies must work harder: Lee. *The Australian*, 19 April, 1.

Sherif, C. W., & Sherif, M. (1967). Attitude as the individual's own categories: The social judgement-involvement approach to attitude and attitude change. In N. Warren & M. Jahoda (Eds), *Attitudes* (pp. 395–422). Ringwood, Vic.: Penguin.

Sherif, M. (1936). *The psychology of social norms*. New York: Harper & Brothers.

Sherif, M. (1956). Experiments in group conflict. *Scientific American, 195*, 54–8.

Sherif, M. (1966). In common predicament: *Social psychology of intergroup conflict and cooperation*. Boston, MA: Houghton Mifflin.

Sherman, L. W. (1993). Defiance, deterrence, and irrelevance: A theory of the criminal sanction. *Journal of Research in Crime and Delinquency, 30,* 445–73.

Sherman, R. C. (1998). Using the World Wide Web to teach everyday applications of social psychology. *Teaching of Psychology, 25,* 212–15.

Sherman, S. J., Hamilton, D. L., & Lewis, A. C. (1999). Perceived entitativity and the social identity value of group memberships. In D. Abrams & M. A. Hogg (Eds), *Social identity and social cognition* (pp. 80–110). Malden, MA: Blackwell.

Sherry, J. L. (2001). The effects of violent video games on aggression: A meta-analysis. *Human Communication Research, 27,* 409–411.

Shopland, A. (2001). Danger: Romantics at work. *The New Zealand Herald,* 13 August, E1.

Shopland, A. (2002). *The New Zealand Herald,* 13–14 April, C11.

Shubik, M. (1986). Cooperative game solutions: Australian, Indian, and U.S. opinions. *Journal of Conflict Resolution, 30,* 63–76.

Shulman, S., Glicker, J., & Sroufe, L. A. (1994). Stages of friendship growth in pre-adolescence as related to attachment history. *Journal of Social and Personal Relationships, 1,* 341–61.

Sidanius, J., & Pratto, C. (1999). *Social dominance: An inter-group theory of social hierarchy and oppression.* Cambridge, MA: Cambridge University Press.

Sillars, A. L., & Wilmot, W. W. (1994). Communication strategies in conflict and mediation. In J. A. Daly & J. M. Wiemann (Eds), *Strategic interpersonal communication* (pp. 163–90). Hillsdale, NJ: Lawrence Erlbaum Associates.

Silva, A. V., & Guenther, H. (2001). Helping behaviour among passengers can contribute to the quality of mass transit. *Estudos de Psicologia, 6,* 75–82 [Abstract in English only].

Simpson, J. A., Rhodes, W. S., & Phillips, D. (1996). Conflict in close relationships: An attachment perspective. *Journal of Personality and Social Psychology, 71,* 899–914.

Simukonda, H. H. M. (1992). The NGO sector in Malawi's socio-economic development. In G. C. Z. Mhone (Ed.), *Malawi at the crossroads: The post colonial economy* (pp. 298–348). Harare: Sapes Books.

Singer, M. (1993). The application of organizational justice theories to selection fairness research. *New Zealand Journal of Psychology, 22,* 32–45.

Singh, D. (1995). Female judgement of male attractiveness and desirability for relationships. *Journal of Personality and Social Psychology, 69,* 1089–1107.

Singh, P., Onglato, M. L. U., Sriram, N., & Tay, A. B. G. (1997). The warm and cold variable in impression formation: Evidence for the positive-negative asymmetry. *British Journal of Social Psychology, 36,* 457–77.

Singh, S., & Vasudeva, P. (1977). A factorial study of the perceived reasons for poverty. *Asian Journal of Psychology and Education, 2,* 51–6.

Sinha, D. (1989). Cross-cultural psychology and the process of indigenisation: A second view from the Third World. In D. M. Keats, D. Munro & L. Mann (Eds), *Heterogeneity in cross-cultural psychology* (pp. 24–40). Lisse: Swets & Zeitlinger.

Sinha, J. B. P. (1984). Toward partnership for relevant research in the Third World. *International Journal of Psychology, 19,* 169–77.

Sinha, J. B. P. (1990). A model of effective leadership in India. In A. M. Jaeger & R. N Kanungo (Eds), *Management development in developing countries* (pp. 252–263). Chippenham, UK: Routledge.

Sistrunk, F., & McDavid, M. W. (1971). Sex variable in conforming behavior. *Journal of Personality and Social Psychology, 17,* 200–207.

Skinner, B. F. (1953). *Science and human behaviour.* New York: Macmillan.

Skowronski, J. J., & Carlston, D. E. (1989). Negativity and extremity biases in impression formation: A review of explanations. *Psychological Bulletin, 105,* 131–42.

Sloan, T. S. (2000). Culture, cognition, and psychological individualism. In J. F. Schumaker & T. Ward (Eds), *Cultural cognition and psychopathology* (in press). Westport, CT: Praeger.

Slovic, P., Fisch, B., & Lichenstein, S. (1982). Facts versus fears: Understanding perceived risk. In D. Kahneman & A. Tversky (Eds), *Judgement under uncertainty: Heuristics and biases* (pp. 463–89). New York: Cambridge University Press.

Smith, B. J., & Carr, S. C. (1997). Selection in equalitarian Australia: Weighted average or motivational gravity? *South Pacific Journal of Psychology, 9,* 7–19.

Smith, B. N., Kerr, N. A., Markus, M. J., & Stasson, M. F. (2001). Individual differences in social loafing: Need for cognition as a motivator in collective performance. *Group Dynamics: Theory, Research, & Practice, 5,* 150–58.

Smith, C. M., Tindale, R. S., & Dugoni, B. L. (1996). Minority and majority influence in freely interacting groups: Qualitative versus quantitative differences. *British Journal of Social Psychology, 35,* 137–49.

Smith, M. K. (2002). Chris Argyris: Theories of action, double-loop learning and organizational learning <www.infed.org>, accessed 9 May 2002.

Smith, P. B., & Bond, M. H. (1999). *Social psychology across cultures.* Boston, MA: Allyn & Bacon.

Smith, P. K. (1997). Bullying in lifespan perspective: What can studies of school bullying and workplace bullying learn from each other? *Journal of Community and Applied Social Psychology, 7,* 249–55.

Snyder, C. R., & Fromkin, L. (1980). *Uniqueness: The pursuit of difference.* New York: Plenum.

Soble, A. (1990). *The structure of love.* New Haven, CT: Yale University Press.

Solomon, S., Greenberg, J., & Pyszczynski, T. (1991). A terror management theory of social behaviour: The psychological functions of self-esteem and cultural world-views. *Advances in Experimental Social Psychology, 24,* 93–159.

Sorrentino, R. M., & Higgins, E. T. (1986). Motivation and cognition: Warming up to synergism. In R. M. Sorrentino & E. T. Higgins (Eds), *Handbook of motivation and cognition* (pp. 3–19). Brisbane: John Wiley & Sons.

Sorrentino, R. M., Bobocel, D. R., Gitta, M. Z., Olson, J. M., & Hewitt, E. C. (2000). Uncertainty orientation and persuasion: Individual differences in the effects of personal relevance on social judgments. In E. T. Higgins & A. W. Kruglanski (Eds), *Motivational science: Social and personality perspectives* (pp. 336–53). Philadelphia, PA: Psychology Press/ Taylor & Francis.

Spears, R., Lea, M., & Lee, S. (1990). De-individuation and group polarization in computer-mediated communication. *British Journal of Social Psychology, 29,* 121–34.

Special Commentary (2001). The study of cross-cultural management: Past, present, and future. *International Journal of Cross-Cultural Management, 1,* 11–30.

Spitzberg, B. H., & Cupach, W. R. (1998). *The dark side of close relationships.* London: Lawrence Erlbaum Associates.

Sprecher, S. (1984). Asking questions in bars: The girls (and boys) may not get prettier at closing time and other interesting results. *Personality and Social Psychology Bulletin, 10,* 482–8.

Sprecher, S. (1994). Two sides to the break-up of dating relationships. *Personal Relationships, 1,* 199–222.

Sprecher, S. (1999). 'I love you more today than yesterday': Romantic partners' perceptions of changes in love and related affect over time. *Journal of Personality and Social Psychology, 76,* 46–53.

Sprecher, S., & Metts, S. (1989). Development of the effects of gender and gender-role orientation. *Journal of Social and Personal Relationships, 6,* 387–411.

Sprecher, S., & Regan, P. C. (1998). Passionate and companionate love in courting and young married couples. *Sociological Inquiry, 68,* 163–85.

Sprecher, S., & Schwartz, P. (1994). Equity and balance in the exchange of contributions in close relationships. In M. J. Lerner & G. Mikula (Eds), *Entitlement and the affectional bon: Justice in close relationships* (pp. 11–41). New York: Plenum Press.

Sprecher, S., Aron, A., Hatfield, E., Cortese, A., Potapova, E., & Levitskaya, A. (1994). Love: American style, Russian style, and Japanese style. *Personal Relationships, 1,* 349–69.

Sprecher, S., Sullivan, Q., & Hatfield, E. (1994). Mate selection preferences: Gender differences examined in a national sample. *Journal of Personality and Social Psychology, 66,* 1074–80.

Staats, A. W., & Staats, C. K. (1958). Attitudes established by classical conditioning. *Journal of Abnormal and Social Psychology, 15,* 1–15.

Stafford, L., & Reske, J. R. (1990). Idealisation and communication in long-distance premarital relationships. *Family Relationships, 39,* 274–9.

Stangor, C. (Ed.) (2000). *Stereotypes and prejudice: Essential readings.* Philadelphia, PA: Psychology Press.

Steele, C. M. (1997). A threat in the air: How stereotypes shape the intellectual identities and performance of women and African-Americans. *American Psychologist, 52,* 613–29.

Stendhal, B. M. (1926). *The red and the black.* New York: Liveright.

Stephens, D. F. (1998). Aggression. In J. L. Duda (Ed.), *Advances in sport and exercise psychology measurement* (pp. 277–92). Morgantown, WV: Fitness Information Technology, Inc.

Sternberg, R. J. (1986). A triangular theory of love. *Psychological Review, 93,* 119–35.

Sternberg, R. J. (1987). Liking versus loving: A comparative evaluation of theories. *Psychological Bulletin, 102,* 331–45.

Sternberg. R. J. (1988). *The triangle of love.* New York: Basic Books.

Sternberg, R. J. (1997). Construct validation of the triangular love scale. *European Journal of Social Psychology, 27,* 313–35.

Sternberg, R. J., Forsythe, G. B., Hedlund, J., Horvath, J. A., et al. (2000). *Practical intelligence in everyday life.* New York: Cambridge University Press.

Sternberg, R. J., & Barnes, M. L. (1985). Real and ideal others in romantic relationships: Is four a crowd? *Journal of Personality and Social Psychology, 49,* 1586–1608.

Sternberg, R. J., & Barnes, M. L. (Eds) (1988). *The psychology of love.* New Haven, CT: Yale University Press.

Sternberg, R. J., & Beall, A. E. (1991). How can we know what love is? An epistemological analysis. In G. J. O. Fletcher & F. D. Fincham (Eds), *Cognition in close relationships* (pp. 257–78). Hillsdale, NJ: Lawrence Erlbaum Associates.

Sternberg, R. J., & Grajek, S. (1984). The nature of love. *Journal of Personality and Social Psychology, 47,* 312–29.

Stewart, D. D., & Stasser, G. (1998). The sampling of critical, unshared information in decision-making groups: The role of an informed minority. *European Journal of Social Psychology, 28,* 95–113.

Stirling Minds (2001). Yawning alert! *Stirling Minds, 4,* 4.

Stodghill, R. M. (1948). Personal factors associated with leadership: A survey of the literature. *Journal of Psychology, 25,* 35–71.

Stone, F. M. (1999). *Coaching for performance: How to choose and use the right technique to boost employee performance.* New York: American Management Association.

Stoner, J. A. F. (1961). *A comparison of individual and group decisions involving risk.* Boston, MA: Massachusetts Institute of Technology (MIT), School of Industrial Management.

Stoner, J. A. (1968). Risky and cautious shifts in group decisions: The influence of widely held values. *Journal of Experimental Social Psychology, 4,* 442–59.

Storms, M. D. (1973). Videotape and the attribution process: Reversing actors' and observers' points of view. *Journal of Personality and Social Psychology, 27,* 165–75.

Stouffer, S. A., Suchman, E. A., DeVinney, L. C., Star, S. A., & Williams, R. M. (1949). *The American soldier: Adjustment during army life,* vol. 1. Princeton, NJ: Princeton University Press.

Streatfield, K., & Singarimbun, M. (1988). Social factors affecting use of immunization in Indonesia. *Social Science and Medicine, 27,* 1237–45.

Stroop, J. R. (1935; reprinted 1992). Studies of interference in serial verbal reactions. *Journal of Experimental Psychology, 18,* 643–62, 15–23.

Strube, M. J., & Garcia, J. E. (1981). A meta-analytic investigation of Fiedler's contingency model of leadership effectiveness. *Psychological Bulletin, 90,* 307–321.

Stumpfer, D. J. (1971). Fear and affiliation during a disaster. *Journal of Social Psychology, 82,* 263–8.

Suemer, N., & Guengoer, D. (1999). The impact of perceived parenting styles on attachment styles, self-evaluations, and close relationships. *Turk Psikoloji Dergisi, 14,* 35–58 [article text in Turkish].

Sulthana, P. (1987). The effect of frustration and inequity on the displacement of aggression. *Asian Journal of Psychology and Education, 19,* 26–33.

Sumer, H. C., & Knight, P. A. (2001). How do people with different attachment styles balance work and family? A personality perspective on work-family linkage. *Journal of Applied Psychology, 86,* 653–63.

Sunstein, C. S. (2001). Boycott the daily me! *Time* (special issue on e-technology), 4 June, 78–9.

Sutton, S. (1998). Predicting and explaining intentions and behavior: How well are we doing? *Journal of Applied Social Psychology, 28,* 1317–38.

Sutton, R. I., & Hargadon, A. (1996). Brainstorming groups in context: Effectiveness in a product design firm. *Administrative Science Quarterly, 41,* 685–718.

Swap, W. C. (1977). Interpersonal attraction and repeated exposure to rewarders and punishers. *Personality and Social Psychology Bulletin, 3,* 248–51.

Swim, J. K., Aikin, K. J., Hall, W. S., & Hunter, B. A. (1995). Sexism and racism: Old-fashioned and modern prejudices. *Journal of Personality and Social Psychology, 68,* 199–214.

Syme, G. J., & Nancarrow, B. E. (1992). Predicting public involvement in urban water management and planning. *Environment and Behaviour, 24,* 738–58.

Tajfel, H. (1970). Experiments in inter-group discrimination. *Scientific American, 223,* 96–102.

Tajfel, H. (1978). *Differentiation between social groups.* London: Academic Press.

Tajfel, H., & Turner, J. C. (1979). An integrative theory of inter-group conflict. In G. W. Austin & S. Worchel (Eds), *The social psychology of inter-group relations* (pp. 33–47). Monterey, CA: Brooks/Cole.

Takahashi, F. (1977). The effect of empathic contact in emotional role-playing on changing and maintaining attitudes and behavior. *Japanese Journal of Experimental Social Psychology, 16,* 99–109.

Tan, D. T. Y., & Singh, R. (1995). Attitudes and attraction: A developmental study of the similarity-attraction and dissonance-repulsion hypotheses. *Personality and Social Psychology Bulletin, 21,* 975–86.

Tan, S. L., & Moghaddam, F. M. (1996). Reflexive positioning and culture. *Journal for the Theory of Social Behavior, 25,* 388–400.

Tattam, A. (2001). The psychology of relationships. *In-Psych, 23,* 16–18.

Taylor, D, M., & Jaggi, V. (1974). Ethnocentrism and causal attribution in a South Indian context. *Journal of Cross-Cultural Psychology, 5,* 162–71.

Taylor, D. M., & Moghaddam, F. M. (1994). *Theories of inter-group relations: International social psychological perspectives.* Westport, CT: Praeger.

Taylor, R., & Yavalanavanua, S. (1997). Linguistic relativity in Fiji: A preliminary study. *South Pacific Journal of Psychology, 9,* 69–74.

Taylor, S. E., & Fiske, S. T. (1975). Points of view and perceptions of causality. *Journal of Personality and Social Psychology, 32,* 439–45.

Taylor, W. (1988). The Grim Reaper: The use of research in policy development and public education. In *Report of the Third National Conference on AIDS* (pp. 543–7). Canberra, ACT: AGPS.

Tembo, K. C. (1991). Evaluation of source of messages on AIDS by college students. *Malaŵi Medical Journal, 7,* 117–18.

Tenenbaum, G., Stewart, E., Singer, R. N., & Duda, J. (1997). Aggression and violence in sport: An ISSP position stand. *The Sport Psychologist, 11,* 1–7.

Tennov, D. (1979). *Love and limerence: The experience of being in love.* New York: Stein & Day.

Terry, D. J., & Hogg, M. A. (1996). Group norms and the attitude-behavior relationship: A role for group identification. *Personality and Social Psychology Bulletin, 22,* 776–93.

Thirer, J. (1992). Aggression. In R. Singer, M. Murphy & L. Tennant (Eds), *Handbook of research in sport psychology* (pp. 365–87). New York: Macmillan.

Thomas, D. R. (1994). Understanding cross-cultural communication. *South Pacific Journal of Psychology, 7,* 2–8.

Thompson, P. A., & Ahn, D. (1992). To be or not to be: An exploration of E-prime, copula deletion, and flaming in electronic mail. *Et Cetera: A Review of General Semantics, 49,* 146–64.

Thornton, B., & Maurice, J. (1998). Physique contrast effects: Adverse impact of idealised body images for women. *Sex Roles, 37,* 433–9.

Thornton, B., & Moore, S. (1993). Physical attractiveness contrast effects: Implications for self-esteem and evaluations of the social self. *Personality and Social Psychology Bulletin, 19,* 474–80.

Thornton, B., Kirchner, G., & Jacobs, J. (1991). Influence of a photograph on a charitable appeal: A picture may be worth a thousand words when it has to speak for itself. *Journal of Applied Social Psychology, 21*, 433–45.

Till, A., & Freedman, E. M. (1978). Complementary versus similarity of traits operating in the choice of marriage and dating partners. *Journal of Social Psychology, 105*, 147–8.

Ting-Toomey, S. (1988). Intimacy expressions in three cultures: France, Japan, and the United States. *International Journal of Intercultural Relations, 15*, 29–46.

Tomada, G., & Schneider, B. H. (1997). Relational aggression, gender, and peer acceptance: Invariance across culture, stability over time, and concordance among informants. *Developmental Psychology, 33*, 601–9.

Tomlinson, J. (1999). *Globalisation and culture.* Chicago, IL: University of Chicago Press.

Tomlinson, M. (2000). Pathways to attachment: The Strange Situation and culture in the South African context. *Southern African Journal of Child and Adolescent Mental Health, 9*, 107–122.

Tood, J., Mackie, J. R., & Dewhurst, K. (1971). Real or imaginary hypophallism: A cause of inferiority feelings and morbid sexual jealousy. *British Journal of Psychiatry, 119*, 315–18.

Towles, S. T., & Fazio, R. H. (2001). On the origins of racial attitudes: Correlates of childhood experiences. *Personality and Social Psychology Bulletin, 27*, 162–75.

Townsend, J. M., & Wasserman, T. (1998). Sexual attractiveness: Sex differences in assessment and criteria. *Evolution and Human Behaviour, 19*, 171–91.

Townsend, P. (1979). *Poverty in the United Kingdom: A survey of household resources and standards of living.* Harmondsworth, UK: Penguin.

Trafimow, D., & Finlay, K. A. (1996). The importance of subjective norms for a minority of people: Between-subjects and within-subjects analyses. *Personality and Social Psychology Bulletin, 22*, 820–28.

Trahair, R. C. (1969). Dynamics for a role theory for the worker's judgement. *Human Relations, 22*, 99–119.

Travis, L. E. (1925). The effect of a small audience upon eye-hand coordination. *Journal of Abnormal and Social Psychology, 20*, 142–6.

Traynor, W. J., & Watts, W. R. (1992). Management development in the Pacific during the 1990s. *Journal of Management Development, 11*, 69–79.

Triandis, H. C. (1977). Theoretical framework for evaluation of cross-cultural training effectiveness. *International Journal of Intercultural Relations, 1*, 19–45.

Triandis, H. C., McCusker, C., & Hui, C. H. (1990). Multimethod probes of individualism and collectivism. *Journal of Personality and Social Psychology, 59*, 1006–1020.

Triandis, H. H. (May 2002). *Culture, conflict, and negotiation.* Research seminar, Auckland University of Technology, New Zealand.

Triplett, N. (1897). The dynamogenic factors in pacemaking and competition. *American Journal of Psychology, 9*, 507–533.

Trompenaars, F. (1993). *Riding the waves of culture.* London: Economist Books.

Tsai, J. L., & Levenson, R. W. (1997). Cultural influences on emotional responding. *Journal of Cross-Cultural Psychology, 28*, 600–625.

Tsoi-Hoshmand, L. (1976). Marital therapy: An integrative behavioural-learning model. *Journal of Marital and Family Therapy, 2*, 179–91.

Tucker, P., & Aron, A. (1993). Passionate love and marital satisfaction at key transition points in the family life cycle. *Journal of Social and Clinical Psychology, 12*, 135–47.

Tuckman, B. W. (1965). Developmental sequence in small groups. *Psychological Bulletin, 63*, 384–99.

Tuckman, B. W., & Jensen, M. A. (1977). Stages of small-group development revisited. *Group & Organization Studies, 2*, 419–27.

Turner, J. C. (1982). Towards a cognitive redefinition of the social group. In H. Tajfel (Ed.), *Social identity and intergroup relations* (pp. 15–40). Cambridge, UK: Cambridge University Press.

Turner, J. C. (1991). *Social influence.* Milton Keynes, UK: Open University Press.

Turner, J. C., & Onorato, R. S. (1999). Social identity, personality, and the self-concept: A self-categorising perspective. In T. R. Tyler & R. M. Kramer (Eds), *The psychology of the social self: Applied social research* (pp. 11–46). Mahwah, NJ: Lawrence Erlbaum Associates.

Tversky, A., & Kahneman, D. (1973). Availability: A heuristic for judging frequency and probability. *Cognitive Psychology, 5*, 207–232.

Tyler, R. R. (1990). *Why people obey the law.* New Haven, CT: Yale University Press.

Tyson, G. A. (1993). Response to Colman's article 'Crowd psychology in South African murder trials'. *American Psychologist, 48*, Comment.

Tyson, G. A., & Turnbull, O. (1990). Ambient temperature and the occurrence of collective violence: A South African replication. *South African Journal of Psychology, 20*, 159–62.

Uleman, J. S. (1987). Consciousness and control: The case of spontaneous trait inferences. *Personality and Social Psychology Bulletin, 13*, 337–54.

Valentino, N. A. (1999). Crime news and the priming of racial attitudes during evaluations of the President. *Public Opinion Quarterly, 63*, 293–320.

Valian, V. (1998). Sex, schemas, and success. *Academe: Bulletin of the American Association of University Professors*, September/October, 50–55.

Van de Ven, A. H., & Delbecq, A. L. (1974). The effectiveness of Nominal, Delphi, and interacting groups discussion. *Academy of Management Journal, 17*, 605–621.

Van de Vliert, E., Schwartz, S. H., Huismans, S. E., Hofstede, G., & Daan, S. (1999). Temperature, cultural masculinity, and domestic political violence: A cross-national study. *Journal of Cross-Cultural Psychology, 30*, 291–314.

Van den Bos, K., & Spruijt, N. (2002). Appropriateness of decisions as a moderator of the psychology of voice. *Journal of Social Psychology, 32*, 57–72.

Van Dyne, L., & Saavedra, R. (1996). A naturalistic minority influence experiement: Effects on divergent thinking, conflict and originality in work groups. *British Journal of Social Psychology, 35*, 151–67.

Vance, C. M., & Ring, P. S. (1994). Preparing the host country workforce for expatriate managers: The neglected other side of the coin. *Human Resource Development Quarterly, 5*, 337.

Vanzetti, N., & Duck, S. (1996). *A lifetime of relationships*. Melbourne: Brooks/Cole.

Vartia, M. A. L. (2001). Consequences of workplace bullying with respect to the well-being of its targets and the observers of bullying. *Scandinavian Journal of Work, Environment, and Health, 27*, 63–9.

Vaughn, B. E., & Bost, K. K. (1999). Attachment and temperament: Redundant, independent, or interacting influences on interpersonal adaptation and personality development? In J. Cassidy & P. R. Shaver (Eds), *Handbook of attachment: Theory, research, and clinical applications* (pp. 198–225). New York: The Guildford Press.

Vecchio, R. P., Hearn, G., & Southey, G. (1997). *Organisational behaviour*. Sydney: Harcourt Brace.

Vinacke, W. E., Shannon, K., Palazzo, V., & Balsavage, L. (1988). Similarity and complementarity in intimate couples. *Genetic, Social, and General Psychology Monographs, 114*, 51–76.

Volk, J. E., & Koopman, C. (2001). Factors associated with condom use in Kenya: A test of the health belief model. *AIDS Education & Prevention, 13*, 495–508.

Von Bertalanffy, L. (1940). Der organismus als physikalisches system betrachtet. *Naturwiseenschaften, 28*, 521.

Voss, N. (1998). Daylight rape on busy Darwin road. *Northern Territory News*, 28 May, 3.

Waeneryd, K. E. (2001). *Stock-market psychology: How people value and trade stocks*. Northampton, MA: Edward Elgar.

Wageman, R. (1997). Critical success factors for creating superb self-managing teams. *Organisational Dynamics*, Summer, 49–61.

Walker, A. E., & Smither, J. W. (1999). A five-year study of upward feedback. *Personnel Psychology, 52*, 393–424.

Walker, I., & Crogan, M. (April 1997). *Academic performance, prejudice, and the jigsaw classroom: New pieces to the puzzle*. Third Annual Conference, Society of Australasian Social Psychologists, Wollongong, NSW.

Wallace, E. P., & Carr, S. C. (2000). Personal correspondences and recollections. March 2000.

Wallace, P. (1999). *The psychology of the Internet*. Cambridge, UK: Cambridge University Press.

Wallach, M. A., Kogan, N., & Bem, D. J. (1962). Group influence on individual risk taking. *Journal of Abnormal and Social Psychology, 65*, 75–86.

Walsh, M. (1997). *Cross-cultural communication problems in Aboriginal Australia*. Darwin, North Australia Research Unit Discussion Paper 7/97: Research School of Pacific and Asian Studies, The Australian National University.

Walster, E., Aronson, V., & Abrahams, D. (1966). On increasing the persuasiveness of a low prestige communicator. *Journal of Experimental Social Psychology, 2*, 325–42.

Walther, J. B. (1993). Impression development in computer-mediated interaction. *Western Journal of Communication, 57*, 381–98.

Walther, J. B. (1996). Computer-mediated communication: Impersonal, interpersonal, and hyperpersonal interaction. *Communication Research, 23*, 3–43.

Ward, C. (1996). Acculturation. In D. Landis & R. Bhagat (Eds), *Handbook of intercultural training* (pp. 124–47). Newbury Park, CA: Sage.

Ward, C. A. (2001). Models and measurements of psychological androgyny: A cross-cultural extension of theory and research. *Sex Roles, 43*, 529–52.

Warr, P. (1982). A national study of non-financial employment commitment. *Journal of Occupational Psychology, 55*, 297–312.

Watson, J. B. (1919). *Psychology from the standpoint of a behaviourist*. Philadelphia, PA: Lippincott.

Watson, J. B. (1924). The unverbalised in human behaviour. *Psychological Review, 31*, 273–80.

Weaver, C. (1972). *Human listening: Process and behaviour*. Indianapolis: Bobbs-Merrill.

Wedenoja, W., & Sobo, E. J. (1997). Unconscious motivation and culture. In J. F. Schumaker, D. Munro & S. C. Carr (Eds), *Motivation and culture* (pp. 159–77). New York: Routledge.

Wegner, D. M. (1999). *The seed of our undoing. Psychological Science Agenda, 1/2*, 10–12.

Wegner, D. M., Lane, J. D., & Dimitri, S. (1994). The allure of secret relationships. *Journal of Personality and Social Psychology, 66*, 287–300.

Wegner, D. M., Schneider, D. J., Carter, S. R., & White, T. L. (1987). Paradoxical effects of thought suppression. *Journal of Personality and Social Psychology, 53*, 5–13.

Weick, K. E. (1996). An appreciation of social context: One legacy of Gerald Salancik. *Administrative Science Quarterly, 41*, 563–74.

Weiner, B. (1995). *Judgements of responsibility: A foundation for a theory of social conduct*. New York: The Guildford Press.

Weinstein, L. (1982). Negative incentive contrast effects with sucrose and rats as due to aggression. *Bulletin of the Psychonomic Society, 19*, 359–61.

Weldon, D. E., Carlston, D. E., Rissman, A. K., Slobodin, L., & Triandis, H. C. (1975). A laboratory test of effects of culture assimilation training. *Journal of Personality and Social Psychology, 32*, 300–310.

Wetherell, M. (1982). Cross-cultural studies of minimal groups: Implications for the social identity theory of inter-group relations. In H. Tajfel (Ed.), *Social identity and inter-group relations* (pp. 207–240). Cambridge, UK: Cambridge University Press.

Wetherell, M., & Potter, J. (1992). *Mapping the language of racism: Discourse and the legitimation of exploitation.* Hemel Hempstead, UK: Harvester Wheatsheaf.

Wetsman, A., & Marlowe, F. (1999). How universal are preferences for female waist-to-hip ratios? Evidence from the Hazda of Tanzania. *Evolution & Human Behaviour, 20*, 219–28.

Wheeler, L., & Kim, Y. (1997). What is beautiful is culturally good: The physical attractiveness stereotype has different content in collectivist cultures. *Personality and Social Psychology Bulletin, 23*, 795–800.

Wheeler, L., Reis, H. T., & Bond, M. H. (1989). Collectivism-individualism in everyday social life: The middle kingdom and the melting pot. *Journal of Personality and Social Psychology, 57*, 79–86.

Wheeler, L., Shaver, K. G., Jones, R. A., Goethals, G. R., Cooper, J., Robinson, J. E., Gruder, C. L., & Butzine, K. W. (1969). Factors determining choice of a comparison other. *Journal of Experimental Social Psychology, 5*, 219–32.

White, G. L., Fishbein, S., & Rutstein, J. (1981). Passionate love and the misattribution of arousal. *Journal of Personality and Social Psychology, 41*, 56–62.

White, J. B., & Langer, E. J. (1999). Horizontal hostility: Relations between similar minority groups. *Journal of Social Issues, 55*, 537–59.

Whitfield, R. (1998). Darwin folk top the honesty poll. *Northern Territory News*, 27 November, 3.

Whitley, B. E. (1993). Reliability and aspects of the construct validity of Sternberg's Triangular Love Scale. *Journal of Social and Personal Relationships, 10*, 475–80.

Whitton, J. L., Kramer, P., & Eastwood, R. (1982). Weather and infradian rhythms in self-reports of health, sleep, and mood measures. *Journal of Psychosomatic Research, 26*, 231–5.

Wiederman, M. W., & Allgeier, E. R. (1992). Gender differences in mate selection criteria: Socio-biological or socio-economic explanation? *Ethology and Sociobiology, 13*, 115–24.

Wilke, H., & Van Knippenberg, A. D. (1990). Group performance. In M. Hewstone, W. Stoebe, J. P. Codol & G. M. Stephenson (Eds), *Introduction to social psychology* (pp. 315–80). Oxford, UK: Blackwell.

Williams, A., Coupland, J., Folwell, A., & Sparks, L. (1997). Talking about Generation X: Defining them as they define themselves. *Journal of Language & Social Psychology, 16*, 251–77.

Williams, C. (1983). The 'work ethic', non-work, and leisure, in an age of automation. *Australian and New Zealand Journal of Sociology, 19*, 216–37.

Williams, D. (1996). *The social impact of arts programs: How the arts measure up — Australian research into social impact.* Working Paper 8. Adelaide: Comedia SIAP.

Williams, K. D., Bourgeois, M. J., & Croyle, R. T. (1993). The effects of stealing thunder in criminal and civil trials. *Law and Human Behaviour, 17*, 597–609.

Williams. L. (1992). Torture and the torturer. *The Psychologist, 5*, 305–8.

Williams, R. (2000). 'Why should I feel guilty?' Reflections on the workings of guilt in White–Aboriginal relations. *Australian Psychologist, 35*, 136–42.

Wilson, D., Zenda, A., McMaster, J., & Lavelle, S. (1992). Factors predicting Zimbabwean students' intentions to use condoms. *Psychology and Health, 7*, 99–114.

Wilson, E. J., & Sherrell, D. L. (1993). Source effects in communication and persuasion research: A meta-analysis of effect size. *Journal of the Academy of Marketing Science, 21*, 101–112.

Wilson, M., Daly, M., & Daniele, A. (1995). Familicide: The killing of spouse and children. *Aggressive Behaviour, 21*, 275–91.

Winefield, T., Montgomery, R., Gault, U., Muller, J., O'Gorman, J., Reser, J., & Roland, D. (2000). The psychology of work and unemployment in Australia today. Discussion paper of the Australian Psychological Society <www.psychsociety.com.au>.

Witte, K. (1994). Fear control and danger control: A test of the extended parallel process model (EPPM). *Communication Monographs, 61*, 113–34.

Witte, K., & Morrison, K. (1995). Using scare tactics to promote safer sex among juvenile detention and high school youth. *Journal of Applied Communication Research, 23*, 128–42.

Woike, B. A., Osier, T. J., & Candelia, K. (1996). Attachment styles and violent imagery in thematic stories about relationships. *Personality & Social Psychology Bulletin, 22*, 1030–34.

Wolff, P. M., & Braman, R. O. (1999). Traditional dispute resolution in Micronesia. *South Pacific Journal of Psychology, 11*, 44–53.

Wong, M. M. L. (1996). Shadow management in Japanese companies in Hong Kong. *Asia Pacific Journal of Human Resources, 34*, 95–110.

Wood, W., Lundgren, S., Ouellette, J. A., Busceme, S., & Blackstone, T. (1994). Minority influence: A meta-analytical review of social influence processes. *Psychological Bulletin, 115*, 323–45.

Woodhall, J., & Winstanley, D. (1998). *Management development: Strategy and practice.* Boston, MA: Blackwell.

Worchel, S., & Mitchell, T. R. 91972). An evaluation of the effectiveness of the culture assimilator in Thailand and Greece. *Journal of Applied Psychology, 56*, 472–9.

World Bank. (1999). Poverty-Net: Data on poverty <www.worldbank.org/poverty/data/regions/data.htm>.

Wright, A. (1997). *Grog war*. Broome, WA: Magabala Books Aboriginal Corporation.

Wright, S. C., Aron, A., McLaughlin, V. T., & Ropp, S. A. (1997). The extended contact effect: Knowledge of cross-group friendships and prejudice. *Journal of Personality and Social Psychology, 73*, 73–90.

Wynn, K. (2001). Kiwis don't care! *Sunday News*, 12 August, 7.

Wyon, D. P., Andersen, I., & Lundqvist, G. R. (1979). The effects of moderate heat stress on mental performance. *Scandinavian Journal of Work and Environmental Health, 5*, 352–61.

X, M., & Haley, A. (1987). *The autobiography of Malcolm X*. Reading, UK: Penguin.

Yan, W., & Gaier, E. L. (1991, April). *Causal attributions for college success and failure: An American–Asian comparison.* Annual Meeting of the American Educational Research Association, Chicago, IL.

Yeal, C. (1996). Basic components of love: Some variations on Sternberg's model. *Revista de Psicologia Social, 11*, 185–201.

Yee, N. K., & Van Dyne, L. (2001). Individualism-collectivism as a boundary condition for effectiveness of minority influence in decision-making. *Organizational Behavior and Human Decision Processes, 84*, 198–225.

Yela, C. (1996). Basic components of love: Some variations on Sternberg's model. *Revista de Psicologia Social, 11*, 185–201 [abstract only].

Yelsma, P., & Athappilly, K. (1988). Marital satisfaction and communication practices: Comparisons among Indian and American couples. *Journal of Comparative Family Studies, 19*, 37–54.

Yerkes, R. M., & Dodson, J. D. (1908). The relation of strength of stimulus to rapidity of habit formation. *Journal of Comparative Neurology and Psychology, 18*, 459–82.

Yoon, S. J., & Kim, J. H. (2001). Is the Internet more effective than traditional media? Factors affecting the choice of media. *Journal of Advertising Research, 41*, 53–60.

Yoshiyama, N. (1991). A time series analysis of minority influence on the majority in a group. *Japanese Journal of Experimental Social Psychology, 30*, 243–8.

Young, H. M., Lierman, L., Powell-Cope, G., & Kasprzyk, D. (1991). Operationalising the theory of planned behaviour. *Research in Nursing and Health, 14*, 137–44.

Yovetich, N. A., & Rusbult, C. E. (1994). Accommodative behaviour in close relationships: Exploring transformation of motivation. *Journal of Experimental Social Psychology, 30*, 138–64.

Yzerbyt, V. Y., Rogier, A., & Fiske, S. T. (1998). Group entitativity and social attribution: On translating situational constraints into stereotypes. *Personality & Social Psychology Bulletin, 24*, 1089–1103.

Zajonc, R. B. (1965a). Attitudinal effects of mere exposure. *Journal of Personality and Social Psychology, 9*, 1–27.

Zajonc, R. B. (1965b). Social facilitation. *Science, 149*, 269–74.

Zebrowitz, L. A., & Collins, M. A. (1997). Accurate social perception at zero acquaintance: The affordances of a Gibsonian approach. *Personality and Social Psychology Review, 1*, 204–223.

Zebrowitz, L. A., Collins, M. A., & Dutta, R. (1998). The relationship between appearance and personality across the lifespan. *Personality and Social Psychology Bulletin, 24*, 736–49.

Zillman, D. (1984). *Connections between sex and aggression*. Hillsdale, NJ: Lawrence Erlbaum Associates.

Zimbardo, P. G. (1968). Cognitive dissonance and the control of human motivation. In R. P. Abelson, E. Aronson, W. J. McGuire, T. M. Newcomb, M. J. Rosenberg & P. H. Tannenbaum (Eds), *Theories of cognitive consistency: A sourcebook* (pp. 439–47). Chicago, IL: Rand McNally.

Zimbardo, P. G. (1982). Pathology of imprisonment. In D. Krebs (Ed.), *Readings in contemporary social psychology* (pp. 249–57). New York: Harper & Row.

Zuccaro, S. J., Foti, R. J., & Kenny, D. A. (1991). Self-monitoring and trait-based variance in leadership: An investigation of leaders' flexibility across multiple group situations. *Journal of Applied Psychology, 76*, 308–315.

Zucker, G., & Weiner, B. (1993). Conservation and perceptions of poverty: An attributional analysis. *Journal of Applied Social Psychology, 23*, 925–43.

INDEX